Touched by Fire

ALSO BY LOUISE BARNETT

The Ignoble Savage: American Literary Racism

Touched by Fire

The Life, Death, and Mythic Afterlife of George Armstrong Custer

Louise Barnett

Henry Holt and Company New York

Henry Holt and Company, Inc.
Publishers since 1866
115 West 18th Street
New York, New York 10011

Henry Holt ® is a registered
trademark of Henry Holt and Company, Inc.

Published in Canada by Fitzhenry & Whiteside Ltd.,
195 Allstate Parkway, Markham, Ontario L3R 4T8.

Library of Congress Cataloging-in-Publication Data
Barnett, Louise K.
Touched by fire : the life, death, and mythic afterlife of George Armstrong Custer / Louise Barnett. — 1st ed.
p. cm.
Includes bibliographical references and index.
ISBN 0-8050-3720-9 (alk. paper)
1. Custer, George Armstrong, 1839–1876. 2. Generals — United States—Biography. 3. United States. Army—Biography. I. Title.
E467.1.C99B27 1996
973.8'2'092—dc20 95-43995
[B] CIP
ISBN 0-8050-3720-9

Henry Holt books are available for special
promotions and premiums. For details contact:
Director, Special Markets.

First Edition—1996

Designed by Paula R. Szafranski

Printed in the United States of America
All first editions are printed on acid-free paper. ∞

10 9 8 7 6 5 4 3 2 1

Frontispiece: George Armstrong Custer, c. 1873 (courtesy of Little Bighorn National Monument).

Grateful acknowledgment is made to the following institutions for permission to reproduce the photographs and images in this book: to the National Archives for images 1, 2, 3, 7, 10, and 11; to the Little Bighorn Battlefield National Monument for images 4, 5, 6, and 8; to the Library of Congress for images 9 and 15; to the Western History Department of the Denver Public Library for images 12, 13, and 18; to the Monroe County Historical Commission Archives for images 16 and 17. Jeffrey L. Ward designed the map on page 290.

To the memory of my parents,

David Wendell

and

Anna Louise Kennamer

Through our great good fortune, in our youth our hearts were touched with fire. It was given to us to learn at the outset that life is a profound and passionate thing.

—Oliver Wendell Holmes
on the Civil War

Contents

Touched by Fire

Introduction

> Life is worth living for—or it would be—if it abounded more in such types as Mrs. General Custer and her husband. There was a bright and joyous chivalry in that man, and a noble refinement mingled with constant gaiety in the wife, such as I fear is passing from the earth. —Charles Godfrey Leland, *Memoirs*

"We can picture what determination, what bravery, what heroism must have inspired this devoted little band of martyrs when surrounded and assailed by a vastly overwhelming force of bloodthirsty, merciless and unrestrained barbarians, and that they manfully struggled to the last, equally void of hope or fear."[1] So George Armstrong Custer had written nine years before the Battle of the Little Bighorn to the father of a young officer killed with his entire party by Indians in Kansas.

Custer might have described the Last Stand fight and his own death with the same words, heavily freighted as they are with polarized emotional language: devoted martyrs imbued with determination, bravery, and heroism overwhelmed by bloodthirsty barbarians, the few against the many *manfully* struggling in spite of the odds, consumed by the struggle to the exclusion of hope or fear.

This might have been Custer's view of himself; many others have emerged over the years. Before his controversial death, Custer lived an equally controversial life. And since 1876, the polemics of fierce partisans and detractors have propelled controversy into his afterlife. Disinterested observation can scarcely find a foothold on the battlefield of Custer's Last Stand.

Custer, it seems, is one of those figures we invest with meanings of our own according to our own politics and predilections. His image has been polarized from the nineteenth-century symbol of the *beau sabreur,* saving the Union in charge after glorious charge during the Civil War, to his contemporary reassessment as the ruthless exponent of white expansionism making unjust war on the Indian.

No detail is too small to engage those opposed armies of Custerphiles and Custerphobes.[2] In their hands, Custer's insistence on taking his regimental band into the field whenever possible can be seen as either an appropriate way of maintaining morale or as a foolish frippery, an example of Custer's love of spectacle for its own sake. About more complicated matters—his severe disciplinary measures, his battle tactics, his character—evaluation often seems to depend more on the attitude an observer brings to Custer than on an examination of relevant circumstances.

Oddly enough, his reputation has replicated his life: days of gold in which the world hailed him as a hero, followed by days of lead in which he seemed to be everything but a hero—a lackluster, unpromoted army officer, a rampant egomaniac, or, in the most revisionist incarnation, merely a maniac—the insane commander of Thomas Berger's novel (and Arthur Penn's movie), *Little Big Man.*[3] Custer seems to have experienced every possible incarnation in the contemporary imagination, from appropriation as a positive icon by Anheuser-Busch to condemnation as a transgressor of community values in the advertising brochure of an organization called the Hartford Lunch Company. Each page of this strange little pamphlet proffers an instructive homily, such as "our duties lie in service to ourselves, and we best serve ourselves by serving humanity"—a noble goal but, according to the company, one Custer failed to achieve: "He did not give an undivided and unselfish service. He did not work for the good of all."[4] Drinkers saw a much different image in the brewery's widely distributed lithograph of Custer energetically brandishing his saber as he fought to the death at the Little Bighorn.

The general's multifaceted personality continues to elude simple definition: the man whose filial devotion and tender sensibility prompted him to cry whenever he parted from his mother or saw a sentimental play thrived on fighting and killing. Deeply uxorious, he nevertheless persistently offered attentions to other women. And he inspired both love and hatred among his officers and soldiers alike. But aside from these complexities of character, Custer obviously attracts us today because of his mysterious end in a battle that, more than famous, became uniquely meaningful in American history—not as history but as myth. Every generation since 1876 has spawned a new group of apprentices dedicated to Custer's legend, amateur and professional historians who never tire of asking how the great Civil War hero could have been killed by Indians, along with every man with him, in the very centennial year that extolled American progress. As fate would have it, the country's leading generals, William Tecumseh Sherman and Philip H. Sheridan, were in Philadelphia attending the centennial exposition, the chief celebration of national accomplishment at the moment the news came—which they, like everyone else, found unbelievable.

For 120 years now, history has questioned how the life and career of this renowned military leader could have met with so abrupt an end on the afternoon of June 25, 1876. How did Custer arrive at that particular hillside above a small stream in southeastern Montana so unaware of the great body of Indians opposing him? If only one man had survived to explain how it happened, we could have buried these dead forever, but lacking that resolution, the image of the Last Stand has stubbornly endured. "Despite all the disabusing histories I read," Andrew Ward confessed in 1992, "George Armstrong Custer has stood tall in my imagination, battling alone among the gallant dead and dying of his doomed command, his long hair blowing in the dust and smoke, his sabre upraised against the lurid horde, gloriously poised on eternity's brink."[5]

This book undertakes the search once again for "a man waiting to be discovered," as one historian has put it, between the extremes of the "Last of the Cavaliers and the Glory-hunter."[6] Beyond or behind that transfixing moment of the Last Stand is another Custer, whose mystery equally seizes the imagination. For the generation of the Civil War he was a compelling image etched into the nation's visual memory: the victorious boy general with the golden locks, dressed in his famous black velvet and gold braid, his long red tie flowing behind him as he led his troops into battle. This is the Custer who graduated last in his class at West Point but went on to phenomenal glory in the Civil War. It's baffling, this success that seems without antecedent. Better, it's inspirational—if so apparently mediocre an individual could suddenly metamorphose into a hero, there may be hope for even the most ordinary of us.

No work about Custer could reveal him as he was without devoting considerable attention to his wife, Elizabeth Bacon Custer—"Libbie"—the woman he loved and depended upon during the twelve years of their marriage. Theirs is an unusual love story.

On June 25, 1926, Libbie Custer, now an elderly, white-haired lady, left her Park Avenue apartment in Manhattan to go to a nearby hotel. She had no radio at home to listen to the fiftieth anniversary ceremonies transmitted from the battlefield of the Little Bighorn, ceremonies that she had been invited to attend. Once again, after wavering, she had decided not to journey to the place where her husband had been killed. Libbie often said that her life had ended on that day fifty years earlier, yet from other points of view she had lived fully and exceptionally. What hadn't she seen and done in her eighty-four years? Married during the Civil War, she became the only woman General Philip Sheridan allowed to stay in his army camp. Determined to continue sharing her husband's life after the war, she traveled with him to the Plains frontier, where she experienced fire, flood, and the threat of Indian attack, double-edged because Custer's officers promised her husband to kill her before allowing her to be captured. Then, when Custer was killed by Indians, Libbie was unexpectedly, and without any vocational preparation, forced to remake her life alone at the age of thirty-four.

Fifty years later she could look back upon a successful career as an author and lecturer, a career whose theme had been her dead husband. And although she always subscribed to the prevalent ideology of domesticity for women, after her husband's death she had also become an adventurous world traveler. She was one of the first Western tourists to visit Japan, she attended a coronation durbar in Delhi, and she was briefly stranded in Europe when World War I broke out.[7] In 1876 news of the battle had taken eleven days to reach the outside world; in 1926, as she listened to the radio, planes flew over the same ground where men on horses had fought. Thousands were marking the semicentennial in a spirit of reconciliation between Indians and whites, a spirit that Libbie Custer had eventually come to share.

There is a kind of perfection about Libbie Custer's life that must arouse, if not suspicion, at the least perplexity. Her devotion to Custer is so absolute, her personality so sweet and self-effacing. In her fear of many things she seems the essence of fragile Victorian helplessness, yet to be with her husband she was ready to dare any danger and suffer any hardship. Against his critics she fought tenaciously and uncompromisingly. She would die a few days short of her ninety-first birthday, having devoted twelve years of marriage and fifty-seven years of widowhood to George Armstrong Custer. Her constant efforts to memorialize him contributed to a myth of Custer as the ideal man and hero, but in the process she was mythicized herself as the faithful widow who was—as one newspaper described her—as much in love with her husband on the day she died as on the day she married.[8] Even severe critics of Custer have regarded the Custer marriage with a certain reverence.

One of the Custers' contemporaries, Henry James, wrote a celebrated tale, "The Altar of the Dead," about a man named Stransom who devotes his life to memorializing dead friends.[9] Fittingly, Stransom meets a woman engaged in the same project, but she has dedicated her life to the memory of one great love, a man whom Stransom regards as unworthy of such devotion. Many had a similar opinion of Custer. When James published his tale in 1895, Libbie Custer had already spent nineteen years living such a story, a story as fascinating in its way as her controversial husband's. Where the unnamed woman in "The Altar of the Dead" mourns privately, Libbie's devotion to Custer's memory was a lifelong labor to keep his name before the public. Her success exceeded her hopes—in part.

Thanks to Libbie's efforts and to the heated controversies of Custerphiles and -phobes squaring off in every generation, Custer's story did not end with his death. In her fifty-seven years of widowhood, Libbie did her best to foster the image of a heroic Custer, but this mythicized ideal could not have taken root through her dedication alone. Her vision spoke to a national need for an anachronistic hero just as our own time has required Custer's refashioning as an antihero. The truth of the historic Custer, unsurprisingly, lies somewhere in between.

PART ONE

Glory

1

Early Days

> I look back on the days spent under the home-roof as a period of pure happiness, and I feel thankful for such noble parents.
>
> —George Armstrong Custer to his father

> When the Custer homestead in New Rumley, Ohio was being converted into a public monument, a large penny was found at the site. One side of the coin had the initials GAC scratched in it and nine indentations, possibly standing for the owner's age.
>
> —*Cadiz Republican*, January 21, 1932

There was nothing exceptional about George Armstrong Custer as a schoolboy, nothing to suggest that he would become the famous Boy General of the Civil War, and, of course, nothing to predict that he would become a legend for being killed by Indians at the age of thirty-six. If he did not appear in any way unusual before his military success, he does seem to have been overwhelmingly representative: the son of hardworking and upstanding midwesterners, the product of a loving family he remained loyal to all his life, a youth who intended to rise in the world and would go East to do so, returning to the West as an enthusiastic booster of American expansionism. He may not have made a list of resolutions for self-improvement like Fitzgerald's Great Gatsby, but according to his brother, he was determined to get an education and equally determined not to be a farmer.[1] As he told his prospective father-in-law, he had "always had a purpose in life."[2]

George Armstrong Custer was the first surviving child of Maria Ward Kirkpatrick and Emmanuel Custer. Each had been widowed young and each brought children to the new marriage. Custer's birth was soon followed by four others: Nevin, Thomas Ward, Boston, and Margaret. By all accounts the Custer family was a nurturing environment for its numerous children.

Maria Custer comes down to us as a woman of fragile health and strong maternal sensibility. An undated letter to "my loveing son" indicates that she gladly embraced the traditional concept of the self-sacrificing mother and saw her duty in life to be the creation of a happy home for her family. Thinking of material things her children needed and lacked had often caused her tears, she wrote, but she had tried to compensate for "the empty spaces" with "little acts of kindness." The letter concludes: "It is sweet to toil for those we love."[3] All evidence suggests that she lived this creed.

Emmanuel Custer is more strongly individualized in the historical record, in part because he was a more public person. In her tribute to him after his death in 1892, Libbie Custer remarked that the two dominant passions of his life, religion and politics, remained intense until the end. After the contested presidential election of 1876, Emmanuel visited his son's widow in New York. When he told her that he could not go home "without seeing Mr. Tilden," the defeated candidate, she advised him to go early to avoid the press of business that would occupy such a public figure. A man of rural habits, Emmanuel appeared at Tilden's home before the governor was awake, but eventually he was received "with great cordiality." He had made the visit to say the following: "Mr. Tilden, I only came to pay my respects to the President of the United States."[4] On another occasion, Libbie recalled, a townsman asked him if it didn't shake his faith in democracy to know that most clergymen were Republicans. "No," he answered. "It don't shake my faith in Democracy, but it makes me rather suspicious of their religion."[5]

He was certainly a solicitous father. A number of his wartime letters to Custer express concern over his son's penchant for exposing himself to danger. "Now my son," one letter reads, "I doant think that it is necessary for you to lead every charge in person you should be more cearful and not run into danger when it is not required."[6] Another letter begins, "You know my darling son that I love you as I love my life."[7]

Emmanuel Custer was also fun-loving. In a theme that would frequently recur in letters and conversations, he once told Libbie, "I was always a boy with my boys." Elsewhere he said that "they knew I was just as good a boy with them as they were."[8] After a trip full of pranks, the family laughed together when the two Custer brothers told their mother about the jokes they had played on their father. In one episode, when Tom and his father shared a train compartment, Tom dexterously lifted Emmanuel's wallet and threw it over the transom to his brother Armstrong, who was waiting outside the door. Emmanuel gave hot pursuit, but when he pounded on the door of the compartment where he thought the culprit had taken refuge, he was greeted by a shower of cold water poured over the transom—and a lady's screams. Custer then appeared and sternly questioned his father's attempt to break into a lady's quarters. Not long after, Emmanuel took his revenge by pretending to a steamboat crowd that his two sons were strangers who had picked his pocket. He had to confess the joke when the crowd began to lay angry hands on them.[9]

Emmanuel's espousal of boyish humor into advanced adulthood was undoubtedly a model for Custer, who seems—even in the report of a doting wife—to have sometimes displayed insensitivity in his pursuit of humor. He was amused when the clothes their maid had just hung out to dry were blown all over and had to be washed again; he thought it a wonderful joke to abruptly pick up a young woman and place her on the giant carcass of a dead buffalo—where she screamed in terror.[10] Some of Custer's harsh juvenile humor was shared by his cavalry cohort, who put a premium on toughness. Libbie once remarked that she felt sorry for men learning how to ride since the custom was to greet even hard and injurious falls with "a roar of derision." She records without comment a ritual of the hunt that required the other officers to rush upon the man who brought down the first deer and smear him thoroughly with the animal's blood.[11]

From the very first, however, Autie, as his family always called him in imitation of his first efforts to pronounce Armstrong, had been a typically active and irrepressible boy.[12] His cousin Mary Custer remembered that when she met Autie for the first time, the nine year old told her that if she was his cousin, he guessed he ought to kiss her—which he promptly did. He was known to be particularly mischievous—not bad—"just full of life and always ready to do anything which had a semblance of daring in it."[13] This sometimes brought him into conflict with his father, whom Mary Custer remembered as a "very strict disciplinarian." On one occasion Emmanuel gave his son a severe whipping for visiting his cousin without permission.

Emmanuel Custer had come to New Rumley, Ohio, in 1806 as a blacksmith, the only one for miles around, but in 1849 he gave up this trade in town for a farm, eighty acres of hilly land that could not easily support his family of nine.[14] Like most Americans, he wanted to own land, if only a subsistence-level farm. He was known and respected in his community, a justice of the peace for many years and a trustee of the New Rumley Methodist Society.[15]

Looking back on his boyhood, Custer would reassure his father that he had not felt the family's poverty: "I never wanted for anything necessary. You and Mother instilled into me principles of industry, self-reliance, honesty. You taught me the value of temperate habits, the difference between right and wrong."[16]

When Autie was thirteen, his parents decided to send him to Monroe, Michigan, to live with his married half-sister, Lydia Ann Kirkpatrick Reed, and take advantage of a good school there. Three years later he was back, having obtained a position to teach in the Beech Point district school. One pupil of the sixteen-year-old Custer remembered him as "socially inclined," jovial, and full of life. Another recalled him as pleasant and well liked by both sexes. His long fair hair made her think "what a pretty girl he would make."[17] At this time he played the accordian, evidently a passing enthusiasm since we never hear of it again.

Custer's students observed the traditional practice of locking out the teacher until he brought them Christmas treats, but when the boys of the class barred the door, Custer refused to play his part. Instead, he went off to protest to the district school directors.[18] This is not an anecdote that turns up in Libbie's loving memoirs of her husband, and the response seems uncharacteristic of a good-tempered young man who played his share of practical jokes. Being bodily ejected from his classroom might have injured the teenaged schoolmaster's precarious dignity.

In November 1855, the McNeely Normal School opened in Hopedale, Ohio, and Custer enrolled for a term while continuing to teach school. His class notebook from that time gives an impression of conscientious application in its detailed outline of every lesson. It also gives some idea of the strongly partisan education he was receiving. A page headed Men of America formulaically invokes national superiority in every category:

> The greatest man take him all in all of the last hundred years—was George Washington an American
>
> The greatest Doctor of Divinity was Jonathan Edwards—an American
>
> The greatest Philosopher was Benjamin Franklin—an American
>
> The greatest living Sculptor is Hiram Powers—an American
>
> The greatest living Historian is William Ch. Prescott—an American
>
> The great Ornithologist was J. J. Audubon—an American
>
> The greatest Lexicographer since the time of Johnson was Noah Webster—an American
>
> The greatest inventors of modern times were Fulton, Fitch, Whitney and Morse—all Americans[19]

It was during the summer of 1856 that Custer decided to apply to West Point, but it was by no means clear at that time that he would commit himself to a military career. For a boy without financial resources like himself, going to West Point was a way of getting a good education at government expense.

Long before the term was coined, Custer's appointment to West Point may nevertheless be considered the first instance of "Custer's luck." Appointments to the military academy were usually political, and Custer was at the disadvantage of coming from a family of Democrats—Democrats of modest means and therefore modest influence—in a Republican state. In pursuit of his goal, he wrote to and then visited Congressman John Bingham, but without a lucky circumstance, he might have had nothing further than a polite reception for his pains. The seventeen-year-old Custer happened to be in love with a young woman named Mary Holland and was speaking to her of marriage, an idea that her father, a Republican, opposed. Alexander Holland may have seen an opportunity to get rid of the unwanted suitor by sending him to West Point, where he would be unable to marry for five years, and so may have furthered Custer's cause with Bingham.[20]

Later, when the one-time candidate had become a famous general, Bingham said that Custer's letter of application had immediately impressed him. Read today, the document seems merely an unvarnished request for information, characterized perhaps by honesty, but hardly by the originality that Bingham also claimed to have found.[21]

In spite of the spirit in which he wrote to his sister early on, saying that he would not leave West Point "for any amount of money, for I would rather have a good education and no money than a fortune and be ignorant,"[22] Custer never distinguished himself academically there: he graduated last in his class of thirty-four. As he himself pointed out, a number of Southern cadets had resigned before graduation—had they stayed, he suggested, one of *them* might have ended up at the foot of the class.[23] Nonetheless, even when the class was complete, Custer was always near the bottom.[24] Former classmates remembered him as the "dare-devil of the class," who rarely studied.[25]

Just over a hundred years later, Tobias Wolff would be taunted with the name of Custer when he finished forty-ninth out of forty-nine in his officer candidate school class, and he would offer a similar assessment: "It wasn't as disgraceful as it looked. There'd been one hundred twenty of us to start with. But it was still pretty bad."[26]

In fact, a poor record at West Point hardly indicated a lack of military ability. The Academy had a reputation for high standards. As its historian, Stephen Ambrose, has observed, "The course of studies was so rigorous that only those with outstanding ability or excellent preparation could stay in the school."[27] In Custer's class, only sixty-eight of one hundred and eight potential students passed the entrance examination.[28] In June of 1858, the completion of Custer's first term as a full-fledged cadet, eight more members of his class were dropped; two years later, only thirty-five of those sixty remained.[29]

Custer's failure to apply himself to academics put him in the company of several other West Pointers who became famous during the Civil War, most notably Ulysses Grant and Philip Sheridan.[30] Grant remarked in his memoirs that he had spent so much of his time at West Point reading novels from the library that he had little time to review his lessons.[31] Anticipating family criticism of his mediocre performance, cadet Sheridan had attempted to explain his low ranking in a letter to his sister. "You may think my standing not very good, but out of the 40 that stand above me in Math., 15 are graduates of other colleges," he told her, adding for good measure, "and 30 of them can speak the French language."[32]

That Custer did not find academic subjects engaging becomes clear in a letter he wrote to his cousin Augusta. He dutifully responded to a question of hers by enumerating all of his courses—drawing, painting, and two foreign languages in addition to such subjects as "natural philosophy" and "sword exercise"—but for only one subject did he offer any qualifying comment: "I take lessons in riding every day, this I enjoy very much."[33] Most of the subjects Custer enumerated would not be predictive of ability in battle. Moreover, the West Point curriculum did not include strategy or leadership, subjects whose lack would soon be felt when war broke out.[34]

At greater length and with more enthusiasm than he wrote of any of his studies, Custer's letter goes on to describe attending a dance, an adventure that involved breaking several academy rules. It was necessary to pretend to go to bed at ten o'clock, then rise, place a dummy in bed in case of a surprise inspection, and sneak out wearing civilian clothes—forbidden attire. After the ball, the cadets sneaked back to their rooms shortly before reveille at 5:00 A.M. Custer told his cousin that he was "in poor humor for hard study during the next day."[35]

Such behavior was in keeping with Tully McCrea's assertion that Custer was "always connected with all the mischief that is going on and never studies any more than he can possibly help."[36] Another contemporary, J. M. Wright, identified Custer as "the rarest man" he knew at West Point. Newly arrived at the Academy, Wright first saw Custer returning from leave: "From a hundred throats went out in various forms of ejaculation 'Here comes Custer.' . . . I failed to note anything in his appearance that warranted the attention he received. I saw only an undeveloped looking youth, with a poor figure, slightly rounded shoulders and an ungainly walk. But this was Custer, then considered an indifferent soldier, a poor student, and a perfect incorrigible." Later, Wright learned that Custer was a "roystering, reckless cadet, always in trouble, always playing some mischievous pranks, and liked by every one."[37] McCrea, at one time Custer's roommate, wrote to his cousin Belle that he "admired and partly envied Custer's free and careless way, and the perfect indifference he had for everything. It was all right with him whether he knew his lesson or not; he did not allow it to trouble him."[38]

One lesson he certainly failed to learn was the translation of a French sentence that read "Léopold duc d'Autriche se mettit sur les plaines de Silesie," a mundane description of Leopold, duke of Austria, positioned on the plains of Silesia. Custer's fanciful version had the leopard, the duck, and the ostrich meeting upon the plains of Silesia.[39] Languages were evidently not Custer's favorite subjects, for another of the few classroom anecdotes preserved for posterity has him asking the Spanish professor how to say "class is dismissed" in Spanish. When that innocent obliged, Custer rose and led the class out.[40]

Those who knew Custer at West Point glossed over his academic performance to remember fondly the escapades he engineered or participated in. Morris Schaff, a year behind Custer, recalled that he "fooled away many an hour that should have been devoted to study" in the company of Custer and his friend Jim Parker.[41] Another classmate recalled a midnight raid on first-year cadets, who were divided into a tall group and a short group. The plan was to switch the clothes of the two groups, but the perpetrators had to escape with the job half done.[42]

Custer had many other ways of getting into trouble besides the honorable custom of deviling plebes. The record of his demerits, contained in the *Register of Delinquencies* for 1856–61, reveals a certain amount of boyish activity such as throwing snowballs or stones and "trifling at formation to march from supper." The gregarious Custer was guilty of inappropriate socializing in the form of "loitering, visiting," and talking. Other offenses are more the result of disinclination than immaturity: his clothing was often in some disarray, although this did not have to be excessive to incur demerits. On one occasion his gun was "grossly out of order."[43]

Long after their West Point days together, Evan Andruss wrote to Libbie that her husband's "boyish—but harmless—frolics kept him in constant hot water," so that he spent most Saturday afternoons doing extra guard duty.[44] Custer himself recalled that if his memory served him right, "I devoted sixty-six Saturdays to this method of vindicating outraged military law during my cadetship of four years."[45] Surveying this record, one Custer partisan concluded that Custer "simply could not obey all the hundred and one petty rules laid down for cadet behavior."[46] Petty or not, cadet rules were designed to inculcate the strict obedience to authority that is the first principle of military organization. That the undisciplined cadet became a field commander who embraced a strict discipline is not necessarily anomalous, however. To seventeen and eighteen year olds, the relationship between polishing one's boots properly at the Academy and winning victories on the battlefield might well appear tenuous, but Custer's military career began under wartime conditions where the value of discipline became immediately apparent, and as an exceptionally young general, he wanted both officers and men to take him seriously. At Bull Run, his first Civil War battle, Custer noticed that even in a chaotic retreat, the regulars maintained their formation: "The value of discipline was clearly shown in this crisis by observing the manner of the few regular troops, as contrasted with the raw and undisciplined three months' men. The regular soldiers never for a moment ceased to look to their officers for orders and instructions."[47]

His early and impressive successes would confirm Custer's belief in the soundness of his own judgment in military matters. By the end of the war severity was such a fixed principle of his leadership that the man who had been indifferent to military discipline at West Point became known as a commander who believed in absolute authority. "To enforce obedience to his authority," he wrote at the beginning of his Civil War memoirs, "no penalty should be deemed too severe."[48] Perhaps his very attitude as a cadet influenced him later; as he had not been deterred from numerous infractions at West Point, he might have felt that only the most extreme measures would make an impression on men inclined to be disobedient. There is also, it might be added, an appreciable difference between following strict orders and imposing them on others.

In any case, demerits were not taken very seriously at West Point, and few escaped them.[49] Philip Sheridan had 189, and most of the fifty-two graduates of his class, the class of 1853, had similarly high scores. Marcus Reno, the man who would later be Custer's second in command at the Little Bighorn, had 61 demerits in his last term alone, while Custer had 52 in his last. Reno's demerits were much like Custer's, the result of a generally undisciplined attitude that could be attributed to immaturity, but Custer's lackluster performance was offset by a quality that Reno did not have—popularity. Reno also went steadily downhill academically: as he moved through four years, his class rank slipped from twenty to twenty-nine to thirty-two to thirty-five. Custer was consistently at the bottom of his class.[50]

Custer was devoted to West Point—he even expressed a wish to be buried there—but he resisted the clubbiness associated with its graduates, perhaps because he was a Westerner and a country boy from a family of Democrats. To someone who solicited his membership in an Association of the Graduates of the United States Military Academy, he responded with a certain passion that while he yielded to none in "love and admiration of our Alma Mater," he was totally opposed to such an organization. He spoke for those officers who had not gone to West Point but had instead received their training in "the best of all military schools"—battle. To make a distinction between the two groups seemed to him invidious.[51]

Although most of the professors at West Point were Easterners, and

Eastern students tended to have the edge there—generally having had better scholastic preparation than those from the South or West—an egalitarian spirit like Custer's was encouraged by the academy's regimen.[52] All lived under the same spartan condition, one cadet wrote: "In a few days after entrance, external inequalities vanish as if by magic. Duties, privileges, dress, rooms, food, all are alike; no one is permitted to have money, or at least to spend it. In a week every sign of external inequality has disappeared."[53] The parents of cadets presented a fairly homogeneous picture as well. In the *Circumstances of the Parents of Cadets 1842 to 1879, No. 1* they were categorized as indigent, reduced, moderate, or affluent (with subcategories of city, town, and country). Of seventy-seven in Custer's class, only five were classified as affluent and four as reduced.[54] His own parents were to be found in the columns headed "moderate" and "country."

Custer graduated from West Point in 1861, but the final episode of his life there was a court-martial for neglect of duty in failing to take the proper steps "to suppress a quarrel" when he was officer of the guard.[55] Instead, he had encouraged it by saying "let there be a fair fight." The two cadets involved testified that the incident had been a mere "scuffle," without injuries or noise, and the officer who broke up the proceedings reported favorably on Custer's previous conduct. Given this testimony and the urgent need for trained officers in the wartime army, Custer was treated lightly, sentenced to be reprimanded in orders. He himself believed that some of his classmates already in Washington used political influence to get him released quickly.[56]

Looking back on his West Point days, Custer candidly wrote that future cadets would not benefit from a study of his career there "unless as an example to be carefully avoided."[57] But it is equally unlikely that Custer would have been a better commander if he had compiled a better record at the military academy. After graduation he went directly to the battlefield, where he became for a time the army's youngest general, consistently distinguishing himself in four years of constant fighting. His difficulties in the postwar army are more probably attributable to the loss of status he had to endure after a success of such magnitude.

2

Libbie Bacon, Libbie Bacon

How I love my name Libbie BACON. Libbie B-A-C-O-N. Bacon. Libbie Bacon.

—Libbie to Custer, January 1864

When plans for her wedding to George Armstrong Custer were being made, Libbie Bacon reluctantly consented to her father's wish that she use the name Elizabeth on the invitations, a name she did not connect with herself. "How I love my name Libbie BACON," she wrote to her future husband. "Libbie B-A-C-O-N. Bacon. Libbie Bacon."[1] She also loved the happy life associated with her identity as the beloved only child of a leading citizen of Monroe, Michigan, Judge Daniel Bacon. As she had written in her diary when she was eighteen, "Our home is very delightful to us and cosy and pleasant to all. We are a very happy family."[2] Her home, she told Custer four years later, was "the spot the dearest to me in the world."[3] As well it might be, for more than the usual reasons. During the critical years of early adolescence Libbie had virtually had no home: when her mother died, her heartbroken father had closed the family house, moved into a hotel, and placed Libbie in a local boarding school. The diary entry that announced her mother's death goes on to record, "our pleasant home will be broken up."[4]

In fact, by many standards, Libbie Bacon had a difficult childhood. She was the only one of four children to live to adulthood; at the age of twelve she lost her mother; and when she was in her late teens, her father remarried, introducing a stepmother into their close relationship.

But Libbie failed to respond negatively to any of these cues: she was happy, secure, and popular. She thought it a pleasant and undeserved benefit that people pitied her for her motherlessness and accordingly made allowances for her. "Poor motherless Libbie Bacon," she recalled them saying, almost relishing the expression that described and yet failed to encompass her condition. Shortly after her mother's death Judge Bacon visited Libbie at Grand Rapids, where she had been sent to stay with her mother's relatives, and reported with some wonderment that she was "without gloom, without a murmur at her sad fate—and even happy!"[5] Such a seemingly quick recovery could have been a measure of Libbie's desire to please her father. On the death of her mother she had confided to her diary her hope that "the Lord will spare me to my father for I am his only comfort left."[6]

Of the lost brother and sisters, the former the apple of her father's eye and a sibling she must have dimly remembered herself, there are no tortured musings or symptoms of survivor's guilt—only the matter-of-fact assessment that their loss doubly endeared her to her father.[7] She eagerly welcomed her stepmother into the family, which became without any painful transition a mutually affectionate unit of three. As he contemplated her approaching marriage, Daniel Bacon wrote to his daughter, "It has been your good fortune to have had two devoted and affectionate mothers, and each have [*sic*] often said to me that their wish and hearts desire was to make your home a pleasant one that when separated from that home you might look back to it with pleasurable feelings and recollections."[8] Libbie always did.

She had the wisdom, a wisdom that at this early stage of her life seems more born than bred, to count her blessings and consider herself fortunate. Her father was socially esteemed and financially comfortable, and she was reputed to be the prettiest girl in Monroe, surrounded by friends and admirers.

A good student with a flair for art and literature, she achieved her ambition to be valedictorian when she graduated from the Boyd Seminary in June 1862. As she wrote to one of her aunts, everyone liked her address, her father was "greatly affected," and the papers "were very kind in their criticism."[9] Libbie's cousin Rebecca, who had come to Monroe for the occasion, sent her parents a glowing appraisal of their niece: "Libbie has a splendid disposition and lovely temperament. I never saw her superior in qualities that go to make up a noble woman. Her parents never restrain her, but encourage her mimicries, drolleries and schoolgirl gaieties."[10]

The next milestone for a young woman in the 1860s would be finding a husband, but Libbie was in no hurry. Confident in attracting others, she could write in her diary, "I don't see the use in stewing as some girls do for fear the fellows won't like them and they won't ever be married. If no one ever comes that I love then I shall be a 'spinster' but to be one from necessity or one from pleasure are different things. I am sure of never ranking among the first named."[11]

This was an honest appraisal rather than conceit. Before George Armstrong Custer decided that he would overcome all obstacles to make Libbie his wife, she had had a number of suitors, some of whom she imagined she was taking seriously. When Custer was just one of many young men who paid attention to the twenty-year-old Libbie, Judge Bacon was also noticing his daughter's suitors. In 1862 he wrote to his sister Charity that "Libbie like her Aunt Harriet has many suitors, many of the mustached, gilt-striped and Button kind, more interesting to her than to me."[12] Once the war broke out he was, in fact, particularly afraid that Libbie would want to marry a soldier.

Libbie's diary reveals an earnest attempt to sort out her feelings about the men who were "licentious," that is, displayed an interest in her. She would always have a light touch with regard to romance, the ability to take in stride a man's attraction to her, even when it was unwelcome or inappropriate. A comment she made about Mr. Highwood, her art teacher, is representative in acknowledging her effect on the smitten man while at the same time placing it in perspective: "I believe him to be *licentious beaucoup*. And if I made the slightest advance he would take me in his arms and kiss me to suffocation! But he is a fine teacher and 'tis a pity we can't have everything good combined."[13] Libbie was romantic, allowing herself to imagine a passionate scene, but she was not silly, nor were her own feelings involved. Since Mr. Highwood's "licentiousness" was unthreatening, it did not affect Libbie's appraisal of him as a "fine teacher." Her last comment is a tidy moral that both forgives and dismisses.

During the holiday season of 1861 she wrote in her journal: "Mr. B's blue eyes followed me about somewhat closely. I believe him to be licentious for he wouldn't look so out of his eyes if he wasn't. Foolish for me to write all this but how could I but be flattered by his marked attentions preferring me to the rest."[14] The entry is typical of Libbie's honest observation and analysis of her own reaction. Firmly situated in the Protestant tradition, she searched her heart repeatedly to discover her own response to such signals.

Mr. Bissell, still another attractive and attracted man, delighted Libbie with his "splendid black eyes, a black mustache and ditto hair. Yes I like him," she wrote forthrightly, "and we became acquainted quickly. He gives compliments under such a garb of beautiful language it makes me swallow them with pleasure." The same social occasion provoked thoughts about two other men: Mr. Brown, who "*looks books full* out of his eyes," and Elliot Slocum, who is "*better, truer, loves me more*."[15]

With all of these splendid eyes and mustaches hovering over her, Libbie worried if she would know the real thing when it came along. Of the young minister Mr. Dutton she confessed, "I am quite taken up with him. Yes indeed I could learn easily to love him. I wish I wasn't so susceptible. I fear I shall never know who I do love!"[16] She frequently found herself reciprocating when she knew that an attractive man liked her: "I cannot be different from what I am. I am so lively and unreserved and talkative, and I can't be cold and dignified and treat them as if they were wood and marble. I must be natural."[17]

But it became clear to Libbie during a two-week period in which she saw Mr. Dutton almost every day that she found the minister a stimulating companion without being in love with him: "I was mighty near loving him but I am just as far away now from it. I never can." When Mr. Dutton declared his love a week later and kissed her, "I knew *then* he loved me . . . but no love was in my bosom for him, simply admiration for his intellect."[18]

George Armstrong Custer was on leave from the war and visiting his sister in Monroe when Libbie was formally introduced to him in November 1862. She was not impressed. "This meeting, which was to change her entire life," an early biographer writes, "is barely mentioned in her journal though one wonders what was written on a small portion of about six lines that was torn out of the book just under her simple statement that she had met him."[19] Possibly Libbie had made some slighting comment about Custer that later embarrassed her: reminiscing after his death, she wrote that "with the critical and hard eye of a girl I decided I would never like him because his hair was light and I despised his military overcoat as it was lined with yellow (which I thought was his choice rather than regulation)."[20] On the first anniversary of that consequential meeting she could not remember what they had said to each other then.

For some time Custer was simply one of many young men who gravitated to the pretty daughter of Judge Bacon. Libbie noticed his persistence, but she was used to such attention: Elliot Bates, for one, had told her that if she did not marry him, he would have no wife.[21] Not long after meeting Custer, Libbie wrote to her good friend Laura Noble, "I *don't care for* him except as an escort."[22] This was soon to change.

Although she had a lively personality, Libbie had always been an obedient and conscientious daughter. In 1859, when she was seventeen, she attempted to evaluate herself in her diary and concluded that "there is *much* to do to make me what I should be, yet I cannot but feel that I have improved much."[23] To her father she wrote in the same year, "I want to be a *good* woman and try and have you *proud* of me."[24] When her father would not allow her to go on a sleigh ride with a party of friends during the Christmas season of 1860, she wrote in her diary, "Father said No for I went last year to my first ride and the company didn't get home till 5 o'clock. . . . 'Tis, of course, all right and Father knows best but its hard and a great disappointment." She also wanted to learn to skate, but "father thinks it not best." At a party at her good friend Nettie Humphrey's, "I wanted to dance so badly that I almost cried several times but I knew father wouldn't like it so I did not."[25]

George Armstrong Custer's aggressive courtship of Libbie would be the first important occasion on which Libbie found herself opposed to her father. She thought she was prepared to be dutiful regardless of her feelings, and she also thought, at first, that she had not fully succumbed to Custer's determined wooing. Her diary entries tell another story, however—that of an earnest young woman committed to resisting her heart in order to please her father, yet failing to understand that she was already in love.

Tully McCrea, who had been at West Point with Custer, described his friend as a ladies' man of the love-'em-and-leave-'em variety, an indication that Custer had had experience in winning the affections of women.[26] Custer's skillful approach to Libbie was commensurate with such experience. First of all, he behaved with decision and determination: he proposed the second time they met and continued to renew his suit at every opportunity. Libbie could be in no doubt about the strength of his intention. He told her "he would sacrifice every earthly hope" to gain her love, convincing her that he loved "with an intensity that few know of."[27] He also communicated a sense of her high value, prizing and remembering every word she said. Before long, Libbie was afraid that Custer had spoiled her for other men: "Certainly I don't believe I shall *ever* find some qualities that C has so admirably combined in his character in anyone else." She reiterated in her diary that Custer has spoiled her: "Everything I said or did was remembered & treasured by him. He was more devoted than I ought to expect in any other man."[28]

One entry confided a passionate fantasy, which is then curbed by her belief that she must renounce Custer's love: "I long so to put my arms about his neck & kiss him & how often I lay my head on his breast—in imagination—and feel how sweet it would be to make him entirely happy. . . . Dear, *dear* man, I never can tell him how deeply I have felt for him, yes & toward him. It is *hard* to crush out the affection I feel for him."[29] Another entry expresses the same desire to abandon herself to her feelings while at the same time obeying her father by not having such feelings: "I wish I could . . . kiss him a thousand times and say everything I desire or think to him & then blot that day out of my mind forever." In March of 1863 she wrote, "I have everything I wish & have had nearly all my life and now one thing is refused me I sometimes almost rebel. But I shall conquer. In time I'll learn not to regret or reprove."[30] A few months later she was still conflicted. "I am trying hard to tear Autie's image from my heart," she told her journal. Then, in her candid fashion, she added, "No, I am not!" followed by "I will too!"[31] Whatever arguments she marshaled against Custer—for example, that they shared no similar tastes—were overwhelmed by the intensity of her love.

Instead of learning in time to give Custer up, when he returned to the army in October of 1863, Libbie realized that her feelings were strong enough to challenge her father. She wrote in her diary, "Dear C—try as I did to suppress the 'fancy' for six months it did no good. The *fancy* I know was more, it was *love*. I do love him and have all the time. He is *dear, dear*. I *tried* so hard to think it was an idle, passing fancy. But I love him." At the same time, her father's wishes were still law: "I cannot go on tho' until I talk to Father. I am going to do so tonight if I can. It is very hard for me to do so but I *must* and, if Father says *no* I shall abide by his decision." In spite of this resolution, she immediately continues, "Oh how dear he is. I love him so. His words linger in my ears, his kisses on my lips. I forget everything sometimes when I think of him."[32] Libbie's conflict was happily resolved by her father's approval of Custer as a suitor.

Despite his early misgivings and hesitations, Daniel Bacon ultimately found himself well pleased with George Armstrong Custer, an opinion he adhered to until his death. When he at last gave the young man his blessing as Libbie's fiancé, he apologized for having kept Custer in suspense for so long, the result of his attachment to "an only offspring." But in the end, what Libbie wanted was all that mattered to her father, "her present and future happiness, for which I have lived." Finally, he concluded, "your explanatory and excellent letter, a full face and personal interview with our reliable and mutual friend Col. ———, to say nothing of incidental interviews with Judge Christiancy, Col. Grosvenor & others as well as letters from the Potomac independent of interviews with as well as the wishes of my daughter perfectly reconciles me to yield my hearty assent to the contemplated union."[33] Custer had passed a demanding test indeed!

Libbie had wanted to be engaged to the man of her choice, but she showed no inclination to rush into marriage. When she was seventeen she had written to her father that she liked acting "*free* and *girl like.*"[34] To Custer she now wrote, "The very thought of marriage makes me tremble. Girls have so much fun." She implored him not to even mention marriage for "at least a year."[35]

Custer overcame her scruples just as he had overridden Judge Bacon's opposition: he and Libbie were married in Monroe on February 9, 1864, little more than fourteen months after their first meeting.

When Daniel Bacon wrote to a sister about the wedding, he pronounced himself satisfied in all respects—by Libbie as a young woman, by the marriage festivities, by the mutual devotion of the couple. Yet he could not help but speculate: "What awaits Custer no one can say. Libbie may be a widow or have a maimed husband."[36]

Libbie moved easily from her father to her husband, both of whom admired and indulged her while exercising authority over her. Yet in her married life, whose beginning was synonymous with her entry into adulthood, psychological demons appeared that may have had their origin in her early experience of bereavement. At the time of these losses she had demonstrated no symptoms of unresolved grief, yet contemporary clinical research suggests that such experience "sensitizes the individual to loss, evoking unresolved grief at subsequent separations."[37] Libbie became a fearful person, hiding under the bed when it thundered, closing her eyes when negotiating difficult passages on the march, and, above all, fearing constantly for her husband's safety. To some degree this was a reasonable response to his dangerous profession, but in Libbie it became excessive, as if those long-buried sisters, brother, and mother remained an active reminder of the pain of loss.

3

"The Honorable and Glorious Profession of Arms"

> It requires no extensive knowledge to inform me what is my duty to my country, my command. . . . "First be sure you're right, then go ahead!" I ask myself, "Is it right?" Satisfied that it is so, I let nothing swerve me from my purpose.
>
> —Custer to Annette Humphrey, October 9, 1863

The American Civil War was intensely fratricidal: the opponents spoke the same language, adhered to the same religion, and could not be ethnically differentiated from each other. Their military leaders had all gone to the same school, the United States Military Academy at West Point, where they had learned to place honor and duty above all else.*

It was a war that set a number of records for carnage. The First Battle of Bull Run "was by far the largest and most costly in American history up to that time"—around 600 were killed on each side.[1] Compared to later battles, these numbers are paltry: in a single day at Antietam "more than twice as many Americans were killed or mortally wounded than in the War of 1812, the Mexican War, and the Spanish-American War combined."[2] At the battle of the Wilderness, the firing was the most constant and rapid ever heard on the North American continent.[3]

*Custer's farewell to troops leaving the army, May 12, 1863, says in part: "The record of their deeds . . . will live in history, and in the memory of their comrades who still continue to serve the country and its cause in the honorable and glorious profession of arms."

Ultimately, some 620,000 would die in Civil War battles—more than the total of all the nation's other wars combined.[4]

Custer's attitude toward warfare was shaped by his education at West Point. He might have been an indifferent student and an undisciplined cadet, but he absorbed the spirit of the institution wholeheartedly. The very principle that brought him trouble on the eve of graduation—allowing two cadets to fight rather than stopping the fight, as his duty required—would govern his behavior in the field: a fair fight, and may the best man win. Custer believed in the Union cause without harboring personal animosity toward his friends and classmates who were on the other side. He respected their defense of their chosen country even as he asserted the superiority of his own choice. Years later, he wrote of his roommate, James Parker, "We separated; he to make his way . . . to the seat of the Confederate Government, and accept a commission under a flag raised in rebellion against the Government that had educated him, and that he had sworn to defend; I to . . . report for such duty as might be assigned to me in the great work which was then dearest and uppermost in the mind of every loyal citizen of the country."[5]

One historian believes that Custer's court-martial was a fortunate fall that prevented him from coming to Washington with the rest of his class, "indistinguishable among so many, and not apt to have been singled out for special attention."[6] The "special attention" he was singled out for as soon as he arrived in Washington—taking a message to the commander in chief, the legendary General Winfield Scott—did not, however, lead to particular advancement. Custer's real break came almost a year after his arrival at the front, when he came to the attention of General George B. McClellan, commander of the Army of the Potomac. In May of 1862 McClellan's army needed to cross the Chickahominy River to continue its progress toward Richmond. With this in mind, McClellan's chief engineer, General John G. Barnard, chose Lieutenant Custer to jump into the Chickahominy and find out how deep it was. Without hesitation, Custer jumped in, exposing himself to the possibility of enemy fire from the opposite bank. On that first plunge, luck got him across the river without attracting enemy attention, and, as he would habitually do during the war, Custer accomplished more than expected: he ascertained the depth of the river *and* scouted the enemy's position, returning with a plan for an attack that he was then instrumental in carrying out. The man in charge of this raid, Lieutenant Nicholas Bowman, reported that "Lieutenant Custer, Fifth United States Cavalry . . . was the first to cross the stream, the first to open fire upon the enemy, and one of the last to leave the field."[7] For this notable effort he was summoned to McClellan's headquarters.

As Custer told Libbie, "McClellan was always careful in dress and not only wore full uniform but expected his large staff to do the same. The foreigners on duty with him—the Duc de Chartres, Count de Paris and Prince Joinville—were resplendent in gold lace and foreign orders." Coming into headquarters in the wet and mud-spattered uniform he had worn into the river, Custer was "painfully aware of the contrast to the glittering perfection of General McClellan and his staff."[8] Perhaps his appreciation of the difference between his own unkempt self and the gold-lace aristocrats led to Custer's cultivation of a distinctive image once he began to receive public attention: before that moment, there is no evidence that he was ever concerned with his appearance.

In retrospect the episode would seem more funny than painful. When Libbie published an account of it in *Tenting on the Plains* she added to the manuscript version that her husband "often laughed" in drawing the "comical contrast between his Rozinante of a horse, rough, muddy and thin, his own splashed, weather-worn clothes, and the superbly equipped men who confronted him."[9] Appearances to the contrary, it would be the "dripping, muddy lieutenant" who became the applauded brilliant general rather than the "superbly equipped" members of McClellan's staff. Like McClellan himself, these men were more decorative than useful when it came to prosecuting the war.

In keeping with the behavior he would display throughout the Civil War, Custer was self-effacing when the commanding general thanked him and asked what he could do for him. McClellan remembered that Custer "replied very modestly that he had nothing to ask, and evidently did not suppose that he had done anything to deserve extraordinary reward."[10] The general, who, incidentally, had noticed that the young man was "carelessly dressed," promptly appointed Custer to his staff as a captain. "In those days," McClellan recalled, "Custer was simply a reckless, gallant boy, undeterred by fatigue, unconscious of fear; but his head was always clear in danger, and he always brought me clear and intelligible reports of what he saw when under the heaviest fire. I became much attached to him."[11] Custer later wrote in one of his articles about the Civil War: "The Chickahominy river, a stream which, however chargeable with some of the misfortunes of the Army of the Potomac, was almost literally a stepping-stone for my personal advancement."[12]

This would be the official beginning of "Custer's luck," that knack for being in the right place at the right time and—equally important—making the most of it. As General Nelson Miles remarked, the real definition of "Custer's luck" was the *judgment* to do the right thing at the right time: being on the scene was certainly a prerequisite, but in and of itself did not guarantee results.[13] Custer's successes were more a product of his ability to profit from opportunity.

In later years a Captain Biddle, who had observed the scene, told Libbie that a number of officers had been standing around, and "any one of us might have done it, one said to me . . . only Custer thought quicker than we did."[14] It was not only a matter of thinking "quicker," but of acting—fearlessly and decisively. Musing on the qualities that led to success in battle, Colonel Theodore Lyman told his wife that there were few officers who would place themselves at risk as a matter of choice: "They will go anywhere they are *ordered* and anywhere they believe it is their *duty* to go; but fighting for fun is rare; and unless there is a little of this in a man's disposition he lacks an element. Such men as Sprigg Carroll, Hays (killed), Custer and some others, attacked wherever they got a chance, and of their own accord."[15] Custer clearly had the disposition that produces effective military leadership: he led charges rather than directing from the rear, his energy never flagged, and—most important of all—he got results. As a general who served under him memorably described him, "unlike many equally brave and skilful officers, he was rarely content to hold a position or drive his enemy: he always gathered the fruit, as well as shook the tree of battle."[16]

Perhaps equally felicitous was Custer's sudden renunciation of alcohol early in the war. When he visited Monroe on leave in October 1861, his sister confronted him after a drunken spree and reportedly persuaded him to take the pledge.[17] Whatever the circumstances, in the future Custer would never meet his fortune with judgment muddled by drink.

Even before the serendipitous encounter with McClellan, Custer had given his allegiance to the general with all the fervor of his youth. "I have more confidence in him than any man living," he wrote to his parents, "and am willing to forsake everything and follow him to the ends of the earth and would lay down my life for him if necessary. I would fight anyone who said anything against him."[18] Custer's language smacks of the religious disciple, but his was, in fact, a fairly common view of the wildly popular general.

Not long after Custer seized the moment at the Chickahominy, a friend recalled running into the newly promoted Captain Custer and asking him how he had risen so rapidly. Custer showed him a group of prisoners he and Captain Brice had just captured "during a brilliant reconnaissance on the south side of the Chickahominy."[19] While Custer's initial crossing of the Chickahominy has long appealed to the imagination of chroniclers, it alone was not the "act of daring gallantry" that purchased McClellan's good opinion: what counted was the more tangible result, the second crossing with the raiding party.[20] Yet, to provide some perspective on this well-known episode, significant only in demonstrating Custer's abilities to the commander of the army—when McClellan later wrote up the raid he made no mention of Custer's part in it.[21]

As a captain on McClellan's staff, Custer seemed to be well positioned to advance. McClellan would soon be relieved of command, however, and Custer would be a lieutenant again, in need of impressing another commander and remaking his fortune. That he did so—that he ultimately succeeded under such different generals as McClellan, Pleasonton, and Sheridan—suggests that his rise was not due to the caprice of one commander or the reward for one chance accomplishment. The qualities of leadership Custer consistently demonstrated during the Civil War would have been as persuasive with almost any military superior.

Custer soon had his second chance for advancement with his assignment to the staff of the new commander of the cavalry, Alfred Pleasonton. As the general's representative, he accompanied a raiding party behind enemy lines in Virginia. The raid accomplished its objective, and in addition, Custer captured two fine horses, one of which he presented to General Pleasonton.[22] Pleasonton, described by Charles Francis Adams as "the bête noire of all cavalry officers,"[23] liked and appreciated Custer, who followed up his gift with a request. He asked the general to recommend him to Michigan's Governor Austin Blair to command a regiment of volunteers. More accurately, Pleasonton was asked to add his name to an impressive list of other generals who had already agreed to support Custer's candidacy: Burnside, Stoneman, Humphrey, Copeland, and Stahl. While this maneuvering showed ambition, it was at the same time no more than routine in the influence-ridden ambience of the wartime military.

Despite the connections Custer had established in the Army of the Potomac, he did not get the Michigan job—perhaps because of his youth, more likely because Governor Blair was paying a political debt with the appointment. As a consequence of Custer's failure however, a Monroe friend and supporter, Judge Isaac Christiancy, would later be able to write to him, "Every step of your remarkable advancement has been due to your own merit, without favor."[24] And before long, Custer would be in a position to reflect with satisfaction that he commanded the Second Michigan Brigade, which included the regiment he had hoped to lead. Eventually he would command an entire division.[25]

The path to this advancement opened unexpectedly when the difficult and much disliked Pleasonton recommended that Custer, along with two other promising young officers, be promoted to brigadier general of volunteers. Custer wrote to Judge Christiancy that he had never been more surprised, undoubtedly a genuine response considering the number of ranks and older officers he had vaulted over. Ambition had led Custer to hope that in the course of time he would be worthy of a star, but "in all my lofty flights I never supposed that in one sudden and unlooked for leap I should change the first lieutenant's shoulder strap . . . for the 'Star of a Brigadier.'"[26] He was twenty-three years old—at that time the Union army's youngest general.

Of the other men who were just as suddenly elevated on June 29, 1863, Wesley Merritt, five years Custer's senior, would continue on a parallel track with Custer for the remainder of the war, his name often coupled with Custer's for cavalry excellence. Captain George Sanford, who served under Merritt, felt that there was no need for invidious comparisons between them: "Both were at this time young men of wonderful brilliancy and great promise and well worthy of the devoted allegiance in which they were held by their troopers."[27]

General Sheridan often referred to Custer and Merritt as "his boys," but Merritt received a division command before Custer and also became Sheridan's chief of cavalry. War correspondent Charles Page wrote that Merritt had "an army reputation as a cavalry officer second to none," while even a partisan like Custer's first biographer, Frederick Whittaker, admitted that Merritt "was held in higher esteem by many, as not being thought so rash and reckless."[28] Whittaker is rather hard on Merritt nevertheless. In analyzing the difference between the two cavalry leaders, he concludes that Merritt lacked some indefinable quality: "It is hard to say what it was, except beauty of person and that chivalrous romantic spirit which pervaded Custer's every look and action"—in short, panache.[29] Instead, Merritt presented a serious, even intellectual appearance, but like Custer he had an iron constitution and a determined ambition.[30]

The two young generals would be friendly rather than bitter rivals during the war, matching each other's achievements through their very different styles. On October 9, 1864, in a battle that became popularly known as the Woodstock Races, Captain Sanford was sent with orders for Custer, arriving at the very moment when Custer was forming his lines for a charge. "I told him that the 1st Division [Merritt's] had captured five pieces of artillery," Sanford related, "and was about to ask him whether he had taken any, when he said, 'All right, hold on a minute and I'll show you six'; and immediately ordered the charge sounded. The division charged with a will and got their six pieces of artillery in less time than it has taken me to write about it."[31]

Custer had a tendency, natural in someone of his youth, to idolize those commanders who had favored him. While officers such as Charles Francis Adams, Jr., heartily rejoiced at Pleasonton's dismissal, it was a blow to Custer when the man who "never lost a battle and who gave the cavalry its character" was sent to obscurity. Pleasonton's replacement, unknown and hence at first distrusted, would turn out to be Custer's greatest patron, the commander closest to him in spirit and the most successful of the generals Custer served under. "Oddly built" has become a cliché in describing Philip Henry Sheridan: he was small, with a bullet-shaped head, and, as President Lincoln described him, was "one of those long-armed fellows with short legs that can scratch his shins without having to stoop over to do it."[32] An early biographer commented that on horseback Sheridan looked like a large man, while "on his feet, he is indeed peculiar."[33] He could be compared to Napoleon in other ways as well: Grant, at least, made the comparison in terms of Sheridan's military genius.[34] "No man would be better fitted to command all the armies in the field," he reportedly said.[35]

After a lackluster career at West Point, where, as an undersized Irish Catholic from the Midwest, he had been a ridiculed outsider, Sheridan began his army career in an unspectacular fashion. But once he saw active field duty, his brilliance was universally acknowledged and he rose rapidly. Those who saw Sheridan in action invariably turned to forceful images to describe his charisma. Unlike McClellan, he was not idolized by his men, but he could inspire them: Captain Henry A. DuBois, a medical officer serving at army headquarters, thought that Sheridan exerted a "magnetic influence" that at times could encompass the entire army.[36] For Sanford, "his influence on his men was like an electric shock . . . a stimulus strong enough to turn beaten and disorganized masses into a victorious army."[37] According to General Joshua L. Chamberlain, Sheridan's style of fighting was "rushing, flashing, smashing," and he communicated great intensity of purpose on the battlefield.[38] When Horace Porter, an officer on Grant's staff, reproached him for recklessly exposing his person at the front, Sheridan replied, "I have never in my life taken a command into battle, and had the slightest desire to come out alive unless I won."[39]

Sheridan would take rightful credit for transforming the Union cavalry from the army's errand boy, wasted in "ornamental service" and picket patrol, into an effective fighting force, capable of meeting and eventually beating the once superior Confederate cavalry.[40] On the same day that Merritt and Custer were vying to see who could capture the most guns from the Confederate cavalry commander General Jubal Early, Early wrote to his commander, Robert E. Lee, to confess that the cavalry of the Army of Northern Virginia, the most splendid fighting force of the first years of the war, could no longer hold its own: "The fact is, the enemy's cavalry is so much superior to ours, both in numbers and equipment, and the country is so favorable to the operations of cavalry that it is impossible for ours to compete with his."[41]

Pleasonton, who once called Custer "one of the finest cavalry officers in the world," regarded the military as the profession in which the character of one man, the commanding officer, stamped itself "indelibly" on the men serving under him. "I have seen men when they have been hesitating or excited," he told a joint congressional committee, "and some gallant, dashing man would come up, and you would see the men brighten up at once. You could see an immediate change to a different state of feeling."[42] Custer had this ability to lead, a charisma similar to Sheridan's in inspiring men to follow him in battle, to make his purpose theirs. W. H. Beebe, a veteran who wrote to Libbie Custer when the Custer monument was unveiled in Monroe, Michigan, remembered his experience as a nineteen-year-old soldier in a regiment of Custer's division: "How his command adored him; how willing we were to follow where he led." Beebe further recalled "the confidence each and all had in his good judgment, and the assurance that when he struck a blow on the enemy, it would be a victory."[43]

In the words of one cavalryman, when Custer took over the Third Division, "Every member felt proud to be known as one of Custer's division."[44] Men rejoiced because they knew it meant "a foremost place in every fight." As one regimental historian put it, "the boys liked General Custer, there was some get up and get to him."[45] This reputation came at a price: while Custer compiled an impressive array of battle victories, matériel destroyed, guns taken, and prisoners captured, his Michigan Brigade suffered more casualties proportionately than did any other comparable unit of federal cavalry.[46]

In the Grand Review of May 23, 1865, General Meade, commander of the Army of the Potomac, led the procession, followed by Wesley Merritt, acting commander of the cavalry in Sheridan's absence, and then Custer. Sheridan did not occupy his rightful place in the procession because of orders to go south immediately. Once again, as an eyewitness described the moment, Custer gave the event his individualistic stamp with a minor contretemps:

> Just as the division was turning the corner of Pennsylvania Avenue and 15th Street, an enthusiastic lady admirer of General Custer, rushed into the street past the guards lining the sidewalks, and presented the dashing cavalry leader a wreath of roses, which he gallantly received on the point of his saber. At this startling and unexpected occurrence, his high spirited and nervous charger took fright and reared, making a plunge and attempted flight, but his skilful rider managed quickly to check him up, and resumed his place at the head of the column.[47]

Since he was known to be a superb horseman, critics have accused Custer of engineering this episode to get attention.[48] Such suppositions seem yet another measure of the feeling that Custer incites rather than an accurate assessment of the incident. According to Libbie, Custer's striker had brought a snaffle bit whereas only a curb bit could control the high-spirited horse, and Custer was simply caught off guard when something startled his temperamental mount.[49] Custer's war record and colorful reputation had already given him the admiring attention of the public; the clumsiness of dropping his hat and sword in front of the presidential reviewing stand would only have detracted from this heroic image.

Writing his Civil War memoirs, Custer stated that he had participated in every battle from Bull Run to Appomattox, except Fredericksburg, "and in most of the important minor engagements and skirmishes."[50] In all that fighting there were many significant moments, among them Custer's contribution to the battle of Gettysburg, where, by soliciting an overriding order, he was able to join General David Gregg in repulsing Jeb Stuart's cavalry and thus prevent that body from acting in concert with Pickett's charge. The encounter was so fierce, one observer remembered, that "many of the horses were turned end over end and crushed their riders beneath them."[51] A man serving under Custer was later responsible for Stuart's death, one of the gravest Confederate losses. And, by the luck of rotation, Custer was in the lead at Appomattox, where he secured the rich prize of Lee's supply trains.[52] His Civil War experience came full circle, for just as he had captured the first enemy flag for the Army of the Potomac, so he received the Confederate flag of truce that marked the end of the war. Such moments, participating as they do in the events that make or break nations, symbolically bear the full weight of history.

4

Libbie's War

> I had rather live in a tent, outdoors with you than in a palace with another.
> —Libbie to Custer, January 1864

The war loomed over, even controlled, Libbie's courtship, marriage, and honeymoon. Autie had wooed her when he was home on various leaves, and on another they married and began their honeymoon. But Libbie received a bitter initiation into her husband's profession when the honeymoon was cut short by an order requiring Custer to report back to the field. He placed her in a boardinghouse in Washington where other officers' wives were living and set off immediately.

Any new bride would have been unhappy to have the war swallow her honeymoon, but for Libbie the anguish of abrupt parting would be felt over and over during the final phase of the war. Because she had invested everything in her husband, nothing ever compensated her for his absence, let alone the dangers he faced. "Promotion and triumph never made up for the days and nights of anxiety," she wrote, "and I could never have posed for the patriotic women in history who buckled on their husbands' swords. All the time I was in Washington the first waking moment was dread of another day."[1]

The newlyweds' desire to be together produced a novel arrangement: when the cavalry had a respite from fighting, usually while waiting for fresh horses to arrive, Libbie was allowed to come to camp. When the troops moved out again, she returned to Washington. Trips in either direction were apt to be at a moment's notice, so much so that her new brother-in-law, Tom Custer, also a cavalryman, joked that she slept with her boots buttoned to be ready to join her husband at any time.

While their interrupted honeymoon and early weeks of marriage gave Libbie her first lessons in the uncertainties of war and the trials of living with a military husband, her true baptism by fire came a little later. What she eventually found out about the mission that had required Custer's return to the front was of another order, for it included a disillusioning discovery about the military. As Libbie recorded it in her Civil War notes, Judson Kilpatrick, the general nicknamed "Kill Cavalry" by his own men for his reckless squandering of their lives, had used political influence to get approval to make a raid on Richmond early in 1864, purportedly to release Union prisoners from the notorious Libby Prison, but "in reality for his own aggrandizement." Custer was assigned the dangerous role of diverting Confederate attention from the major Union force. Supposedly, Kilpatrick said that Custer's life was a price he would willingly pay to attain the great end of freeing the prisoners.

Custer had told Libbie from the first that he did not want her to know official business, not because he distrusted her—he said diplomatically—but because "cunning staff officers" would ask her leading questions and learn from her blushes. But Libbie discovered the secret of the expedition anyway, probably from Custer's cook, Eliza, "to whom the officers told everything."

The knowledge shattered her "first ideal in military life." She had previously imagined that the courage to go into battle could be found only in company with other "equally glorious traits." To find instead that it could coexist with jealousy and "heartless indifference as to the lives of others" was a stunning blow, one that still resonated more than thirty years later. When she wrote her retrospective account on February 28, 1895, she made a grim observation: "The wind sighs through the prairie grass waving about the scattered stones on a Montana plain and moans over the sod that covers the bones of men who fell because they were deserted by dim cowards. So my military life began and ended with the actual knowledge of perfidy in officers."[2]

Newspaper reports gave Kilpatrick much credit. On March 3, 1864, the front page headline of the *New York Times* announced "Kilpatrick's Brilliant Cavalry Movement against Richmond." The army knew better, however: Custer's diversionary raid had been a success, but the main effort was a wretched failure.[3] The major objective had been to free the thousands of Union prisoners in Richmond jails, but after significant

Union losses of 340 men, 583 horses, and much weaponry, they still languished there.[4] It was also an enemy propaganda coup, for in addition to robbing and mutilating the body of Colonel Ulric Dahlgren, the Confederates removed his written orders, which their newspapers inaccurately reported to be the burning and sacking of Richmond.[5] Colonel Theodore Lyman, a member of General Meade's staff, more than shared Libbie's low opinion of Kilpatrick. He described him as "a frothy braggart, without brains and not over-stocked with desire to fall on the field. . . . He gets all his reputation by newspapers and political influence."[6]

When Libbie referred to the incident in her second book of memoirs, *Tenting on the Plains*, she made no mention of the behind-the-scenes politicking that produced the raid, Kilpatrick's indifference to Custer's fate, or her own outrage when she learned of these circumstances. Although she had decided opinions on matters affecting her husband, her books tend to ignore or downplay the underside of military life: the ambition that turned officers into bitter rivals and the personal animosities that often flourished in the close quarters of an army camp or frontier post. What she wanted to remember above all else was the happiness inspired by her husband's "joyous temperament, which would not look on the dark side."[7]

Beginning her marriage not only in wartime but in a war zone required a "sudden maturing" in the twenty-two-year-old girl who thought of herself as having grown up in "a sheltered home in a quiet town where I was spared all anxieties and cares." In her life as a newly married woman, she was always terrified about something: "I had to fight out many a battle whether to yield and run or face whatever awaited me. I had double terrors from real dangers and from imaginary ones." At the same time as she confronted unaccustomed sources of fear, she consciously understood that she must replace indulgence with self-control in order to share her husband's life as fully as possible: "It never occurred to me that a camp should be made any more comfortable on my account. I was impressed with the desire to obliterate myself as much as possible and also to prove my superiority to all the roughness of the life." If she complained, she knew she would be barred from camp, since Custer's bachelor commander, General Philip Sheridan, regarded the personal attachments of his officers as detrimental to good military service: "He groaned when they became engaged and was utterly discouraged when they married."[8] Once when Custer was sent into the field, leaving Libbie in camp, General Sheridan and his staff came to ask if they could do anything for her. She thanked them and declined assistance although—now alone in the Stevensburg, Virginia headquarters—she badly wanted to ask them to stay nearby. In time even Sheridan told his young general, "Custer, you are the only man whom matrimony has not spoiled for a charge," and Libbie became the only woman he allowed in camp. She would be there whenever the cavalry was idled between engagements, and when their orders came to move out, she returned to Washington, heedless of whoever saw her tears—"but oh, it was a *land* of tears then."[9]

After his wife had been commuting between Washington and camp for five months, Custer wrote enthusiastically to his sister, "Libbie is a true soldier's wife."[10] A few weeks later he again wrote to Ann that "it is all I can do to keep her [Libbie] from coming right out to camp in the govt wagons that come with our forage and rations. She likes the army about as much as I do."[11] Perhaps she did, but it is seldom clear how much Libbie liked anything for itself as opposed to liking it because of her husband. Living in an army camp could not have been comfortable or convenient for a woman as gently brought up as Libbie, but from the beginning to the end, she maintained that her husband's presence made any place the most desirable spot to her.

The conditions that war imposed on the young couple intensified the romantic fervor they brought to their marriage. Custer felt that no marriages were happier than those of the army because the recurrent separations meant repeated honeymoons. Each meeting was informed by the knowledge that it might be their last. When Libbie, terrified and miserable in her Washington boardinghouse, heard Autie's step on the stair, her happiness was overwhelming: "Nothing in the English language can describe the joy and relief of heart I had once more I saw my husband unharmed." Their partings were equally emotional: she would try to conceal her sobs as he, also overcome, would rush out and fling himself into the saddle—"oh these awful hours for women! How they blister the heart!" she wrote, remembering. Her father had urged Libbie to keep a diary, but she found it impossible: "All my strength and every nerve in me was taxed to the utmost while at the front and when I was obliged to return to Washington alone I was too broken hearted to do anything with a purpose."

Their wartime correspondence, however, confirms what Libbie recalled as "the rapture of fulfilled love." Elsewhere, in notes written in 1917, she spoke of "the marvel of it all and the mystery of two souls discovering in each other the mystery, effulgence, exultation." Both were ardent, but Libbie's style is more open and direct, while his is often formal and literary. "Neither tongue nor pen can express the intensity of my love," he wrote to her. One letter concluded: "Need I repeat to my darling that while living she is my all, and if Destiny wills me to die, wills that my country needs my death, my last prayer will be for her, my last breath will speak her name and that Heaven will not be Heaven till we are joined together. . . . Yours through time and eternity, Autie."[12]

Early on in the marriage a telling incident revealed the dynamics of the Custers' relationship. His army wagon, containing Libbie's letters along with his other personal effects, was captured by Confederates at Trevillian Station. In his somewhat stiff style Autie wrote to Libbie that he did "not relish the idea of others amusing themselves with them [her letters], particularly as some of the expressions employed . . . Somebody must be more careful hereafter in the use of *double entendu*."[13] For Libbie, news that Autie had survived still another dangerous battle eclipsed all else. She replied that the idea of "some rebel . . . devouring [her] epistles" was of little consequence, and defended what she had written because "there can be nothing low between man and wife if they love each other."[14] In taking this position Libbie simply embraced a standard Victorian belief: women were expected to be purer than men, but the purity of a married woman was not required to be asexual or passionless.[15] At the same time, her utter lack of concern for the violation of their intimate communications would be unusual, except in light of how unimportant everything else seemed to Libbie next to Custer's safety.

Receiving her unrepentent response, Custer apologized for his gentle criticism and retreated, commenting that her letter "would afford equal amusement to my Southern acquaintances as those now in their hands. Now do not think me exacting or too particular." The effect was surprising: where Libbie's reaction to the initial chiding had been to assert an opposite view, Custer's apology caused her to capitulate entirely. She next wrote, "I am glad you are so particular with me. With my much loved and honored parents I felt indignant at reproof, but when you express yourself as ever so slightly displeased I feel grieved and try to do better."[16]

As Libbie described her behavior at the time, "I was eternal vigilance for even with the rapture of fulfilled love came the adjusting of differences of opinion." The exchange of views on the language of her letters indicates that Libbie believed it to be her responsibility to be flexible, even when her husband showed himself willing to be accommodating, too. But Libbie could not always restrain her passionate nature. Just as during their courtship she had yearned to give him a thousand kisses, so a few months after the issue of propriety in correspondence was settled, supposedly on his terms, she wrote: "I don't care if fifty rebels read this letter. I miss your kisses."[17]

What Libbie probably did not know was that Custer had suffered a similar loss at Buckland, Virginia, on October 19, 1863. At that time, prior to their marriage, some letters written to him by an unidentified woman were published in the Richmond papers, "and afforded some spicy reading, though the most spicy parts did not appear."[18] These were not letters written to Custer by Libbie, for she had only received her father's permission to correspond with her intended that very month. During the time Custer had declared himself the serious suitor of Libbie Bacon but lacked her father's blessing, he had continued to keep alive the hopes of Fannie Fifield, Libbie's quondam rival. In her diary Libbie had appraised the situation shrewdly, writing that Custer, "like others, takes all she gives which I sometimes think is *everything*, but when a man has all he desires in one he rarely desires the girl for his wife."[19] Fannie, whom Libbie regarded as a "low-minded girl," might well have written something "spicy" to Custer: he had given his sister explicit instructions that if anything should happen to him, to burn his correspondence, mentioning in particular a long letter from Fannie.[20]

The war was omnipresent in the city where Libbie waited for news. For women like her, the day began with running to the window. If the War Department was flying a battle flag, they went out, "wearing the simplest clothes, veiled so as to escape attention in that lawless city," seeking the list of wounded and dead. Such a journey was frequently difficult and unpleasant: "In the lower quarter of the city there was not a piece of sidewalk," one soldier wrote. "Even Pennsylvania Avenue, with its sidewalks, was extremely dirty; the cavalcade of teams, artillery caissons, and baggage-wagons, with their heavy wheels, stirred the mud into a stiff batter for the pedestrian."[21] At the War Department many of the clerks were women dressed in black—widows and orphans of "dead heroes" compelled to work. Later, when she herself became a young widow in need of a job, Libbie would remember those clerks and consider government employment.

If their loved ones were still unharmed, the women returned to their boardinghouses to wait once more.

As spring turned to the "dreadful heat" of a Washington summer, most of the women went back to their home states, yet Libbie "implored" her husband to be allowed to stay. She also implored her father, for she had been married only a few months, and the habit of obtaining her father's permission was ingrained. It must have been clear to both father and husband that Libbie wanted to be near Custer above all else: she was allowed to stay in the rapidly emptying city. Beginning the search for new lodgings, Libbie found doors firmly closed in her face, a bewildering experience for an appealing young woman accustomed to admiration and social inclusion. In a city that seemed "to belong to nobody," a woman alone was considered suspect. Eventually, Libbie had to seek help in the form of a letter of recommendation from the vice president. This secured her a new room. The importance of influence was another lesson of the war years, learned reluctantly.

So Libbie stayed on, finding Washington "the saddest city on earth." Accustomed to the pleasant summer weather of Michigan, she remarked what generations of newcomers to Washington have discovered with dismay—that in summer the temperature may drop only one degree from day to night. In the summer of 1864 it was as impossible to escape the war in Washington as the heat: "In every street were ghastly men with bandaged heads, an arm pinioned to the side, or painfully hobbling with crutches." The sounds of war were omnipresent as well: "Through open windows one heard the groans of the sufferers as long trains of ambulances traveled through the city." It was also impossible to seek refuge from the "blistering city" in the parks or riverboats, as these places were off-limits for decent women. Washington at that time was Gomorrah to the young bride.

New recruits passing through Washington noted evidences of the war on every hand and were appropriately chastened. One wrote that "the long streets seemed lined with the offices of surgeons, undertakers, and embalmers. Coffins, artificial limbs, and the like ghastly articles greeted the eye wherever it turned."[22] For Mason Tyler, a recruit from Massachusetts, Washington was a catalog of injuries, "here and there a soldier limping on crutches or a cane or with his arm in a sling, or his head or some part of his body bandaged." He added, somewhat unnecessarily, "It was very depressing to those just entering the service."[23]

To another volunteer soldier, Washington was "a vast military camp, full of hospitals and squalid in appearance."[24] Hospitals could not be built fast enough, and they were appallingly understaffed. At the beginning of the war Dorothea Dix had demanded that nurses be over thirty years old and plain, in order to establish nursing as a profession for respectable women, but this requirement eventually gave way to the pressing needs of a huge and continuing medical emergency.[25] Patriotic women felt a strong need to serve, and, having little to fill her anxious hours, Libbie thought of becoming a nurse. But when she was told that she would have to remain until the end of the war, she could not commit herself—she wanted to be free to go to her husband whenever possible.[26] Instead, she visited regularly at Armory Square Hospital, where Custer's Michigan soldiers were sent, schooling herself not to weep.

During her little more than a year in Washington Libbie saw President Lincoln several times. On the first occasion he stopped a White House reception line to ask if she was indeed the woman whose husband went into battle "with a whoop and a shout." That would have been enough to make her his firm supporter, but in addition Libbie responded to his obvious empathetic concern for the feelings of others, a quality she had as well. In spite of the burdens of office, the president seemed always to have time for "black robed women" who came in an endless procession to ask something of him for their sons or husbands. Libbie often glimpsed him walking alone near the White House at the end of the day, "always sad, his head bowed . . . for the sorrows of the Civil war were ever present with him."

Once she was taken to a more private meeting with Lincoln by the Custers' Michigan congressman. They made their way through a number of corridors in the War Department until they reached a room where they found the President alone. He held Libbie's hand for a moment, seeming to scrutinize her deeply—"I felt his benevolent gaze but was disturbed (girl-like) for fear that he would not think me worthy of the youngster to whom he had ventured to give such high rank and who had made good."

Libbie's vivid fear of being unworthy of her husband would endure through twelve years of marriage and fifty-seven years of widowhood.

On their honeymoon visit to West Point she had suddenly become aware of Custer's importance: "Until we reached West Point I received all the attention and accepted the homage as a matter of course exactly as if the glory of wifehood was greater than that of war. . . . I gradually realized that his own profession had placed him on a pedestal and that I must begin to take in the fact." In Washington the realization deepened. "I cannot tell you with what attention Armstrong is treated," she wrote to her parents. "And though I have no desire to put on airs it is very agreeable to be the wife of a man everyone knows and respects."[27] Libbie was just short of her twenty-third birthday when she wrote these words, a young woman married two months and suddenly transported at a moment of national crisis from a midwestern backwater to the center of government.

Although Libbie enjoyed the gala events of officialdom, to which she was frequently escorted by Michigan friends of Custer's, she lived for opportunities to be with her husband. Once she accompanied a congressional party on a steamer trip, unaware that Custer had been informed of their arrival and would meet the ship. He approached romantically, "standing in a small boat shouting and waving his hat." The party cheered as he bounded on deck and rushed to her. Libbie "forgot everything but that I was again with my husband."

When Richmond fell, Libbie was invited by the Committee on the Conduct of the War to visit the city on an excursion with their wives. When the committee continued on to Charleston, Libbie remained in Richmond, waiting for Custer to join her from the front. Left alone with a hostile Confederate housekeeper in Jefferson Davis's mansion, she spent a terrifying night sleeping in his large four-poster bed, fearing that Confederate soldiers might be hidden in the house or that the housekeeper might decide to murder her ("one Yankee less"). Early the next morning, though, Custer was there, taking the stairs three at a time, saber clanking. In this latest reprieve from her fears and his danger, she cried and laughed.

Because the protocols of military life seemed both strange and absurd, she could not at first take them seriously. Custer had been right about "cunning officers" attempting to make use of Libbie. One tried to enlist her influence with Custer by confessing that a leave of absence would be especially helpful to him at that time. Libbie replied that she didn't imagine it would be any trouble, and when her husband returned, she mentioned it casually. His reaction was unforgettable:

"Such a look of amazement came over his face I began to get a glimmer of some mistake—." Custer ushered her into their private room and closed the door, reminding her of those occasions in her school days when the principal of the seminary she attended would solemnly invite a student to come to his office. He "begged me to confine myself to the care of the household and not lay myself open to the accusation that I commanded the regiment. It was my first and last essay at commanding."[28] Libbie made mistakes—and that was a serious one—but, unlike her husband, she had been a diligent student in school, and she continued to be one in her marriage.

The hundreds of pages of Libbie's Civil War reminiscences reveal instance after instance in which she subjected herself to frightening and distasteful experiences in order to be with her husband. Her job at the front was "to enter into all the frolic and be jolly as I could over my numerous mistakes in military affairs." Knowing the importance of playing the expected part, she developed a persona to do so, while underneath she remained secretly appalled. Shocked by the death of a handsome young Michigan officer, she "was mystified by the men around me dwelling on the misfortune of dying in a skirmish and missing the glory of open battle—Death was death to me and the distinction I could not at first understand." Although she came to understand, Libbie never shared these feelings: the formative experience of Kilpatrick's ambition wantonly jeopardizing her husband's life was definitive.

At Stevensburg, she rode near enough to the skirmish line to see the enemy's pickets and the smoke of cannonballs. An eager officer asked if she would like to see a battle, but she promptly replied, "The smoke will do." They returned to camp and to the report of the battle: "And what horror after our merry ride's end to know that an officer to whom I had been presented and admired had been killed in that very fight."

Three prisoners, one of whom was a murderer, were kept in the cellar of the house the Custers lived in at Stevensburg. They were New Jersey men, actually German immigrants who, according to Libbie, had enlisted "for the bonus only." There must have been many such soldiers in the Union army, but these men had deserted to go to the Confederate army and betray their own troops. They were captured by Union scouts, tried in the office next to the Custers' bedroom, and condemned to death. Libbie remembered the rattling of their chains when they were brought up from the cellar and the great solemnity of their execution—the band playing the Dead March from *Saul*, the condemned men cloaked in black cambric gowns. The sensitive Libbie climbed into bed and required the maid to pile pillows and bedding on top so that she would not hear the "fatal shots"—but whatever the unpleasantness, there would never be any question in Libbie's mind about her choice to be with Autie.

Libbie's most treasured war relic revealed the high opinion in which both Custers were held by his commanding officer. After the historic peace was signed at Wilmer McLean's house, McLean offered to sell the furniture. General Sheridan paid twenty dollars for the table where Grant had written the terms of surrender, then presented it to Custer for Libbie with this note: "My dear Madam—I respectfully present to you the small writing-table on which the conditions of the surrender of the Confederate Army of Northern Virginia were written by Lt. General Grant—and permit me to say, Madam, that there is scarcely an individual in our service who has contributed more to bring this about than your very gallant husband."[29]

The token of Sheridan's esteem for both Custers was gratifying, but as an elderly widow, Libbie most remembered from her Civil War days the joy of reunion with her husband, heralded by the clank of his saber: "The rattle of a sabre rings through the years as clear to me as half a century since."

5

Knight sans Peur et sans Reproche

> Mr. Steadman, [*sic*] who sought for an introduction to me, told me that during and since the war I had been to him, and, he believed, to most people, the beau ideal of the Chevalier Bayard, "knight sans peur et sans reproche," and that I stood unrivaled as the "young American hero." I repeat this *to you alone*, as I know it will please you.
>
> —Custer to Libbie, 1871

Whatever Custer had become by 1871, Clarence Stedman's graceful compliment—the tribute of a man of letters to a man of action—was an accurate description of the Civil War Custer. Primary records, both private and public, all reveal a modest and gallant young man whose great popularity was won fairly and worn lightly.[1] Captain George Sanford remembered that Custer was reputed to be ambitious, "but as far as I could see, or can now judge, his ambition seemed to be more to surprise and startle both friend and foe with the brilliancy of his deeds than anything else, and his claims for special honor were always for his Division rather than for his personal account"[2]—this from someone in his rival's camp, an officer serving with Wesley Merritt.

Custer had no need to sing his own praises; others did that in abundance, and not only after the fact. At a presentation of captured enemy flags in Secretary of War Edwin Stanton's office, a soldier named Sweeney suddenly interrupted the secretary's compliments to the division to say that "it was all owing to General Custer; if Gen. Wilson had commanded us the rebs would have driven us to hell."[3] Stanton turned to Custer and said to him, "General, a gallant officer always makes gallant soldiers." A reporter covering the ceremony wrote that "the embarrassed looks of General Custer, as he bowed his thanks, showed that his modesty was equal to his courage."[4]

According to another battlefield reminiscence, Custer was similarly self-effacing when General Sheridan sent a message complimenting him for a successful action at Yellow Tavern. He modestly expressed his thanks, Theodore W. Bean reported, "saying he deemed the 'honorable mention' of his brigade a most pleasing and fortunate episode of his life."[5] A *New York Herald* article about Kilpatrick's failed attempt on Richmond noted that "General Custer's command was made up of detachments of troops who were nearly all strangers to him, and yet he declares that men never behaved more gallantly in the world. To them he awards all praise."[6]

Custer's official reports throughout the war are filled with generous praise of those serving under him, praise that noticeably diminishes in length and enthusiasm during his service on the Plains. Of one subordinate at Gettysburg, he wrote: "The gallant Major Webber [Peter A. Weber] . . . kept me so well informed of the movements of the enemy that I was enabled to make my dispositions with complete success." The report goes on to encompass the entire unit: "I cannot find language to express my high appreciation of the gallantry and daring displayed by the officers and men of the First Michigan Cavalry. They advanced to the charge of a vastly superior force with as much order and precision as if going upon parade; and I challenge the annals of warfare to produce a more brilliant or successful charge of cavalry than the one just recounted."[7] The annals of warfare were probably equal to Custer's challenge, but rather than overweening egotism his exaggeration suggests a twenty-four year old's natural exuberance over a victory as heady as Gettysburg.

When Custer was transferred from the first to the third division of cavalry, the majority of the officers he had commanded petitioned, unsuccessfully, to be transferred as well. One of the men left behind grumbled that the First Division had accomplished nothing since Custer left: "Now, all you hear about is the 3rd Division. The 3rd Division captured so many battle flags, nothing but the 3rd Division, while the 1st Division is scarcely heard of. The fact is you have Custer now."[8]

Custer's concern for others also manifested itself in a direct and personal way: he was unfailingly kind to his former classmates when he encountered them as prisoners. The son of James Washington remembered that when Custer saw his father a prisoner at General McClellan's headquarters, he immediately took out his wallet and thrust a roll of bills into Washington's hand—not bothering to count them first.[9] Custer's letters to his sister reveal other instances of his solicitude. Recognizing a badly wounded prisoner as a former classmate, Custer "took care of him and fed him for two days." He also provided stockings and money to his friend: "This he had not wanted to take, but I forced it on him."[10]

Custer could be just as generous to an unknown enemy soldier. Once, while occupying Charlottesville, his troops captured a Confederate captain and brought him to headquarters, which turned out to be the prisoner's own house. After an affecting reunion with his wife in Custer's presence, he was taken aside by the general and, rather than being confined, was "placed upon his parole of honor that he would not attempt to escape." Relations were most cordial between Custer's staff and the enemy captain and his wife during the three days that the headquarters occupied the house, but when the time came to move on, the wife was desolate. Just as the captain was about to resume his prisoner status, Custer intervened, addressing the man's wife: "Madam, I am under great obligations for your kindness during our stay with you. To show my appreciation, and as the best return which I can make, allow me to present you your husband." He then lifted his hat with a flourish and bowed low to the couple before riding on, master of the gallant gesture.[11] Another of his memorable displays of gallantry occurred at Appomattox, where he instructed his band to play "Dixie" while reviewing some surrendered troops.[12]

Custer also exhibited a notable concern for his own men, visiting them in the hospital at the front and commending them to Libbie's attention when they were transferred to Washington. On one occasion he fought until midnight and then rode to the hospital to visit his wounded.[13] The first sergeant of the Fifth Michigan Brigade remembered that after the battle at Yellow Tavern, Custer's "words of cheer and sympathy to the wounded were deeply appreciated."[14]

Almost fifty-three years later, a veteran wrote to Libbie to tell her of an incident that had remained in his memory. He had received a summons to report to the general but was not told why. When he appeared, Custer informed him that his mother had written to say that she had not heard from him: "I mumbled something about postage. Go to your quarters and the first thing you do write to your mother. That will do. And to this day I dont [know] whether I wrote or not." The man added,

"This is just to show that Gen Custer took an interest in his men. Other Generals would have thrown the letter in the waste basket and that would end it."[15]

In 1876 when a farmer who had fought under Custer learned of his former commander's death, he recalled for the *New York Herald* a day of fighting during the Shenandoah Valley campaign. He had been struck in the leg by a bullet, and according to the *Herald*, "Gallant General Custer gave him his arm to lean upon, looked into his eyes with all a mother's tenderness and sympathy, and said:—'Let me help you to the rear; you're a brave man!'" No wonder, the reporter wrote, this former member of the Michigan Brigade had exclaimed, "I would have given my right arm to save his life—aye, I would have died in his place!"[16]

That Custer the compassionate commander was also the Custer who had boundless enthusiasm for the work of fighting has been difficult for some to accept. The military is a peculiar profession, whose practitioners, since we dislike the idea that anyone might enjoy an activity associated with death and destruction, are often expected by civilians to have no love for their work. The evidence of our senses, or common sense, should tell us otherwise, particularly when battle is justified as answering a perceived threat to the nation and lauded as a high form of patriotism. General Grant once described himself as a reluctant warrior who never went into battle with enthusiasm.[17] This exemplary attitude, showing as it does a proper concern for the suffering and loss caused by war, did not prevent Grant from pursuing his objectives as tenaciously and with as heavy casualties as any commander who welcomed armed conflict. Professional soldiers are trained to fight, and not coincidentally, promotion is much quicker when they do. The annals of warfare are littered with pronouncements such as the popular toast of Civil War officers: "To promotion—or death."[18]

Society's ambivalent attitude is fleetingly captured in *They Died with Their Boots On* (1947), a popular film of Custer's life. In a brief scene the commandant of West Point threatens to expel Custer for having a fistfight with another cadet. Custer replies with genuine wonder, "I didn't know that you could get fired from the army for fighting." Phil Sheridan actually had a similar experience at West Point when he was almost expelled for a fight he began with a cadet who had ridiculed him. Someone had second thoughts, probably along the lines later suggested by the movie, and the expulsion became a year's suspension.[19]

Tully McCrea also remarked the conflict between what military men were supposed to do and the ordinary rules of society. He wrote to his father that he had just returned from church, "where I heard a sermon from the text, 'Thou shalt not kill,' and I thought that it was a singular one for a minister to select to preach to officers and cadets."[20]

The battlefield is not the only theater of human strife and suffering, but it is among the more dramatic, in purpose and practice a killing field. Officers lead their men into battle where some will likely die, and we expect such actions to have their attendant scruples. When Falstaff calls recruits "food for powder"—that is, cannon fodder—we recognize it to be a measure of his cynicism and not simple realism. Yet an officer who is so concerned about loss of life that he cannot bring himself to act will probably go the way of General McClellan, who was so fearful of battle casualties that he was ultimately relieved of his command. McClellan's business should not have been "wandering around a battlefield crying over the dead," one historian has written. "It was his business to win victories, and if men died in the process, that was war."[21]

That Custer was a war lover or took a sadistic pleasure in killing, as some of his critics have asserted, is not borne out by contemporary accounts of his behavior.[22] While still at West Point he was already reflecting on the possibility of opposing his classmates in battle. He wrote that he and his Southern roommate esteemed each other as brothers but might end up meeting in battle on opposing sides: "We often think of this," he told his sister, "and hope we may never be compelled to aim a blow at each other."[23]

Custer did say early in the war that he would be "willing, yes glad, to see a battle every day during my life," but as he was not yet twenty-three years old when he wrote these words to a female cousin, in the first flush of success on the battlefield, he might be allowed some hyperbole. In any case, his complete statement reads differently, providing a thoughtful explication of the problem that career military men face rather than the facile assertion that the words taken out of context suggest:

> You ask me if I will not be glad when the last battle is fought. So far as my country is concerned I, of course, must wish for peace, and will be glad when the war is ended, but if I answer for myself *alone*, I must say that I shall regret to see the war end. I would be willing, yes glad, to see a battle every day during my life. Now do not misunderstand me. I

> only speak of my own *interests* and *desires*, perfectly regardless of all the world besides, but as I said before, when I think of the pain & misery produced to individuals as well as the miserable sorrow caused throughout the land I cannot but earnestly hope for peace, and at an early date.[24]

Why should it be in Custer's interest or desire to fight? It was what he had been educated to do in four years at West Point, what his country had called upon him to do at that moment in history, and what—he was discovering—he did well. Not surprisingly, he enjoyed the testing of his abilities in this challenging sphere and he was pleased to be successful. Success was both individual and national, the highest of patriotic duties. That he might have such feelings while disliking the suffering and death around him is neither contradictory nor unreasonable: he was not a civilian reluctantly putting aside his ordinary vocation to answer his country's higher call; he was a career soldier, a professional.

Five months before his letter to cousin Augusta, Custer described his feelings when the dead were buried after a skirmish: "Some were quite young and boyish and, looking at their faces, I could not but think of my own younger brother." He wrote to his sister that one man had been married the day before he left home:

> Just as his comrades were about to consign his body to the earth, I thought of his wife, and, not wishing to put my hands in his pockets, cut them open with my knife, and found knife, porte-monnaie and ring. I then cut off a lock of his hair and gave them to a friend of his from the same town who promised to send them to his wife. As he lay there I thought of that poem: "Let me kiss him for his mother . . ." and wished his mother were there to smooth his hair.[25]

He was similarly moved by news of the death of a West Point friend, LeRoy Elbert. "Poor fellow!" he wrote to his sister, "He was one of my best and truest friends. . . . no one was with him when he died, no one knew him, his body was thrust on shore among strangers and by accident was recognized by some one and sent to his friends."[26]

Libbie maintained that her husband "could never get hardened to suffering. The dead on the battlefield, the wounded in the hospital moved him so that it was impossible for him to even look upon them calmly."[27] Custer visited his wounded and mourned the dead, but he also understood, as General McClellan did not, that excessive concern could lead to fatal hesitation. Leadership required action, and this was always Custer's forte.

Custer's appearance turned heads, though not always approvingly. The dress he adopted and made famous as a general was clearly contrived to be distinctive, and it established an image that the men serving under him rallied around and in part adopted. By war's end, all the men in his division were wearing his trademark red tie. Captain James Kidd, who served under Custer as part of the Michigan Brigade and became what can only be called a Custer worshiper, remembered the first impression he had of his commander's dress. He had heard an unfamiliar voice giving orders:

> Looking back to see whence it came, my eyes were instantly riveted upon a figure only a few feet distant, whose appearance amazed if it did not for the moment amuse me. He was clad in a suit of black velvet, elaborately trimmed with gold lace, which ran down the outer seams of his trousers, and almost covered the sleeves of his cavalry jacket. The wide collar of a blue navy shirt was turned down over the collar of his velvet jacket, and a necktie of brilliant crimson was tied in a graceful knot at the throat, the long ends falling carelessly in front. The double rows of buttons on his breast were arranged in groups of twos, indicating the rank of brigadier general. A soft, black hat with wide brim adorned with a gilt cord, and rosette encircling a silver star, was worn turned down on one side giving him a rakish air. His golden hair fell in graceful luxuriance nearly or quite to his shoulders, and his upper lip was garnished with a blonde mustache. A sword and belt, gilt spurs and top boots completed his unique outfit. A keen eye would have been slow to detect in that rider with the flowing locks and gaudy tie, in his dress of velvet and of gold, the master spirit that he proved to be. That garb, fantastic as at first sight it appeared to be, was to be the distinguishing mark which, during all the remaining years of that war, like the white plume of Henry of Navarre,

> was to show us where, in the thickest of the fight, we were to seek our leader.[28]

To an officer who did not serve with Custer but merely observed him at General Meade's headquarters, his costume was ludicrous, "like a circus rider gone mad!" But, Colonel Theodore Lyman continued, "his aspect, though highly amusing, is also pleasing, as he has a very merry blue eye, and a devil-may-care style."[29]

Was Custer vainglorious to dress in this fashion? Tully McCrea anticipated this objection when he described the outfit to his cousin: "You may think from this that he is a vain man, but he is not; it is nothing more than his penchant for oddity."[30] Custer's uniform was distinctive, was in fact unique, but it was not for that reason more ostentatious than many military uniforms. Custer was never immaculate like General McClellan, or swathed in gold lace like the French aristocrats on McClellan's staff, but, like many generals, he made his uniform an expression of individuality.[31] There was wide latitude in battle dress at the time, and generals had the prerogative of designing their own uniforms. Aside from this, one need only look at a chronological series of photographs or portraits of military men to see that plumes, epaulets, gold braid, aiguillettes and fourragères, sashes, chevrons, and fancy buttons—among other embellishments—have long been the familiar stuff of military apparel.[32]

The cavalry was especially known for a showy appearance: on the Confederate side Jeb Stuart had a costume that rivaled Custer's, "a uniform brilliant with gold braid, golden spurs, and a hat looped with a golden star and decorated with a black plume."[33] Elevated on horses, cavalrymen were seen to greater advantage than those soldiers who trudged the earth. They exemplified Lord Herbert's dictum that "a good rider on a good horse is as much above himself and others as the world can make him."[34]

In his eloquent farewell to the men he had led to so many victories Custer once again shifted the glory from himself to them: "When the war is ended and the task of the historian begins, when these deeds of daring, which have rendered the name and fame of the Third Cavalry Division imperishable, are inscribed upon the bright pages of history, I only ask that my name be written as that of the Commander of the

Third Cavalry Division."[35] Through circumstances he could hardly foresee at the time, Custer's name would indeed be inscribed upon the pages of history, but not as he wished in this address. He was correct in one way, however: there would be nothing in his remaining eleven years of life to warrant a revision of his desire to be remembered as the commander of the Third Cavalry Division.

PART TWO

Transition

6

Postwar Doldrums

Military law is very severe and those who overstep its boundaries must abide the consequences.

—George Armstrong Custer to Minnie St. John, August 7, 1857

I can say that I never saw troops so badly managed and provided for, both in regard to outfit and rations, as this division of cavalry was while it remained under the command of General Custer, or such a lack of common sense in orders and in the exercise of discipline, as was displayed by its command.

—Lt. Col. Alexander G. McQueen, First Iowa Cavalry, January 25, 1867

When the Civil War ended, Custer was, at the age of twenty-five, one of 135 major generals.[1] He might have embarked on a new career altogether, and he seems to have considered it: his name was valuable, and any number of patriotic men of business would have been happy to give him an office with a title on the door and a prominent place on the company's letterhead. While he was in New York exploring opportunities, he went to a "clairvoyant," who told him that he was thinking of changing his business "to railroads or mining." Custer wrote to Libbie that this was "strictly true."[2] Perhaps he did seriously investigate the possibilities of a career in these fields, but what he had been educated to do at West Point, and what he wanted to do, was to remain where his strongest talents lay. In the Civil War he had demonstrated over and over again an extraordinary ability to lead men into battle and inspire them by his own example of fearlessness and endurance.

Unfortunately, nothing else that the clairvoyant predicted came to pass. As Custer related her words, "I would prosper, my children would never know want. I was *always* fortunate since the hour of my birth and always would be."

At Custer's moment of uncertain direction, the dying Judge Bacon was astute in telling his daughter that she should not try to make her husband give up the army.[3] Given this deathbed injunction from her beloved father, Libbie's desire to remove Custer from the dangers that had poisoned her peace of mind during the Civil War reluctantly gave way to the duty to support her husband—although the thought of further separations from him was unbearable.

In truth, remaining in the military was a logical and sensible choice for Custer. He loved soldiering, and he flourished under the harsh conditions and extreme physical exertion that life in the field demanded. Coming back after an enforced absence of nine months, Custer wrote to Libbie from Fort Leavenworth, "I experienced a home feeling here in garrison that I cannot find in civil life."[4] It was a young man's game, and he was still young. Moreover, he had emerged from the Civil War with an impressive record to build on and a celebrity status in the press. General Sheridan, who would himself continue to rise, was a powerful and zealous patron. The army was the source of Custer's identity, the place where he had distinguished himself and where he could continue to be best appreciated.

In the contracted peacetime army there were many officers like Custer with fine Civil War records and further ambitions. George Crook, a classmate of Sheridan's, returned to the regular army as a colonel but was quickly promoted to brigadier general because of his success in the Southwest against the Apaches. Ranald Mackenzie, who was Custer's age, was regarded by Grant as the most promising young officer to emerge from the war.[5] He had achieved a higher rank than any man in his West Point class, and a "higher rank than any other officer whose military life began in the second year of the war."[6] Before insanity claimed him at the age of forty-three, he compiled an enviable record on the frontier. Nelson Miles, General Sherman's nephew-in-law, struck Sherman as more insufferably ambitious than all other officers put together. As he later wrote to Sheridan, "I know no way to satisfy his ambitions but to surrender to him absolute power over the whole Army with President & Congress thrown in."[7] Miles would achieve what was arguably the army's best record as an Indian fighter.

Even in military life, Custer was to discover after the Civil War that moments requiring his greatest talents were rare. During the war

"Custer's luck" meant having qualities suited to the opportunities for distinction that came his way; those qualities would continue to be valuable, but without opportunities, Custer could not replicate the brilliant performances he had become accustomed to. After participating in over a hundred engagements in the Civil War and achieving the rank of division commander, he would go to the frontier as the second in command of a single cavalry regiment—and be lucky to get it. In fact, quite a few young Civil War heroes first suffered a period of disappointment and adjustment as they tried to continue their military careers. As one partisan wrote,

> When the fighting was over and the Army once again reorganized, the brilliant young *temporary* generals (*i.e.,* of volunteers)—those who did the hard fighting and campaigning and won the war for the Union—with a few exceptions, stepped down to permanent ranks as low as captain and started their upward climb all over again, while the "old regulars"—officers whom, for the most part, no one ever heard of before or since—came out of the Army's woodwork to assume command of the regiments."[8]

There were many stories like that of Alfred A. Torbert, who had commanded the First Division of Cavalry and then become the Army of the Potomac's chief of cavalry, commanding three divisions. Descending to the rank of captain in the postwar army, he chose to resign.

For the youthful rising stars who continued military careers, euphoric early success placed a heavy burden of expectation on the remainder of their lives. As a graduate of West Point immediately plunged into a major war, Custer had hoped to be a general one day; he was completely surprised when he suddenly became the youngest general in the army at the age of twenty-three. Another young man, an English poet traveling in France at the time of the French Revolution, wrote of himself, "Bliss was it in that dawn to be alive, but to be young was very Heaven."[9] Custer, at a similarly critical moment in his own country's history, had even more reason to feel bliss than had Wordsworth: he was not only young but famous as a hero, a notable participant in the history of his time.

Custer brought his own style and insouciance to that role, but there is no evidence that he became subservient to his own image: what he did succumb to, rather, is too confident a belief in his own judgment and invulnerability—in Custer's luck. During the Civil War years he had led a charmed life: everything confirmed a high opinion of his abilities, and he escaped harm in fighting remarkable for its great loss of life. This shaped an attitude that persisted into a far different context.

Charles Hofling, a psychiatrist, has described Custer's life in terms of an oscillation between periods of success coupled with self-control and periods of failure marked by lack of control, predictably climaxing in a wild loss of control at the Little Bighorn.[10] I find instead one major period of great stress and lack of control in Custer's life, the postwar years of adjustment from 1865 to 1867. This culminated in his court-martial and suspension, a low point followed by an enduring recovery. Whatever disappointments and difficulties Custer experienced from his return to the army in 1868 until his death on the battlefield of the Little Bighorn, he met them with equilibrium—as an adult. Willful, at times naive in his rapport with power, and prone to making mistakes because he was most comfortable in the world of direct action, he was nevertheless in control of himself from 1868 to the last that we know of him, riding off in the direction of the Indian village on June 25, 1876.

Custer's postwar transition years were made particularly difficult by his quickly and unexpectedly going from the zenith of his lauded Civil War performance to the nadir, from the center of national activity to the periphery of Alexandria, Louisiana. And what a periphery! Hot, humid, full of unhappy troops and hostile locals—it was the quintessential miserable environment and the ultimate backwater. The volunteers Custer came there to command had joined the army to save their country. After the war was over, they felt entitled to return to civilian life as quickly as possible; instead, these Northerners found themselves in the Deep South on an ambiguous mission.

The Custer of Alexandria and Texas, where he had to march his disaffected troops, channeled his energy and tenacity into a harsh discipline that bordered on the inhuman—the refuge of the insecure. Although he enjoyed hunting and riding with Libbie and the local gentry and playing pranks on his father, who had been put on the army payroll, his military decisions during this time were so controversial that he was forced to defend them to the secretary of war. The situation was never resolved or overcome; it simply ended when the troops and Custer himself were mustered out in late 1865 and early 1866.

When he moved on to the plains, his service as lieutenant colonel in the newly formed Seventh Cavalry should have been more satisfactory—almost anything would have been after the Texas experience. But at first it was not. Custer was unsuited to subordinating his own desires and ideas to higher authority—ordinarily a severe, even fatal defect in the military—but one that had not shown itself during his Civil War service. When Custer respected a superior and thought as he did, and when that superior gave him both confidence and leeway—as Phil Sheridan had done—the problem could be controlled.

Neither of these conditions obtained when Custer first arrived in Kansas. He came as a subordinate to commanders he did not admire. Moreover, Indian fighting would never offer the unmixed satisfactions of Civil War battles, nor would he command the loyalty and respect that he had once received almost effortlessly. Libbie anxiously observed the situation, but Custer counseled patience, reminding her that "as yet, he had done nothing to win their regard or command their respect; he had come among officers and men as an organizer, a disciplinarian, and it was perfectly natural they should chafe under restraints they had never known before."[11] In the past he had invariably won the admiration of men he led into battle, but he lacked this avenue of leadership altogether in Texas, and—because Indian fighting was so different from the great Civil War battles—it would not work especially well on the Plains.

Unlike the unrewarding duty in Texas, the assignment to the Seventh Cavalry promised to be long-term. Custer had another painful transition episode, worse than his experience in Louisiana and Texas because he could not blame conditions: his turmoil was self-generated. During this crisis he was away from Libbie, even, at times, out of communication with her. In desperation he risked sacrificing his career completely by abandoning his command to seek her out.

When he wrote his Civil War memoirs, Custer attributed the fall of his hero, General George McClellan, to his appointment to high command "without first having had an opportunity to prepare himself by apprenticeship, as his successors had, by working their way up, step by step, through intermediate grades, from colonels or captains to that of general commanding-in-chief, and thus acquiring a self-confidence and resolution which sudden elevation to high and supreme command was not calculated to give."[12] Custer gave no indication that he sensed any parallel between his own situation and McClellan's, but the two men shared the condition of "sudden elevation" followed by a precipitous deflation. The opposite of the cautious McClellan, Custer had his elevation repeatedly validated by success on the battlefield: unlike McClellan, he did acquire self-confidence and resolution. This may have made his transition to a lower status all the more difficult, for in the lesser venues of frontier duty he was not recognizable as the man he had been—the popular Civil War general. The change in circumstance seemed to produce a change in character that supplanted the solicitous commander with an aloof and unfeeling martinet, still admirable in the eyes of his friends but unappealingly self-absorbed to others.

Several weeks before the Grand Review marked the ceremonial end to the Civil War, Custer had received a note from Sheridan: "It is possible that I will go west and up Red River and through Texas in command of a large force and of the interior country to the Rio Grande. Would you like to go with me should I go—If so answer by telegraph, by saying yes."[13] Texas had quickly become a source of concern now that the war was over and the government was able to turn its attention to other matters. The Confederal general Kirby Smith held fast with his troops there, refusing to surrender and serving as a magnet to other disgruntled Confederates. Across the border in Mexico the French had ignored the Monroe Doctrine to place Maximilian on the throne. Grant and Sheridan hoped that massing federal forces in Texas would deter French ambition, but if not, they were contemplating an invasion of Mexico.[14]

Kirby Smith surrendered before Custer could join Sheridan at his headquarters in New Orleans, but the government still regarded the French in Mexico as a serious threat. Custer's orders were to assume command of some 4,500 volunteer troops gathering at Alexandria, Louisiana—the First Iowa, Twelfth and Fifth Illinois, Second Wisconsin, and Seventh Indiana Cavalry regiments—and march them some 250 miles to Hempstead, Texas.

When he met the troops at the end of June, Custer must have felt entirely equal to the assignment. He was a seasoned commander and bona fide hero who had overcome any doubts about his youth by fearlessly leading his men into battle. The preemptive nature of battle had swept all before it; the petty irritations of thousands of men living at close quarters became mere background details for soldiers engaged in one critical battle after another in what they believed to be a great cause. The men who followed Custer to victory in the Civil War, wearing the same red tie that individualized his own uniform, adored their Boy General.

Without the overriding nature of a life-and-death struggle to aid him, Custer had no means of gaining his men's affection in the postwar years. Alfred B. Nettleton, one of Custer's officers during the Civil War and later a general, wrote that he and others had at first regarded Custer as an adventurer, a view confirmed by his idiosyncratic dress. However, Nettleton continued, "One engagement with the enemy under Custer's leadership dissipated all these impressions."[15] Unfortunately, there was no battle in Louisiana, no obvious enemy, no winnable war, and—in the opinion of the volunteers—no cause worth fighting for. Custer tried to be philosophical about the loss of his men's affection, probably making a virtue of necessity when he later wrote, "I never expected to be a popular commander in times of peace."[16]

No one could have changed the miserable weather; perhaps no one else could have secured better supplies in the immediate postwar confusion; however, a more experienced officer or a man of a less absolute and less confrontational temperament—a man who set his sights lower—might have avoided some of the trouble that followed. Just as he never experienced the highs of Custer's career, Wesley Merritt, made a general at the same time as Custer, also missed the lows: he too was instructed to march volunteer troops into Texas and did so without incurring the violent opprobrium that Custer attracted. Merritt's march of 5,500 men—1,000 more than Custer had—over 600 miles, as opposed to Custer's 250 miles, turned out to be a "model march."[17]

Custer also exacerbated a bad situation by a fundamental error of judgment. Thomas Cogley, who wrote the history of the Seventh Indiana Cavalry Volunteers, identified that error as his failure to distinguish between a regular soldier and a volunteer: "He did not stop to consider that the latter were citizens, and not soldiers by profession—men who had left their homes and families, to meet a crisis in the history of their country, and when the crisis was passed, they had the right to return to their homes."[18] Ulysses S. Grant said much the same thing when he described the soldiers who fought the Civil War as men who "could not be induced to serve as soldiers, except in an emergency when the safety of the nation was involved."[19]

While Custer's forces passed five restless weeks in Alexandria, enduring wretched weather, mosquitoes, and the hatred of the local population—all without having any idea of why they needed to be there—an incident occurred that crystallized the relationship of the commanding officer to his command. On July 7 a petition calling for the resignation of Lieutenant Colonel N. H. Dale of the Second Wisconsin Cavalry Regiment was signed by fifteen commissioned and seventy-five noncommissioned officers of that regiment. According to Charles Lothrop, who wrote the history of another regiment under Custer's command, the intention of the petition was simply to allow the officer next in line to be promoted to lieutenant colonel before being mustered out (and thus presumably secure a higher pension).[20] Since Dale was generally disliked, the plan may also have had a less benign motive, but in any case Dale took the matter to Custer, who had no choice but to regard it as gross insubordination. Custer directed that commissioned officers be arrested and noncommissioned officers reduced in rank. This had the intended effect of producing retractions, and the officers were restored to rank and duty.

Had all the petitioning officers retracted, the episode would have ended with a tidy confirmation of Custer's view of discipline: prompt severity produces reform and discourages further infractions. But one officer, the young Lieutenant Leonard Lancaster, refused to retract. Faced with open defiance, Custer again had no choice but to act according to military law and turn the lieutenant over to court-martial proceedings on grounds of conspiracy and insubordination. Certainly Lancaster had not intended to "incite mutiny"; nevertheless, given his insistence that he understood his action and continued to approve the petition, he could only be found guilty. The court sentenced him to execution. None of Custer's critics suggests that he attempted to influence the decision.

A new petition was immediately circulated, this time by Dale on behalf of Lancaster. It was signed by all the commissioned officers of the regiment *and* by Custer's own staff officers, who were mostly his longtime friends. At this juncture a more flexible commander might have realized that the interests of discipline had been satisfied and the time to temper justice with mercy had arrived. Custer did in fact have something like this in mind, but the means he chose to carry out his decision were unfortunate. He thought a dramatic pardon, enacted on the field of execution at the last minute, would be more effective than simply acquiescing to the petition for clemency. More important, it would make clear that he was in control, not simply swayed by pressure.

Preoccupied by his own role, Custer misjudged badly: during the interval between the request for mercy and the execution date, the men, hearing nothing from Custer, became increasingly bitter. Disaffection spread from the Second Wisconsin to the other regiments, which were already angry over their prolonged service in a broiling and god-awful backwater of the Deep South. Custer received death threats but regarded them merely as a further opportunity to demonstrate his courage under duress.

Emmet West, a quartermaster sergeant and author of the history of the Second Wisconsin Regiment, wrote that when Lieutenant Colonel Dale presented his clemency petition, Custer told him that he wanted to shoot Lancaster.[21] Given Custer's belief in harsh punishments and Lancaster's stubbornness, it may have been true, but it might just as easily have been a calculated way of intensifying the dramatic reversal he was plotting.

In any event, Custer's careful orchestration of the episode backfired: when the last-minute reprieve came, after the firing squad had already heard the commands "ready" and "aim," the men who had formed a hollow square around the waiting grave judged Custer to be a monster. Their feelings of horror and injustice were by then too strong to be dissipated by what they saw as a cheap, insensitive trick.

In any military organization there are instances in which men hate their superiors far more than they hate the enemy. Lieutenant Lancaster, who was prepared to die for the cause of getting his commanding officer to resign, seems to have regarded it as a moral crusade. His intransigence when everyone else knew it to be a lost cause appears to be foolish or naive, but perhaps in the close quarters of combat, Dale had come to be an obsession, a symbol of the abuse of authority.[22] In a book written by a friend and neighbor, Lancaster is described as turning down some would-be rescuers with this ringing speech: "I'll stay here; I am guilty of no crime and I would die a hundred deaths rather than play the part of a coward and I'll never be called a deserter. I shall be shot tomorrow night. Let them shoot me if they want to. I shall die with clean hands and a clear conscience."[23]

Instead of the martyrdom Lancaster envisioned, his sentence was commuted to a dishonorable discharge and three years' imprisonment with hard labor on the Dry Tortugas—hardly a slap on the wrist. Several months later General Sheridan quietly issued an order that he be released, an indication that the army was embarrassed over the matter. Lancaster returned to his home in Eau Claire and began a long campaign to clear his name. Reversing the dishonorable discharge was done quickly, but it took twelve years to get a bill passed in Congress granting him back pay. With evident satisfaction West concluded his story of the affair by pointing out that at the time of writing (his book appeared in 1904), Custer and Dale were long dead, but Leonard Lancaster was still flourishing in Eau Claire, a respected citizen and member of Eagle Post No. 52.[24]

Since Lancaster did not die, after all, even the damage Custer sustained by bungling his pardon might have been contained and forgotten had he made no further mistakes in handling the command. But the obstinance Custer demonstrated in the face of criticism during the Lancaster incident was to become only more self-righteous and obdurate. On the march into Texas he enforced a series of rigid orders that, combined with a paucity of rations, kept anger against him white-hot. As one volunteer wrote to his hometown newspaper in Iowa, the *Lyons Mirror*, "the march from Alexandria to this place [Hempstead] was the most severe and uncomfortable, and attended with more suffering than any of the regiment has experienced during its four years' service in the field."[25]

General Orders No. 15, which Lothrop pronounced "a military curiosity and a disgrace to its author," were issued on the eve of departure.[26] The first paragraph required that the command "move in columns of four, omitting the usual interval between companies, squadrons and regiments"—a recipe for extreme discomfort. To Lothrop it revealed an "utter want of knowledge of the manner of conducting a march of a large body of cavalry in midsummer. . . . packed together like sardines in a box . . . under a broiling Louisiana August sun, the roads dusty and 'dry as powder,' with no armed enemy in the entire Department of the Gulf."[27] The orders further required that an enlisted man not be permitted to leave the ranks except on duty or when accompanied by an officer. If on duty, he had to be furnished with "written authority." No foraging would be allowed since the supply train would provide "all needed supplies," and it was particularly important to respect the "rights and property" of the country's inhabitants, whom Custer described euphemistically as having "been beyond the control of the Government for four years." And so on for fifteen paragraphs, all of which contained rules that had to be "strictly observed."[28]

These orders, in part designed to maintain control over a military population that Custer knew to be disaffected, created unnecessary misery. Conditions of the march were hard enough in the terrific heat, and sickness, especially diarrhea, was rampant. Animals suffered along with the men. Lieutenant Colonel Alexander G. McQueen of the First Iowa Cavalry wrote in his account of the journey that men who did not have saddles were required to ride their horses bareback:

> The result was that after a few days the horses' backs thus ridden would become scalded, raw and fly-blown. On numerous occasions those faithful dumb brutes were turned loose by my orders and abandoned, with a foot or more of their backbones entirely exposed, and their living flesh being eaten up by large clusters of maggots that were embedded in the flesh and under the skin. . . . It would have been an act of mercy to have shot the animals, but the regulations forbid such.[29]

Special Orders no. 2, which announced that depredations against the person or property of local inhabitants would be punished promptly and severely, without benefit of court-martial proceedings, had been in effect since Custer's arrival at the end of June, before—as critics have pointed out—Custer had any experience with his troops and hence any reason to believe such orders were needed. It, too, applied to the march. Any enlisted man found violating this order would "*have his head shaved, and in addition . . . receive twenty-five lashes upon his back, well laid on.*"[30] Theoretically, treating the conquered foe magnanimously in order to win back their allegiance to the Union was a reasonable policy. In practice, it alienated Custer's own troops. Once again, to men who already felt injured by having to remain in the army when the war was over, such an order added the proverbial insult. Congress had abolished flogging on August 5, 1861; to the indignant volunteers, their commander quickly assumed the guise of "hero of the lash."[31]

For Custer, well supplied and well mounted, comfortably dressed for conditions and accompanied by his family, the concerns of the men he commanded but had never led in battle must have seemed remote. He was preoccupied by a larger consideration: marching his force without incident through what had recently been enemy territory. As a leader during the war, Custer had diminished the distance between himself and his men, sharing the dangers of battle and visiting them in the hospital. They had reciprocated with affection and emulation. On the march to Texas, the men perceived a great gulf between their own circumstances and their commander's: because they felt themselves treated badly and unfairly, they resented every perk of rank that Custer assumed. Twenty-five years later it still rankled Dr. M. P. Hanson, the surgeon for the Second Wisconsin, that "the best ambulance teams were taken to transport the General's camp equipage, staff and hunting dogs, while sick men were transported on unloaded provision wagons without springs."[32] This charge would recur throughout Custer's career. Cogley also notes that "Custer's wife accompanied him on the march to Texas, and he compelled soldiers to perform menial services for her and himself, which was in express violation of the law."[33]

Writers favorably disposed to Custer tend to move quickly over the march from Alexandria to Texas and the sojourn there, emphasizing the pleasant memories that Libbie records in *Tenting on the Plains.* As she pointed out, her young husband had the difficult task of playing many roles, "expected to act the subtle part of statesman and patriot, and conciliate and soothe the citizen; the part of stern and unrelenting soldier, punishing evidences of unsuppressed rebellion on the part of the conquered; and at the same time the vigilant commanding officer, exacting obedience from his own disaffected soldiery."[34] Custer was not suited to subtle and diplomatic roles: his means of winning respect from his soldiers had always been his exemplary leadership in battle.

Libbie assumed (rightly) that the men hated Custer, but she saw it as an example of "the penalty the commanding officer generally pays for . . . the privilege of rank and power," rather than as a specific response to a specific commander and his actions.[35] Libbie's correspondence stressed instead what would always be her paramount consideration. She wrote to her cousin, "You know Rebecca how the horror of the coming spring campaign used to steal over me in my gayest moments last winter. *Now* I have no fear—I let the future go and enjoy the present. And it is so delightful to be free from fear of a coming separation."[36] Twenty-two years later she recalled that "our life in Texas after the war went easily enough as it had no anxieties, no partings, no separations."[37]

In *Tenting on the Plains* Libbie concentrated on what she knew best: the details of the Custers' life together and her own experience. On the march to Texas, she remarked, "there was no hour or circumstance out of which we did not extract some amusement," and so it seems in her account of hunting, horse racing devoid of the attendant evils of gambling her father disapproved of, lighthearted pranks and family pastimes, and beloved pets.[38] Surrounded by Custer's staff of good friends and gracious Texas planters who liked her husband so much "he could be elected to Congress,"[39] Libbie inhabited an alternate universe from the undersupplied and hostile environment in which the volunteers marked time, governed as if they were all malefactors.

Lothrop's history reported that when Custer's horse was beaten in a race the men cheered the winner resoundingly and made rude remarks about Custer ("couldn't steal the race this time!").[40] Their jeers must have been a painful reminder of a better time, the other side of Libbie's nostalgic reminiscence about an incident in the Civil War when Custer came upon the Fourth Michigan Infantry at night, "and when it was daylight, and they recognized him, how glad they were to see him."[41] Mustered out on November 15, 1866, the men of the Second Wisconsin Cavalry left camp two days later on foot. According to one, "Custer was not with us on that march and we did not have to march by fours, and for slight offenses have heads shaved and receive twenty-five lashes. We never saw more of Custer nor had any desire to."[42]

Custer's official statement about his leadership of the Wisconsin, Indiana, and Iowa Volunteers was actually an apologia, a defense and justification against complaints lodged with the army by political figures in those states.[43] It was challenged point by point by Lieutenant Colonel McQueen of the First Iowa Cavalry. McQueen, too, in the words that Custer used in his own statement, described himself as having "been in command of troops almost continuously since the commencement of the war, frequently in much larger numbers than at present."[44] He stated that he did not speak merely in passion or without regard to what might be the consequences of his speech because he was prepared to prove his accusations.

McQueen lived up to his word, meeting every assertion of Custer's with facts, particulars, and vivid details that convincingly refuted his commander. Custer, for example, claimed that there was no excuse for a private to steal a cow from a civilian because "whatever deficiencies existed in the commissary department, the supply of beef was always ample and of the best quality."[45] On the same subject McQueen countered with damning specificity:

> The full rations of fresh beef were generally issued at this time, but not any more than the legal ration of beef, while all other rations were damaged and unfit for use, especially the hard bread, which was full of worms and bugs. I have seen the soldiers at this time compelled to rob their horses of part of their rations of corn and spend a greater portion of the night in boiling and parching it to get enough to appease their hunger. Enlisted men whom I knew well in citizen life came to me imploring for relief, saying they were actually becoming weak and emaciated from starvation, "and would be glad to eat what their fathers fed to their dogs." This was not said to me in a captious spirit of mutiny, but imploring for relief, which I was unable to render.[46]

Furthermore, according to McQueen, the circumstances in which the rations of beef were issued on that painful march were unnecessarily awkward, even cruel:

> After getting into camp the men were required to graze their more than half-starved horses and attend to other duties. Rations were issued almost every day, but not until late at night, after the arrival of the supply train, when the men should be asleep. . . . Fresh beef was issued every night, which would be killed after the arrival of the supply train, and not allowed time to cool, either before or after slaughtering. After being driven behind the supply train all day, and furnished often at such a late hour at night, it was impossible to cook it properly for want of vessels, salt, and time to procure necessary rest and sleep, while these evils could have been remedied very easily by having the beef cattle and forage train move one day in advance, there being no enemy at this time to molest them. The attention of the commanding General was called to these irregular practices, but without effect.[47]

Custer defended his position with the bare assertion that beef rations were issued regularly. As the particulars of McQueen's rebuttal make clear, however, the rations were only one aspect of a more complicated situation. Custer was not simply unaware of the problems—Lothrop reproduces the documents that establish how often he was informed of them. Such complaints, and the men who voiced them, could not get Custer's attention: he had made up his mind in Alexandria how to treat these men, and his attitude did not change on the march.

Were McQueen one voice crying in the wilderness, it might be possible to dismiss his version of events in favor of Libbie's idyllic recollections. But all three of the regiments that accompanied Custer to Texas left their histories, and all agreed that Custer was a bad commander. Their accounts were supported by a number of official communications, most tellingly by Custer's own orders and, in the case of Lieutenant Colonel McQueen, by the many documents sent to Custer requesting redress.

It might also be tempting to conclude that Custer was willfully unjust, but it is part of the complexity of the man that he was not. When, for example, it was brought to his attention that some saddles and other equipment belonging to individual men had been confiscated as government property, he promptly ordered these items restored to their owners. Regarding his use of severe punishment, that such means are a valuable and at times necessary deterrent, and that Custer's situation required such a deterrent, is certainly arguable. Texas had no civil law at the time of the march, and Mexico seemed to threaten. Moreover, Custer was not the only commander to have dissatisfied volunteers on his hands: units posted to other Southern areas at war's end were also unhappy.[48]

Where Custer placed himself squarely in the wrong was in his attitude of indifference toward the men under his authority. He might have eliminated a number of gratuitous difficulties and spared these troops additional hardship by adapting their marching orders to local conditions. Instead, Custer accepted his alienation from his men and doggedly enforced his will.

Although the governors of both Iowa and Wisconsin had protested to the secretary of war, who in turn had ordered Sheridan to investigate Custer's behavior and correct any abuses, Custer emerged from the episode professionally unscathed. Secretary Stanton, who had known Custer's father in Ohio, had always been well disposed to the Civil War hero. He may well have remembered the ceremony he presided over the year before when he complimented the general on his leadership after Custer's men presented the secretary with Confederate flags they had captured at the battle of Cedar Creek. At any rate, Stanton was willing to pass the matter on to Sheridan without becoming personally involved.

Sheridan, who would have his own troubles in the postwar South, shared Custer's philosophy of command and supported him fully. On November 13, 1865, he sent Custer a handwritten note, saying that Custer's disciplinary measures had been "mentioned to me in several communications to the Sec. of War."[49] They had been more than mentioned: when the second telegram from the governor of Iowa had arrived, Secretary Stanton had forwarded it to Sheridan with a peremptory order to take "prompt measures to prevent the infliction of the punishment mentioned in Gov. Stone's telegram."[50] Nonetheless, Sheridan's note to Custer continued: "Your acts are my acts on any question of discipline."[51]

There was, however, one repercussion that Custer knew nothing about. The matter of his postwar conduct had come to the attention of General Grant. On October 17, the former commander of the Second Wisconsin Cavalry, Cadwallader Washburn, wrote to Grant and to Representative Elihu B. Washburne of Galena as well. Congressman Washburne promptly wrote to Grant himself, repeating the contents of Washburn's letter, which included the information that while Sergeant Lancaster languished in the Dry Tortugas, his family was now dependent upon public charity. He concluded: "I do not know but it is necessary for Custer to do all these inhuman and barbarous things to maintain discipline, but I have observed that it was not necessary for *you* to do such things in any Command *you* ever had."[52] Grant in turn sent a telegram to Sheridan on December 14: "There is great complaint of cruelty against Gen. Custer. If there are grounds for these complaints relieve him from Duty."[53] Once again, Sheridan emphatically defended his protégé, writing to Grant that there was no foundation for complaint, that he had given the matter his "personal attention" and knew that the troops had suffered no "unusual hardship or discipline." He concluded: "If anything he has been too lenient."[54]

Was Grant convinced? In a recommendation he wrote for Custer at Sheridan's behest at the end of the war he stated, "There is no officer in whose judgement I have greater faith than in Sheridans."[55] Less than two years later Custer's court-martial would cross his desk, again accompanied by a plea for leniency from Sheridan: "There was no one with me [in the Civil War] whom I more highly appreciated than General Custer. He never failed me, and if his late misdeeds could be forgotten, or overlooked on account of his gallantry and faithfulness in the past, it would be gratifying to him and to myself, and a benefit to the service."[56] This time Grant was not disposed to mitigate the punishment; on the contrary, his official statement of review remarked its mildness.

7

Joining the Frontier Army

> Once when General Sherman was serving in that region, some one remarked to him that "it was a fine country and all that it needed was plenty of water and good society." To this the General is reported to have replied very brusquely, "That is all hell needs."
>
> —Frances Carrington, *My Army Life and the Fort Phil Kearny Massacre*

Part of the difficulty of Custer's post–Civil War adjustment may have been his rude initiation into the frontier army, a body of men that neither military historians nor the general public have held in much esteem. One newspaper described the ranks of postwar enlisted men as "human driftwood—men who have committed crime elsewhere, and are hiding in the service under assumed names . . . men who are disappointed, disheartened, and ambitionless, and find the lazy life of a soldier a relief."[1] And the son of an immigrant to Dakota Territory in 1873 observed that "in those days it was a common belief that the only men who would enlist in the regular army were those who were either too lazy or too shiftless to accept regular employment."[2] Historian Robert M. Utley regards the *New York Sun*'s stern charge that "the Regular Army is composed of bummers, loafers, and foreign paupers" as "only partially accurate; there were other undesirables as well: criminals, brutes, perverts, and drunkards, to name a few."[3] For many the army was not a profession of choice but the employer of last resort, and as such, it was not held in high regard by the general public.[4]

Summing up the state of the army as late as 1897, Colonel Anson

Mills found that "the pay of the men is too niggardly to entice any one into any kind of employment in this country, save the unfortunate or the idle and vicious, seeking temporary relief from suffering for food, shelter and raiment."[5] Charles King, who served with General Crook during Custer's years on the Plains, estimated that in the twenty-five years following his retirement he was asked by at least a hundred former soldiers for help in finding jobs, but he had been able to find places for only three. One prospective employer told him, "You see, it's this way. We naturally reason that a man couldn't have been of any account if the best he could get for himself all these years was a job at soldiering."[6]

If these soldiers were already inferior in every respect to the men who fought the Civil War (they were even a half inch shorter!),[7] the army reciprocated by provisioning them poorly and punishing them harshly. A staggering one-third of the men recruited between 1867 and 1891 deserted; for every five men who died from wounds or accidents, eight died from disease and countless more were plagued with scurvy.[8]

Suicide and homicide rates were high, as an embarrassing comparison of American and British data revealed. In the six year period of 1866–71, American army homicides were "strikingly in excess of the proportion" in the English army, while suicides—62 per 1,000—"even exceed the ratios reported during the same years for the troops serving in India, which averaged 55/1000." Accidental drownings were also "very greatly in excess of those reported in the English army."[9]

The enlisted man on the frontier, Utley writes, "would live in dark, dirty, overcrowded, vermin-infested barracks, sharing a straw-filled mattress with a 'bunkie.' He would eat bad food, badly prepared. . . . He would find them [his fellow soldiers] profane, contentious, and addicted to gambling and whiskey."[10] As venereal disease was the primary ailment treated by army doctors, sex—when obtainable—could be added to the list of vices.

And theft: privates made thirteen dollars a month, a pittance, approximately 20 percent of which was lost in exchanging the paper money for gold and silver, the only recognized currency on the frontier. The theft of horses was rampant, and besides horses, "the men would steal tents, canvas wagon covers, ammunition and arms. . . . It was not a very difficult thing for the soldiers to dispose of anything they could steal."[11] So wrote First Sergeant John Ryan, who spent ten years in Custer's Seventh Cavalry and later wrote about it in a series of articles for his hometown newspaper. He might have paraphrased the Civil War soldier who replied to a reprimand for drinking too much that "you must not expect all the moral virtues for thirteen dollars a month."[12]

As for drinking, Custer wrote to Libbie from Fort Dodge, which he described as the "lowest post" he had ever known, that she would be "horrified" to know "the vast quantity of liquor drunk by the officers. Even some of the temperate (?) ones dispose of one canteen full each day and whiskey costs $3.75 per canteen."[13] In a similar vein, Captain Albert Barnitz, one of Custer's officers, wrote to his wife that there appeared to be "a premium offered for drunkenness in the army!"[14]

At any rate, hard drinking was often a matter-of-fact accompaniment of soldiering: witness C. J. Bascom's recollection of a trip he made with General Sheridan in 1868. Bascom was superintendent of the water service for the Kansas Pacific Railroad (later the Union Pacific), and in that capacity he accompanied Sheridan and ten officers from Fort Hays to personally inspect a pumping station that had been burned by the Cheyenne. Sheridan's party had five gallons of whiskey, but on the way back the whiskey gave out six miles before the coach reached Hays. "Such a tongue lashing as Sheridan gave to Captain Jones, quartermaster, is seldom heard," Bascom remembered. "All Jones could say was that he didn't think they would be gone so long."[15] It was a four-hour trip, and before it was over, eleven men had consumed five gallons of whiskey! Yet Sheridan was notorious for hard drinking, and C. J. Bascom seems to be a sober enough witness.

Libbie Custer soon had occasion to see for herself the dimensions of the problem. When she and her Monroe companion, Anna Darrah, traveled from Fort Hays to Fort Harker, they were escorted by two officers and ten enlisted men. At the first stage station the troopers were able to procure whiskey. One by one they passed out and were put in the supply wagon, eventually leaving the apprehensive women without a functioning escort.[16]

Were a man to escape indulgence in liquor when he was well, he would be likely to find it prescribed when he was sick: whiskey, quinine, and cathartics were the chief "medicines" of the army doctor, although liquor was more often deleterious than healing.[17] The abundant use of alcohol in all forms took its toll. On his first command in Kansas Custer had the unpleasant experience of having an officer in delirium tremens commit suicide, leaving behind a young wife about to give birth.[18] In Sergeant Ryan's memoirs drinking had particularly serious consequences when the regiment was stationed near that "row of saloons on the Kansas and Pacific Railway called Hays City," where pistol shots could be heard "almost any hour during the night" and there were enough deaths from violence to warrant a separate cemetery.[19] The monotony of routine army life caused such dangerous places as Hays City to beckon, and more than a few soldiers of the Seventh died with their boots on on the floor of Drum's Saloon, a favorite hangout. Two were dispatched there by the famous Wild Bill Hickok, who sometimes scouted for the army.

There must have been many more who led lives of quiet desperation like that of a German shoemaker described by Ryan. This man would work hard and save his money until one day he succumbed to the urgings of fellow soldiers to join them in a saloon, where he would get drunk and spend everything he had saved. Sober again, he would "get so mad that he would jump up and pitch all his tools into the fire. He would then settle down to work again, and keep sober until he had another sum of money saved up," when the same events would be predictably reenacted.[20]

Louis Laurent Simonin, a French visitor to a frontier army post in 1867, shortly after Custer's arrival on the frontier, observed the chief pastime of the officers and asked philosophically, or perhaps only rhetorically, "What can one do in the desert if he doesn't drink?"[21] The readiest answer would have been "gamble." When Dr. James DeWolf arrived at Fort Abraham Lincoln to accompany the Dakota column against the Sioux in 1876, he wrote to his wife that "the officers of this post are all fine Gamblers." Several weeks later he ended another letter, "it is long after taps & I hear the I raise it two dollars in a tent close by."[22] A twentieth-century Custer buff, Dr. Lawrence Frost, said that he had seen dice from Fort Lincoln that "literally had round corners as the result of long periods of service."[23]

In this, too, the habits of the enlisted men were similar to those of their officers. Sergeant Ryan recalled that gambling was especially heavy from the first to the tenth of each month because at the beginning of the month the men received their allotment of tobacco, which they used as gambling currency.[24] In fact, tobacco had long served as a medium of exchange in military life. As a cadet at West Point, Custer had sought the parental permission necessary to obtain tobacco, not because he wanted it for himself—he thought chewing was filthy and possibly unhealthy—but for his roommate, who in turn would "get me things I want."[25]

Throughout his adult life Custer seems to have had no trouble keeping his promise to sister Ann not to drink as much as a drop of liquor, and when he decided to do so, he was able to give up profanity as well. Gambling remained a weakness in spite of repeated resolutions to conquer it.

In keeping with its history as a conservative institution, the army met all violations of its code of conduct with a firm discipline that in practice often resulted in brutality. Drunkenness especially inspired inventive torments such as having to bury the bottle (in a hole 10 feet by 10 feet by 10 feet), being bound and gagged with revolting yellow army soap, or carrying a heavy log uninterruptedly for a half or full day. This latter punishment was in effect until 1887.[26]

In the frontier army Custer continued to believe that strict discipline, enforced by harsh punishment, was the best medicine for the ills of desertion, insubordination, and unruly behavior. Many officers held similar views, and even an army wife, Teresa Vielé, related an incident in Comanche country whose moral is the salutary effect of severe measures with soldiers who were showing signs of insubordination. When the men began to exhibit symptoms of intoxication, it was discovered that their canteens contained whiskey: "One man, more bold and intoxicated than the rest, refused to pour his out. He was tied to the back of his horse with a rope and dragged nearly a mile. The rope finally broke, leaving him behind. He eventually straggled into camp, sober and bruised. Afterwards he was always 'a model specimen of military discipline.'" This brutal treatment of the rebellious soldier was necessary to save the rest, Vielé felt: "Prompt and decided measures were absolutely requisite."[27]

One day at Fort Harker, Kansas, during Custer's absence from the Seventh, the district commander, a Colonel English, observed some men with shaved heads and the mark of the brand being marched around the post and kicked by black troopers. He put a stop to the kicking and found out that the officer responsible was Major Joel Elliott. Sergeant Ryan comments that "no one especially approved of this procedure," but his is a noncommissioned officer's view.[28] Elliott could have cited Custer, his absent commander, as his exemplar in such matters.

Instances of the barbarous treatment of enlisted men were innumerable since in practice there was little to check the behavior of an officer in wielding discipline. A frontier army wife with the imposing name of Mrs. Orsemus Bronson Boyd recounted in her memoirs that she discovered many things in the army that cried out for change: "One which greatly troubled me was the power extremely young officers exercised over enlisted men. If the latter were in the least unruly, most fearful punishment awaited them, which in my opinion was not commensurate with the offense, but depended entirely upon the mercy and justice of the offender's superior officer, who usually but a boy himself had most rigid ideas of discipline."[29]

George Bird Grinnell's instruction to his white American readers that Indians "are just as human as ourselves. . . . In all respects they are men of like passions with us" might have been directed with equal profit toward army officers on the subject of their men.[30] As Colonel Mills observed, "Nothing . . . in our Republic, is so un-American as the great gulf that is maintained by laws, written and unwritten, between the commissioned and non-commissioned."[31] In his diary of the Seventh's Black Hills expedition of 1874, Private Theodore Ewert also remarked on the officers' lack of compassion: "Humanity is something that is foreign to their feelings and a little kindliness is but seldom or never shown to one of the rank and file. The officer of the U.S. Army has no respect for a man under his command."[32]

A few years later, a new recruit to the Seventh had similar feelings. Ami Frank Mulford, who joined the Seventh in the spring of 1877, wrote that he believed the principal cause of desertion to be "the manner in which many of the harsh officers treat enlisted men. . . . Bad officers are sure to spoil good soldiers."[33] In 1891 a survey of deserter-convicts in the military prison at Fort Leavenworth found that the most often reported specific reason for desertion was "tyrannical superiors," a reason conspicuously absent from Custer's discussion of the causes of desertion in his book *My Life on the Plains.*

Because the army maintained an impassable gulf between officers and enlisted men, officers seldom recognized "the fact that enlisted men have any rights or attributes to be respected."[34] This distinction even extended to death. Vielé described the graves of enlisted men in the barracks graveyard as marked with only small numbered sticks. The two officers buried there had wooden crosses.[35] Custer's troops followed a similar practice on the 1873 march from Yankton to Fort Rice, when seven men died within a short period, possibly from some epidemic disease that the regiment wanted to conceal from the communities along its line of march. The men were secretly buried, one grave serving to accommodate six soldiers, the other reserved for one officer.[36]

The frontier soldier's life seemed to alternate between hard and dangerous work on the one hand and vicious amusements on the other, the second as likely to do him in as the first. Between the lines of the grim descriptions of frontier army life, however, more innocent pleasures can be glimpsed: on Custer's Black Hills expedition of 1874 the men pursued the great American pastime vigorously, organizing into two clubs, the Actives and the Athletes, and playing a series of match games.[37] On many field expeditions enlisted men were able to hunt and, especially, fish. As Lieutenant James Calhoun noted on the Yellowstone expedition of 1873, "one singular characteristic of a soldier is that no matter what his surroundings are he is in some mysterious way able to make himself comfortable and to have a pleasurable time." Calhoun enjoyed hearing his men joke together—one joke that he recorded in his diary concerned mosquitoes so big and noisy that a soldier had mistaken them for a stampeding heard of mules.[38] It shows the ability of at least some of the men to transform the hardships of the environment into humor.

In addition to the internal problems that generally plagued the military, a severe limitation to effective frontier performance was the overextension of the army, systematically reduced by Congress from a postwar strength of fifty-seven thousand officers and men in 1866 to a mere twenty-five thousand in 1874—far too few to police the immense frontier region.[39] "Perhaps never in American history," one historian wrote, "were army men asked to solve such widespread military problems with so few men."[40] The many forts, some of which General Sherman once characterized as deserving the name of "fort" as much as prairie dog villages did, tended to be ad hoc responses to local pressures rather than parts of a total frontier strategy: they "encouraged settlers to move beyond the range of military protection, stirred up the Indians, and led to still more forts—many beyond effective logistical support."[41]

Often the buildings in these outposts were thrown together quickly by soldiers inexperienced in construction: memoirs of frontier army wives are eloquent on the subject of leaky roofs and walls that could not keep out the unrelenting prairie wind. When Colonel Delos B. Sackett made an inspection tour of some frontier posts in 1866, he found most of them simply unfit for occupancy. At Fort Randall the quarters were "built of cottonwood logs, the lower logs of the buildings rotted out; every crack and crevice swarms with bed bugs, fleas, rats, mice, spiders, etc." At Fort Sully there was not a single inhabitable building.[42] Eight years later nothing had changed. No less a person than the secretary of war offered a similar critique in his report for 1874:

> As long as the Army is in many localities badly sheltered, living in huts and adobe buildings sadly in need of repair, the roofs leaking, and the walls open to the inclement weather, I must repeat what I have so often insisted upon, that the appropriation for "barracks and quarters" . . . are, as for some years they have been, entirely inadequate to the necessities of the service and the health and comfort of our troops.[43]

Characterized by extremes of heat and cold, bitter winters and constant wind, the flat and treeless Plains were a hostile environment for the frontier army. Libbie remarked the "extreme heat of the summers on the barren plains, the long, snow and ice bound winters in poorly built quarters and no protection of lives from the blasts that swept over hundreds of miles of arid desert that surrounded us."[44] Bureaucrats in Washington often showed little sensitivity to the exigencies of weather. During the severest part of winter, when temperatures of fifty degrees below freezing were not uncommon, Colonel Henry Carrington was ordered to leave Fort Phil Kearny, Wyoming. On the journey, his wife reported, the driver of her wagon knocked at the little window in front to ask to be relieved: "'His feet had gone to sleep.' When the man was lifted from the saddle he was unable to stand for he was frozen almost to his knees."[45] He did not survive the amputation of both his legs when the party arrived at Fort Reno two days later.

In miserable, far-flung outposts, troops endured the endless Plains winter often removed from almost all outside contact. Aside from the inadequacies of frontier forts as physical structures, they offered little in the way of culture. Testifying before the House Committee on War Department Expenditures, Custer remarked of Fort Buford that "except the civilization that he [an officer] takes with him, there is none whatever there."[46] Like many frontier posts, Buford was entirely surrounded by hostile Indians who exhibited "the most intense hatred for the whites," and as a result, its men were confined to the precinct of the fort even during the summer, and to "fighting a losing battle with the bottle."[47] General Holabird wrote bitterly in his annual report of 1869 that "troops buried in snow, afflicted with scurvy, have the misfortune to be cut off from their fellow men about half the year, as at Fort Buford [South Dakota]. . . . The morale of the troops at Fort Buford has never been good; much of it has no doubt arisen from neglect and *the great isolation of the Post.*"[48] At the equally isolated Fort Union one soldier wrote, "As far as hearing what is transpiring on earth is concerned we might as well be in the heart of the Atlantic ocean."[49]

The impossibility of operating effectively under such conditions was clear to General Sherman, who wrote to his brother, Senator John Sherman: "I have good Department Commanders, but the country is so large, and the Indians so scattered, that we cannot foresee where they will turn up."[50] Sherman's frustration is evident in the use of the word *scattered* to describe the Indians three times in a short letter as well as his insistence that the subject of frontier defense is "as important as Reconstruction."[51] "Scattering" became a key idea in the army's approach to Indian warfare: Indians could never be found in large numbers because they "scattered," both during a battle and afterward. Soldiers, in contrast, went to war in organized units. As a newspaperman described one of Custer's battles on the Yellowstone expedition: "There was no scattering or flagging. Every man keeps in his place."[52]

A year after Sherman's worried letter, he would receive a plaintive telegram from the acting governor of Colorado, who reported that Indians had obtained possession of the country to within twelve miles of Denver: "Captain Graham whom General Sheridan sent to our relief, has lost nearly all his horses, and his command is powerless. . . . Cannot a trusted officer of the army be sent here to overlook and represent the situation. Many outlying districts are being abandoned, entailing untold loss to the country."[53] Sherman ignored the request: he received such pleas all the time, and he was convinced that large centers of population like Denver were not the most needful of his meager resources.

8

Frontier Army Wives

A fort in the midst of the wilderness surrounded by crafty and savage Indians is not the place for a lady.

—Tully McCrea to Belle McCrea, October 27, 1860

I had cast my lot with a soldier, and where he was, was home to me.

—Martha Summerhayes, *Vanished Arizona*

As a young officer preparing himself for frontier duty, Custer's former roommate Tully McCrea had strong feelings about subjecting women to such a life. He wrote to his cousin Belle that "the idea of taking a young wife from the midst of civilization and refinements to some fort in the western wilderness, where she would be surrounded by savages and deprived of everything that is desirable, friends, society, literature, and amusements of every kind is not only repugnant to me, but also I think that no man is justified in doing it."[1] In a similar vein the reporter Theodore Davis marveled that women were willing to endure such a life, whose drawbacks he thought would be enough "to deter the most energetic female from the trip; but no! nearly every post has its ladies."[2] While the army agreed with Lieutenant McCrea, the reality was as Davis noted—nearly every post had its ladies.

During the Civil War Libbie Custer was the only woman allowed in General Sheridan's army camp, but on the frontier she was one of a number of officers' wives who braved all manner of daunting conditions to be with their husbands. The ideology of the day may have valued women as wives rather than as workers outside the home, but marital status gave women nothing in the army. Not the least of the hardships these wives endured was army policy, which did not officially acknowledge their existence—although as early as 1802 Congress had made provision for laundresses at army posts. The laundresses, who received "housing, a daily ration, fuel, and the services of the post surgeon in addition to their pay," invariably became the wives of enlisted men.[3] In spite of the institution's failure to recognize or provide for them, though, the wives of officers were welcomed into the community of the frontier post and treated with courtesy. The reporter Theodore Davis expressed the common attitude of his time when he remarked that they "undoubtedly do much to keep up the respectability of the place, and restrain the too free licence which is common at posts where there is no 'lady of the army.'"[4]

The courtesy offered these army dependents did not extend to housing, where rank alone governed. A newly arrived bachelor major could commandeer the quarters of a captain with a wife and numerous children, never mind that the captain's family would have to cram themselves into an insufficient space so that the major might have a number of rooms to himself. Dislocations caused by rank were so numerous that in the 1870s one five-year period at Fort Clark, Texas, saw at least fifty such moves.[5] Those army wives who accompanied their husbands to the frontier had to accustom themselves to turning out and being turned out, but as one veteran told a novice, "After you've been turned out once yourself, you will not mind turning others out."[6]

According to army regulations, a second lieutenant was allowed only one room and a kitchen.[7] Even a dozen dependents would not alter his allotment, since the army did not recognize their existence. Martha Summerhayes, whose husband languished as a lieutenant in the frontier army for twenty-two years, wrote that she "could never get accustomed to the wretched small space of one room and a hall. . . . The forlorn makeshifts for closets, and the absence of all conveniences, annoyed me and added much to the difficulties of my situation."[8] Mrs. Boyd and her husband arrived at their assigned post to find only three houses—all occupied. Like the Custers and other frontier couples, the Boyds spent some time living in tents, which were no doubt preferable to some of the wretched structures designated officers' housing at many posts. The standard officers' quarters were two-family houses with a hallway in the middle: "Children and chickens were a never-failing cause of disturbance."[9]

Given such a system, there were bound to be outrageous inequities. Frances Roe, a young woman with many opinions and a great capacity for indignation, was particularly indignant about receiving a note at 10:00 A.M. to vacate quarters by 1:00 P.M. that same day. To compound the inconvenience, the soldier who had been serving as the Roes' cook was ordered back to his company by Lieutenant Roe's company commander because "he was much needed there," but a day later the commander transferred the man to his own kitchen. The Roes' ejection set off a chain reaction causing six other households to move—which was some satisfaction to the put-upon Frances.[10]

Complaints about the quality of housing abound in almost any army wife's account of her life on the Plains, for these accommodations were often hastily and poorly constructed. Libbie, who tended to express herself mildly, imagines an army wife saying to the quartermaster, "When you build the next post, Major, have the goodness not to trust to your own ideas of kitchens please; let a woman give you a hint or two."[11] Rain could bring disaster to these flimsy buildings. In Alice Baldwin's quarters the ceiling was once converted into a waterfall: "In bed, surrounded by basins, pails, tubs, cups, and dripping pans—any available container to catch the water—I lay motionless, not daring to move for fear of upsetting the various receptacles."[12] Lydia Lane reported that after fifty-seven hours of rain, every roof on her Texas post was leaking.[13]

At Fort McKinley the quarters were built with perfectly aligned windows so close to one another that it was easy enough to look through the entire row. One day a woman did exactly this and saw her neighbor "with an apron wet with mud while an old towel on her head leaked mud drops from its ends." When she rushed to investigate, she discovered that the neighbor was giving a party that evening for the departmental commander, a number of officers, and their wives. In the midst of her preparations, however, a heavy rain had brought the ceiling down, depositing a load of mud on the table already set for dinner. In exemplary army wife style, the woman cleared away the mess and went ahead with her entertaining.[14]

Roe was most eloquent on the subject of these difficulties. "This country itself is bad enough," she wrote decisively, "and the location of the post is most unfortunate, but to compel officers and men to live in these old huts of decaying, moldy wood, which are reeking with malaria and alive with bugs, and perhaps snakes, is wicked."[15]

Whatever the ordinary discomforts, worse conditions were always waiting in the wings: according to the published recollections of frontier army wives, fire, flood, sickness, and Indians were constant threats that chronically burst forth to claim victims. And if their husbands chanced to become casualties of these scourges, the wives were turned out unceremoniously. "In civil life a poor widow can often live right on in her old home," Roe commented, "but in the Army, never!" Of a new widow who was also a new mother, she added, "Mrs. White will have to give up the quarters just as soon as she and the little baby are strong enough to travel."[16]

Even the determinedly sanguine Libbie admitted that things could be bleak: "Sometimes when it rained persistently and we camped on wet ground it was cheerless."[17] Writing to her absent husband from Fort Concho, Texas, on August 7, 1877, Alice Grierson gave him news of the post that must have done little to lift his spirits:

> Dr. Buells sickness is a very tedious, and discouraging one, and their prospective journey . . . rather forlorn. . . . The Gasmans had, and still have their own troubles. Capt. Kennedy, was quite awhile on the sick list, Lt. Ward was sick in the hospital the latest news. It is said that Dr. King made that servant Harriet stop eating dirt, which caused her to become insane. . . . Lt. Smither has lost his father, is troubled about his little boy, and not very well. Capt. Little has been in quite a [lot of trouble], the boy had a dangerous fever, and Mrs. Little had had hemorrhages of the lungs."[18]

Teresa Vielé noted that the cemetery at Ringgold Barracks contained "long dismal rows of graves of victims of cholera and massacre," while Frances Carrington's first sight when she arrived at Fort Phil Kearny was the wood train returning with the scalped and naked body of a soldier murdered by the Indians a short time before.[19] It was an ominous greeting: her own husband would soon be brought back in a similar condition.

Nevertheless, it was a convention of the life, or at least of the memoirs written about it, to treat hardships lightly. Women who could not stand the generally harsh conditions went back East; those who elected to remain learned to make the best of it, determined as they were to be with their husbands. Libbie had quickly learned as a Civil War bride that the role of a woman in camp was to lift spirits, not create additional difficulties for the army. Martha Summerhayes learned the same lesson on the postwar frontier when her husband admonished her not to cry at the funerals of enlisted men: "It would not do for the soldiers to be sad when one of them dies. Why, it would demoralize the whole command." An experienced army wife stopped Martha's recital of grievances one day to advise her that "there's no use in fretting about little things."[20]

All of the wives recounted disasters with aplomb, but no one illustrates the ethos of the army wife quite as well as Margaret Carrington, the wife of the commander of Fort Phil Kearny during the late 1860s.[21] The Carringtons' house had burned to the ground shortly before they left to construct the new fort: "some *best chairs*, bedsteads, and mattresses (all properly packed), with a half hundred beef tongues, some potatoes, and selected groceries, were prematurely consumed; but as this was only an incident very possible in army life, the fun of the affair made up for its losses."[22] Carrington's straightforward account of the journey to the remote place where the fort was to be constructed reveals more of her startling adaptability. A "sirocco-like wind" wore the party down as they made their way through a dismal and monotonous country, unrelieved by any tree. Then they encamped at Mud Springs "just in time to receive the full benefit of a thunder-storm and small tornado, which grappled sternly with our canvas, and for a time threatened to unroof as well as drown us."[23]

And all of this was simply a prelude to living in a desolate and dangerous outpost, surrounded by Indians of a piece with other aspects of the hostile environment. Predictably, much went amiss. While the fort lost its turkey hen to the wolves, and half the chickens died, Indians drove off the cattle that had been brought six hundred miles. Fort Phil Kearny was particularly displeasing to Chief Red Cloud and his Oglala Sioux, who virtually held the small number of inhabitants prisoner, inflicting casualties whenever they ventured out to cut wood. During Margaret Carrington's residence at the fort, Captain Fetterman and eighty men were killed by the Indians, after explicitly disobeying Colonel Carrington's orders not to go beyond a certain point. Their bodies were mutilated, with muscles removed from the thighs, calves, and arms, to incapacitate them in the spirit world—a compelling reminder of what could happen to the undermanned garrison if the Indians decided to attack it.[24]

"Yet," Carrington somehow writes, "with all these sacrifices and losses from repeated change, there were real cosey times in tents, houses, or in cabins."[25]

Frontier assignments varied considerably, depending upon the climate, the political and geographical context, and the size of the post. A "one-company post" was dreaded because it did not offer a critical mass for social life—or for the support and companionship that women needed to receive from other women. In some places a wife might find herself virtually the only woman, a situation that never seemed to bother Libbie, but would have made a difference had she found herself facing childbirth. Marian Russell's memoirs recount how, as the only army wife at Fort Bascom, she had to depend upon a pioneer woman who lived nearby, the mother of four children, when she gave birth to her first child. The army doctor she described as "helpless."[26] Another army wife gave birth in a tent "in the wilds of Texas, far from any post or settlement. Having no woman to give her the care she required nor to tell her what was necessary to be done, she became totally blind from the glare of the sun on the white canvas walls. . . . Her baby died."[27] Elizabeth Burt's husband was sent to Omaha unexpectedly when their baby was three weeks old, a separation that left her with a heavy heart.[28] Yet she was fortunate not to be the one traveling, as many wives did with infants or small children.

Even without children, moving could be difficult enough. There was seldom much time in which to make the necessary arrangements, and auctions of household goods were common on frontier posts. During ten days' notice before moving, Frances Roe complained, "we are expected to sell, give away, smash up, or burn about everything we possess, for we have already been told that very few things can be taken with us."[29] When things were transported, there were other hazards: worldly goods were smashed in transit, burned up, or destroyed when they were carelessly left out in the rain.[30] After a long, arduous journey Martha Summerhayes arrived at Camp Apache to find that her barrel of china was missing, having been in a wagon that had plunged off the mountain trail during the journey. She was still a new army wife at the time and "cared then a good deal about my belongings."[31]

• • •

As the army wives recounted such difficulties, however, their memoirs frequently had in common a double and, in a sense, paradoxical vision: the chronicle of deprivation and hardship on the frontier reveals a subtext of liberation from the complexities of civilization. On the one hand, they lamented the many inconveniences and dangers of frontier life; on the other, the shedding of superfluities led to a new appreciation of elemental things—especially the magnificent landscape—and to the satisfying exercise of ingenuity as they learned to improvise and substitute. The wives documented a learning experience in which the supposed necessities of civilized life were stripped away and—most of the time—revealed to be dispensable. But they were a self-selected group, after all; women who consciously chose to be on the frontier with their husbands and were determined to make it work.[32]

At first the unfamiliar world the wives entered seemed characterized by absence: "As far as the eye could reach, vast stretches of vacant land, blank and nothing in sight."[33] But eventually the power of the landscape and the insistent presence of nature captivated them. Alice Baldwin, who had had no interest in the "dreary, wind-swept Plains," found herself charmed when springtime produced an array of wild flowers: "There were varying shades of the wild hyacinth, with its purple clusters, the yellow daisies, the foxglove and the spring blossoms of the thorny cactus, while the green plains made all a scene of floral beauty which was most pleasing to the eye."[34] Martha Summerhayes at first seemed determined to find no redeeming qualities in her surroundings—she was lukewarm about the Grand Canyon and hated the desert. Gradually she allowed herself to open to the landscape until one day she discovered that its wild grandeur was "beyond all that I had ever dreamed."[35]

The beauty of nature counterbalanced its horrors in these women's writings about lovely wildflowers and magnificent panoramas, vicious insects, and violent weather. "Everything in nature is so beautiful, and the climate is so restoring and healthful," Margaret Carrington wrote, adding with no sense of irony, "one could look upon such frontier life with something like complacency were it not for these savages."[36]

There was a popular army story about a soldier stationed in Arizona who died and went to hell, only to return for his blankets because hell was cold after Arizona.[37] Nevertheless, most of the exceptions to the rule of learning to love the country were found in Texas. Lydia Lane described her journey from Corpus Christi to the western frontier as "through a dreary, desolate country, where nothing lived but Indians, snakes, and other venomous reptiles." Arrival at Fort McIntosh was little better and by her account could have qualified as one of Melville's Encantadas, those accursed islands whose only population was poisonous vermin: "Back of our quarters was quite a large yard, but there was not a living thing in it, except tarantulas, scorpions, and centipedes, with an occasional rattlesnake for variety." Lane said she had seldom experienced such a "dreary-looking place" as Fort Fillmore, and Camp Lancaster was "the worst station I had seen in Texas." Yet when her husband was forced to retire in 1870 for reasons of health, she wondered if she could ever settle down to civilized life again and remain in the same place "year after year."[38]

Given the dismal condition of the forts, most of the wives would have agreed with Libbie Custer's dictum that "the one that goes is happier than he who stays behind."[39] The women left in garrison while their husbands took to the field were confined to a daily routine that one described as "baking, brewing, stewing, and sewing."[40] In the summer of 1875, when Elizabeth Burt's husband, Andrew, accompanied the Yale paleontologist Othniel Marsh on a fossil-hunting expedition, he seemed far less disturbed by their separation than his wife was. Andrew liked being in the company of the famous scientist and the other notable men with him, and the party returned in great good humor over their discovery of numerous fossils.[41] Ellen Biddle asserted that officers on the frontier had more interests in their lives than their wives did: in addition to their military duties, "they could swing a gun over their shoulders and go hunting, which is the greatest pleasure a man knows."[42]

At the same time, the very hardships of life in frontier army posts contributed to an intimacy that compensated in human warmth for material deprivations. Leaving a congenial post, Martha Summerhayes felt a grief that was peculiar to the army life of continual displacement: "Two years together, in the most intimate companionship, cut off from the outside world, and away from all early ties, had united us with indissoluble bonds,—and now we were to part."[43]

When there were no women present, the officers had few innocent pastimes: they drank and gambled. With women, socializing at the post became less lethal, and in addition to visiting, there might be charades, readings, music, and drama.[44] Women also required lessons in riding, shooting, and hunting, although Libbie noted that officers regarded teaching visiting women to shoot at a mark more dangerous than making a cavalry charge.[45]

At a larger post, the social calendar might be as crowded as that of a resort hotel, an endless round of visits, rides, croquet, walks, singing, dancing, hunting, and picnics.[46] A typical entry in Annie Gibson Roberts's diary of her 1870 visit to Fort Hays described her ride with Wesley Merritt to the cavalry camp where they found Libbie and a friend "fixing up for a little entertainment to which we ladies of the post are invited." They rode back to the post, where she was staying with her uncle's family, and then went to the dance. Annie danced until midnight and then stayed the night with a friend.[47] A visitor a few months earlier, Libbie's cousin Rebecca Richmond, wrote to her mother that a party of music and dancing at the Custers' house lasted until 3:00 A.M. Five days later, another letter informed Rebecca's parents that she was out until 5:00 A.M. at a masquerade party.[48]

Since the wives were primarily occupied with domestic matters, their memoirs are filled with the problems of procuring decent food. Fresh produce was often unobtainable, and canned foods prohibitively expensive. At the same time that the Palace Restaurant in Tucson provided a full meal for a quarter, an army wife was paying two dollars for a can of peaches.[49] In her desperation to vary the monotonous diet of the post, Libbie once made a trip to a nearby town "largely inhabited by outlaws and desperadoes." While she was marketing, the bridge was swept away by a flash flood, and Libbie and her escort, an officer and a sergeant, were stranded until they could arrange a precarious passage in a small boat.[50]

Eggs were particularly unobtainable and particularly prized. Perhaps because she never did any cooking herself, Libbie wrote appreciatively of powdered eggs.[51] Not all wives were so easily mollified by substitutes, though. When Jack Summerhayes cavalierly told her wife to cook without eggs, it was the last straw: she almost wished her husband, his commanding officer, and the soldier assigned to help with the cooking "at the bottom of the Rio Colorado."[52]

But cooking was not always spartan on the frontier. Libbie's cousin Rebecca, who frequently visited the Custers, described a dinner she ate at Colonel Sturgis's house: "The first course consisted of soup, and the second of fish; the third of turkey and oysters with a great variety of vegetables, the fourth of birds and veal, with jellies and pickles; the fifth of ham and salad; the sixth of charlotte russe, with cream, blancmange, and cake; concluding with nuts, oranges, and coffee."[53]

When Eveline Alexander had the honor of entertaining General of the Army William T. Sherman during his visit to Fort Stevens, Colorado, she decided to make a blancmange for the dinner. In the midst of preparations a sudden gust of wind completely destroyed the fragile pudding, but in true army fashion she refused to be discouraged. The general clearly enjoyed the meal she served, saying that "he had not tasted so fine a saddle of mutton since he left Saint Louis." Noticing that he had a third helping, Eveline took him at his word.[54]

The social distinctions of civilian life might seem beside the point in the army, where rank was sovereign, but Eveline Alexander's diary is memorable for its social appraisals of everyone she met. When she joined her husband at Fort Smith, Montana Territory, she found the women already there "a queer set." The decidedly middle-class Eveline pronounced one mother and daughter "very common"; she noted that another officer's wife was a former laundress and two others were Mexicans, applying these labels as if they spoke for themselves. A bride of nineteen was "not highly educated, but well behaved," while another bride was only fourteen—utterly ignorant, but, Eveline thought, with some potential.[55]

Army wives mirrored the society they came from in regarding people of other races as inferiors who merited only patronizing interest, if any. They were usually both fearful and curious about Indians, the proportion depending upon their circumstances.[56] When Frances Roe first arrived on the frontier, she confessed that she had always longed to see what the experienced would recognize as a Cooper Indian, a "real noble red man—dressed in beautiful skins embroidered with beads, and on his head long, waving feathers." Instead, "they were simply, and only, painted, dirty, and nauseous-smelling savages!"[57] The commanding officer's wife told her that Indians were all alike: "When you have seen one you have seen all. And she must know," Roe concluded, "for she has lived on the frontier a long time, and has seen many Indians of many tribes."[58] Libbie noted matter-of-factly that many of the Kansas teamsters were Mexicans, "short, swarthy, dull, and hardly a grade above the animal."[59]

Emily Fitzgerald, at Fort Lapwai during the Nez Percé troubles, always expressed an unmitigated hatred of the hostiles in her letters home. Even before the war broke out, she wrote of a meeting between peace commissioners and the dissatisfied Indians, "I wish they would kill them all," then added to make certain of being understood, "the Indians, not the commissioners."[60]

Army wives tended to see Indian women as degraded by heavy labor and bereft of those courtesies accorded to women by American society.[61] Elizabeth Burt was indignant at the sight of a squaw toiling with heavy sacks while her "lordly" husband walked unencumbered, occasionally prodding her with a heavy stick when she faltered. When Burt described this "outrage" to her husband, he complacently replied that "squaws were accustomed to this kind of treatment."[62] Libbie minutely chronicled the attentions that the "one pretty squaw" among the Indian women at Fort Lincoln paid to her warrior husband, combing and braiding his hair, strapping on his leggings, adjusting his warbonnet. On one occasion Libbie saw him running along the riverbank after bathing, "his wife waving a blanket behind him to keep off the mosquitoes!"[63] Libbie clearly perceived no kinship between herself and this "faithful slave," yet, with some allowance for cultural differences, she might have seen the woman's devotion to her husband as similar to her own. As a bride she had quite happily helped her husband put on his dress uniform.[64]

The most extreme and unfavorable descriptions of Indian women were made by men. An early visitor to the Plains frontier, Pierre-Antoine Tabeau, observed of the Indian tribes he encountered that the women were "beasts of burden of these inhuman monsters . . . loaded with all the work."[65] His would become the stereotypical view. Custer's brother-in-law, Lieutenant James Calhoun, puzzled over the mourning customs of Indian wives: "Why they should feel sad to lose their lords and masters is a conundrum I cannot answer, for their lives are spent in a continual state of servitude, and their masters are of the most brutal order."[66] Commenting in the 1870s on a White House reception for some visiting Indians, Captain DeWitt Clinton Poole was strongly impressed by the contrast he observed between the white and Indian women mingling there, "the former lithe and graceful, delicately formed, with finely cut features, the peers and companions of man; the latter heavy and awkward, coarse featured and over-worked, the menials and slaves of their male companions. The elevation of women by civilization and enlightenment, and her low estate under the rule of savages were here boldly outlined."[67]

Mexican women fared almost as badly as Indians in the condescending observations of Lydia Lane. It was rumored that one could see Mexican "beauties" at Mexican dances in Santa Fe, so the army wives, escorted by officers, occasionally went to these dances in the hope of glimpsing these women. Oddly enough, they never did. The beauties were "unavoidably absent," and Lane reported with considerable satisfaction that she was still waiting to see "the first really pretty Mexican woman."[68] Lane's insensitivity extended to her amusement over the fears of her Mexican servant girl, who "almost had a convulsion" the first time she heard a train whistle, and who had particular difficulty with the steps: "she was not used to going up- and down-stairs in the adobe shanties at home." The girl's hesitation exasperated the Lanes, who were "ready to shake her for her delay."[69]

Martha Summerhayes, a descendant of the Puritan divine Jonathan Edwards, is an arresting exception to the rule of frontier prejudice. Her Massachusetts upbringing was seasoned with a stay in Germany, where she fell in love with the romance of the army, a quality that would be in short supply in the desolate outposts of her story. While Summerhayes ignored the standard decorum of army wives in allowing herself the luxury of complaining about the tremendous heat (up to 122 degrees), the heavy dust, and the desolate landscape, she had a greater ability than most wives to accept all sorts of people. After her husband upbraided her for crying at a soldier's funeral, she made an effort but found it impossible to repress her natural feelings: "Visions of the poor boy's mother on some little farm in Missouri or Kansas perhaps . . . would come before me, and my heart was filled with sadness."[70]

It was undoubtedly more of a leap to feel rapport with the dark-skinned people of her new environment, but Martha was capable of this as well. Libbie Custer praised the handsome physique of Wild Bill Hickok in a distanced and stylized way, but it is difficult to imagine her, or any of the other army wives who penned memoirs, frankly relishing the physical attractiveness of a male Indian as Summerhayes does: the association of Indians with savagery, and Indian men with particular danger, was too strong a barrier. When the Apache chief Diablo came to visit, however, Summerhayes noticed his "extraordinary good looks." On his second visit, she made the observation again.[71]

Before long the couple acquired an Indian servant, whom Summerhayes described appreciatively: "Tall and well-made, with clean-cut limbs and features, fine smooth copper-colored skin, handsome face, heavy black hair . . . this was my Charley, my half-tame Cocopah, my man about the place." Charley's scanty loincloth costume, which a scandalized visitor objected to, revealed his body to advantage. As she tried to tell her visitor, within his own culture Charley was perfect as he was: "I explained to her that the Indian's fashion of wearing white men's clothes was not pleasing to the eye, and told her that she must cultivate her aesthetic sense, and in a short time she would be able to admire these copper-colored creatures of Nature as much as I did. But she never recovered from her amazement at Charley's lack of apparel."[72]

More than simply accepting native peoples without condescension, Summerhayes, an early cultural relativist, came to value their philosophy of life. When her San Francisco aunt objected to her constantly wearing white dresses because people would think she was Mexican, Summerhayes replied, "I almost wish I were. . . . Look at the tired faces of the women in your streets. . . . one never sees that sort of expression down below." She had asked her Mexican servant, who had never seen a tree or green grass, if she did not want to see these things: the woman simply shook her head no. Summerhayes found this incomprehensible at first, but she came to envy the Mexicans' ability to accept their environment. The women dressed comfortably while she, at the behest of her husband, "sweltered during the day in high-necked and long-sleeved white dresses, kept up the table in American fashion, ate American food in so far as we could get it, and all at the expense of strength."[73]

In this environment, American civilization became for Summerhayes *"a whirlpool," "a struggle"—"fetters."* Not that she was unhappy to go back East after four years in the West; she simply felt that the Mexican mode of life was more suited to the desert than her own culture's.

The wives who wrote memoirs did so in the frontier army spirit of chronicling difficulties while maintaining a positive spirit. They also tended to defer to their husbands, even in such domestic matters as cooking without eggs. And beyond the dictates of their husbands and the unspoken law of facing hardships without complaining lay the vast body of military law and usage that governed their conduct. Even in a frontier fort surrounded by wilderness there were rules applying to everything, as Frances Roe found out when she thought to compliment the post commander on his furniture—made by soldiers—by saying that she would like to have the same pieces made for her own quarters. Rather than acting pleased, the officer appeared uncomfortable: he finally muttered something about the post having no good carpenters at present. Later, Roe found out that only senior officers were allowed to have their furniture made by soldiers. Her husband, a mere second lieutenant, did not qualify.[74]

Because group decorum was so strong in the tiny societies of frontier army posts, and because surrounding dangers furnished a rationale for controlling the behavior of women altogether, those rarely chronicled instances of individual assertion are all the more memorable. Alice Baldwin recorded an incident at the preliminary peace talks of 1867 when an unnamed army wife joined a circle of Indians and officers who were passing the pipe and silently smoking. When the pipe reached the woman, "she took a whiff herself, to the surprised consternation of her husband and the indignant chiefs."[75] Annie Sokalski, a controversial army wife renowned for her fine riding and shooting, was another singular personality. One day during General Sherman's visit to Fort Phil Kearny she appeared on the parade-ground in her wolf-skin riding habit, "with wolf-tails at the bottom of the skirt almost sweeping the ground, and a fur hat from which floated another bunch of wolf-tails." As she galloped past Sherman, he acknowledged the strangeness of what he had seen, raising his hands in a gesture of astonishment and saying to the post commander: "What the devil of a creature is that? Is she a wild woman, a Pawnee, or a Sioux, or what?"[76] A woman with a penchant for self-assertion like Annie's could expect such categorization.

Another violation of accepted behavior was venturing too far from the post, an experience Elizabeth Burt and Libbie Custer described in almost identical terms. Probably many others had similar close calls—even women who tried to adhere to the rules would sometimes become restive under a numbing regimen of confinement due to Indians or bad weather. At Fort C. F. Smith, Burt and several other women were forced to run for their lives, chased by Indians when they left the precincts of the post. A soldier had told them about a lovely spring with wildflowers nearby, and "the temptation to gather those flowers and to see the spring was great."[77] Accompanied by an officer, Libbie and her friend Anna Darrah walked outside the prescribed limits of their post, returning only after dark. The sentry fired on them, and they were forced to cower in fear until the officer could creep away to get help.[78] Both writers were chagrined at the danger incurred by their violation of the rules, and both vowed never to break them again—although Libbie would have similar episodes from time to time, followed by the same remorse and vows to be more careful.

As they contemplated their frontier experiences from the vantage point of many years later, army wives were inclined to be nostalgic. They had braved a great deal to be with their husbands, including, very often, long separation from their children. Absorbed in coping with their situation, they did not realize then what came to be the case, that the memories of discomfort would pale and only "bright and glowing recollections" remain.[79] Martha Summerhayes, whose reminiscences were otherwise so different from those of most army wives, begins her final page conventionally with a bow to the salutary nature of hardships and with the usual twinge of nostalgia for the past. But instead of ending on a saccharine note, she dismissed the images called up by memory: "The army life of those years is past and gone, and Arizona, as we knew it, has vanished from the face of the earth."[80]

Even now, except for a ribbon of road, vast stretches of the Great Plains seem much like they must have been in the time of the frontier army: a desolate, unmarked expanse of violent climatic extremes, still unfriendly to settlers. But Summerhayes was right: everything else that constituted the life of these wives on the frontier—the great herds of buffalo, the hostile Indians, and the army itself—has indeed vanished from the face of the earth.

9

The Plains Indians

> The Great Spirit did not make us to work, but to live by hunting. You white men can work if you want to. We do not interfere with you, and again you say, why do you not become civilized? We do not want your civilization! We would live as our fathers did, and their fathers before them. I am no white man! —Crazy Horse

> Of course, the march of civilization cannot be impeded. The white man is destined to drive the aboriginal Indian from his haunts, his hunting-ground, and his lodge. It seems hard that this should be so, but it is the destiny of nations. —*Chicago Tribune,* April 21, 1876

Like everyone else on the frontier, Custer held James Fenimore Cooper responsible for misleading his postwar countrymen about the real nature of Indians.[1] He criticized Cooper's romanticized image of the "noble red man," yet the counterimage Custer offered in his own writing could also have come straight from Cooper—a version of Cooper's Indian villains, the evil Iroquois. "Inseparable from the Indian character," Custer wrote, ". . . is his remarkable taciturnity, his deep dissimulation, the perseverance with which he followed his plans of revenge or conquest, his concealment and apparent lack of curiosity, his stoical courage when in the power of his enemies, his cunning, his caution, and last, but not least, the wonderful power and subtlety of his senses."[2]

Whether or not Custer believed in his own literary description, he did consciously attempt to acquire firsthand knowledge of Indians. Just as he prided himself on getting to know everything about his surroundings and on finding unusual animal specimens, which he kept as pets, sent to eastern zoos, or killed and preserved himself—so he studied Indians, becoming proficient in Indian sign language and learning Indian customs. As the Arikara scout Red Star said, "If we ever left out one thing in our ceremonies he always suggested it to us."[3]

Many army officers were neither so interested nor so astute. Colonel John Gibbon, a well-meaning person who felt that he understood Indians and spoke up for treating them decently, could nevertheless be curiously obtuse about what he observed. Early on in Gibbon's march down the Yellowstone as part of the operation that would end for Custer at the Little Bighorn, his Crow scouts lost their entire pony herd to their traditional enemy, the Sioux. Gibbon wrote:

> The scene which followed was absurd in the extreme. The Crows assembled at their camp and *cried* like children whose toys had been broken. There is nothing unnatural in a crying child, and the manly grief of a broken heart excites one's sympathy, but to see a parcel of great big Indians standing together and blubbering like babies, with great tears streaming down their swarthy faces because they had lost their horses, struck every one as supremely ridiculous.[4]

Gibbon made a facile assumption that the weeping of white and Indian males is the same behavior, but what he contemptuously described as a demeaning loss of control in public was actually a ritual response appropriate to the great humiliation administered by the enemy. Such a pronounced public display suited not only the indignity experienced by the warriors but the loss itself: horses were the chief material possession and source of wealth of the Plains tribes, and their theft was rightly lamented. That the loss had been inflicted by their foremost enemy intensified the blow.

Unlike Gibbon, Custer was a careful observer, and he knew how to make his Indian scouts feel valued. When he was given a group of Crow scouts who had been with Gibbon, he told them that he had heard that the Crow Indians were "the bravest scouts and the best horsemen among all the Indians, and that was the reason he had asked General Terry to send them to him."[5] The scouts responded in kind, telling Custer that they had heard that he never abandoned a trail, that when the food gave out, he ate mule: "That was the kind of a man they wanted to fight under; they were willing to eat mule too."[6]

In terms of relating to Indian scouts, there was also a telling difference between Custer and his second in command at the Little Bighorn, Major Marcus Reno. While assembling the scouts for a reconnaissance that General Terry had assigned him, Reno instructed a scout named High Bear that he could not go because his horse was galled. High Bear replied: "You see the sun there, if you say it does not move I will not dispute you," an Indian way of politely expressing his utter disagreement. Reno made matters worse by instructing the interpreter to tell High Bear that "any man who is not a fool would agree with me, and that he will show himself a soldier by agreeing with me without question." High Bear became incensed at this insulting pomposity, both men went for their weapons, and another scout had to intervene to restore peace.[7]

Custer also intended to forbid a scout with a disabled horse from going with him, but he had the wisdom to relent when the Indian, Howling Wolf, made a spirited reply: "See, he is sound under the saddle. He can out-travel any horse but yours and should he fall I will keep up with you on foot." Custer laughed and said, "Since you are a wolf you may go."[8]

Like other Americans imbued with a spirit of progress, Custer believed that those Indians who renounced their traditional culture could be assimilated. He was therefore particularly pleased with a group of reservation scouts that accompanied his 1874 reconnaissance of the Black Hills. After the expedition he sent them back with a letter that stated in part, "I do not say, simply, that they have been good soldiers, for I doubt if any village in our country could turn out thirty more exemplary men." He went on to add that one Sunday he heard the familiar strains of "Rock of Ages," and, wondering where the singing was coming from, left his tent to look. No cavalrymen were singing, only the "sons of those who had roamed over the prairies in barbarous wildness," and he concluded, "May the good work go on."[9]

Since Indians who scouted for the army and celebrated the Christian Sabbath more fervently than whites were rare on the Plains, settlers generally had no patience with the approach of "good work" rather than firepower. Samuel J. Crawford, who resigned the governorship in order to lead his Kansas volunteers against the Indians, described the situation from the settler's point of view:

> There, under the same Government, was the War Department, with an army in the field, endeavoring to suppress Indian hostilities, and at the same time, the Interior Department, furnishing the same hostile Indians with supplies & munitions of war. Back of the Interior Department was a gang of thieving Indian agents in the West, & a maudlin sentimentality in the East, derived from James Fenimore Cooper's novels & impressed upon that department by ignorant but well-meaning humanitarians.[10]

When a professor at Eastern University, Nathaniel P. Hill, visited Colorado in the summer of 1864, he reflected the views of the frontier's ordinary white citizens. "There is no sentimentality here on the frontier respecting Indians," he wrote to his wife. "Indians are all the same, a treacherous and villanous set. I would rejoice, as would every man in Colorado, to see them exterminated."[11] It was a common enough view. Teresa Vielé, an army wife in Texas before the Civil War, also favored extermination. "Nothing less," she wrote, "will render many portions of the State of Texas a safe abode for white settlers."[12]

Individual instances aside, the white and Indian cultures that met on the Plains frontier could not coexist, nor did they want to. Crazy Horse's emphatic words to his friend, the Sioux agent Dr. Valentine McGillycuddy, ring through history as the definitive statement of the Indian position: "We do not want your civilization! . . . I am no white man!"[13]

Another famous Sioux, Sitting Bull, left a letter for white soldiers along the Yellowstone River that said "I want to know what you are doing on this road. You scare all the buffalo away. I want to hunt in this place." Weigh his forthright statement against one of General Sherman's equally direct pronouncements: "The more I see of these Indians the more convinced am I that they have all to be killed or be maintained as a species of pauper."[14] Apart from the other cultural differences that separated them, whites and Indians inhabited the land so differently they could not share it. Indians wanted to use the land for hunting, whites for cultivation and settlement. Meeting Sitting Bull for the first time, General Nelson Miles found himself treated to a lecture on the subject. "God placed me here and he gave me this great country, and I want to live here," the chief said pointedly. After listening "for some time," Miles told his audience at an Order of Indian Wars banquet, "I finally made up my mind that talking would do no good."[15] It seldom did when Indians and whites met to resolve their conflicts.

The old Puritan-colonial rationale for taking Indian land remained persuasive in Custer's time: Indians made no use of land, neither cultivating it nor extracting its valuable underground resources. They roamed over it like wild animals whereas whites, in a cliché often applied by whites to their settlement of North America, "made the wilderness bloom," establishing communities with such permanent structures as homes, stores, churches, and schools. Nineteenth-century Americans took satisfaction in bringing about changes of this sort, which they invariably called progress. Voicing the prevailing view, an enlisted man in the Seventh Cavalry wrote in his diary in 1869, "Plenty of wood and water and the very best of land, very rich. Too good to let the Indians have. They ought to be driven off and the land given to the poor white man of different states."[16] Similarly, a writer for the *Sioux City Times* in 1872 protested that "the Government should donate such a country to a race of degraded thieves as a park, for they want it for nothing else."[17] Such opinions merely restated in blunt language the more elegant formulations of the nation's political fathers. In the late-eighteenth century Benjamin Franklin had speculated that rum might be the means of fulfilling "the design of Providence to extirpate these savages in order to make room for the cultivators of the earth."[18] John Quincy Adams asked rhetorically in 1800, "Shall the exuberant bosom of the common mother, amply adequate to the nourishment of millions, be claimed exclusively by a few hundred of her offspring?"[19]

In 1921, looking back on the long resolved issue, Walter Camp remarked with satisfaction that the lesson to be learned from the white-Indian struggle for possession of the continent was that "no people or class of men, generally speaking, shall dominate some portion of the earth if there be others who will take it and make better use of it."[20] This belief, whether phrased directly in the language of an enlisted man or in the more abstract rhetoric of an after-dinner speaker, was the heart of the matter. Certain that they made better use of the land, whites were equally certain that they deserved to have it.

A voice like that of William H. Hare, missionary bishop of Niobrara, was truly crying in the wilderness when he wrote to the *New York Tribune* protesting the proposal to buy the Black Hills from the Sioux.

Apropos of the assertion that "barbarism has no right to hold back vast areas of land from the tillage of the needy settler," Bishop Hare argued that common opinion erred in its view of the problem. "The chief sinners in this line are not Indians," he wrote, "but white speculators, who have bought up land and hold it by the ten-thousand acres, to the exclusion of the needy."[21] A similar point might have been made concerning the huge tracts of land given to the railroads rather than made available to small homesteaders.

Even if whites wanted to understand Indians—and some on the frontier did—there were serious barriers to doing so, first and foremost that of language. Frontier interpreters usually had only a limited practical vocabulary; complexities and nuances escaped them. Substantive issues aside, the account of almost any Indian-white negotiation embodied radical misunderstandings, as much the result of inept translation as of extreme cultural difference.

Miscommunication was rampant. In General Hancock's first meeting with the Cheyenne and Arapahoes he made a long speech, but according to the mixed-blood witness George Bent, "he did not know how to talk to Indians and the chiefs did not understand him at all."[22] The three interpreters were similarly at a loss. Bent did not record what they conveyed to Hancock about his speech, but the twentieth-century scholar Stanley Vestal assumed that on many occasions an interpreter, "rather than lose his pay, would converse with the chief about the weather, and then tell the eager white man a yarn made of whole cloth."[23] He might also spin such a tale to the Indians: a few months after the battle of the Little Bighorn an informant learned that an interpreter at the Cheyenne Agency was telling the Indians that "the whites are going to do something terrible with them."[24]

No one has ever satisfactorily explained the most famous mistranslation of Plains Indian history. After Crazy Horse's surrender in 1877, General George Crook asked his band of Oglalas to serve as scouts against the rebellious Nez Percé. According to a bilingual scout who was present, Crazy Horse replied: "We are tired of war; we came in for peace, but now that the Great Father asks our help we will go north and fight until there is not a Nez Percé left." Frank Grouard, the official interpreter and someone who knew Crazy Horse well, rendered the final part of the speech rather differently. By his account, the famous warrior said, "We will go north and fight until not a white man is left."[25] Had a simple error of idiomatic usage been made, one might assume that the interpreter had done so in good faith, but Grouard, who was fluent in Sioux, could not have innocently confused the dissimilar nouns for "white man" and "Nez Percé."[26]

Crazy Horse and Grouard had been friends when Grouard lived with the Sioux, but he abandoned them to become an army scout. It is possible, then, that Grouard feared some reprisal when this most formidable of war chiefs became a reluctant agency Indian.[27] Yet this explanation would contradict the observation of Captain John Bourke, who saw Crazy Horse about this time and described him as "gloomy and reserved" to all but Frank Grouard: "When talking to Frank his countenance lit up with genuine pleasure."[28] Crazy Horse, it seems, did not change his feelings for his friend. Grouard, who had seen which way the wind was blowing some time before, may have changed his.

Almost ten years later, in 1886, faulty translation was still hobbling communication between the two cultures. When a number of Indians and army veterans came together for a reunion of participants in the battle of the Little Bighorn, it was an optimum chance for whites to hear Indian accounts of the battle. Some of the army veterans began asking questions of Gall, the renowned warrior who had played a major role in the fighting. Gall's English was rudimentary. According to Vestal, the theme of his speeches was usually "'when do we eat,' though sometimes he varied this military formula by threatening to kill anyone who disagreed with him."[29] On this occasion, however, Lieutenant Edward Godfrey wrote that from the volubility of the answers related by the interpreter, "nearly all, including Gall, became satisfied that the interpreter was 'padding.'"[30] Similar instances are repeatedly encountered in the history of Indian-white interaction because on the Plains frontier it was almost impossible to find a genuinely bilingual interpreter—or a disinterested speaker.

Aside from the technical problems of translation, Indians had ways of expressing themselves that inevitably misled whites. As the sensitive observer Thomas B. Marquis noted, to the Indians who had fought at the Little Bighorn, "Custer" meant the army they encountered rather than its leader: "When Indians claimed to have killed Custer, this meant 'I was at the battle. I saw the Custer soldiers, shot at them, helped in the killing of them.' None of the Indians claimed to have seen Custer and recognized him."[31] Whites hearing the assertion "I killed

Custer" naturally assumed that an individual was claiming responsibility for Custer's death.

Miscommunication was a two-way street. If it happened at all, Custer's widely cited declaration to his Ree scouts—reported by one of them long afterward—must have been an instance of Indian failure to understand a white man. Supposedly Custer told the scouts that after a victorious campaign against the Sioux, he would go to Washington and become their Great Father.[32] Some critics have eagerly seized upon this as evidence of presidential ambition; others have thought that Custer expected to become Indian commissioner. Perhaps Custer had such a secret ambition that never revealed itself in any of the voluminous records left by himself or others.[33] More likely, he merely said that he would see the Great Father and make certain the Rees were well taken care of. Although he had learned the basic sign language of the Plains Indians, Custer did not speak Ree, nor were his scouts proficient in English. When the Ree narrative was published, many years after the events it describes took place, an enlisted man who served with Custer wrote to Libbie to express his misgivings about the account, some of which he found "impossible to accept." He concluded delicately: "I believe the Indian is naturally as truthful as the white man, no more and no less, but sometimes their interpreters for reasons best known to themselves make the Indians say some strange and improbable things."[34]

The personal names of Indians also suffered distortion in translation. In Custer's time there were no scholars of Plains Indian culture who could tell the general public, for example, that the press's mocking rendition of Sitting Bull as "Slightly Recumbent Gentleman Cow" was far from the mark. The more accurate translation of Tatanka Iyotake was "Buffalo Bull Who Resides among Us." Since the buffalo was the center of Sioux life—their primary source of food, shelter, and clothing—such a name conferred honor on its possessor and pointed to his value to the tribe, a value akin to that of the buffalo.[35] Tashunka Witko, known to whites as Crazy Horse, is more accurately translated as "Untamed Horse."[36]

Already erroneously subsumed under a common rubric that blurred their tribal distinctions and thus failed to reflect their own sense of identity, Indians were further removed from proper designation and a recognition of individuality by being referred to mockingly as "Lo," or

"Mr. Lo," a deliberate misreading of a famous passage in Alexander Pope's *Essay on Man*: "Lo, the poor Indian! whose untutor'd mind / Sees God in clouds, or hears him in the wind" (1.99–100).[37] Pope regarded the Indian as poor because he was an uneducated heathen, but his poem also intimates that this example is not entirely negative: the Indian lives according to nature, happy with his lot. The reader Pope addressed directly is "wiser," but misled by pride to sin.

For white settlers, the verse—in which "the poor Indian" is read as if it were an apposition to the proper name "Lo"—simply described a superstitious, hence lesser being: at best for nineteenth-century Americans, Indians were "an inferior breed of men."[38] In addition, the term is a sarcastic reference to those eastern humanitarians whose idea of "the poor Indian" was so at variance with the frontiersman's bloodthirsty scalping savage. The *Leavenworth, Kansas, Times and Conservative*, for example, commented indignantly on the story of Thomas Alderdice, whose wife was captured and killed by Cheyennes: "We wish some of the philanthropists who talk about civilizing the Indians, could have heard this unfortunate and almost heart-broken man tell his story. We think they would at least have wavered a little in their opinion of the Lo family."[39]

Misleading and demeaning names for Indians were only one manifestation of a common attitude. Plain lack of interest—the automatic dismissal of things Indian as savage and inferior, therefore unworthy of white attention—largely accounts for the failure to understand cultural differences. This attitude was reciprocated by the Indians, who were ethnocentric as well. When a Paiute Indian first saw white men, he told his family that "they were not like 'humans.' They were more like owls [a bird of bad omen to the Paiute] than anything else."[40] Toward an enemy Indians could be relentless. On the Black Hills expedition Custer's favorite Indian scout, Bloody Knife, made a speech whose point was the wrongful lenience of the whites toward some Indians who had been in their power. "The chief of the whites had captured 27 Sioux—He had let them go—This was wrong," Bloody Knife complained. "It was wrong to the Rees. . . . They returned to Fort Lincoln without a single scalp—They had told their squaws that they would bring their belts full of scalps."[41]

Whites regarded their Indian enemies with equal callousness. It says a great deal that long after he should have known better, General Sheridan confessed that he had assumed "Sitting Bull" to be a generic term for "hostile."[42] Sheridan is the source of the most famous remark about Indians: "The only good Indian is a dead Indian." This was not exactly what he said, and the context of the actual remark suggests he was making a joke at the expense of an Indian who identified himself to the general as "Tosawi, Good Indian."[43] Nevertheless, the saying's notoriety reflects the preference of a sizable number of white settlers.

The history of the "Indian problem" on the Plains is often starkly dichotomized between "humanitarians" and others, or between those who favored Grant's peace policy and preferred to keep Indian affairs in the Department of the Interior and those who saw military force as a better policy and accordingly wanted to transfer the Indian Bureau to the Department of War. But the polarization was not as stark as it may seem with religious figures and former abolitionists ranged against army officers and frontier settlers. However much reformers and humanitarians, as they were variously called, wanted to settle and civilize Indians—turning them all into Custer's model scouts—few preached the complete integration and equality of nonwhite peoples.[44] Most nineteenth-century Americans believed that heredity, which they identified with race, was a more powerful explanation for character than was environment: such a premise suggested to them that nonwhite peoples would always be inferior to whites.[45] What liberals envisioned for Indians was articulated by President Rutherford B. Hayes: "We owe it to them as a moral duty to help them in attaining at least that degree of civilization which they may be able to reach."[46] The degree of civilization attainable and the best way of achieving it were open to debate.

The noisy controversy over the best means of dealing with the Plains Indians obscured a salient fact: everyone agreed that they had to be dealt with in some fashion or other. No matter how outraged prominent people were about injustices committed against the Indians, no one seriously suggested the obvious solution of complete withdrawal from their land. Few even suggested not taking any more of it. On the contrary, territory supposedly guaranteed the Indians first by treaty and then, after 1871, by agreement continued to shrink—steadily and inexorably. The consequences of the Dawes Act of 1887 might be taken as representative of all governmental efforts to help the native inhabitants of the United States—well-meaning but doomed to failure because most Indians were unready to embrace white culture. Over a period of forty-seven years the Dawes initiative to establish and encourage individual Indian ownership of reservation land led to the transfer of two-thirds of Indian land to whites.[47] "History, and here cited without comment," as Herman Melville might say.[48]

During the Custers' years on the plains the two competing authorities, the departments of Interior and War, awkwardly shared the duty of implementing official policy toward Indians. It was not the black-and-white dichotomy that partisans of each have described: each side had its credible and humane spokesmen, but each had its share of irresponsible representatives as well: venal and inept Indian agents on one side, practitioners of indiscriminate slaughter on the other. Moreover, the rivalry between the two departments was bound to have negative effects on the objects of contention—the Indians. Libbie Custer related an all too typical instance in which a delegation of Sioux from a nearby reservation came to ask for food at Fort Abraham Lincoln. Although their condition of near starvation would have made it understandable, the Indians were not begging: they simply wanted an "advance" on their own supplies, which had been held up by bad weather. Custer telegraphed to Washington for permission to feed them—which was denied by the Department of the Interior, jealously preserving its prerogative to manage Indian affairs.[49]

And quite aside from the politics and partisanship that made every issue a contest, powerful economic interests—often referred to as the "Indian ring"—worked to maintain the lucrative business of supplying the government's Indian wards. Few commentators on the period failed to express indignation at the corruption of the "Indian ring."[50] In 1869 Sheridan had written to Grant that "thieves and robbers of the Public monies extend from the lowest agent to the halls of Congress connected with the present Indian management."[51] Some two years later, General Crook made the same point in a letter to Rutherford B. Hayes, then governor of Ohio. "The fact is," he told his good friend, "there is too much money in this Indian business, for these people to die without a hard struggle, and I am particularly anxious that the honest and good people of the country should understand what a gigantic fraud this Indian ring is."[52]

Few cases reveal this corruption as clearly as that of the Indian chief and the Yale professor, Red Cloud of the Oglala Sioux and Othniel

Charles Marsh, the country's first professor of paleontology. In 1875 the professor accompanied an expedition whose purpose was to settle the question raised by Custer's 1874 reconnaissance of the Black Hills; namely, was there a significant amount of gold in the region? Since the expedition was launched from the Red Cloud agency, the reservation allotted to the Oglala Sioux, the professor had a chance to see for himself how the Indians were treated, and he was scandalized. He wrote a long letter to President Grant detailing abuses that he described as "a natural result of the present loose and irresponsible system of furnishing the Indians with goods and supplies, a system that tends directly to invite fraud."[53]

Professor Marsh began his complaint by bluntly stating his lack of confidence in both Secretary of the Interior Columbus Delano and Commissioner of Indian Affairs John Quincy Smith: "In all my intercourse with these two officials, their object has manifestly been to find out, not so much what the frauds actually were, as the extent of my information concerning them, so as to prevent, by every means in their power, all publicity or exposure of them."[54] Red Cloud himself had shown Marsh an array of shoddy rations, samples of which the professor took East. In every case the discrepancy between what the government paid for goods and the quality and quantity received by the Indians was astounding. The blankets given to the Indians, for example, were too few and of poor quality: "The brand U.S.I.D. on these blankets injured the cloth, so that, after a short wear, holes replaced the letters."[55] Moreover, the Indians complained that the blankets were too small to be used by adults.[56] The government paid for and shipped thirty-seven bales of blankets; eighteen bales were distributed and then only on November 12, in the middle of a snowstorm.

Several months before Marsh saw these conditions for himself, Lieutenant W. L. Carpenter, who had been stationed at the agency all winter, wrote of Red Cloud's Sioux: "The poor wretches have been several times this winter on the verge of starvation, through the rascality of the Indian Ring. They have been compelled to eat dogs, wolves, and ponies."[57]

Receiving this detailed missive from a distinguished—and disinterested—citizen, President Grant ordered an investigation. It was all he could think of to do, in spite of Marsh's having told him that "no less than five special Commissioners, or other officials, appointed and paid by the Department of the Interior, had personally investigated this agency before my visit, and given that Department information indicating the bad state of affairs there."[58]

Unsurprisingly, the reservation agent and his suppliers put up a vigorous defense of their comfortable arrangements, and the commission rather naively accepted their explanations: "One of the largest cattlemen in Wyoming assured the commission that no man living could estimate the weights of cattle on the hoof, yet all these cattlemen were making their living largely through their ability not only to estimate the weights of the cattle they bought but to estimate what the animals would weigh after being on good range for six months."[59]

The commission took Marsh to task for making no effort to determine if the samples given to him by Red Cloud were truly representative. It concluded that they were not, although it also found that the general run of rations was inferior in quality to what was specified. It recommended that several contractors not be used in the future and that the inspector who had certified the rations as acceptable be fired. But ultimately the well-publicized investigation changed little.[60]

This was business as usual for the government and its Indian contractors, but it must have been disillusioning to the public-spirited professor. No doubt nothing but sharp practices could be expected from those involved in the profitable racket of Indian supply, but what must have been Professor Marsh's surprise—and chagrin—to hear Red Cloud deny in his presence that he had complained or given him the incriminating samples! The savvy chief, in the interval between Marsh's visit to the reservation and the meeting with President Grant in Washington, had reconsidered the advisability of making such an accusation, or possibly had judged the government officials involved to have more power than the professor. In any event Red Cloud's main priority had become replacing the agent for his reservation with one who, he said with simple eloquence, was already wealthy and would not attempt to fill his pockets at the expense of the Oglalas.[61]

Indians like Red Cloud whom the government regarded as important were sometimes invited to travel East and observe the impressive cities there in the hope that they would realize the superiority of American society to their own. (Usually they returned home with more distaste than admiration.) On one such visit the Sioux chiefs Spotted Tail and Swift Bear were invited by General Sherman to spend an evening at the general's home. "Mrs. Sherman and her daughters showed these two chiefs every attention and courtesy, gave them strawberries, ice cream and cake."[62] It may have been these desserts that Spotted Tail was thinking of when he later remarked that white men had many good things to eat and drink that they had never sent out to the Indians. The Shermans and the chiefs finished the evening by spending several hours looking over the general's "collection of Indian curiosities, weapons and trinkets."[63] This is a peculiar moment to imagine. Since Indians have always been extremely sensitive about their sacred objects falling into the hands of outsiders, this part of the evening could have been highly offensive to the Sioux chiefs, the counterpart of an Indian asking Sherman to admire his collection of white scalps. If so, the chiefs observed a courteous silence, and Sherman was left with the impression that he had entertained his guests well.

White-Indian relations were studded with such anomalous encounters. At the 1867 peace conference at Medicine Lodge Creek, many of the Indians "wore clothing stripped from the bodies of slain troopers."[64] And a widespread complaint along the frontier was that United States citizens were being killed with firearms furnished the Indians by the United States government. Libbie Custer and many others would believe with some justification that her husband's troops had been killed not only with government-issued guns but with a better quality gun than the firearms furnished the soldiers by the army.[65]

After entertaining Spotted Tail, Sherman wrote to Sheridan, "I saw Spotted Tail and treated him kindly because he has gone on his reservation and behaved himself well." Another prominent Sioux in the delegation did not receive such favorable attention from the army's four-star general. "Red Cloud," Sherman's letter continues, "I have declined to see. [He] has been impudent and insolent in the extreme demanding the removal of Fort Fetterman and both removal of all roads and people from his country, which he construes to be wherever he pleases to go."[66] Never mind the possible justice of Red Cloud's claims to land the Sioux had long regarded as theirs: Red Cloud's Oglalas had killed the very officer that Fort Fetterman had been named after, along with his entire force of eighty men. Moreover, as the chief had also demanded and gotten the abandonment of three frontier forts, Red Cloud had some basis for his "impudent and insolent" behavior.

Red Cloud failed to appreciate what Spotted Tail had immediately grasped on his visit to New York in 1870—demography was against the Indians. (In fact, Red Cloud had refused to go to New York, feeling that he had already seen enough in Washington.) When Spotted Tail saw the ships full of immigrants in New York harbor, he marveled that more new white people entered the port in a year than comprised the entire Sioux nation—although the Sioux were numerically superior to all other Plains tribes. In the decade after 1860 a million white settlers had moved beyond the Mississippi; in the decade after 1870 some two and a half million joined them.[67] Spotted Tail went back home convinced of the painful necessity of coming to terms with the white man.[68]

National purpose required that all Indians be confined to places where they would not impede the settlement of the West, but beyond this action there was little in the way of a plan.[69] Few important people cared much about Indian affairs.[70] The policy devised, the reservation system, was merely a form of containment on tracts of land where Indians could live out of the way of whites.

The "hostiles," those Indians who rejected confinement and continued to fight, are stereotypically described as "hot-headed young men." While there was a generational difference of opinion about dealing with the white intruder, it was not a simple matter of hot-headed youth versus wise age. Plains Indians established identity and gained personal distinction by their behavior as warriors, and this was done when they were young.[71] Like the post–Civil War officers who languished in the army without promotion, they saw their chance for achievement diminish with an enforced peace. If these young men were to acquire respect and reputation, they had to distinguish themselves in battle. The "old chiefs," their identities comfortably established, could afford a more pacific view.

Boards of inspection, committees, commissions, fact-finding groups—the government kept launching bureaucratic initiatives, first to solve the Indian problem by removing the native inhabitants to reservations, and then to deal with the new set of problems that reservation life created. But when white Americans thought about the future of their country, they found it convenient to imagine the Indian question resolved in the easiest way by the disappearance of Indians, a disappearance that had no specific agent because it was simply inevitable. Samuel Bowles earned the peculiar title of "humanitarian exterminator" from one historian because Bowles felt that the white man's only role vis-à-vis the Indian was "to smooth and make decent the pathway to his grave."[72] "Barbarism," asserted Lieutenant-Colonel George Forsyth, "must necessarily give way before advancing civilization."[73] Or, as another military man wrote, "no human hand could stay the rolling tide of progress."[74] Most formulations of this sort were expressed in similar impersonal terms that mantled the bare face of dispossession and its attendant brutalities in grandiose abstractions. Custer as a West Point cadet was no exception to this general rule although his language is more colorful. In a composition for his ethics class he described the Indian "on the verge of extinction, standing on his last foothold, clutching his bloodstained rifle, resolved to die amidst the horrors of slaughter, and soon he will be talked of as a noble race who once existed but have now passed away."[75]

Even Secretary of the Interior Columbus Delano, a proponent of Grant's peace policy, told a delegation of visiting Indians that the process of white settlement was unstoppable. Perhaps he thought he had found an especially effective argument when he stated that "the Great Spirit has decreed it."[76] Captain William Ludlow, who explored the Black Hills as part of the Custer expedition of 1874, had the soothing thought that the Indians themselves were reconciled to the inevitable. "The more far-sighted," he wrote, "anticipating the time when hunting buffalo, which is now the main subsistence of the wild tribes, will no longer suffice to that end, have looked forward to settling in and about the Black Hills as their future permanent home, and there awaiting the gradual extinction which is their fate."[77]

Thomas Henry Tibbles, an advocate for Indians in the last quarter of the nineteenth century, believed that their generosity would work against accepting the culture of "a race of sordid people who were subordinating every noble instinct to a ruling passion for accumulating property."[78] Tibbles's point was neatly illustrated when a reporter asked Sitting Bull the source of his influence with his people. He was answered with a question: "Your people look up to men because they are rich; because they have much land, many lodges, many squaws?" The reporter answered yes. "Well," Sitting Bull continued, "I suppose my people look up to me because I am poor. That is the difference." Whereupon the reporter wrote that "in this answer was concentrated all the evasiveness natural to an Indian."[79]

Tibbles's passionate involvement was inspirational: on a lecture tour he made with two Indians on behalf of the Ponca tribe, a woman in the audience was so impressed that she immediately joined the cause. Helen Hunt Jackson went on to write a book, *A Century of Dishonor*, that became the most compelling voice of her time on the side of justice to Indians.[80]

But white sympathizers could only do so much. While newly freed slaves had in Frederick Douglass an eloquent spokesman for their interests, Indians had no comparable figure at home in the white world and able to command its respect.[81] Where former slaves could make common cause, Indians were fragmented into hundreds of tribes who were seldom able to perceive a common interest in opposing whites. In this vacuum of concerted effort and leadership, Indian policy was made entirely by whites who felt that, as President Grant said to a delegation of Sioux, "we know what is for your good better than you can know yourselves."[82]

10

Indian Fighting

However vigilant the troops may be, the Indian on his raid is more so—however well mounted the trooper, the Indian has three mounts to his one. Whatever care may be taken to secure the best arms and ammunition to the troops, the Indians finds means through his friends to be fully his equal in that respect, and in his entire familiarity with the country vastly his superior.

—General Christopher Augur, *Annual Report for the Department of Texas, 1873*

In one of the magazine articles that Custer wrote for *Turf, Field and Farm*, he described Indian warfare as "a distinct and separate species of hostilities, requiring different talent, different *materiel*, as well as *personnel*, and different rules of conduct."[1] With the element of surprise, superior mobility, and a commanding knowledge of the region in their favor, warriors could raid at will on the sparsely settled frontier. They tended to be, Acting Governor Hall of Colorado wrote bitterly to General Sherman, "better armed, mounted, disciplined, and better officered than our men."[2] This was an exaggeration on the part of a desperate territorial governor: the Indians might be better mounted, but they were seldom better armed, and in the army sense had no discipline or leadership. However, it was true that the army, badly undermanned to secure such a vast expanse of territory, was often ineffectual. It could not catch the Indians in the act of committing violence against whites, and when it caught up with Indians suspected of doing so, political opponents might keep it from inflicting punishment.

Trained to fight battles against conventional forces, the army was poorly prepared to meet the conditions of frontier combat. Simply encountering Indians in battle for the first time was likely to be a significant shock for whites. As a survivor of the 1862 Sioux uprising in Minnesota wrote, "There is something so fiendish in their yells and terrifying in their appearance when in battle that it takes a good deal of time to overcome the sensation that it inspires."[3] The history of Monroe, Michigan, which both Custers imbibed as schoolchildren, offered a similar example. During the War of 1812 two hundred Americans, mostly soldiers, were killed there in one fell swoop by Indian allies of the British. As they attempted to retreat, the soldiers were routed "from some unexplained and unaccountable reason, but probably on account of an irretrievable panic caused by the terrible cries and war-whoops of the savages."[4]

For professional soldiers, there were other aspects of Indian fighting that distinguished it from fighting more conventional enemies, most profoundly the sense of the enemy as alien. Americans had shared with other opponents in battle "an awareness of their common participation in one civilization" that did not apply to Indian warfare.[5] As one frontier army wife put it, "War is dreadful anyway, but an Indian war is worst of all. They respect no code of warfare, flags of truce, wounded—nothing is respected! It is like fighting to exterminate wild animals, horrible beasts!"[6]

The common code of warfare most often referred to, that of the officer and the gentleman, seems to crop up everywhere in Civil War annals, sometimes in a fantastic form. Henry Edwin Tremain recalled a Confederate officer taken prisoner at Sailor's Creek who appealed to his Union counterpart because his watch had been stolen. The officer replied, "That is to be regretted, sir; if it can be found, it shall be restored and the thief punished." This against a backdrop that Tremain describes as "scattered bleeding horses, wrecked artillery, ghastly human corses [sic] . . . smoking ruins of burning baggage wagons—while for acres the grounds were strewn with side-arms, muskets, and other tokens of defeat."[7]

Custer, like many West Point graduates, had had numerous friends who fought on the other side in the Civil War, and his kindnesses to those he found captured or dying are well known. In a letter to his sister he described accompanying a Confederate colonel under a flag of truce inside rebel lines, where he met some officers who knew his classmates: "We had social chat for more than an hour, discussed the war in a friendly way, exchanged cards, etc. Before leaving them I wrote several little notes to my different friends who were on the other side."[8] This experience was not confined to officers. Mason Tyler wrote home about the lively intercourse that followed when his company found itself across the river from the enemy. The rebels were eager to talk and extremely friendly. They regularly sent over their Richmond newspapers, "came over one day of their own accord and played euchre with some of the regiment above us, and were very anxious to trade tobacco and sugar for coffee, etc."[9] Such fraternization "according to the rules" was impossible *and* unthinkable in Plains Indian warfare.

When men fight in groups, the fighting itself can serve as a common denominator. Recalling the eulogy of a Civil War officer whose saber was always covered with blood after a charge, William Bisbee commented: "So the veneer of so-called civilization is sometimes very thin, and in combat the red and white man may not be so very far apart."[10] Kill or be killed could potentially eclipse all other rules and ideologies on any battlefield, but despite any such similarities in actual combat, cultural difference proved stronger in shaping whites' and Indians' perceptions of each other as foes.

Since the methods required to fight Indians did not conform to traditional ideas of warfare, the enterprise seemed lesser to the American public, yet this attitude did not accurately reflect the reality of the experience. After the wearying Sioux campaign of 1876 limped to its close, General George Crook, one of the army's most prominent and experienced Indian fighters, told his troops with considerable eloquence,

> Indian warfare is, of all warfare, the most dangerous, the most trying, and the most thankless. Not recognized by the high authority of the United States senate as war, it still possesses for you the disadvantages of civilized warfare with all the horrible accompaniments that barbarians can invent and savages execute. In it you are required to serve without the incentive to promotion or recognition; in truth without favor or hope of reward.[11]

Ten years later he was to tell a reporter frankly that Indians "don't fear the white soldiers, whom they easily surpass in the peculiar style of warfare which they force upon us."[12] One aspect of the "peculiar style" created the persistent dilemma of Indian warfare; namely, that taking enough troops to be effective against a large force of Indians meant moving too slowly to encounter a large force of Indians.

Custer, and other members of Sheridan's command in the Shenandoah Valley, had experienced some elements of this "peculiar style," otherwise known as guerrilla warfare, in the person of Colonel John Singleton Mosby and his notoriously effective rangers, men who infiltrated the Union lines, often wearing federal uniforms, and killed pickets and couriers. Sheltered by the civilian population, they could rarely be pursued successfully, to the great exasperation of the Union army. Sheridan was so incensed by the murder of his engineering officer by Mosby's men that he ordered Custer to burn all the houses in a five mile area.[13]

The animus that the Union side felt against the irregularities of Mosby's Irregulars lingered. Thirty-eight years after the Shenandoah Valley campaign Edward W. Whitaker, Custer's chief of staff during the Civil War, wrote a letter to the *Washington Post* in which he referred to Mosby's men having put to death prisoners and wounded men. "Soldiers of the Army of the Potomac," he wrote indignantly, "believe 'Mosby's Men' were not heroes, but a gang of outlaws, robbers, and cowardly murderers, who never fought openly. . . . Where is the battlefield that Mosby and his men ever saw?"[14]

Indians waged war in the same manner as Whitaker attributed to the Confederate guerrillas, perpetrating atrocities against civilians behind the backs of the army and avoiding battle unless they had the advantage of numbers.[15] They killed the wounded and took no prisoners. Like Mosby's men, they did not "stand and fight." The positive side of this method from the army's point of view was the small scale of Indian operations. With what sounds suspiciously like contempt, Harry Turney-High wrote that "a great majority of American tribes behaved towards their enemies like modern game laws regard deer: If you kill them all now, what fun will there be in the future? They consistently failed to pursue and exploit a victory."[16]

Just as Union soldiers and civilians resented Mosby's tactics, frontier soldiers regarded Indians as violating the proper or "civilized" practice of war.[17] After writing "civilized warfare," Custer had the grace to add, "if the solecism may be allowed."[18] Morally speaking, "civilized warfare"—which in the nineteenth century comprised soldiers slashing other soldiers with bayonets and blowing them to bits with ordnance—is an oxymoron.[19] Presumably, it meant to white Americans of Custer's time "warfare as we ourselves practice it," as in General Sherman's admiring description of the Nez Percé: "They [the Indians] abstained from scalping, let captive women go free, did not commit indiscriminate murder of peaceful families which is unusual, and fought with almost scientific skill, using advance and rear guards, skirmish-lines and field-fortifications."[20] In short, the Nez Percé fought like an ideal white army.

Specific battle tactics aside, white and native Americans tended to approach the fight with different goals and from different mindsets. In the late-nineteenth century the United States was a capitalistic society committed to technological progress and industrial development; it did not exalt militarism, nor did it—after the Civil War—give its shrunken army the resources needed to police the frontier effectively, let alone wage aggressive war. General Sherman remarked in a letter to Libbie Custer that "the object of war is not to kill, but to produce results."[21] By results he meant accomplishing tangible objectives, defeating the enemy. The style involved in making war, like the killing, was superfluous. For Indians, an enemy was rarely defeated in the sense understood by whites. Style was everything, or almost everything, in the Indian way of fighting: the demonstration of courage *was* the result. As George Bird Grinnell described the reasons the Cheyenne made war, "the chief motive was the love of fighting, which was instilled into them from early youth. From their earliest days boys were taught to long for the approbation of their elders, and this approbation was most readily to be earned by success in war. The applause of their public was the highest reward they knew."[22]

White American warfare has always been enamored of statistics and of results: the killing of a certain number as efficiently as possible is a means to the end of imposing the will of the state upon the enemy. For the Plains Indians, a battle death was cherished as an individual experience, part of the ritual of the fight. Theirs was a warrior culture with an elaborate code of battle exploits in which "counting coup" on the body of an enemy, that is, touching him under dangerous circumstances, could be more prestigious than some ways of killing him.[23] Counting coup honored daring and courage: it had its counterpart in the army's commendations for meritorious service, in the universal admiration for the warrior who is fearless. Reporting the death of one of his officers in the Shenandoah Valley campaign, Custer wrote: "I believe I am correct in stating that he fell farthest in advance of those who on that day surrendered their lives in their country's cause."[24]

Indians often killed in a way that seemed far more terrible to white Americans than their own methods of slaughter. Scalping and the mutilation of the genitals are usually prominent in white accounts of Indian killings; along with torture, which was known to be part of Plains Indian war culture, they were the practices that came to epitomize Indian warfare and to evoke a lively dread. Examples abound: in full sight of the Seventh Cavalry at Fort Wallace, Kansas, "a powerful warrior was seen to pick up the bugler, Charles Clark, who had been pierced by three arrows, and strip him as he rode along; after taking off all his clothing he mashed the head to a jelly with his tomahawk, and then threw the body under his horse's feet."[25] This incident was reported to readers of *Harper's Weekly* as an example of "unheard of atrocities" under the heading of "Late Indian Outrages."

Many of the men who fell at the Little Bighorn and elsewhere in Indian warfare were killed by hand—either clubbed or knifed—and their bodies were then intentionally mutilated, scalped, and sometimes partially dismembered—in some cases while they were still alive. At the Little Bighorn and elsewhere, fallen soldiers were definitively "rubbed out," in the Indian expression: after death, their bodies were stripped and insulted, their defeat total.

Who could forget Kate Bighead's matter-of-fact recital of an episode she observed at the end of the battle of the Little Bighorn: "I saw back along the ridge a living soldier sitting on the ground, in plain view. He was just sitting there and rubbing his head, as if he did not know where he was nor what was going on in the world. While I was watching him, three Sioux men ran to him and seized him. They stretched him out upon his back. They went at this slowly, and I wondered what they were going to do. Pretty soon I found out. Two of them held his arms while the third man cut off his head with a sheath-knife."[26]

Men killed by ordnance do not look good either, and they may well suffer as much. An account of almost any Civil War battle of consequence contains stories like the narrative of Dr. Moses Gunn, chief surgeon for the Fifth Michigan at the outset of the Civil War. On May 7, 1862, he wrote to his wife: "Captain Le Farren was brought back with the end of his nose shot off and his cheek horribly mangled; then in they came constantly—terribly shot and maimed."[27] The victims of Indian warfare were typically mangled in similar fashion, but, although the end result might be the same, the *intentional* prolongation of suffering and dying was regarded as a peculiar horror of Indian warfare. Conventional battlefields might be strewn with the bodies of thousands of men who had died in agony, but these bodies would not have spoken to the living of extended suffering as vividly as the individually dispatched and mutilated bodies of Indian victims. The impersonal nature of their own means of engineering human destruction was more palatable to the white imagination, as the idea of instantaneous death in an explosion is less terrifying to contemplate than a painfully drawn out death at the hands of a sadistic killer. The apprehension of an excruciating death was such that officers on the frontier might feel no shame in resolving to commit suicide if all hope was lost rather than allow themselves to fall into the hands of the Indians.[28]

Although Indians learned to respect the power of artillery, it would have seemed boring and unrewarding to them to blow up a huge number of their enemies in one action. The contempt that whites had for the Indians' individualistic style of fighting was reciprocated by Indian opinion of white warfare. It was "just shooting," Sitting Bull said. He thought the white soldiers did not know how to fight: "They stand still and run straight; it is easy to shoot them. They do not try to save themselves."[29]

Like combat and killing, the spoils of war meant different things to the two opposing forces on the Plains. In the interest of producing the "results" that were their object, as General Sherman had explained to Libbie, white Americans had a penchant for counting everything and often destroying it after it was counted. The principle of quantification, so much a part of military records, continued to be supremely important on the frontier as it had been in the Civil War. During the Shenandoah campaign, for example, the cavalry alone captured 2,556 prisoners, 71 guns, 29 battle flags, 52 caissons, 105 army wagons, 2,557 horses, 1,000 horse equipments, and 7,152 beef cattle. It destroyed 420,742 bushels of wheat, 780 barns, and 700,000 rounds of ammunition.[30] In his memoirs, General Sheridan wrote with satisfaction of Custer's accomplishments at Beaver Dam Station: he destroyed the station, 2 locomotives, 3 trains of cars, 90 wagons, from eight to ten miles of railroad and telegraph lines, some 200,000 pounds of bacon and other supplies, amounting in all to about a million and a half of rations, and nearly all the medical stores of General Lee's army.[31] One becomes inured to the specifics of these endless litanies, except, perhaps, for the last item—"nearly all the medical stores of General Lee's army." *Lacrimae rerum*: this particular destruction must have caused more suffering than the loss of the bacon and other supplies.

A member of General Sheridan's staff, George Forsyth, later wrote that at the battle of Cedar Creek, when he was making his report to the general on enemy guns captured, Sheridan asked him, "How do you *know* that we have that many of the enemy's guns?" Forsyth satisfied his commander by replying: "I have placed my hand on each and every gun."[32] Fortunately, Sheridan did not require Forsyth to be so certain of all the supplies that fell into the army's hands.

On the frontier the army continued its tabulations, although at times, lacking the certitude a Forsyth could confer, the numbers were probably grossly inflated. Theodore Davis, the reporter who accompanied the 1867 Hancock expedition, described a typical occurrence: "The village was burned, but not before a careful inventory had been taken of all the property to be destroyed. I have heard some estimates of the value of the property that were ludicrously large. The loss inflicted upon the Indians could easily be made good by them in a single summer."[33] It was seldom that provisions captured from the Indians were regarded as useful to whites; they were usually destroyed wholesale to deny them to the enemy.

Indians quantified, too, but on a rudimentary or human level: their greatest exploits were in "counting coup" (or, as Turney-High would have it, "the child's play of *coup*-counting").[34] Property in and of itself was usually secondary: while Indians took pride in numbers when they were stealing horses, there were two motives at work that were not quantitative—the skill and daring required to steal the enemy's horses and the usefulness of what was captured. After the Battle of the Little Bighorn, Wooden Leg told Thomas Marquis, "Indians were saying to each other: 'I got some tobacco.' 'I got coffee.' 'I got a soldier saddle.' 'I got a good gun.'"[35] No systematic inventories were taken in the manner of white battles, and anything that was not useful was thrown away. Their migratory lifestyle deterred the Plains Indians from accumulating unnecessary possessions.

The individualistic manner in which Indians fought also allowed an element of spontaneous, disorganized play that seems to be worlds apart from the systematic destruction of a conventional military force.[36] A Cheyenne warrior recalled for Grinnell a well-known incident in Kansas in 1867. The Cheyenne had derailed a Union Pacific freight train, giving themselves far more plunder than they knew what to do with: "The boys and young men in sportive mood tied ends of the pieces of calico to their horses' tails and galloped wildly over the prairie, while the cloth, as it unrolled, swung out behind them in great curves."[37]

John Stands in Timber's grandmother told him a similarly playful anecdote about the Sioux at the Little Bighorn dressing up in captured uniforms and holding a mock parade: "They were just having fun, showing off. . . . They came down along the camp in line, wearing the blue uniforms and soldiers' hats on their heads with the flag and the bugle and the gray horses. But none of them had pants on. They had no use for pants."[38] From a distance this ludicrous parody of white soldiers was thought to be part of the Seventh Cavalry by the approaching troops of the Montana column. The Boy General, at that time lying dead and undiscovered on the hillside of the Last Stand, might have appreciated such shenanigans. When he captured General Thomas Rosser's personal effects during the Civil War, he paraded among his troops wearing his old West Point classmate's coat, which was several sizes too big for him. Later he sent a note to Rosser requesting that his next uniform be made smaller to fit Custer better.[39]

11

Nadir

I am almost determined that, come what may, you must and shall join me wherever I am this summer.

—Custer to Libbie, April 22, 1867

I almost feel tempted to desert and fly to you.

—Custer to Libbie, May 6, 1867

I am ready to set out for Hays, or any point where I can see you at fifteen minutes' notice. Remember, I am not afraid of Indians, or anything else, if you are at the end of the trip.

—Libbie to Custer, June 27, 1867

Between February of 1866, when he was mustered out of the volunteer army, and his arrival at Fort Riley, Kansas, that fall as a lieutenant colonel in the regular army, Custer had an unpleasant taste of the vagaries of politics. Having written to President Andrew Johnson requesting an appointment as a colonel, specifying only that he did not want to command black troops, he received an invitation to accompany a presidential tour in which Johnson would explain his Reconstruction policy to audiences violently opposed to it.[1]

A journey with the president and his entourage of notables must have appeared to be a desirable opportunity to the Custers. General Grant also went along, and he and Custer always received more applause than President Johnson did.[2] If this was gratifying to Custer at first, it soon became embarrassing. As the trip progressed, heckling of the president intensified; often he could not be heard because he was shouted down. On other occasions he lost his temper and engaged the hecklers on their own level.

For Custer the worst incident occurred in Scio, Ohio, the closest railway point to his birthplace. Although he himself received a warm welcome as a native son, the discourtesy to the president—by now a cumulative burden—caused Custer to yell at the crowd: "I was born two miles from here, and I am ashamed of you."[3] The Custers left the presidential train at the next stop and went home to Monroe, from which they would join the newly created Seventh Cavalry regiment in Kansas.

From September of 1866 to March of 1867 Custer was stationed at Fort Riley, shaping up the newly created Seventh Cavalry regiment under the direction of the veteran commander, Colonel Andrew Jackson Smith. At the end of this period Smith wrote to General Grant to support the confirmation of Custer's appointment as lieutenant-colonel of the Seventh: "He is a worthy officer and an accomplished cavalry soldier. I can't well do without him."[4] On March 1, 1867, the same day that Smith described his subordinate so favorably, Smith's own commander, General Winfield Scott Hancock, left Fort Leavenworth, Kansas, to launch his spring campaign against the Indians.[5] Hancock was accompanied by the press—the young Henry Morton Stanley, representing the *New York Herald*, and Theodore Davis of *Harper's*. Stanley would later become famous for finding Dr. Livingston in Africa while Davis, who was an admirer of Custer, was nevertheless regarded by Libbie as an "insufferable bore."[6]

Throughout his brief and ineffectual campaign, the cavalry officer who was known in the Civil War as "Hancock the Superb" would behave imperiously toward the Indians, giving them peremptory orders and ultimatums and constantly threatening to bring his troops to their villages, a prospect that was bound to alarm them under even the best of circumstances. For every Indian on the Kansas plains, the recollection of the Chivington Massacre of a peaceable Cheyenne village at Sand Creek in Colorado little more than two years before was still vivid, and there were in addition the usual sources of conflict between the two cultures: for the Indians, the construction of the railroad brought an increasing number of white settlers who were disrupting the game, and the settlers, in turn, had to contend with depredations by the Indians.

The real subject of contention, possession of the land, always lay concealed behind such specific grievances. The country simply could not be shared by two such different peoples. *Infest*, the revealing term whites commonly used to describe the occupation of an area by Indians, has a sinister significance: like an infestation of vermin, Indians represented a nuisance that spoiled the country for white habitation. Through persuasion or force, General Hancock intended to clean out this infestation and make Kansas safe for white settlement and railroads. Like Custer himself, Hancock was a displaced war hero, seeking to keep his reputation burnished on the Plains.

During the Hancock campaign Custer would see his first Indians, see the bodies of men who had been killed and mutilated by them, and—in the harsh environment of the endless, treeless Plains—lose his bearings to the extent of abandoning his command and undertaking a hard and desperate journey to reach the comfort of Libbie. The result was arrest and court-martial.

Historians have long been aware that from the middle of June 1867 until his arrest little more than a month later Custer's paramount concern was to be with Libbie rather than to carry out his orders.[7] But earlier than they have realized—in fact, from the very beginning of the campaign—the famous Civil War fighter was determined to view the Indians as peaceful and to avoid war, thus rejoining Libbie as soon as possible. Throughout the month of April his letters have this common theme. On April 8, he wrote, "The Indian agents here say the Indians desire peace; if so, they can be accommodated. I am certain I never felt more peaceful in my life. Particularly do I desire peace, when I know that war means separation."[8] On April 15, after the Indians had fled, Custer wrote to Libbie that he would try to overtake them to "at least try to disabuse their minds of an idea of harm, so that you need not fear war. I am strongly for peace."[9] On April 22, he wrote that a note from headquarters indicated that "General Hancock was moderating in his desire for war. God grant it may be true!"[10] A letter of May 2 told Libbie that Custer had written "a very strong letter" against an Indian war: "I regarded the outrages that have been committed lately as not the work of a tribe, but of small and irresponsible parties of young men, who are eager for war. The stampede of the Indians from the village, I attributed entirely to fear. . . . My opinion is, that we are not yet justified in declaring war."[11]

Libbie, for her part, confessed in her letters that "our separations grow more hopeless to me."[12] She described herself as "very unhappy. . . . I am tormented with anxieties that I cannot overcome."[13] After their long period together, it was difficult to regain the discipline of Civil War days. "I am going at myself with whip and spur, and shall take up such work as will keep me from being utterly forlorn," she wrote, adding: "But, oh, what thoughts get sewed into my work!"[14] The Custers had had no such anxious separations since the war ended two years before, and neither adjusted well.

The Seventh Cavalry, commanded by Colonel Smith and Lieutenant Colonel Custer, had joined General Hancock's command when it came to Fort Riley. But after the first unsatisfactory encounter, in which the Indians had abandoned their village instead of remaining for a parley as had been agreed, Hancock dispatched Custer and his force to pursue them. Custer never caught up with the Indians—a pattern that would be repeated for the rest of the campaign—but he did find a series of deserted and burned stations along the Smoky Hill River stagecoach route. From the employees who remained, huddled together for safety in every fourth station or so, Custer learned that large numbers of Indians had recently been seen going north. Only fifteen miles west of Fort Hays, riding in advance as he liked to do, Custer came upon the still smoking ruins of Lookout Station, where he found the bodies of three men, "so mangled and burned as to be scarcely recognizable as human beings. The Indians had evidently tortured them before putting an end to their sufferings. They were scalped and horribly disfigured."[15]

It was shortly after this that he gave Libbie some inkling of his developing state of mind:

> The inaction to which I am subjected now, in our present halt, is almost unendurable. It requires all the buoyancy of my sanguine disposition to resist being extremely homesick. Hitherto I have been comparatively contented, and able to divert my thoughts from home to incidents and occurrences of the march, but even that poor pretext is denied me here. You little imagine how great the sacrifice is to me. . . . I can hardly devote the proper time and attention to my daily duties.[16]

"Home" meant wherever Libbie was: the longest the Custers would remain in one house would be their final period of less than three years at Fort Abraham Lincoln, Dakota Territory.

Two weeks later Custer was more dependent than ever on hearing from Libbie. There had been a period without letters from her. "In all my life I do not remember anything that has been so unceasingly on my mind," he wrote, "but to-day Richard was himself again: I received your letter of Tuesday."[17] It was an ironically apt allusion: Custer was actually no more himself again than the character he quoted, Shakespeare's villainous Richard III, who was rushing pell-mell to disaster. The recoveries occasioned by the arrival of Libbie's letters were fleeting, and, in the intensity of their preoccupation, indicative of his failing grip. When the division superintendent and express messenger brought the mail, Custer "could hardly wait till they took their departure, so eager was I to devour my letters."[18] A few days later when more letters came he used language of excess and hoarding to describe the strength of his feelings: "No miser with his gold ever gloated over his possession as I do to-day."[19]

Theodore Davis, who traveled with Custer's command while Stanley accompanied Hancock, described Custer at the time as depressed and moody, a changed man from the "jovial, and entirely happy young man" who had been assigned to escort Davis during the latter's first visit to West Point.[20] Yet, in spite of an endless rainstorm, he seemed to recover his good spirits, bursting into Davis's tent one evening when the reporter had been whistling and singing. "Stop this cheerfulness in purgatory," he ordered, "or I'll have you out here in the flood walking post." Davis told him some amusing anecdotes of his experience on the Plains and soon Custer's "hearty joyous laugh" had served as a bugle call to attract other officers, as many as could squeeze into the tent.[21]

When General Hancock received Custer's report of the hostile activities along the Smoky Hill, he decided to destroy the abandoned village. It had not been possible from the evidence at the station to implicate any particular tribe, but it seemed probable to both Custer and Hancock that the Indians Custer had followed from the village to the stage trail had been responsible. In any case, the frustrated Hancock felt that they should be punished for fleeing—that the "bad faith practiced by the Cheyennes and Sioux who occupied the Indian village" was reason enough to destroy it.[22] With this less than satisfactory and far less than victorious action, Hancock retired from the field. Stanley commented sarcastically, "When General Hancock's expedition first set out from the Missouri River, it was generally expected that there would be a good deal of fighting; but the General's disposition and management of the Indian chiefs were such that he had only to conduct a series of tactical marches through the red men's domains."[23] Custer was hardly alone in suffering the malaise of the Civil War hero deposited in the foreign and far less definitive world of Indian warfare.

The epilogue to the campaign was also less than glorious. Returning to Fort Larned, Hancock met with the Kiowas and, though he fancied himself a veteran Indian fighter and stern disciplinarian of the Indians, he nevertheless allowed himself to be seduced by the powerful oratory of the notorious Satanta, a Kiowa chief later described by his Texas prosecutor as "the arch fiend of treachery and blood."[24] In action Satanta was one of the most hostile of Indians, raiding and killing at will in Texas, which had long been Kiowa country. In speaking to whites he was equally formidable: Hancock was so impressed that he gave Satanta a uniform coat with all the insignia of a major general, a yellow silk sash, and a plumed hat. Shortly thereafter the chief raided Fort Dodge dressed in his new finery: "He had the politeness, however, to raise his plumed hat to the garrison of the fort, though he discourteously shook his coat-tails at them as he rode away with the captured stock."[25]

Custer and his command rested and resupplied at Fort Hays, allowing him a few weeks' interlude with Libbie before he marched out again on June 1 to make another futile sweep of a thousand miles of hostile Indian territory. Stanley, who had not yet spent any time with Custer, described him at this moment in terms of a widely held view of his military skill: "He is to commence active and offensive operations against the Sioux and Cheyenne tribes. Custer is precisely the gentleman for that job. . . . From all we hear from persons qualified to judge, he must be a first-rate cavalry officer, and will no doubt perform any task allotted to him to the entire satisfaction of the western people."[26]

A different view prevailed in the journal of Albert Barnitz, a captain in Custer's command. On May 17, 1867, Barnitz described an instance in which Custer ordered the heads of six men half-shaved and then paraded the men through camp, "to their own great humiliation, and the exceeding mortification, disgrace, and disgust of all right-minded officers and men in camp. . . . No man but an incarnate friend could take pleasure in such an abuse of authority, & I have greatly missed my guess if the 'Brevet Major General commanding' is not fast losing whatever little influence for good he may have once possessed in the Regiment."[27]

Custer had also made a bad impression on General Hancock. Not long before Stanley hailed him as the coming hero of the expedition, Custer had written to Hancock to apologize for what the superior officer had taken to be Custer's avoidance of him. "I regret exceedingly," he wrote, "that you should consider me lacking in cordiality. . . . Since my first entry into the service it has been my rule not to visit Superior Headquarters unless upon duty or in obedience to a command. My reasons are, that I consider the proper post for every officer is, when in the field, with his command."[28] Custer apparently did not realize that his explanation could be construed as an oblique rebuke to Hancock for expecting him to dance attendance upon headquarters. In light of what followed, Custer might have preferred to offer some other excuse than adherence to his troops since the expedition would end with Custer's court-martial trial for abandoning his own command in the field.

General Sherman, commander of the Division of the Missouri, which included Kansas, had been disappointed with the Hancock expedition's ineffectuality, and he now placed his hopes in Custer. A few months earlier Sherman had written to his brother, Senator John Sherman, about Custer's appointment to the Seventh, "I think he merits confirmation for military service already rendered and military qualities still needed (youth, health, energy and extreme willingness to act and fight)."[29] Acting and fighting were what Sherman expected from the energetic young Civil War hero; what he got was the same fruitless pursuit and parley that had characterized Hancock's campaign. In fact, before long he would personally upbraid Custer for treating with the notorious Sioux warrior Pawnee Killer rather than fighting him.[30] Sherman, who was all business when he was on the job, had no idea that at the present time Custer's "extreme willingness to act and fight" was blunted by longing for his wife.

At the first stop on his tour of his division—Fort McPherson on the Platte River—Sherman paid a visit to Custer and gave him further orders. When the command needed to be resupplied, it was to report to Fort Sedgwick, roughly a hundred miles southwest of McPherson in Colorado Territory. Nevertheless, as Tom Custer testified at his brother's court-martial trial, Sherman had verbally given Custer latitude "that if he wished he could go to Denver City or he could go to hell if he wanted to. That he could go to any post he wanted to."[31] The words sound like Sherman's, but what he must have had in mind was the effective discharge of the mission, not the personal considerations that actually caused Custer to go elsewhere.

In his memoirs of this time in Kansas Custer wrote contemptuously that the forces of another Indian fighter, General Alfred Sully, "had marched up the hill and then, like the forces of the king of France, had marched down again," yet his own movements during the Sherman scout were just as much an exercise in futility.[32] He engaged no Indians in combat; worse, he scarcely pursued any. The Custer of the Civil War who could not rest until he had won back an advantage lost to the enemy seemed indifferent to checks administered by his new opponents.

Like many Americans, he found it difficult to regard Indians as worthy enemies. The mutilated bodies of the stage line employees might well have been "one of the most horrible sights imaginable," as he wrote to Libbie, but it was small scale compared to the monumental carnage of the Civil War. He described the failure of his plan to follow the Indians in a matter-of-fact tone that indicated his sense of their unimportance: "A pursuit of a few hours proved our inability to overtake them, and we returned to camp."[33] Furthermore, the spur of a competing military unit, such as Wesley Merritt's provided during the Civil War, was absent: Custer was alone in a vast wilderness.

In spite of the restorative powers of Libbie's company in May, the superbly self-confident and eternally optimistic Custer was gradually succumbing to a situation that offered little hope of even modest accomplishment. There were problems of resupply, a high rate of desertion that threatened the safety of the command, and, above all, an elusive target. As the mixed-blood scout George Bent described the summer, the Indians were in control: they raided as they pleased, "easily avoiding the large bodies of troops sent against them and attacking the small detachments."[34] Custer found himself experiencing once again the frustration he had felt with this style of warfare in the Shenandoah Valley. Just as when he had vowed to get the Confederate irregular Colonel John Singleton Mosby, "all he accomplished, pursuing false leads and chasing wraiths, was to wear out scores of horses."[35]

It seems that on the Plains, Custer vented his frustration on his officers and men. Captain Barnitz's letters and journal for the first two weeks of May are full of references to the commanding officer's high-handed behavior, using such terms as "obstreperous," "injudicious," and "obnoxious." Barnitz had been an admirer of Custer's during the Civil War, so much so that he had written a rather awkward poem about Custer at Appomattox that praised his commanding officer extravagantly:

> *Over his shoulders his scarlet scarf*
> *Floated and flamed as he held his course;*
> *Never a leader so buoyant as he*
> *Fell on the foe with such measureless force!*[36]

Barnitz had been eager to serve under Custer in Kansas, but now he wrote to his wife that she would be "filled with utter amazement" if he were to give some examples of Custer's "cruelty to the men, and discourtesy to the officers." He was such a "complete example of a petty tyrant" that Barnitz feared he could not continue in the same regiment with him.[37]

Undermining Custer's equilibrium more deeply—since ultimately he felt himself equal to any professional problem—was the difficulty of being separated from Libbie. In spite of the almost constant pressure of battle during the last year of the Civil War, which had been the first year of their marriage, Custer had always been fairly close to Washington: either he dashed to Libbie for brief visits or she came to his camp during those lulls in the fighting when the cavalry waited for fresh horses. When General Sherman sent word that Libbie had best remain "quietly" at Fort Riley because Custer would be in the field all summer, she seized upon the word and commented passionately: "Quietly! He may talk about living quietly, but I cannot."[38]

Usually when they were apart, a copious flow of letters provided emotional sustenance, but mail delivery became uncertain when neither one knew the movements of the other. Custer had written to Libbie to go to Fort Wallace and join a wagon train for his camp. Disregarding his orders to obtain supplies from Fort Sedgwick, he accordingly sent a company of his men to Wallace to bring back the supply train and his wife. He proceeded to dispatch a second company to scout Beaver Creek, where the experienced scout Will Comstock expected to find Indians, and he then detached still another group to communicate with Sedgwick. At that point, bereft of a third of his command, Custer was attacked by a party of Sioux. Instead of fighting, he offered to parley, a response that would have disgusted Sherman, but which Custer justified in *My Life on the Plains* as a necessary measure to protect the three small parties he had sent out.

Although Custer intended to stay on the Indians' trail, they easily shook off their unwelcome escort. Whenever any small body of men was separated from the command, however, they made their presence known. The command's doctor somehow found himself alone and had to make a mad dash of four miles back to camp with Indians in hot pursuit. He attributed his success in outrunning them on a tired mount to the fact that the horse was as frightened of Indians as its rider.

All of this finally convinced Custer that the Indians were committed to war, and that he should send reinforcements to the supply train bringing his wife from Fort Wallace: "The mere thought of the danger to which she might be exposed spurred me to decisive action," he wrote candidly.[39] On June 25 he sent out another company with instructions to join forces with the scouting party on Beaver Creek and proceed together to the supply train. The very next day the rapidly moving rescue force found the train under sharp attack by several hundred Cheyenne and Sioux.

Now guarded by three companies, the supplies reached Custer's camp on June 28, but Libbie was not along—a circumstance that must have increased his anxiety immeasurably. He had written her on June 22, "You cannot imagine my anxiety regarding your whereabouts, for the reason that if you are now at Wallace, you can join me in about six days, and we can be together all summer."[40] In the meantime Libbie had made a vain tour of the Kansas forts, going from Riley to Leavenworth to Harker to Hays and back to Riley without seeing her husband. On June 27, just as Custer was expecting her arrival with the supply train in a day or two, she was writing to him: "I am ready to start for you at a moment's notice."[41]

Soon thereafter they fell out of communication, with Custer not knowing where Libbie was or why she had not followed his instructions, and she ignorant of the specific plan to bring her to camp. His book explained that she had never received his urgent letter instructing her to go to Fort Wallace, although, since she quoted from it in her own book, *Tenting on the Plains,* she must have received it eventually. Her book says instead that General Hancock had forbidden her to accompany the supply train.[42] Characteristically, when the subject was separation from Autie, she wrote that "the memory of my disappointment has not departed after all these years."[43]

It may have been around this time, late June or early July, that Libbie received two letters she refers to in *Tenting on the Plains*, letters "strangely in contrast to all the brave, encouraging missives that had cheered my day. . . . there were desperate words written, which, had he not been relieved by news of my safety, would have ended in his taking steps to resign. Even he, whom I scarcely ever knew to yield to discouraging circumstances, wrote that he could not and would not endure such a life."[44]

Just as Custer was reaching the psychological point where he would abandon his command, desertion by his own troops was becoming a more pressing problem than the Indians. Men were bleeding away at night, often taking the best horses with them. On the night of June 6 a particularly large group of between thirty and forty deserted.[45] There was a good reason for not pursuing them—Custer's priority at the time was to find Lieutenant Lyman Kidder and his escort of ten men (including a Sioux scout), who had been sent from Fort Sedgwick to join Custer and were now overdue—but undoubtedly this suggested to those eager to leave that they could walk away with impunity.

On June 7, during the midday pause in the march, another group of twelve did just that, seven on horseback and five on foot. Custer ordered the officer of the day, Henry Jackson, to pursue the deserters and kill them. Jackson was joined by other officers—Tom Custer, Joel Elliott, and William Cooke—who were close at hand. The men on horseback got away, but the five on foot were overtaken and brought back, three of them wounded. Custer had the wounded men placed in a bare army wagon and publicly announced that they would receive no medical attention. One died of his wounds ten days later.

Like his powerful patron Phil Sheridan, and like many other officers of the time, Custer genuinely believed that severe discipline was a proper deterrent. He had carried out the execution of deserters during the Civil War and in Louisiana, but in those cases the men had been tried by court-martial and condemned to death. They had received "due process" as the army understood it.

Still, there was every reason to regard the command's situation as critical and extreme measures necessary. Months earlier, when another forty men had deserted from the Seventh "in an organized body," General Hancock had sent a telegram to General Sheridan saying that "all possible means have been ordered to kill or capture the deserters."[46] Custer's command was a relatively small force isolated in enemy territory, aware that they were surrounded by hostile Indians who constantly probed their vulnerabilities. Davis recounted that "during the afternoon march it was discovered that a general émeute had been arranged by the men to take place that night. As it did not occur, it was evident that the summary measures of the afternoon had a salutary effect. For days after this there were no more desertions in the Seventh Cavalry."[47] Davis did not mention that in addition to the example made of the daytime deserters, Custer took special precautions to thwart another mass exodus that night by requiring all officers to share guard duty. Moreover, the fifteen miles the command had marched after the incident took it farther away from the road to the Colorado mines that had been a preferred escape route.

As time passed, hopes of finding the Fort Sedgwick party alive diminished, but the command pressed on. One day circling buzzards and an accompanying stench led them to the horrific remains of the Kidder party. The bodies were stripped and some partially burned. Skulls had been scalped and crushed, limbs slashed, noses cut off, and, Custer wrote, "the features otherwise defaced so that it would have been scarcely possible for even a relative to recognize a single one of the unfortunate victims." His subsequent comment unconsciously revealed the rigid compartmentalization of the military caste system, even in death: "We could not even distinguish the officer from his men."[48]

The day after burying the Kidder party the command reached Fort Wallace, where Custer made the decision that would lead to his court-martial and arrest. Since there were insufficient supplies at Wallace—not surprisingly, as he had been expected to resupply at Fort Sedgwick—Custer decided that a detachment of seventy-five men should ride for Fort Harker, two hundred miles away. In *My Life on the Plains*, Custer explained that he decided to accompany the detached force rather than stay with the men at Fort Wallace, who would have nothing to do but recuperate from their recent exertions. Simply waiting at Wallace would have been unbearable to Custer under ordinary circumstances because he hated inactivity, but in this case, the rationale he constructed for his behavior is less persuasive than the motive of reuniting with Libbie.

The men and horses had already been marched hard in the hope of saving the Kidder party. Custer no longer had a compelling professional reason to continue at a brutal pace, but by now he was obsessed with getting to Libbie. When six of his men were attacked by Indians close to Downer's stage station, and four returned with the information that the other two had been killed, he neither went back to bury the bodies nor bothered to ask Captain Carpenter, the officer in charge at Downer's, to do so. As Carpenter wrote to his parents, when Custer heard the news of the attack, with the report of two men killed, he remained unconcerned, "finished his dinner, and moved on without saying a word to me about the bodies, or thinking of hunting the Indians."[49] Custer wrote that the six men "had without authority halted some distance behind."[50] This, as he knew, was not the case. Noticing that his mare Fanchon was missing, Custer had himself sent a sergeant with a detail of men back to investigate her absence.[51]

Furthermore, when Captain Louis Hamilton asked to spend the night at the station because the men were upset and demoralized about the Indian attack, Custer simply told the young captain, a great-grandson of Alexander Hamilton, that they would be moving on.[52] Since it was convenient to his purpose, Custer assumed that Captain Carpenter would take care of burying the dead troopers. As it turned out, one of the men had only been wounded.[53] Fortunately, the Indians had not seen him and the burial detail brought him back to the station, where he recuperated.

The command pressed on to Fort Hays, arriving around three in the morning. Here, Custer told Hamilton to bring the troops up at a more reasonable pace while he took a few men on to Fort Harker, one step closer to Libbie. From his own testimony, Custer's first act after arriving at Harker at two A.M. was to find out when the train left for Fort Riley. His next was to go to the headquarters of Colonel Smith, the commander of the Seventh, and rouse him out of bed. This visit had to be paid immediately because the train that would take him to Libbie left at three A.M. Smith was courteous, as always, and sent his regards to the ladies (Libbie and her friend from home, Anna Darrah) when Custer announced his imminent departure for Riley.

Thomas Weir, serving as Smith's adjutant, accompanied Custer to the station and waited with him until the train arrived. Many years later, however, Lieutenant Edward Mathey told the researcher Walter

Camp that "it was reported that when Custer met Weir a scene was enacted and Weir 'got down on his knees to Custer.'"[54] Supposedly, the confrontation was over Weir's excessive interest in Libbie, brought to Custer's attention by an anonymous letter,[55] but this vague, third-hand story makes little sense. Weir and Libbie were not newly acquainted, since the officer had also served with Custer in Texas. Moreover, Libbie had never made any secret of what both she and Custer regarded as an innocent attraction: Weir was good company when he wasn't in his cups. Although Weir's lively companionship must have been welcome during the troubling time of the Custers' separation, Libbie's letters and actions demonstrate clearly that reunion with her husband occupied her entirely. Weir and Libbie had not been at the same post for most of the time Custer had been away, and if Weir had reason to fear Custer's wrath, he would hardly have volunteered to accompany him to the depot, purely for reasons of sociability, as he testified at Custer's court-martial.[56]

Custer had lightly demurred at what he considered to be Libbie's overvaluation of Weir, a man who apparently socialized with women easily and was a good conversationalist. Perhaps after hard riding and little sleep he became irrational and turned on Weir, but if the melodramatic scene did take place, it was quickly forgotten. A month later Weir wrote to Custer about his upcoming court-martial trial, "Will any little favor I may be able to give be kindly received? I am anxious in the affair to go on your side."[57]

While Autie and Libbie began what she would later describe as "one long, perfect day," Colonel Smith was reconsidering the events of the middle of the previous night. Once he had sorted out the situation, he realized that Custer had had no authority to go to Fort Riley and immediately ordered him back to his command. When Custer arrived on July 21, he was placed under arrest.[58]

The court-martial trial began on September 15 at Fort Leavenworth, where, as a pointed indication of his support, General Sheridan allowed the Custers to use his vacant quarters. The charges were absence without leave from his command and conduct to the prejudice of good order and military discipline, which comprised the rapid march "upon private business and without proper authority or any urgency or demand of public business," the misappropriation of ambulances and mules to get from Hays to Harker, and the Downer's Station incident. An officer of the Seventh, Captain Robert M. West, preferred an additional charge of conduct prejudicial, based upon the treatment of the deserters on July 7.

The army hierarchy, as represented by Colonel Smith and General Hancock, was primarily concerned with those actions taken "without proper authority," a phrase that occurs in the formulation of the first two charges. Had Custer had authority, had he been able to convince the court that he had acted upon "public business," the long marches and exhausted horses that received so much attention in the trial would have become insignificant. A cavalry historian has concluded that far more army horses died of poor conditions than of battle—they were overworked, underfed, and in many cases, literally ridden to death.[59] This was part of the cost of doing business, as it were.[60] But since the accusation maintained that Custer had *not* been engaged in public business, he was personally responsible for misusing government property.

Had there been a valid reason for Custer's urgency in leaving Downer's Station, his response to the Indian attack would not have attracted any special attention outside his own command. It was perfectly true, as he asserted, that going back to pursue the Indians would have been futile. This was a lesson Custer had learned over and over again in his first Indian campaign. It also seems clear that Captain Hamilton, to whom Sergeant Connelly reported about the attack, had told Custer that two men had been killed, not that one had been left behind alive.[61] What was disturbing about the incident was Custer's attitude of contempt and lack of sympathy for the six men attacked by, Connelly estimated, fifty Indians. In the long statement Custer submitted to the court he wrote, "Had they offered any defense this would not have occurred, instead however they put spurs to their horses and endeavored to escape by flight."[62]

Although the army had not brought charges against Custer for his treatment of the deserters, it was this offense that produced the most damning testimony. Whereas Custer testified that he had given to Sergeant Jackson alone the order to bring no one back alive, the other officers—his brother Tom, Joel Elliott, and William Cooke—all testified that he had used similar language to them. Custer's own notes written the day after the event corroborate their account: "I directed Major Elliott and Lts. Custer, Cook & Jackson, with a few of the guard, to pursue the deserters . . . and to bring the dead bodies of as many as could be taken back to camp."[63]

Two of the men had clearly surrendered before they were shot; about the third, Johnson, the man whose wound was ultimately fatal, there was conflicting testimony. Elliott said that Johnson had raised his carbine as if to shoot: "I was riding at a gallop and rode on to him, and whether he threw down his arms before my horse struck him, or just at that time, I could not tell; it was all done so quickly I don't know." Yet Lieutenant Jackson testified that the arms of the three men were forty to fifty yards from where they were lying down when they were shot.

The wounded men, who appeared to be in "a good deal of pain," were placed in an army wagon which some of the soldiers tried to make more comfortable by lining with their overcoats.[64] Although Custer initially forbade the deserters medical attention, once the march resumed and the men were no longer in earshot, he gave Dr. Coates permission to treat them. The doctor recalled Custer saying, "Doctor, my sympathies are not with those men who are wounded, but I want you to give them all necessary attention."[65] Coates also reported that Custer asked about the men's condition from time to time and that he told Custer that the wounds were not serious.

The doctor proved to be an able witness, arguing skillfully for his point of view—that the wounded men had received all necessary attention—and that his own judgment on such matters was superior to that of the court's. Questioned about the trajectory of the bullet that wounded Johnson, the doctor replied, "A shot at that distance might have taken the exact course it did. A very slight thing will turn the course of a ball." He continued with a climactic illustration: "If you will allow me, it is recorded in medical history of a ball having struck the breast bone, and to have been found lodged in the testicles."[66]

Like Shakespeare's arrogant general, Coriolanus, Custer did not help his own case. By objecting to each and every member of the court at the beginning of the proceedings he made it clear that these were not the men who should be judging *him.* During testimony he made numerous objections, most of which were overruled. Then, in a written statement of forty-four legal-size handwritten pages, Custer presented himself in a style that must have been exceedingly irritating to the members of the court. The mere use of the word *Gentlemen* at the beginning of many sections subtly suggested that the court and the defendant were on an equal footing, that he saw them as considering the case together. At the same time Custer implied that he had a better understanding of what happened.

His approach was both grandiose and outrageous, seeking to redefine the terms upon which he was to be judged. First, he asked to be judged on the quality of sincerity, or good faith, since honorable individuals might differ as to means and methods: "By the degree of good faith and sincere desire to discharge well and faithfully the responsible duties devolving upon me which I hope to be able to make evident to your mind, I claim to be judged." Self-justification and indignation held sway in equal measure, especially in his testimony concerning the deserters:

> I place here on record the expression of my indignation that anyone should have been found in the service to prepare these charges, to defeat the purposes of discipline, and to set facts that received the unanimous approval of all my officers and right minded enlisted men . . . in such array against me as to excite the apprehension in the mind of many that I was not only arbitrary but even inhuman.[67]

(In a letter at the time he wrote with satisfaction that Captain West, the instigator of that particular charge, "is drinking himself to death, has delirium tremens.")[68]

Custer did not confine himself to the outraged rhetoric of injured innocence, a posture that would at least have had the virtue of consistency. He undercut this effect by some shabby plea bargaining, for immediately after the ringing defense of his treatment of the deserters he told the court that the order to shoot to kill that four officers heard and acted upon was "for effect" and not to be taken literally. He also indicated that only when he happened to learn about the train leaving for Fort Riley did he think "of asking permission of Genl Smith to visit my family at Fort Riley."[69] Custer had not merely happened to learn of the train's departure, however; it had been his first concern when he arrived at Fort Harker. And he had specifically *not* asked permission: he had *told* Smith that he was going, allowing him to assume that Custer, who had been operating under direct orders from General Sherman, had received permission elsewhere.

Custer was found guilty of all charges and sentenced to a suspension from service for one year and forfeiture of pay proper.[70] As a reviewing officer, General Grant wrote that the court, "in awarding so lenient a sentence for the offences of which the accused is found guilty, must have taken into consideration his previous services."[71]

What exasperated army men even more than the charges of which Custer was found guilty was his petulant behavior after receiving the verdict. Judge Advocate General Joseph Holt wrote to General Grant on February 14, 1868, objecting to Custer taking his grievances with the court-martial proceedings into the public forum by writing a letter to the *Sandusky Register*, which appeared in the December 28 issue of the newspaper. Holt concluded that Custer,

> in the manner of his thus appealing from his sentence to the public, in his misrepresentations in regard to the evidence in his case, in his attacks upon the impartiality and justice of the members of the court, in his criticism of the course pursued by Genl. Hancock, and in the language with which he assails one of the officers who preferred charges against him, must be deemed to have been at least guilty of *conduct to the prejudice of good order and military discipline.*[72]

Sheridan, even while pleading for Custer's reinstatement, acknowledged that "he has done many things which I do not approve of—especially the letter he wrote and had published, reflecting on the court that tried him." He added, "He held high command during the Rebellion and found some difficulty in adapting himself to his altered position."[73] This was no more than the truth: perhaps it is the essential truth explaining the difference between the Civil War and the postwar Custer.

When he was sentenced, Custer was almost twenty-eight years old.

Philippe Régis de Trobriand, an articulate and cosmopolitan Frenchman who made a career in the American army, summed up Custer's first year on the Plains in this way: "Certainly General Custer is a good cavalry officer, brave, energetic, intelligent. He served brilliantly during the war and accomplished a good deal against the Confederate cavalry. What has he done against the Indians? Nothing. Vainly he exhausted men and horses, pursuing the Indians without making contact with them, and his best reports amount to four or five men killed to one of the enemy." An evenhanded observer, Trobriand was simply using Custer to point out the difficulty of Indian warfare: "The problem is to pursue them and to get at them on the desert plains, their natural haven of escape from punishment for their depredations."[74]

Had he not been court-martialed, Custer's first year in Kansas still would have shown a lack of success tantamount to failure. Whether he was justified in the actions for which he was court-martialed, as he insisted, no frontier military man had reason to be impressed with Custer's first tour of duty on the Plains. De Trobriand, writing in his journal at Fort Stevenson, Dakota Territory, knew this, and Custer himself knew it, although it could be argued that Custer did not know it well enough. He had received a salutary check, but—as his arrogance at the court-martial revealed—his own self-confident temperament rejected the idea of fault too thoroughly to read the verdict as other than political: he saw himself as the scapegoat for General Hancock's failed campaign. In this attitude he found support in his powerful mentor's indulgence. General Sheridan, while no doubt wishing that Custer could stay out of trouble, believed him to be a commander he could always rely on in battle.

Yet however much Custer extenuated his court-martial, he knew as he began his enforced exile from the army that he needed to become a winning commander once again.

PART THREE

Recovery

12

Victory on the Washita

> I can whip the Indians if I can find them, and I shall leave no effort untried to do this. I have a difficult task before me but I am confident that if the Indians can be found I can do it as well as most persons could.
>
> —Letter from Custer, correspondent unknown, Fort Dodge, Thursday, October 8, 1868

The Custers retreated to Monroe, Michigan, for Custer's year of suspension from the army. Nine months later, dinner was interrupted one evening by the happy arrival of a telegram from General Sheridan, which Custer proudly reproduced in *My Life on the Plains*:

> Headquarters Department of the Missouri
> in the Field, Fort Hays, Kansas
> September 24, 1868
> *General G. A. Custer, Monroe, Michigan*:
>
> Generals Sherman, Sully, and myself, and nearly all the officers of your regiment, have asked for you, and I hope the application will be successful. Can you come at once? Eleven companies of your regiment will move about the 1st of October against the hostile Indians, from Medicine Lodge creek toward the Wichita mountains.
>
> (*Signed*) P. H. Sheridan, *Major General Commanding*[1]

With his usual sanguine response to events Custer chose to overlook the detail that his own regimental officers had not *unanimously* asked for his return. He preferred to regard the premature recall as a vindication of his behavior on the Plains and a victory over those officers who had approved his court-martial.

At the same time, the period of eclipse—if not out-and-out disgrace—had had some effect. The Custer who eagerly started for Kansas as soon as he received Sheridan's telegram was determined to succeed, but he also had a more realistic sense of what the coming campaign would involve. The letter that he wrote to a friend shortly after his arrival combines his usual confidence with a sober assessment. Beginning with an announcement of determination—"I can whip the Indians if I can find them, and I shall leave no effort untried to do this"—he finished with a more cautious restatement: "I have a difficult task before me but I am confident that if the Indians can be found I can do it as well as most persons could."[2] The words "as well as most persons" hardly embodied the high standard Custer had set for himself in the Civil War; they suggested instead the chastening effect of recent experience.

After ten months out of uniform, Custer was exhilarated to be back in what he now recognized as his natural home environment. He wrote to Libbie that Sheridan had expressed pleasure and relief at seeing him: He "has said to me twice already, 'Custer I rely everything upon you and shall send you on this expedition without giving you any orders leaving you to act entirely upon your judgment.'"[3] Three days after this he again informed Libbie of his warm welcome: one of General Sheridan's staff had told him that all the officers of the regiment were glad to have him back. All told, the letter contains three references to the pleasure others took in his return, but, he added, "I would not repeat this even to you only I want you to see that even my enemies ask to have me return. General Sheridan also said that now he could smoke a cigar in peace once more as Custer had never failed him."[4]

If General Sully, who was no longer very successful in the field, had truly expressed a desire for Custer's return, he soon had reason to regret it. Sheridan sent him back to his post at Fort Harker and gave the command of the expedition against the Indians to Custer.

Custer's letters to Libbie during the preparation for the campaign emphasized his satisfaction at once more being highly regarded and entrusted with significant responsibility. After condemnation, suspension, and inactivity, it was sweet to be openly prized by the departmental commander, and by his enemies as well, as the man of the hour. Midnight, November 22, a few hours before his command moved out in search of Indians to fight, Custer wrote to Libbie: "Am to be my own master as General Sheridan trusts to my judgment." A page later he returned to this pleasing aspect of affairs: "He told me . . . that he would not restrict me by orders on the coming scout but would trust everything to my judgment."[5]

Sheridan had received a similar free hand from his own superior, General Sherman, and he accordingly wrote to Custer on October 15, 1868, to indicate that he would block "any efforts that may be attempted in your rear to restrain your purpose or check your troops."[6] The expedition would be Custer's game to win or lose.

Custer had roughly six weeks at Sheridan's base of operations, Camp Supply, to prepare his fighting force. To make it more professional he ordered two drills at target practice each day and then selected the top forty out of his eight hundred men to form a corps of sharpshooters under the leadership of Lieutenant William Cooke. Another, more controversial measure was "coloring the horses," so that each troop had horses of only one color. Custer, who regarded spectacle and appearance as important elements in esprit de corps, was well pleased with the result; others resented the substitution of new horses for their customary mounts. Captain Albert Barnitz's journal entry for November 12 reads: "Have felt very indignant and provoked all evening in consequence of General Custer's *foolish, unwarranted, unjustifiable* order with regard to the new horses."[7]

Another decision Custer made at the time was to appoint California Joe Milner chief of scouts. Joe had caught his fancy through a picturesque appearance and frontier speech that Custer delighted in reproducing at length in *My Life on the Plains*, but since by his own admission he was personally unacquainted with any of the scouts, his selection was both random and precipitous. Joe proved unequal to this unexpected elevation and enlarged responsibility. On a night march when he was supposed to be operating in advance of a body of soldiers, he imbibed too much and drifted off on his own, turning himself around so that he was facing the oncoming troops. His befuddled brain then imagined the approaching soldiers to be Indians, and he charged the column wildly, yelling and striking out in imaginary battle with the enemy. Amazingly, Joe was recognized before anyone could take a shot at him, but he was so possessed of his delusion that he had to be completely bound and tied to his mule.[8]

Although Custer did not say so in his narrative, after the California

Joe debacle he reappointed Ben Clark as chief scout, the man who had served in that capacity while Custer was suspended from duty. The incident is telling. Clearly attracted by California Joe's humorous individuality, Custer impulsively made him chief of scouts, a promotion that neither the scout nor anyone else had anticipated. Fortunately, the mistake was discovered before there were serious consequences, but it could easily have been otherwise.

The dramatic conclusion to Joe's brief tenure as chief scout did not end Custer's fondness for the man "whose droll sayings and quaint remarks had often served to relieve the tedium of the march or to enliven the group about the campfire."[9] At the end of *My Life on the Plains*, he expressed his pleasure at having recently heard from Joe and reproduced the scout's letter.

Both men were to die violently—of gunshot wounds—in 1876, Custer fighting Indians and California Joe in an obscure private quarrel at Fort Robinson, Dakota Territory, with a man named Tom Newcomb. Whatever the dispute, and accounts differ, Joe must have thought it had been resolved when his opponent was willing to shake hands, but this turned out to be a ruse: Newcomb later returned with a rifle and shot in the back "a man who, a short time before, had spared his life."[10] The etiquette of personal combat on the frontier differed from standard dueling about as much as frontier Indian fighting differed from Civil War battles: a couple of months earlier another colorful figure, Wild Bill Hickok, was also dispatched from behind.

Matters of law also differed: Dr. Valentine McGillycuddy, agent at the Red Cloud Sioux reservation, was in Fort Robinson at the time of Joe's death and performed a postmortem examination on his body. He later wrote to Joe's grandson that when the murderer was arrested, "the nearest civil authorities four hundred miles away were notified to come and get the prisoner; but they not appearing at the end of four days, we had to under the law, turn him loose; and there being no frontier town near by there was no one to lynch him. So he went free."[11]

Thirty-four years later, Libbie Custer received a letter from a stranger who described himself as the son of California Joe. He said he had been taken captive by Indians as a boy and then ransomed; he returned voluntarily to live among them until the age of twenty. At the time of his letter he was a Presbyterian minister, seeking information about his father.[12]

. . .

The famous mountain man Jim Bridger had been so alarmed when he heard of Sheridan's plan for a winter campaign that he had visited the general personally to argue that the severe winter weather on the Plains would make such an attempt disastrous. "Blizzards don't respect man or beast," the legendary old hunter told the general.[13] But, like many mountain men, Bridger had lived like an Indian for so long that he had forgotten that whites preferred to bend the environment to their will rather than change their own plans. Sheridan knew that a winter campaign was the army's only chance: during the summer the Indians' expert guerrilla tactics gave them every advantage. Their immobility during the winter, and their expectation of safety, leveled the playing field. In addition, although the command would itself come close to starving on occasion, it could always be resupplied. In the winter the Indians operated under an economy of scarcity: if their stores were destroyed, they could not easily be replaced.

Another proponent of the winter campaign was the governor of Kansas, Samuel J. Crawford. He regarded it as "the only way to bring the hostile Indians to a sense of their duty," a curious concept to apply to the Indians, who would not have understood it, and would have rejected it if they had.[14] Governor Crawford meant that the Indians who had been laying waste to the settlements of the Solomon and Saline river valleys the previous spring and summer needed to be taught by force to accept the reservation system, that is, to confine themselves to a limited and specified territory set aside for them by the American government. As Crawford wrote in his proclamation to recruit a regiment of volunteer cavalry, "Longer to forbear with these bloody fiends would be a crime against civilization, and against the peace, security and lives of all the people upon the frontier."[15] For some time he had been sending such apocalyptic messages to Washington, where some political figures felt that the real crime against civilization was its *lack* of forbearance with the Indians.

While Custer was readying his troops, the thousand volunteers drawn from the indignant citizenry of Kansas prepared to march to a rendezvous with the Seventh. The zealous Crawford had resigned the governorship in order to lead them into battle. Of the thousand-odd horses that carried these men out of Topeka on November 5, not one would still be alive three months later: the Nineteenth Kansas would become a regiment of foot soldiers.

Jim Bridger had been right about the weather, but in addition to deep snow followed by deep mud—neither conducive to cavalry travel—the Nineteenth was poorly guided and got lost. John McBee, a seventeen-year-old volunteer, heard later that their guide, Apache Bill, might have lost the way on purpose because he had a Cheyenne wife he was trying to protect. If Bill was a terrible guide, fired the minute the regiment finally straggled into Camp Supply, he wasn't half bad as a doctor. He asked McBee if his teeth were sore from eating buffalo meat: "They were very sore and painful. Bill told him to eat the fat of the buffalo (the fat from about the kidneys) like bread and that that would cure his sore teeth. McBee did so and his teeth got all right."[16]

When the Kansans finally arrived at Camp Supply after a hard march of twenty-four days on only seven days' forage, their horses dying steadily along the way, they were disappointed to find that four days earlier the impatient Custer had persuaded Sheridan to let him move out: "They feared the enterprising Custer would strike so vigorously that the Indians would roar for peace," thus depriving them of vengeance.[17]

Custer and the Seventh had marched off on the morning of November 23 in the middle of a blizzard that had already deposited more than a foot of snow on the ground. In *My Life on the Plains* Custer represented himself as reassuring the dubious that conditions were optimum for their purposes: the cavalry would be on the move while the Indians remained immobile, and when they least expected army operations. For all Custer's cheerfulness about the storm, he had to admit that it was "a serious obstacle encountered quite early in the campaign."[18]

He also wrote in his stiff way that breakfast that first morning of the campaign was more a matter of form than substance, "for who, I might inquire, could rally much of an appetite at five o'clock in the morning, and when standing around a camp fire, almost up to the knees in snow?"[19] If scout Ben Clark is to be believed, this might be a sportive reference to Custer's younger brother, Tom, who lingered overlong at the breakfast table that morning, "to the disgust of Custer, who told him repeatedly to hurry and finish his breakfast. The Colonel [Tom's brevet rank] still lingered, however, and brought on an explosion of wrath from Custer, who charged into the tent, kicked over the mess table and sent dishes and victuals flying in all directions."[20] Rather than receiving greater privileges, the commanding officer's younger brother had a special responsibility to live up to the commanding officer's exacting standards. Tom once asked Libbie to intercede with Custer for him, "to see that he quit jumping on him for every little damned thing just because 'I happen to be his brother.'"[21]

Custer might well have been tense. A lot was riding on his performance: first and foremost, the rehabilitation of his army career. Sheridan was counting on him as well.

In spite of the falling snow, when the command marched out, its accompanying band played the familiar rollicking tune of "The Girl I Left Behind Me." One critic is disgusted that Custer took along "a pack of tootlers" when he should have been all business.[22] "When the weather, the situation, and the fact that the use of a brass instrument for playing at such a time could only be torture to the player," another writes indignantly, "the vainglory of the thing is no less apparent than its lack of sensibility [*sic*]."[23] In fact, when the moment of attack came, the band began Custer's favorite tune, the Irish drinking song "Garryowen," and then suddenly stopped: saliva had frozen in their instruments.[24]

Was the band's presence on the march a valuable morale booster or a foolish gesture? A brass band riding off into unknown territory on an Indian hunting expedition in the middle of a blizzard is a bizarre image, but, latter-day critics to the contrary, there is no evidence that anyone objected at the time. The fighting force must have been reassured by the normality of having their band along.

On the Plains, Custer acquired a reputation for charging to the tune of "Garryowen," but music had been an important part of his sense of military operations from the beginning. In 1863 he attempted to mislead the enemy as to the strength of his command by directing fires to be built and the band to play at different points.[25] Libbie remembered that during the Civil War her husband's Michigan Brigade band were the only musicians always at the front. They were fired upon for the first time at Brandy Station and forced to retreat, but they proved their dedication that night when they gathered outside Custer's tent and began to play "exactly where they had left off that morning."[26] Years later, scout Luther North would recall that Custer's Black Hills expedition "was the first and last expedition that I was ever on in an Indian country that had a band along."[27]

While the Seventh was getting underway, some Cheyenne and Arapaho chiefs led by Black Kettle appeared at Fort Cobb on November 20 to meet with Colonel William M. Hazen, whose job was to provide rations for friendly Indians in the area of the fort.[28] Black Kettle, whose Cheyennes had been unexpectedly attacked and butchered by Colonel John M. Chivington at Sand Creek, Colorado, in 1864, was a recognized advocate of peace. Nevertheless, he candidly admitted to Hazen that his young warriors had raided last spring over his objections: "Some will not listen, and, since the fighting began, I have not been able to keep them all at home. But we all want peace, and I would be glad to move all my people down this way. I could then keep them all quietly near camp."[29]

Black Kettle's honest confession that he could not always control his young men may have determined Hazen's decision not to help the Indians. Hazen, a bit like Pontius Pilate, seemed anxious only to dissociate himself from the matter and justify his own position. He told the chiefs, "You must go back to your country, and if the soldiers come to fight you must remember they are not from me, but from that great war chief [Sheridan], and with him you must make peace." In conclusion he said, "I hope you understand how and why it is that I cannot make peace with you." All the chiefs politely replied that they did.[30]

It is unlikely that the Indians truly understood the convolutions of white authority that awkwardly divided responsibility for Indian affairs between the army and the Department of the Interior. Sheridan himself constantly complained that this structure of competing government bureaucracies was an anomaly: "I am ordered to fight these Indians, and General Hazen is permitted to feed them."[31] Moreover, Hazen had been less than forthcoming with the Indians who sought, and according to his instructions should have received, his protection. As he reported to Sherman, he favored their punishment because the young Cheyenne warriors would raid again unless they were made to feel the power of the army.

The Indians were thus dismissed without the promise of protection they had come for. They returned to their camp on the Washita River the night before Custer's attack.

The goal of the Custer expedition was Indian Territory (present-day Oklahoma). From Camp Supply, on the north fork of the Canadian River in northern Oklahoma, Custer marched first west and then south to the South Canadian, heading toward the Antelope Hills, a location favored by the Southern Plains Indians for winter camping. On the morning of November 26, 1868, after a conference with his Osage Indian and white scouts, he sent Major Joel Elliott and three of his eleven companies to explore westward up the river. A courier returned after only a short time to inform Custer that Elliott had struck an Indian trail of 150 warriors twelve miles out. Custer sent back word that Elliott was to pursue the trail; the main command would hasten to join him. He summoned his officers, told them the situation, and gave his orders: the baggage train would remain behind, along with extra blankets and tents, and the troops would take only what they could carry—a risky decision in the fierce Plains winter. Taking out his watch, Custer told the assembled officers that they would begin to move out in twenty minutes.[32]

It was a long day. Spurred on by Custer's determination, his command did not halt for rest or nourishment until 9:00 P.M. when it was reunited with Elliott's three troops. After an hour for the men to feed their horses and have a quick meal of coffee and hardtack themselves, the reunited troops continued their pursuit. The Osage scouts led the way with Custer close behind, clues leading them inexorably toward the Indians, excitement mounting.

By then it was well after midnight. When the scouts sighted a large body of animals, Custer looked at them "long and anxiously . . . but was unable to discover anything in their appearance different from what might be presented by a herd of buffalo under similar circumstances."[33] Then three separate sounds confirmed beyond any doubt that they were close to human habitation: one of the scouts heard a dog bark, and soon Custer heard it too. He then heard the tinkling of a bell, which he interpreted as that of the herd's lead pony, and—the culminating evidence—the cry of an infant. The Seventh had found Black Kettle's winter camp on the Washita River.

Custer's plan was to surround the village and, at daybreak, four hours later, make a concerted attack from all sides. To this end the command was divided into four units, approximately equal in strength according to Custer, although the one he chose to lead contained not only four troops, but all the scouts and the squad of sharpshooters. Nothing remained but to wait in the bitter cold and snow without making a sound.

Before the attack, the already chilled men of Custer's personal command were instructed to remove their overcoats and haversacks for greater freedom of movement in the freezing air. The band was to play "Garryowen" when the order to charge was given. As everyone waited expectantly, a shot suddenly rang out from the far side of the village, followed immediately by Custer's order to attack. It was the beginning of the Battle of the Washita in which the Seventh Cavalry captured the Cheyenne village and, by Custer's report, killed 103 Indians, including the chief and his wife; captured 53 women and children; and destroyed an enormous amount of Indian property.

Custer wrote in his field report to Sheridan that "the Indians were caught napping"[34]—in retrospect ominous words, for they would recur in Custer's last reported speech to his men as he looked across the Little Bighorn almost eight years later, perhaps thinking of the surprise attack at the Washita. On that future occasion he would be mistaken.

In spite of their surprise, the Indians fought vigorously and inflicted serious casualties, the extent of which the command would not realize until later in the day. The popular young Lieutenant Louis Hamilton was killed instantly in the first moments of the battle. Another officer, Captain Albert Barnitz, was seriously wounded and expected to die: he managed to recover but was incapacitated for further army service. Most disturbing was the disappearance of Major Elliott. Late in life, the scout Ben Clark said that Custer had asked him during the battle if he knew where Elliott had gone. Clark gestured eastward. It was all that he or anybody knew at the time.[35]

Other matters were more pressing. Throughout the morning Indians had been gathering on the surrounding bluffs in increasingly worrisome numbers. J. M. Pickens, an enlisted man in company M, had been designated one of the horse-holders, a group who remained outside the village guarding the cavalry horses. They could see nothing of what was happening, but when it became clear from sound alone that the battle was over, he recalled, "we men then began to clamor for a move to the scene. Our Corporal in charge made a feeble objection at first but on second thought yielded and we moved down into the valley. . . . By the time we were in camp the Indians were swarming on the bluffs around us, and if we hadn't become restless our corporal might have held us there just a little too long."[36] He mused that he had not realized the narrowness of their escape until many years later.

During a lull in this second phase of the battle Custer ordered the lodges and all captured property piled up and burned. One of the enlisted men had brought to Lieutenant Edward Godfrey a beautiful dress made of antelope skins "as soft as the finest broadcloth" and decorated with beads and teeth. Godfrey, who was in charge of the operation, fleetingly thought of asking Custer for permission to keep the dress, but then, he said to himself, "orders are orders" and threw it into one of the bonfires. After his long career of Indian fighting, that beautiful dress still stuck in Godfrey's memory as a senseless sacrifice. "I have never ceased to regret that destruction," he wrote.[37] (Custer did exempt a handsome lodge for himself, which some of the women captives erected for him on the return to Camp Supply.)

Soon "all that was left of the village were a few heaps of blackened ashes," but what had been destroyed would live on in the public record, proudly cataloged and enumerated to validate the extent of the victory.[38] According to Custer's field report there were "241 saddles, 573 buffalo robes, 290 buffalo skins for lodges, 160 untanned robes, 210 axes, 140 hatchets, 35 revolvers, 47 rifles, 535 lbs of powder, 1050 lbs of lead, 4000 arrows and arrowheads, 75 spears, 90 bullet moulds, 35 bows and quivers, 12 shields, 300 lbs of bullets, 775 lariats, 940 buckskin saddle bags, 470 blankets, 93 coats, 700 lbs of tobacco," and all foodstuffs. As Custer summed it up, "We destroyed everything of value to the Indians."[39] After selecting a number of mounts for the prisoners, Custer also ordered the 875 Indian ponies killed.

Custer's account of what happened next seems unbelievable at a time when the Seventh was surrounded by hostile warriors, when the second-ranking officer and the sergeant major were unaccounted for, and when Custer was in need of extricating his command from a spot becoming tighter by the minute. Nevertheless, he pauses in his account of the battle in *My Life on the Plains*, as he says he paused during the battle, for some comic relief—spun out in a leisurely fashion in his narrative but possibly lasting only a few minutes in real time. Entering the tepee where the captives were being held, Custer engaged in an elaborate bit of byplay with some of the women, allowing Black Kettle's articulate sister Mahwissa to make two long speeches while placing in his hand the hand of a young Indian girl. According to his interpreter, Raphael Romero (called "Romeo" throughout the regiment), this was a marriage ceremony—and a good joke on Custer, who suddenly remembered his responsibilities and made his escape. He did not escape so readily from persistent rumors that he later acted the role of husband to the beautiful young woman, Monahseetah.

Custer at last learned from a captured squaw that the village was only one in a series strung out along the river; his weakened force, running low in ammunition, would be seriously outnumbered. Just as the situation became more threatening, quartermaster James Bell arrived with several thousand rounds of ammunition, but the additional supplies could be only a temporary reprieve.

Concerning Major Elliott and the other missing men, Custer faced a terrible dilemma: by the time their absence was noticed, they were probably beyond help, but frontier army policy was unequivocal: You did not abandon your men to the Indians. The five troops accompanying Custer had sustained the loss of their overcoats and rations when the place where these articles had been left was overrun by the enemy. This blow, the tightening noose of an unknown number of hostiles, and the unwieldy numbers of captured and wounded compelled Custer to turn his attention to withdrawal. He made some search for Elliott and his men, but it yielded nothing, and so, as darkness approached, Custer set his command in motion, marching boldly toward the next Indian village. The warriors withdrew in haste, assuming that Custer intended to attack their own women and children, but once darkness had fallen, the command turned and retraced its steps, arriving back at the battleground around 10:00 P.M. The countermarch was only a bellicose false front for the benefit of the Indians; in reality, Custer's greatest desire was to reach his baggage train.

The following day Custer found the train, unmolested by Indians, and could then turn his attention to the gratifying duty of informing his commander of the successful engagement. Not only did Sheridan fire off a communication to Custer generously commending the officers and men and tendering his "special congratulations to their distinguished commander," he immediately wrote to Libbie: "My dear Friend, I have only time to tell you of your husbands [*sic*] proud services in killing 103 Indians and capturing nearly 1000 horses and much other property. . . . God bless him for his efforts."[40]

James Albert Hadley, an officer with the Nineteenth Kansas, recalled the Seventh's return to Camp Supply on December 1 as a splendid show staged for full effect by Custer before an admiring audience. The five troops who had lost their overcoats and overshoes—this last detail not mentioned in Custer's account—"were wrapped in many-colored blankets with their feet tied up in grain sacks."[41] With the

Osage scouts in full warpaint, the band (or "tootlers"), the Indian captives, and the ranks of cavalry, the exotic spectacle must have resembled a Roman triumphal march.

Like the other Kansans, Hadley was eager to see the famous commander of the Seventh. At the head of the column he glimpsed "a young man of medium height, slender, wearing buckskin hunting shirt and leggings much befringed."[42] To his surprise, this unprepossessing figure was Custer. Another young volunteer, David Spotts, wrote in his diary on December 2, "we are anxious to hear all about the fight and get a better view of Gen. Custer, as he was dressed like a scout yesterday and we did not recognize him." He added that Custer's men described him as "a fine fellow, kind to them and will share with a private who is in need"—a rather different picture from the imperious Custer of '67.[43]

A few days later Spotts recorded, "We got to see Gen. Custer today at close range. He is of medium size, light complexion, long curly golden hair, wears a light colored hat and buckskin suit, the same as the scouts wear, the leather fringe on the seams of arms and legs. His men all like him."[44]

Custer had once again demonstrated that he could inspire men in battle. Long years later the son of a trooper who had fought with Custer at the Washita wrote that he had never heard his father "say a harsh word of General Custer, but always spoke of him as a brave and fearless commander, and one who would not send his men into an engagement that he was afraid to go into himself. . . . I never heard father speak of Gen. Custer as being harsh and domineering toward his men."[45]

Custer had also accomplished his mission. As he stated in the conclusion of his official report to Sheridan, "We have taught the Indians that they are safe from us at no place and at no season, and also, what some of our own people may doubt, that the white man can endure the inclemencies of winter better than the Indian."[46] What Custer attributed to the hardiness of his race was more a matter of adequate supply. In the winter of 1868 Black Kettle's band had been rendered destitute, dependent upon the charity of other Indians to survive the harsh winter, while white society was able to keep its armies resupplied.

Apparently Custer had recovered the balance that he so demonstrably lacked in his disciplinary measures during the Louisiana-Texas interlude and his first year on the Plains. On December 6, he wrote to Libbie exuberantly,

> General Sheridan's letter contains some words to me that will delight you. He says in congratulation "the Battle of the Washita River is the most complete and successful of all our Indian battles and was fought in such impossible weather and circumstances as to reflect the highest credit on yourself and Regiment." Oh is it not gratifying to be so thought of by one whose opinion is above all price and whose friendship is to be so highly prized?[47]

Libbie, by then settled at Fort Leavenworth, could only rejoice along with her jubilant husband.

The matter of Major Elliott and eighteen other missing men was the one blot on Custer's victory. Elliott was the second in command, yet he had ridden off without orders, impetuously pursuing some Indians. This behavior was so "entirely exceptional," in the opinion of Randolph Keim, a newspaperman in Sheridan's camp, that he wondered if Elliott's horse had run away with him, causing a number of troopers to mistakenly accompany him.[48] Unbreveted and under a cloud, the major supposedly called back to Lieutenant Hale as he rode off, "Here goes for a brevet or a coffin!"[49] In keeping with the military ethos, he wanted to distinguish himself, but he may have been overeager because he had *not* made the most of his opportunity when he commanded the Seventh during Custer's absence. Sheridan, hardly the man to soft-pedal his judgments, had voiced his displeasure.

What Elliott *had* excelled in was the commissioned officers test given after the Civil War to place officers in the regular army. Although he had finished the war as a captain, Elliott had scored so high on the test that he had been elevated to the rank of major. But theoretical knowledge isn't everything in military success. Generals like Lee and Sherman combined exceptional academic performance with brilliance in the field while Grant, Sheridan, and Custer had been indifferent students at West Point but distinguished field commanders during the war. Elliott may have been simply a good test-taker.

One officer of the Seventh would use the fate of Major Elliott and the others who went to their deaths with him to do immeasurable harm to Custer within the regiment. Captain Frederick Benteen had hated Custer ever since the two first met during Custer's difficult period of adjustment to the frontier. In the way that such things happen, Benteen disliked his new superior officer instantly: they were both strong-willed, opinionated, and loyal to their heroes. Custer spoke contemptuously of Benteen's hero, General James Wilson, and this might have been enough. It seems likely that Benteen, who had a well-developed sense of his own abilities, was jealous of Custer—the West Point graduate, the younger and better-rewarded man.

These are all understandable motives, but they hardly seem enough to explain Benteen's dogged hatred. E. A. Brininstool, a Custerphobe, wrote to Custer biographer Frederic Van de Water that Benteen's son Freddy had closed off discussion by claiming to have no idea why the two men were enemies. Brininstool noted that the younger Benteen did not like to talk about his father and ignored inquiries: "I sent him a batch of letters written by this human skunk W. J. Ghent of Washington [a Custer partisan], in which he brands the old man as a liar and drunkard, and yet that damnable son refuses to take any action or even to get mad over such defamation of character."[50] Perhaps Freddy, the only survivor of five children, had found his father difficult to live with, too, or perhaps he was merely immune to the virus of conjecture over the Last Stand that others found so infectious.

Whatever the cause, Freddy's silence resonates against a letter his father wrote to the *Army and Navy Journal* seven months after the Little Bighorn disaster. He was commenting on Frederick Whittaker's public accusation that he had failed to go to Custer's aid, as ordered: "I have one child—a ten-year-old boy; if he learns from his father's daily life, what his character is, as he must, will it make much difference to him in after years, in stumbling across Whittaker's book to see his father quoted as having neglected the first duty of a soldier?"[51] Benteen's question was meant to be rhetorical, but perhaps Freddy's later failure to defend his father indicates that the true answer was "yes."

According to Ben Clark, who had been at Custer's side throughout the battle, Benteen approached him a day or two later and asked if he would be willing to make a statement that "Custer knowingly let Elliott go to his doom without trying to save him." Clark "refused to have anything to do with the matter." He flatly asserted in an article in the *New York Sun* that Custer had known nothing of Elliott's going, a position he maintained in an interview with the researcher Walter Camp years later.[52]

In old age David Spotts could not recall ever having heard a word of criticism of Custer for returning without Elliott's body: "I conversed with a number of the boys of the 7th U.S. Cavalry and [heard] only praise for their commander."[53] The diary that he kept during the campaign of 1868 recounted the episode without any hint of controversy. The entry for December 2, the day after the Seventh marched into Camp Supply, recorded that "it was found during the late afternoon that Maj. Elliott and about twenty men were missing. After hunting around where the fighting had taken place, their bodies could not be found, and the searchers had to leave them behind, knowing they had been killed at some place not far away."[54]

The truth of Spotts's last phrase was verified when the Seventh returned to the battlefield some two weeks later, accompanied by General Sheridan and the Nineteenth Kansas regiment. Moving in the direction in which Elliott had last been seen, they discovered the place of his massacre some two miles from the site of Black Kettle's village. Lieutenant Colonel Horace L. Moore, second in command of the Kansans, remembered that "the throat of every one of them had the appearance of having been cut. This was caused by the Indians having cut out the thyroid cartilage."[55] Moore recalled no other mutilations or any scalpings. Custer's more detailed description of the gruesome remains, based upon the examination of the individual bodies conducted by the regimental surgeon, included both. Badly outnumbered and on indefensible terrain, Elliott and his men had been able to do nothing but "sell their lives dearly."

The wound of Elliott's loss might have healed without consequence had Benteen not been determined to keep it festering. He wrote a letter to his friend William DeGress in St. Louis, upbraiding Custer for abandoning Elliott and the men with him in language worthy of the most melodramatic captivity narrative:

> Who can describe the feeling of that brave band, as with anxious beating hearts, they strained their yearning eyes in the direction whence help should come? What must have been the despair that, when all hopes of succor died out, nerved their stout arms to do or die? Round and round rush the red fiends, smaller and smaller shrinks the circle, but the aim of that devoted, gallant knot of heroes is steadier than ever, and the death howl of the murderous redskin is more frequent. . . . Soon every voice in that little band is still as

> death; but the hellish work of the savages is scarcely begun, and their ingenuities are taxed to invent barbarities to practice on the bodies of the fallen brave.[56]

On February 9, 1869, DeGress had the letter published anonymously in the *Missouri Democrat*, a St. Louis newspaper; the *New York Times* reprinted it on February 14. Since then, the reason for Elliott's fate has been in the public domain—a source of continued controversy.

Another issue that would linger unpleasantly but more predictably was the degree of culpability of Black Kettle's tribe. Custer added a postscript to his letter of December 19 to Libbie, telling her not to mind that newspapers would condemn the battle: "You know how little such trifles affect me."[57] His orders, which he had carried out, had been to "destroy their village and ponies; to kill or hang all warriors, and bring back all women and children."[58]

Sheridan, in his report to Sherman dated two days after the Seventh's return to Camp Supply, contended that tangible evidence of raiding had been found in the Indian village, including the scalp of an "expressman killed and horribly mutilated just before I had left Fort Dodge,—the mail on his person was found in 'Black Kettle's camp."[59] A month later his report to Sherman was far more detailed:

> Mules taken from trains, mail matter carried by our murdered carriers, photographs stolen from the scenes of outrage on the Solomon and Saline, were found in the captured camp; and, in addition, I have their own illustrated history found in their captured camp, showing the different fights or murders this tribe were engaged in—the trains attacked, the hay parties attacked about Fort Wallace, the women, citizens, and soldiers killed. It is at the service of any one desiring information on the subject.[60]

Sheridan's description of this book is the only trace of an invaluable Indian artifact that seems to have vanished from history, perhaps consumed in the great Chicago fire that took its toll on Sheridan's headquarters a few years later. In any case, it did not turn up in the various bequests that the Sheridan family would later make to the Smithsonian, nor is there any word of it in private hands.

Sheridan's annual report to the secretary of war was still more precisely detailed with regard to proof of Indian raids: clothing and bedding were added to the list of incriminating evidence and the mail he originally mentioned became "the mail which I had sent by the expressmen, Nat Marshal and Bill Davis, from Bluff Creek to Fort Dodge, who were murdered and mutilated."[61]

Immediately after the battle, Thomas Murphy, superintendent of Indian affairs, had protested to the commissioner of Indian affairs that Black Kettle was "one of the best and truest friends the whites have ever had, amongst the Indians of the Plains." Murphy argued that Black Kettle had ransomed white captives with his own ponies, and even after the atrocities inflicted on his people at Sand Creek had "used all his influence to prevent the Cheyennes from going to war to avenge this wrong."[62] His point of view was shared by Major Edward W. Wynkoop, former agent for the Cheyennes and Arapahoes, who wrote to the commissioner of Indian affairs that he knew Black Kettle to be innocent:

> In regard to the charge that "Black Kettle" engaged in the depredations committed on the Saline river during the summer of 1868, I know that same to be utterly false as "Black Kettle" at the time was camped near my Agency on the Pawnee Fork. . . . There have been Indians deserving of punishment but unfortunately they have not been those who received [it] at the hands of the troops at the "Battle of the Washita."

Wynkoop went on to question the "evidence" Sheridan found in Black Kettle's village, asking, "How did they know that those evidences existed previous to the assault?"[63]

George W. Manypenny, a former commissioner of Indian affairs and chair of the Sioux Commission of 1876, may have been the first person to notice that "Custer's detailed report says nothing of such things." Surely, he continued, "if the damning evidence Sheridan described had been found, Custer would have announced the fact."[64] It was a curious omission from an account full of implausibly quantified data on captured Indian property.[65]

Custer may have omitted any evidence of Indian raids because his primary interest was to emphasize the battle's success in depriving the Indians of goods that they needed both to survive and to make war. It never occurred to him to question or verify the guilt of the tribe since the Seventh had found white captives in the village and since Black Kettle's sister, the loquacious Mahwissa, had confirmed that "frequent raiding and war parties . . . from time to time had been permitted to go forth and depredate upon the settlements of the white men."[66] The chief himself had admitted to Colonel Hazen only a few days before the attack that he had not been able to restrain his young men from raiding. However, by the time Custer published an account of the battle, the army had been bitterly criticized for attacking the "peaceful" Black Kettle, and the mail carriers' bloody scalps and other evidence of Indian aggression would have been politically useful.

While white accusations against the Indians were the trees that obscured the forest, the overriding issue was their appropriation of Indian land without a concomitant assumption of responsibility for the inhabitants of it. The problem on the Plains in 1868 and 1869 was the dispossession of the Indians from their territory before the new reservation system was equipped to care for them.[67] Writing only a few days after the Washita victory, Thomas Murphy speculated that if Congress had speedily enacted the Medicine Lodge Treaty of 1867, the Indians would have received the treaty provisions they expected during 1868:

> I believe we could have kept them at peace, and that by this time they would have been quietly located on their new reservation, where we could control and manage them, gradually wean them from their wild and wandering life and in doing which it would not have cost the Government as much per year as it is now costing per month to fight them, and this cause would have been far more humane and becoming a magnanimous and Christian nation.[68]

This view was echoed by George Manypenny, who noted that Sheridan's 1868 winter campaign had been exceptionally well provisioned. The general had sent ahead four hundred thousand rations to Fort Dodge, three hundred thousand to Fort Lyon, and three hundred thousand to Fort Arbuckle: "one-tenth of this amount of food given to these homeless Indians, would have accomplished all that was necessary . . . the simple performance of an obligation, under the treaties of Medicine Lodge creek."[69] Manypenny's position was borne out in the field by Colonel Benjamin Grierson, commander at Fort Sill, who wrote to Sheridan's headquarters on April 7, 1869. Grierson argued that the reservation system would work if the Indians were properly fed, but that most of the time rations were insufficient. This forced the Indians to leave the reservation to hunt or else starve. The conscientious Grierson went on to say that his instructions called for using force to keep the Indians "where they belong,—yet I feel that it is unjust to *hold* them here and not feed them."[70]

Given the central importance of warfare in Plains Indian culture and the need of young warriors to establish their reputation by fighting, it is by no means certain that payment of the agreed-upon provisions would have prevented all raids. Weaning the Plains Indians from a nomadic life would take far more time and effort than Murphy or anyone else envisioned. But critics were on unassailable ground in one respect: it should have been a sacred duty for a nation that assumed moral superiority to honor the treaty obligations it had not only freely accepted but proposed. Furthermore, as partisan interests swayed both outraged settlers and equally incensed warriors, leadership in this area was surely the responsibility of the national government, one its badly divided bureaucracy failed to meet.

13

Save the Last Bullet for Your Wife

Degradation unspeakable; the brutalities of the men, the venom of the squaws. . . . People in civilized conditions cannot imagine it. But we who have seen it know. Death would be merciful in comparison.—Libbie Custer to her aunt Eliza Sabin, from Fort Hays, Kansas

A white woman has just come into our camp deranged and can give no account of herself. She has been four days without food. . . . I can only explain her coming by supposing her to have been captured by the Indians and their barbarous treatment having rendered her a lunatic.—Custer to Libbie, November 7, 1868, Camp Supply, Kansas

The old-time rule of the Plains: "When fighting Indians, keep the last bullet for yourself."
—Thomas B. Marquis, *Keep the Last Bullet for Yourself: The True Story of Custer's Last Stand*

The Battle of the Washita was the stunning victory the frontier army needed so badly to maintain credibility—with politicians in Washington, with settlers, and with those Indians who still felt that they could raid and escape punishment. But Sheridan saw it as only a beginning. "If we can get in one or two more good blows there will be no more Indian troubles in my department," he wrote.[1] Accordingly, he visited the site of the recent battle with Custer, then ordered the Seventh Cavalry and the Nineteenth Kansas to pursue any recalcitrant Indians and herd them to their reservations. The expedition accomplished this objective, but it was most memorable for dramatically rescuing two captive white women from the Cheyenne when Custer boldly took several tribesmen hostage until the women were released. The young women evoked both horror and compassion in their rescuers, for they were popularly regarded as having survived "a fate worse than death," one that Custer, with Libbie's full agreement, had made provision to spare her.

In *Tenting on the Plains* Libbie described the first time she felt the reality of an injunction commonly heard on frontier army posts: in the case of an attack, women were to be killed rather than allowed to fall into Indian hands. During the period when the separated Custers were frantic to see each other, Custer had sent instructions for Libbie to join a wagon train bringing supplies to his command. The train was attacked by Indians, but because the post commander had considered it too dangerous for her to go, Libbie was not on it. As she recounted,

> The first time I saw Colonel Cook [Cooke, the wagon train commander] after this affair, he said: "The moment I found the Indians were on us, and we were in for a fight, I thought of you, and said to myself, 'If she were in the ambulance, before giving an order I would ride up and shoot her.'" "Would you have given me no chance for life," I replied, "in case the battle had gone in your favor?" "Not one," he said. "I should have been unnerved by the thought of the fate that awaited you, and I have promised the General not to take any chances, but to kill you before anything worse could happen."[2]

In a fictional version of this episode, Cooke tells another officer,

> When the attack developed I said to myself, at once: "If Mrs. Custer were here, in my charge, the first thing I must do would be to ride to her ambulance and mercifully shoot her. That is my solemn promise to the general." "Whew!" sighed the other officer, gravely. "That would be horrible. But not so horrible," he added, "as to let her or any other white woman fall alive into the hands of the Indians."[3]

According to Libbie's account, Cooke admitted that he would get her killing out of the way so that he would not have to keep worrying about her, but Libbie showed no sign of resentment. Describing another incident in which she and an officer escort unexpectedly came upon a group of potentially hostile warriors, she wrote of her awareness that the danger was twofold: "I was in peril from death or capture by the savages, and liable to be killed by my own friends to prevent my capture. . . . While I knew that I was defended by strong hands and brave hearts, the thought of the double danger always flashed into my mind when we were in jeopardy."[4]

The idea of killing women to save them from the Indians was such a commonplace in the frontier army, so widely reiterated, that it begins to seem not only unremarkable but obligatory.[5] William Cody, beginning his career on the same Kansas plains as the Custers, related an episode in which he was chased by Indians and, while urging the horse on with one hand, held a loaded gun to his wife's head with the other in case they were overtaken.[6] Small wonder that Mrs. Cody decided to go back to St. Louis to live while her husband became famous as a scout and buffalo hunter.

At the constantly besieged Fort Phil Kearny, the commanding officer did not hesitate to prescribe emergency mercy killings for all women and children: "If, in my absence, Indians in overwhelming numbers attack, put the women and children in the magazine with supplies of water, bread, crackers and other supplies that seem best, and, in the event of a last desperate struggle, destroy all together, rather than have any captured alive."[7] His own wife and children were part of this group. One of Ellen McGowan Biddle's first instructions as an army wife was "never let an Indian take you alive." Her husband was not the only one to shift the burden to the woman herself.[8] Perhaps most unnerving was Lieutenant Jack Summerhayes's command to his wife, Martha, when their small force approached a pass frequented by hostile Indians. Jumping out of their coach to defend it, he hurriedly thrust a pistol into Martha's hand and told the young mother, "Don't let them get the baby. . . . *Don't let them get either of you alive.*"[9]

Fairfax Downey gave the frontier army's standard view of the subject when he wrote that army women were instructed that captivity meant "one long agony of horror and shame til death as the victim of the lust of successive chiefs and the slave of their jealous squaws. . . . There was, consequently, never any doubt in the Army as to what must be done in the last resort."[10] Custer, as his instructions to fellow officers indicated, shared the common view. Describing what happened to a young woman who fell into the hands of the Kiowas, "a beautiful girl just ripening into womanhood," he said that she was exposed to "a fate infinitely more dreadful than death itself. She first fell to one of the principal chiefs, who, after robbing her of that which was more precious than life, and forcing her to become the victim of his brutal lust, bartered her in return for two horses to another chief." The girl was passed from one captor to another, "undergoing a life so horribly brutal that, when meeting her upon her release from captivity, one could only wonder how a young girl, nurtured in civilization and possessed of the natural refinement and delicacy of thought which she exhibited, could have survived such degrading treatment."[11]

Given the values of Victorian America, women tended to concur with the army's assessment of the matter. Lydia Spencer Lane's description of the situation she might find herself in as a frontier army wife is typical of the vague but suggestive horrors usually invoked:

> Men were generally put to death by slow torture, but they were allowed to live enough to witness the atrocities practiced on their wives and children, such things as only fiends could devise. Babies had their brains dashed out before the eyes of father and mother, powerless to help them. Lucky would the latter have been, had they treated her in the same way; but what she was forced to endure would have wrung tears from anything but an Indian.[12]

A brief news item in *Harper's Weekly* for December 22, 1866, tersely reported the same paradigmatic circumstances: a husband killed and scalped, an infant thrown onto rocks and killed, and a mother and three daughters taken into captivity, where "the mother and the two eldest daughters were subjected to the most unheard-of cruelties and outrages by their brutal captors."[13]

When Camp Cooke, Montana Territory, was threatened by Indians, it is not surprising that Sarah Canfield wrote in her diary that the women "held a 'council of war,' and decided if the Ft. could not be held that we preferred to be shot by our own officers rather than to be taken captive."[14] Mary Manley Parmelee, a child at Fort Abraham Lincoln at the time of the cavalry's defeat at the Little Bighorn, wrote matter-of-factly that in case of an attack on the post, women and children were to gather in the post trader's store, and, "if worst came to worse [*sic*], it was agreed that they were to be killed there by their own husbands and fathers, rather than that they should fall into the hands of the Indians."[15]

There seem to have been few dissenters from the prevailing view that death was preferable to the chance of undergoing such horrors. One exception was Sallie Tallmadge, a spirited young woman who went hunting in a party headed by the famous Indian fighter Major Eugene Carr. After she became lost on the first day of the hunt, Major Carr wanted her to promise that she would shoot herself if the Indians appeared in sight. She refused, whereupon he said, "Very good; then I shall shoot you if they appear."[16] (Fortunately they didn't.)

Women who returned from Indian captivity reinforced the emotional reaction that death was the preferable fate. A year after Libbie escaped the Indian attack and possible death at the hands of one of her husband's officers, Custer freed the two young Kansas women who had been in Cheyenne hands for a number of months. Patrolling the same territory of the wagon train fight in search of marauding Indians to punish, he was now in the company of the Nineteenth Kansas Volunteers, who, having missed out on the Washita victory by their tardy arrival at Camp Supply, were anxious to avenge the killing and rape of their fellow Kansans along the Solomon and Saline Rivers. They were more than eager to do battle.

When the Indians were found, instead of gratifying the combined forces by attacking, Custer opted to negotiate for the release of the two captive white women. The dramatic scene of their restoration has been variously described by eyewitnesses, of whom the Kansas volunteer David L. Spotts is probably the most reliable. He wrote in his diary that the women's unsmiling faces revealed the hard life they had led: Mrs. Morgan, who had been captured as a bride of one month, "appeared to be 50 years old, although she was less than 25."[17]

Custer, anxious to justify his "better judgment" and "humanity" in resisting the urge to seek revenge, reported that the captive women were "bright, cultivated, and good-looking."[18] Yet he also wrote in his official report that "the story of their captivity and their treatment by their captors is a recital of such barbarous cruelties and enormous indignities, that it is surprising that civilized beings could endure it and still survive."[19] Libbie's description of the two women was more like that of Private Spotts: "The young faces of the two . . . were now worn with privation and exposure, and haggard with the terrible insults of their captors, too dreadful to be chronicled here."[20]

Too dreadful to be chronicled at all in those times. Government records and other sources all use *outrage* as a code word for rape; captivity in which repeated sexual violation was assumed to have occurred is often referred to as "a fate worse than death."[21] Yet Richard Irving Dodge, an army officer who made some study of the Plains Indians during this period, was remarkably explicit:

> Either the character and customs of the Indians have greatly changed, or Cooper and some other novelists knew nothing of Indians when they placed their heroines as captives in the hands of these savages. . . . No woman has been taken prisoner by any plains Indians who did not as soon after as practicable become a victim to the lust of every one of her captors. . . .
>
> No words can express the horror of the situation of that most unhappy woman who falls into the hands of these savage fiends.
>
> The husband or other male protectors killed or dispersed, she is borne off in triumph to where the Indians make their first camp. Here, if she makes no resistance, she is laid upon a buffalo robe, and each in turn violates her person, the others dancing, singing, and yelling around her. If she resists at all her clothing is torn off from her person, four pegs are driven into the ground, and her arms and legs, stretched to the utmost, are tied fast to them by thongs. Here, with the howling band dancing and singing around her, she is subjected to violation after violation, outrage after outrage, to every abuse and indignity until not infrequently death releases her from suffering. . . .
>
> If she lives, it is to go through the same horrible ordeal in every camp until the party gets back to the home encampment.[22]

Colonel Dodge went on to say that he could provide numerous "well-authenticated instances of outrages as bad, and many far worse, than any here described." But, he concluded, "I am glad to leave this sickening and horrible subject. I would infinitely prefer to suppress all mention of these fearful atrocities, and I only mention them in the interest of truth."[23]

Colonel Dodge objected to the large sums sometimes paid to ransom such captives since he regarded kidnapping as a profitable Indian racket that the government should not encourage. But, in keeping with his gruesome description of captivity, he ultimately concluded that the policy of paying ransom was proper, "no amount of money being too great to weigh against the delivery of a woman from the horror of such a situation."[24] As early as 1867 General Sherman wanted the practice of ransoming captives discontinued, but officers on the frontier could seldom resist when an opportunity to rescue white women and children presented itself.

Given the horrific picture of captivity that was widely diffused on the frontier, restored captives were assumed to have been severely affected by their experience. Whether or not they had suffered any part of the abuse so graphically described by Colonel Dodge, they had known the complete powerlessness that is the most devastating of human circumstances. And since the Indians often separated captives from each other, they usually had to endure their lot in isolation, an isolation that would continue in some measure even if they returned to their former world.

Having endured "a fate worse than death" without in fact dying, the woman who survived captivity was not seen as a positive role model of hardships overcome so much as a repugnant anomaly, albeit one deserving of Christian charity. One writer about frontier captives also remarked that many seemed to die quickly upon returning to white society, although he was uncertain whether to attribute this to the emotional trauma or the physical hardships of the experience.[25]

The story of Matilda Lockhart, a thirteen or fourteen year old recovered from the Comanches, fulfilled the expectation of frontier ideology: "The once sprightly, joyous young girl, whose presence had been everywhere like a gleam of sunshine penetrating the gloom of the wilderness, was a mere wreck of her former self. Her health was almost utterly ruined by the privations and hardships she had undergone and the brutal treatment to which she had been subjected by her savage captors."[26] Covered with scars, Matilda lingered a few years and then died.

Returned captives like Matilda may have internalized their culture's message that they were better off dead, or they might not have been able to adapt to their condition of alienation in a place where they once belonged. In the account she wrote of her captivity among the Sioux, Fanny Kelly found it necessary to explain why she had chosen to keep herself alive:

> Many persons have since assured me that, to them, death would have been preferable to life with such prospects, saying that rather than have submitted to be carried away by savages, to a dark and doubtful doom, they would have taken their own lives. But it is only those who have looked over the dark abyss of death who know how the soul shrinks from meeting the unknown future. Experience is a grand teacher, and we were then in her school, and learned that while hope offers the faintest token of refuge, we pause upon the fearful brink of eternity, and look back for rescue.[27]

Fanny Kelly *was* rescued, and lived to write about her experience, but except for a few celebrated captives, we know too little about the later lives of most of these women. Many people of both sexes had at the very least ambivalent feelings about bringing such "damaged" women back to white society. One eyewitness observing the freeing of Sarah White and Anna Morgan wondered "what must their feelings have been . . . rescued from a living death to the warm embrace of friends and kindred."[28] Yet beyond the initial welcome, what kind of future might they have? Captivity narratives usually ended with the victim's restoration to white society because the exotic experience, the one seen as worth recounting, was the captivity. After the former captive had been reabsorbed into her own culture, there was no more story—except possibly a sentence or two to dispose of the rest of her (ordinary) life. Deliverance from captivity was the climax, the presumed happy ending.

Abbie Gardner-Sharp, who was captured at the age of thirteen in the Spirit Lake massacre of 1857, described the experience some twenty-eight years later, a delay occasioned by her frail health. "Never have I recovered from the injuries inflicted upon me while a captive among the Indians," she wrote. "Instead of outgrowing them, as I hoped to, they have grown upon me as the years went by, and utterly undermined my health."[29]

Because of David Spotts's continuing interest in the women freed by Custer, we know something more about their later life. An anonymous biographical sketch appended without comment to Spotts's memoirs reported that Morgan's mind became weak, and she was sent to the Home for the Feeble Minded in Topeka, where she died in 1902, some thirty-four years after her captivity.[30] The account strongly implied causality, but it did not relate how soon after her return she was incarcerated. In fact, she was admitted to the asylum on May 31, 1901, because of an "attack of insanity" of two months' duration. She died there little more than a year later.[31]

Libbie wrote that a few years after Custer had recovered the Kansas women, a "little Indian boy" playing in front of a house drew the attention of some of the Seventh's officers. They discovered there one of the former captives, who told them that her husband, "instead of trying to make her forget the misery through which she had passed, often recalled all her year of captivity with bitterness, and was disposed to upbraid her, as if she had been in the least responsible for the smallest of her misfortunes."[32] The woman must have been Anna Morgan, who gave birth to one child by an Indian father and then to two sons and a daughter by her husband. The Indian child survived several years.

According to later information provided by Spotts, the two rescued captives had very different attitudes and histories after their release.[33] The incident Libbie described was characteristic of Morgan, who seemed unable to keep from talking about her treatment as a captive, "telling how she was traded around among the different chiefs." This was "very annoying to her husband who insisted that she refrain from speaking about it to any one." Fourteen years after her return from captivity the couple separated, Morgan taking her two younger children and moving to western Kansas to farm. When her house was destroyed by a cyclone, she went first to Kansas City, then back to Delphos, the town she had originally lived in with her family. After her daughter married, they all moved to Colorado, where her younger son enlisted in the army and was sent first to Cuba, then to the Philippines. Evidently, he never rejoined the family. Morgan went to California but later returned to her elder son with "her mind gone." She ended in the Topeka asylum, then, after a series of misfortunes and removals.[34]

Miss Sarah C. White, on the other hand, was described as having quickly recovered her cheerfulness. According to her biographer, she had "had the Christian's assurance that she would be protected. . . . When the Indians heard her talking with the 'Great Spirit' they were afraid to harm her, fearing some punishment would befall them, but to have her with them would bring protection to them as well as to her."[35] This comforting story was probably invented to spare White embarrassment. Captives who had the good fortune not to become pregnant were well advised to say that they had not been sexually abused.

In fact, Sarah White refused to talk about any aspect of her captivity, even to her family and even late in life. She was eighty when Spotts wrote to General Godfrey cautioning him not to mention her captivity "or she will not answer your letter. Many have got in bad by doing so."[36] She married happily a year after her release and had a large family. At eighty Mrs. Brooks, the former Miss White, was healthy and active; at eighty-two she was hoping to get some belated compensation from the government for the cruelties of her captors, of which Spotts mentions only feet frozen so badly that she lost all her toenails. He otherwise concluded vaguely that "in many instances she was mostly brutally treated."[37]

These stories are more meaningful in juxtaposition than in isolation. Anna Morgan needed some outlet to talk about her sexual experience as a captive, but she was unable to communicate with a husband who preferred to ignore her captivity, and community mores denied her any other audience. Yet she could not restrain herself from telling her intimate story inappropriately, as she did to the officers of the Seventh Cavalry who happened by. Obtaining no help in overcoming her trauma, Morgan seems to have had a restless, unhappy life in contrast to the settled and happy life that Sarah Brooks led after her similar captivity. Brooks, who *never* spoke of her experience, was thus able to avoid becoming an anomaly and embrace the role of a traditional housewife and mother. Through what must have been a tremendous act of will, she reconstituted herself as the person she was before, a posture she maintained for the rest of her life. This denial served her well, allowing her to lead the normal life of her world.

It may be that Custer made rescuing the two Kansan women his priority because on some level he had been affected by the death of another captive and her child in the fight on the Washita. Mrs. Clara Blinn had tried to call attention to her plight and obtain release. Through a friendly Indian visiting the camp where she was held she sent a desperate plea back to the Fort Cobb trader, whose Indian wife had been known to arrange the release of captives. "Kind Friend," she wrote.

> Whoever you may be, I thank you for your kindness to me and my child. You want to know my wishes. If you could only buy us of the Indians with ponies, or anything, and let me come stay with you until I could get word to my friends, they would pay you back, and I would work and do all I could for you. It is not far to their camps, and you are not afraid to come. Pray you will try and do so. They tell me, as near as I can understand, they expect traders to come and they will sell us to them. Can you find out by this man and let me know whether they are white men or Mexicans? I am afraid they will sell us into slavery into Mexico. If you can do nothing write W. T. Harrington, Ottawa, Franklin County, Kansas, below Fort Lyon. I cannot tell whether they killed my husband or not. My name is Mrs. Clara Blinn, my little boy is Willie Blinn. He is two years old. Do all you can for me, and God will bless you. . . . Write my father and send him this.[38]

When Indians were attacked, it was not uncommon for them to kill their captives. Returning to the Washita site several weeks after the battle, Sheridan and Custer discovered the bodies of a young white woman and an emaciated child they judged to have been eighteen months old—the hapless Clara and Willie. Custer wrote: "Upon our attacking and routing Black Kettle's camp her captors, fearing she might be recaptured by us and her testimony used against them, had deliberately murdered her and her child in cold blood."[39] It is more likely that the killing was done in retaliation for Custer's attack since the traffic in captives was well established by the time Custer came to the Plains.

Sometimes a woman turned up to tell a grim story. One reappeared in Texas who had been captured as a child and sold several times during a fourteen-year captivity, once to a group of Missouri traders who kept her for some time and then sold her to a man by the name of Chinault. By chance he brought her back to the region she had been abducted from. She had forgotten her name, but on the basis of her story she was eventually identified as a Putnam.[40] On the other hand, Cynthia Anne Parker, the mother of the famous Comanche chief Quanah Parker, had been captured as a child, raised as an Indian, and happily married within the tribe where she wished to remain. After living with the Comanches for twenty-three years, she was forcibly separated from her husband and children and returned to white society against her will.[41]

There were undoubtedly occasions when women disappeared without a trace: a wagon train on the Plains was attacked, the men killed, and the women captured. If there were no free survivors, as frequently happened when the party was small, no one would have been in a position to report on unaccounted-for women. If those attacked were recent immigrants, without friends or relatives, or without *zealous* friends or relatives with the resources and will to conduct an investigation thousands of miles from home, no one might come forward to ransom them, and these women vanished definitively. "I saw one party which was massacred up west of Dodge," Lee Herron writes of Kansas in 1868. "Not a soul was left to tell who they were or where they were going, and no doubt their friends looked for them for many years and at last gave up in despair."[42]

Mary Smith Jordan was one woman who disappeared altogether after setting out to hunt buffalo with her husband, her brother-in-law, and the husband's male employee. [43] When the party failed to return as planned, a search discovered the remains of the men, clearly the victims of an Indian attack, and a sunbonnet of Mary's. A telegram was dispatched: "Have found three boys, Mary missing. Suppose she has been carried off by the Indians." No one was eager to inform Mary's mother, "for everyone knew what Indian captivity meant."[44]

Finally, as the fatal telegram was passed from hand to hand, Mrs. Smith screamed, "Read it!" Jennie, at eighteen the family's youngest daughter, describes a reaction of grief and horror that was either expressed in or remembered in terms of the clichéd gestures of nineteenth-century melodrama: "Mother stood up straight for a moment then threw her hands over her head and giving a piercing scream, fell to the floor in a dead faint." Jennie and her sister responded more idiosyncratically:

> My sister never moved out of her chair until someone helped her up. I managed to get out of the house and went to the east side and lay down on the ground, face as near to the house as I could get. I was not unconscious, just stunned. Some of our friends asked me if I wanted anything and urged

> me to get up. I lay there about two hours and then let my friends take me into the house.[45]

Search parties found nothing, and so General Ord, the local commander, wrote to General Sheridan for permission to take the next step—offering a reward for Mary's return. With his usual decisiveness Sheridan replied that "after having her husband and friends murdered, and her own person subjected to the fearful bestiality of perhaps the whole tribe, it is mock humanity to secure what is left of her for the consideration of five ponies."[46]

Could it be that five ponies was too high a price for a woman? Theodore Davis said that "the general run of [squaws] may be purchased for a pony, a small quantity of flour and sugar, a little tobacco, and a bottle of whisky."[47] Raphael Romero, a scout who took a Cheyenne wife, told Custer that he had given her father two of his best ponies.[48] But if the price was high, objectively speaking, it was one that Mary's family would have gladly paid, for they did not share Sheridan's assumption that it would have been "mock humanity" to ransom her. While her husband and one of his five brothers had been killed, Mary's widowed mother and six brothers and sisters were alive and tormented by the thought of Mary in Indian hands. In fact they had proposed the ransom although the disposition of such matters was in the power of the military.

General Sherman concurred with Sheridan's decision not to offer ransom although there is a noteworthy difference in his reason for doing so. Where Sheridan seemed preoccupied with the individual woman as being too damaged to be worth ransoming, Sherman responded pragmatically: "So long as ransoms are paid to Indians, so long will they steal women, to use, and sell."[49] He sent orders "forbidding the practice of ransom in future cases."[50]

Occasionally there were false signs of hope with respect to the missing woman. The spring after Mary's disappearance a dignified young Indian woman came to the Smiths' door accompanied by three warriors who prudently carried a white cloth on a stick. The woman said that she belonged to a small, friendly tribe, the Otoes, who had had nothing to do with what had become known as the Jordan massacre. Government officers had visited their reservation and informed them of all that had happened. The woman had come to express sympathy: "I want to help you and I hope you get your daughter back," she told Mary's mother.

Some time later the army rescued a captive woman that many hoped would turn out to be Mary. She was not Mary, nor could she be of any help: "That she had been tortured was evident from the scars on her body and the haunted look in her eyes. But her mind was a complete blank."[51]

Jennie concluded her account of her sister's disappearance by saying that the government "kept up the search among the Indians for ten years but never saw or heard a word of her."[52] What she did not know, apparently, was that a year after the massacre the superintendent of the Cheyenne and Arapahoe Agency informed the commissioner of Indian affairs of the episode's sorry conclusion: "They [a band of Cheyenne] run on the Jordans, murdering the men and taking captive the Mrs. Jordan whom I believe they kept a day or two for the purpose of gratifying their fiendish desires and after having exhausted their animal desires in outraging her person, killed her."[53] Evidently no one passed this report along to the grieving but still hopeful Smith family.

When she arrived in 1870 to cook for the railroad crews stationed in Ellis, Mrs. Smith had been the first woman to make her home there. In 1885 a party was held to celebrate her fifteen years of residence, and a Dr. Watson presented her with a bouquet made from twenty different kinds of grain and vegetables that had not been growing in the area when she arrived. The party seems to have been pleasant, but an observer noted that "as always, the subject that lay closest to Mrs. Smith's heart was the mysterious disappearance of her daughter."[54]

Significantly, when he rejected the appeal to ransom Mary Smith Jordan, Sheridan suggested that one reason she was not worth reclaiming was the death of her husband. For whites, the abuse of those women belonging to men made the most compelling case against Indians. As Roger Mills of Texas told Congress, "While you sit in council and gravely deliberate as to what is humanity to the savage, he burns down the house of the settler over his head, scalps his children, and carries into captivity his wife to satisfy the lusts of demons."[55] This violation of hearth and home is clearly meant to be climactic order: the wife's ongoing sexual abuse by "demons" repeats the outrage to male honor over and over again.

Sheridan consistently invoked the specter of Indians violating white women to marshal support for an unaccommodating policy toward the Indians. "The wife of the man at the center of wealth and civilization and 'refinement,'" he wrote to Sherman, "is not more dear to him than is the wife of the pioneer of the frontier."[56] Although single women were just as likely to be abducted as married women, the use of the word *wife* was talismanic, more forcefully evoking male interests.

While whites on the frontier constantly demonized the Indians, describing their "lust" as fiendish, the practice of raping an enemy's women was hardly unique to Native Americans. Indian women captured by enemy tribes were treated in the same fashion as white captives, and Indian women were also frequently abused by whites. Several sources report, for example, that the Cheyenne women captured in Custer's battle of the Washita were forced to submit to officers of the Seventh Cavalry.[57]

The *Annual Report of the Commissioner of Indian Affairs, 1866* exposed the underlying economic motive of captivity when it attributed to a Plains Indian the statement "that stealing white women is a more lucrative business than stealing horses."[58] Withholding these women from their own men was both insulting and financially profitable. During the time of captivity women were sometimes used sexually, but not in a manner that suggested they were valued by the Indians: they were commonly traded and shared rather than jealously retained as an exclusive possession. On one occasion some braves told S. T. Walkley, acting agent of the Comanches and Kiowas, about a recent raid in which they had captured two white squaws "whom they ravished as much as they wanted, and then threw them away."[59] This behavior expressed a twofold contempt for the enemy, who was proven unable to protect his women and whose women were not worth keeping anyway.[60]

In his portion of the secretary of war's report for 1869 Sheridan referred to clergymen who champion the Indian as "the aiders and abettors of savages who murdered, without mercy, men, women and children; in all cases ravishing the women sometimes as often as forty and fifty times in succession, and while insensible from brutality and exhaustion forced sticks up their persons, and, in one instance, the fortieth or fiftieth savage drew his saber and used it on the person of the woman in the same manner."[61] In an official document of 1869 this was plain speaking indeed—if not an expression of prurient interest.

The image of multiple rape persisted in Sheridan's mind. On several other occasions he wrote in a similar vein, always referring to women "ravished sometimes 50 to 60 times in succession, then killed and scalped, sticks stuck in their persons, before and after death."[62] Ensnared by Sheridan's heated rhetoric and vivid detail, contemporary readers might have failed to raise the question that a keen student of Indian affairs asked of the report's author, namely: "How did he know that the Indians ravished women forty and fifty times in succession?"[63]

The fact is that we have no way of recovering precise numbers of white women captured, or captured and raped, by Indians on the Plains frontier. There were many reasons why such figures might be distorted in either direction. How real was the threat?[64] A great deal depended upon time and place. The *Annual Report of the Commissioner of Indian Affairs for 1846* took note of what would be a persistent problem on the southern Plains into the 1870s: "They [Commanches and Kiowas] have not only committed numerous murders and carried off and destroyed much property, but they have been in the habit of taking captive women and children with the view of obtaining a ransom for them, and when this has not been realized, the situation of these captives has been deplorable; being subjected to a life of much hardship, and but too frequently to great cruelty and outrage."[65]

The Minnesota Historical Society, which precisely figures the dead in the Sioux uprising of 1862–63 at 664, could say only that hundreds, mostly women, were taken captive. After the Battle of Wood Lake, 269 women and children were recovered; others were rescued here and there, but the report concluded that "the record of those who were never heard of again will never be complete."[66] Carl Rister states that between 1835 and 1875 hundreds of captive women and children were taken along the southern plains border, and he adds the unsavory detail that some white traders were involved as well, no doubt receiving fees as intermediaries when they arranged ransoms.[67] In fact, statistically speaking, few women on the frontier were captured by Indians. Nonetheless, all lived with the frightening possibility. Of those who became captives, there were probably more Anna Morgans than Sarah Brookses, women whose lives were permanently damaged or shortened by the experience as opposed to women who recovered fully. Women were expected, even encouraged, to be afraid, and more than one must have been intentionally threatened with the specter of Indian torture and rape. In 1849 the captain of Catherine Haun's wagon train announced an Indian attack for a drill, causing the women in the party to become hysterical: "Some screamed, others fainted, a few crawled under the wagons," Haun wrote. "All of us were nearly paralyzed with fear."[68] Julia Sinks, a pioneer woman in Texas, believed that such false alarms were the work of men who wanted to excite "a host of fears for the pleasure of allaying them."[69]

Custer was himself expert at arousing his wife's fears. On April 14, 1867, he wrote to her about his experience of sitting with a group of Indian warriors in their tepee: "I could not but wonder what your sensations would be, if you could peer through the smoke of the Indian fire and see me dressed as at home, surrounded by a dozen or more of these dusky and certainly savage-looking chiefs. I smiled silently as I thought of the strange position in which I found myself." But then his thoughts took a sudden turn: "Neither could I help a shudder running through me, as a thought darted into my mind, 'What if Libbie should ever fall into the hands of such savages!'"[70]

Custer knew that Libbie was anxious and sensitive, yet he did not spare her a grisly description of some Indian victims that his command found along the trail: "The hair was burned from their heads. It could not be determined whether they had been burned alive or after being killed. The flesh was roasted and crisped from their faces and bodies, and altogether it was one of the most horrible sights imaginable."[71] Disregarding Libbie's strong objections, he insisted that she visit a man who was "as nearly a madman as can be" after the murder of his children and the abduction of his wife. As Custer could have anticipated, the encounter disturbed Libbie profoundly, inducing repeated nightmares of little blond heads "clotted with blood, and their sightless blue eyes."[72]

Libbie also wrote that her husband "had only to refer to the captives I had seen soon after their release to elicit promises of caution from me."[73] As if compelled to relive a horrific memory, she recalled, "The girl, then nineteen years old, in the captivity which was worse than death, had lost all traces of girlhood. Had she been retained as the property of one chief her fate would have been more deplorable than any that a woman ever endures, but even this misery was intensified, for she was traded from one chief to another. . . . The suffering of these poor captives made a lasting impression on me."[74] Describing her fear of Indian attack years later when the Custers were stationed at Fort Abraham Lincoln, Libbie wrote that death was not thought of "so much as the all-absorbing terror of capture. Our regiment had rescued some white women from captivity in Kansas, and we never forgot their stories."[75]

Libbie's reluctantly acquired knowledge of what she called "the horrible fate which every woman in those days considered worse than death" rendered her for some time the victim of exaggerated terrors: "I could not even ride out of camp with an escort without inward quakings, and every strange or unaccountable speck on the horizon meant to me a lurking foe."[76] Predictably, in such an environment exaggeration and panic were the order of the day. Anything that moved might be taken for Indians: tumbleweeds, animals of various sorts, even—on one occasion—a flock of geese.[77] Shortly after coming to Kansas, Libbie wrote to her husband that the Washington *Chronicle* had reported a massacre at Fort Buford, Dakota: "When it was no longer possible to make a further stand, the colonel shot his wife, and the command were finally all killed."[78] Some time later she wrote that the story had been only a rumor.

Like Libbie, countless women on the Plains lived with the same fear: "Rumors of Indians on the rampage became a part of every pioneer's experience."[79] In Ellis, where her mother had been the first woman settler, Jennie Smith remembered that it had been "one scare after another. . . . We lived night and day with the fear they were coming."[80] One pioneer woman recalled that "the one dread of our lives was Indians. . . . although they had never molested us, we feared them intensely."[81] However unlikely the possibility of Indian attack, living in such terror must have been a stifling and deforming experience for many women on the frontier. Irrational fears can be just as powerful as rational fears, and these particular fears had some foundation.[82]

Much like Herman Melville's emblematic picture of the harpooner Queequeg suspended on a rope between the teeth of the predatory sharks and the well-meaning but equally dangerous knives of his shipmates, a white woman on the frontier was caught between groups of warring males, either of whom might find reason to kill her on short notice. It must have been easy enough to hate and fear the enemy, but she was further required to acquiesce in her killing by her protectors, to *believe* in the desirability of such a death for her own good. In the absence of a male relative or husband, any man could assume this "duty" toward her.

When Custer was on the Yellowstone Expedition of 1873, he wrote to his wife about the advantages to young men of "this great enterprising western country, where the virtues of real manhood come quickly to the surface, and their possessor finds himself transformed from a mere boy to a full-fledged man almost before he realized his quick advancement."[83] The great twentieth-century historian of the Plains, Walter Prescott Webb, wrote in the same vein: "Men loved the Plains. . . . There was zest to the life, adventure in the air, freedom from restraint; men developed a hardihood which made them insensible to the hardships and lack of refinements."[84] Ironically, the vast Plains frontier that proved such an inviting space for male achievement—for great feats of riding, hunting, and fighting on the part of Indians and whites alike; for the heroic exploits of Kit Carson, Wild Bill Hickok, Buffalo Bill, George Armstrong Custer, and countless others—often seemed to be simply another place of confinement for women.[85]

14

Libbie and Autie, or a Companionable Wife

> Don't spend more money than you can help at the Sutler's, drinking and card playing. Don't be influenced by the badness around you. Oh, Tom, if I find that the boy I have loved, and prayed over, has gone downhill. Oh, if only you had a companionable wife.
>
> —Libbie to Tom Custer, December 1875

The rhythm of separation and togetherness that intensified the Custers' passionate relationship during the Civil War persisted into the early years on the frontier, culminating in Custer's reckless dash for Libbie in July of 1867. In the remaining nine years of their marriage, however, the absences due to battle would become less frequent and the urgency would accordingly diminish. During the eight years between Custer's victory on the Washita and his defeat and death on the Little Bighorn he had encounters with Indians but no major battles—not surprisingly, since there were few such battles in all of Plains Indian warfare.

After Custer returned from the Washita campaign, the couple settled into the mature phase of their marriage. Although some strains became more noticeable when external threats subsided, Autie and Libbie remained mutually devoted and dependent upon each other, constructing a solid and satisfying world within the instability of military life. As one observer described them on a buffalo hunt at this time, "General Custer was the hero of all who knew him, and Mrs. Custer, who attended in a carriage, was like a queen, surrounded by her court."[1] Each had a sphere of influence in which the other took pleasure.

In the years before his death, the primary components of Custer's professional, social, and marital life would remain relatively static. Foremost was nonpromotion, in itself no disgrace since so many worthy officers were competing for so few places in the downsized postwar army. But it must have galled the couple nevertheless: Libbie, who tended to airbrush her recollections of army life, did comment negatively on the cutthroat nature of military competitiveness.[2] On the positive side, Sheridan's continued patronage had the tangible benefit of giving Custer de facto command of the Seventh Cavalry by keeping the regiment's colonel on detached duty.

The Custers were also surrounded by a close-knit group of fellow officers and their wives, called by a resentful outsider "the royal family."[3] Annie Roberts, a young woman who visited the Seventh and later married into it, left several memorable images of the Custer marriage in the summer of 1870. On one occasion Custer "gently rocked his wife's hammock, every so often bending over to whisper something to her that made her blush"; then they looked toward Annie and smiled, "as if to say, 'this is love,' and I smiling back said to myself, 'will it ever come to me like this?'"[4] In another of Annie's artfully composed pictures, Libbie "sat with her sewing while surrounded like a young queen in her court by the officers of the 7th Cavalry. . . . They seemed to love and admire her and to wait upon her slightest wish. The General, not far away, in a folding chair or cast upon the ground at her feet, seemed happy in having her appreciated and admired."[5] During one of those pleasant interludes Custer turned to Annie and told her that he was the happiest man in the world, that he "would not change places with a king," a sentiment he often expressed to his wife, as well.[6]

Yet there was something that might have marred this idyllic picture. Autie and Libbie were a young and attractive couple, but after five years of marriage they had had no children. They at first took for granted that in due course children would arrive, as indicated by Custer's comment to his bride that "we are just entering on life's journey with all its cares, and, I hope, in a short time its *responsibilities*."[7] It was a conventional expectation in a nineteenth-century marriage and, indeed, "to be fruitful and multiply" was regarded as a Christian duty. Libbie's parents had four children while in two marriages each, Custer's parents, Emmanuel and Maria, had a total of eleven children survive infancy. The average American woman of Libbie's age would be "the mother eventually of five or six children."[8]

Early on, Libbie expressed an eagerness for children that the era regarded as inborn in women.[9] Four months after their wedding she wrote to Autie, "I think of the days of peace when little children's voices will call to us. I can hardly wait for my little boy and girl."[10] When they had been married for eight months, Libbie wrote to him that during a church service "I prayed that I might be given a child that I might try and make it a cornerstone in the great church of God—and Autie, if God gives me children I shall say to them: 'Emulate your Father! I can give you no higher earthly example."[11]

Marguerite Merington, Libbie's literary executor, recounted that a subsequent letter "voices the young wife's grief and self-reproach that their hope of children showed no signs of fulfilment."[12] Evidently Merington regarded this letter as too personal to publish, and unfortunately it is not to be found in her papers. One would like to know exactly how the element of "self-reproach" was expressed, but most likely it was in conventional terms. By reproaching herself, Libbie behaved according to the nineteenth century's incomplete knowledge of human fertility: she assumed that she alone must be at fault. Admonitions against female masturbation during the nineteenth century gave special prominence to the consequence of failure or inadequacy in child-bearing.[13]

After the initial phase of disappointment, the Custers appear to have reacted sensibly to their childlessness. Although the prominent American gynecologist James Marion Sims was at the height of a career devoted to helping women conceive, primarily by correcting minor uterine abnormalities through surgery, there is no evidence that the Custers consulted any medical specialist.[14] It would have been an extraordinary, and most likely futile, step. For serious Christians like Libbie, God was the arbiter of family size, and the human role was one of acceptance—of many children, of the death of children, of barrenness. In the official ideology of Victorian America the reproductive processes were not to be tampered with; even in 1914 when Margaret Sanger began her long campaign to remove "the stigma of obscenity" from contraception, she was harassed and vilified.[15]

In a time when the army's policy toward dependents was so unenlightened that no provisions were made for their existence, it was obvious that a family was especially burdensome in military life: Frederick Benteen remarked that he had "lost four children in following that brazen trumpet around."[16] Other negative consequences of having children could be observed everywhere: many women died in childbirth or suffered broken health through repeated childbearing; parents might have to endure the heartbreak of losing children at any age, and even middle-class families might be faced with destitution when the provider suddenly died. In a nineteenth-century medical textbook a woman physician purported to describe the changing feelings of a representative patient, a young woman who fell in love and quickly married: The patient had believed marriage the summit of human happiness. Within a year, however, she became pregnant "and such pains as accompanied this [birth] she had never before believed that woman could endure." Many pregnancies followed the first, "until ten, twelve or even fifteen children have been born, with an accumulation of troubles to correspond." She begs her young friends to pause and consider before they leave home at so early an age: for "marriage and maternity are not a romance."[17]

Anyone in the Custers' world would have had cautionary tales at hand. Alice Grierson, another frontier officer's wife, had a sister-in-law who was left a widow without means of support when she was pregnant with her eleventh child.[18] Benteen's experience in losing four of his five children was not uncommon; Libbie's father had lost three out of four, and Bill Cody—born in the same year as Libbie—also outlived three of his four children. Had he lived only one more year, all four would have predeceased him. Libbie's own childhood experience of losing all three of her siblings is likely to have left her with some impalpable sadness associated with childbearing.

Even the constant bother of children might have seemed a deterrent. When Libbie visited the Custers' affluent friends the Barkers, people who could certainly afford all the amenities of child care, she must have made some negative comment on the familial situation in a letter to Autie. His excessive response indicates a desire to transform their childlessness into an asset:

> I am delighted and overjoyed that my little darling bride is having an opportunity of really seeing and determining how troublesome and embarrassing babies would be to us. Our pleasure would be continually marred and circumscribed. You will not find in all our travels a married couple possessing and enjoying so many means of pleasure and mutual happiness as you and your boy. Our married life to me has been one unbroken sea of pleasure.[19]

Yet three days before, he had written her in a quite different vein—to propose that they adopt his nephew and namesake, "Autie Kirkpatrick," the ten-year-old son of his half-sister Lydia Ann Kirkpatrick and her husband, David Reed.[20] The request followed an elaborate prologue, establishing the seriousness of the matter while giving Libbie every opportunity to refuse in good conscience:

> Now I want to ask you a question and before you answer it weigh it fully in your own mind and answer me just as you feel. If you answer in favor of it, well and good; if you from any cause or reason are not inclined to the idea, be frank enough to tell me, and you disapproving of the proposition shall not in the slightest way ruffle my feelings or cause me to think one jot less of you. Your wishes shall be law and I hope you will tell me your views with your usual candor.[21]

After making this weighty proposal, Custer must have received the letter from Libbie recounting some exasperation or inconvenience involving the children of the Barker household, because he immediately shifted gears to extol their child-free life. The two letters were not contradictory, however. Both stressed the drawbacks of *babies*: the letter suggesting the adoption of young Autie made the specific point that he was past the age when children were a nuisance.

For all of his tactful phrasing and solicitousness for his wife's feelings, Custer clearly desired to adopt his nephew—to have a son. His childhood within a large, close-knit family had been happy, and he remained strongly attached to his parents and siblings, a dutiful son and a man who throughout his adult life enjoyed vigorous horseplay and teasing with his father and brothers. He had also taken a strong interest in his sister Margaret's education, paying her tuition at a good private school. It was natural that he would want to replicate this affection and family camaraderie at his own hearth. Libbie, on the other hand, had been for all practical purposes an only child, pampered in some respects, but after her mother's death deprived for many years of an actual family home and regular parental warmth. The one point of stability and continuity in her life had been her father; then it became her husband.

In the Custer marriage it often seemed that Libbie not merely acquiesced to but heartily embraced everything her husband proposed, yet in this instance she must have refused. No further mention of adoption was made, and the Custers remained without children.

Among Libbie's manuscript papers is an undated drawing of a family tree with many children in its branches, apparently the Yates family.[22] Below the tree and off to one side is a barking dog labeled "GAC," and this verse:

> *Too oft indeed we feign dislike*
> *For what we* most have tried *to win*
> *But not succeeding, then to say,*
> *"The grapes are sour," is too thin.*

The drawing is most likely Libbie's own, and it could have been a response to the sentiments of Custer's letter about the advantages of childlessness, as if Libbie were determined to face the situation squarely, accept it as her religion counseled, and then make a humorous drawing to encourage the same attitude in her husband.

Libbie's decision not to adopt the son her husband wanted but that she could not bear appears to have had no negative repercussions in their marriage but may well have returned to haunt her late in life. As for Autie Reed, he remained Custer's favorite nephew and achieved his own modest place in the annals of the Little Bighorn, memorably glimpsed by Benteen's men as he eagerly galloped off to join his uncle in what turned out to be the Last Stand. Autie Kirkpatrick, Autie Custer, Autie Reed—whatever possibilities any of these identities represented were cut off at the age of eighteen at the Little Bighorn, where the battlefield memorial oddly lists his name as "Arthur Reed."

Since women were chiefly responsible for raising children and had no profession outside the home, some commentators have seen the Custers' childlessness as exclusively Libbie's concern, although in terms of temperament it was probably Custer who felt the loss more fully.[23] His parental impulses found some outlet in the large amount of time and attention he devoted to nurturing his dogs. His favorite he referred to as resembling a "well-cared for and half-spoiled child, who can never be induced to retire until it has been fondled to sleep in its mother's arms.

Tuck will sleep so soundly in my lap that I can transfer her gently to the ground and she will continue her slumber, like a little baby carefully deposited in its crib."[24] When a puppy was sick, "he walked the floor half the night, holding, rubbing, trying to soothe the suffering little beast," and searching his book of dog medicine for a remedy.[25] When a dog was injured on a hunting trip, he "would not take time to get off his hunting clothes nor go near the fire until he had called the dog into his room and extracted the painful quills."[26]

One schoolmate and boyhood friend remembered the young Custer as always surrounded by "magnificent specimens of both horses and dogs," while another recalled that "hounds and setters shared his room and often his bed."[27] From her visit to Fort Abraham Lincoln, Katherine Gibson has left behind a memorable picture of a mature Custer always accompanied by at least eight or ten dogs: "He had a habit of throwing himself prone on the grass for a few minutes' rest and resembled a human island, entirely surrounded by crowding, panting dogs."[28] And Libbie pronounced her husband "as courteous in responding to his dogs' demonstrations, and as affectionate, as he would be to a person."[29]

On the Plains, Custer indulged his love of animals in general by acquiring almost anything as a pet—squirrels, field mice, wolves, horned toads, a pelican, a beaver, and a wildcat were represented in his collection at one time or another—and he was remarkably relaxed about their behavior. Once a pet raccoon found his pocketbook and washed the money within it so zealously that nothing was left but a heap of unidentifiable bits of paper. Custer was amused. His pack of hunting dogs, in addition to running riot in the community, seized many a piece of meat intended for the Custers' dinner and often left muddy paw prints on their bedspreads. Libbie and the maid might be dismayed, but Custer was tolerant of these antics and of the inconvenience to other people—neither was he bothered by the resentment of enlisted men when he appropriated an ambulance for his animals' transportation. It was usually left to Libbie to smooth over whatever trouble was made by the dogs and to pacify the maid's indignation on the domestic front.

Beyond a pragmatic concern to take good care of a valuable property, Custer was clearly fond of his dogs: he felt deeply the accidental death of Maida, a favorite staghound. "Words fail to express the grief occasioned by the untimely death of so faithful a companion," he wrote, and then went on to commemorate Maida's loyalty in lines plagiarized from Byron:

Poor Maida, in life the firmest friend
The first to welcome, foremost to defend;
Whose honest heart is still your master's own,
Who labors, fights, lives, breathes for him alone.

Custer's elegy concluded with another unacknowledged borrowing, this time from William R. Spencer's "Beth Gelert: or The Grave of the Greyhound."[30]

Custer's letters were always full of prideful accounts of the dog's hunting exploits. Attracted to extraordinary specimens, he wanted his hunting dogs to reflect his self-image, that is, to be exceptionally courageous, proficient in battle, and tireless in pursuit. So it hardly seems coincidental that affection for particular dogs was correlated with outstanding performance. In Kansas he was delighted that Maida and Blucher killed a wolf: "Of the many dogs that are in this regiment," he wrote to Libbie, "there is but one that will attack a wolf, and he needs to be encouraged."[31] On the Yellowstone Expedition of 1873 he kept Libbie informed of all canine triumphs. "Regarding the dogs," he wrote on one occasion, "I find myself more warmly attached to Tuck then to any other I have ever owned. Did I tell you of her catching a full-grown antelope-buck, and pulling him down after a run of over a mile, in which she left the other dogs far behind?"[32]

Just as Custer's love of animals seemed to indicate his greater need to fill the absence left by the couple's lack of children, Custer—unlike Libbie—had had his share of attachments to children before their marriage. His young Civil War bugler Joseph Fought regarded him as a father figure, as did the waifish Johnnie Cisco, who had attached himself to Custer during the war and followed him to the frontier.[33] Even at Fort Abraham Lincoln, in the last year of his life, Custer can be glimpsed through the eyes of a visiting reporter giving lessons to the children of his household servants: "He sat on a low stool by his desk, with a spelling-book in his hand; before him were two little girls, one white and the other colored. . . . I have found that this has been his custom for several years, and all these little people of his household know of written words is what he has taught them."[34]

On October 26, 1868, a month after Custer had returned to Kansas at the peremptory summons of Phil Sheridan, he wrote to Libbie, who was still in Monroe, expressing a view of their marriage in keeping with the romantic idealism of his time. As he sometimes did in their correspondence, he addressed her in the third person:

> She has been to him more than his fondest hopes ever pictured a wife could be. She has disappointed him in nothing material to our mutual happiness and today he is a better, truer man for having had her society and love. And he owes her a life of devotion, of pure unbounded and undivided affection for the pure love she bears him, for his [*sic*] unselfish devotion to him and to his interests, and for the perfect type of a true, pure and loving wife she is and ever has been to him.[35]

It was no accident that this letter extolling Libbie's wifely virtues repeated the word *pure* three times in one sentence. Nineteenth-century America, following Victorian England, regarded purity as a paramount virtue in a woman.[36] After seeing a performance of Shakespeare's *Winter's Tale* on one of his trips East without Libbie, Custer wrote to her that it had aroused the same emotions in him as *Othello*—both powerful studies of the effects of male jealousy. He then quoted lines from *Othello* that had evidently made such a strong impression on him that he remembered them almost exactly: "'I'd rather be a toad and live upon the vapors of a dungeon than keep a corner in the thing I love for others.'"[37] The letter continues with his musing: "A fear from which I am free, for if ever husband had unlimited confidence in his wife's purity . . ."[38] It was evidently not necessary to complete the sentence, but three days later the subject was still on his mind. He wrote to Libbie about an officer who had become a drunkard because of his wife's infidelity: "How blessed am I that I am united to a pure, virtuous and devoted wife and I feel immeasurably thankful for it."[39]

Could Libbie be similarly confident of her husband's sexual fidelity? There is no hard evidence to the contrary, but a great deal of innuendo and some legitimate suspicions, particularly about Monahseetah, the young Indian woman captured at the Washita, whom Custer described at length in *My Life on the Plains*. There he wrote appreciatively that "added to the bright, laughing eyes, a set of pearly teeth, and a rich complexion, her well-shaped head was crowned with a luxuriant growth of the most beautiful silken tresses, rivaling in color the blackness of the raven and extending, when allowed to fall loosely over her shoulders, to below her waist."[40] Considered the prettiest girl in Monroe when Custer won her, the feminine and sweet-faced Libbie had little curls framing a lovely oval face with rounded cheeks. Monahseetah, as Custer saw her, had sex appeal.

The lovely captive, daughter of Chief Little Rock, already had a dramatic marital history, having disliked her husband enough to shoot him in the knee. By then divorced, she was nevertheless well advanced in pregnancy when the Battle of the Washita took place, giving birth little more than a month after entering captivity.

In the months following the battle, Custer came to rely on Monahseetah as a negotiator with the Cheyenne, a circumstance that some commentators have regarded as prima facie evidence of an illicit relationship. After all, Monahseetah spoke no English, and Custer did not know her language. In spite of this, there would have been good reason to have employed her: as a chief's daughter she was a woman of status—and besides, Custer had learned Indian sign language.[41] Beyond this, Monahseetah was evidently willing to be very accommodating, unlike the elderly captive Mahwissa, who, when sent on a mission to her tribe, did not return. Attractive and useful, Monahseetah seemed to serve as yet another incarnation of the Indian princess embraced by American culture for her helpfulness to white males.[42]

On one occasion Custer sent Monahseetah at night from the army camp to a nearby Indian village. When she sensibly feared that the sentries might shoot her by mistake, Custer conducted her through the picket line, "she clinging to my hand." In writing about the incident he felt it necessary to counter the reader's surprise that a captive could be trusted to undertake such a mission to her own people and return to captivity: "She had become a great favorite with the entire command, not only this, but she believed she would in due time be given up to her own people, and that until then she would receive kind treatment at our hands, and be exposed to less personal danger and suffering during hostilities than if with her village." In his final mention of Monahseetah, Custer noted her "marked feelings of regret when the time for her departure arrived."[43]

Whatever Monahseetah's usefulness as a go-between, various sources do report that she shared Custer's bed while the Seventh remained in the field away from Libbie. Custer's persistent enemy, Frederick Benteen, not surprisingly offers the fullest version of events in a letter to a man who joined the Seventh much later: "Of course you have heard of an informal invitation from Custer for officers desiring to avail themselves of the services of a captured squaw, to come to the squaw round-up corral and select one! (?) Custer took first choice, and lived with her during winter and spring of 1868 and '69."[44] The oral tradition of the Cheyenne supported this version,[45] as did the scout Ben Clark in an interview with Walter Camp. According to Camp's notes, after stipulating that he was not to be quoted, Clark said that Custer "picked out a fine-looking one [squaw] and had her in his tent every night."[46]

When Monahseetah gave birth early in January Custer immediately conveyed the news to Libbie; when the captives were brought to Fort Hays he insisted on taking Libbie to visit them in spite of her fear.[47] Could Libbie have suspected that the young Indian woman had been her husband's mistress? Not consciously, perhaps, but her description of Monahseetah—based at this time exclusively on what Custer had told her—is nevertheless suggestive. After praising Monahseetah's ability in reading a trail, Libbie wrote: "Mo-nah-see-tah had in many other ways made herself of service to the command. She was young and attractive, perfectly contented, and trustful of the white man's promises, and the acknowledged belle among all other Indian maidens." Recalling the story of Monahseetah's crippling of her husband, Libbie wondered with some trepidation if she might suddenly produce a hidden weapon now "and by stabbing the wife, hurt the white chief who had captured her."[48] Since Monahseetah had already demonstrated fidelity to Custer as a willing negotiator with her own people, returning to captivity rather than escaping, her motive for stabbing Libbie could only have been sexual rivalry, an idea Libbie does not entertain explicitly.

When the two women actually met, Libbie's description of Monahseetah was a curious variation on her husband's. She did not find Monahseetah's features attractive—the features of Indian women are seldom attractive, she told the reader—but then Monahseetah "let the blanket fall from her glossy hair, her white, even teeth gleamed as she smiled, and the expression transfigured her."[49] As for Monahseetah's child, it was Libbie's idea of any Indian baby, objectified as "a cunning little bundle of brown velvet, with the same bright, bead-like eyes as the rest."[50] Once again the Custers had an opportunity to acquire a son, for Monahseetah offered to leave her baby with them. Libbie was spared from accepting this "somewhat embarrassing gift" by Custer's tactful refusal.

Monahseetah's reluctance to return to her people might have been motivated by her desire to remain with Custer more than by the loss of her easy life as a captive (Cheyenne tradition has it that she grieved like a widow when Custer died), but Custer experienced no break in conjugality as a result of their affair, and—as far as we know—never saw Monahseetah again.[51] If, as contemporary Custer historians believe, he slept with Monahseetah during the period of separation from Libbie, she served as no more than a convenient sexual partner. His infidelity was of the same sort that Southern slaveholders were notorious for, an exercise of the double standard that entailed no responsibility for the man and had no aftermath.[52]

If Monahseetah did not disrupt the Custer marriage, there were other women who did. A letter of May 10, 1867, written long before Custer set eye on the chief's daughter, indicated that he had promised Libbie never to give her "fresh cause for regret by attentions paid to other girls." Feeling desperately lonely for Libbie during his first Kansas tour of duty, he wrote that his love for her had driven all thoughts of women he had previously been attentive to from his mind. He signed the letter "Yours and yours only I would not be another's if I could."[53] However, his resolution to give Libbie "no fresh cause," was evidently no more enduring than his resolution as a new husband to forgo gambling.

The crisis in the Custer marriage came in 1870, documented in a long, soul-searching letter that Custer wrote to Libbie from the East, where he had gone without her for the second Christmas season in a row.[54] Unique in their preserved correspondence, his letter of December 20, 1870, begins by discussing the long-term strain that his inveterate gambling had put on their relationship.[55] Announcing his intention not to play cards for money in the future, "so long as I am a married man," he indicated that the subject had been one of contention between them: "You may laugh at me, perhaps taunt me with the remark that I am unable to carry out the resolution I have formed but . . . do it I will." Libbie's presumed lack of confidence in his ability to keep such a vow obviously rankled Custer, for moments later he reiterated: "As to my ability to carry out this resolution, it gives me not a thought although I have often heard you express the idea that I was incapable of doing it. It was natural perhaps that you should feel so. But you do not know me. I can do almost any thing of my own will except stop breathing, if I so desire it."[56]

When he addressed their relationship directly, Custer described himself as scarcely able to write—"my eyes are blinded with tears." He referred to "distressing words" Libbie had spoken on their trip to St. Louis as

> merely the culmination of thoughts which have long filled your mind against me. I have long felt it, even in your best moments I could discover the absence of that fervor, that enthusiasm and joy which once characterized the manner with which you gave or accepted little attentions to or from me. In your manner you have been more or less mechanical, apparently not inspired to act from any powerful emotion. I perceived it. Silently hoped and prayed for the return of your accustomed warmth.[57]

In the face of this devastating change Custer wrote of his hope that

> time would convince you that you were wrong and that however erratic, wild, or unseemly my conduct with others may have been you were still to me as you always have been—the one great all-absorbing object of my love. I will not pretend to justify my conduct with others. Measured by the strict law of propriety or public opinion I was wrong. . . . I will only say what you ought to have known that through it all my love for you passed like gold through the furnace only to be purified.[58]

Having accepted his guilt, albeit with some equivocation, Custer announced his intention of living "such a life that I at least may have no further reproach to answer for. The satisfaction of aiming to do right will be sufficient." He concluded with many protestations of his love, but protestations that suggested their origin all too readily: "No woman has nor ever can share my love with you. As there is to me but one God Supreme and alone, there is also but [one] woman who in my heart reigns as supreme as does that God over the universe. It has been so. It is and will be. You are and ever will be that one single object of my love."[59] Ordinarily Custer closed his letters to Libbie with endearments, but the word *faithful*, which he now used, styling himself "Your faithful and dearest Autie," was unusual.

Custer's own behavior and the comments of others seem to have led

Libbie to suspect her husband of infidelity. Benteen, who is often unreliable on Custer, accused him of an affair with a married woman and one with a young woman visiting the Custers, yet, given Custer's fame in the twentieth century, it is odd that no corroborating documents have come to light.[60] It was one thing to take an Indian mistress in the field; quite another to carry on in the restricted space of an army post with women known to Libbie.[61] Such activity would hardly go unnoticed. Custer's own words admitted to some sort of impropriety that almost certainly involved another woman, despite his eloquent assertion that Libbie was the only woman he would ever love. These were, of course, words that any man wanting to save his marriage under similar circumstances might say.

What was perhaps most remarkable about Custer's letter, though, was his focus on his own pain and deprivation without the slightest acknowledgment of or apology for *Libbie's* suffering. In fact, his admission of wrongdoing was almost buried in surrounding verbiage that subtly shifted the blame to Libbie: however he behaved, *she* should have understood and continued to treat him well. Moreover, he phrased his intention to reform only in abstract terms: he would alter his behavior because it was the right thing to do, not because he had hurt her.

Whatever the truth of the matter—no evidence survives other than Benteen's allegations and Custer's letter—the Custers apparently found a satisfactory way to re-create their marriage. The previous April both husband and wife had filled out a questionnaire on sentimental matters that predicted how Libbie, at least, might react to a marital crisis. Custer had answered the questions humorously, but Libbie responded seriously. She stated that "to love, with heart and soul" was "the sublimest passion." The "sweetest words" were "would I were with thee every day & hour," and her definition of happiness was "no separation from my other self."[62]

This view was the bedrock of Libbie's existence. Little wonder that she was ultimately predisposed to accept her husband's anguished protestations and vow to reform, accompanied as they were by his extravagant reassurances that she remained the one love of his life. Alone at Leavenworth, she must have mentally entertained the possibility of life without Autie and found it unthinkable. After all, Libbie had also told the questionnaire that her greatest fear was "having to take care of myself."[63] Much later in life she would write in her diary, "Every woman needs a keeper."[64]

Both Custers were prone to idealize their relationship, Custer praising Libbie as the perfect wife who, in true Victorian fashion, had made him a better man; Libbie extolling his virtues as fervently. In 1866 she had written to her cousin Rebecca that she was at a loss to know how her husband could get any better. "But," she concluded, "I shall have innumerable tales of his goodness to pour into your ear when I see you."[65] Such utterances were commonplace in her correspondence of the pre-crisis period, evidence that Libbie had invested her being in the image of an ideal husband and marriage. There was a long silence after Libbie received Custer's confessional letter, but then she wrote him a "nice warm loving letter," to which he responded in kind.[66] He, too, had invested a great deal in the idea of their mutual devotion and singularly blessed union.

Custer had resolved to turn over a new leaf, but the major accommodations in their relationship would always be Libbie's. Both before and after the crisis, his letters reveal a manipulative pattern of behavior: he would do as he pleased in a way that was bound to cause Libbie some pain, then disarm any anticipated criticism by protesting his love for her and his regret that they were not together. Traveling in the East in December 1869, he wrote to tell Libbie that he was postponing his return in spite of having written to her repeatedly that he was leaving on a certain date. Custer's influential friend Kirkland C. Barker had insisted that he visit him in Detroit:

> Barker I could see felt hurt to think I had not been with him more. He has done so much for me and is still doing so much that I felt I could not wholly disregard his wishes; besides, I reasoned that you would prefer to have me satisfy my friends here if I could do so by prolonging my visit one week more. . . . I hope my darling will not blame me for the change, for I would much rather be with her, oh so much rather, it seems so very long since I saw her.[67]

Libbie must have been disappointed, but without appearing selfish she hardly could have challenged Custer's artful argument, an argument that even enlisted her on its side. Besides, it was a fait accompli.

However much Custer might have missed Libbie when they were apart, he always had many things to occupy his time. Called away to Washington or New York by professional duties and business affairs, he would profit from the occasion by socializing with friends and enjoying the metropolis. Lacking such diversions, Libbie felt a corresponding desire to be with him that was more single-minded and intense. She wrote from the backwater of Elizabethtown, Kentucky, where the Custers were stationed from 1870 to 1872, "it is only another proof of how you brighten every spot to me, when I attempt to be contented in the same places without you. . . . When you are away it is so very lonely and so long. I can't stand it here without you Autie. . . . But with you here it will seem sunshiny and bright."[68] Libbie's attitude toward her surroundings was not changed simply by the presence of the husband she loved. His curiosity about his environment, whatever environment, could transform it, and his energy demanded constant activities that swept Libbie up as well.

Custer's letters from the East typically related encounters with women who found him attractive coupled with declarations of his love for Libbie, the latter—he must have felt—excusing his admission of the former. When an attractive young woman forthrightly lamented to Custer, "Oh, why are you married?" he told Libbie that he had replied, "Well, I found a girl I loved. And if you knew her you would love her too." He went on to say that he had made no advances toward this young lady: "Girls needn't try to get her dear Bo away from her, because he loves only her, and her always."[69] So, in spite of the flirtatious badinage, Libbie was supposed to be reassured.

This same pattern of confession and reassurance went back as far as 1859, when he wrote from West Point to his then sweetheart and intended wife, Mollie Holland: "You wished to know whether I had any Lady love here or not. Of course I have. I will describe her to you." A detailed and highly attractive description followed, concluding with Custer's assertion that she is so beautiful that half of the cadets tried to obtain her smiles, but I turned out to be the favored one." About another woman he wrote that "I know more about her than any other person and have done more with her or *rather to* her and she to me than any other one . . . and if she had a husband he could not have done but one thing more than I did, and I shall leave you to guess what that was—(can you guess? if you cannot—I will tell you)." After all the talk about other women, Custer nevertheless signed his letter "Your true and devoted H——d."[70]

Certainly Custer intended to impress Mollie with evidence of his attractiveness to other women and was instead overzealous. His immature attempt to promote himself may have been the natural consequence of her parents' opposition to his courtship, but the letter nonetheless exhibits a striking lack of awareness that its confessions about other women are too enthusiastic (indeed, it appears that Mollie never wrote to Custer again). With only a little modification, the nineteen year old's epistolary habit persisted into adulthood. He did become a shade more politic, tempering his obvious need to brag with more palliating avowals of love for Libbie alone, but the basic pattern remained. At one social function he wrote to Libbie that he had sat next to a baroness: "The Baroness wore a very handsome satin, and oh so low. I sat beside her on a sofa and 'I have not seen such sights since I was weaned' and yet it did not make my angry passions rise, nor *nuthin* else."[71]

Even as an adult and a married man, Custer sometimes went too far. On one occasion he even sent Libbie a picture of a woman he had met in New York. Whether Libbie tore it up out of real or feigned jealousy, Custer was flattered by her reaction and hastened to give her one of his characteristic reassurances.

Determined to preserve her marriage, not as a diminished thing but as the ideal union she wanted it to be, Libbie seemed to accept Custer's version of events—that women pursued him and that he responded courteously to their interest, but nothing more. A scant two months after she learned of her widowhood, she wrote a graceful note of thanks to Captain McCaskey, who had brought her the devastating news. Every word testified that Libbie was still under the spell of her initial overwhelming grief, but the last thought was especially revealing of her priorities. Speaking of McCaskey's wife, Libbie wrote, "I am glad that she has been blessed with God's best gift, a devoted and faithful husband."[72] Both Custers prized devotion, and, while Custer's sexual fidelity may have been questionable, Libbie could have had no doubt that he had been devoted to her.

As the years passed, Libbie would continue to feel that she herself had been blessed with, and tragically deprived of, "God's best gift." Almost six years after Custer's death she wrote to a recently married woman, "You know without my telling you what a paradise is yours, to love and to be loved as you are! The world is so empty, so unsatisfactory and life is *not* worth living to a loving woman without such love!"[73] Late in Libbie's widowhood the comforting rationale of the sought-after but faithful husband had become dogma: she told a reporter that Custer was so handsome in his famous Civil War uniform she was not at all surprised that "the ladies all fell in love with him. But I didn't mind that at all, because I knew he wasn't interested in anyone but me."[74]

While Libbie could be reassured about her husband's love, her fears for his safety were not as easily overcome. Annie Roberts praised her for "the nobility with which she has always calmly endured such terrors, and repressed any verbal utterance of them in the unselfish desire never to mar the enjoyment of others," yet Annie went on to record an incident in which Libbie had not been able to restrain her fears. A group of officers and women from Fort Riley had gone out for a day's excursion on the plains when some unidentified horsemen were seen in the distance, and Custer, accompanied by a few of his officers, rode off to investigate. Once they were out of sight shots were heard, and, Annie wrote, "Mrs. Custer fell on her knees exclaiming, 'Autie will be killed.'" As it turned out, the "unidentified riders" were actually scouts, and the shots had been a ruse contrived by Custer to spice up the outing—even though he knew the terror it would cause Libbie.[75] As a confirmed lover of practical jokes, Custer could be insensitive to the effect they had on others.

In addition to Libbie's fears of such physical threats, she also had internal anxieties springing from a deep-seated insecurity. The Custers' longtime cook, Eliza, might have scoffed that Libbie took her husband's part no matter what, but Libbie's preoccupation was entirely in the other direction: she worried that she was not a good enough wife. Among her papers there was an article entitled "True Love," which states that a woman loved by a man "knows that he overrates her virtues, but determines to realize as nearly as possible his estimate of them. . . . True love exalts, purifies, sanctifies."[76]

After Custer's death, Libbie wrote to a close friend about the "notions" that people who live alone must fight off: "one of mine is that I wasn't more of a success as the wife of the man I loved—tho' God knows I tried."[77] In the same vein she would frequently confess an almost pathological sense of inadequacy to strangers who complimented her performance on the lecture circuit. She felt she could never do enough as a widow to perpetuate Autie's memory, perhaps in this way expiating her perceived failings as a wife.

While Custer was by her side, these self-doubts remained in check, in large part because he understood her needs as well as she understood his. She once described how he would sense her discomfort in a crowd and disengage himself from a surrounding throng to seek her out and whisper "the word that made my evening radiant after that—Perhaps only this. 'Well old lady I've been looking 'em all over and I think you'll do.'"[78] The rapport between the two is obvious here, as is Custer's joking reminder that he did look over other women even if he preferred Libbie.

In the summer of 1873 Custer wrote Libbie from the Yellowstone that he enjoyed her society more and more each day, "and yet I am sure we have not reached the acme of our enjoyment in each other. I think that both our facilities and our abilities for enjoyment will increase in the future." The letter concluded by addressing Libbie as "apple of my eye—joy of my life and the dearest and truest of wives."[79] Their old story, he wrote in another letter from the Yellowstone, "in ten years has not lost its freshness."[80] Certainly this is a more mature affection than the passion of their correspondence as newlyweds, but its deep satisfaction and appreciation are unmistakable.

Libbie fully reciprocated these sentiments. One of her last letters to Custer commented that his putting in a full day on the march and then writing articles for publication at night was "perfectly wonderful." She asked: "How can I praise you enough?"[81] The question would shortly become the theme of Libbie's fifty-seven-year widowhood, and it would have been a fitting inscription on her tombstone, a modest tablet in the shadow of Custer's at West Point.

15

The Great Buffalo Hunt

It is utterly useless to attempt the description of a buffalo hunt—the enjoyable part of it must be seen, not read.

—George Armstrong Custer

Custer's tour of duty in Kansas ended in 1871 when he received a leave of absence, eventually extended to eight months' duration, and then reported to his new post, Elizabethtown, Kentucky, on September 3. Only two companies of the Seventh followed Custer to Elizabethtown. The others, which had been dispersed among several forts in Kansas, were now reassigned to police duty in a number of southern states. Custer's new assignment was a boring one in a backwater whose liveliest inhabitant, according to Libbie, was a pig.[1] For most of the period when he was stationed in Kentucky, Custer was on detached duty, inspecting horses purchased for the army and thinking, Libbie said, that he would like to be a horse breeder himself. In January of 1872 he was temporarily rescued from this quiet life by a summons from General Sheridan to take part in a special buffalo hunt for a visiting foreign dignitary. It was a chance to be at the center of things again, a meaningful interlude in a life that for the moment was going nowhere.

The Grand Duke Alexis had arrived from Russia on November 20, 1871, for a tour of the United States. The fourth son of the Russian czar, he was a celebrity of some magnitude and was treated as such—feted and acclaimed—wherever he went. Each city tried to outdo the rest in giving him a lavish welcome, and he listened to (or endured) many flowery speeches made by public officials. On December 11 in Boston, for example, he was treated to a "brief" address by James Russell Lowell that managed to incorporate quotations from Swift, Madame de Staël, D'Alembert, and Cervantes.[2]

The press avidly tracked his progress through the country. "The rumor that the Grand Duke Alexis prefers little women," one newspaper announced, "is exercising a marvelous effect among the stately young ladies of fashion, who are knocking the high heels from their shoes and eschewing lofty coiffures."[3] When Alexis had a free day in a St. Louis hotel, vigilant reporters noted that "more than the customary number of young ladies gossipped and promenaded in the parlors."[4]

Whether they went to these extremes or not, young women were most interested in the Grand Duke. It undoubtedly helped that in addition to being young, handsome, and aristocratic, he was a romantic figure—Libbie cited a report that "he was sent from Russia to break up an affair with someone not acceptable at court," a story that apparently whetted feminine interest and admiration throughout his visit.[5] The *Omaha Tribune* wrote that ladies described Alexis as "perfectly handsome," and went on to give some particulars: six feet, two inches tall, with a "high white forehead," "light golden" hair, "very large hands" and "immense" feet.[6] Libbie added that he had blond side-whiskers "which we women seeing him afterwards believed to be his first effort, they appeared so downy and so immature."

When General Sheridan, the army's second ranking general, was seated next to this paragon at an official dinner in Washington, he discovered that what excited Alexis more than being lionized up and down the eastern seaboard was the prospect of seeing wild Indians and hunting buffalo. Sheridan, who had just a few months before provided a highly successful expedition for a group of affluent New York businessmen, offered to arrange a hunt for the royal visitor.

In the early seventies parties like this took place all the time, the cachet of hunting buffalo on the Great Plains attracting foreign noblemen as well as American sportsmen. Hunters frequently turned up at army posts, with or without invitation: Libbie complained that in one season the Custers had entertained some two hundred of them.[7] Sir St. George Gore, a British aristocrat who traveled with the considerable retinue of 40 men, 112 horses, 12 yoke of oxen, 14 dogs, 6 wagons, and 21 carts, killed 2,500 buffalo on one hunting trip.[8]

On January 12 in Chicago Sheridan's private railroad car—including an entourage of Generals George A. Custer, J. W. Forsyth (Sandy), and George A. Forsyth (Tony), surgeon Morris J. Asch, and Colonel Michael V. Sheridan (Phil Sheridan's brother)—was joined to the end of the Grand Duke's train. Except for Custer, all the military men were members of Sheridan's staff. At Omaha still another general, E. O. C. Ord, joined the party. The Grand Duke was accompanied by his own top brass: the Russian vice chancellor; the commander of the navy, Admiral Poisset; three counts; and a number of lesser officials.[9]

Autie and Alexis seem to have immediately discovered themselves to be kindred spirits. Libbie, who acquired her information about the hunt from her husband, said that they were like two boys, "wrestling, dancing, singing 'If ever I cease to luf' all the way to McPherson," the fort where the party left the train and proceeded forty miles south by army ambulance and horse. At their campsite on Willow Creek, a great deal of work had been done to clear away the layers of snow and ice from many storms in order to lay out some thirty or forty tents.

Here, four years before their dramatic clash on the Little Bighorn, Sioux Indians and whites cooperated in a quintessential Plains Indian event: on January 15 visiting royalty with its glittering attendants, generals galore, scouts, soldiers, Indians, caterers, and reporters came together at the camp on the Nebraska plains to hunt buffalo. It was an exclusively male experience of hunting seasoned with danger, hearty eating and hard drinking, colorful rituals and dances performed by "wild" Indians, and even the romantic embellishment of an Indian princess, "Miss Spotted Tail."

Sheridan had appointed Custer to lead the hunt, but to make certain that buffalo were found, he had engaged the services of a particular favorite of his, the renowned scout and hunter William Cody, or "Buffalo Bill." Spotted Tail, the friendly chief of the Brulé Sioux, had agreed to bring a number of his warriors and their families from their reservation in return for tobacco and other desirable provisions. The *Lincoln Daily State Journal* reported that "no servants, carriages, or luxuries will be indulged in, the design being to rough it,"[10] but while this would have been the proper spirit for a serious male retreat, the "design" was not observed too scrupulously: the Grand Duke's tent was carpeted, champagne was offered all around whenever he brought down a buffalo, and his high-ranking officers wore uniforms resplendent with gold and lace. Moreover, Alexis traveled with his own bed since it was difficult to find one adequate to his large frame. Sheridan, capable of the most rugged campaigning, was known to like his luxuries when hors de combat—although, as it turned out, the hunt produced a moment very much like combat.

The weather was wonderfully mild, far from the negative temperatures and howling blizzards that can settle on the Plains in January. Perversely, however, some aspects of the hunt that should have been under control went awry. Miguel Otero, a young man whose father was a caterer in the nearby town of North Platte, ran into some trouble when he accompanied a driver and another employee to the camp to oversee the delivery of some provisions. Since he was inside the carriage and they were outside driving, Otero paid no particular attention to the men; he only noticed that they became increasingly noisy as the trip progressed. But after a small keg of whiskey was delivered to Sheridan, "the General came rushing out, looking hotter than a boiled owl." The keg, as it turned out, was considerably lighter than it should have been. Like most people who experienced Sheridan's profanity, Otero was significantly impressed: "In all my life I never heard one man bestow on another such curses as the General used on the poor driver."[11] It would not be the last time on the hunt that Sheridan, famous for the energy and inventiveness of his foul language, had occasion to let loose.

True to his reputation, William Cody found the buffalos for the Grand Duke's hunt. Bill had received his sobriquet and earned his renown during an eight-month period in 1867–68 when he worked for the Union Pacific railroad as a buffalo hunter. For five hundred dollars a month, a munificent salary at the time, he contracted to provide at least 12 buffalo a day for railroad workers, but he was credited with a total of 4,280, by no means an unrealistic figure. For the Grand Duke's hunt he led out the somewhat unwieldy party, which included two companies of cavalry and the Second Cavalry band.

It had been agreed that the first kill belonged to the distinguished visitor; after that, anyone could shoot. Alexis, because of excitement, unfamiliarity with buffalo hunting, or inexperience with the firearm that had been thrust into his hand, failed to bring down his first quarry—or his second. In fact, he squandered the ammunition in two six-shot revolvers without connecting with a target. As the guest of honor, he had been given the best horse available, Cody's Buckskin Joe, a trained buffalo hunter, but this might have contributed to the problem. Since Bill never took more than one shot to fell a buffalo, Joe was accustomed to moving on the minute his rider fired a gun. Finally, the combination of the excellent buffalo horse, the world's best buffalo hunter, and the buffalo hunter's special gun, "Lucretia Borgia," produced the longed-for result: Alexis made a kill.[12]

The Russians went wild. They ran to their prince to formally embrace him in turn and then to embrace each other. Alexis, meanwhile, had cut off the buffalo tail for a trophy. As it was passed from hand to hand, distributing blood and dirt on the fancy uniforms, an ambulance arrived with champagne, and the cavorting stopped in order to toast the Grand Duke. In addition to everything else, it was his twenty-first birthday.

Ultimately, everyone had a satisfactory day. Alexis brought down another buffalo, this time making a shot so good that it surprised everyone, including himself. He sent a cablegram to his father, recalling the time two years before when the Czar had watched Alexis kill his first bear. The first buffalo was clearly another such milestone. Evidently the exchange of hunting exploits was a dominant theme in father-son communications, since the Czar replied that he had shot a wild boar on the same day as Alexis was killing his first buffalo. Libbie noted that "the soldier who volunteered to take the dispatch to the station was enriched by more dollars than he had ever seen at one time."

Next, the Grand Duke turned his attention to the other attraction of the hunt—the Indians. Since he had expressed skepticism about the value of bow and arrow shooting, Custer arranged for the Indians to demonstrate their skill by driving a buffalo into camp and killing it literally under Alexis's nose. The Duke pronounced himself impressed and gave one warrior a twenty-dollar gold piece. More gold changed hands to provide Alexis with the Indian's bow and a quiver of arrows as a souvenir.

Dinner that first night was heavily carnivorous: buffalo tail soup, broiled fish, salami of prairie dog, stewed rabbit, fillet of buffalo with mushrooms, roast elk, antelope chops, buffalo calf steaks, blacktail deer, wild turkey, broiled teal, and mallard.[13] Following the meal the Indians performed a war dance in front of the Grand Duke's tent, "illuminated by a great camp fire and Chinese lanterns hung on nearby trees."[14] Well pleased with the spectacle, Alexis distributed liberal presents to the Indians, who also received the promised rations of sugar, coffee, and tobacco—staples of white culture that Indians had universally embraced.

No one may have realized it at the time, but the exchange represented an increasingly common pattern in the Indians' changing economy. Instead of performing their traditional activities for reasons intrinsic to their culture, they performed for spectators, who would pay for the experience. It would not be a fair exchange, as Sitting Bull later observed.[15]

Sheridan invited Spotted Tail and the other tribal leaders, along with their families, to join the officers for a late supper that included "luxuries unfamiliar to the uneducated taste of the Indians, but of which they readily approved, particularly the champagne."[16] In the atmosphere of evening conviviality and comfortable fraternization among representatives of three very diverse cultures—Russian aristocracy, American military, and Brulé Sioux—Custer clearly enjoyed becoming the center of attention. The scout James Hadley wrote to Libbie that "Custer's description of the grand-duke's first buffalo was one of the funniest things ever produced."[17] He did not mention another aspect of Custer's performance—flirting with Spotted Tail's daughter.

Working together as a boyish twosome, Alexis and Custer entertained the rest of the party with their attention to some of the Indian girls. Custer addressed himself to the chief's daughter, who is referred to in contemporary accounts only as Spotted Tail's daughter or "Miss Spotted Tail." Alexis, who throughout his visit was attentive to all the young ladies who came his way, needed no more encouragement than Custer's example to select a similar object of attention. While the two men vied with each other in extravagant gestures and whisperings, the young Indian women giggled with pleasure and the onlooking officers commented and teased.

As the *Daily State Journal* delicately put it, Miss Spotted Tail "was not averse to admiration." Others entered the game, including Lieutenant Clark of the Second Cavalry, who gave her a present of jewelry. The newspaper account continued:

> Gen. Custer, who had been profuse in his attention to her, stepped forward and, taking advantage of his knowledge of the Indian sign language and vernacular, entered into conversation with her and requested the privilege of putting rings in her ears, which she graciously accorded. He consumed much more time in this pleasant occupation than was necessarily needed, and having adjusted one of them in her ear, without changing his position put his arms around her

> neck in order to adjust the other. As she made no objection to this proceeding, he claimed the only reward he could request for his pleasing liberty, and the scene ended by him kissing her. It was done so graciously that old Spotted Tail had no cause to scalp him for his temerity.[18]

This was clearly seen by all who left a record of it as a piece of good-natured fun in which Miss Spotted Tail became a willing prop for a Custer performance under the tolerant eyes of her father. Yet Custer's opportunistic fondling of the young woman has the unpleasant aftertaste of something society casually tolerated for too long.

Spotted Tail might have made his daughter's person unavailable—as it ordinarily would have been according to the customs of his own culture—but he was preoccupied by his own agenda: more than the presents his people received for their participation, this astute chief wanted to make the most of his proximity to power by extracting certain long-range benefits from General Sheridan. When his turn to speak came, Spotted Tail alone gave a substantive speech. He asked Sheridan directly for two things: to be allowed to hunt south of the Platte until the Indians had become self-supporting from farming, and to have more than one trader at his reservation. In Washington, he said, he had seen that the white man was not compelled to trade at a single store. This he regarded as a system superior to the monopoly that traders typically enjoyed on Indian reservations.[19] Sheridan immediately granted the first request but acknowledged that he would have to speak with the Great Father about the second. Since corruption in the Indian Bureau was at its zenith during the Grant administration, and since traders paid for the privilege of monopoly—which enabled them to offer inferior goods at exorbitant prices—the chief's reasonable request was doomed.

There is no record of Custer's reaction to Spotted Tail's petition, but the fates were alert. Four years later one of the threads that led to the Little Bighorn was Custer's public protest against just such a trading monopoly on army posts. Had he not angered President Grant by his outspoken criticism of this practice, which benefited both Grant's brother Orvil and Grant's personal friend, the secretary of war, Custer would not have been replaced by General Terry as commander of the expedition against the Sioux. In that position he most likely would not have found himself on that hillside above the Little Bighorn with a mere two-hundred-odd men.

What might Custer have told Libbie about the episode with Miss Spotted Tail? Libbie left copious notes on the hunt, including the following topic headings:

DISTRIBUTION OF PRESENTS
MISS SPOTTED TAIL

This is chronologically accurate because presents were given to the Indians before Miss Spotted Tail became the center of attention, but the juxtaposition of the chief's daughter and the presents also suggests Miss Spotted Tail's assimilation to the rewards handed out. She became the culmination of the evening's entertainment.

Libbie had only one comment, later in her notes, to flesh out the topic of Miss Spotted Tail: "Young, shy, and pretty as the Indian girls often are until they become married drudges, she received many compliments and gifts." Libbie wrote nothing that indicates her husband's attentions or their prominence. Provided she had not heard about the physical contact, Libbie might have simply been amused, as she was when Custer told her that an elderly Cheyenne woman had tried to marry him to a young and attractive tribeswoman after the Battle of the Washita.

It was important to both Custers that they share their lives completely, that whatever happened to one when they were apart be recounted to the other in their constant and detailed correspondence. Once in New York, Custer wrote to Libbie, "a beautiful girl, eighteen or nineteen, blonde . . . walked past the hotel several times trying to attract my attention. Twice for sport I followed her."[20] Such episodes were always treated lightly in Custer's letters, as if they were only a matter of "sport" or exaggerated public performance.

In the case of Miss Spotted Tail, however, there is no evidence that Custer told his wife about his flirting. Had he done so, Libbie might have been reminded of their first married quarrel, which occurred when they visited West Point on their honeymoon trip:

> The general had been called away, his intimates asking me to spare him for a time. One of his oldest professors came to join us, was introduced, looked me over curiously, apparently approvingly as far as outward appearances, and said he would take one of the privileges with a bride—whereupon he kissed me. I blushed, naturally, but as he seemed like a methuselah to me, there was nothing to do but accept (or submit).[21]

As soon as they were alone, Libbie told Autie that the professor had kissed her and said "lovely things" to her. Her husband listened with increasing gloom: "I begged to know what was the trouble. Had I done anything that he disapproved? Possibly this innocence might have been misunderstood for a girl's duplicity—I wondered whether I was to be 'returned with thanks' to my father, and before the cloud lifted I was—in army terms—*ready* myself to 'apply for a leave of absence' of indefinite length. I was so discouraged, so unhappy."[22] The young couple eventually straightened the matter out, but Custer's reaction made it clear that he regarded the kiss as a usurpation for which he held Libbie at least partially accountable.

The flirting and badinage with the Indian girls ended a day crowded with exotic experiences for the Grand Duke. Another day of hunting followed in which he shot nine buffalo and then, since the buffalo in that area had scattered, the party decamped to Denver. There Chalkley Beeson took up the story. He was an engaging combination of talents, a frontiersman and a violinist, hired to play at the ball given in the Grand Duke's honor. Custer sought him out there because Beeson had been bragging about the great herds of buffalo to be found around Kit Carson, a place in Colorado close to the Kansas line.[23] This revived everyone's appetite for a second round of hunting, and they organized an expedition on the spot, with Beeson as a guide.

The first hunt had been carefully prepared in advance, but on this impromptu hunt the only mounts obtainable were inexperienced cavalry horses that stumbled into prairie dog holes right and left, sending their hapless riders tumbling. As the party approached a huge herd of buffalo, Custer—with his usual desire for attention and his penchant for boyish pranks—stopped and said, "Boys, here's a chance for a great victory over that bunch of redskins the other side of the hill." Addressing the mayor of Denver, he instructed: "Major Bates, you will take charge of the right flank, I will attend to the left. General Sheridan and the infantry will follow directly over the hill. Ready! Charge!" He and Alexis galloped away, but a complete lack of organization resulted in pandemonium as soon as the "enemy," the buffalo herd, was engaged. Bullets began whizzing close to the "infantry," which scrambled to get out of range. Sheridan was ill-suited to such an emergency: "He threw his short legs and fat body to the ground, telling himself perhaps that this fool charge was putting him in greater peril than he had known in the Battle of Winchester."[24]

Beeson yelled at the hunters to stop firing, "but they were so excited that it looked for a little bit as though they would wipe out the entire command of 'infantry.'"[25] As James Hadley remarked, "It was a miracle that nobody was killed or crippled that day."[26]

When things finally calmed down, Sheridan was furious. He gave the men "a liberal education in profanity," not sparing Custer and Alexis. Custer must have at least feigned contrition to his patron, but the Grand Duke did not seem to care: "He was having the time of his life."[27]

The party dispersed at St. Louis on January 23, but Custer and Alexis had become comrades, and, at the Grand Duke's request, Sheridan allowed both Custers to accompany the royal party for the brief remainder of their tour. Libbie, too, was happy to exchange the monotony of Elizabethtown for the glamor of a royal progress with the charming Grand Duke. She soon observed that "chasing the buffalo did not comprise all of the hunting of his highness." As newspaper accounts had intimated, women did indeed flock to the Grand Duke's presence, and he reciprocated their interest. On their excusion to the Mammoth Cave, for instance, a group of mothers sent their daughters along under Libbie's chaperonage. "They were so fascinating," she wrote, "I don't think that on our arrival the Grand Duke knew whether he was in a cave or on top of a mountain."

During Alexis's encounters with an enthusiastic democratic public, there were trying occasions, but he seems never to have lost his royal aplomb. Libbie wrote that people insisted on telling him "local jokes or side splitting stories," which were bound to be incomprehensible to him in spite of his good command of English. Worst of all, they "clapped his imperial back or dug his royal ribs in emphasis." All reports agreed that the Duke was always affable, although it was unimaginable that a commoner in his own country would have been able to approach him as Americans constantly did—let alone touch his person.

The nation's democratic principles must have been evident to Alexis throughout the tour in the form of the crowds that claimed his attention. In Omaha the governor of Nebraska hosted him for dinner in his home, an occasion on which he undoubtedly met the city's elite. Afterward, however, the public was allowed in to shake his hand: "all sorts and conditions of men and women and a host of children marched through the house," including teamsters with whips in their hands. The weather was stormy: "All brought more or less mud into the house, to the ruination of beautiful carpets that covered the floor."[28] When Alexis reboarded his special train, a voice in the crowd called out with American informality, "Goodbye, Alec," to which the Grand Duke responded from his own tradition by lifting his hat and replying, "Goodbye, sir."[29] Yet in spite of the perfect manners, which Libbie said were put to good use with the mothers of all those attractive young ladies, there were times when the man's essential self showed through, that of an excited twenty-one year old who had temporarily escaped some of the constraints of his social position. How else explain what Libbie mentioned twice in her notes, that Alexis was so happy over the hunt that "he picked General Sheridan up and carried [him] through the entire train." Sheridan may have been reminded of the Union victory at Cedar Creek, when an exuberant Custer, his Boy General, had picked him up and whirled him around.[30]

At New Orleans the Grand Duke and his entourage were met by the Russian fleet and sailed for home. Alexis became titular head of the imperial navy, lived in Paris most of his life, and never married. Nor did he ever return to America. History does not reveal how he remembered his tour or what happened to those souvenirs—the buffalo hooves, the bow and arrows—the artifacts that Alexis took away with him. Were they immediately forgotten and laid aside or kept on display, a sometime evocation of that carefree time? Did they come to rest in some corner of the vast imperial domain to be eventually discovered and destroyed by irate revolutionaries, or were they preserved and passed on to future generations in some White Russian collection?

For Custer it had been a unique interlude, a carefree time of hunting and carousing with army top brass and foreign dignitaries who appreciated his expertise and applauded his clowning. Sanctioned by Alexis's approbation and Sheridan's favor, he was able to indulge his boyish capacity for fun and momentarily escape Kentucky, where Libbie languished and his career stagnated.

Only a few years later, Custer would be dead and Libbie would receive a letter of condolence written by Baron N. Schilling for the Grand Duke: "His Highness remembers with great pleasure the time he passed in your society. About your heroic husband, the late general Custer, the Grand Duke speaks always in terms of the highest esteem and admiration, and the news of your sorrows afflicted him so much, that he could not resist the wish to express his sincere regrets."[31]

Of the men brought together for the Grand Duke's hunt, the one whose star would rise the highest was Buffalo Bill. Although it was another ten years before he officially invented the Wild West show that made him world famous, the 1872 buffalo hunt contained many of the same elements, including the hunt itself, feats of riding and shooting, and Indian performances. These were packaged and presented in much the way as in the show, that is, not as authentic, spontaneous experience but as contrived spectacle for payment. As the real frontier disappeared, a created image took its place, appealing to the residents of those long-settled Eastern cities who were relatively uninterested in the phenomenon of the West as reality. As spectacle, however, Buffalo Bill's Wild West was enormously popular, not only in the East but in England and Europe as well.[32] Up until his death in 1917 Cody made a fortune with it nearly every season, although he lost money through generosity and poor management almost as regularly. Libbie Custer, who attended a number of performances, thought that Cody's Wild West was the "most realistic and faithful representation of a Western life that has ceased to be."[33]

Much has been written about Indian and white attitudes toward animals as a contrast between respect for nature and a ruthless assault upon it, yet these different behaviors proceeded quite logically from different economies: for whites an economy of multiplicity and abundance, for Indians one of dependence on a single product and scarcity. Whites often killed wild animals casually and wastefully because, wrong as this seems today, they saw no reason not to: game was so plentiful that on the Plains in the immediate postwar period it was impossible to imagine it otherwise. Herds of antelope and elk would sometimes run through an army camp or graze alongside of army horses, while flocks comprising hundreds of wild turkeys were commonplace. And above all, there were buffalo in the millions, the great staple of the Plains. But animals were seldom merely observed in the nineteenth-century West: descriptions of huge numbers of whatever wild animal are invariably accompanied by descriptions of wonderful hunting. One appreciative English visitor wrote: "For men, or rather for sportsmen, America offers an unrivalled field."[34] Although the Indians also believed the supply of game was inexhaustible—unlike whites, they were almost completely dependent upon it for their food supply and so were more cautious.

The buffalo offered the most forceful example of white society's unthinking destruction of a huge animal population, one that once extended from the Potomac River to the Rockies. From the beginning of New World colonization, the herds were steadily pushed westward at the rate of ten miles a year, until, at the end of the Civil War, some seven or eight million, out of a population of several times that size, remained on the Great Plains.[35] This still enormous number would diminish rapidly. As they crossed the Plains, men would often fire wildly at the herds from moving trains: this was hunting at its most minimal, with no interest in using any of the animal or concern for finishing off the wounded. In a more positive vein, buffalo became a staple of the frontier diet. Peter Robidoux, who in 1868 worked in a boardinghouse that catered to Kansas Pacific passengers and employees, recalled the following bill of fare: "Buffalo roast, buffalo steak, buffalo stew, buffalo rump, buffalo heart, buffalo tongue and more buffalo if you wanted it."[36]

Hunting for sport, hunting for meat, and hunting for hides all flourished in the years the Custers spent on the Plains, but it was the annual traffic in two or three million hides during the early seventies that did the real damage. In 1871 a Pennsylvania tannery discovered that buffalo hides could be used for commercial leather; as a result, from 1872 to 1874 three million buffalo were killed yearly, primarily by hide hunters.[37]

The Indians understood that the buffalo were disappearing, but could do nothing. "My heart fell down," a Plains Indian named Pretty-Shield remembered, "when I began to see dead buffalo scattered all over our beautiful country, killed and skinned, and left to rot by white men, many, many hundreds of buffalo. . . . The whole country there smelled of rotting meat. . . . And yet nobody believed, even then, that the white man could kill *all* the buffalo."[38]

Beyond the straightforward motives of pleasure and profit that drove the killing of the buffalo—a destruction that the white man could indeed accomplish—lay the larger issue of Indian policy. In 1874 Secretary of the Interior Columbus Delano testified before Congress: "The buffalo are disappearing rapidly, but not faster than I desire. I regard the destruction of such game as Indians subsist upon as facilitating the policy of the Government, of destroying their hunting habits, coercing them on reservations, and compelling them to begin to adopt the habits of civilization."[39] *Destroy, coerce, compel*—these verbs tell it all.

General Sheridan informed the Texas legislature, which had been thinking of curbing the traffic in buffalo hides, that the buffalo hunters were doing "more to settle the vexed Indian question than the entire regular Army has done in the last thirty years"—quite an admission for a general who played a key role in frontier army policy. Sheridan continued with his usual ruthlessness: "For the sake of lasting peace let them kill, skin and sell until the buffaloes are exterminated." Congress allowed a bill forbidding the killing of buffalo in the territories to die in committee in 1876, at which time it was already too late.[40]

Professional hunters slaughtered enormous numbers of buffalo for profit, but when there were no more buffalo, they moved on to the other enterprises that a growing and diversified economy provided. And, in countless Wild West shows—of which Buffalo Bill's was only the most famous—they turned the buffalo into an exhibit of the Old West. For the Plains Indians, when there were no more buffalo, their way of life was over: they had no choice but to become "coffee-coolers," reservation Indians dependent upon government rations for subsistence.

One of those moments crystallizing the differences between the two cultures occurred in April of 1891 in Sioux Falls, South Dakota. Anticipating the crowds of Indians and whites drawn to a celebrated Indian trial, "an imaginative entrepreneur had built a corral and succeeded in assembling a herd of seventeen buffalo." Whites were attracted to the unfamiliar sight of the impressive animals, as they would be to some exotic specimen in a zoo, but the Sioux went wild with joy. They "scampered about, although at the risk of their lives, and in general made so free with the animals that the latter looked around as though dazed at the proceedings."[41] For the white entrepreneur, the buffalo was a source of profit; for the white spectators, it was a source of casual entertainment; for the Indians, it was *the* source—the center of their traditional and by then vanished way of life.

The epilogue belongs to Chalkley Beeson, reminiscing some thirty-five years after the buffalo hunt for the Grand Duke. "In my short span," he wrote in 1907,

> I have seen this whole western country settled up. . . . There are hundreds of prosperous towns and even cities on the very ground where I have killed buffalo and dodged Indians. It was a wild country, a wild life, and they were gallant men that lived it. All or most of them are gone. . . . But it is better now, better all around. The buffalo, like the Indian, took up too much space. It took too many acres for him to live on, and he had to give way to those who could do with less."[42]

16

Heroes of the Plains

Three such long-haired show-offs as Custer and the two Bills could never work together. Who would do the admiring, the applauding?

—Mari Sandoz, *The Buffalo Hunters*

The Plains were a landscape and a space ideally suited to Custer's boundless energy, his love of outdoor life, his avid horsemanship. Numerous descriptions of him on horseback testify that he easily met one of the Kiowa criteria for leadership, "to be handsome on a horse," making a heroic impression on the men he commanded, accompanying journalists, and others—among them the Cheyenne woman Kate Bighead, who remembered him as a handsome man she had seen in the South.[1] Forty-seven years later, another woman's memory of seeing Custer in the Grand Review was still vivid. His "commanding figure," she wrote to Libbie, was "a sight to climax all that had gone before in my girlish admiration."[2]

In time Custer would develop a reputation as a skilled plainsman and Plains Indian fighter, but where he had been exceptional as a field cavlary commander in the Civil War—reaching the very pinnacle of his profession at a surprisingly young age, finding himself worshiped by his men and extolled to the public by an admiring press—on the Plains he could never achieve unique distinction. This was reflected in the obvious disappointment of a reporter who compared his visual memory of Custer at the height of his glory with a picture of him taken in 1872. "It is not the same General Custer that we saw years ago," he wrote.

> It was in the closing hours of the war, and the name of Custer was linked with deeds of heroism and daring. He was the *beau ideal* of a cavalry leader, and as he stood that night in front of the crowd that blocked up Main street, his long hair falling down his shoulders, his face bronzed but nearly beardless, his form tall but thin and sinewy, flags floating over his head, and lamps flaring and casting mystic shadows, he looked more youthful than he really was, looked a knight of bold adventure, a spirt of dash and courage. The General has grown stouter, more rugged since then, and, in the picture at least, his flowing beard robs his face of much of its old boyish look.[3]

Custer would have been hard-pressed to live up to the reporter's memory of the romantic young cavalier, but it was an image that had been etched into the memories of many who had seen him during the Civil War. During those years Custer had attracted attention for his idiosyncratic appearance, characterized by his long blond curls and gold-braided velvet jacket. The woman who wrote to Libbie forty-seven years after seeing Custer exclaimed, "Will I ever forget the beautiful sight!—And how the people *cheered*. I see his smile now as the sombrero was gallantly lifted."[4]

Like two other men he knew on the Plains, Buffalo Bill and Wild Bill, Custer had a presence that enhanced his physical appearance and made him memorable. All three legendary figures were physically striking and became famous at a young age. Each was admired for shooting and riding and was well known to a large public because of media attention—newspapers in Custer's case, Ned Buntline's dime novels in Cody's, and one notorious magazine article in Hickok's. Custer and Hickok would die young and at the hands of familiar enemies—with some help from their own actions. Of the three, only Buffalo Bill made the transition from a violent way of life to entrepreneurial success, old age, and death from natural causes.

Heroes are usually thought of as tall, and there has always been some uncertainty about Custer's height. He measured five feet, eight inches when he arrived at West Point, but he was only seventeen, an age when many boys have not attained their full growth. Libbie said that he was "nearly six feet," which would have been noticeably taller than the average frontier army soldier, who at five feet, seven inches was two inches shorter than soldiers measured ninety years later and a half inch shorter than Union soldiers of the Civil War.[5] George B. Sanford, a young cavalry officer during the Civil War, remarked that Custer's "great height and striking countenance made him a very imposing figure." But Sanford may be suspected of some hyperbole, since he went on to describe his subject's "great mass of blond curling hair falling almost to his waist."[6] Two observers who first saw Custer in Kansas described him as "slender"—which was not surprising since he led a life of vigorous physical activity that kept him trim and at times thin.[7]

As a cavalryman, Custer had the advantage of being seen on horseback, and as a commander, he chose to ride in another position of preeminence—at the head of his troops. Describing his first view of Custer during the Civil War, J. H. Kidd said that he heard orders being given and turned to see "an officer superbly mounted who sat his charger as if to the manor born. Tall, lithe, active, muscular, straight as an Indian and as quick in his movements, he had the fair complexion of a school girl."[8] Most Civil War descriptions of Custer were similarly admiring, although this one was unusual in not mentioning what many regarded as Custer's most striking feature, the long blond curls that caused the *New York Herald* to dub him "the Boy General with the golden locks."

It comes as something of a shock then for a frontier army doctor to have found Custer less than prepossessing when he saw him for the first time at an officers' dance: "I watched him with a good deal of interest, for at that time he was a distinguished man in the service," Dr. R. H. McKay writes,

> and I must say that I was rather disappointed in his appearance. He seemed to me to be under-sized and slender, and at first blush to be effeminate in appearance. Maybe his long hair, almost reaching to his shoulders, gave this impression, but the face was something of a study and hard to describe. Something of boldness or maybe dash, a quick eye, and he was intensely energetic, giving the impression that he would be a veritable whirlwind in an engagement. He did not convey the idea of a great character.[9]

Whatever the meaning of his final sentence, the doctor was astute: what Custer lacked in physically impressive attributes, he compensated for with energy and "boldness." Like many American heroes, he was to some extent self-invented, consciously living up to an image that he had fashioned for himself, an image preserved in an unusually large number of photographs.

As these photographs reveal, Custer did not have classically handsome features: while the prominence of his nose and cheekbones, and a shapely forehead, gave his face strength and interest, and his eyes were a piercing blue, his chin was weak and his nose long. Libbie wrote fondly that someone had told her that "distinguished men of strong character had almost invariably big noses. I noted that, and counted noses when we found ourselves in an assembly at the East with people of note, and as my husband passed me, I was guilty of whispering that I had gone over the assembly, and noted the number down in my memory, and that ours out-shone and out-sized them all."[10]

What was most attractive about Custer was his vitality, his buoyancy and unfailing optimism. He was famous for boundless energy, not only the energy to endure long marches—in that respect he was no different from other prominent Indian fighters, men like George Crook, Eugene Carr, and Nelson Miles—but an energy that he brought to every occasion, from the battlefield to the dance where Dr. McKay observed him with curiosity. As McKay surmised, Custer was a "veritable whirlwind" in battle, but he was a whirlwind off the battlefield, too—always planning activities and setting personal goals, always in motion mentally and physically.

To his supporters, this energy was an admirable quality; to his critics, it was the part of his makeup that led him to be insensitive to and even abuse those of more typical limitations. "When he set out to reach a certain point at a certain time," an officer who knew Custer told T. M. Newson, "you could be sure that he would be there if he killed every horse in the command. . . . He would overshoot the mark, but never fall short of it."[11] Custer biographer Frederic Van De Water, who regarded his subject as "a martinet who expected all to possess his own inexhaustible energy and spirit," even cast his late-night letter-writing to Libbie in a sinister light as still another example of a tirelessness that was used against others.[12] Custer often ended a letter with the information that he had to go to bed since reveille was only two or three hours away.

Such ceaseless activity may simply have been an expression of egotism, Custer's desire to continually engage the world, impress himself upon it, and reap the admiration of others. To people of ordinary energy it may well have appeared ostentatious and more—an intentional reminder of their lesser capacities. Custer's tireless enthusiasm is associated with a boyishness that persisted even in his adult character, a quality that, like so much about Custer, can be read both positively and negatively. His ready delight in experience and his capacity for wholehearted fun were appealing, yet the accompanying devil-may-care impulsiveness and self-indulgence had the potential to wreak havoc. On Custer's first march in Kansas he recklessly pursued a buffalo miles from his troops. A sudden movement of his horse as he fired caused him to shoot his own mount instead of the buffalo, leaving him alone and on foot in unfamiliar and dangerous country. On that occasion Custer's luck held—the regiment found him before any Indians did—but the incident exemplified a quality that could be dangerous.

Already well known in Kansas at the end of the war, James Butler Hickok, "Wild Bill," was to achieve national fame in 1866, the year of Custer's arrival there, when George Ward Nichols published an article about him in the February issue of *Harper's New Monthly Magazine*. Just as Buffalo Bill never needed more than one shot to bring down a buffalo, Wild Bill was described by Nichols as never needing to shoot twice at the same man. According to the reporter, Wild Bill told him that he had always shot well, but he came to be perfect by shooting at a dime "at bets of half a dollar a shot." To the awestruck Nichols, Bill's was "the handsomest *physique* I had ever seen. In its exquisite manly proportions it recalled the antique. . . . He appeared to me to realize the powers of a Samson and Hercules combined."[13]

In the opinion of Wild Bill's biographer, Nichols's hero-worshiping description proved to be a death warrant, "for from that day until his death a scant nine years later, he was besieged by journalists and others eager for more details, most of them not interested in the truth. He was constantly obliged to prove himself the equal of all comers."[14]

Nichols's article was as much tall tale as interview, but on one point there was much agreement. The young English reporter Henry Stanley, who knew Wild Bill in 1875, described him as "as handsome a specimen of man as can be found," an assessment Custer agreed with in *My*

Life on the Plains, where he called Bill "one of the most perfect types of physical manhood I ever saw."[15]

Like Nichols, Libbie Custer remembered Wild Bill as

> a delight to look upon. Tall, lithe, and free in every motion, he rode and walked as if every muscle was perfection, and the careless swing of his body as he moved seemed perfectly in keeping with the man, the country, the time in which he lived. I do not recall anything finer in the way of physical perfection than Wild Bill when he swung himself lightly from his saddle, and with graceful, swaying step, squarely set shoulders and well poised head, approached our tent for orders. . . . I do not at all remember his features, but the frank, manly expression of his fearless eyes and his courteous manner gave one a feeling of confidence in his word and in his undaunted courage.

Wild Bill reminded Libbie of a thoroughbred horse: "He looked as if he had descended from a race who valued his body as a choice possession, and therefore gave it every care."[16]

Evidently he did give it every care, somehow overcoming the difficulties that restricted other people's toilet on the frontier. Theodore Davis recalled with some wonder that when "ordinary mortals were hustling for a clean pair of socks," Wild Bill would appear in "an immaculate boiled shirt, with much collar and cuffs to match—a sleeveless Zouave jacket of startling scarlet, slashed with black velvet" and other accoutrements to match, including French calfskin boots that were polished "as if the individual wearing them had recently vacated an Italian's arm chair throne on a side street near Broadway. The long wavey hair that fell in masses from beneath a conventional sombrero was glossy from a recent anointment of some heavily perfumed mixture."[17]

A man who walked around the frontier dressed like a dandy and reeking of perfume had to have a great deal of personal authority to survive. Often Bill's commanding physical presence—he was reported to be six feet, two inches—was enough to defuse a situation, but if it was not, he never walked away from trouble. Once he became legendary, he was careful not to literally turn his back on trouble either—until a fatal lapse at a poker game in Deadwood.

. . .

If Wild Bill was regarded as the most impressive physical specimen of his time and place, an image he emphasized by his elaborate self-presentation, the six-foot-tall William Cody was the most handsome. Dr. George Kingsley, who accompanied the earl of Dunraven on some of his hunting expeditions to the Plains, pronounced Buffalo Bill "one of the handsomest and the best built men I have ever seen."[18] General Nelson Miles remembered that the day Cody "first reported to me he was the handsomest man I had ever seen. . . . His features were as perfect as if chiseled out of marble."[19] Queen Victoria evidently shared General Miles's opinion. When Cody presented his Wild West show for her 1887 Jubilee, the queen had not attended a public performance since her consort's death in 1861. Given the importance of the occasion, she made an exception—and then asked for a second, unscheduled performance.[20] Her favors to the showman thereafter aroused the jealousy of Cody's wife, Louisa, who spitefully named the queen in her petition for divorce. (The judge ordered this testimony expunged from the record as "manifestly unjust, preposterous, false, and brutal.")[21]

In addition to being handsome, Buffalo Bill seems to have been the most likable of men, at least to everyone but his wife. Their severe incompatibility kept them at odds and usually apart, although after the judge had reprimanded both parties for seeking a divorce on insufficient grounds, the Codys lived together amicably until Bill's death. Away from Louisa, Bill struck an army officer as "one of the most contented and happy men I ever met."[22] Henry Davies wrote that on a hunting trip Cody guided, "he at once attracted to him all with whom he became acquainted."[23] Like everyone else, Davies remarked on Cody's "strikingly handsome features."[24]

Biographers document that Bill was openhanded to a fault, always propping up old friends and business associates financially and maintaining a great number of relatives. And in spite of his celebrated proficiency as a marksman, hunter, and scout, he was not known for braggadocio, at least not until fairly late in life when—famous and sought after—he had many temptations to remember his past more expansively.[25]

When Libbie described the hunt that General Sheridan arranged for the Grand Duke Alexis of Russia, she praised Cody generously. Although Custer had been put in charge of the expedition and thus might have played the leading role, especially in his doting wife's account, Cody was in fact the hero of Libbie's narrative, while her own husband was barely mentioned. As Libbie's knowledge of the hunt must have come primarily from Custer, her manuscript suggests that he was not the rampant egotist his detractors portray, for nothing would have been easier for him than to have given himself center stage in recounting events to Libbie. Instead, he must have been responsible for the admiring details about Buffalo Bill that turned up in her account. General Sheridan, Libbie wrote, knew that Cody was the only man who could influence the Brulé chief Spotted Tail to come to the hunt: "The scout was known to all the tribes, not only for his courage but for his inviolable word." She reported that he received many gifts from all the foreign guests "for having made the hunt such a success."[26]

In Libbie's telling Custer seems to have been amused rather than annoyed when a little girl in Denver asked him: "Are you Buffalo Bill or Wild Bill or Spotted Tail?" Had Custer envied or belittled Buffalo Bill's or Wild Bill's accomplishments, Libbie—her husband's fiercest partisan—would not have written of either man with such unrestrained enthusiasm.

Contrary to Mari Sandoz's assumption that three such "show-offs" could not get along, they did in fact respect each other and work together harmoniously. Cody and Hickok were good friends, and each scouted briefly for Custer. Apparently Custer acknowledged the merits of both men, neither of whom was a military competitor. But it may tell us something that Custer did not mention his first meeting with Cody in *My Life on the Plains*. It was an occasion when, according to Cody's memoirs, the newly arrived Custer thought his horse would be a better mount than Cody's mule for the journey they were taking together. On the difficult terrain—territory that Cody already knew—the mule outperformed Custer's horse, a fact that must have been irritating to Custer, who loved to excel and to be right. Nevertheless, in Cody's telling, Custer took it in good spirit.[27]

When it came to shooting, one of the necessary skills of a hero on the Plains frontier, all three men were admired, but in different contexts. Wild Bill was *the* acknowledged master of shooting at a moving target with a pistol.[28] This skill made him a successful sheriff of Ellis County in 1869 (site of the notorious Hays City) and marshal of the equally notorious Abilene in 1871. In Abilene, a boy named Andrew Platner told about the time he was on his way to school and saw Wild Bill kill two escaping murderers who were fleeing in opposite directions. To the schoolboy it seemed that the marshal killed both men simultaneously. The pistol had been fired in opposite directions with such speed that he thought he had heard the sound of only one shot.[29]

There were countless stories of Wild Bill's proficiency to illustrate his descriptive epithet, "the Prince of Pistoleers." Robert Kane saw him in the early 1870s when Hickok and Cody were in Milwaukee for an engagement of the play they were touring in together. One afternoon they were persuaded to do some shooting for interested locals. Kane later remembered that Wild Bill never seemed to hurry: he had that perfection of motion that makes performance seem effortless. "Standing midway between the fences of a country road, which is four rods wide," Kane wrote, "Mr. Hickok's instinct of location was so accurate that he placed a bullet in each of the fence posts on opposite sides. Both shots were fired simultaneously."[30]

Unlike many notorious gunmen, Wild Bill was neither a sadistic killer nor a braggart. In Custer's opinion Bill's various homicides were all justifiable, and he seems to have been made uncomfortable by acclaim.[31] Libbie described some Eastern friends of the Custers, undoubtedly readers of the extravagant *Harper's* article, who arrived for a visit and immediately begged to see Wild Bill: "They gave flowers to any bystander whom they saw, requesting that they be given to the renowned scout. But the more he was pursued with messages the more he retired from sight, hiding in the little back room of one of the drinking-saloons opposite. He was really a very modest man and very free from swagger and bravado."[32] Finally, Custer himself was persuaded to go in search of Wild Bill, and he returned with his man.

In 1902, when he was sixty years old and many years removed from the frontier, Buffalo Bill could still hit a tin can thrown into the air twice before it hit the ground and, using a Winchester, kill five mountain sheep at fifteen hundred yards, two of them with one shot apiece.[33]

Custer was always esteemed for his riding and shooting, but he could not match the feats—let alone the legends—of such men as Wild Bill and Buffalo Bill. On the great buffalo hunt, for instance, Custer put on an impressive display of riding for the Grand Duke Alexis. Throwing aside the reins on an almost unbroken horse he had commandeered, he applied knee pressure to force the spirited animal in a circle while using his hands to fire two revolvers continuously "with as much accuracy as though he were standing on the ground."[34] The Grand Duke declared it was the finest exhibition of horsemanship he had ever seen and applauded every shot, but what might he have said if he had seen the race between Buffalo Bill and Lieutenant Edward Spaulding in which Cody bet the lieutenant that he could jump off of and back onto his horse, Tall Bull, eight times in a mile and still win? He won the bet.[35]

In a letter to Lieutenant Cooke's mother after her son had been killed at the Little Bighorn, Captain Thomas French wrote that Custer's late adjutant was, "excepting myself perhaps and General Custer—the best shot in the regiment."[36] This was not necessarily great praise, however, as soldiers, including officers, had the reputation of being indifferent shots. George Bird Grinnell remarked that everyone had seen soldiers shoot, "and we know that they can't shoot well. . . . Most of them just fire in the general direction of anything they're trying to hit."[37] This mediocrity was understandable: the frontier army "plodded along with an allotment of ten rounds for practice per man each month, which many never got, general indifference to the condition of the rifles and ammunition, and no training for the range."[38] In a letter of June 21, 1876, Dr. James DeWolf told his wife that he and Dr. Porter had gone out pistol shooting with Lieutenants Harrington and Hodgson. The two doctors came in first and second. "So you see," the doctor concluded, "some of the cavalry cannot shoot very well."[39]

Most likely Custer *was* a good shot: his eyesight was excellent, and he had both the resources and the will to practice. Richard Roberts, a young man whose sister Annie married into the Seventh, described Custer target shooting with such determination that he ignored mosquitoes so numerous that they blackened his hands. Lieutenant James Calhoun observed on the Yellowstone expedition that "General Custer was probably the most fortunate hunter in the command and many a time have I seen him bring down an antelope running at great speed across his front, and three or four hundred yards distant."[40]

Such accomplishments might have set Custer apart in the regiment, but on the Plains frontier his world included not only the two celebrated Bills, but a number of well-known sharpshooters, among them the North brothers, Frank and Luther. In a story Grinnell told, Custer once saw a mother duck with a row of ducklings swimming behind her and announced that he would shoot the heads off a few of the ducklings. "I looked at Luther North," Grinnell related,

> and made a sign to him and he dismounted and sat down on the ground behind the general. General Custer fired at a bird and missed it and North shot and cut the head off one of the birds. Custer shot again and missed and North cut the head off another bird. Custer looked around at him and then shot again and again missed and North cut the head off a third duck. Just then an officer rode up over a hill near the pond and said that the bullets after skipping off the water were singing over the heads of his troops. The general said, "We had better stop shooting"; and mounted the horse and rode on without saying a word.[41]

Taking Grinnell's comments on Custer as a whole, one suspects that he disliked Custer's self-proclaimed prowess as a marksman and hunter. He preferred men like his friends the North brothers, crack shots and reticent men.

Writing to Libbie from the Black Hills expedition of 1874, Custer announced triumphantly that he had achieved the hunter's greatest desire—he had killed his first grizzly. Grinnell and North, peacefully picking wild raspberries on a hill nearby, heard enough shooting to bring down a regiment of bears and wondered what was going on.[42] Captain William Ludlow, the Arikara scout Bloody Knife, and Custer had shot simultaneously at the bear, so perhaps Custer was entitled to only one-third credit, although he claimed pride of place in the photographs taken on the spot. To deflate the accomplishment even more, that sour enlisted man, Private Theodore Ewert, insisted in his diary that the bear was not a grizzly at all; it was simply an old cinnamon bear. General Custer, he wrote with his usual acidity, "wishes to magnify his discoveries to the fullest extent."[43]

As the necessary setting for the adventurous lifestyle of men like the two Bills, the Great Plains inevitably changed with increasing settlement. With the destruction of the immense herds of buffalo by the mid-1870s, they became, in the scornful words of the Kansas frontiersman James Hadley, "the plains of the Texas cow . . . wholly devoid of that subtile and chivalrous atmosphere inciting men to unrecorded battles, tragic sacrifices and nameless graves."[44] James Buel, a newspaperman who knew Wild Bill in Kansas City, when the town was a lively place of thirty thousand, remembered one evening in 1872 when he was assigned to report on three murders and one suspicious death. "But today," he wrote with satisfaction, "the infamies and demoralizing characters which once filled the streets of Kansas City exist only in the history of her progress, and the hum of her commerce has long since displaced the sonorous voice of the keno caller and the death-crack of the revolver."[45] That was in 1891, almost the end of the forward-looking, progress-minded nineteenth century. Had Buel lived another hundred years, he might have heard once again "the death-crack of the revolver" and other sounds of an urban violence he had imagined gone forever.

In a brief stint with the army after the Battle of the Little Bighorn, Buffalo Bill "took the first scalp for Custer" with suitable publicity. He was thirty-five when he had this last genuine adventure on the Plains, although he would narrowly miss being at the scene of Sitting Bull's death in 1890. In the following years, however, he would take advantage of the copious material from his early life to become a showman, a celebrity throughout the United States and Europe. The buffalo, which had supported the Plains Indians and given him his famous sobriquet, were gone, but being a white man, and a particularly gifted one, he adapted to changing conditions.

Cody had had a successful stage career for ten years before he moved on to an even more successful career as the man who brought the Wild West back East. He and Wild Bill and some other authentic frontiersmen had been persuaded to tour in "Scouts of the West," a weak drama written by Ned Buntline. The nonactors were terrible but loved by audiences for their very ineptitude: the forgotten lines and stammered ad-libs emphasized their genuineness. Buffalo Bill started out as awkwardly as the others, but he quickly learned how to give a crowd-pleasing performance. Wild Bill, on the other hand, could never accept the illusion necessary to acting. "He insisted that we were making a set of fools of ourselves," Cody remembered.[46] Before the tour was over, Wild Bill gave it up and went back to Kansas.

Although Buffalo Bill became the more polished performer, he remained, like his friend, wedded to an idea of authenticity. As if he could bring the real thing to his audiences, he insisted on calling his creation "the Wild West" without the addition of the word "show."[47] The Deadwood stagecoach was "real," as were many of the performers—sharpshooters, genuine cowboys, and Indians, even, for one season, Sitting

Bull himself. A man who lived in the area in those days remembered that Bill would come each spring to collect Indians for his show: "They left in paint and feathers and returned, after a year, in Prince Albert coats, Stetsons, patent leather shoes and long, well-groomed glossy hair."[48] What they did with this apparel once they returned to the reservation he did not say.

Of course, the entire production was contrived—as it had to be. Cody commanded attention by shooting eighty-seven balls out of a hundred thrown from a trap while he rode a horse at full speed.[49] A disgruntled old-timer wrote to Custerphobe E. A. Brininstool that "yokels were impressed by Cody's riding around the ring shooting balls thrown in the air, such wonderful shooting, I told them his cartridges were loaded with fine shot and a kid could hit them with his eyes shut, but it was no use to talk."[50] The yokels preferred to be impressed with the fakery of a man who had at one time been the real thing, a frontier adventurer.

Traveling shows like Buffalo Bill's were the first phase of re-creating the West as artifact and entertainment for the ordinary, stay-at-home citizen. The second, when Americans became mobile, would reverse the process: rather than taking the show to them, it would bring the audience to the actual or reconstructed Western sites, where they could admire the chair Wild Bill was sitting in when he was killed, the Deadwood stagecoach, and other memorabilia of the vanished frontier.

This form of entertainment continues to this day. In 1929 Dr. Thomas B. Marquis, a Custer buff who lived in the vicinity of the Little Bighorn battlefield, wrote to Libbie Custer that he could not "foresee a time when interest in the Little Bighorn battle will cease. Tourists visit the place by the scores and hundreds all through each day of the summer season. They increase in number year after year."[51] The doctor, regarded as an eccentric in his community, was certainly prescient. In his remote corner of southeastern Montana, the Little Bighorn Battlefield National Monument, until 1992 the Custer Battlefield National Monument, draws huge numbers of visitors every year—over a quarter of a million in recent seasons. It is an especially busy place during the annual reenactment of the battle, an event from which the Crow Indians—whose land it is—make a modest profit.[52]

The same summer that Custer died at the Little Bighorn, Wild Bill Hickok, the man whose physical grace had impressed Libbie Custer so indelibly, was shot from behind in Deadwood, Dakota Territory, by an unknown twenty-two year old whose motive was never adequately established. If Wild Bill's killings were the stuff of legend, his own death at the hands of Jack McCall had its farcical side. McCall seems to have been somewhat less than unprepossessing. Most contemporary observers refered to him as small and cross-eyed, although one, perhaps simply for good measure, gave him a broken nose as well.[53] The unheroic killer approached from the rear, put a gun to Bill's head and shot, then attempted to make a quick getaway. However, when he ran out the saloon door and tried to mount his horse, the saddle girth turned and deposited him on the ground.[54] Desperate, he continued down the street and into a meat market, where he tried to conceal himself behind a side of beef.[55]

As it turned out, there was no need to hurry or worry. Deadwood was little more than a thriving mining camp in those days and had no real law: as inexplicably as McCall had killed Wild Bill, a self-constituted jury found the murderer innocent. After a while McCall moved on and unwisely bragged about his feat in Wyoming, where he was arrested, tried, found guilty, and hanged on March 1, 1877.

In the aftermath of Bill's murder there were some who speculated that a dark conspiracy of gamblers and lawbreakers had killed him out of fear that he would become the marshal and clean up Deadwood, but this theory is unlikely. Bill had slowly but inexorably slid downhill, from law officer to "inoffensive gambler," the next thing to derelict. Then, because of increasingly serious eye trouble, he began to lose his one great talent and could no longer count on being the best shot around. Given his notoriety, this was a danger to his life and health. At that point he did a sensible thing in marrying the retired circus owner Agnes Lake, a capable woman eleven years his senior. Agnes had met Bill years before when her circus came to Abilene at the height of his reputation. Apparently there was mutual admiration at the time, but each was at the height of a busy career in which, evidently, sentimental inclinations were not a priority. Shortly after their reacquaintance and marriage in 1876, the lure of Black Hills gold, or perhaps masculine pride, caused Bill to go back to the frontier with the intention of prospecting some easy gold.

Bill's last letter to his bride, addressed to "my own darling wife Agnes," was optimistic: "I know my Agnes and only live to love her. . . . I am almost sure I will do well here."[56] The "almost" was a prudent hedge. Instead of prospecting, Bill had instinctively gravitated to the more comfortable pastime of saloon poker. Like Custer, he died with his boots on, and like Custer, he died as he lived. The hand he was holding, aces and eights, would be known thereafter among gamblers as the dead man's hand,[57] and the chair he was sitting in would be preserved against the future, when Deadwood became a tourist attraction. Agnes Lake's daughter, a circus performer, later toured with Buffalo Bill's Wild West under the stage name Emma Hickok.

Pondering his relationship with horses, William Faulkner once remarked that he had learned from them "to have sympathy for creatures not as wise, as smart, as man, to have pity for things physically weak."[58] One cannot imagine Custer similarly moved either to or by thoughts of weakness: in all things he loved the exceptional performance that could be assimilated to his own standard of hard-driving achievement. Where the two Bills seem to have been cool personalities, cultivating the nonchalance that validates mastery and most demonstrates it, Custer retained throughout his life a boyish eagerness for challenges, for competitions, for victories. Did he want achievement and recognition more than they did? Not necessarily: he was only more obviously pleased by the opportunity to excel.

All three men revealed an individuality that made them memorable figures to those who even briefly encountered them, and each measured up to Hemingway's definition of courage as "grace under pressure." Understandably, when the pressure ended, they were apt to fall off to some extent—to be less than heroic but still more than ordinary, trailing clouds of glory into their decline. Of the three, Custer had the most resources to refashion his life meaningfully, although Buffalo Bill had the greater success. Yet it is hardly fair to compare them in this respect: had Bill died at Custer's age, he would have been only at the beginning of the career that ultimately made him famous.

Much later, Colonel Edward C. Little, a congressman from Kansas, wrote indignantly that the heroes of the frontier actually surpassed those of antiquity, whose advantages were all in the telling:

> Homer sang Achilles into thirty centuries of renown. The deeds of many frontiersmen excel those of the Greeks. . . . Ivanhoe in his iron kettle with his long lance killing the

> neighbors for love of God and lady never surpassed the courage and sacrifice of Wild Bill and his comrades. But the dime novelist has been their biographer and cheap notoriety their reward. They deserve a statelier history and a sweeter requiem. . . . Walter Scott would have made this great scout and peace officer a hero and a prince of the border.[59]

The fault, dear Brutus, is not in us, but in our scribes.

17

Farther West

> Of all our happy days, the happiest had now come to us at Fort Lincoln.
> —Libbie Custer, *"Boots and Saddles"*

In 1873 the tedium of service in the South ended for Custer and the Seventh Regiment with a return to active field duty in Dakota Territory: their assignment would be to escort and protect an engineering party of the Northern Pacific Railroad. After this summer expedition, the regiment's new home base would be Fort Abraham Lincoln, a few miles downstream from Bismarck on the Missouri River—and on the cutting edge of conflict with the increasingly agitated Sioux. It was a welcome move: Libbie described in her book *"Boots and Saddles"* how Custer celebrated the happy news with "wild hilarity" and how she surreptitiously consulted an atlas to see where they were going—as far as Lapland, it seemed.[1]

The Yellowstone expedition of 1873, the first order of business once the regiment had moved to Dakota, would give the Seventh its last Indian fighting before the Battle of the Little Bighorn. This clash on the Yellowstone River with some of the same Lakota Sioux who would be at the Little Bighorn three years later would reinforce Custer's belief in his regiment's superiority and the concomitant inferiority of Indians as a fighting force.

During this period of transition, while the regiment lingered in Yankton, Dakota Territory, and then marched the 495 miles to Fort Rice, several contretemps occurred that place in perspective the now mature

Custer. Eight years after the end of the Civil War, he was, at the age of thirty-three, largely through his turbulent adjustment to a diminished career. Unlike those of the earlier postwar years, the difficulties Custer encountered at this time were of less consequence, but were also unnecessary, engendered by his lack of judgment in dealing with subordinates.

Custer again managed to gratuitously annoy his superiors as well. Even before the Seventh left Yankton, he went over the head of his immediate commander, General Alfred Terry, with a telegram to Washington informing the War Department that a severe snowstorm had immobilized the regiment.[2] This impolitic action produced a pointed response from Terry: "Send here [Terry's headquarters] copies of your orders for approval and confirmation."[3] Custer again became high-handed on the two occasions when his initial request for steamboat passage for some of his force was refused. At Yankton his quartermaster, Lieutenant Nowlan, hailed the steamboat *Western* because "Colonel Custer had ordred that his laundresses and sick be provided with cabin passage . . . to Fort Rice."[4] The boat was already under contract to the government to service the upper Missouri posts, but the captain would not agree to Custer's demand. Nowlan detained the boat in his commander's name, and when Custer appeared, he was handed a letter from the company agent indicating the terms of its contract with the government, specifically, "10 days notice in providing transportation." The letter pointed out—reasonably, if not helpfully—that "the contractor cannot, of course, be required to perform that which he has not agreed to perform, and he has not contracted to carry any soldier or laundress in the cabins or to furnish cabin passage to any except 'commissioned officers.'"[5] After a fairly lengthy negotiation, a compromise was reached.

Six weeks later, well into the march, Custer flagged down another passing steamer, the *DeSmet*, because he wanted his troops ferried across the river. Captain Joseph LaBarge agreed to transport the command, but the next day Custer added the condition that the Seventh's wagon master had to supervise the loading. LaBarge flatly refused, whereupon Custer threatened to arrest him! Before the threat could be carried out, LaBarge steamed away.[6]

In both cases Custer's aim was unobjectionable, but when he encountered the will of someone who had reasonable grounds for opposing his plans, he exacerbated the situation rather than seeking resolution. The long negotiation with the *Western* should have been fresh enough in his memory to temper his response in the *DeSmet* incident, but it obviously did not have that effect.

These flare-ups of Custer's will did not prevail against civilians who were outside his authority, but they were indicative of the trouble he had within his own officer corps. A young and articulate lieutenant serving in the Seventh, Charles Larned, wrote to his mother in terms reminiscent both of Captain Barnitz's criticism of Custer in 1867, and of the more serious criticism of his immediate postwar assignment: "Custer is not making himself at all agreeable to the officers of his command. He keeps himself aloof and spends his time in excogitating annoying, vexatious, and useless orders which visit us like the swarm of evils from Pandora's box, small, numberless, and disagreeable."[7]

One of Lieutenant Larned's letters asserted that Custer's hard-driving manner during the Yankton stay was causing concern among his officers: the men were fatigued and demoralized by "ceaseless and unnecessary labor. The police of camp, stables twice a day, water call (involving a five mile ride) twice—mounted guard mounting (a guard of sixty-five men), drills twice, and dress parade composes an exhaustive routine. We all fear that such ill advised and useless impositions will result in large desertions when the command is paid off."[8] If Larned was accurate, that is, if a number of officers shared his assessment of the situation, it may explain the sudden arrival of Colonel Samuel Sturgis to assume command of the regiment.

Four years earlier, in 1869, Colonel Sturgis had replaced the Seventh's original colonel, Andrew J. Smith, thus filling a position Custer had undoubtedly coveted for himself.[9] But with his Civil War record shadowed by the march into Texas and the court-martial of 1867, Custer's expectations had been unrealistic. Unable to achieve his protégé's longed-for promotion, General Sheridan kept Sturgis on detached duty as a conciliatory measure, leaving Custer de facto commander of the Seventh. There is evidence that the two men maintained a friendly professional relationship: on August 13, 1869, Sturgis described his subordinate generously in an official communication to headquarters. "There is, perhaps, no other officer of equal rank on this line," he wrote, "who has worked more faithfully against the Indians, or who has acquired the same degree of knowledge of the country and of the Indian character."[10] Still, the ongoing situation was bound to have created some awkwardness between them: each must have seen the other as the obstacle to unencumbered command of the Seventh.

Why at that particular moment without apparent cause or warning Sturgis should have descended on the Seventh remains mysterious. No explanatory paper trail has yet been discovered, but someone may have complained to Terry about Custer's behavior in terms that alarmed the general. Moreover, Custer's arrogance in bypassing Terry to communicate directly with the War Department may have suggested to him the value of placing Custer under observation for a period.

Whatever the intention, Sturgis made no changes during what turned out to be a short visit to the Yankton encampment. Custer retained command, effectively marginalizing the Seventh's colonel, who must have left the regiment with a keen appreciation of that fact.[11] Nevertheless, their friendly relationship seems to have survived this strange episode: Sturgis's only son joined the Seventh right out of West Point in the summer of 1875, and the colonel wrote a long chatty letter to Custer thanking him and Libbie for the kind interest they had shown in Jack.[12]

When the Seventh arrived at Fort Sully, Custer forced another confrontation with his officers. General Terry had ordered a general court-martial, whose proceedings began in the cavalry camp but quickly shifted to Fort Sully, where the court could utilize the more comfortable facilities of buildings with tables and chairs. Since the officers expected to spend several days conducting the session, their decision was sensible. Custer, however, ordered the court back to camp, possibly because he did not want the regiment's business conducted in the more public venue of the fort.[13] The court returned in a frame of mind that can easily be imagined, since their only action was to repeat what they had already done, namely, adjourn once again in order to move to Sully. Lieutenant Larned, who was serving as judge advocate, wrote to his mother that Custer was "making himself utterly detested by every line officer of the command . . . by his selfish, capricious, arbitrary and unjust conduct."[14]

The court prevailed, but Custer was not graceful in defeat. He continued to harass it until the officers unanimously protested to General Terry.[15] On June 11, 1873, Larned wrote that the court-martial proceedings were "the source of endless annoyance and trouble to all concerned. Custer undertook to bully and insult that body at the start, and, finding that his efforts at control were powerless, did everything in his power to hector and annoy its members. The court has made an indignant protest against his assumption."[16]

Once again Custer had countered reasonable opposition with stiff-necked authority, creating a contest of wills that alienated his officers over an insignificant matter. Six years after the low point of his court-martial, Custer was showing signs of the same behavior that had made so few willing to testify for him then. His actions seem perverse, but the march to Dakota was the beginning of a new phase for the recently re-united Seventh—a fresh start in a new place—and Custer, as always, was concerned with maintaining the regiment's positive image. After its dispersal in various southern locations, the Seventh would have a chance to work as a fighting unit in the most significant military theater available at the time—the territory of the most hostile and warlike Indians remaining on the North American continent. This opportunity may have prodded Custer's ambition, causing him to make determined efforts to raise the efficiency of his men and to apply his authority too heavily to his officers.

Custer was dealing with a recurrent problem: once again his men failed to immediately live up to his expectations—expectations that had been set during the Civil War, when his troops had matched his own zeal and accomplishments. After what was essentially police duty in the South, the regiment needed to be brought up to fighting condition, but Custer wanted to move too quickly, and in his frustration tightened the screws too much. Although his expectations were impossibly high, his method was not without results. Even Larned had begun his critical letter of April 30 with the admission that "the command presents a splendid appearance under arms and is in magnificent condition."[17] All of the discipline and drill had borne fruit in Yankton when, in the presence of General Terry, the regiment put on a full-dress field review for the admiring townspeople. It was a fine spectacle, eliciting much praise from the *Yankton Press*. In Custer the paper saw "the beau ideal of the soldier and Commander."[18]

A few days later another incident bore out the need for stern measures, when, on the morning of May 17, the regiment discovered that Indians had stolen halters, lariats, and side lines from their horses and mules—this on a march that Custer intended to be a trial run for the expedition itself.[19]

During the Civil War Custer had not had to worry about the ineffable quality of esprit de corps: he had effortlessly induced it in all the units he commanded simply by leading them into battle. On the frontier he made many attempts to re-create the same spirit that had animated his Civil War troops—taking the band into battle, coloring the horses, encouraging officers and men alike to live up to his own exacting standards—but essential ingredients were missing. Charles King, a frontier officer, felt that army policy during this period discouraged esprit de corps: in the understaffed frontier army, the integrity of a regiment could not be maintained because regimental companies were parceled out over a wide area and often merged with troops of other commands.[20] Generally speaking, the men who served in these fragmented units were not men imbued with the desire to save their country, and the times when Custer could function as an inspiring leader were too few. Undoubtedly, his measures did accomplish a certain amount of shaping up, but at the cost of satisfaction with his leadership that would ultimately prove more counterproductive.

A number of reservation Indians were seen along the march, tribes belonging to the famous Lakota Sioux, who dominated the northern Plains. The names by which these Indians became known to whites reflected the two sides of their policy: *Lakota* meant "allies," while *Sioux* was an abbreviated corruption of the Algonquian word *Nadoessis*, meaning "enemies."[21] When the Lewis and Clarke expedition had passed through Sioux territory, Meriwether Lewis had been unfavorably impressed. He regarded the Sioux as "the vilest miscreants of the savage race" because he rightly perceived that they would be intractable to white purposes. "Unless these people are reduced to order, by coercive measures," he wrote prophetically, "I am ready to pronounce that the citizens of the United States can never enjoy but partially the advantages which the Missouri presents."[22]

That the Sioux, themselves an expansionist people, would clash with white expansionism on the northern Plains was only to be expected. As early as the mid-1660s a French priest, Father Allouez, wrote that the Sioux had "conducted hostilities against all their enemies, by whom they are held in extreme fear."[23] Altogether, in a two-century period that ended in the 1870s, the Sioux fought against at least twenty-six other tribes.[24] Those tribes in the region that allied themselves with the United States in the post–Civil War period did so because the Sioux were their "most feared enemy," relentlessly driving westward and pushing smaller and weaker tribes off their land.[25] The Crow chief Plenty Coups, in discussing why he had made the decision to ally his people with the whites, explained that there had been little choice in the matter: "We plainly saw that this course was the only one which might save our beautiful country for us. When I think back my heart sings because we acted as we did. It was the only way open to us."[26]

The Sioux were fearsome, yet they were often described as exceptionally attractive as well. Henry Boller, a young man on the Missouri as a fur trapper, wrote in his journal that "men and women, the wild prairie Sioux have no superiors among the Indians in appearance and domestic virtues."[27] They were tall and straight—and healthy, because their nomadic life spared them the ravages of epidemic diseases that decimated tribes living in populous agricultural villages.[28] Boller also noticed "a great many handsome women among the Sioux," as did Lieutenant Larned, who wrote for the readership of the *Chicago Inter-Ocean*: "[They] are by no means repulsive. Rich eyes, low, liquid voices, and a pleasant modesty of demeanor atone for their defective toilets. The vermillion on their cheeks is laid on with a liberality worthy of a higher degree of civilization."[29] Indian women made a less favorable impression on Libbie Custer, who asserted that "only extreme youth and its ever attractive charms can make one forget the heavy square shape of Indian faces and their coarse features." Nevertheless, she gave one village beauty a good notice: "Her bright eyes, the satin smoothness of her hair, and the clear brown of the skin made a pretty picture."[30]

While the regiment marched from Yankton to Fort Rice, the eight accompanying officers' wives traveled the distance by steamboat, cooped up in small cabins for thirty-four days. Lieutenant Larned wrote to his mother that "during this time they have succeeded in discovering each other's failings with astonishing distinctness, and, from all I hear, have made the atmosphere pretty warm."[31] Larned was especially concerned about the condition of Annie Yates, a young woman whose admiration for Libbie Custer as the model army wife was so strong that she may well have tried to follow Libbie's example despite her very different situation as a young mother. "Poor woman!" he exclaimed. "You cannot imagine how badly she looks. She had a chill nearly every other day all the way up, and is emaciated almost to a skeleton. Her baby wears her out and the drain on her constitution in nursing it has been very severe."[32]

The wives hoped to stay at Fort Rice while the regiment continued on to the Yellowstone to protect a party of railroad surveyors from the Sioux. To their intense disappointment they were told that the post was not equipped to house more women, although the real reason might have been otherwise. Libbie intimated that the officers of Fort Rice refused to allow the Seventh's wives to stay because, of the three women already there, "no two of them spoke to each other."[33] Libbie and the other disappointed wives had to return to their homes in the East for the time being.

The summer expedition getting underway would surely involve some fighting, since its purpose was to extend the railroad through the very heart of Indian country. A similar effort to protect surveyors for the Northern Pacific Railroad had been forced to turn back the year before in the face of Indian harassment. In the spring of 1872 the government had sent two separate forces to accompany the railroad surveyors, led by General David Stanley from Fort Sully, Dakota, and Major E. M. Baker from Fort Ellis, Montana. When Baker had a fight with Indians, the engineers decided to abort the survey. Baker returned to Fort Ellis, and Stanley, not finding him at the agreed-upon meeting place, waited a few days before he, too, abandoned the field. "The savages claimed a victory," George Kingsbury wrote, "because they had defeated the object of the expedition by their attack of Baker, thus preventing the uniting of the forces."[34]

The 1873 surveying party was headed by Custer's old West Point friend and Civil War opponent, Thomas Rosser. Rosser's rise from a position of menial labor to chief engineer of surveyors struck Custer as emblematic of the American character. "His determined and successful struggle against adversity," he wrote, "presents a remarkable instance of the wonderful recuperative powers of the American character."[35] During the three-month march, the two men were constantly together—riding, climbing, taking their meals at the same table, and sitting around the campfire hashing over the battles in which they had opposed each other.[36]

General Stanley would command the 1873 expedition, but because his leadership had frequently been impaired by drunkenness the year before, Rosser warned him that his incapacity would not be tolerated this time: Custer, he said, would not hesitate to relieve him of command if it became necessary.[37] It seemed as if it might indeed become necessary, since early on Lieutenant Calhoun wrote in his diary that

Stanley was "surrounded by a crowd of admiring frauds who flatter his vanity and take advantage of his love for the rosy which is inordinate and are thus enabled to carry out their own ends."[38] Later, he remarked on Stanley's unfairness in having some of his officers arrested for drunkenness: "The commanding Officer of the Expedition sets the example, his officers follow him, and while they are placed in arrest he goes unpunished."[39]

On June 20, 1873, the Yellowstone expedition set out from Fort Rice. All told, there were over a thousand fighting men—317 infantrymen in addition to 810 members of the Seventh Cavalry—accompanied by 4 surgeons, 39 scouts, 1,000 horses, 2,500 mules, 500 citizen employees, 2 correspondents, and 2 English noblemen with an American friend.[40] Like other British aristocrats to be found on the Plains, the young noblemen were along for hunting and adventure.[41]

Stanley seems to have expected to quarrel with Custer, and before long he did, once even placing Custer under arrest for a brief period. In every instance, however, Custer was in the right. One complicated incident arose when Stanley ordered Custer to provide a horse for Lieutenant P. H. Ray, chief commissary of the expedition. On his own initiative, Custer also furnished a horse to Fred Calhoun, a civilian employed by the railroad party.[42] Since the horse given to Ray had "foundered and broken down," Stanley's order of July 7 to Custer went on to specify that the horse furnished to Calhoun be returned immediately. As Stanley perceived matters, Custer had given one of Stanley's officers a useless mount, but "in violation of law and regulations" had provided a civilian with a good government horse.[43] Custer executed Stanley's order immediately, but he could not resist adding an impertinent endorsement to the effect that he saw no difference between furnishing a horse to one civilian (Calhoun), as he had done, and to another (the newspaperman Barrows), as Stanley had done.[44]

The next day, thinking further about his language, Custer wrote to Stanley that he had intended no disrespect: "What I intended and what I adhere to was to cite the decision of the Colonel Commanding in a parallel case as a precedent which I might be justified in following."[45] This failed to pacify Stanley, who called Custer to his tent, placed him under arrest, and, for good measure, ordered him to leave his Sibley stove behind.[46] Apparently, the stove had become an obsession with

Stanley, who repeated the order six times. He was convinced that the Seventh's delays in getting underway some mornings could be attributed to the stove, since a Sibley stove needs a certain amount of time to cool down before it can be packed up. One historian has suggested that the delays were actually caused by oversleeping officers who, in keeping with the Seventh's reputation, had been up late gambling the night before.[47] Their tardiness in the morning delayed breakfast, which in turn delayed the packing up of the stove.

Writing to Stanley again, Custer explained that the horse he had loaned to Fred Calhoun for a few days was the government horse provided for his own use, since he himself preferred to ride his own horses. "Nothing was farther from my intention," he protested, "than to do ought which would admit of being construed as an act of disrespect."[48] Yes and no: Custer had undoubtedly not thought that giving his horse to a member of the railroad party was in any way blameworthy. On the other hand, he had not been able to resist a retort in response to his commanding officer's admonition although he certainly knew that military orders are not intended to be the object of commentary.

Custer was released the day after his arrest, and once the record had been set straight, Stanley was apologetic. For the rest of the expedition he and Custer had good relations, to the extent that on August 1 Stanley named a new creek discovered by the expedition "Custer's Creek."[49] (Eventually there would be at least one of almost everything in the West named for Custer: a forest, a highway, a county, a town, and—until recently—a battlefield.)

While Stanley's expedition report remarked that "for the first seventeen days of our march it rained fourteen days, in some instances three or four heavy rain-falls in twenty-four hours," Custer's correspondence made no allusion to bad weather.[50] As usual he gloried in the open-air activity of a march, the experience of new country, and the opportunities for good hunting.

The expedition proceeded under the angry eyes of hostile tribes of Sioux, who, at this late stage of Indian-white relations, understood that the railroad scared away game and brought endless numbers of white settlers to threaten their way of life. Seeing Indians looking down on them from the surrounding bluffs, the expedition did not at first realize that a large village was fleeing in its path. Stanley identified the Indians as Hunkpapa Sioux, who had "at no long time since come from that center of iniquity in Indian affairs, Fort Peck."[51]

On August 4 Stanley's report noted that he "had sent Lieut. Col. Custer ahead to look up the road, a service for which he always volunteered."[52] Initially, Custer's two companies spotted only a few Indians, who appeared eager to lead them into a stand of timber. Custer resisted following, whereupon some three hundred burst out of the trees, "as if they had suddenly been shot into the world."[53] The eighty cavalrymen at first fought defensively and then turned to the attack. Although the Indians outnumbered Custer's force significantly, four hours of hard fighting inflicted losses and wore them down. They were completely routed, leaving behind battle paraphernalia and clothing in their haste to get away.[54] Custer's report of the battle referred to their abandonment of the field as "cowardly."[55]

On August 8 Custer received orders to go after the Indians, accompanied by "all the adventurous spirits in the command that could be spared," including the two young Englishmen and their American friend.[56] Since the Indians had fled precipitously, it was easy to follow their trail of cast-off articles, many of which identified them to the command as agency Indians. Some undoubtedly were, but since there was much fraternization between reservation and nonreservation Indians, the hostiles might also have obtained government goods from their agency relatives.

Pursuit abruptly ended at the river, which was too wide and too swift at that point to be crossed. Custer fumed, but the next day the battle came to him. On August 11 the cavalry woke to find itself already under fire. Correspondent Samuel Barrows would later cite this battle when he wrote of Custer, "Fear was not an element in his nature. He exposed himself freely and recklessly."[57] (Custer had given Libbie repeated assurances that he would not expose himself "freely and recklessly," but this was a common observation of his behavior in battle.) With the help of the infantry and the guns, the Indians were again defeated at little cost to the army. James Calhoun observed in his diary that the Englishmen, who had participated in the fight, thought that "Indian fighting was the best sport in the world."[58] The Seventh Cavalry had reason to share their view: nothing in these last fights before the Little Bighorn suggested that they should worry about meeting Indians on the field of battle. On the contrary, Custer's article about the expedition, published almost simultaneously with his death, revealed a sense of mastery and control in Indian fighting. About the battle of August 4, he wrote: "The troopers, most of them being thoroughly accustomed to Indian fighting, preserved the most admirable coolness from the moment the fight began. Some even indulged in merry-making remarks tinctured at times with the drollest humor."[59]

In the midst of their success, however, they were reminded once again of the dangers of "straggling." August 4 had been "an awful day for heat," and the men's throats were parched. Two men, August Baliran, the sutler, and Joseph Honsinger, the veterinarian, succumbed to a longing for water and rode off to a creek a short distance from the regiment, where they were surprised and killed by Indians.[60] These deaths would have ramifications.

The rest of the expedition was uneventful, but one small detail touches the imagination. On August 19 three head of cattle were found. They were "in fine condition and thought to be part of Major Baker's herd of last year."[61] Although Lieutenant Calhoun had noted in his diary that wolves prowling around the expedition's cattle had been a constant nuisance, these cows had inexplicably survived wolves, Indians, and a Montana winter.[62]

The Yellowstone expedition of 1873 was successful both in achieving its goals for the railroad and for Custer personally. The engineers mapped a better route than the one considered the year before, a route that would save many miles of track and make the extension of the railroad more financially feasible. With the conclusion of the expedition Custer was poised to assume command at the new post of Fort Abraham Lincoln, which was situated across the river from the young town of Bismarck, a bustling community whose residents had increased from two hundred to twelve hundred in a year. Founded as the terminus of the Northern Pacific, and originally named Edwinton after a railroad surveyor, the town was later renamed Bismarck to attract German capital to the railroad.[63] It had eighteen saloons and two churches, giving it a shade more respectability than the Hays City of Custer's time, which had twenty-two saloons and no churches.[64] An old-time resident maintained that a respectable woman could always go about on the streets safely, fearing neither insult nor molestation.[65] Conveniently located across the river from the fort, an unsavory area of brothels and gambling dens called Point Pleasant, or sometimes simply "the Point," attracted soldiers to various kinds of vice and death. Shootings were common, as were accidental drownings when, after an evening's inebriation, men attempted to return to their barracks by crossing the river on moving cakes of ice.[66]

After overseeing the final arrangements for the imposing house that he and Libbie would occupy at Fort Abraham Lincoln, Custer went East to visit his parents and bring back Libbie and her friend Agnes Bates. The three were royally welcomed to the post, where the Custers would have a real home together for fewer than three years. In fact, the newly built commander's quarters lasted only a few months. On February 6, 1874, typical of those cataclysmic misfortunes that pepper the memoirs of frontier army wives, the Custers' first home burned to the ground, costing Libbie and Agnes their wardrobes and destroying some cherished Custer memorabilia as well. The house was swiftly rebuilt, grander than ever.

Domesticity would come to the fore in this last period of Custer's life. Between the two Sioux campaigns of 1873 and 1876, the only official duty that took him away from Libbie and their happy days at Fort Lincoln was a reconnaissance expedition into the Black Hills in the summer of 1874. This was more of a leisurely male retreat specializing in hunting and science than an army exercise, and after that he stayed put until the Sioux campaign of 1876. Long leaves would give him a chance to pursue his business interests—unsuccessfully.

George Bird Grinnell, who occasionally visited the Custers at Fort Lincoln while waiting for the Black Hills expedition to assemble, left a brief but memorable picture of the Custer marriage, Custer "delighted to relate his hunting exploits" and Libbie "extremely kind and hospitable."[67] Other comments Grinnell made indicate that he disliked what struck him as Custer's bragging about his prowess as a hunter. Custer, who kept meticulous records of his achievements on the hunt, might have annoyed guests with these stories while Libbie palliated their annoyance with her charm and hospitality.[68]

Luther North, who came along on the Black Hills expedition as Grinnell's assistant, recalled that "Custer was quite sociable and did a good deal of talking. He was a very enthusiastic hunter, and was always telling of the good shooting he had done." But, he added, "He didn't seem to care much about hearing of any one else doing good shooting."[69]

Just as he tallied the number of Indian dead and captured, the number of lodges destroyed, and other such data in his official report on the Battle of the Washita, Custer tallied what he killed hunting. Summing up the Yellowstone expedition of 1873, he gave Libbie the following totals: "forty-one antelope, four buffalo, four elk, seven deer (four of them blacktails), two white wolves, and one red fox. Geese, ducks, prairie-chickens, and sage-hens without number completed my summer's record." He added: "No one assisted me in killing the antelope, deer, or elk, except one of the latter."[70]

Custer was not only an avid hunter, he studied taxidermy to preserve what he had killed.[71] In cataloging the furnishings of her husband's library, Libbie unconsciously revealed a monument to killing, a museum of Plains' species in which the glassy eyes of stuffed specimens looked out at the Custers from every direction. She mentioned the heads of buffalo, bear, black-tailed deer, and antelope. Of the smaller animals, the room contained a jackrabbit, a yellow fox, and a "tiny fox with a brush—called out there a swift." Birds were represented by a sandhill crane, a mountain eagle, and a great white owl. Other animals existed only as skins—an enormous bearskin rug in front of the fireplace, beaver and cougar skins on the chairs. Military accoutrements such as spurs and riding whips were hung on antlers, a further reduction of animal to artifact, and one corner of the room was reserved for Custer's collection of firearms, the means of bringing down even more specimens. Having described it all, Libbie commented thoughtfully: "The firelight reflected the large, glittering eyes of the animals' heads, and except that we were such a jolly family, the surroundings would have suggested arenas and martyrs."[72]

Although a newcomer might be forced to hear the Custer hunting stories, according to Libbie, her husband generally preferred to avoid the ordinary social circle and spend his evenings in his library: "His own studious habits made it a deprivation if he gave up much of his time to entertaining."[73] The child is not always father to the man, for certainly none of Custer's West Point classmates would have recognized the studious individual Libbie described, a man who shunned company and marked the course of the French and English armies on a map as he read book after book on Napoleon.[74] Nor did his habit of weighty reading begin at Fort Abraham Lincoln. The chaplain from Custer's service at Fort Hays wrote to Libbie after the publication of *"Boots and Sad-*

dles" to say that Custer had borrowed Carlyle and Frederick the Great from him.[75]

The spring of 1875 found Custer riding into Bismarck with a company of cavalry to repossess army grain that had been stolen from Fort Lincoln. The grain and two persons involved in its theft were taken back to Fort Lincoln, where the civilian thieves were imprisoned along with Rain-in-the-Face, the Hunkpapa who had bragged of killing Honsinger and Baliran during the Yellowstone expedition. In the same way that he had marched into Bismarck and arrested two of its citizens, Custer sent a party of the Seventh Cavalry under Captain George Yates to Standing Rock Agency to bring in the guilty warrior. However satisfying emotionally, from a legal point of view they were both dubious actions, more kidnappings than otherwise. Later, the incarcerated thieves—and Rain-in-the-Face along with them—mysteriously made their escape.[76]

Their cameo roles in the life of Custer over, the grain bandits drifted back into their world, not to be heard from again; the Hunkpapa warrior Rain-in-the-Face, on the other hand, became a legendary actor at the Battle of the Little Bighorn, endowed with all the bloody-minded revenge that white mythmakers and his own braggadocio could give him.

PART FOUR

1876

18

Prelude

"Don't you ever get mixed up with these politicians, Jack," he said, with a forced smile, "they've killed many a good man before you and me." —Custer in *The Master of the Strong Hearts,* a novel for boys

During his final years at Fort Abraham Lincoln, Custer remained unpromoted, a disappointment to him, but not a bitter one. When he had time on his hands in Elizabethtown, he had begun writing an account of his early years in Kansas, articles that were first published in *Galaxy* magazine and then issued as a book, *My Life on the Plains,* in 1874. This was one new occupation; another was taxidermy; still another paleontology, as the indifferent student of West Point was replaced by a man who worked to master his environment through knowledge, returning from each foray with prize specimens. Yet while he developed an intellectual potential that had not been stirred by formal education, his keenly sensuous apprehension of life, his ability to savor the moment, was undiminished. In 1873 he wrote from the Yellowstone River that "each step was a kaleidoscopic shifting of views, sublime beyond description."[1] Letters from the following year's exploration of the Black Hills were equally ecstatic, describing his hunting exploits and the wonders of the new terrain with equal measures of enthusiasm. Custer pronounced the country "rich and beautiful" and the expedition "a success, exceeding the expectations of the most sanguine."[2]

While his interests were constantly expanding to include new areas, he did not at the same time deepen his knowledge of human behavior, especially in the political arena. He was always more concerned with testing himself against his surroundings—learning the land. Far from

Eastern centers of power, with a brother, sister, brother-in-law, wife, and a circle of devoted friends sharing his life, Custer lived in a world removed from his enemies and remote from day-to-day political considerations. But the expedition into the Black Hills in the summer of 1874 brought him into the public eye once again. When he publicized the finding of gold, a politically sensitive issue and one that had not been his expedition's concern, Custer created a dilemma for the government, committed by treaty to Indian sovereignty in that region but responsive to the pressure of white mining interests. As a result of his indiscretion, the follow-up expedition of 1875 was assigned to another officer.

When a campaign against the Sioux was planned for 1876 with Custer expected to be the field commander of a large force, it looked like the last chance to win an impressive victory over the Indians—and the long-sought promotion for Custer. Many Sioux were already on reservations: after the mopping-up operation of 1876, it was assumed that there would be no further need to fight them.

Eighteen seventy-six was a milestone year for the country, capped by a lavish Centennial Exhibition in Philadelphia celebrating the achievements of the nation's first hundred years, its growth from four to forty million inhabitants and from thirteen to thirty-eight states. In 1854, Samuel Colt, the inventor of the famous six-shooter, had told the British Parliament, "There is nothing that cannot be produced by machinery."[3] This was the spirit embodied in the giant Corliss steam engine that was the centerpiece of the Exhibition, but in terms of posterity more accurately represented by Alexander Graham Bell's new and as yet unappreciated invention, the telephone. In the Exhibition's six months its 450 acres were visited by eight million people, including—not long before his death—George Armstrong Custer.

Custer could not have foreseen a few months before that he would be brought East by his involvement in the gathering scandals of the Grant administration. Grant, who had voted only once before he ran for president, was arguably the least qualified as well as the youngest man to hold that office. His ignorance of governmental institutions and political process was equaled only by his complacency about this lack of knowledge. As president, he behaved as he had as general: in addition to his trademark whiskey and cigars, he brought to the office a penchant for favoring his friends and an expectation that his orders would be obeyed. Had he had better judgment, these proclivities need not have damaged his presidency, but as William Cullen Bryant concluded after Grant's first two nominees for the Supreme Court were rejected, he lacked "the discernment necessary for putting proper men in their proper places."[4]

By 1876 it had become clear that the proper place for some of the men to whom Grant had assigned high office was jail. The year opened with the exposure of a major scandal, the Whiskey Ring's large-scale conspiracy to defraud the government. Grant's friend John McDonald had masterminded a scheme to divert huge sums of whiskey tax money into his own pockets, and those of his coconspirators—who included Grant's confidential secretary, Orville Babcock. The ring had been so powerful and well connected that the secretary of the treasury, Benjamin Bristow, had had to conduct a secret investigation in order to gather the necessary evidence for public prosecution.

It is obligatory in any discussion of the scandals of Grant's administration to acknowledge that the president himself was an honest man. But it should be added that Grant must have been the most credulous and inept of honest men, choosing as friends and associates so many dubious characters whose misuse of government office and influence escaped his notice. Not long before Bristow's perseverance had brought the Whiskey Ring to light, both the president and Babcock had accepted expensive presents from its chief malefactors. James G. Blaine, the well-known Republican senator from Maine and a contender for the presidential nomination, was widely quoted that spring when he said, "I have no influence with the present administration. No man has who is not a thief by instinct."[5]

The public was already sufficiently alarmed by the extent of corruption revealed in a series of scandals that had recently come to light. In addition to the Whiskey Ring scandal, the Crédit Mobilier fraud had charged the public ninety-four million dollars for railroad trackage that cost forty-four million to lay, and in the process enriched a number of public officials—including Custer's first patron, John Bingham.[6] Many people must have felt as Mabel Hubbard did when she wrote to her fiancé, Alexander Graham Bell, about the latest example of government corruption: "Belknap's iniquity, coming after all those other stories and scandals, makes us feel as if there were no justice in such a sink of corruption as Washington."[7] Hubbard referred to William Belknap, another military friend of Grant's, who served in the cabinet as secretary of war. Only six days after the end of Babcock's trial, in which the bribe-taking secretary was acquitted but not vindicated, the sensational Belknap affair claimed the public's attention.

At his own post Custer had discovered that goods that could be bought for much less in the nearby town of Bismarck were sold by the trader at exorbitant prices. He instructed his officers and men to make their purchases in town, only to have an irate trader appeal to Belknap, who in turn instructed Custer that all business must be done through the trader. Custer fumed at the patent injustice to the poorly paid troops, who were nevertheless forced to enrich the secretary of war's appointee, and at the bridling of his own authority. He was so annoyed that when the secretary paid a visit of a few hours to Fort Abraham Lincoln, Custer violated protocol by not meeting him at the boundary of the post, although apparently Belknap was unaware of this slight.[8]

Custer was probably pleased to see Belknap caught in trouble typical of the Grant administration, although in this case the involvement of Belknap's wife added an extra fillip of scandal. During the Civil War Belknap had met two Kentucky belles, the beautiful, vivacious, and extravagant Tomlinson sisters, each of whom captivated Washington society in turn. Carrie became Belknap's first wife, but the younger sister, Amanda—known as Puss—also became a part of her brother-in-law's household after she was widowed and her sister took sick. The first Mrs. Belknap died in 1870, leaving an infant whose care was undertaken by her sister.

This sister, described by a contemporary as "the most beautiful woman I ever saw in Washington or anywhere . . . perfect," soon became engaged to her former brother-in-law.[9] She did not immediately marry him, however, preferring to go to Paris for a year to purchase an elaborate trousseau. When she returned with a high-fashion wardrobe, including forty pairs of shoes, she was ready to emerge as the most dazzling woman in Washington society.[10]

Underpinning the glitter and glamor so freely indulged in by the second Mrs. Belknap was a sordid arrangement for post tradership kickbacks, one of which had been originated by the enterprising first Mrs. Belknap. The lucrative Fort Sill tradership had been procured for William Marsh, whose wife was a girlhood friend of the Tomlinson sisters. Marsh remained in New York City, having nothing to do with the Fort Sill tradership other than collecting the agreed-upon sum of twelve thousand dollars a year from the man who continued to be the trader.

He divided this money equally with the first Mrs. Belknap, and then, after her death, with the second Mrs. Belknap and Belknap himself. Profits dwindled, and eventually Marsh was disposed to tell his tale to the House Committee on Expenditures in the War Department. His testimony, on February 29, 1876, spelled the end for Belknap.

The morning after the world learned these details, Belknap rushed to the White House to resign, thinking in this fashion to avoid impeachment and save his wife from public scandal. Not having the facts of the case did not deter Grant from accepting his friend's resignation; the Victorian impulse to shield women from dishonor, as Major Reno's court-martial a year later would demonstrate, was still a powerful component in the male code of behavior.

Congressional Democrats were not so easily moved. They continued their investigation, or rather their efforts to embarrass the president, since they lacked the two-thirds vote necessary for impeachment. It was the summons to testify at these hearings that brought Custer to Washington in the spring of 1876.

Accounts vary as to how the House Committee headed by Heister Clymer obtained Custer's name. Custer critics assume that he volunteered out of antipathy for Belknap and love of publicity, but the historian John Gray offers another view. He believes that Captain George A. Armes, a perennial thorn in the flesh of the army, provoked the investigation of Belknap by giving an exposé to the *New York Herald* and persuading Clymer to take up the matter. Gray further asserts that Custer's name turned up on a list of witnesses compiled by Colonel William Hazen, an outspoken critic of post tradership corruption.[11] In any case, the summons was a command performance.

Custer always appreciated an opportunity to come in from the periphery of his remote frontier post to the center of political power. Such a visit gave him a chance to renew old acquaintances, hear the latest news, and enjoy theater and music. Possibly he felt safe because he had the approval of General Sherman and the active support of General Sheridan, the two most powerful generals in the army. Lacking political skills himself, Custer may not have noticed that Sheridan never endangered his own position for anyone else. Nor, apparently, was he aware of what everyone in Washington knew by now: that Grant was loyal to his friends and vindictive to his, and their, enemies.

Well before this scandal broke, neither General of the Army William Tecumseh Sherman nor Lieutenant Colonel George Armstrong

Custer regarded Belknap as a satisfactory secretary of war. Sherman's resentment at being bypassed in the decision-making process by a man he had commanded in the Civil War had caused him to leave Washington and establish his headquarters in St. Louis. Custer, as the commanding officer at Fort Abraham Lincoln, felt similarly bypassed by the secretary's policy of appointing post traders from Washington rather than continuing the traditional practice of allowing local commanders to make the appointments.

Congressman Clymer, once Belknap's Princeton roommate, now his prosecutor, realized that in Custer he had a star witness. Although the renowned Civil War hero and Indian fighter had no startling revelations, just logical suspicions based on meager firsthand knowledge, his testimony could generate bad publicity for the administration. Clymer insisted on recalling him for a second appearance.

The transcript of Custer's participation in the committee hearings suggests a conscientious attempt to be truthful and professional coupled with a complete failure to understand the political implications of his testimony. "No one who witnessed the earnest manner in which he gave his testimony," the pro-Republican *New York Times* wrote, "doubts the sincerity of his convictions," yet there was little of real help to the committee and almost every utterance had something in it that could make the president furious.[12]

The unscathed survivor of so many fierce military battles, Custer must have imagined that he was invulnerable in the political arena as well. His behavior at the Little Bighorn has often been attributed to this sense of being untouchable, but it is equally germane to his incautious testimony in the congressional hearings on the sale of post traderships. Revisionist biographer Frederic Van De Water scarcely exaggerated when he wrote that "no man determined on self-ruination could have gone further."[13]

When Custer was asked about furnishing the president's brother, Orvil Grant, with transportation to visit trading posts, he replied: "I told him I would not give it to him as a trader but that to any member of the President's family visiting there, out of courtesy to the President of the United States, I would render any facility I could."[14] Such nice distinctions must have seemed ludicrous to Washington insiders, or to anyone who had been following the revelations of gross corruption in the administration.

Asked a leading question, how the secretary of war's preemption of the power to appoint post traders had affected the morale of the army, Custer failed to take the hint. He replied that in his opinion it had not affected morale. It had, more mundanely, "greatly increased the inconveniences and expense of living on the frontier."[15] Custer elaborated earnestly on this point, a great wrong in his mind but less than incendiary compared to the huge inflation of prices engineered by the Crédit Mobilier schemers and the millions pocketed by the Whiskey Ring—both government scandals that the public had been familiar with for some time.

Custer told an undoubtedly bored committee that he "had known the post-trader at Fort Lincoln to go out and stop an officer's wagon, driven by his servant, and inspect the wagon to see what was in it, and threaten to use his influence with the Secretary of War because we traded with a town five miles distant, where we got things about half his prices."[16] An irritation to the post commander and the personnel of the fort, to be sure, but hardly the stuff of scandal, let alone impeachment!

The hearings were a minefield for Custer, but his political naïveté was so extreme that he wrote to Libbie that he was being careful when he was actually setting off charges right and left. His testimony bristled with contempt for Belknap and with references to fraud and corruption that could only be embarrassing to the now beleaguered Grant administration.

At the same time, and this is probably what Custer meant in his letter to Libbie, he was meticulous in distinguishing between fact and hearsay in his own responses. About kickbacks he said carefully that "it was a matter of common report and common information among the officers and men, that the trader had to pay a tax to outside people; but it was impossible to trace this tax."[17] He said that it was "the general impression along the river" that the creation of the Great Sioux Reservation had been for the benefit of traders.[18] When asked if the reservation had dispossessed any whites, he replied precisely: "I cannot say that it dispossessed people who had acquired title because I am not sufficiently familiar with the legality of their title, but I know that it dispossessed people who claimed that they had a title."[19]

One incident he discussed would later require a specific retraction, the case of a shipment of corn in sacks marked "Indian Department." Custer had refused to accept the corn, he told the committee, believing that it had already been paid for as provisions for the Indians. He reported his suspicion to General Alfred Terry and in due course received an order from Terry to accept the corn, which, following orders, he did. When he was asked if he had any doubt that the corn had been paid for twice by the government, Custer responded both carefully and forthrightly: "I believe that it was paid for twice; but I cannot prove it any better than I have told you, because when they gave me the order to receive it, I considered that I was relieved from all responsibility in the matter."[20] This, of course, cast some doubt on his immediate superior, General Terry.

All told, Custer's assessment of the corn transaction was reasonable, but it turned out to be at least partially wrong. When Terry explained to Custer that the transaction had been aboveboard, Custer promptly sent a telegram to retract that part of his testimony. Lost in the exchange was the fact that, however valid the purchase by the army, the corn had been significantly underweight—a widespread form of fraud in the furnishing of provisions.

When asked why he had not spoken out against the various abuses about which he had testified, Custer told the committee that the secretary of war's "gag rule" of March 15, 1873, required any officer's statement to be first vetted by the secretary. Moreover, he noted that Colonel Hazen, the officer who *had* spoken out, was presently languishing in a very undesirable post—the desolate Fort Buford.[21]

The Grants were very fond of the Belknaps, and Grant had become increasingly irritable during the hearings.[22] His brother Orvil and brother-in-law John Dent both enjoyed the profits from post traderships in exactly the way that Caleb Marsh and William Belknap had done. The freewheeling Custer was a convenient focus for Grant's anger over the entire affair: when Custer applied for leave to return to his post, the president would neither see him nor allow him to join the campaign against the Sioux. Custer was treated shabbily, denied access to the president, and then arrested for having left Washington without seeing him.

A number of newspapers excoriated Grant for, as the *New York World* put it, "a scandalous performance."[23] This bad publicity may have been as influential as the intercession of Generals Sherman, Sheridan, and Terry on Custer's behalf.

In supporting Custer's petition Sheridan nevertheless chided him for having attacked "his brother officers," an inaccurate description since neither the secretary of war nor the president's brother were fellow army officers at the time. On the contrary, Custer had spoken *on behalf of* "his brother officers," forced to pay inflated prices to support the system of tradership kickbacks and muzzled by Belknap's order. That Custer fell to his knees and with tears in his eyes begged his superior, General Terry, to help him regain the Sioux campaign may be an invention of Terry's aide and brother-in-law Colonel Robert Hughes, a man ever ready to laud Terry at the expense of others. A persistent story has it that Terry actually composed Custer's telegram to Grant, pleading for his reinstatement, but this also seems implausible since Custer wrote with facility. Terry may have made suggestions or edited Custer's draft; certainly he was disposed to be helpful, not simply because he was a decent man whose sense of fair play inclined him to take Custer's part, but because he believed that Custer would be essential to the campaign's success.

Custer's telegram appealed to the president "as a soldier to spare me the humiliation of seeing my regiment march to meet the enemy & I not to share its dangers."[24] With much of the press criticizing Grant for his treatment of Custer, and with Terry, Sheridan, and Sherman supporting a reconsideration, the president relented to the extent that he allowed Custer to command his regiment. Terry was still required to take the field as commander of the entire force, however. In as short a time as practicable after this decision, the expedition would begin its march from Fort Abraham Lincoln toward the historic moment on the Little Bighorn.

Retrospectively, it is tempting to view the last period of a life as culminating in some sense other than its literal ending, and in Custer's case, his dramatic death was preceded by other climactic events. In several respects it was a turbulent time in his life: even before he became unwittingly embroiled in the politics of the Grant administration, he had suffered the most serious financial reverses of his life. There would be no time to remedy the situation before he marched off to his death, but this may have been just as well: even a cursory familiarity with Custer's life makes clear that the famous "Custer's luck" did not extend to business. His plans for recouping losses invariably led to greater losses.

The reporter Theodore Davis, who accompanied Custer on his first Indian expedition, said that Custer "did not swear, drink whisky or use tobacco in any form—But he drew the line at cards."[25] With the exception of occasional periods of remorse Custer was an inveterate gambler, an enthusiastic horse racer and poker player who was capable of losing larger sums than a man of his means could afford. These peccadillos might have informed the testy response he once made to the accusation that some of his officers were addicted to gambling:

> Exactly what meaning is intended to apply to the word "gambling" which is construed differently by different persons I am at a loss to understand. If by gambling the act of betting money or risking it on games of chance or contests of speed between horses and if among games of chance are included that usually known as poker, and similar games, my answer is that so far as my knowledge and belief extends none of the officers of this command are "addicted to gambling" except the Commanding Officer and he is addicted to it only so far as it neither interfere with his duties, violate any rule of propriety nor meddle with other people's business.[26]

This last was undoubtedly a pointed remark.

According to John Burkman, Custer's striker, Custer once gambled away money saved for a holiday trip to New York, then made it back by arranging a horse race that he handily won. At other times the Custers were forced into drastic economies on their holidays, probably because of his gambling. If Burkman, who worshiped Custer, is to be believed, Custer bet as much as a thousand dollars in the above game.[27]

Libbie's memoirs portray a lighthearted husband who cared nothing for money, a statement she supports—significantly—by saying that no one so incapable of holding on to it could be assumed to care for it. In spite of this description, Custer was constantly making efforts to supplement his modest salary, and these invariably ended badly.

An early experience might be regarded as predictive. On September 20, 1864, Custer's father wrote to say that a horse his son had sent had arrived: "He looks bad. He is prety thin and his Main is spoiled it is about half off. Mr. Wallis says that he has been prety sick. . . . I wish you had told me what the horse cost you and what the cost was for bringing him out. I should not like to loose any money on him. I have always been afraid to deal in high priced horses."[28] Without doing so directly, Emmanuel Custer seemed to be advising his son to be more careful about his horse purchases, a lesson that Custer was unable to learn.

None of Custer's racehorses ever distinguished itself except Don Juan, an excellent stallion captured in Virginia during the Civil War and bought from the army for a mere $125. When Custer checked its record in the turf register at the office of the racing journal, *Wilkes' Spirit of the Times*, he learned that it had a superb pedigree and a value of $10,000. The record for the mile was 1:44. Don Juan had run it in 1:46 and could be considered, Custer was told, the sixth fastest horse in the country.[29] But Don Juan died unexpectedly.

Frederick Whittaker, Custer's first biographer, claims that Custer lost $10,000 trading horses during the period he was stationed in Elizabethtown, Kentucky: "No sooner had he paid his money for a valuable mare, than the mare would be kicked by another, and get a broken leg, or fall sick or die; and in this way, horse ventures all came to grief."[30] Custer had also bought property in Kansas, but it, too, promised no great return. His house remained unrented; the land did not appreciate.

During a four-month leave in 1871 Custer went to New York with the explicit purpose of obtaining venture capital for an investment proposed to him by Colonel Jarius Hall, a Monroe veteran of the Michigan Brigade. The western half of the Stevens silver lode near Georgetown, Colorado, already belonged to the Crescent Silver Mining Company of Cincinnati, but the eastern half could be bought for $100,000. Shares were $50, and Custer was listed in the amount of $35,000, a sum that most historians agree he could not actually have put up.[31] In March Custer wrote to Brigadier General E. D. Townsend, adjutant general of the army, requesting an extension of his leave because it would "secure to me the sum of about thirty thousand dollars which I am liable to lose if called away at the expiration of my present leave.[32] This was probably a commission for the use of his name and for his promotional efforts: he did, in fact, sign up some of the New York financiers he had met socially after the war. Among others, August Belmont invested $15,000 and John Jacob Astor, $10,000.[33] Characteristically, Custer was optimistic. He wrote to Libbie, "Can it be that my little Standby and I who have long wished to possess a small fortune, are about to have our hopes and wishes realized? If I succeed in this operation as now seems certain, it is to be but the stepping stone to large and more profitable undertakings."[34]

A series of letters from Hall revealed that little by little these grandiose hopes had to be relinquished. The letters repeatedly attempted to reassure Custer, but as time passed without any more tangible proof than Hall's good intentions, even the optimistic Custer must have become disheartened. "I have delayed writing three or four days," Hall wrote in 1872, "that I might if possible tell you of a favorable report, but the fact is matters are badly mixed and I must ask you to wait another week at least."[35] Two years later, it was the same story, the prospect of good news in the future mixed with entanglements in the present. Hall hinted that "some dispute with the Crescent Company is liable to arise"—hardly surprising since the lode had been divided between Crescent and the Hall-Custer interests—but, he continued assertively as always, he would maintain his rights and "protect the trust deed held by our New York friends." He further reminded Custer that "it [the Stevens mine] is regarded as one of the rich mines of Colorado, at least that portion belonging to us."[36]

Over the course of Hall's correspondence (Custer's letters are missing) it became apparent that the mine had been seriously undercapitalized. "If we can clear off the indebtedness on the mine, raise a few dollars for our pocket and raise a working capital," Hall wrote to Custer in 1875, "we will some day have a mine that we can keep or sell. The mine is a good one and is all that has been claimed for it."[37] This letter implied that a substantial part of the amount of purchase had not been raised in 1871, but borrowed. The happy prospects Custer had envisioned for Libbie depended upon raising still more money. Two months later, little more than a year before his death, Custer's request to sell his interest in the mine produced this confession from Hall: "I hardly know of anything to say, or suggest in regard to the Stevens but will do the best I can in Colorado and try to sell it to another party. Your interest in the profits shall be equal to my own and I will do the best I can. The debt against the property cripples it, but I trust that it can be paid off and leave a small margin for us."[38] There had been no bad faith involved in this venture, simply an eagerness to rush ahead without the necessary capital. In later years, for other owners, the Stevens mine justified Hall's sanguine predictions.[39]

With the collapse of his hopes for a mining fortune, Custer began a series of railroad stock speculations that would leave him owing $8,578 to the stockbrokerage firm of Justh and Company. On February 10, 1876, he signed a six-month promissory note for this debt at 7 percent.[40] When the note fell due after Custer's death, it was a shock to Libbie, who was already struggling with an estate of less than $3,000 and liabilities totaling over $13, 000.[41]

Seven years later, dissatisfied with the Custer estate's settlement of only ten cents on the dollar, Justh would seek to recuperate the remainder from Custer's cosigner, Ben Holladay, a Western transportation magnate. This resulted in an embarrassing public exposure of the debt in 1883 when the suit came to trial. Justh won at first, but the Supreme Court of the District of Columbia reversed the decision on the grounds that it was a gambling debt.[42] By prevailing standards, such an assumption was unduly harsh. As the court itself remarked, "the extent of this form of speculation now rife in our country is unprecedented."[43] Citing "financial authorities," the court stated that an "enormous total of 128,162,466 shares . . . representing the prodigious sum of twelve billion eight hundred and sixteen millions two hundred and forty-six thousand dollars" had been sold during 1881 alone, the majority of which transactions were no different from other forms of gambling. The court viewed this practice as "pernicious traffic," demoralizing the community and often ruining the humble along with the mighty. It obviously intended its verdict in *Justh v. Holladay* to serve as an object lesson to speculators.

In the opinion of Mr. Justice Hagner, Custer's language in his correspondence with Justh was evidence of "an illicit business, with which Custer was rather ashamed to be connected." Nothing in the letters seems to support such a pejorative reading. In both, Custer acknowledged his debt emphatically, but the first letter may be regarded as simply the reassurance an impecunious man gives his debtor that he is in good faith: "I have acknowledged to you verbally and in writing that I am indebted to you, and should you deem it your interest to resort to law, I will certainly, if placed upon the stand, acknowledge the same fact in open court." The second letter is equally earnest and reassuring, but it introduces another element: "The circumstances under which this debt was contracted render my obligation concerning it peculiarly binding, and I consider my honor pledged to effect the discharge of my indebtedness to you at the earliest date practicable."[44]

The "circumstances" Custer alluded to might have been his recommendation to Justh by a mutual friend, Rufus Ingalls, which in turn disposed the stockbroker to give Custer particularly favorable terms. Such circumstances would have colored their business relationship and intensified Custer's chagrin when he found himself owing an amount that he had no means of repaying. Ingalls was a military man, Grant's assistant adjutant general, whom Custer had met and become friendly with early in his career on the Plains.[45]

Justice Hagner was also suspicious of a note Custer had sent to Justh ordering a stock purchase and stipulating that if Justh was unwilling to carry out the transaction, he should write to Custer but have his message delivered by someone "not connected with your office." The justice observed that "the poor man showed more caution and strategy in this communication than he displayed in his last fatal campaign." Why do all this, he asked rhetorically, "unless he was engaged in a gambling stock transaction, which he was unwilling should be known?"[46] The justice's assumption seems highly speculative itself since the mere fact of receiving a message from a legitimate brokerage would hardly constitute evidence of wrongdoing in anyone's eyes. Only one person might have warranted such precautions—Libbie. By the time of the "suspicious" note, Libbie had joined her husband in New York, and secrecy would have been advisable to conceal the precarious nature of his stock dealings from her. Her letters from New York at the time are full of pride that her husband was so much in demand socially; there is no hint that she knew of his increasingly troubled financial affairs. Had she known, her holiday would have been spoiled by anxiety about the magnitude of Custer's losses.

Justice Hagner's last animadversion on the subject concerned the disparity between Custer's slender resources and the "immense amount" of business he had undertaken with Justh. Custer was always optimistic that his ventures would succeed, and he probably reported his assets to Justh in the best light. Ben Holladay, who cosigned the promissory note that Custer eventually signed, had at one time controlled a considerable fortune but by then was ruined. Surely it was the responsibility of Justh to assess the situation objectively and limit his backing. Most likely, in the all-too-lax environment of the Gilded Age, he failed to do so because Holladay, too, was a friend and business associate of Ingalls. That Custer intended to defraud the broker in any way is not supported by any evidence.

Justh's case was not helped by his own unforthcoming testimony. Although he testified that his transactions for Custer did not differ from any other margin transactions, and that he trusted his client (an assertion he made twice), the court seemed determined to regard the case according to its own prejudices: "His testimony abounds throughout in . . . expressions from the vernacular of the stock market, which would naturally be used in describing illicit purchases and sales upon margin."[47] It seems in the court's eyes that sales upon margin were always illicit purchases. In fact, in the Wall Street of the time, it was difficult to separate the two kinds of transactions. "The vast majority," as one historian has written, "were virtually gambling."[48]

The court's reasoning in the case of *Justh v. Holladay* was more in keeping with its own conviction that stock speculation was a pernicious evil than with actual law. At that time speculators were bound by no rules other than "the natural ones of the market."[49] As Custer had written, the word *gambling* is construed differently by different people, and had he been alive at the time of the suit, he would have argued that he had been engaged in a legitimate speculation.[50] Certainly his correspondence suggests the condition of bona fides that constituted one test of legitimacy. The 1865 *Manual of the Stock Exchange* in effect at the time states that "when a speculator cannot pay over the full value of a stock, the broker may favor him with a loan."[51] The amount of the loan was left to the individual broker's discretion. Until the stock market crash of 1929, buying stocks on margin with very little money down was neither illegal nor uncommon.

It was also, as the court clearly and censoriously realized, enormously attractive. As one history of the New York Stock Exchange commented wistfully, "If the customer would buy, only in such amounts, and only of such stocks as will leave him a sufficient reserve, all troubles from margin calls would be escaped. However, the desire to make a large profit is often very alluring—all business men meet it, and all salesmen take advantage of that desire."[52] That Custer had such a desire is undeniable; that he received a special dispensation because of his connections would have been in no way exceptional. The resulting series of transactions was certainly a prime example of the evils of untrammeled speculation on margin, the kind of thing that would later be regulated, but it was hardly as Judge Hagner described it, "an illicit business, with which Custer was rather ashamed to be connected."

More serious charges of influence peddling and illegitimate manipulation have recently been raised against Custer, based entirely on a letter to Custer from Rufus Ingalls. Referring to himself and Ben Holladay, Ingalls wrote:

> We want to do a big thing in Black Hills, and we can have half a million money put up to carry it through—We have any amount of Sioux and Valentine Scrip besides—Ben wants to put in stages and be Sutler to new Posts. He has promise of Interior for Indian Trade. He hopes a Depot. . . . Now, what think you! Ben counts much on you—he can put on Stages from Union Pacific also. Now, what should he do to be in right *place*, right *time*? . . . If I can have control over whole subject of horse shoes &c, I mean to ask a Board with yourself as President. The Goodenough and Elastic Companies want an officer to go to Europe. It can be easily managed—if-if-if their shoes are actually the *best*—about which I am doubtful more than half the time. What think you? . . . Let me know what I can best do.[53]

On the basis of this letter alone historian Richard Slotkin concluded that Custer "was capable of countenancing and participating in a scheme to deliberately defraud the Army on the buying of horseshoes of dubious quality." He goes on to say, "The letter also suggests that Custer, for all his public opposition to the 'Indian Ring' and to Belknap's granting of post sutlerships, was not adverse to profiting from such enterprises himself."[54]

Yet there is no evidence that Custer acted upon any of the propositions made by Ingalls, nor does the letter itself support the idea that Custer was being asked to do something fraudulent. Ingalls intimated that the horseshoe manufacturer might give Custer a trip to Europe if it was awarded the army contract by a board headed by Custer. But he *did not* suggest that Custer throw the contract to Goodenough if the horseshoes were not in fact "good enough." On the contrary, he wrote, "It can be easily managed *if-if-if their shoes are actually the best—about which I am doubtful more than half the time* [my emphasis]." If truly fraudulent arrangements were being made, the quality of the product would have been irrelevant.

A prominent military figure like Custer, who had commanded the first army expedition to the Black Hills, could have been helpful to men seeking business in the region, but Ingalls and Holladay did not need to rely on Custer. Holladay, a well-known figure in the field of Western transportation,[55] already had influence in the Department of the Interior, according to Ingalls's letter. Furthermore, neither stage lines nor post traderships were in Custer's gift, nor did he have influence in government quarters that would have been helpful to his prospective business associates. Just the opposite: he had already quarreled with Secretary of War Belknap, who had overruled him on the trader's practices at his own post. The most he could do would be to direct Ingalls and Holladay to the proper place to pursue their projects, and he may well have done so.

In February of 1876 Holladay cosigned Custer's note to Justh and Company, but it is difficult to see this as a pay-off rather than a courtesy between friends or business associates. Financially precarious himself, Holladay must never have expected to be held liable for the sum. It is unlikely that he or anyone else knew how slender Custer's financial resources actually were: Custer associated with some very rich men when he came to New York, and it was commonly, though erroneously, believed that Libbie had inherited a sizable estate. Besides, had Custer lived, the note would have continued to be his responsibility. Since Holladay's financial difficulties were common knowledge,[56] Justh, too, must not have questioned Custer's ability to pay—or to stay alive.

As for Custer himself receiving kickbacks from post traders, this accusation was made by his bitter enemy, Frederick Benteen, and has never been substantiated by any other source.[57] Had he participated in the corruption associated with the provisioning of the military or the Indians, we should expect to find some mention of it on the part of others: the world of the military frontier where Custer spent the last nine years of his life was exceedingly small and gossipy; as Dr. William Gorgas wrote of a typical frontier post, "a whiff of scandal came as an occasional godsend."[58] Custer, as he well knew, had a number of detractors who would have enjoyed exposing him had he been guilty of any such impropriety. Instead, he went on record against the practice in a public congressional hearing, an inexplicably foolhardy action if he himself was implicated.

That Custer was in fact an inept or unlucky businessman is indisputable according to the ultimate criterion of the bottom line: his modest estate was swamped by debt. That he was, as Slotkin contends, "a direct and active participant in the corruption of the Gilded Age" is another matter, and one that has not been proved.[59]

As he prepared to go on the summer campaign Custer was already considering a new financial opportunity, one that promised more certain rewards than the risky ventures he had always pursued. The Redpath Lecture Bureau had offered him a speaking tour of five nights a week for the handsome sum of two hundred dollars a performance.[60] He had intended to accept the contract when he returned from the expedition against the Sioux.

What began the chain of events that culminated in Custer's disaster on the Little Bighorn? The underlying cause was the constant and increasing pressure of white immigration onto Indian hunting grounds and the faithlessness of white agreements made to preserve Indian rights to that land. The consequence of such a force meeting an intractable object was predicted well in advance by a man with the proven capacity to assess situations realistically, William Tecumseh Sherman. As Sheridan's major campaign against the Indians was getting underway in 1868, Sherman wrote to his brother the senator:

> The Indian War on the plains need simply amount to this. We have now selected and provided reservations for all, off the great roads. All who cling to their old hunting grounds are hostile and will remain so till killed off. We will have a sort of predatory war for years, every now and then be shocked by the indiscriminate murder of travellers and settlers, but the country is so large, and the advantage of the Indians so great, that we cannot make a single war and end it.[61]

As an afterthought, he added that the Indians held another great advantage over the army—they could steal horses when they needed new ones.

A year earlier Sherman had written to his brother about the penetration of the West by railroads: "Whether right or wrong, those roads will be built, and everybody knows that Congress, after granting the charts [charters] and fixing the routes, cannot now back out and surrender the country to a few bands of roving Indians."[62] "Whether right or wrong": Sherman's words would accurately characterize the state of affairs on the Plains until the late 1870s, when outrage over the Custer fight led to a more vigorous effort to break the "hostiles," those Indians who had never signed any treaties and who refused to live on reservations at all.

As for the Sioux, so often described by the epithet *warlike,* the final straw was undoubtedly the infiltration of whites into their most sacred and beloved land, Paha Sapa—the Black Hills.[63] For white Americans, it was one thing to consign to Indian occupation vast tracts of land unsuitable for white development, quite another to refrain from advancing into such an oasis of timber, vegetation, and water set in the arid plains. According to General Terry, a former lawyer, the Indians were given "no just offense" by the army's 1874 expedition into an area set aside by treaty for the Sioux because the motive of the expedition was merely benign reconnaissance: "It seeks neither gold, timber nor arable land.[64] Seeking or not, it found all three, and when they were found, the Black Hills—predictably—became overwhelmingly desirable to white Americans. William Ludlow, the expedition's chief engineer, thought it was inevitable that the Black Hills would eventually be "the home of a thronging population." He concluded with words that resonate ominously to readers today: "To this, however, the final solution of the Indian question is an indispensable preliminary."[65]

The irresistible magnet was gold, officially discovered by Custer in 1874 and confirmed by a follow-up expedition of 1875. "At the news of gold," frontier newspaperman John Finerty wrote with appropriate drama,

> the grizzled '49er shook the dust of California from his feet, and started overland . . . the Australian miner left his pick half buried in the antipodean sands . . . the diamond hunter of Brazil and of "the Cape"; the veteran "prospectors" of Colorado and Western Montana; the "tar heels" of the Carolinian hills; the "reduced gentlemen" of Europe; the worried and worn city clerks of London, Liverpool, New York or Chicago; the stout English yeoman, tired of high rents and poor re-

> turns; the sturdy Scotchman, tempted from stubborn plodding after wealth to seek fortune under more rapid conditions . . . in short, every man who lacked fortune, and who would rather be scalped than remain poor, saw in the vision of the Black Hills, El Dorado.[66]

Some lost their scalps, but there were always more prospectors to take their place. For a while the army tried to enforce the government policy of keeping prospectors out, but it simply could not be done. As James Calhoun had written in his expedition journal, even before Custer publicized the presence of gold, "the excitement in the western settlements is so intense, that if the government does not take the matter in hand, the settlers will penetrate into this country on their own responsibility. . . . It is supposed in the vicinity of the Black Hills there are vast treasures of immense wealth."[67]

If the less than compelling evidence of the Custer expedition had been enough to attract hordes of miners, a dry report from the geologist accompanying the 1875 expedition was sufficiently arresting to confirm their wildest expectations. Walter P. Jenney wrote that he had surveyed the Black Hills area systematically, region by region. His soberly stated conclusion: "The deposits of auriferous gravel in the Black Hills may generally be said to be favorably situated for working, and . . . the gold can be very cheaply extracted, with the expenditure of but comparatively little time or capital in opening the deposits."[68] Gold, to be "cheaply extracted"—Jenney could not have crafted a more tempting invitation to a mining rush. Two months before Custer began his last march, there were already eleven thousand white men in Custer City, the Black Hills town named after him.[69] Eventually, the Homestake Mining Company, the largest operating gold mine in the Western Hemisphere, would take $1.5 billion worth of gold out of the Black Hills.[70]

Once again a tribe of Indians was simmering over flagrant violations of their territory, and once again the government was faced with the unpalatable business of removing Indians from land promised to them forever in order to make way for white enterprise. The government strategy was to put the Indians in the wrong. Giving them an ultimatum to be on reservations by January 31, 1876, it defined any who did not obey as "hostiles," against whom the army would make war. This plan, devised in a secret conference at the White House on November

*E*volution of an Image.

(above left) Brigadier General Custer in 1864. Still showing some of the fullness of youth, his face lacks the prominent cheekbones that would characterize his maturity.

(above right) Brigadier General Custer later in 1864. There is more facial definition and some scruffy whiskers, but Custer has not yet achieved a memorable self-presentation.

(left) Major General Custer in 1865. The full-blown image—mustache, long hair, long trademark tie, and a posture of easy dominance: he would be comfortable inhabiting this vision of himself for the remainder of his life.

*L*ibbie, age 22, at the time of her marriage in 1864. She was known as the prettiest girl in Monroe, Michigan, and she attracted attention in Washington as well. Her sweet-faced beauty would endure over the course of a long life.

*T*he Custers and Eliza. While Custer stares purposefully away, as if his mind were fixed on more important matters, Libbie looks into the camera with a slightly upturned mouth, and Eliza looks down as if she is stoically enduring the experience. The arrangement is emphatically hierarchical.

*S*our Grapes" Family Tree Sketch. Libbie's sketch of the fox labeled GAC barking at the child-laden family tree of Captain Yates, addresses the Custers' childlessness. Libbie uses a light touch to counter Custer's envy of the prolific Yateses. The verse at the bottom right reads:

Too oft indeed we feign dislike/For what we most have tried to win/But not succeeding, then to say,/"The grapes are sour," is too thin.

*H*eroes/Villains of the Battle of the Little Bighorn

*F*rederick Benteen and the Fort he didn't build. Hailed as a hero of the Little Bighorn, Benteen was later court-martialed for his behavior at Fort DuChesne. Sent there to replace the tents with buildings, he began to drink heavily and failed to get the building done, although—as might be expected from such an opinionated and self-righteous person—he defended himself vigorously at his trial. He is the last figure on the right in the back row; his wife is the middle figure in the front row.

*M*ajor Marcus Reno. We search Reno's appearance in vain for a clue to his character. He seems to have had no friends before the battle of the Little Bighorn; certainly he had none afterward. Whatever his culpability on the battlefield, his later years were miserable and poverty-stricken.

*W*illiam Tecumseh Sherman. *(left)*
Ulysses S. Grant. *(below)* The difference in posture is suggestive. Grant's academic record at West Point was mediocre, Sherman's distinguished, but they were both brilliant generals and good friends during the Civil War. After the war, Grant took up politics and the presidency while Sherman adamantly shunned both.

Philip H. Sheridan. In this Civil War photograph Sheridan looks into the camera without fear of revealing his essential self, determined and unflinching in the face of whatever war demanded of him. He favored and defended Custer until Custer's run-in with the President in 1876.

***P**ulchritude on the Plains*

James Butler Hickok *(left)*. William Frederick Cody *(right)*. "Wild Bill" Hickok and "Buffalo Bill" Cody were both widely described as handsome. Like Custer, the two scouts knew how to fashion a compelling self-image of which the most obvious parts—height, distinctive dress, and long hair—seemed to reflect their daredevil reputations.

Custer in his element on the plains, with his dogs and pet pelican (Fort Dodge, 1868).

*S*itting Bull. After the Little Bighorn, his name invoked for the public all that they hated and feared about Indians. He was assumed to have masterminded the battle and to be responsible for all Indian resistance to white hegemony. Far-fetched rumors circulated about him—that he had gone to West Point and was proficient in Latin and French. Without such exaggerations he was formidable enough: his face reveals the force of will and determination that helped make him a great leader of his people.

*C*uster cigar band. Custer has had an ongoing existence in numerous popular artforms and artifacts such as this late nineteenth-century cigarband.

Libbie Custer in old age. She remained as she had always been—handsome and dedicated to her husband.

Edward Settle Godfrey. Even for the time Godfrey's mustache was enormous, either a sign of vanity or an attempt to conceal a weak lower jaw. When others proved unable to stay the course, Godfrey became the chief commentator on the battle of the Little Bighorn and was eventually recruited by Libbie Custer to defend her husband's actions on the battlefield.

3, 1875, would allow the government to attack those Sioux who had remained outside the reservation system as admitted enemies of white expansion. In this ambitious campaign, originally planned for early spring, the Indian problem would be settled once and for all.

Regardless of their inclinations, it would have been impossible for the targeted Indians to meet the deadline. As Colonel Charles Francis Bates wrote, "The order reached them in the dead of winter and with a time limit so short that it was impossible for them to comply. The intense cold and deep snow, together with the weakened condition of their ponies, prevented them from making the long trips even if they had wished to do so."[71]

But they did not wish to do so. Their leaders—most notably, Sitting Bull and Crazy Horse—were bitterly opposed to any accommodation of whites. Moreover, they were on land recognized as theirs by the American government. Why should they leave it? Whites were, in Crazy Horse's words, "the only people who make rules for other people, that say 'if you stay on one side of this line it is peace, but if you go on the other side, I will kill you all.'"[72] Indians had always had some difficulty understanding white logic.

19

The Little Bighorn

Forty years after a battle it is easy for a noncombatant to reason about how it ought to have been fought. It is another thing personally and under fire to have to direct the fighting while involved in the obscuring smoke of it. —Herman Melville, *Billy Budd*

These Wasichus wanted it, and they came to get it, and we gave it to them. —Iron Hawk

Three hundred to three thousand!
   They had bravely fought and bled;
For such is the will of Congress
   When the white man meets the red.

The white men are ten millions
   The thriftiest under the sun;
The reds are fifty thousand,
   And warriors every one.

So Custer and his loyal men
   Lay under the evening skies,
Staring up at the tranquil heavens
   With wide accusing eyes.

—John Hay, "Miles Keogh's Horse"

The 1876 expedition to teach the Sioux that they must be reservation Indians was fraught with bad omens from the start. First of all, it was supposed to get underway much sooner, and this late start was one of the most crucial *ifs* of the Little Bighorn disaster. If it had, the Indians would have been a much weaker force, since by June 25 the "hostiles"—Indians who refused to live on reservations at any time—had been considerably augmented by the "summer roamers," those Indians who lived at their agencies during the harsh winter months but drifted away to hunt during the summer.

Custer's unexpected political troubles provided other history-altering circumstances. Because of them, General Terry was ordered—by President Grant himself—to command the expedition. Had Custer commanded the combined Montana-Dakota column as originally planned, whatever he might have decided to do would probably have been an improvement on the ill-fated Terry plan.

An unenthusiastic Terry and an exuberant Custer marched the Dakota column out of Fort Abraham Lincoln on May 17, headed for a rendezvous on the Yellowstone River with the Montana column, commanded by Colonel John Gibbon. At the same time, General George Crook was moving against the Indians from the south: presumably the enemy would be cornered between these armies. To the armchair strategists in Washington this may have seemed like a sensible and effective plan, but since Crook and Terry were not required to coordinate their efforts, in practice it was neither. Battle historians have referred to a three-pronged attack, but there was never any realistic possibility of the Terry or Terry-Gibbon forces acting in conjunction with Crook's command. Sheridan had recognized this, apprising Sherman that he had "given no instructions to Generals Crook or Terry, preferring that they should do the best they can under the circumstances . . . as I think it would be unwise to make any combination in such a country as they will have to operate in."[1] He was entirely right in the sense that the country and the position of the hostiles in it were both unknown, making precise coordination impossible. In his postmortem of the disaster, Sherman wrote to Sheridan that they had been responsible for allowing two departmental commanders (Crook and Terry) in the same field, whereas "one officer should have unlimited control of all the troops."[2]

As the column rode away, a strange meteorological phenomenon caused its reflection to appear marching in the sky, a ghostly double of the flesh-and-blood men that could not help but upset the already emotional wives.[3] Libbie was always a worrier, but about this expedition she appears to have had more forebodings than usual. On June 21, four days before the fatal encounter at the Little Bighorn, she wrote to her husband: "I cannot but feel the greatest possible apprehensions for your safety on this dangerous scout. Oh Autie I feel as if it was almost impossible for me to wait your return with patience. I cannot describe my feelings. I have felt so badly for the last few days."[4] She, at least, had a more accurate sense of the danger facing her husband than anyone on the expedition had.

Dr. James DeWolf, a contract surgeon attached to the Seventh Cavalry, did not know Terry, but he wrote to his wife around this time that "we can stand the expedition as well as Genl Terry he don't enjoy it much I think." A few days later a similar statement followed: "I can stand as much horseback riding as any of them. I guess General Terry gets about the most tired of anyone except Lt. Gibbs who is a poor rider & does not enjoy it much." He added mysteriously, "the trip is not pleasant to some high in rank for several reasons which I will tell you when I come home."[5] He may have been referring to the uneasy rapport between Custer and Terry, between Custer and Terry's officious aide and brother-in-law, Colonel Robert Hughes, or between Custer and his second ranking officer, Major Marcus Reno, who had been eager to replace Custer in leading the Seventh. Any number of possibilities might have fleshed out DeWolf's enigmatic remark, but it suggested that localized tensions in the command structure were all too obvious.

As the Dakota column made its slow and uneventful progress through rain, mud, and even a freak snowstorm on June 1, the smaller Montana column, which had been in the field since the beginning of April, was impatiently awaiting them on the Yellowstone River. There was a good deal of exasperation in this quarter, too. When the Montana column learned that neither Crook nor Custer had yet taken the field, and that both were expected to be delayed for another month, they quite naturally felt abandoned. "We were to have acted in conjunction with these forces," Lieutenant James Bradley wrote, "but we are now, when well advanced in the Sioux country, left unsupported."[6] This apparently didn't bother his commander. On April 21 Gibbon wrote to Terry that he was "strong enough to defy the whole Sioux Nation should they feel inclined to come this way."[7] He had a force of 450 men. Fortunately for Gibbon, the Sioux felt inclined only to harass his column, picking off stragglers and—to the intense humiliation of the Crow scouts—stealing all their ponies.

Bradley was Gibbon's chief of scouts, a reliable and astute observer, and a man who had the bad luck to be surrounded by people of lesser mettle. He would become the first person under Terry's command to discover the Sioux and form some conception of their strength, but when he did, both his subordinates and superiors reacted foolishly. His diary entry for May 16, when his scouting party discovered a Sioux village on the Tongue River, a tributary of the Yellowstone, recorded how he wanted to creep closer at night to estimate accurately the number of Indians. His Crow scouts were absolutely opposed: "Finding that I could not rely upon them to assist me in the execution of my night enterprise, I resolved to accept their advice and return."[8] Gibbon was informed of the location of the enemy and made plans to attack, an intention that could be carried out only by crossing the cold and swift-flowing Yellowstone.

Lieutenant Edward J. McClernand, Gibbon's chief engineer, described what happened next:

> To get horses to cross, a number were tied head to tail, with a lariat fastened into the halter ring of the first horse. The other end of the lariat was held by a man in a row boat . . . and the fastened animals were thus led into the stream, but as soon as the horse on the lariat entered the main current he pulled loose from the soldier in the boat and turned downstream, followed, of course, by those in rear. To make a long story short they were soon swimming in a circle and six or eight were drowned, when the attempt to cross was reluctantly given up.[9]

This mishap was avidly observed by some hostiles on the other side of the river, who must have had their own opinions of the commander's competence. According to Bradley, the expedition's Crow scouts assumed that the botched crossing was an excuse for calling off the attack, "a device to conceal our cowardice."[10]

At the time of Bradley's first scouting trip, the Indian village was around thirty-five miles from Gibbon's command. On his next scout of May 24–26, Bradley discovered "an immense Indian camp," which he took to be the same village earlier sighted, now a mere eighteen miles away on another tributary of the Yellowstone, the Rosebud. Bradley wanted to bring up other officers of his party to see the village because "upon our return from our first scout there had been some parties ungenerous enough to deny that we had found a village," but once again his Crow scouts were anxious to leave immediately.[11]

And once again Gibbon found a means of avoiding battle. Dr. Holmes Paulding, the column's accompanying physician, wrote to his mother that "our C.O.'s excuse was that he had rec'd orders from St. Paul to guard *this* side of the Yellowstone. There's literal obedience for you. This whole trip has been a miserable farce and everything has been as disagreeable as idiotic, pig headed stupidity could make it."[12]

Bradley was more restrained, but he, too, could not help but ponder the failure to engage the Sioux in the light of later events. He thought that their force of 350 men (100 men had been temporarily detached) would have found between 800 and 1,000 warriors—"pretty big odds, but I imagine the majority of our officers would not have hesitated to give them a trial, and there are some who assert confidently that we would have gained a rousing victory, dispersed the village, and prevented that tremendous aggregation of force a month later that made the massacre of Custer's command possible."[13] A reasonable scenario, and one that would have changed history.

Some of Bradley's overt exasperation was captured by Dr. Paulding, who noted in a journal entry of May 29 that when he joined a gathering of officers,

> Bradley was saying as I went in that some officer, he heard, had said things to the effect that he, Bradley, had not seen Indians or a village as he reported from his scouts, and that though he didn't Know who the officer was, he wished to remark in the presence of 9 officers there at the time that whoever said so was a liar and a scoundrel. Freeman reproved him for intemperate language—but he said that he had nothing to retract.[14]

One of the strands woven into the expedition's fabric of disaster was Gibbon's failure to make use of the information brought to him by Bradley; worse, he concealed this intelligence from Terry although he continued to send him insignificant messages. The Crow chiefs who had met with Gibbon when he came looking for scouts early in the season had accurately taken his measure. One of them told Bradley, "The old man [Gibbon] is only talking. You have already been down below, our young men went with you, and you turned back after awhile without doing anything. We are afraid that you will do it again."[15]

While Gibbon temporized and prevaricated, Crook, taking full advantage of the free rein granted him by Sheridan, remained out of communication with Terry's command during the critical period before the Custer fight. As it turned out, the knowledge of his clash on the Rosebud with a large band of Sioux on June 17 would have been precious intelligence to Terry and Custer.

O. L. Hein, an officer who revered Crook, described him as a striking figure, although it is clear from his description that the general's physical attributes were not responsible for this impression so much as the spirit that imbued them. He was, according to Hein, "of medium height and slight build, his hair and beard were light brown, his eyes gray and piercing, his face long and narrow, his nose aquiline and his mouth large and firm. His look was determined."[16]

John Bourke, who served with Crook for forty years and was also a strong partisan of the general, said that he was as "plain as an old stick and looked more like an honest country squire than the commander of a war-like expedition."[17] In fact Crook looked more like "an honest country squire" because he eschewed military dress, but it may be disputed that this plain appearance betokened modesty and reticence. Custer's image, the Boy General with golden locks, was not something Crook could imitate, but his plainness was in itself striking and attention-getting. An observer less partial than Bourke might also have seen Crook's long, showy whiskers as a sign of personal vanity, and, in fact, a doggerel of the time suggests that Crook's appearance was susceptible to an altogether different interpretation than Bourke's:

I'd like to be a packer
And pack with George F. Crook,
And dressed up in my canvas suit
To be for him mistook.
I'd braid my beard in two long tails
And idle all the day

In whittling stick and wondering
What the New York papers say.[18]

Although Crook supposedly abhorred publicity, at the time that Custer was being admonished to take no correspondents on the Sioux campaign, Crook's army was accompanied by five.[19]

Crook and Custer actually had much in common. Both were avid hunters who enjoyed riding far ahead of their troops. Crook, like Custer, had been repeatedly warned of the danger of this practice, but—also like Custer—he paid no attention to the advice.[20] Crook had a strong abstemious streak: he never used tobacco or profanity, although he went farther than Custer by eschewing tea and coffee as well. Like Custer, he made an exception for cards. In Bourke's admiring description, Crook "endured heat, cold, marching and every species of discomfort with Indian-like stolidity. If he felt weariness, he never made anybody the wiser. . . . He was ever and always an officer to do, and do without pomp or ceremony, all that was required of him, and much more."[21] Custer liked a certain amount of pomp and ceremony, but in other respects the description fits him as well.[22]

John Finerty, one of the correspondents who accompanied Crook, had wanted to go with Custer. His editor told him, "Custer is a brave soldier—none braver—but he has been out there some years already, and has not succeeded in bringing the Sioux to a decisive engagement. Crook did well in Arizona."[23] This favorable judgment of Crook's ability would require some revision after the close of the campaign of 1876: Crook did manage to stay alive, but it was the Sioux who brought a "decisive engagement" to him, and the decision was in their favor.

On May 29 Crook left Fort Fetterman in eastern Wyoming and marched northward, with a column that stretched four miles.[24] He established a base camp on Goose Creek near the present-day city of Sheridan, Wyoming, and on June 16 led some fifteen hundred men—including friendly Crow and Shoshone Indians and civilian packers—north along the Rosebud River, so named for the wild roses growing along its banks. According to the account of Captain H. R. Lemly, a member of Crook's army, the Indian allies did little but delay the column's progress. When the column came across buffalo, the Indians took this as a sign of the Sioux: they insisted on stopping to perform their war dance while scouts went out to locate the enemy. The scouts returned with news of a recently abandoned lodge, which required more singing and dancing. On June 17 the march got underway again, but was again halted by the scouts' report of Sioux nearby: "Immediately the Indians began to strip themselves and their ponies and, amid great excitement, to dance and sing."[25]

The soldiers had become somewhat inured to these performances and were thus taken by surprise when bullets suddenly rained down into the camp. General Crook was playing cards with some of his officers at the time.[26] The Indian allies dashed up the adjacent ridges, but dashed back down just as quickly, with the Sioux hard behind them. "Every hill appeared to be covered with their swarming legions," one of Crook's commanders wrote, "and up from every ravine, and out of every little vale, more seemed to be coming."[27] In the opinion of Captain Mills, "our friendlies were worthless against them; we would have been better off without them."[28] Correspondent Finerty agreed. He believed that "the timidity and obstinacy" of the Crows destroyed Crook's plans.[29]

The behavior of the Indian allies may not have helped, but Crook's plans were also open to criticism. The warriors attacking Crook under the direction of Crazy Horse were probably no more than 750 against Crook's 1,300 fighting men: the army might have carried the day if it had been used properly, but Crook began fighting on the defensive before the day was half over.[30] Convinced that a large village lay just ahead, he split his force, just as Custer would do a week later, in order to send eight companies down the Rosebud canyon in search of the village. Mills described himself as approaching the village when Crook's adjutant general galloped up with the order to return: so close to achieving the objective, Mills could not believe he was being pulled back. He asked if the messenger was certain of his message. When it was confirmed, Mills returned—and found Crook the picture of dejection. The general said that it had been "a more serious engagement" than he had thought.[31]

The Sioux eventually broke off the fighting, undoubtedly satisfied by having stopped Crook in his tracks. The army remained on the battlefield that night but then retreated to Goose Creek with the wounded, hors de combat during the next critical period of the campaign.

Why did Crook, having discovered a large force of hostile Indians, do nothing further? Possibly because of the influence of Washakie, the

Shoshone chief who stuck close to the general and counseled him to caution. James Irwin, the agent at the Shoshone Wind River agency, wrote to the commissioner of Indian affairs, "[Washakie] tells General Crook to hold on, make a connection with General Terry and get all the outside troops he can before he risks another battle or he will be badly whipped."[32]

Crook never admitted that he had lost the Battle of the Rosebud, but the facts spoke for themselves. The Sioux accomplished their objective and, having done so, went back to their village. Crook achieved nothing. An editorial in the *Daily Independent* concluded with a reassessment of Crook's success in Arizona: "He may out-General the indolent Apache, but he is no match for the daring and aggressive Sioux."[33]

General Sherman agreed. Exactly eight months after the battle, he wrote to Sheridan that Crook should not have abandoned the field:

> Instead of moving back to his train, he should have brought his train up to him and kept up the pressure . . . and had he done so the Custer massacre was an impossibility—the moment he turned back to his train the Indians were free to turn with their aggregate force upon each or either of the other columns. This in my judgment was a terrible mistake and I cannot shut my eyes and understanding to it.[34]

Long before the Dakota column assembled at Fort Abraham Lincoln to march under Custer and Terry, Dr. DeWolf wrote to his wife that there was some scuttlebutt about the expedition being called off because "Genl Crooks [*sic*] reports that the number of indians off the reservation has been greatly exagerated."[35] That Crook was the source of this misinformation is ironic since he had already been effectively defeated by a large band of Sioux in a controversial winter battle and would be defeated by them again on the Rosebud.

In the businesslike field diary that General Terry kept, mostly brief references to times and distances covered, and in the correspondence he maintained with his large family, he expressed some irritation with the independent-minded subordinate who had tried his patience on more than one occasion. On May 27 Terry wrote to his sister Fanchon from the difficult terrain of the Badlands that the column needed to find the Davis Creek pass, the only place in the vicinity where the wagons could get through: "General Custer, who had been over the country before, undertook to guide us to it, but he went astray, and passing close to it led us far to the Southward of it."[36] On May 31 Terry's diary noted that Custer rode behind, "playing Wagon Master." The column had been underway about two miles when Terry received a message from "Lt. Col. Custer, who left the column early in the day without any authority whatever."[37]

Custer's show of energy might have seemed ostentatious to his less active commander, who was "preoccupied with comfort, the word appearing endlessly in his letters."[38] Jacob Horner, a member of the Seventh, recalled that Custer would pitch in and help build crossings for the teams: "Terry and his staff would be standing on the bank of the stream looking on while Custer was among the men helping to build the crossings."[39] Terry had more enthusiasm for the good food his cook was preparing on the march. He wrote to his sister Elizabeth that he had had "a very good dinner of roast beef, mashed potato, warm biscuit, and raw onions in vinegar for salad. The beef was very good, but the onions were *beyond praise.*"[40]

This thoughtful, intelligent man knew that in the campaign against the Sioux it would be easy to fail and difficult to succeed. Terry's last communication from Sheridan before setting out from Fort Abraham Lincoln was not calculated to produce optimism about the likelihood of engaging the Sioux in meaningful numbers. Instead, Sheridan reminded Terry of "the impossibility of any large numbers of Indians keeping together as a hostile body for even a week."[41] "I did hope," Terry confessed to Fanchon, "and I had reason to hope, that we should find the Indians here in force, prepared to fight, but now I fear that they have scattered and that I shall not be able to find them at all. This would be a most mortifying and perhaps injurious result to me."[42] *Scattered* was the word that Sherman and other Indian fighters used repeatedly in describing the experience of pursuing their quarry. Their choice of words was highly ironic in the context of the 1876 campaign against the Sioux and the disaster of the Little Bighorn. Four days before the battle and his own death at the hands of the Indians, Dr. DeWolf wrote to his wife: "I think it is very clear that we shall not see an Indian this summer. . . . It is believed that the Indians have scattered and gone back to their reservations."[43] No one could imagine that the target Indians were not going to scatter this time.

Far from scattering, the Indians these three major military expeditions sought within an area of nearly 100,000 square miles constituted the largest gathering known to Plains Indian history.[44] No one on the march would have suspected such a concentration, and certainly Custer did not entertain such a thought. Two weeks into the campaign he wrote to Libbie that a reconnaissance he undertook established "beyond a doubt that all stories about large bodies of Indians being here are the merest bosh."[45]

Terry had not reprimanded Custer for his unauthorized forty-five-mile scout, but on June 10 he gave to Major Reno the reconnaissance that Custer had undoubtedly expected to command. The instructions were as specific as the purpose was unclear: Reno was to scout the Powder River but under no circumstances to go on to the Rosebud. Had he followed orders, he would have come back with nothing. He chose to disobey orders and returned with valuable intelligence that allowed Terry to construct a better plan.[46] Oddly enough, Terry was indignant. When he sent Colonel Hughes to meet Reno, "Reno gave him no reason for his disobedience of Orders."[47] Yet there was an excellent reason for Reno's conduct, and it seems strange that Reno, who often put himself forward and overrated his abilities, would have failed to make this case. Possibly Reno's pompous manner annoyed Hughes, who then gave his own distorted account to Terry. Hughes's defense of Terry and his plans tended to be so zealous that on more than one occasion he may have been guilty of actually falsifying documents.[48]

On June 22 Terry held a conference on the steamer the *Far West* and gave his commanders their orders. The plan he had devised—of two columns covering the major avenues of escape and trapping the Indians between them at the northern end of the valley of the Little Bighorn—was theoretically satisfying but empirically flawed. It made no provision for the unknown terrain, unknown position, and unknown force of the enemy. Terry himself decided to accompany Gibbon, who Terry had every reason to believe was less capable on his own than Custer.

Terry's written orders to Custer walked a fine line between freedom and restraint. He began with the obvious circumstances of the situation and continued with a graceful compliment: "It is, of course, impossible to give you any definite instructions in regard to this movement; and were it not impossible to do so, the department commander places too much confidence in your zeal, energy, and ability to wish to impose upon you precise orders, which might hamper your action when nearly in contact with the enemy."[49]

At the same time, Terry wanted Custer to follow his plan: "He will, however, indicate to you his own views of what your action should be, and he desires that you should conform to them unless you shall see sufficient reason for departing from them." Custer was to follow the Indian trail discovered by Reno up the Rosebud. Should the trail lead into the valley of the Little Bighorn, Terry thought Custer should still "proceed southward, perhaps as far as the headwaters of the Tongue, and then turn toward the Little Horn, feeling constantly, however, to your left, so as to preclude the possibility of the escape of the Indians to the south or southeast by passing around your left flank."[50]

As an afterthought, and a clear indication that he assumed Custer would bear the brunt of the fighting, he offered him significant reinforcements: Gatling guns and four companies of the Second Cavalry. Custer rejected both. In refusing the guns, he was thinking of speed; in the rough country of his proposed march the guns, pulled by condemned cavalry horses, would have slowed him down significantly and made it easy for the Indians to evade his force. His refusal of additional cavalry was less reasonable. According to Lieutenant Godfrey, Custer felt sure that the Seventh Cavalry could "whip any force that would be able to combine against him; that if the regiment could not, no other regiment in the service could; if they [the Indians] could whip the regiment, they would be able to defeat a much larger force, or, in other words, the reinforcement of this battalion could not save us from defeat."[51] Another four companies might have made the difference, though, and the ponderous Gatlings, which would indeed have been of little use against the Indians, might instead have slowed Custer down enough to prevent the Last Stand.[52] More likely, Custer would have left the guns with the pack train to catch up when they could while he dashed ahead to get the Indians before they scattered.

On June 21 Terry had written to Sheridan, "I only hope that one of the two columns will find the Indians."[53] Only after the fact did Terry imagine that his plan had required a precise rendezvous between the two columns. At the time of its formulation it was assumed that either one of the forces could engage the Indians successfully, with the other serving to block any escape. *Scattering* remained the central concept and the operative fear.

Because Custer would command only cavalry as opposed to the slower mixed cavalry and infantry in the Montana column, which was also left to drag the Gatling guns, it was clear that he would have the best chance of engaging the enemy. Having been twice denied battle by their own commander, Gibbon's officers were somewhat dashed to think that they were to be denied once again by the disposition of forces. "It is understood," Bradley wrote glumly, "that if Custer arrives first, he is at liberty to attack at once if he deems prudent. We have little hope of being in at the death, as Custer will undoubtedly exert himself to the utmost to get there first and win all the laurels for himself and his regiment."[54]

Something similar must have been in Gibbon's mind when he called out to the departing Custer words that the Sioux might have found quite funny: "Now Custer, don't be greedy. Save some Indians for us." Custer responded, "I won't," probably addressing Gibbon's first comment—or facetiously addressing the second. The exchange later proved embarrassing to Gibbon, who went to great lengths to explain what seemed to be a perfectly straightforward remark: "I meant nothing in that except that I wanted Custer to know that I knew he was always ready to fight and that I wanted him to know that if there was anything I could do, I was ready and willing to do it."[55]

So Custer headed off with the Seventh at last, having agreed or not agreed, depending on how you read the exchange with Gibbon, to share some of the Indians and the glory of defeating them. After Libbie's sense of foreboding and the strange heavenly double of the departing column, ominous signs continued to punctuate the journey along the Rosebud—the remains of an enormous encampment, the recently lifted scalp of a white man, and then, the grounds where the Indians had held a Sun Dance called by their great spiritual leader, Sitting Bull. A pictograph left in the sand inside a sweat lodge showed his dream that soldiers would fall into the Lakota camp and be killed. Custer's Ree and

Crow scouts must have read this and similar signs of the enemy's confidence with increasing gloom.

On the night of the twenty-fourth, after the officers had met at Custer's tent for their orders, some remained behind to sing softly—"Annie Laurie," "Little Footsteps Soft and Gentle," "The Good-bye at the Door," and the Doxology. W. O. Taylor pauses in his narrative of the battle to muse on the strangeness of it: "Was it not something in the nature of a prayer, coming from those generally lighthearted cavalrymen and born of an unconscious premonition of the sad fate that so soon awaited many of them?" His was one of those questions that would never have been asked if the next day had taken a different course, but in any case, the officers' sense of premonition did not linger: they concluded their singing with "For He's a Jolly Good Fellow."[56]

Because Custer wanted to cross the Wolf Mountains as soon as possible and then rest his troops on the other side, the march resumed around 11:00 P.M. Having left the main command two hours earlier, a group of Indian scouts led by Lieutenant Charles Varnum arrived at a lookout called the Crow's Nest around 2:30 A.M. on the twenty-fifth. The scouts insisted that they could see a vast pony herd ahead in the valley of the Little Bighorn, but Custer rode to join them and see for himself.

According to Varnum, Custer was irritable because his brother Tom and brother-in-law James Calhoun had left the column to follow him without obtaining permission. He sent them back peremptorily. Succeeding events must have increased his irritability, for he, too, was unable to see what the scouts had seen, even with some borrowed field glasses. While some commentators have conjectured that by the time he arrived, morning haze had obscured the clear view the scouts had had, Lieutenant Varnum, who was there at the same time as the scouts, had also been unable to see anything. It may be, of course, that the two officers did not have eyesight as keen as they believed.

After the sighting, Varnum reported the tension in a conversation between Custer and Mitch Boyer, the half-Sioux guide acquired along with the Crows. Custer told the scout, "'I've got about as good eyes as anybody and I can't see any village Indians or anything else' or words to that effect. Boyer said, 'Well General, if you don't find more Indians in that valley than you ever saw together you can hang me.' Custer sprang to his feet saying, 'It would do a damned sight of good to hang you, wouldn't it.'" Varnum remembered this, he wrote to Walter Camp, because "the word damn was the nearest to swearing I ever heard him come, and I never heard him say that but once before and that was in an Indian fight on the Yellowstone August 4th 1873."[57]

On their way to the Crow's Nest, Varnum and his scouts saw some hostile Indians, who, Varnum felt sure, would soon be aware of the presence of soldiers. While Custer was at the Crow's Nest, it was discovered that a box of hardtack that had dropped off the pack train had been found by Indians, who were certain to give the alarm to the village. When Custer heard that hostiles were close by and presumably aware of the Seventh's presence, he acted with the same dispatch he had shown when scouts brought news of an Indian trail along the Washita: thinking he'd lost the element of surprise, he decided that the Seventh would attack the enemy as soon as possible.

At their last camp before the battle the water was so strongly alkaline that it was undrinkable by man or beast, a circumstance that would have serious consequences during the long hot day that followed. When the Indian war veteran Henry R. Boynton enumerated the "almost unbelievable" hardships encountered in frontier service, he began with thirst.[58] In the heat and dust of that June 25 the lack of water at the beginning of the day would both contribute to the suffering of the men and horses who retreated to the bluffs and delay the pack train, whose thirsty mules could not be hurried out of the river and on to join the command. And a final indignity in an army that ran on coffee and hardtack was the deprivation of the former on what would be the last morning of their lives for 263 of the men, including the coffee-loving Custer.

An anonymous letter written by Custer to the *New York Tribune* illuminates his strategy on that final day. His words condemn Reno's failure to pursue the Indians on the Rosebud scout, and although unjust to Reno, they provide a key to his own actions at this critical moment: "Had Reno, after first violating his orders, pursued and overtaken the Indians, his original disobedience of orders would have been overlooked. . . . Few officers have ever had such a fine opportunity to make a successful and telling strike and few ever failed so completely to improve their opportunities."[59] In similar circumstances Custer was determined to make a "successful and telling strike" and not waste "a fine opportunity."

Not long after the column was underway again, Custer made the first division of his command. Mindful of Terry's instructions to interdict an Indian escape southward, he sent Captain Benteen and three companies—D, H, and K—off on a "scout to the left." If he found no Indians, Benteen wrote in his report of July 4, he was to return to the trail the command was following *and* communicate the results of his scout to Custer.[60] An enlisted man later wrote that he overheard Benteen say to Custer at this time, "Hadn't we better keep the regiment together?"[61] Although Benteen's propensity for taking credit is evident whenever he discusses his military career, his unfinished narrative on the battle makes no such claim.[62]

After marching westward along the main Indian trail for two hours, Custer arrived at the "lone tepee," a Lakota burial lodge erected for a casualty of the battle with Crook. By then it was early afternoon. The site had been occupied by a small band of Indians glimpsed fleeing by the scouts. Custer immediately ordered Major Reno to take companies A, G, and M—splitting off another 25 percent of his force—and pursue this village. Custer's adjutant, Lieutenant William Cooke, told Reno "to move forward at as rapid gait as [he] thought prudent, and to charge afterward, and that the whole outfit would support [him],"[63] although, since one quarter of the whole outfit had already departed with Benteen, that might have been understood to refer only to the remaining five companies under Custer's direct command (company B, the last of the twelve, was assigned to guard the pack train).

Custer and companies C, E, F, I, and L briefly followed Reno, then, after crossing the Little Bighorn, turned north. Later, Reno would maintain that after promising support, Custer had in fact abandoned him.[64] In his first field report, however, Reno wrote: "After following over his trail it was evident to me that Custer intended to support me by moving farther down the stream and attacking the village in flank."[65] In short, Custer envisioned a pincers movement squeezing the Indians between Reno and himself, while Benteen stayed off to the south to preclude escape in that direction—a reasonable strategy if the number of Indians had been smaller.

When Reno suddenly found himself approaching a gigantic village, his position was untenable, and he managed it badly. The Indians he

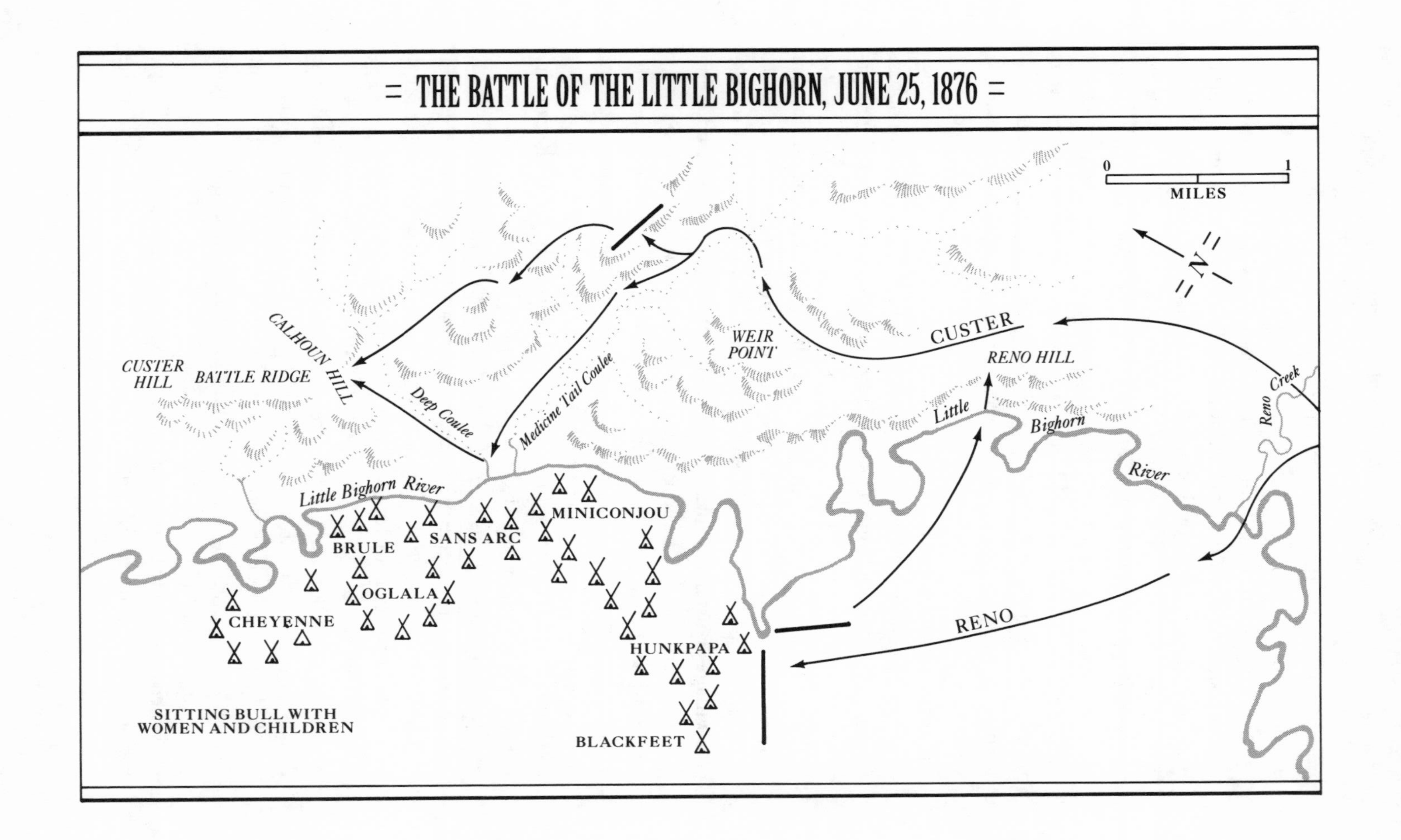
THE BATTLE OF THE LITTLE BIGHORN, JUNE 25, 1876
0
1
MILES
N
CUSTER
RENO HILL
Reno Creek
WEIR POINT
CALHOUN HILL
CUSTER HILL
BATTLE RIDGE
Deep Coulee
Medicine Tail Coulee
Little Bighorn River
Little Bighorn River
MINICONJOU
SANS ARC
BRULE
OGLALA
CHEYENNE
HUNKPAPA
BLACKFEET
RENO
SITTING BULL WITH
WOMEN AND CHILDREN

was pursuing did not seem either terribly worried or terribly hurried, and he began to suspect that he was being drawn into a trap: "I could not see Custer or any other support, and at the same time the very earth seemed to grow Indians, and they were running toward me in swarms, and from all directions."[66] Instead of riding into the village and wreaking havoc as he was supposed to do, Reno stopped short and set up a skirmish line. Since he was badly outnumbered, this might have been prudent, but it wasn't glorious. The skirmish line lasted only around fifteen minutes before the left flank was turned by the hasty departure of the Indian scouts. These men were supposedly eager to fight their traditional enemies, the Sioux, but they were paid only for their services as scouts. They took the low road and survived.

Reno and his men hastily retired to a nearby stand of cottonwood where the Indians hotly besieged them. Opinion differs sharply about whether or not Reno should have kept his battalion in the timbers: it was a good position that provided cover, and had Reno been able to anticipate the arrival of Benteen, he might have held out there. But at this point "every element [of Custer's attack force] was moving in different directions without coordinated purpose or contact," so he had no way of knowing when and if Benteen would arrive.[67] The pack train, bearing the much-needed extra ammunition, could not have gotten into the timbers and might well have fallen into the hands of the Indians.

Probably Dr. Porter was most accurate in describing Reno's state of mind as the Indians applied more pressure in the timbers. "I think," he told the court of inquiry in 1879, "he did not know whether it was best to stay there or leave."[68] He first ordered the troops to mount, then quickly to dismount, then to mount again, finally getting underway—in George Herendeen's opinion because of a volley of fire in which Custer's favorite scout, Bloody Knife, was killed and a soldier was heard to scream, "O, my God! I have got it."[69] Bloody Knife's brains spattered Reno's face, no doubt shaking him further, for he neither ordered a bugle call nor arranged to cover the retreat. Some men had to rush to catch up with the departing column; seventeen were stranded and had to hide in the timbers for a day or more.

Everyone in Reno's battalion that day agreed that the retreat was hasty and disorderly, a "stampede" in the words of Herendeen. It was also costly: before leaving the timbers, the battalion had suffered losses of two dead and two wounded. Crossing the river and negotiating the steep bluffs on the other side took the lives of thirty-seven, with seven wounded.[70]

Sometimes, what accounts for the difference between living and dying can only be called luck: the two doctors, Porter and DeWolf, crossed the river together. On the other side, Porter rode up one ravine; DeWolf inexplicably chose another and was killed. DeWolf had avowed a strong commitment to prudence in letters to his wife, often repeating that he would take no foolish chances. Luck canceled out his habitual caution.

When the court of inquiry asked Reno to "state what became of the wounded men that were left in the timber," he answered, chillingly, "I suppose the Indians killed them." To the question "What steps were taken to bring them out of there?" he gave a stark reply, "I could not make any efforts; none were made."[71]

The hilltop where Reno reunited his shattered forces was not readily defensible, offering neither cover nor superior altitude, and the command was soon under attack again. The arrival of Benteen and his three companies at this time appeared providential. Benteen had received urgent orders along the trail to join Custer, but as he was pondering this message, Reno came up and implored him: "For God's sake, Benteen, halt your command and help me. I've lost half my men."[72]

Benteen became the undisputed hero of the siege that followed, but his conduct in other respects could be criticized. After the scout to the left, which had uncovered no Indians, he came back to the main trail and followed it in what some of his subordinates regarded as too leisurely a fashion, lingering to water the horses until made aware of his officers' impatience. Then he received the message from Custer, brought by trumpeter John Martin, a recent immigrant from Italy, where he had been born Giovanni Martini. Martin had been given a hastily scrawled note by Custer's adjutant. It read: "Benteen: Come on. Big village. Be quick. Bring packs. W. W. Cooke. P.S. Bring pacs."[73] Custer had already dispatched Sergeant Daniel Kanipe to the pack train to bring it up. It is likely that what Custer wanted from Benteen was not the unwieldy and slow-moving pack train in its entirety but the extra ammunition packs.

Although the urgent order from his commander outranked Reno's plea for help, Benteen disregarded it and remained with Reno. His testimony on this point to the court of inquiry had to have been a lie. He said that Martin's "language conveyed the impression to me that they were in possession of the village, that the Indians were all skedaddling, to use his own words."[74] Martin stated in an interview with Walter Camp that Benteen had asked him if Custer was being attacked, and he had responded yes without elaboration. He was positive that he had not used the term *skedaddling*, a word of recent coinage that seems unlikely in the vocabulary of a man with little English, but one in keeping with Benteen's own distinctive verbal style.[75] Moreover, Martin had been sent back before Custer was anywhere near the village. He would have known of its existence and nothing further.

Reno hill provided the first opportunity for many in the Seventh Cavalry to assess the behavior of their fellows under fire, men they had known well in other circumstances. Later in life they tended to remember the extraordinary incidents—Benteen striding around the hilltop scorning cover as if he was impervious to bullets; Captain French, "cool as a cucumber."[76] In a bizarre moment remembered by Lieutenant Edgerly, supplies from the newly arrived pack train were immediately utilized as breastworks: "When the first box of hard bread was put down on Benteen's line a man threw himself down behind it very eagerly. He had hardly gotten his head against the box when a bullet came tearing through it, killing him instantly. Strange as it may sound here, every man who saw this, laughed!"[77]

Edgerly also noticed that Private Saunders "had a broad grin on his face altho' he was sitting in a perfect shower of bullets." Under fire there was no time to ask for an explanation, but the next day, when the Indians withdrew, Edgerly asked Saunders why he had been laughing. He replied with an enviable sense of humor, "I was laughing to see what poor shots those Indians were; they were shooting too low and their bullets were spattering dust like drops of rain."[78]

Years later, Lieutenant Edward Godfrey was to recollect vividly the only two recruits of his company who participated in the battle. They took positions next to each other on Reno hill. Soon after sundown one of them, a man named Hellman, was shot in the abdomen:

> His sufferings were intense. . . . I went to him and told him that as soon as it was safe I would have him taken to the hospital, or doctor. He was quiet for awhile, but as his suffering increased he began to yell and scream at intervals. Every time he screamed a volley came in that direction. . . . Finally

> Captain Weir said to Hellman: "Don't scream, my man. The noise gives direction to the shooting and may cause the death or wounding of others." This was about dusk. Thereafter not a sound came from him. After a bit I went up to him. His comrade was sobbing and in reply to my summons to help carry Hellman to the rear, he said, "He is dead!"[79]

Not long after the consolidation of the Reno-Benteen forces, the Indians suddenly withdrew to the west. They were obviously drawn to the Custer battle some four miles away, but the men on Reno hill, who had fought hard and taken heavy casualties, who by this point in the waning afternoon were beginning to feel their exhaustion and even more their thirst, preferred to ignore the evidence of their senses. Some, in spite of their own experience that afternoon, could not imagine Custer in serious trouble. Mindful of the unwritten law of military operation that you march to the sound of the guns, both Reno and Benteen would deny to the court of inquiry hearing any significant firing, although Reno's field report stated that firing was heard in the direction of the village, and we "knew it could only be Custer."[80]

Lieutenant Varnum, in a letter to his father written July 4, 1876, said that the men on the bluffs had known "from the fearful firing at the other end of the village that some one was getting it hot and heavy up there."[81] To the court of inquiry he described himself as saying to Lieutenant Wallace, "Jesus Christ! Wallace, hear that! and that! . . . It was not like volley firing, but a heavy fire—a sort of crash, crash! I heard it only for a few minutes." George Herendeen, the scout who remained in the timbers, heard "a great many volleys fired; then between the volleys, and after the volleys ceased, there were scattering shots." Edgerly also heard "heavy firing, by volleys."[82]

Captain Thomas Weir showed the most initiative in interpreting and acting upon the sounds of battle. He told Lieutenant Edgerly that Custer was engaged and that the Reno-Benteen command should go to his aid. Edgerly agreed. When he saw Weir move out, incorrectly assuming that Reno had given him permission, he followed suit and thus was able to see the Custer battlefield from a hilltop now called Weir Point. He saw Indians firing at objects on the ground, undoubtedly the bodies of Custer's command.[83] Neither group was able to approach Custer's position, however. Less than three miles from the Last Stand battlefield, Weir's men were forced to retreat, as was the entire Reno-

Benteen column when it, too, ventured out. The hill remained under siege for another day until, late in the afternoon of the twenty-sixth, the Indians mysteriously left. Fearing their return, the men clung to their position until the Terry-Gibbon column reached them around noon on the twenty-seventh.

While Benteen was still scouting off to the south, and at the moment when Reno moved west to attack the village that had been glimpsed fleeing, Custer turned north, probably seeking a vantage point from which to get a view of the enemy and then attack from this third direction. He expected Benteen's battalion to return to the main trail after determining that no Indians were escaping over the southern route, but he had also given Benteen orders to "pitch into anything you find," meaning that if there *had* been Indians, Benteen might have been engaged for an indefinite period of time. Benteen sent no message to confirm either of these possibilities.

Custer himself sent two messages back, the first to Captain Thomas M. McDougall, in command of the pack train, and the second to Benteen. Most likely he sent no message to Reno because there was no change in orders: Reno was to engage the Indians at the eastern end of the village while Custer prepared to attack at the western end. Reno, on the other hand, sent two messages to Custer, the first merely informing him that the Reno battalion was poised to attack. The second, with its news of the overwhelming number of the enemy and the urgent need for reinforcement, may have arrived too late to be acted upon, or Custer might have felt that his own attack would be the best reinforcement of Reno. Both of Reno's messengers got through and were found dead on the Last Stand battlefield.

Sergeant Kanipe, the first messenger sent by Custer, believed that the sighting of some sixty to seventy-five Indians on the bluffs on the north side of the Little Bighorn caused Custer to leave Reno's trail and turn north. These Indians were probably not an intentional decoy, a favorite Indian strategy, but they had the same effect on Custer—who knew about this Indian trick and in the past had warned others about it. Pursuing the Indians along the bluffs, the command at last came to a place where the village could be seen, not in its entirety but enough to suggest its enormity.

In addition to his message for McDougall to hurry up with the pack train, Kanipe carried a verbal message added by Tom Custer: "And if you see Benteen tell him to come on quick—a big Indian camp."[84] Kanipe delivered both messages.

The second messenger, trumpeter Martin, was Custer's orderly on June 25. Like Kanipe, he was able to describe Custer's progress along the bluffs and his halt to observe the village, after which Custer told his men that they would go down and capture it. The whole command pulled off their hats and cheered at the news.

In the early afternoon heat the village appeared to be barely stirring: only women and children could be seen, leading Custer to think that he had "caught the Indians napping," not literally as had been the case on the Washita, but figuratively. The officers discussed the possibility that the warriors were off hunting buffalo and would have to surrender if they returned to find their women and children captured.[85] No one with the Seventh could know that the Indians had spent three nights feasting, dancing, and celebrating their recent victory over Crook—they were actually in their lodges resting.

About a half mile beyond the place where the command had halted to observe the village, Martin was given his famous message ordering Benteen to "be quick" and sent on his way. Significantly, when he delivered it, neither Reno nor Benteen asked Martin for particulars on the whereabouts of Custer.[86]

Custer rode off to attack the enormous village with his tiny force, thinking, as he made his final plans, that Reno was engaged on the eastern flank of the village, that Benteen would soon be on his way to join him with more ammunition, and that there appeared to be no warriors in the camp to oppose him. Whether or not he reached the river has always been disputed since the evidence is contradictory.[87] But what happened in an overall sense is crystal clear: the Custer command was crushed by an overwhelming force of Indians who, in addition to superior numbers, had the advantage of terrain and possibly weaponry. Counting only the repeating rifles, they had nearly fourteen bullets for each of the men who died with Custer. And although the Springfield rifles that the cavalry had were superior in "stopping power, range, and accuracy . . . the repeating rifles would have been very effective, perhaps even superior in firepower to the single-shot Springfield carbines, as the Indians drew progressively closer to the cavalry positions."[88]

The effect weaponry had on the Last Stand lends new significance to a sentence in Custer's official report on the Battle of Gettysburg. On

August 22, 1863, Custer attributed the success of the Fifth Michigan against superior numbers to the fact that they were armed with the Spencer repeating rifle, which is, "in my estimation, the most effective fire-arm that our cavalry can adopt."[89] At the Battle of the Little Bighorn the Indians had the Spencer; Custer's troops had new issue single-shot Springfields.

The Indians squeezed the Custer command between two renowned warriors, Gall on the east and Crazy Horse on the west. After the battle, they did not at first shed a great deal of light upon their movements, since they were not accustomed to thinking in terms of American military formations and had reason to be cautious about what they said to whites once they were dependent upon them. Archeological data, however, has confirmed much of the Indians' account of what happened at the Little Bighorn.[90]

Early on, the hard-pressed men of the Last Stand must have waited for the kind of relief that Custer had described in the battle of August 4, 1873, on the Yellowstone, when the two troops of the Seventh eagerly expected the arrival of the rest of the command:

> All eyes were turned to the bluffs in the distance, and there were to be seen, coming almost with the speed of the wind, four separate squadrons of Uncle Sam's best cavalry, with banners flying, horses' manes and tails floating on the breeze, and comrades spurring forward in generous emulation as to which squadron should land its colors first in the fight. It was a grand and welcome sight.[91]

Instead, the scenario must have been more like the one Custer pictured after the demise of Lieutenant Lyman Kidder's party, all of whom were killed by Indians in Kansas while bringing orders to Custer. As Custer wrote to Lieutenant Kidder's father, "They manfully struggled to the last, equally void of hope or fear."[92] Some of those with Custer must have feared, and all must have hoped until the last that the Reno-Benteen forces would finally appear and save the command, but the idea in the condolence letter is the brave man's scorn of any emotional crutch as well as his repudiation of ignoble fear. In that life-and-death contest, all of a soldier's efforts were to be engaged in doing the job "to the last."

After their great victory over Custer on June 25, the Indians' abandonment of the next day's battle against Reno is an ironic counterpart to a series of actions taken by the soldiers opposing them: neither side knew enough about the other to make informed decisions. When the Indians learned of Terry's approach, they decided to leave, although they easily outnumbered the combined forces of the Terry-Gibbon column and the remnant of the Seventh Cavalry.

James McLaughlin, who knew Gall well, said that the ardent warrior never gave him satisfactory reasons for the withdrawal; some may be adduced nevertheless.[93] Since the Reno-Benteen force occupied a defensible position, further fighting would have cost the Indians losses they were not prepared to accept: "Deliberately to incur losses for strategic ends was wholly repulsive to Indian ideas," and, as now seems likely, Indian losses already sustained in the Custer fight were not negligible.[94] The Indians had achieved two sizable victories, over Crook on the Rosebud on June 17 and over Custer on June 25. The approach of still another army was probably decisive since Indians never chose to fight in the vicinity of their villages.

American Indian scholar Stanley Vestal reported that on the second day of battle, Sitting Bull made the following speech to his warriors: "Let them live, they are trying to live. They came against us, and we have killed a few. If we kill them all, they will send a bigger army against us."[95] Whether the great Hunkpapa Sioux made this sensible statement, it was true enough, and the Indians must have known it. Invariably in their experience, an attack on white soldiers sooner or later brought more soldiers. They had come to the Little Bighorn in the first place to hunt, as they did every summer, and to celebrate their traditional way of life; now that the game had moved on, they were ready to move on, too, leaving the battlefield to new opponents—history and myth.

For the white soldiers who first came upon the site, the battlefield was like a Rorschach inkblot in which they might read their own desires or predispositions. One of the earliest observers, Lieutenant McClernand, thought that at the end Custer was thinking "clearly, fast and courageously." McClernand thought that the line Custer established on Last Stand hill (the northern end of a ridge) "showed more care taken in deploying and placing the men than . . . was shown on any other part of the entire field—including, of course, Reno's several positions."[96] Benteen, predictably, thought there was no evidence of organization at all, but archeological investigation has tended to support McClernand. According to the most recent fieldwork, "it is clear that at least the final positions of the Seventh Cavalry troopers represented a V-shaped formation."[97]

Had Custer survived, one writer suggests that he would have been remembered as a figure of the magnitude of General Nelson Miles, that is, as someone with a respectable niche in military history but not known to the general public. If other writers are correct, he would have been court-martialed and cashiered for the disaster to his regiment at the Last Stand, escaping with his life but not his reputation.[98]

Writing to his wife after the battle, Lieutenant Godfrey exclaimed simply, "O God, the horrors of that field!"[99] The memory remained vivid: in 1896, he wrote to E. S. Paxson, who planned to do a painting of the scene, that he would never forget what he had witnessed on the battlefield of the Little Bighorn, June 27, twenty years before:

> The marble white bodies, the somber brown of the dead horses and ponies scattered all over the field . . . and the scattering tufts of reddish-brown grass on the almost ashy-white soil, depict a scene of loneliness and desolation that "bows down the heart in sorrow." I can never forget that sight! . . . The naked, mutilated bodies, with their bloody fatal wounds, were nearly all unrecognizable and presented a scene of sickening, ghastly horror![100]

A manuscript found among Major Reno's effects after his death showed that the same image had imprinted itself on his mind. "Even now, after the lapse of nearly ten years," he wrote, "the horror of Custer's battlefield is still vividly before me, and the harrowing sight of those mutilated and decomposing bodies crowning the heights on which poor Custer fell will linger in my memory till death."[101]

Everyone seemed struck by the nakedness of the bodies, which the Indians had stripped of clothing. Captain Weir exclaimed, "Oh, how white they look!" Turning to Godfrey, he added, "My, that would be a beautiful sentiment for a poem!" and seemed to be quite overcome by the strange thought.[102]

Bradley, the more dispassionate observer, reported little mutilation. In his opinion visible blows had been inflicted by hatchets or clubs in order to finish off wounded men. Custer he described as naked but unmarked, with a peaceful countenance as if he had simply fallen asleep. He had been struck by two bullets, either of which would have been fatal, one in the left side, the other in the left temple, the latter possibly a coup de grâce, since it had not bled.[103] In an anonymous manuscript among Libbie's papers, probably one of the many reminiscences of her husband that she solicited, the writer described telling Custer that (s)he had dreamed of him being shot from his horse by an Indian. He had replied, "I cannot die before my time comes, and if by a bullet in the head—why not?"[104] Clearly, he had fallen, as he described an officer in a Civil War battle, "as the warrior loves to fall, with his face to the foe."[105]

Rumors persist that Custer also had an arrow in the groin, a detail publicly suppressed out of respect for Mrs. Custer. Both the existence and cover-up of the wound are possible, even likely; Indians often shot arrows into their dead victims as a further token of disrespect, and private parts were a favorite target. Technically, this is mutilation, but a single arrow, even tellingly placed, seems little compared to the extensive violence performed on the remains of Tom Custer, unidentifiable except for a tattoo. In addition to George Armstrong Custer, his younger brothers Tom and Boston, nephew Autie Reed, and brother-in-law James Calhoun died at the Last Stand. All told, the regiment that came limping back to Fort Lincoln had lost 51 percent of its strength.[106]

One of the dead, Captain Myles Keogh, achieved an enduring posthumous fame simply because his horse survived the battle. He had fulfilled his name (the Latin *miles*, meaning "soldier") by leaving his home in Ireland at an early age and fighting for the pope before coming to the United States. The handsomely turned out but alcoholic career soldier, who rode a horse "like a Centaur," had written his brother in June of 1869 that he regarded Indian fighting as "the most worrying service in the world."[107] He also said that the month of June had never passed since he left home without something unpleasant occurring to him. "Let us see what it will bring forth this time," he concluded the letter.[108] Though not for another seven years, his appointment in Samarra did indeed take place in June.

Custer voiced no premonition that we know of, but the Cheyenne liked to think that they had had some hand in his doom. Eight years before on the Kansas plains, one of their chiefs had deliberately poured ashes on Custer's toes from the pipe they had smoked together as a way of indicating disrespect and bringing bad luck.[109]

. . .

At his Goose Creek camp, where he had been hunting and fishing since the Battle of the Rosebud on June 17, General Crook received the news of the Seventh Cavalry's defeat as he returned from a hunting trip, "his pack mules loaded down with elk, deer and big horn sheep." He read the dispatch, Captain Mills writes, "and while all of us were horrified and oppressed with mortification and sympathy for the dead and wounded, there was with all, particularly in General Crook's expression, a feeling that the country would realize that there were others who had underrated the valor and numbers of the Sioux."[110]

When General Terry returned to his base camp on June 30 he found a telegram that General Sheridan had sent to him on June 6. It read as follows: "Couriers from the Red Cloud Agency reported at Laramie yesterday that Yellow Robe arrived at the agency, six days from the hostile camp. He said that 1800 lodges were on the Rosebud and about to leave for Powder River below the point of 'Crazy Horse's fight' and says they will fight and have about three thousand warriors. This is sent for your information."[111]

If white encroachment on land guaranteed to the Sioux "as long as the grass shall grow" led the Indians to fight at the Little Bighorn, and the government's ultimatum to be on reservations by January 31, 1876, or be considered hostile provided immediate justification for the army's presence there, the battle took the shape it did for lack of military intelligence and efficient communication.

No one in any of the three commands marching to engage the Sioux had an accurate idea of the number of Indians massing in southeastern Montana Territory. General Sherman's postmortem began with some history: in 1864 the commissioner of Indian affairs had written in his annual report that only seven to ten thousand "hostile" Indians remained, "and the hostiles themselves were so scattered and divided in cliques and bands that, except under extraordinary provocation, or in circumstances not at all to be apprehended, it is not probable that as many as five hundred warriors will ever again be mustered at one point for a fight."[112] By November 1, 1875, the number of remaining hostiles had been reduced to three thousand—at least in the commissioner of

Indian affairs' annual report. When General Sheridan ordered three distinct columns to move to a common center, Sherman continued, it was felt that none of the three could encounter more than five hundred to eight hundred warriors.[113]

Responding to an early writer's statement that "it was well known that thousands of Indians had left their agencies," Lieutenant Godfrey flatly asserted, "it wasn't known to us." He went on to describe attending Custer's final meeting with his officers on the evening of June 24, in which Custer told them he had made "every endeavour" to determine the strength of the hostiles. He thought it was likely to be between eight hundred and one thousand, although "young warriors from the agencies might bring the total to 1,500."[114] At that same meeting, Custer also told his officers that he had rejected Terry's offer of four troops of the Second Cavalry. One writer who was not at the battle described Benteen saying "we will regret not having them," an assertion that Godfrey emphatically annotated "not so!" in his copy of the article.[115]

Because the two armies were in communication only by a two-thousand-mile line around the rear, no one in the combined Custer-Gibbon force under General Terry knew, as they plotted strategy in the cabin of the steamboat the *Far West* on June 21, that four days earlier Crook's army of a thousand men had been defeated on the Rosebud some thirty miles to the south, or, for that matter, that this army was still nearby and largely intact on Goose Creek.[116]

Either piece of crucial information—the number of Indians gathering on the Little Bighorn, or their defeat of Crook—would have made a great difference to General Terry's combined Montana-Dakota column; both together would have made all the difference.

Shortly after Custer learned that he would be allowed to join the expedition, while he was still in St. Paul, he supposedly told Captain William Ludlow that "he had gotten away from Stanley and would be able to swing clear of Terry" without any difficulty.[117] It is highly debatable that Custer ever said this: the source is not Ludlow but the partisan and untrustworthy Robert Hughes, ever loyal to his brother-in-law, General Terry.[118] But had Custer said such a thing, it hardly would have been an announcement of insubordination. The expression "swing clear" is vague enough, nor would Custer have been unusual in hoping to claim credit in the field, as evidenced by the Montana column's disappointment when it looked as if Custer would have the best opportunity to do so.

Furthermore, Custer's sedentary, comfort-loving superior was a man inexperienced in fighting Indians, and, at the age of forty-nine, had hoped that his days in the field were over. In a sense Terry himself wanted Custer to "swing clear"—that is, to play the active role, to put his renowned energy and experience as an Indian fighter to good use, to carry out Terry's plan, but to make whatever decisions were necessary according to the circumstances of the moment—in short, to be a responsible field commander. After all, Custer's success would also be Terry's.

Did Custer disobey Terry's orders? This has been a fiercely contested point since the battle, although attention to the actual words of the document given to Custer should have precluded this particular controversy from the start. According to the written orders, if Custer saw "sufficient reason" to depart from Terry's orders, he might do so. And Custer did indeed have grounds to disregard Terry's purely theoretical construct. That the battle turned out badly does not change the basis upon which Custer acted. As General Sherman declared in reviewing the findings of a court of inquiry on a Civil War battle:

> It would be an unsafe and dangerous rule to hold the commander of an army in battle to a technical adherence to any rule of conduct for managing his command. He is responsible for results, and holds the lives and reputations of every officer and soldier under his orders as subordinate to the great end—victory. The most important events are usually compressed into an hour, a minute, and he [the commander] cannot stop to analyze his reasons. He must act on the impulse, the conviction, of the instant, and should be sustained in his conclusions, if not manifestly unjust. The power to command men, and give vehement impulse to their joint action, is something which cannot be defined by words, but it is plain and manifest in battles, and whoever commands an army in chief must choose his subordinates by reason of qualities which can alone be tested in actual conflict.[119]

Although his superiors all had reservations about his conduct off the battlefield, Custer had already been tested in actual conflict and won their clear confidence in that arena.

The events of Custer's final day bear some comparison with those of Custer's only other significant Indian battle, the attack on Black Kettle's village on the Washita. There, too, Custer rapidly followed a trail to an Indian village of unknown size and divided his forces to encircle the enemy. In both instances the Indians were taken by surprise, "caught napping," as Custer said. Ironically, in the case of the Little Bighorn, the Indians glimpsed early on the day of the battle who had precipitated Custer's attack had not carried the news to the village before the arrival of the troops themselves.

The differences between the two battles, between victory and defeat, are more instructive. First and foremost, Custer scouted properly on the Washita: Ben Clark and several other scouts were sent to reconnoiter the village. After receiving their fairly specific report, Custer "held a council with his officers, outlining his plan."[120] This well-thought-out and well-communicated plan enabled the divided forces of his command to act in concert effectively, and when he needed more ammunition, it arrived providentially. Fortunately for the Seventh, the Indians in Black Kettle's village were no match for the soldiers in numbers, and the Indian women and children taken captive protected the Seventh from a counterattack by the warriors of other nearby villages. At the Little Bighorn the command was divided before a precise plan had been formulated, neither other troops nor ammunition reached the beleaguered Custer force, and the Indians—at least fifteen hundred warriors—were more than a match for the Seventh in numbers and firepower. The caption of a map tracing the routes of Reno, Benteen, and Custer asks the reader to note "with what comparative ease Custer's defeat was accomplished by feeding his command piece-meal to the Sioux at hours most convenient to them."[121] To conduct a successful defensive operation against the Indian force, it was essential that the regiment be reunited.[122]

Historical accounts have conflated the small village of Indians that Reno was sent to run down with the huge encampment that he stumbled into, as if Custer had knowingly sent a terrier to bark at the heels of an elephant.[123] At the same time, it will not do to simply excuse Custer's supposed ignorance of the enormous village lurking behind a bend of the river, for Custer knew full well that one small band of Indians did not constitute the extent of his quarry. At the time of the lone tepee decision no one had seen the great village, extending for over three miles along the Little Bighorn, but the trail Custer was following indicated a large number of Indians ahead, as did his scouts, who had seen an immense pony herd in the valley.

General Sherman would later say that Custer had had no choice but to attack once he found the Indians, a debatable point in and of itself and one that obscures the more critical issue—would Custer have attacked *in the same way* had he known the number of Indians the Seventh faced? It seems obvious that he would not have done so. As Lieutenant Edgerly wrote, "Nobody thought that any hard fighting would take place. . . . his plan all along was to have his troops disposed to head them off in all directions."[124] "Plan" in terms of the Little Bighorn must be understood in the loose sense of an overall design rather than in the more specific sense in which Custer had formulated a plan for the battle on the Washita.

Custer's sharp exchange with Mitch Boyer suggests that he thought his scouts were exaggerating the size of the enemy. He knew that Indians were never eager to attack an enemy of superior force. If Indian scouts did not want to fight, for whatever reason, they might exaggerate the dangers in their reports to white commanders. On both of Lieutenant Bradley's scouting forays, the Crows had discouraged him from approaching the Sioux camp closely, where he might have made a more accurate determination of its size.

There had never been such a gathering of Plains Indians in history, so no one imagined that the Indians would be too many for the army. White military men were accustomed to assuming that their superior organization, discipline, and weaponry would offset even significant disadvantages in numbers. Consider some other famous encounters with Indians in which victorious whites were greatly outnumbered: the Wagon Box Fight may have had a ratio as high as 75 to 1; the battle of Adobe Walls, 41 to 1; and Beecher's Island, 19 to 1. On Last Stand hill, the ratio was probably no higher than 15 to 1.[125]

Moreover, there was the guiding principle of *scattering*, to which frontier military lore was wedded.[126] When their vulnerable villages were discovered, conventional wisdom dictated, Indians ran away; they did not stand and fight. Even after their decisive victory at the Little Bighorn, a white man as sympathetic to the Indians as George Bird Grinnell could not imagine it otherwise. "Of one thing we may be sure," he wrote, "that if Reno and Custer had kept on and charged through the village from opposite ends, *the Indians would have scattered* and there would have been no disaster [my emphasis]."[127] Grinnell seems to have envisioned the precise coordination of the Washita rather than the lack of communication that obtained among Custer's separated forces at the battlefield. As it happened, neither Reno nor Custer came close to charging the village because of the compelling circumstance that was radically different from the Battle of the Washita—numbers.

An example that should have been instructive, the annihilation of Captain William Fetterman by a large force of Sioux, was well known throughout the frontier army, but Fetterman was a novice (and a fool) with only eighty men; Custer had an entire regiment, and he was an experienced and intelligent commander who had in fact gotten the better of some of these same Indians on the Yellowstone in 1873—where he was outnumbered 5 to 1. He would have seen no reason to equate his own well-grounded confidence with the foolhardiness of Fetterman. Yet that very conclusion is inescapable: by thinking like Fetterman that he could handle any number of Indians, Custer led his men into the same death trap.

The steamer *Far West* arrived at Fort Lincoln during the night of July 5, loaded down with bad news and wounded men. At a council of officers held to discuss what needed to be done, Captain William McCaskey, commanding in Custer's absence, took upon himself the difficult assignment of going to the Custer residence at first light to break the news to Libbie and the relatives staying with her—Custer's sister, Margaret Calhoun, and his niece Emma Reed.[128] After the initial shock, Libbie wrapped herself in a cloak and accompanied McCaskey to inform the other bereaved wives. Some commentators have taken this cloak as a sign of trauma, evoking the image of a woman shivering in the intense summer heat.[129] It was only 7:00 A.M., however, and at Fort Abraham Lincoln, where a wind blows unceasingly off the prairie, even a hot summer day can begin on the cool side.

Of the day that followed, Captain Yates's son remembered that he was playing in his yard when another small boy called to him, "Hey, George. Your father has had his head cut off by Indians." Soon this boy, too, learned that his own father was dead.[130] There were twenty-four widows at Fort Lincoln, and many children like George and his two sisters left fatherless.[131]

After hearing the terrible news, those at the post were shocked and apprehensive, so that when the cannon on the watchtower went off a few days later—the signal for an Indian attack—the soldiers immediately sprang to arms. A sentry in the tower had been found shot, it was at first believed, but it turned out that he had merely fallen down in an epileptic fit, discharging his gun as he fell. The man who found him assumed the worst and fired the cannon.[132]

Several days later, Libbie sent a message to Captain Marsh of the *Far West*, requesting that he visit her and the other widows. But, his biographer tells us, "he could not bear the thought of witnessing their grief, and declined."[133] When the Dakota column had marched from Fort Lincoln, Libbie had asked to accompany the expedition on the *Far West*, but had been told by Marsh that it had no accommodations suitable for women. What scrap of comfort did she now hope to obtain from the captain? The *New York Herald* reported on July 17 that Libbie's condition "continued to be alarming. During divine service at her house yesterday she fainted, and remained in a swoon for nearly an hour." Lieutenant Colonel Nelson Miles, a good friend of the Custers, wrote to his wife on July 23 that Libbie "seemed so depressed and in such despair."[134]

A fuller account of her grief during the time she remained at Lincoln was left by an otherwise unknown young man. Milan S. Harmon, a civilian working at the fort in July of 1876, wrote a letter to his sister and brother-in-law, the Reverend and Mrs. William Jenkins, in which he described visiting Mrs. Calhoun and Mrs. Custer after the tragedy. Libbie told him, "I have lost all, I have nothing more to suffer." She added that she had smiled, no doubt ruefully, "to see that I did not shudder at the storm, I was always such a coward in the storms but today I watched it without fear."[135] It was her way of expressing hopelessness, for Libbie had feared storms so much that Custer had once run across an open parade ground with "hailstones pounding down on him like a shower of lead" in order to reassure her.[136] He had found her under the bed. Subsequently, he had assigned a soldier to stay with her in the event that he could not be there himself.

In spite of Libbie's grief and anomie, by the time she left Fort Lincoln with the other widows, the purpose that would motivate the rest of her life was clear, if not yet articulated. When the post children came to say good-bye to her, she gave each one a small photograph of her husband.[137]

Among Libbie's papers there is a sheet headed simply "from June 25 to July 5, 1876"—that period of time in which she had not known about the battle. Below is this unsigned verse:

God pity the wife who is waiting at home
with her lily cheeks and violet eyes
dreaming that old dream of love
while her lover is walking in paradise[138]

20

Survivors

> We transformed by our service this howling wilderness into a civilization. . . . When I came up some three or four years ago on the Burlington up to Sheridan, where we fought the Indians, Crazy Horse's great camp was over here in the Wolf Mountains. As I was climbing those hills, looking over the field where we had fought that battle, I looked down in the valley and I saw farmers cutting their alfalfa and cutting their wheat. Oh! I thought, what a wonderful change.
>
> —Honorable Luther Barker, commander,
> Kansas Indian War Veterans

Of the 647 men who marched to the Little Bighorn on June 25, 1876, 384 returned alive.[1] Surviving is less romantic than dying heroically: Thomas Rosser said that as a soldier he would prefer to lie with the dead at the Battle of the Little Bighorn than live with the survivors.[2] It would be tidy to find that the survivors Rosser spoke of, the soldiers, were marked by their experience in some singular way like the archaeologists who opened Tutenkhamen's tomb. But they reveal, after the Last Stand, a variety of life stories. Thomas Weir, in his thirties like most of the officers killed at the Little Bighorn, died a few months after the battle, probably of alcohol-related causes; Charles Windolph, an enlisted man who would become the last army survivor, lived to be a hundred. Lieutenant Edward Settle Godfrey, who covered up an undistinguished face with an almost grotesquely enormous mustache, became a general, as did handsome Lieutenant Winfield Scott Edgerly.

• • •

One of the most poignant histories connected to the Little Bighorn disaster belongs to the young widow of Lieutenant Henry Harrington, whose body was never found. The *Detroit Evening Journal* of December 2, 1887, told the story of her gradual obsession with the idea that her husband had not died but had been taken captive by the Indians. On the way back from a visit to Texas in 1885, she disappeared. "Some believe," the paper reported, "that she was impelled by her belief in the existence of her husband to go in search of him. But she has never since been heard of."[3] Major Reno thought that Harrington had been burned at the stake. In the lull on Reno-Benteen hill when the Indians mysteriously withdrew, Reno later said that through his field glasses he saw the Indians engaged in a war dance around three captives tied to stakes, one of whom, he thought, must have been Harrington.[4] One can understand why Mrs. Harrington took refuge in the conviction that her husband survived as a captive.

The most interesting stories belong to the two men who shared the command of the seven companies at the Little Bighorn that did not join Custer, Major Marcus Reno and Captain Frederick Benteen. Embittered by controversy over their actions there, each saw the deterioration of the army career that had been his livelihood and life.

Both Benteen and Reno had high opinions of their own ability, the difference being that most people agreed with Benteen's estimation of himself and completely rejected Reno's. Reno seems to have been a man who was stubbornly blind to his own mediocrity. According to Hugh Scott, who joined the Seventh right after the Little Bighorn, Benteen was then "the hero of all America, credited with saving the remnant of the Seventh Cavalry," and Reno's reputation "was being pulled apart all over the United States."[5] For Reno, the crucial event of the battle's aftermath began two and one-half years later, on January 13, 1879, when a court of inquiry convened at Chicago to consider his conduct at the battle. This had been called by President Hayes in response to Reno's own request: he needed an official forum to counter the public charges raised by Frederick Whittaker, the successful dime novelist and biographer-hagiographer of Custer. On June 13, 1878, Whittaker had released a letter to the press asserting that Reno's failure to carry out his order to charge the village, "owing to his cowardice and disobedience," caused the army's defeat. Moreover, after being joined by Benteen and the pack train, "he remained idle with this force while his superior officer was fighting against the whole force of the Indians, the battle being within his knowledge, the sound of firing audible from his position, and his forces out of immediate danger from the enemy."[6]

Two months after the battle a headline in the *New York Herald* asked, "Was It Rashness of the Dead or Prudence of the Living?" and continued pointedly, "Seven Companies Inactive While Custer was Slaughtered."[7] Years later General Nelson A. Miles, who became the army's most renowned Indian fighter after Custer's death, wrote of the battle that no commander can win "with seven-twelfths of the command remaining out of the engagement when within sound of his rifle shots."[8] The final phrase went beyond the suggestion that the seven companies were culpable for unwittingly remaining hors de combat to imply that they intentionally ignored their comrades in distress, a key point at issue in the proceedings of the court of inquiry.

It has been commonly held that after the Battle of the Little Bighorn the army closed ranks at the court proceedings to preclude criticism damaging to itself: further scrutiny of the campaign—which had been a waste of time, money, and men—could only reinforce the public's antimilitary sentiments. In interviews with Walter Camp, the interpreter Frederic F. Gerard said that "the general understanding among all whom he talked with confidentially was that any officer who made himself obnoxious to the defense would incur the wrath of certain officers in pretty high authority in certain department headquarters farther west than Washington and not as far west as St. Paul"—in other words, Phil Sheridan, whose office was in Chicago.[9] As Gerard told Camp, "it was made the business of certain ones active for the defense to get hold of all the doubtful witnesses before they were called and entertain them well. On such occasions they were cautiously sounded and discreetly primed."[10]

Indisputably, the three colonels who comprised the court would have had reason to be deferential to the army's lieutenant general, and one—Wesley Merritt—was a particular favorite of Sheridan's. Almost twenty years later the court recorder, Lieutenant Jesse M. Lee, wrote to Libbie that he had been influenced "by the prejudicial opinions of those whose motive I did not then understand, and whose sources of information I then had no means of testing."[11] At that late date it must have seemed futile to Lee to specify what or whose prejudicial opinions he had in mind; at any rate, he did not elaborate.

Reno was officially exonerated of wrongdoing by the court of inquiry, but when witnesses were offered the opportunity to commend him, few gave more than halfhearted approval and some considerably less. With the exception of Colonel John Gibbon, who was not present at the battle, each one was asked the same question: "State whether the conduct and example of Major Reno as Commanding Officer was such as tended to inspire the men of his command with courage, coolness and confidence, or the reverse, describing his conduct fully as it came under your observation during the engagement."

A conscientious answer addressing all parts of the question could hardly be given in a few words. For an engagement that covered more than two days and three different venues, a response of some length would have been expected, even—one would think—mandatory. Benteen answered this long, involved question merely with "I think it was all right, sir."[12] Young Lieutenant Luther Hare struggled. After saying that he had seen no evidence of cowardice, he felt impelled to add: "It is very hard for me to answer the question. That was the only action I was ever in of any prominence and I don't know whether he rose equal to the emergency or not. I have not much to go upon in making an estimate." Most finessed the question by saying that they had seen little of Reno during the siege—hardly a tribute to his leadership.[13]

If the Seventh had been counseled to avoid criticizing Reno, some of the witnesses had clearly turned a deaf ear. Lieutenant Edward Mathey's was perhaps the most damaging testimony. After indicating that he had rarely seen Reno during the battle, so that it was not surprising that he had observed "no action on his part to indicate want of courage, or indicating cowardice," he described discussions held since the battle that made it clear how unfavorably Reno was judged by his fellow officers. According to Mathey, one had said, "If we had not been commanded by a coward we would all have been killed."[14]

Time and again as a new witness took the stand, Reno must have hoped to hear the inevitable question answered with a staunch affirmation of his conduct, but if the men of the Seventh refused to condemn Reno outright, keeping in mind that they had survived along with him, they had no stomach to defend him either. The disastrous retreat from the timbers was assailed from almost every point of view: because no bugle call had been given, many of the men failed to hear the command to move out; because no rear cover was provided, casualties were heavy; Reno *led* the retreat rather than bringing up the rear; and, most crucially, the movement itself was a tactical error—the position in the timbers was more defensible than the open space the command moved to. Describing his own behavior toward his men, Sergeant Edward Davern commented: "I think it is the duty of an officer on a retreat to be the last one out, and on a charge to be the first one." Even Captain Myles Moylan, the officer who supported Reno most strongly, refused to do so on the issue of leading the retreat—which Reno had ludicrously characterized as a charge.[15]

Colonel Gibbon, who had arrived with General Terry to rescue the remainder of the Seventh Cavalry on June 27, was an irritatingly gratuitous witness from Reno's point of view, since he had not been present at the battle. Over Reno's objection, he testified at length to the weakness of the hill position that Reno retreated to. "The country was quite broken by a succession of little rolling hills and valleys," he told the court, "behind which attacking forces could conceal themselves. Then the manner in which the animals were exposed was very bad for the command . . . and then the fact of them being cut off from water."[16] He went on to extol the abandoned position in the timbers as far more defensible.[17]

Reno's anger might have been even stronger if he had known anything about Gibbon's decisions during the Montana column's march down the Yellowstone or if he had had access to the comments of some of the officers under Gibbon's command. He would have discovered in what low esteem this know-it-all witness was himself held by his subordinates. But Gibbon's bungling was not the subject of the court of inquiry, and until recently it has received little attention.[18] Similarly, Terry's mistakes were obscured as the Little Bighorn debate quickly became a battle between Custer partisans and critics.

By the time the court of inquiry verdict exonerated Reno, he was already on the slippery slope. As early as September 26, 1876—on the evening of the day the Seventh returned from their disastrous campaign—he had been involved in an altercation with another officer. An exchange of insulting remarks led to a fistfight with Lieutenant John A. Manley, in which Reno "did roll on the floor of the Officers Club room at Fort Abraham Lincoln, Dak. Ty. [Dakota Territory] in the slops and filth caused by spittle and the spilling of liquor upon said floor.[19] Lieutenant Charles Varnum tried to mediate and was repulsed by Reno.

Captain Thomas Weir then attempted to get Reno and Varnum to shake hands, only to see Reno slap away Varnum's hand.[20] These charges brought by a group of officers did not lead to court-martial proceedings because the Seventh's commanding officer, Colonel Samuel Sturgis, refused to support them, but they give some idea of Reno's relations with his fellow officers in the aftermath of the battle.

On March 8, 1877, Reno was brought up on charges of conduct unbecoming an officer and a gentleman for actions committed the previous December when he had commanded Fort Abercrombie, Dakota Territory.[21] The transcript of these court-martial proceedings shows Reno's folly in making rather sedate advances toward another officer's wife and then taking absurdly petty measures to punish her lack of interest. The time the alleged events occurred may be material. It was the holiday season, a period that often exacerbates loneliness. Reno's wife had died suddenly two years before and his only child was in the East. He was generally disliked. On an occasion when Lieutenant James Bell was away from the post, Reno concluded a social call on Mrs. Bell (as she is referred to throughout the proceedings) by taking both of her hands and attempting to pull her toward him. She easily freed herself and offered him a handshake instead. He failed to respond in the conventional manner and instead ran his hand up Mrs. Bell's arm—to the small extent her sleeve would permit.

Her next move was an attempt to bring things back into the realm of acceptable social interaction and discourage further familiarities on the major's part. "Is that the Masonic grip?" she asked. "Yes," Reno replied, "I have a book at home that tells all about it; would you like to read it?"

After further rebuffs by a woman he believed to be accessible to others, Reno was quoted as saying to the post trader, "This means war! Mrs. Bell has thrown down the gauntlet, and I will take it up. Perhaps these people do not know the power of a commanding officer." To a minister who had come to the post to hold a holiday religious service, and, incidentally, to stay at the Bells' house in spite of Lieutenant Bell's absence, Reno allegedly remarked that Mrs. Bell was "notorious in the regiment as a loose character." On this charge, Reno was found not guilty of saying "as a loose character," leaving Mrs. Bell with the dubious consolation of being acknowledged merely as "notorious in the regiment."[22]

Reno was found not guilty of an additional charge, the attempt to bribe a "colored servant" to support his version of events. In the substance of the other specifications, all of which end ritualistically with the solemn phrase "to the scandal and disgrace of the military service," Major Marcus Reno was judged guilty and sentenced to be dismissed from the service. Mitigation to a two-year suspension from rank and pay was recommended and became his sentence.

Shortly after the verdict, Frederick Benteen wrote to his wife that he had seen the announcement in a Bismarck newspaper. "He can congratulate himself in getting off thus easily," Benteen added, "and can now visit Turkey, where the 'scrouging' of women is not attended with as fatal consequence."[23] Benteen evidently knew that Reno hoped to go abroad, a plan that General Sherman vetoed as a means of stripping the punishment "of all effect."

A year later found Reno writing to the president to request immediate reinstatement: "The anguish and humiliation which I underwent at the promulgation of the sentence and the publication in the newspapers spreading it over the country was, to me, an extreme punishment."[24] If it was, it was not salutary: when he returned to the army after serving the entire sentence, Reno was in trouble again only a few months later.[25] The first charge, saloon brawling, was fairly straightforward. Reno was accused of hitting Lieutenant W. J. Nicholson with a billiard cue, "with the manifest intent of inflicting serious bodily injury." He did not deny it, but said that he had picked up the cue in "a fit of passion" after their argument over a gambling debt. According to Nicholson, he had told Reno that he could "lick him in two minutes in any way he wanted." Reno remembered it as "I can knock the stuffing out of you." On another evening he was drunk and disorderly in the billiard saloon, knocking money out of the hands of the saloon keeper ("wantonly and in a riotous manner") and smashing a couple of windows with chairs ("in a wanton and riotous manner"). One wonders about the slight variations in formulaic language, but evidently such phrases were taken seriously by the court. One member argued that the breaking of windows was wanton, if not riotous, and protested when the court's verdict removed the parenthetical expressions.

The third instance of drunken behavior referred to a dinner at the post trader's house where several men had been present and only one bottle of whiskey. Reno argued that since no one had regarded him as drunk when he arrived, and since several other people were being accommodated by the same bottle, it was impossible that he could have drunk enough to become intoxicated. This theory withered, though, when the trader's wife described Reno at her table: "He swayed in his chair, his utterance unintelligible as he hiccuped." She was apprehensive, she told the court, thinking he would vomit at any moment.

Worse than these instances of drunkenness, egregious but hardly uncommon in the frontier army, Reno had incurred the enmity of his commanding officer by frightening his daughter so much that she twitched as if, according to both her and her father's testimony, she had "St. Vitus dance." The charge accused Reno of peeping into the window of his commanding officer's house late one night, "approaching so near (and so stealthily) as to (very seriously) affright and alarm that portion of the family of the said Colonel S. D. Sturgis, 7th Cavalry, which had not yet retired for the night." The words in parenthesis throughout the charge all served to place this bizarre incident in the worst possible light for Reno, who maintained that he had impulsively moved toward the lighted window on his forlorn late-night walk.

Twenty-year-old Ella Sturgis was a dramatic witness. She testified that she had seen Reno's face gradually appear at the window, his eyes fixed on her. "My impression at first," she told the court, "was that I should be shot if I moved. His face was very pale and he looked as if he was about to do something desperate. . . . I was trembling all over and frightened nearly to death." Colonel Sturgis, who had already gone to bed, heard his wife call excitedly, "come quickly Major Reno," a cryptic utterance that must have conveyed very little to a man just roused from sleep. Sturgis's first thought in this emergency was to find some clothes to put on, but when his wife called again more urgently, he came downstairs in his nightdress. There he found his daughter "cowering in the farther corner of the sitting room alone." The word *alone* suggests that Sturgis was prepared to find Major Reno in the house. He immediately asked, "Where is he?" and the prostrate Ella pointed feebly to the side window. Sturgis grabbed a cane and ran outside, but found no one. He came back in and got dressed, with the idea of continuing the search, but his wife and daughter, who feared that Reno might still be lurking about the house, would not let him leave.

Frederick Benteen's testimony that in his opinion Reno "was dead in love with the young lady" did nothing to moderate Sturgis's outrage or help Reno with the court. Reno must have known that he could not realistically aspire to Ella Sturgis; his own explanation of being drawn from his loneliness and unhappiness to the lighted window and the family life it represented seems more plausible.

Reno was found guilty on all counts, although the strongly pejorative language—"wantonly and riotously," "surreptitiously," "stealthily," et cetera—was stricken from the charges. One member of the court objected to removing the word *disgusting* from the description of Reno's behavior at the post trader's home: "At a lady's dinner table he presented the appearance of being about to vomit, so this should be characterized as 'disgusting.'"

A sentence of dismissal was mandatory, but Colonel Thomas Barr, the judge advocate; General Terry, the first reviewing officer; General Sherman, the army's commanding general; and five of the seven members of the court all recommended mercy. Colonel Barr felt that "there was some excuse for the assault" on Nicholson since "the accused appears to have been repeatedly and grossly insulted by that officer." General Terry remarked that "the sentence is manifestly excessive as a punishment for the acts of which Maj. Reno was found guilty." Unexpectedly, President Hayes—neither a drinker nor a Peeping Tom—ignored the recommendation for clemency, and in 1880, after twenty-three years of service, Reno was dishonorably discharged from the army.[26] Compared to Custer's one-year suspension for abandoning his command and ordering deserters summarily shot, it was a harsh punishment, but then, Reno was not a Civil War hero—he was an embarrassment, blamed by many for the defeat at the Little Bighorn.

On leaving the army he wrote to request copies of any letters of commendation on file in the War Department, but unknown to him, there was not much help there. When he had applied for a job on the adjutant general's staff in 1869, a letter addressed to the adjutant general claimed that the writer knew Reno some years ago "and from my recollection [I] do not think that either in point of character or of ability he would add strength to the department."[27]

Few people ever spoke of him with enthusiasm: a fellow cadet at West Point noted in his diary that "Reno is not very popular."[28] Charles Windolph, a private at the time of the Little Bighorn, recollected that most of the enlisted men did not know or care a great deal about Reno: "He didn't seem to be very popular with either the men or the officers."[29] The easygoing Dr. DeWolf, who found everyone he met pleasant and likable, wrote to his wife that "Reno who commands my wing I cannot like."[30] Joining the regiment immediately after the Little Bighorn disaster, E. A. Garlington found it easy to see that Reno was not popular: "There was no gathering around his camp-fire at night as was the custom with a popular c.o."[31] And Hugh Scott, who joined the Seventh at the same time, reminisced that his initial unfavorable impression of Reno "was not improved by observation."[32] Even the mild and humane Terry could not stand him: the August 14, 1876, entry in Godfrey's *Field Diary* reported that Terry had said that "if he had not so much respect for the officers of the Regt. he would put some other field officer on duty with the Regt." Godfrey commented: "It seems that Reno's self important rudeness makes him unbearable."[33]

As long as he had the means, Reno tried to obtain reinstatement by getting bills introduced into Congress. Strongly opposed by Secretary of War Robert Lincoln, these were always pigeonholed or rejected. In 1890 Reno died, a victim of cancer and a pauper. Only long after his death would Custer haters like E. A. Brininstool, Frederic Van De Water, and Fred Dustin give his actions at the Little Bighorn the kind of sympathetic defense Reno had always felt they deserved.[34]

Much later, in 1967, the case that had been repeatedly shunted aside by Congress during Reno's lifetime was brought before the Board for the Correction of Military Records, and his dishonorable discharge was revoked. The board concluded that "the recent loss of his wife, his state of bachelorhood in a desolate frontier fort and in the field and the attendant primitive conditions, were not conducive to producing 'plaster saints.'"[35] It further noted that Reno had become controversial after the battle: "This experience had a traumatic effect on his personality and conduct, and the resulting stigma led to a rapid decline in his prior exemplary conduct."[36] Posthumous justice, perhaps, but, for the very reasons offered by the board, it seems unlikely that a favorable verdict in the final court-martial could have halted Reno's self-destructive course.

As if Reno didn't have reason enough for his personal decline, an enterprising researcher has suggested that the effects of tertiary syphilis, commonly appearing some twenty years after the original infection, could have contributed to the erratic behavior that characterized the last phase of Reno's army career.[37] Reno was treated twice for syphilis at West Point, which could mean that the first treatment was unsuccessful; the symptoms of paresis described in a medical textbook include "defective judgment, lack of insight, confusion, and often depression or marked elation."[38] Moreover, although Reno died of cancer of the tongue, erysipelas—which may occur with tertiary syphilis—was listed as a secondary cause of death.[39]

. . .

Benteen's was a more interesting case, as Benteen was the more interesting man. Most likely Custer seldom thought of the tiresome Reno—other than Custer's strong condemnation of Reno's reconnaissance for General Terry, there is no evidence of any friction between them.[40] Benteen, on the other hand, must have been a chronic irritant, always outspoken, always needling, and yet, because of his ability as an officer, impossible to write off. A few days before the Battle of the Little Bighorn, Lieutenant Thompson, an officer on Terry's staff, overheard a heated argument between Custer and Benteen about the Battle of the Washita, eight years before. Benteen castigated Custer for "abandoning" Major Elliott, while Custer twitted Benteen about shooting a young Indian boy. "It was plain to be seen that Benteen hated Custer," Thompson observed, but significantly he did not say that Custer hated Benteen.[41]

Benteen not only hated Custer, he was obsessed with him until his own death. The bulk of his most virulent condemnation occurred during the 1890s, his own final years and a quarter of a century after Custer's death. Benteen's sense of Custer's overvaluation continued to grate on his equally strong belief in his own undervaluation. Although there was no monstrous and demonstrable wrong to explain Benteen's vicious and enduring hatred, the clash of personalities within the confined space of a cavalry regiment, aggravated by petty irritations and a disposition to be envious, may be enough to account for it.

In annotating a copy of Custer's *My Life on the Plains*, Benteen made the comprehensive declaration: "Gen. Custer did me many wrongs, but I never bore him any malice, but on every occasion offerred [*sic*], rendered him valuable service, and supported him far better than the boot-licks who thronged around him."[42] It was a telling statement of Benteen's hunger for recognition and his complete delusion about his feelings for Custer. In the very act of savaging the long-dead object of his hatred, he habitually presented himself as more sinned against than sinning; yet in his letters, in notes for his son Freddy, and in certain public incidents, the record is the opposite.

Benteen's own account cites Custer's major wrong to him as borrowing a hundred dollars and taking over a year to pay it back. This was irresponsible, of course, but hardly on a par with Benteen's efforts to blacken Custer's reputation and sow dissension among the officers of the Seventh Cavalry over the death of Major Elliott at the Battle of the Washita.[43] How much harm the accusation did to Custer within the regiment can only be conjectured since Custer's own behavior was divisive as well, but Benteen clearly intended the charge to be poisonous to his commander. It further showed Benteen's willingness to sacrifice the truth to his obsession.

Where Benteen took an initiative to discredit Custer over Elliott's death, there was no evidence of comparable plotting on Custer's part. Benteen, however, saw such motives everywhere in Custer's behavior. He suggested that the coloring of the horses before the campaign of 1868, in which each company was required to ride horses of the same color, was not only "criminal, unjust and arbitrary in the extreme," but an act directed primarily against himself because his command ended up with the inferior mounts.[44] He further maintained that Custer deployed his forces in the Battle of the Washita with the intention of getting Benteen killed, a contention apparently without substance since all of the forces were to attack at the same time.[45] Even after the Little Bighorn, Benteen asserted that he was sent on the "scout to the left" at the battle to keep him from getting a share of the glory Custer envisioned.[46]

Had Custer been Benteen, eager to turn the tables on a successful adversary, this kind of highly subtle plotting—for which there is no material evidence—might have been true. As is, it seems far-fetched. Custer's forte was direct action: a cavalry charge, a buffalo hunt, a hard march. The measures he took against others were overt, such as his harsh punishments of deserters and the transfer of officers he did not like—including Benteen—away from his own post. But, most important, nothing indicates that he shared Benteen's preoccupation with their relationship.

Another way that Benteen attacked Custer was to critique *My Life on the Plains* by the standard of unvarnished chronicle rather than any more ambitious literary genre. Obviously Custer had no incentive to discuss his court-martial in a book about his adventures with Indians on the Plains, and since he was writing about *his* life on the Plains instead of a general history of that time and place, any number of people—including Benteen—may well have felt that their contributions had been slighted. In his assessment of the book, Benteen constantly returned to the same points: the omitted court-martial received at least a half dozen annotations, and Custer's failure to mention that A. J. Smith was colonel of the regiment at the time was also noted several times. Custer's references to officers by their brevet ranks, a courteous form of address in widespread use, were systematically corrected to their actual rank in Benteen's notes, although from time to time Benteen signed his own name with brevet rank.

On other matters Benteen's accusations may have had substance. That Custer took the attractive Cheyenne captive Monaseetah into his bed, for example, was supported by Ben Clark's remarks to Walter Camp. Clark should be considered a reliable witness: had he simply wanted to discredit Custer, he might have supported Benteen's version that Custer had intentionally abandoned Major Elliott. Instead, he vigorously defended Custer on the more serious issue of Elliott's death and thus seems evenhanded in confirming the dalliance with Monaseetah.

That Custer made deals with various sutlers to receive kickbacks, another charge Benteen levels, was possible, but there is a suspicious lack of corroborative evidence. Moreover, if he *had* been blatantly guilty of this practice, to the extent that a fellow officer like Benteen knew of it, Custer would have been taking an exceedingly foolish chance in presenting himself as an opponent of such deals when he testified before the Clymer Committee, and the nation, in the spring of 1876. Any report tarring him with his own brush would have ruined his career.

In short, given Benteen's strong desire to find fault with Custer, and his highly subjective renditions of events, his unsupported word must always be regarded as highly suspect.

Despite his obsessive hatred of his commander, Benteen had the reputation of being a good officer. The opinion of his leadership during the siege of Reno hill at the Little Bighorn was close to unanimous: he had been the hero who saved the day. Private William Morris of M Company pronounced him "unquestionably the bravest man I ever met."[47] Sergeant John M. Ryan, who had once been reduced to the ranks by Benteen, nevertheless had this to say of his conduct: "Too much cannot be said in favor of Captain Benteen. His prompt movements saved Reno from utter annihilation, and his gallantry cleared the ravines of Indians."[48] Young Hugh Scott adopted Benteen as his model of the ideal cavalry officer, often watching "his every movement to find out the secret of his quiet steady government, that I might go and govern likewise."[49]

Benteen's decline, when it came, was precipitous. To be promoted to major he had transferred out of the Seventh and into the Ninth Cavalry. Then he was sent as commander to Fort DuChesne, Utah, with the mission of replacing its tents with buildings, but he did not get anything built. General Crook, his exasperated superior, finally instructed his inspector general, Major Robert H. Hall, to investigate. "Probably the principal cause of delay," Hall wrote in his report of December 7, 1886,

> has been the conduct of Major F. W. Benteen, 9th Cavalry, the officer in command. I was informed that he is frequently unfitted for duty through the excessive use of intoxicating liquors, and this for periods of two or three days at a time. During these attacks he is said to be obstinate and unreasonable, and so abusive to those about him as to make it impossible to transact any business with him. These attacks it is said have increased in frequency during the last two months, so that now he is very often thus disabled.[50]

The court-martial proceedings amply confirmed Hall's findings. Most of the testimony documented instances of Benteen's intoxication—drunken blusterings and threats to various men he encountered about the post—and on one occasion in his tent he offended a group of women who were paying a social call. Without ceremony he suddenly went outside and urinated, at some length, against the tent, as could be clearly heard within it. In this episode, however, the officer who had been so lauded for bravery at the Little Bighorn, and pronounced "the finest soldier and the greatest gentleman I ever knew" by the battle's longest-surviving enlisted man, Charles Windolph, deserves some pity.[51] He had developed a painful prostate condition that demanded frequent relief, a condition that must have been worsened by alcohol. He was probably unable to help himself; certainly there is no evidence that he was being intentionally offensive.

Like Custer before him, he took an active role in his court-martial, no doubt hurting his case by his insinuations. Also like Custer, he could not take the charges with equanimity, at one point addressing the court with a mixture of accusation and self-pity: "Now that I have gotten in the way of a Sutler and a Contracter, why, perforce an attempt is made to push me to the wall, charged with being found drunk, and this after twenty five years of terribly severe service."[52] In keeping with his character, he felt himself to be a victim of conspiracy.

Benteen did receive clemency after the court found him guilty and was thus able to take an honorable discharge for medical reasons. Unlike many reluctant retirees, he was fortunate in having the means to live comfortably, on property in Atlanta, until his death a decade later. During this time he soured considerably, becoming more caustic about his former commander in letters to an old friend, the photographer David Barry, and—more remarkably—to Theodore Goldin, a former enlisted man of the Seventh Cavalry who insinuated himself into an epistolary acquaintance. Benteen told Goldin that he was unwilling to make public charges, but he wanted someone to know his opinion of Custer, an opinion that he constantly buttressed with references to "the truth," "affidavits," "proof," and "common knowledge," but no actual supporting data.

The Indians who were surprised by Custer at the Little Bighorn were soon harassed by the armies of the original campaign against the Sioux, augmented by as many other troops as Sheridan could provide. The soldiers suffered long, exhausting marches and in some instances severe deprivations, but, despite their efforts, they predictably produced no decisive victories: Crook's Battle of Slim Buttes, in which he accidentally came upon a band of Sioux, was another episode of bungled opportunity in his lamentable record against them. Like other Indian campaigns, the 1876 campaign against the Sioux signally failed to demonstrate that white soldiers could outfight Indians. It proved instead that whites could bring tremendous resources to bear against the Indians when they had the will to do so. And it confirmed that Indians could generally avoid contact with the enemy, but could not do so and hunt enough game to live on at the same time. Those two preeminent military men, Generals Sherman and Sheridan, had been right in acknowledging that it would not be their army that would tame the hostile Indians: it would be the disappearance of the buffalo.

In their memoirs both generals would write with satisfaction of this denouement. Sherman spoke of replacing the wild buffalo with herds of tame cattle, and of "substituting for the useless Indians the intelligent owners of productive farms and cattle-ranches."[53] Sheridan, who tended to be more verbose and emotional when he considered such topics, wrote that

> the majority of the wasteful and hostile occupants of millions of acres of valuable agricultural, pasture and mineral lands, have been forced upon reservations under the supervision of the Government; some Indian children have been placed in schools, under instruction in a better life than the vagabond existence to which they were born, and the vast section over which the wild and irresponsible tribes once wandered, redeemed from idle waste to become a home for millions of progressive people.[54]

Eventually, the Sioux were coaxed and coerced onto their appointed reservations, where, before long, they were being asked to sell their most cherished and sacred earth, the Black Hills. Their adamant refusal had no bearing on the outcome. As the *Annual Report of the Board of Indian Commissioners* (1879) stated, "It is evident that no 12,000,000 acres of the public domain whose hills are full of ores, and whose valleys are waiting for diligent hands to 'dress them and keep them,' in obedience to the divine command, can long be kept simply as a park, in which wild beasts are hunted by wilder men."[55] "Diligent hands," "divine command," "wild beasts," and "wilder men": the language made it clear who the white Indian commissioners thought deserved those twelve million acres.[56]

The instructions given to the white negotiators of the Grand Council who were called to discuss buying the Black Hills from the Sioux unintentionally defined the problem of all such efforts to adjudicate conflicts between Indians and whites. The commissioner of Indian affairs instructed the government's representatives at the council that "in negotiating with these ignorant and almost helpless people you will keep in mind the fact that you represent them and their interests not less than those of the Government, and are commissioned to secure the best interests of both parties, so far as practicable."[57] Aside from the weasel words "so far as practicable," these were impossible instructions: it was indisputably in the Indians' best interests *not* to sell the Black Hills for any price. It was the government's intention to buy the hills regardless. Given such utterly opposed positions, how could men committed to white culture as a superior form of life, and to American expansion and development of an area rich in minerals and suitable for agriculture, weigh the interests of both parties equally?

Appropriately, the Indian whose name had always been synonymous with intransigence, Sitting Bull, held out the longest, staying in Canada until his band was reduced to a fraction of its original size and had no more food. Mindful of the destitution of his followers, but still with much reluctance, he surrendered on July 20, 1881.[58] Motioning to his five-year-old son, Crow Foot, to hand over his rifle to the officer in charge, he made the following speech:

> I surrender this rifle to you through my young son, whom I now desire to teach in this manner that he has become a friend of the Americans. I wish him to learn the habits of the whites and to be educated as their sons are educated. I wish it to be remembered that I was the last man of my tribe to surrender my rifle. This boy has given it to you, and he now wants to know how he is going to make a living.[59]

With his usual keenness Sitting Bull had articulated the most important issue: now that they had capitulated, how were the Sioux to live?

Crow Foot's own tragedy would spare him the collective tragedy of many Indians of his generation. Sent to the famous Indian school in Carlisle, Pennsylvania, they were educated as whites, only to be returned to the reservation world of "blanket Indians," a life without opportunity or hope. When Sitting Bull prepared to go peacefully with the contingent of forty-four Indian police who had come to arrest him in the winter of 1890 acting on the government's fear that he was lending his still enormous prestige to the Ghost Dance, the fourteen-year-old Crow Foot urged resistance. No doubt he had heard many times about his father's exploit in counting coup against the Crows at the age of fourteen, and like a typical young man, he, too, longed for the glory of such early achievement. Probably his urging his father to resist was not decisive; one of the angry crowd of Sitting Bull's followers fired the first shot, killing a policeman; after that, a general fight broke out that left Sitting Bull and thirteen others dead. Crow Foot had hidden under a pile of blankets in the house, where he was discovered by the police and, while begging for his life, executed. He had been his father's favorite.[60]

When Indians did not simply fade away as white Americans had hoped and expected and even lamented, the government entertained a number of desperate schemes, fantasies that had no relationship to real circumstances. The most visionary was the idea of using former slaves to instruct the Indians, thus economically handling the problem of two different nonwhite peoples whom the dominant society did not wish to assimilate. Another foolish idea was the plan to pay the travel expenses of any German immigrant who would agree to train two Indian apprentices upon arrival. Those who regarded reservations as not sufficiently remote dreamed of buying Baja California from Mexico and settling Indians there.[61] Toward the end of the nineteenth century official policy held that Indians must either conform to white civilization or, as one commissioner of Indian affairs said, bluntly, "be crushed by it."[62] To achieve the desideratum one of assimilation, advocate of the Indians earnestly asserted, they must learn to be greedy, to wear trousers with "a *pocket that aches to be filled with dollars*."[63]

Indians and whites alike gathered to observe the anniversary of the Battle of the Little Bighorn with increasingly elaborate ceremonies, a ritual that celebrated the new harmony between the two peoples. On another ceremonial occasion, the presidential inauguration of 1905, the longtime Sioux agent James McLaughlin positioned himself close to the Seventh Cavalry to watch the parade. When the band from the Carlisle Indian School marched by the Seventh, it struck up the regimental favorite, "Garryowen." "Among the Carlisle students," McLaughlin reflected, "were boys whose fathers had been in the forefront of the red swarm that came up out of the ravine and overwhelmed Custer that day in June of the centennial year." McLaughlin could not help but think with satisfaction that "the men, red and white, who made history in the days when there was a frontier in this country had given way to another and happier people, living in better and happier times."[64] But what were the Indian cadets thinking as they played the tune the Seventh had marched to in their various Indian battles, the tune that for Custer more nearly suggested the trampling and roar of a cavalry charge than any other?[65]

In 1992 the British periodical *The Economist* sent one of its reporters to the largest Sioux reservation. The story, "What Hope for Pine Ridge?" describes a society as deprived and dysfunctional as any in the United States:

> Housing is scarce and flimsy; many homes have no indoor toilets. Suicide rates are twice the national average, as are deaths from influenza and pneumonia. Infant-mortality and murder rates run at three times the national average, and deaths from alcoholism are ten times as high. . . . There is no bank, no clothes shop, no pharmacy. In the town of Pine Ridge, the closest thing to a restaurant is a small taco stand.[66]

Over this sorry panorama we might hear the voice of Sitting Bull, as he spoke to a newsman more than a century before *The Economist*'s reporter visited Pine Ridge:

> White men like to dig in the ground for their food. My people prefer to hunt the buffalo as their fathers did. White men like to stay in one place. My people want to move their tepees here and there to the different hunting grounds. The life of white men is slavery. They are prisoners in towns or farms. The life my people want is a life of freedom. I have seen nothing that a white man has, houses or railways or clothing or food, that is as good as the right to move in the open country, and live in our own fashion.[67]

Custer would have agreed. "The Indian," he wrote in *My Life on the Plains*,

> cannot be himself and be civilized; he fades away and dies. Cultivation such as the white man would give him deprives him of his identity. . . . If I were an Indian, I often think I would greatly prefer to cast my lot among those of my people adhered to the free open plains rather than submit to the confined limits of a reservation, there to be the recipient of the blessed benefits of civilization, with its vices thrown in without stint or measure.[68]

Although the spiritual leader Sitting Bull may have been a more significant leader of the Sioux, he has been replaced in the collective imaginations of whites and Indians alike by the great Oglala warrior, Crazy Horse. Seventeen miles from Mount Rushmore a gigantic sculpture of Crazy Horse is slowly taking shape in the mountain face. When completed, it will surpass in size the presidential heads. The name of Crazy Horse also lives on in legend: just as the paratroopers of World War II yelled the name of an Apache warrior as they plunged to earth, so the modern Seventh Cavalry chose "Operation Crazy Horse" as the name of a summer campaign in the Vietnam War.[69]

The Battle of the Little Bighorn made such a claim on the American imagination that even one of the surviving animals from the Seventh Cavalry was adopted as an important symbol of the conflict. Captain Myles Keogh's horse Comanche, named after the Seventh's fight with the Comanches on the Cimarron River, would become part of the history of the Last Stand.[70] According to popular report the only survivor of that battlefield, Comanche lived on as not only the pet of the regiment but the subject of at least three nonfictional books and a number of poems, novels, and paintings—not to mention countless references in battle literature.[71]

Too badly wounded for the Indians to bother with, Comanche was nursed back to health by the doting regiment and became their living witness to the famous battle. On April 10, 1878, Colonel Sturgis, whose only son had died at the age of twenty-two at the Little Bighorn, issued an order conferring official status on the horse, in part to protect him from those who sneaked souvenir hairs from his increasingly threadbare tail and in part to protect himself from constantly having to decide who got to ride him:

> The horse known as "Comanche" being the only living representative of the bloody tragedy of the Little Big Horn, Montana, June 25, 1876, his kind treatment and comfort should be a matter of special pride and solicitude on the part of the 7th Cavalry, to the end that his life may be prolonged to the utmost limit. Though wounded and scarred, his very silence speaks in terms more eloquent than words of the desperate struggle against overwhelming odds, of the hopeless conflict, and heroic manner in which all went down that day.[72]

Edward Luce, a superintendent of the battlefield national monument, chronicled the comfortable but degenerate life that Comanche led until his death at the age of twenty-nine in 1891. Accustomed to a "whiskey bran mash" given to him regularly during his convalescence, Comanche became a drunk and a nuisance. He appeared at the post canteen on payday to panhandle beers from the soldiers, and when he wasn't sleeping off these sprees, he roamed at will, overturning garbage cans and trampling gardens.[73]

After his death, the Seventh voted to have him preserved, and he became one of the most popular exhibits at the University of Kansas's Natural History Museum in Lawrence. Famous relic that he was, he appeared at the World's Fair in 1893.

The boom to transform the Old West into a series of tourist attractions produced a fierce contest for the possession of Comanche. Fort Riley, Kansas, wanted him for its Cavalry Museum; Miles City, Montana, for its Range Riders Museum on the site of Fort Keogh, named in honor of his fallen master. Since Comanche had marched out of Fort Abraham Lincoln on his way to the Battle of the Little Bighorn, North Dakota felt that it had a claim, as did the place he marched *to*, the Montana battlefield. Residents of Sturgis, South Dakota, another place where the living Comanche had set foot, told the university that in addition to finding many members of the Seventh buried there, and many places named for Seventh cavalrymen, the horse would be close to "Comanche Court where over forty houses are built in one unit named for him."[74]

All of these seemingly irresistible arguments failed to persuade the university to relinquish its valuable property. Only one group of Kansans failed to appreciate Comanche's presence—a militant contingent of Native American students at the university. In the 1970s they organized a protest that failed to remove Comanche but resulted in a rewriting of his descriptive plaque.[75]

If, as Colonel Sturgis wrote, the very silence of Comanche speaks more eloquently than words, it has nevertheless been a provocative silence, inspiring numerous efforts to provide him with a voice. It seems that Comanche has evoked in most people a sentiment not unlike that of Captain Ahab in *Moby-Dick* when he addresses the head of a sperm whale hanging at the side of his ship: "Speak, mighty head, and tell us the secret thing that is in thee. . . . thou hast seen enough to split the planets and make an infidel of Abraham, and not one syllable is thine!"[76] Even Colonel Sturgis followed his pronouncement with a modest attempt to articulate what Comanche's eloquent silence speaks *of*—the overwhelming odds, the hopeless conflict, the heroic deaths, including that of Sturgis's own son, Jack.

• • •

All of the men who accompanied Custer to the Last Stand died there, but this did not prevent "sole survivors" turning up from time to time to tell their stories in local newspapers, enjoy their brief moment of publicity, and then—duly discredited—disappear. One writer collected over seventy such stories.[77] On December 8, 1937, close to the ninety-eighth anniversary of Custer's birth, the *Sheridan*, *Wyoming*, *News* printed an item headlined "Is General Custer Alive Today?" with the subheading "Believe Custer Visited Local Attorney's Office Last Year." The article described a speaker at the local Lions Club who related his encounter with the putative Custer to an "enraptured" audience, a final embodiment of the persistent desire for a survivor.[78]

21

Mystery

> The great Campaign of 1876 is destined to become and remain the most romantic, epochal, tragic, mystical and definitive of all race conflicts known to the history of the New World, and, as the great American Epic, to take rank perhaps with the Iliad itself.
>
> —Charles Edmund DeLand, *The Sioux Wars*

> The entire Custer story has been surrounded in mystery and I recall an elderly Colonel telling me once of a story that used to circulate in army circles that there were men who knew an unpublished truth about the story, but who were pledged never to reveal it.
>
> —Ronald Reagan to John A. Minion, July 15, 1965

Art is long and life is short, Horace said, or, we might say, the time of spilled blood is short and the time of spilled ink goes on forever. Writers often marvel at the disproportionate attention the Battle of the Little Bighorn has received: 263 deaths is an insignificant number in the annals of warfare, and a ridiculously insignificant number in comparison with almost any Civil War battle. At Cold Harbor, where 9,000 men in blue went down in eight minutes of battle, it would have taken only fourteen seconds to arrive at the number of Little Bighorn dead.[1]

All of the Indian Wars produced paltry statistics. Don Russell estimated that between 1789 and 1898 Indians killed 7,000 soldiers and civilians and lost 4,000 of their own, but these figures may be conservative.[2] Let us double them, then, and say that over the 109-year period Russell delimits Indians killed 14,000 soldiers and civilians while losing 8,000: in less than *one month* of 1864 the Army of the Potomac lost 50,000 men to Lee's 32,000.[3]

While making a ritualistic gesture toward the vast amount of writing already generated by the Battle of the Little Bighorn, authors do not hesitate to spill still more ink over yet another theory, another aspect, another figure with a brief walk-on part. But even judging this industry in the harshest terms is not proof against its seductiveness. John S. Gray, a professor of physiology who took up Western history as a serious hobby, announced at the beginning of his book on the Sioux war of 1876 that "the reams of melodramatic and partisan verbiage written from derivative sources and confined to a single hour in a year of warfare offended my scientific training. I vowed to steer clear of that example of caricaturized history."[4] Nevertheless, he went on to write his own book on the battle, which is widely regarded as definitive for its time.[5]

Not long after the battle Dr. Holmes Paulding, the physician accompanying Gibbon's Montana column, wrote to his mother that "the facts are indisputable & all bound to come out."[6] How wrong—or merely optimistic—he was! In a scientific-technological age we have an urge to cherish what small amounts of old-fashioned mystery survive, hoping that an as-yet-unsounded corner of the deep loch will yield the world's last sea serpent, that a remote Himalayan peak will someday bring forth the elusive yeti. The possibility of something new under the sun, or something old and long buried brought to light, has a peculiar power. The mystery of the Little Bighorn is of a different but equally compelling sort, a "what happened" mystery akin to the Kennedy assassination in spawning endless hypotheses and conjectures, but satisfying the same need for the concealed and inexplicable. Like the Kennedy assassination, it has produced its share of the bizarre and the fantastic, the sinister and the absurd. And like the Kennedy assassination, it has created its determined cadres who scour history for explanations. But even in the process of chipping away at the mysteries of the battle, dedicated battle buffs will undermine their own work by insisting that the mystery will endure, *must* endure, forever.

Although the aura of mystery has some basis in the fact that all of the participants are long dead, its stubborn persistence has an element of willfulness. Almost immediately after the battle General Sheridan gave an explanation that might be elaborated on at length, but would remain sound. Showing no foreknowledge of the mountain of commentary and disputation the future would hold, he began, "The history of the battle of the Little Big Horn can now be told in a few words." The description that followed was perfectly straightforward—and, as far as it went, accurate:

> The Indians were actually surprised, and in the confusion arising from the surprise and the attempt of the women and children to get out of the way, Colonel Custer was led to believe that the Indians were retreating and would escape him; furthermore, from the point he left Major Reno he could see only a small portion of the Indian encampment, and had no just conception of its size, consequently he did not wait to close up his regiment and attack with its full strength.

He concluded that Custer's actions on June 25, 1876, were due neither to "recklessness or want of judgment, but to a misapprehension of the situation and to a superabundance of courage."[7]

Another famous general, long out of the command loop, took the same commonsense approach when he reviewed the battle in 1887. For George B. McClellan, Custer

> simply repeated the tactics that he had so often successfully used against large bodies of Indians; and it is probable that he was deceived as to the strength and fighting capacity of his opponents, and that, from his want of knowledge of the details of the ground where the tragedy occurred, he was suddenly surrounded by overwhelming masses of well-armed warriors, against whom the heroic efforts of his command wasted themselves in vain.

Like other military men who spoke up, McClellan commented that "those who accused him of reckless rashness would, perhaps, have been the first to accuse him of timidity if he had not attacked, and thus allowed the enemy to escape unhurt."[8] General Sherman, still in bondage to the traditional idea of Indians "scattering," went on record as saying that once Custer discovered the Indians, he had had no choice but to attack.

The difficulty of getting Indians to stand and fight was indeed a pillar of wisdom in the frontier army: in imagining that he must strike quickly before the Indians escaped, Custer had thought as any other experienced frontier commander would have thought. When McClellan commented that Custer only repeated a strategy that he had employed successfully in the past, he might have expanded his remark to note that the tactic of envelopment was standard in Indian fighting: in addition to Custer's own victory on the Washita, it had been used successfully by Chivington at Sand Creek, Reynolds at Powder River, and Mackenzie at McClellan Creek.[9]

Mystery, having spread its wings over the battle, could not be routed by such sensible interpretations as Sheridan's and McClellan's. It has endlessly hatched small mysteries, a seemingly inexhaustible quantity of analysis and criticism concerning why Custer did what he did at every juncture: why he refused Terry's offer of a Second Cavalry battalion and the Gatling guns; why he did not scout Tullock's creek and send a messenger back from there as Terry had instructed; why he did not continue south along the Rosebud, again as instructed; why he attacked on the twenty-fifth rather than waiting until he could be assured of Terry's presence; why he divided his forces into four units: the pack train—with 25 percent of the entire command, three companies under Captain Benteen conducting a scout to the left, three companies under Major Reno attacking one end of the village, and his own force of five companies—promising to support Reno's attack but marching off, never to be heard from again.[10] Or, more precisely, to be heard from twice again. Two messengers arrived bearing explicit and urgent commands: Sergeant Kanipe to bring up the pack train, and John Martin to give Benteen the hastily scrawled message that all battle buffs know by heart—"Come on. Be quick. Big village. Bring packs. PS. Bring pacs."

There was one sad little secret that did eventually come out, as undoubtedly any other such secret would have; namely, Major Reno's desire to abandon the wounded on the night of June 25 in order to get away.[11] We scarcely need this detail to form an accurate assessment of Reno's capability as a commander under fire, however, nor is it in any way relevant to what happened to Custer's command.

Captain Thomas Weir wrote to Libbie that he had much to tell her about the battle—rather a natural comment since they were good friends and he had been there—but he died before seeing her again. Weir undoubtedly could have given Libbie an eyewitness account of the battle as he experienced it from his position as an officer riding with Benteen, but it is hard to imagine what he could have told her that would have shed light on her husband's last moments. Weir had wanted to ride to the sound of battle but had not received permission to do so from Reno. He tried to go anyway, arriving at an outlook now called Weir Point less than three miles from Last Stand hill.

Most historians of the battle agree that by the time Weir moved out, the Custer battle was over, so whatever he did see was irrelevant to the command's fate. Possibly he saw enough to intuit what had happened; at the court of inquiry in 1879 the vehemence with which most survivors denied hearing any firing from the direction of the Custer battlefield, and denied ever suspecting that the Custer command had been wiped out, was probably the product of retroactive embarrassment. The truth is probably contained in Lieutenant Francis Gibson's letter to his wife, Katherine, written on July 4, 1876: "We heard Custer's command fighting about 3 miles off, in our front, but it was impossible for us to join him as we could neither abandon our wounded men nor the packs of the whole command."[12] In retrospect, Lieutenant Godfrey was convinced that the two emphatic volleys the men on Reno hill heard were signals of distress, but at the time it was just as plausible to assume that their dashing commander was giving the Indians a good fight.

Every minor choice, every tiny detail on the road to catastrophe, takes on a disproportionate significance, becomes portentous and weighty in retrospect. Had the Seventh not been decimated at the Little Bighorn, the commanding officer's decision to wait to distribute their pay on the march rather than at Fort Lincoln, where the iniquities of Bismarck were within easy reach, would have seemed like a sensible plan. As it turned out, the decision now seems like a gratuitous cruelty to men who might have enjoyed a last spree. In light of the imminent disaster, the last words Mark Kellogg sent to his newspaper before setting out with Custer were all too accurate: "I go with Custer and will be at the death."[13] Had Terry required the reporter to remain with his column instead of accompanying Custer, Kellogg would have been sorely disappointed—until the morning of June 27, when the bodies of all who did go with Custer were discovered. Similarly, one of the indelible images of the Last Stand is John Martin's memory of crossing paths with

Custer's youngest brother, Boston, as Martin rode to safety with the last message and Boston hurried to join his two older brothers and be "at the death."[14]

Lieutenant Godfrey, bringing his field diary up to date a month after the battle, described an incident of June 24: "While the officers were separating at the "Sundance" camp Genl Custer's guidon fell down to the rear. I picked it up and stuck it in the ground. Soon it fell again to the rear; this time I stuck it in some sage brush and ground so that it stuck. I never thought of it again till after the fight when my attention was called to it by Lieutenant Wallace who seems to have regarded it as a bad omen."[15] Had Custer won, however, it is unlikely that Wallace would have remembered the incident at all or that Godfrey would have bothered to note it in a belated diary entry.

Had Custer won, there would have been no mystery at all, for white Americans expected him to win. The Battle of the Little Bighorn was a historical anomaly, a shocking throwback to an earlier era when the struggle for the continent was still undecided, not to mention an unthinkable conclusion to the career of the Civil War general who claimed to have captured every enemy gun turned against him. Mystery cannot be chased from the battlefield because the locus of mystery is not the physical site but the psyche of white America. Its source is racism, the pure and simple conviction that a body of white soldiers like the "fighting Seventh" could not be overwhelmed by even an overwhelming number of Indians. For the typical Custer buff, mystery is preferable to this stark fact.[16] It is a credential of the committed battle enthusiast to assert the permanence of mystery over the unpalatable reality of the Indians' achievement.

The Plains Indians, with their superb horsemanship and knowledge of the terrain, were masters of the lightning guerrilla attack. They suddenly swooped down upon an isolated homestead or stage station and massacred its unsuspecting residents, or they ambushed small groups of soldiers traveling through the wilderness, particularly when they had a strong numerical advantage. Then they disappeared. This form of fighting, which Mosby had used so effectively against Sheridan and Custer in the Shenandoah Valley, was not merely unconventional; it appeared to nineteenth-century whites to be cowardly and unmanly. Indians, notoriously, did not stand and fight. They "scattered"; they "skulked" or "sneaked." When it looked like they would lose, they "turned tail and ran."

As a decade of post–Civil War Plains warfare had made abundantly clear to the current generation of military leaders, it was difficult to find Indians to fight. Most of the army's Indian campaigns were punitive marches in which the chief enemies actually encountered were harsh natural conditions—weather and terrain and the evils they engendered: hunger, disease, and desertion. The enemy body count was so low that taxpayers and Eastern politicians grumbled with some justice that the army spent a million dollars killing each Indian. Historically, clashes with Indians in large numbers involved either the killing of women and children or, as in Crook's campaign against the Sioux, blunders that seriously qualified any claim to victory. Plains Indian warfare had a few satisfying victories—given exaggerated treatment by the press—but as a strategy for solving the problem it addressed, it was neither glorious nor efficacious.

There is a genuine mystery here beneath the spurious one of what happened on the Little Bighorn battlefield—the mystery of white America's collective refusal to accept the obvious explanation for the defeat of the Seventh Cavalry and the annihilation of Custer's five companies on that hot day in June of 1876. White Americans have clung to the supposed mystery of the Last Stand as a way of continuing their allegiance to the stubbornly rooted belief that whites could always outfight Indians.

There had to be some aberration, some unknown circumstance, some flagrant departure from reason or plan to account for what was otherwise unimaginable, hence mysterious. And so we have had, down through the years, Reno's cowardice, Custer's ambition, the raw recruits, the jamming rifles.

Immediately after the battle, Sitting Bull came to prominence as the Indian blamed by the newspapers for the catastrophe, so much so that one paper referred to President Grant as "the Sitting Bull of the White House."[17] A subheadline of the July 29 *Chicago Times* described "Sitting Bull's Savages in High Glee Over Their Victory and Confident of Making Quick Work of the Remainder."[18] The *Fort Benton Record* of July 28 featured a "History of the Noted Red" by a Major Maginnis. The major's account suggested that Sitting Bull was personally responsible for every Indian attack.[19]

The equation of Grant to Sitting Bull evidently made an impression on one interested observer. In the 1880s a woman visiting Monroe wrote about meeting Emmanuel Custer: "Old Mr. Custer says he has as much respect now for 'Sitting Bull' as for Gen. Grant—he thinks Grant purposely stationed his son out there in Montana in danger, because of some personal grudge or jealousy."[20]

Anything and everything has been suggested as the fatal flaw that produced the catastrophe, but perhaps the most ludicrous, as well as the most revealing in terms of what the mystery is really about, is the rumor that Sitting Bull went to West Point, a widely circulated story at the time.[21] In keeping with this absurdity was the fraud perpetrated by R. D. Clarke, an officer on General Crook's staff who was surreptitiously responsible for the publication in 1878 of *The Works of Sitting Bull in the Original French and Latin*. As a later catalog description remarked, "Because the army and the public at large could not believe that a group of 'savages' defeated and massacred an entire command, this work tried to picture Sitting Bull as a *cum laude* graduate of Oxford, and the epitome of the 'Noble Red Man.'"[22] This in spite of Sitting Bull's flat denial of any white education or attainments in an interview given in 1877.[23]

Ascriptions of the Sioux victory to the presence of renegade white men in their camp were similarly misguided and similarly motivated, beginning with Major Reno's field report that the command had been fighting not only "all the Sioux Nation," but "all the desperadoes, renegades, half-breeds, and squaw-men between the Missouri and the Arkansas east of the Rocky Mountains."[24] A *New York Herald* reporter interviewing the Sioux warrior Kill Eagle asked three different times about the presence of whites on the Indian side of the battle. In each instance Kill Eagle patiently denied the charge.[25] Stories of army deserters who had masterminded the battle—"a cashiered West Pointer" who had drilled and instructed the warriors, and a bugler who had deserted and taught them army signals—all turned out to be figments of white imagination.[26]

On June 25, 1876, the Sioux and their Indian allies had no need of whites, either as masterminds or foot soldiers, nor did Sitting Bull need to go to West Point to defeat the Seventh Cavalry. But this was simply unthinkable. When a reporter asked Sitting Bull if "the whole command had kept on fighting until the last," he replied diplomatically, "Every man, so far as my people could see. There were no cowards on either side." The mere idea provoked indignation in the reporter, who commented, "Cowards! One would think not."[27]

As the news from the battlefield made its way to the world beyond, it was met with disbelief at every stage. When the Terry-Gibbon army in the field ran across Custer's Crow scouts, they assumed that the fleeing Indians were exaggerating, perhaps as an excuse to justify their withdrawal from the battlefield. Edward J. McClernand, the chief engineer with Gibbon's troops, wrote in his journal:

> Many in our column were willing to admit that Custer's advance guard might have been driven back, but scoffed at the idea of his entire regiment being beaten. In fact Custer commanded the admiration, and excited the enthusiasm of most of the young men in the army. His well known reputation for courage and dash was contagious and caught the fancy even of those among us who had never met him.[28]

McClernand's commander, Colonel Gibbon, had called out those words destined to reverberate ironically down through history: "Now Custer, don't be greedy. Save some Indians for us." Custer seemed to agree to Gibbon's half-humorous request and rode off to join his command. Reflecting on this exchange when he wrote his account of the expedition a few months later, Gibbon remarked, "I do not suppose there was a man in the column who entertained for a moment the idea that there were Indians enough in the country to defeat, much less annihilate, the fine regiment of cavalry which Custer had under his command."[29]

Soldiers shared the attitude of their officers. An enlisted man with Gibbon, William White, later said that when the news of the disaster came, many of the men did not believe it: "The idea that all or even a large number of his men had been killed was totally out of rational consideration, according to our views. As we believed, there was not in existence then and never would be any aggregation of Indians who could wipe out or do any great damage to the Seventh Cavalry—or to our own forces."[30] These words and sentiments that echoed Gibbon's can be found over and over again in records of the army's first reactions to the news of the Little Bighorn disaster.

On June 29 at the base camp at the mouth of the Powder River on the Yellowstone, Major Orlando H. Moore of the Sixth Infantry received the news from the scout Charlie Cross and two Ree Indians. Everyone thought that their story was preposterous and that they were in fact deserters: "So strong was the belief in the invincibility of Custer that Maj. Moore sent the three scouts back to General Terry under guard and if their story proved untrue they were to be shot."[31]

During the siege of June 25 and 26, the remnant of Custer's regiment confined to Reno hill wondered, at times bitterly, where Custer was and why he had not supported them as planned. No one ever came forward later to say that he had anticipated the news brought by Lieutenant Bradley on the morning of June 27. Lieutenant Godfrey reported, "We were simply dumfounded. This was the first intimation we had of his fate. It was hard to realize; it did seem impossible."[32]

In Philadelphia the army's ranking generals, Sherman and Sheridan, were visiting the Centennial Exposition when they received the first news. Both dismissed it as preposterous. Officially confirmed, it was still hard for them to believe. There was, at least, this exquisite irony: the exposition where the generals learned of the battle contained an exhibit of "plains warriors made from papier-maché."[33] While the American public admired this display in the self-congratulatory mode in which it experienced the centennial, the models for the exhibit proved they were not yet ready to be turned into museum artifacts.

Long before the annihilation of the Custer command, army officers had freely asserted the superiority of their forces to the Indians. As Libbie wrote in some manuscript notes, "It was always estimated that one white man was equal to 25 Indians."[34] Custer's brother-in-law Lieutenant James Calhoun related an even more grandiose version in his account of his first frontier experience, chasing some Indians who had stolen a herd of horses:

> I was just beginning to think that probably as there was a force so largely superior to us, the best thing to do would be to quietly retire, without intercepting, when I suddenly remembered having been informed by an officer who had served many years in Arizona, that with ten men he could whip all the Indians in the territory, and as we had our instructions and a desire to then and there do something that would equal any of the Cavalry charges during the war, I abandoned my first thought, and gladly and earnestly longed for glory.[35]

Calhoun was lucky that day: the Indians outran the soldiers, and he had another eight years of life before his thesis was tested and found wanting on the Little Bighorn.

Four days after Custer's death, but well before the news reached the outside world, the *Ellis County Star*, a newspaper in Hays City, Kansas, hailed the reunion of Buffalo Bill and Major Eugene Carr. An enlisted man wrote that when the old soldiers of the regiment saw the two together, they "expressed themselves to the effect that with such a leader and scout they could get away with all the Sitting Bulls and Crazy Horses in the Sioux tribe."[36]

In the most famous instance of racist braggadocio, Captain William Fetterman, who arrived at Fort Phil Kearney in 1866 with no frontier experience, expressed the opinion that a "single company of Regulars could whip a thousand Indians, and that a full regiment . . . could whip the entire array of hostile tribes."[37] Frances Carrington, who heard the captain's comment, said that it was "warmly seconded by Captain Brown and Lieutenant Grummond," her first husband.[38] Disobeying the most explicit orders not to pursue the Indians beyond Lodge Trail Ridge, Captain Fetterman led a body of eighty men, including those two like-minded officers, in pursuit of some Sioux who had been harassing the post's wood train. All eighty were killed, Brown and Fetterman possibly by their own hands. Wiring the news to General Grant in Washington, Sherman expressed his bafflement: "I do not understand how the massacre of Colonel Fetterman's party could have been so complete."[39] The government found it convenient to blame the post commander, who had done his best to prevent such an outcome.

Custer, like every officer on the frontier, knew the Fetterman story and considered it a prime exemplum of how Indians decoyed the inexperienced. Five months after the Fetterman disaster he cautioned Captain Keogh, then serving as commander of Fort Wallace, "as to your pursuing Indians, while it is not strictly forbidden, in doing so you must exercise the greatest precaution against stratagem and surprise, remembering that it is the Indian's *'ruse de guerre'* to decoy small garrisons away from their positions of defence.'"[40] In an attempt to provoke pursuit, Indians would allow the soldiers to see only a few of their number. When the pursuers had followed to the point where escape would be difficult or impossible, they suddenly found themselves confronting a much larger force. This fate that Custer cautioned Keogh against, the fate that had already befallen Captain Fetterman, would also claim Major Joel Elliott and eighteen men of the Seventh at the Battle of the Washita.

Yet for all of his awareness and experience, Custer himself had always been supremely self-confident—and not without reason. His account of an Indian fight on the Yellowstone expedition combines an appreciation of the danger posed by the Indians to his badly outnumbered troops with a belief in the soldiers' superiority. He writes of the Indians, "Had they been willing, *as white men would have been* [my emphasis], to assume greater risks, their success would have been assured."[41] As he went to headquarters to get the latest news on the morning of June 25, Lieutenant Godfrey overheard the Ree scout Bloody Knife tell Custer that enough Sioux would be found to keep his command fighting for two or three days. Godfrey wrote: "Genl remarked laughingly that he thought we would get through in one day."[42]

In a sense, then, Custer became the most notorious victim of white America's collective belief in racial superiority, the representative of countless numbers who incorrectly assumed that they would be able to outrun, or outwit, or outfight the Indians they encountered—whatever the number. When Custer marched out of Fort Abraham Lincoln on the expedition that would bring him to the Little Bighorn, the *Bismarck Weekly Tribune* described him as "full of perfect readiness for a fray with the hostile red devils, and woe to the body of scalp-lifters that comes within reach of himself and brave companions in arms."[43] The white readers for whom this was intended would certainly have preferred this kind of rhetoric to one warrior's observation that the soldiers looked like a stampede of buffalo or Sitting Bull's comment that they were shot down like pigs.[44]

Racial as well as national prestige was invested in a catastrophe that could *not* be explained. This is the abiding mystery of the Little Bighorn.

Civilians, motivated by the same sense of racial superiority that fueled army braggadocio, routinely created their own catastrophes on the frontier by ignoring clear and present dangers. The Museum of New Mexico has a photograph of a five-year-old child, Charlie McComas, whose careful haircut and clothing suggest a genteel upbringing; in fact he was the son of a judge. The child's expression seems vaguely troubled, as if he already knew his life would be cut short by his own father's contempt for Indians as adversaries.

In the spring of 1883 the Apaches went on the warpath. At the same time, in order to hold court, Judge McComas needed to drive from Silver City, New Mexico, to Leitendorf, a small mining camp in the general vicinity of the outbreak. Given the real possibility of danger, the judge might have elected to travel without his family, to procure an armed escort, to postpone the court session. He did none of these things. Evidently convinced that he could handle any contingency, he took his wife and young son on the trip.

The judge and his wife were found murdered on the road, victims—it was later determined—of Chiricahua Apaches they had encountered, neither party seeking the other. Indians often took young children captive, but the hope that Charlie would be recovered eventually died; no trace of him was ever found.

Surfacing repeatedly in battle annals is the comment of an unidentified member of the Seventh hinting that he knew more than he would reveal out of respect for Mrs. Custer. Many have guessed at what he might have withheld: that Custer was not well liked, that he gambled, that the officers had no confidence in his judgment. None of these possible revelations would have been extraordinary, but more important, nothing any such man might have said would have elucidated the Last Stand. Custer communicated no battle plans beyond what we have long known: he sent Benteen off on a scout to the left; he commanded Reno to attack the village ahead; he called for Benteen to join him and for the (ammunition) packs to be brought up. Then he and everyone with him disappeared into silence.

Of course, large numbers of Indians who had participated in the battle survived, but the failure to understand Indian culture and language made it unlikely that white Americans could learn from the Indians what they badly wanted to know: that is, what happened to produce Custer's unimaginable defeat. As one Indian said, "Many different men told me about that battle. If a person kept listening he would hear a great deal."[45] But the majority of whites were unwilling to listen to the Indians. According to one Cheyenne story, Indians recognizing Custer's body on the field punctured his eardrums because he had not listened to them in the past.[46] This is no doubt apocryphal, but it is emblematic of the imperfect communication that obtained between the two cultures.

One of the reasons the mystery of the Last Stand refuses to yield was the lack of even a single army survivor—someone, anyone, who had shared those final hours—hence the fetishizing of Comanche, who was, at least, the horse of a white soldier. Beyond the racist assumption that white soldiers could automatically defeat much larger numbers of Indians was the further assumption that Indian testimony about the battle could be dismissed as inaccurate, although, as the Cheyenne story implied, whites made little effort to truly listen, to understand what they were hearing. For one thing, they attempted to elicit testimony within standard white paradigms—such as clock time or cavalry formations—that were unfamiliar to Indians.[47] When their conventional expectations were not met, they then dismissed what they heard. The assertion "I killed Custer," for example, a declaration of personal responsibility for whites, meant "We killed the soldiers" to Indians. *Custer*, in fact, might refer to anything from the entire battalion to some portion of it rather than to the man himself, an ironic parallel to General Sheridan's comment that he believed "Sitting Bull" to be a generic name for hostile Indians.[48]

Further complicating matters, early Indian accounts tended to tell whites what they wanted to hear because the speakers were fearful of being held responsible for the deaths of white soldiers. Because of cultural differences, this strategy often backfired. Thomas Marquis, a doctor who, as an early victim of Little Bighorn Battle fever, spent a great deal of time talking with Indian battle participants, was repeatedly told that the soldiers had committed suicide en masse, an accusation that was so unpalatable to most whites that his manuscript on the subject could not be published until long after his death.[49] It seems likely that the Indians thought that suicide would be an explanation that exculpated them while accounting for the death of Custer's command. Concerned with escaping blame, they did not consider or realize that the idea of suicide, with its implication of cowardice, would be far worse from the white point of view than honorable death in battle.

Such patently false narratives reinforced the white belief that Indians were unreliable informants and led to the widely held conclusion that the true story of the battle could never be told. As one old-timer wrote to a battle buff, "If only one soldier had escaped from Custer's five troops so as to have told the story . . . Custer's name would have been forgotten a few years after the tragedy."[50] The astute Sitting Bull was more diplomatic. He claimed that all of the soldiers fought bravely and at first said little else about the battle. Only later, when he was forced to live among whites, did he embellish his tale a little.

If, from the white perspective, those who could truly tell what happened were dead, and those who were alive were unreliable, what remained? Although it was not thought of in the immediate aftermath of the battle, science would ultimately prove to be authoritative in providing some of the answers. Like the partial views of individuals, the scientific narrative was a reconstruction from limited evidence, but unlike those views, it appeared to be objective and dispassionate.

In the early 1980s painstaking and thoughtful scholarly research, coupled with a large-scale archaeological dig, systematically dispelled most of the lingering mysteries of the battle. We now know from these investigations that many of the reasons originally offered to explain the cavalry's defeat actually had little or no bearing on the outcome: the percentage of "raw recruits" in the battle was negligible;[51] the defective extraction of the empty cartridge shells from rifles was responsible for only an insignificant number of misfires, most of which occurred on the Indians' side; and neither the army horses nor the soldiers were in especially poor condition.[52] Most important, thanks in large part to John Gray's meticulous analysis of the battle, we know that Custer did not make inexplicably foolish decisions: he made reasonable military decisions on the basis of incorrect information, certainly a less striking explanation for failure in battle than overweening ambition or insanity.[53]

Other than the persistence of racism, it would be hard to explain the ongoing notoriety of the Battle of the Little Bighorn, a battle that resulted in only a small number of dead and wounded and did nothing to change the final outcome of the historic conflict between Indians and whites for possession of the West. Those in the grip of mystery have endlessly measured and timed and plotted the battlefield movements of what was a relatively simple military action—compared to, say, Gettysburg—in an effort to uncover a hitherto ignored explanation of how a small, mediocre fighting force could have been annihilated by a well-armed and determined enemy at least several times its number and consisting of men raised from birth to be warriors.

Like Custer's, the folly of Captain Ahab in *Moby-Dick* brought about a disaster that claimed many lives, but his misfortune was reported back to the world by a survivor. The remnant preserved, the catastrophe explained: it is a satisfying ending—and a fiction. There was no such consolation or clarification to emerge from the messy historical reality of the Last Stand. Whether Custer was considered culpable or blameless, he became a name synonymous with fatal error. Thus, when Norman Maclean wrote, in a book published in 1992, "He might as well have run into General Custer and the Seventh Cavalry on June 25, 1876, on their way to the Little Big Horn,"[54] his readers could be expected to understand that the hapless "he" in the sentence would soon be dead. Maclean went on to make other analogies between the Mann Gulch fire, in which thirteen smoke jumpers died, and the Custer fight: the two events share the circumstance of young men led into battle and suddenly and unexpectedly meeting death. Whether the commander was a gallant hero or a lunatic, the situation continues to be a compelling image with the power to fascinate and appall.

Today an antiheroic Custer is firmly established in the popular imagination—an imagination that in the post–Vietnam War era no longer sees anything romantic in losing and, from the safe distance of over a hundred years, can also wholeheartedly repudiate the dispossession of the Indian. The image of the antihero has evolved with the times, however. Whereas the first version of Custer as loser was a monster of recklessness fueled by egotism—the predatory "glory hunter" of Frederic Van De Water's revisionist biography—the second, in keeping with our diminished times, is merely an incompetent fool.[55] The magnitude of Custer's delusion about the force he confronted on his final battlefield has been preserved in numerous jokes. An Indian favorite, I'm told, is Custer's last order to his command: "Take no prisoners."[56] What John Martin reported Custer as actually saying—"Hurrah, boys, we've got them!"—is almost as good.[57]

No longer the face on the cigar band or the saber-waving figure of the barroom lithograph, Custer is most frequently encountered in contemporary humor and advertising as a blunderer, the foolish and inept architect of his own ruin. Maclean's use of Custer to invoke tragedy is a rare exception; today he is usually a comic allusion, as in Mark Russell's 1993 anecdote: "At the last minute, a reporter had to remind NASA not to launch the Discovery shuttle in the middle of the big meteor shower. As Gen. Custer said to his lieutenant—"Indians! What Indians?"[58]—or, without the humor, merely an example of unpreparedness. Next to an actual photograph of Custer, a 1994 Lotus Development Corporation ad in the *New York Times Magazine* warns, "The competition is organizing around you. Does your E-mail system give you all the ammunition you need?"

Such interpretations of Custer, which steadily gained ground from the publication of *Glory Hunter* in 1934, would seem to be antithetical to mystery. Yet a demythologized battle and a comprehensible commander are clearly not what white Americans want from the Little Bighorn. There must be some face-saving way of making sense of the temporary triumph of "them" over "us," but at the same time, a frank clarification of the mystery would tell us more than we want to know.

PART FIVE

Endless Devotion

22

"I Longed to Die": The Long Widowhood of Elizabeth Custer

> Mrs. Custer has no nearer relative than Mrs. Kendall [her cousin], having neither father, mother, brother, sister, nor child and now no husband. —*Topeka Commonwealth*, July 14, 1876

> How I longed to die. But I knew I had to live my allotted term, live for Autie's memory, for the life that he was not permitted to live out to its full. —EBC to Marguerite Merington

> To lose him would be to close the windows of life that let in the sunshine. Other windows there are from whence comes light but oh it is sunshine and the radiant sunshine of love that we women crave. What I have is like . . . the little patch on our carpet that came about 11 in the old cardinals palace at Rome. I can't do much basking or growing but it serves to keep me in remembrance of rooms in my life where every corner was resplendent with sunshine.
> —EBC, unpublished diary, 1891–92

If Custer had returned from the 1876 expedition against the Sioux to find that a sudden illness had carried off Libbie, leaving him a widower, his emotional and domestic life would have suffered deep trauma, but her death would have left intact his salary, his spacious house at Fort Abraham Lincoln, his career, the army "family" that both he and his wife valued so much, affectionate parents, numerous other kin, and his customary hobbies. How he might have responded to such a loss is only speculation, of course, but given his strong will and natural buoyancy, it seems unlikely that he would have been destroyed. In 1870, at the lowest point of their relationship, he wrote to Libbie that most men, "feeling . . . that the love of the one person whose love alone was desirable was surely but slowly departing from them, would endeavor to hide or drown their troubles by drink or dissipation. I am not so inclined."[1] Whatever Custer's reaction to Libbie's death—whether he would have remained a widower who substituted other interests for conjugality or established a second intimate relationship—he would have faced this radical change supported by a reassuring framework of continuity.

When Libbie lost her husband, she also lost the only life she had known as an adult—the army, and with it, home, social life, and means of support. Every aspect of her life was transformed. Few middle-class women in America in 1876 could earn their living in a remunerative fashion, and Libbie had not been equipped to be one of them.[2] Nor had she ever wanted independence, a career, or an interest other than her husband's life.[3] As she had written to Custer early in their marriage, "I wish to look to my husband as superior in judgment and experience and to be guided by him in all things."[4] At thirty-four she was suddenly alone. "Others thought and acted for me," she once wrote. "Only once [did I act for myself] and that was when I realized for myself that I had met the man who was to be my destiny."[5] This one important decision—to marry George Armstrong Custer—had been made thirteen years before.

As a young widow she was not alone, either in her immediate context—where the Battle of the Little Bighorn had brought widowhood to twenty-four women at Fort Abraham Lincoln—or in late-nineteenth-century America.[6] And in many respects, her situation was superior to that of her immediate cohort, women whose struggles after the disaster of June 1876 took place in undocumented obscurity. Many had children to support on grossly inadequate army pensions, and their unsung grief was not necessarily less agonizing than Libbie's more public anguish.[7] Little more than a month after the news reached Fort Lincoln, Nettie Smith, the widow of Captain Algernon Smith, wrote to Libbie:

> Last night I found a diary kept by Smithie on the other Yellowstone Expedition [1873] in which he so often writes of his "little wife." In one place he says, "These are hard

> marches, but it is consoling to know that we are marching towards my little wife Dudds. God bless her! Only about a month separates us." Oh if that last part could only be true now. I realize the terrible truth more and more every day. How can we have the strength to endure it.[8]

Many must have felt what Libbie's sister-in-law Margaret Custer Calhoun expressed: "Now that Bubbie is gone I feel myself such a nonentity for I know that he did consider me necessary to his happiness, but . . . I do not feel that mentally I am fitted to fill any position of *usefulness* to others."[9]

The great achievement of Libbie's widowhood would be her continued usefulness to her dead husband, her success in bringing her heroic vision of him to a large public. Within a month of Custer's death Libbie had told a young man working at Fort Lincoln that her story was all she had left. "She opened out for my gaze," he wrote to his sister and brother-in-law, "a picture of domestic happiness and true companionship of husband and wife that was marvelously beautiful."[10]

Promulgating a story of conjugal bliss and heroic endeavor to a wide audience was an occupation and a satisfaction that most of the widows could not have hoped for, yet might very well have wanted. Margaret wrote to Libbie to thank her for praising Margaret's dead husband, Lieutenant James Calhoun: "Your sweet, beautiful expressions about Bubbie are so precious to me. Some time won't you tell Miss Davis how lovely and noble he was? I should like her to know—as I feel I would like the whole world to know—but especially those whom I like—though she may not be much interested to hear of any one but Autie—he being her ideal hero."[11]

Margaret, the youngest of the Custer children and the only daughter born to Emmanuel and Matilda, did what most widows had no choice but to do: she went home to her family, in her case to the small town of Monroe, Michigan, with little money and few prospects. Libbie returned to Monroe, too, but she left within a year to make her life in New York City. When Margaret received the news that Libbie had landed her first job in the metropolis, she wrote forthrightly: "Life seems much more unendurable than it did before your letter came. I know I am selfish, I can't help it and yet my selfishness is not so great that I would sacrifice your desires to my wishes, but I grieve for myself, that is all."[12] A lively young woman who would establish her career as a dramatic reader only after her parents' death, Margaret struggled with the monotony of life in Monroe and her uncomfortable feeling that she was different from most of its residents: "Almost any body else to read this would think me a conceited thing—but you will understand me and know that it is not that I do consider myself superior either mentally or morally—but I do consider my *aspirations* superior to those of most of the people with whom I am associated here."[13]

The first anniversary of their common loss was a particularly bleak period for Margaret. She wrote to Libbie that many times she had wanted to write of her "heart sufferings which seemed too great to bear," but restrained herself to keep from adding another burden to Libbie's grief: "I do not want to be selfish, but Libbie, the past week has been the hardest in all the long, sad year. It seems that never before have I suffered such agony. My life seems so desolate."[14] Not surprisingly, Margaret had long periods of ill health, "disgusting sinking spells," as she characterized them, and debilitating headaches that sent her to bed for several days at a time and did not respond to treatment. As her letters indicate, she conscientiously struggled against "selfishness," but who could blame her for wanting to escape, as her sister-in-law had, a life that offered so little.

Libbie, on the other hand, probably experienced her own difficulties in admitting her need for income and searching for work, since at that time employment outside the home for any middle-class woman was unusual.[15] She had caring relatives and friends, none dearer than her closest friend and cousin, Rebecca Richmond, but Rebecca must have unintentionally contributed to Libbie's painful situation by her ignorance of the Custers' slender financial means. Assuming that Libbie had been left comfortably provided for (as she herself was), Rebecca wrote to her cousin that of course Libbie would not want any sort of regular job, that it would be undignified for the widow of a well-known general. Rebecca remarked that a family friend had read in the newspapers that Libbie was seeking work and had found the idea of her employment in any "public position" unseemly. He told the Richmonds that he would never allow his own sister, wife, or daughter to occupy "any public office." Rebecca assured him that Libbie sought occupation "only for mental and spiritual needs and not from any financial necessity."[16]

Rebecca's next letter, perhaps in response to a carefully worded reply from Libbie, is similarly preoccupied with Libbie's efforts to find a job, but there is also a hint that she is having some unexpected thoughts: "You did not write what your income would probably be. I hope that you did not feel it *necessary* to have a paid position in order to support yourself comfortably!"[17]

Libbie had been left nothing but debts, however. Eventually, after prolonged litigation, Custer's estate paid ten cents on the dollar, leaving Libbie with $118.63 to pay her lawyer.[18] It was abundantly necessary for her to supplement her meager army pension of thirty dollars a month, and she received a great deal of advice from Rebecca, who meant well but was not in possession of all the facts regarding either Libbie's financial situation or the job market. "Mother and I do not look upon such an employment for you with any favor," she wrote when Libbie was considering a career as a nurse. "You have talents that ought to be cultivated," her letter continued, "and, after a brief schooling in the Metropolis, your ready wit would make them lucrative. Your income will, I know, support you comfortably, and your pen and pencil would, ere long, furnish you with desirable luxuries in the way of travel, lessons in the languages, treats in the way of fine concerts, exhibitions of painting, etc."[19]

Rebecca was amazingly prescient. The rosy picture she painted, which must have seemed fantastic to the grief-stricken widow of 1877, was a strikingly accurate description of the life Libbie would come to enjoy a decade later as a successful writer and lecturer.[20]

Although Libbie was not old when she was widowed, she followed the pattern of older women in American society by not remarrying. Like Irene Rucker Sheridan, who in the fifty years that she lived after her husband's death often remarked that she "would rather be Phil Sheridan's widow than any living man's wife," Libbie exemplified the "deeply ingrained preference to maintain one's established identity" that characterized older women in an earlier period of American history.[21] After all, Libbie's identity was established nationally as well as personally; it was, as Frederick Benteen said ungenerously, her "whole stock in trade."[22]

Writing in the 1890s, Benteen was thinking primarily of how financially profitable Libbie's role as Custer's widow had been in the twenty-odd years following his death. However, her emotional commitment to her husband and her desire to honor his memory were always far more influential in her decisions: whatever monetary rewards were waiting to be reaped, Libbie could not bring herself to write about Custer for nine years.

Libbie would have been aware of a contemporary and very visible instance of dedicated widowhood. Beginning in 1862, Queen Victoria had set a formidable example of rigorous devotion to the memory of her consort. There is no evidence that Libbie saw herself as emulating this exemplary figure, but a literate adult living in the last quarter of the nineteenth century could hardly escape knowledge of the queen's impressive mourning. Libbie had her own strong reasons to memorialize her dead husband, but whether or not she needed it or consciously considered it as a model, the culturally powerful icon of Victoria as the grieving and faithful widow validated her own choice.

Libbie may have imagined in the first shock of her husband's death and her sudden change of circumstance that she would remain in Monroe permanently. She wrote to a good friend, Sallie Saxe, "I came home to Autie's old parents to try and be a blessing to them. Autie loved them so dearly they can never cease to be my special charge. Autie's sister Maggie and I try to forget ourselves in comforting them."[23] Such a life, however well intentioned, must have quickly become intolerable: in a household of two young widows and bereaved elderly parents—parents who had lost three sons and a grandson—grief would have fed upon grief without respite.

When Libbie first left Monroe to stay with some relatives in Newark, New Jersey, the trip was regarded by her Custer in-laws as simply a visit. Libbie was testing the waters, however. She did not know what employment opportunities she might find or what living arrangements she would be able to make in the metropolitan area, but she must have recalled that when boardinghouse doors were closed in her face in wartime Washington, the influence of a powerful friend found her a place to live. In New York, where Libbie and Autie had spent many holidays and been feted by prominent people, she might enjoy a similar advantage.

Letters from Margaret Calhoun to Libbie show that at first Libbie was expected to return to Monroe and make her life there. In May of 1877 Margaret wrote, "We all miss you so much, and when you come back you will find me a full blown angel . . . for the self sacrifice and unselfishness that I intend to display in regard to your absence, not urging you to hurry home, etc."[24] Libbie must have realized that she had to inform the Custers of her actual plans, as Margaret's letter of June 5 referred to Libbie's new job and spoke of having broken the news to Father Custer. Her letter of June 14 remarked, "Mother & Father miss you so much—speak of you so often—as though you were their *very own.*"

A hint of criticism crept into Margaret's letter of June 24: Mother "feels very badly to think you have left home for good as it were—excepting visits—and that you are out in the world *alone.*" Two months later, the criticism was full blown.

> I do everything in my power to present the matter to mother in a favorable light. It is really because she is so fond of you that she feels so badly about your going away, and though she is so good and unselfish and lovely *she* cannot understand as well as I just why you can not or do not remain at home. You know she has a sensitive heart and I rather think she feels that home is not as congenial as you would wish. . . . Then too I am dreading . . . the remarks that people will be mean enough to make—and to mother too."[25]

Although she betrayed ambivalent feelings about Libbie's escape from a place that she herself found close to unbearable, Margaret could not criticize her beloved sister-in-law directly: comments that might have been construed as criticism were always presented as emanating from Mother Custer. Her letters were sad but admirable attempts to put aside her own bleak life and show generosity toward a person she loved and respected. As a daughter who was also a highly religious young woman, Margaret was duty-bound to remain with her parents, providing what comfort she could for their profound loss.

For Libbie it was a delicate situation. She could hardly admit to Custer's parents that he had not provided for her—or them—sufficiently. Beyond that, as Margaret's letters made abundantly clear, life in Monroe was stultifying, and this, too, would have been a difficult revelation to make to her in-laws. It was unavoidable that tongues would wag in Monroe. In no time at all Margaret found that gossip transformed her news of Libbie's visits to the wards of Bellevue Hospital into Libbie's having sole charge of two hospitals, and—for good measure—living under an assumed name![26]

. . .

In 1876 an energetic and public-spirited woman named Candace Wheeler had been struck by an exhibit of needlework at the Centennial Exposition in Philadelphia. The product of the newly founded Kensington School of Art Needlework in London, it represented an attempt to provide a livelihood for "decayed gentlewomen," an ominous term for women who were living in reduced circumstances because they no longer had men to support them. Appreciating that the same need could be found in her own country, Wheeler returned to New York to found the Society of Decorative Art. A skillful organizer, she eschewed the presidency for herself and chose a proven fund-raiser, Mrs. David Lane. Her board of directors consisted of prominent citizens, including some—such as John Jacob Astor and August Belmont—who had known Custer.

Besieged by the numbers of "decayed gentlewomen" who were eager to sell their wares, the two women quickly realized that the society needed a paid secretary. Lane had recently read that Libbie Custer had come to New York to seek employment, although Wheeler was initially skeptical of Libbie's qualifications: "I am as sorry for her as I can be, but we must have a business-like and useful secretary." As she evidently did in all things, Lane prevailed, and Libbie arrived for an interview, "a pathetic figure in widow's weeds, which seemed to hold the shadow of a heart-rending tragedy. So modest in her estimate of herself, so earnest in her desire to do something for our enterprise, and so fixed in her determination to do something practical for her own needs!"[27]

Wheeler immediately warmed to Libbie. She was hired in 1877 "at the modest salary we could afford" and began her labor of correspondence for the society, which consisted primarily of letters to the great number of women whose work had to be rejected. Wheeler found that "the capacity and sympathy she developed seemed made for our needs."[28] Over the years the working relationship became a genuine friendship, and eventually—by then a respected and affluent author rather than a modestly paid secretary—Libbie was absorbed into the Wheelers' artsy and affluent social circle.

In a letter written to Frances Kingsley, widow of the English clergyman and novelist Charles Kingsley, Libbie gave her own account of this first phase of her life as a widow:

> I left my Michigan home at the earnest desire of a noble woman who tried to inspire me with a wish to do something with my wrecked life, and entered a philanthropic society here modelled after the Kensington School of Needlework. It was a blessed haven for me and I found a place where I was needed. But after five years and half of overtaxing, the confinement of a basement room which was especially trying to my strength because I had lived out of doors so long—I was done for and had to leave. I went with tears, with almost murmurings for I thought I should be turned in upon my own life and its anguish and I knew I couldn't face it even then. But some faithful English friends of my husband's . . . sent me passes and I went to Europe for nine months and again my life was spared.[29]

It was spared, she continued, so that she might take up her true life's work. "I feel sure," she told her friend, "that our Heavenly Father will use me yet to do further honor to a man sacrificed by his country."[30] After nine years of widowhood, she felt strong enough to begin the memoirs that would promulgate her image of Custer for the public and for posterity. Libbie would be possessed by this newfound mission until her death in 1933: no letter about her husband would go unanswered, no matter concerning him would be too trivial to escape her attention. As she wrote to Mrs. Kingsley in 1886, "I have several hundred letters from every corner of our land—such letters no woman ever had it seems to me. Breathing such sympathy and a sort of *possession* of me which is very dear to me, alone as I am."[31] She invariably answered these letters by hand, fearing that correspondents—especially admirers or former associates of her husband—would take offense at a typed response.

In addition to such private efforts to maintain her husband's memory, Libbie responded to every public challenge. When an article on the Battle of the Little Bighorn was forthcoming in the *Century* magazine, she worked to arrange some newspaper editorials in conjunction with its appearance. Writing to the editor of the *Century* about this plan, she exclaimed: "Oh if you knew how I think and think and plan at night in the still hours, ways to have the world see my husband as he should be known!"[32] What she had in mind was her own description of Custer as a perfect hero:

> He revered religion, and was so broad that every one's belief was sacred to him. He dearly loved the society of children when they were able to chatter with him; his deference for the aged was inborn, and intensified by his love for his aged parents; he honored womankind; and he loved animals with such devotion that he was never without having them about him if he could help it.[33]

Yet, as the *Century* article illustrates, Libbie rarely succeeded in getting the world to accept completely her view of a Custer without blemish. She had persuaded Edward Godfrey, a lieutenant at the battle, to write an account that would definitively rebut all criticism of her husband. But even the tractable Godfrey proved unsatisfactory. His article quoted a damaging comment made by Captain Myles Moylan to the effect that Custer had "made the biggest mistake of his life" in dividing the regiment before the attack.[34] Although Libbie wrote to the *Century*'s editor in an attempt to get the passage removed before publication, her effort failed.[35] Sixteen years later, Godfrey withdrew the offending Moylan citation in a pamphlet reprint of his article, but in spite of Libbie's unceasing efforts, questions about the battle continued to be raised, and Custer remained controversial.

Devoting herself to her husband's memory was the satisfaction of Libbie's widowhood, but she did not confuse it with happiness. When she returned to Monroe in 1910 for the dedication of a statue to Custer, she replied to the reporter from the *Detroit Free Press* who had asked about her present life, "Can a woman be happy out of whose life has gone the best and dearest it possessed?" If the answer to this question was a decisive "no," it was not unqualified. Publicly gracious as always, she hastened to add to her response, "I cannot but feel a thrill, though, when I think how the people of Michigan and Monroe have honored the general."[36]

Libbie remained alone, and lonely. An undated phrase in one of the journals she sometimes kept says simply: "Sad season for those who have their memories only where once they had their loved ones."[37] Although surrounded by friends and well-wishers, she would never again, by her own choice, have a sustaining intimate relationship. As she wrote to Mrs. Andrew Carnegie in 1890, "I have no one and am indeed on the outside of everything."[38] The image of being outside looking in recurs. In another letter to Mrs. Carnegie she described herself as "on the outside of everybody's windows now . . . [getting] the shine of the fire light on other people's hearths."[39] Similarly, a journal entry written during a lecture tour in 1892 shows her as a transient who momentarily shares the normal life of others and then moves on: "Like the 'flying dutchman' I sail my bark into a port, look into the glow of someone else's window, and the wind takes my sails and I am carried off to another shore—only to cast anchor long enough to see a land that is not mine and that I never can have."[40]

She could never have her own land again, but she had the consolation of believing she had known a complete world in her marriage. Her choice would be to preserve it as much as possible. Rebecca knew her cousin well when she wrote in her condolence letter, "Libbie, how much rather would you be the early widow of such a man than the life-long wife of many another! Your life with Armstrong has been intense, concentrated, three or four, or a dozen ordinary lives in one, and those you can live over again quietly, thoughtfully, and I will say, pleasurably, for his is a spirit which will always be near you."[41] More than fifty years later, Libbie noted with pleasure a passage in a letter sent to her by N. C. Perkins: "He told me he was never in the same room with me that he was not conscious of Autie's presence."[42]

Libbie's endless devotion to her husband's memory was not a pose, nor was it always or entirely a morbid wallowing in grief: it gave her life a purpose, a structure, and a stature that she could not, or would not, find elsewhere.

How normal it was is open to debate. Ordinarily, resolution of grief is measured by the bereaved's ability to put grieving aside and return to a productive life, one that allows loving again. For many persons, however, this kind of ideal or total resolution never takes place, especially when "the acute grief reaction is intense or there is difficulty accepting the fact of the loss."[43] While it has been customary for clinicians to regard identification with the deceased as a symptom of unresolved grief, research indicates that such a constant attachment may actually be a healthy adaptation to bereavement.[44] Certainly Libbie's world validated her behavior entirely: widowhood was a respectable and dignified condition, nor were widows under great pressure to marry again. Libbie's widowhood gave her a great work, one that she could hardly have pursued had she remarried.

But if dedication to her husband's memory was the central and defining principle of her widowhood, it was not the whole story. Her later years included frequent trips to Europe, ambitious travels in India and the Far East, and active participation in the Cosmopolitan Club of New York. "The excitement of fresh contacts with leaders of my sex is the delight of my old age," she told an interviewer in 1927.[45] She may not have wanted to describe her life as "happy" in a newspaper article, but it was certainly comfortable and pleasurable.

Nonetheless, no matter how many achievements and diversions Libbie accumulated, her grief was always an integral part of her existence. A condolence letter she wrote in 1905 asserted that "the yearning in all of us to have a home all our own and someone in it with whom we are ever first, is too deeply rooted to suppress."[46]

In a journal where she jotted down scraps of poetry and sermons that caught her fancy, she once copied two stanzas from a poem entitled "He Never Came." They reflect her sense of her life after Custer's death, the private emotional life that she seldom allowed others to glimpse:

He died a glorious death—oh yes!
His praises ring through all the land;
But oh, for one fond, sweet caress,
One pressure of his loving hand!

. . . .

I watch the months grow into years,
And mark the dreary weeks go by,
And bear in sorrow and with tears
The life from which I cannot fly.[47]

23

Literary Careers

> "That is nice," said Nettie, kissing her mother, "when I get to be a woman shall I write books, mamma?"
>
> "God forbid," murmured Ruth, kissing the child's changeful cheek; "God forbid," murmured she, musingly, as she turned over the leave of her book; "no happy woman ever writes. From Harry's grave sprang 'Floy.'"
>
> —Fanny Fern, *Ruth Hall*

Libbie would have agreed with Fanny Fern's protagonist Ruth Hall, a woman who, finding all other employment closed after her husband's untimely death, takes up writing under the pen name "Floy" to support her young children. Like Fern, whose autobiographical novel *Ruth Hall* was published in 1856, Libbie might well have said that her own writings had sprung from Autie's grave. Had he lived, she would have continued in a supporting role, contentedly encouraging his own literary work.

Where Custer's writing was a completely acceptable adjunct to his military career, hers was intensely problematic, a threat to her feminine image and her emotional equilibrium. During the years before she began her first book, *"Boots and Saddles," or Life in Dakota with General Custer* (1885), she had determinedly kept herself busy, dreading, as she wrote to Frances Kingsley, the moment when she should be "turned in upon [her] own life and its anguish." To Kingsley, like herself the devoted widow of a well-known man, Libbie described the effort involved, not so much in writing as in confronting her grief so single-mindedly: "I took up my pen to pay my small tribute to my loved one. The actual writing was not so hard but looking in his letters to make extracts for the appendix and preparing the few brief pages for the final chapters cost me such anguish that I well nigh never came to myself again." Similarly, writing her second book, *Tenting on the Plains, or General Custer in Kansas and Texas* (1887), was emotionally lacerating because "Kansas was so full of anguish I cannot write of it without exhaustion."[1]

The debilitation Libbie suffered, so severe that she often had to stop working completely and recoup her strength, had more than one source. Her preoccupation with the lost past would sometimes absorb her in an unhealthy way, producing sad dreams and daytime musings, but more crucial was the weighty responsibility of living up to what she felt to be her "one absorbing duty and privilege," that is, doing justice to her husband in her writing. "I need your prayers," she told Kingsley, "for I tremble so when I touch my pen if it is to speak of Autie."[2]

Libbie's sense of the high nature of her calling was only a little short of Harriet Beecher Stowe's frequent assertion that God had written *Uncle Tom's Cabin*. As she confided to Kingsley, she felt that writing about her husband was a divine mission: "I am so thankful to have been the instrument in God's hands of having in a measure mirrored my husband to his people."[3] On Custer's behalf Libbie could be grandiose; consciously or otherwise, she saw her work for him as her only legitimate reason for self-assertion.

To J. M. Wright, one of his classmates at West Point, the "greatest surprise in Custer's whole career in life was that he should turn out to be a literary man." His West Point cohort would not have been surprised by Custer leading a cavalry charge or even by Custer riding to his death against the Sioux, for he daily risked himself in activities requiring physical daring. "But," Wright continued, "if any one had said in the four years before the civil war that Cadet Custer would in fifteen years be a scholar of artistic tastes and a writer of graphic contributions to the magazines, the prediction would have been derided."[4]

Since Custer had been notorious for his neglect of academics at West Point, his military colleagues often teased him by saying that Libbie must have been writing the articles that later appeared as his book, *My Life on the Plains*. He took the joke in good humor, telling Libbie that when General Sherman said to him, "Custer, you write so well, people think your wife does it, and you don't get the credit," he had replied,

"Well, General, then I ought to get the credit for my selection of a wife."[5]

The *Detroit Journal* compared the books written by the Custers and announced that in spite of Libbie's "well known literary faculty," it was obvious that Custer had done his own writing. In those times of clear gender demarcation, the *Journal* found Libbie's books "filled with womanly personality," while her husband's had "the directness of a military dispatch."[6] With regard to Custer, however, this was an oversimplification. He was accustomed to writing military reports that had this quality, but in his work for publication he attempted—not always successfully—a more literary style.

Although *My Life on the Plains* sold reasonably well, had Custer lived and continued to write, it is unlikely that he would have enjoyed as much popularity as a writer as Libbie did. Nor would he have had the problems she did in dealing with this role. Libbie was, in fact, the more readable writer, with a supple, informal style and a disarming, self-effacing persona. Of the numerous army wives from this period who penned their memoirs, she is the most accomplished writer. Her husband's style was more consciously literary and formal, and although he attempted to be disarming by occasionally showing himself at a disadvantage—when he shot his horse instead of a buffalo, for example, or had to make a difficult military decision—the Custer who inhabits his own pages tends to be a distant figure, in control of his feelings at all times.

Custer's first biographer, Frederick Whittaker, had given Libbie good advice when she decided to write about her husband: "Don't be afraid to write of yourself. It is through *your* memories that Custer's best traits will gradually and unconsciously expand to the world. . . . Write away, just as you talked to me."[7] Libbie did not intend to write of herself directly, but "the unconscious revelation of her own character as a heroic woman and the perfection of a wife" charmed readers and critics alike.[8]

Once she brought herself to begin, Libbie produced three books within a relatively brief period, 1885–90. All three were dedicated to Custer, and all described their life together on the Plains. The first, "*Boots and Saddles*," took up Libbie's most immediate and painful memories, those of the Custers' Dakota years, which ended abruptly at the Little Bighorn. In the next volume, *Tenting on the Plains*, she went back to the immediate postwar episode in Texas, followed by their arrival in Kansas. Her last book, *Following the Guidon*, fleshed out the Kansas years in more detail.

Acclaim for Libbie's three books of memoirs was almost universal among reviewers, but not for the reason she must have hoped. "Its charm," the *Current Literature* reviewer observed of *Tenting on the Plains*, "lies not in the picture which we get of General Custer, but in that of the author by herself. Anything more free from egotism than these pages would be impossible to imagine. Yet Mrs. Custer has drawn herself in a way that is delightful."[9] For reviewers, the most appealing story Libbie told was that of the devoted wife, "willing to share all dangers with him to whom her heart belonged."[10] The word *unconscious* recurs frequently in these reviews to describe Libbie's presumably unintentional depiction of herself as a paragon of wifely virtues. Whether reviewers questioned her adoring portrait of Custer is not always clear, but in any case it is immaterial: what pleased them was *her* acceptance of it, her "perfect and utterly unselfish devotion."[11]

While Libbie's work required her increasing participation in the masculine world of business, she wanted to maintain the image that appealed to her reading public, that of the timid and retiring widow. The friction between these two roles surfaced briefly in a frank letter written to Clarence Edmund Stedman in connection with her publishing affairs. Charles L. Webster, the publisher of *Tenting on the Plains*, had fallen into financial difficulties and failed to market her book well. She had wanted to buy it back in order to go to another firm, but Mark Twain, who had a financial investment in Webster's, had convinced her to give Webster another chance.[12]

This turned out to be a mistake that Libbie attempted to rectify by carrying out her original idea: *Tenting on the Plains* would be removed from Webster's and assigned to Stedman's firm, Harper's. "I cannot help but regret that my agreeable friendship with you should have this very disagreeable element mixed in," she wrote to Stedman, "for you will see me in a light few people have ever seen me—that is, I feel myself an injured woman and cannot help but protest." Clearly this was an uncomfortable position for Libbie, one she felt she must explain:

> On one occasion not connected with your firm, I submitted amiably and quietly and was *dreadfully* wronged. I do not feel willing to keep silent now. I feel that I have rights and

> will endeavor to explain them to Mr. Hall in turn. But as I said I am very sorry to have . . . you drawn into a painful discussion. However I shall hope that you will realize that the author has a side as well as the publisher.[13]

Couching her demands in protestation and apology seemed necessary to Libbie because she was violating the feminine decorum of quiet amiability that had proved itself a liability in her negotiations with Hall (Webster's partner). Yet for all of her determination, she was uneasy at the unfamiliar role and sorry that Stedman, a friend, should see her in this light.

To a great extent the success of Libbie's books depended upon the contrast between a dependably heroic husband and a wife who epitomized the Victorian view of femininity, forthrightly confessing her own fear, vulnerability, and weakness. Taken at face value, he is always admirable and right, but her fallibility is more recognizable as the human condition. The interaction of his greatness and her humanity is as predictable as any television sitcom, and just as satisfying: with each episode the reader looks forward to seeing these familiar characters coping with a new situation that calls for ingenuity within their expected roles. Beyond this, the life the Custers led on the Plains frontier was the stuff of romance: there were encounters with Indians, both friendly and hostile, colorful characters like California Joe and Wild Bill, and an untamed natural environment that seemed fiercer than anything back in the States. Fire and flood assailed their dwellings, soldiers lost their lives not only in battle but on the streets of Hays City and Point Pleasant, and carefree recreational rides could suddenly become perilous adventures.[14] In these incidents and in her descriptions of the routine, Libbie memorably re-created the vanished world of the frontier army.

Libbie had taken no notes at the time of these adventures, nor did she profess to have her husband's excellent memory, but what she remembered was vividly rendered and infused with emotion. Unlike Custer, who—however he might have felt—was constrained by a code of male behavior to write from a vantage point of rationality and control, Libbie freely expressed the horror and desperation that normal people feel in moments of high drama and risk. She noted this difference when she described Custer's efforts to control himself as he took final leave of his Civil War troops. "How glad I was," she wrote, "as I watched the set features of my husband's face, saw his eyes fixed immovably in front of him, listened in vain for one word from his overburdened heart, that I, being a woman, need not tax every nerve to suppress emotion, but could let the tears stream down my face."[15]

Her finest writing is in her long second book, *Tenting on the Plains,* where she introduces her most popular character, the black cook Eliza, a runaway slave who had attached herself to Custer during the Civil War and remained a part of the Custer household for many years.[16] Where *"Boots and Saddles,"* building as it does to the tragic climax of Custer's death, has little room for other people, *Tenting* is more expansive. Custer's brother Tom and his father, Emmanuel, are both individualized, Wild Bill Hickok is tellingly sketched, and, above all, Eliza's voice constantly enlarges and enlivens the narrative with a dimension of comic realism. If the Custers seem all too saintly—he in his buoyant optimism, she in her deference to him—Eliza speaks for the rest of us: exasperated at paw prints on white bedspreads, laundry that gets blown over into the mud, and dinners that must be produced out of nothing.

The most dramatic and effectively presented episode is the storm and accompanying flood at Big Creek, Kansas, in 1867. While Custer was away on an Indian hunting expedition, Libbie and Eliza remained in tents in the cavalry camp near Fort Hays. During the night the water in Big Creek rose thirty-five feet, placing the entire camp in peril. Lightning split the sky and strong winds menaced the tents, throwing the camp into a confused state of emergency. Suddenly two ferocious dogs who had long been enemies broke their chains and began a fight to the death. While the storm raged, soldiers struggled to separate the dogs. Then, the bizarre interruption over, they returned to their work of securing the tents: in one gale seventeen men held down one guy-rope to prevent a tent from being swept away.[17]

Not knowing when and if they themselves would be engulfed by the turbulent expanse of water rushing toward both sides of their narrow spit of land, Libbie and Eliza suddenly heard "sounds that no one, once hearing, ever forgets"—the cries of drowning men. They not only heard but saw, when the lightning flashed, men "waving their arms imploringly" as the current carried them off. In agony at her helplessness to aid them, Libbie rushed to the tent for ropes, only to find that they were so stiff from moisture and tied so elaborately that it was impossible to unfasten them. As Libbie frantically bruised her hands and tore her nails on the unyielding ropes, Eliza thought of the clothesline, yet hesitated to take it. Her paralysis—"I can't do it, I can't do it!"—is an anomalous hiatus in the work of survival, whose full poignance is not comprehensible until Libbie explains that the former slave, with the "inveterate habit of protecting our things," could not bring herself to sacrifice the clothesline, for "where will we get another?" As the mistress, Libbie was of course spared this indecision and hurried to get it. With the line the two women laboriously succeeded in saving three men. Seven others, too far out to catch the rope, swelled the army's lamentably high total of drowned men.[18]

To Libbie's surprise and pleasure, she discovered in the 1890s that as a popular author, she could command handsome fees as a lecturer. Although she eschewed the commercial lecture circuit in favor of the more genteel milieu of women's clubs and colleges, lecturing brought her a measure of affluence.

The journal that Libbie kept for her engagements in 1892 and 1893 contains more direct self-revelation than her other writings because it is so narrowly focused on details of the moment: for once the dominant figure of Custer is reduced to an occasional allusion. For this same reason the journal is generally dull, a repetition of similar experiences in different places with little significant variation. Libbie describes herself as constantly complimented for her reading and her attractive appearance by a changing cast of people she gratefully renders in saccharine. Her hosts are unfailingly "sweet and dear," "delightful," "sympathetic," demonstrative—immersing her in an affectionate appreciation that she can scarcely get enough of. When a veteran asked her after one performance if everyone told her how they liked *"Boots and Saddles,"* she records her frank reply as "not half enough to suit me for I never tired of hearing it said."[19]

Libbie's warm reception wherever she spoke assuaged the persistent stage fright she battled. It was her habit to single out a particularly attentive and sympathetic face in the audience and read to that person, drawing confidence from the encouragement she received. At times an indifferent listener could have the same effect. On one occasion she fixed upon such a person, "reading and talking to him though he didn't know it," and had the satisfaction of gaining his interest.

Part of Libbie's fear was undoubtedly inspired by her unease at public performing, a role that was still difficult to reconcile with feminine respectability.[20] Like Fannie Fern's Ruth Hall, Libbie enjoyed a public success without believing that women should have public roles. While usurping the male prerogative of public performance, she maintained a feminine image through her timidity, which impressed her genteel audience favorably. In Cambridge two pillars of the community, Mrs. Charles Eliot and her sister, Mrs. Parke Godwin, told Libbie they were glad she had no "platform ways." The stage fright that affected the beginning of all her performances pleased them because they were "weary of women who stood unmoved before thousands even."[21]

On another occasion a woman told her that her paper was "such a womanly paper," and Libbie confided to her journal that she was always glad "to escape being classed with the platform woman who has always grievances and seeks perpetually to reconstruct something."[22] In keeping with this attitude she often told the people she met at her lectures that she intended to give up such appearances, only to be met with protests and more of the compliments that she treasured. A "fine looking lawyer" who praised Libbie after one of her lectures must have been surprised at her response when he asked her if she always felt—as he did in court—that it would be possible to do better next time. Libbie told him that *she* always felt that she would never do it again on any account because she was so frightened each time.[23]

Although her hesitancy and shrinking demeanor on the public platform successfully confirmed her femininity in a male world, they were not for all that a calculated pose. Underlying her need to elicit compliments and reassurance was a deep-seated sense of inadequacy that was not merely assumed for the occasion. After overhearing a group of admirers surrounding Libbie for more than an hour, a Mrs. Tullidger wondered how she could stand such adulation without having her head turned. Libbie's reply revealed her constant need for reassurance: "I told her I could not remember {for} 12 hours anything said to me and that I was too conscious of my own deficiencies to believe them—And the dear thing for whom these pages are written {Libbie's close friend Agnes Bates} *knows* how constantly I have the feeling of my own failings and how disappointed I."[24] The entry breaks off abruptly, but at another time when Libbie was complimented for levelheadedness amid so much flattering attention, she finished the thought: "I told them there was always a next morning with me when no one but myself knows how disappointed I am that I can do no better justice to Autie's name."[25]

Libbie's grief was also an integral part of her public persona. Always close to the surface, it produced tears whenever a man who had served with her husband made himself known to her. One veteran told her after hearing her talk that he had wanted to approach her before the lecture but had heard that she became so unnerved at seeing the old soldiers that she could not read or speak. Both cried when he revealed that he had been at the Battle of the Little Bighorn.[26]

Although Libbie in her youth had been a highly prized young woman, with doting parents and many suitors, when she married she became the wife of a famous man to whom she willingly deferred. As the surviving partner of her marriage, she felt ambivalent about returning to the center of attention. She loved being praised, but in Libbie's mind Custer was still the only proper recipient of attention, and she could justify her role only as a contribution to his memory.

Long after she stopped making extensive reading tours, Libbie continued to give occasional talks, especially close to home at the New York women's clubs. One New Year's Day program, testifying to the gradual relaxation of her enmity toward Indians, has her telling "anecdotes of the American Indian" after Oskenonton, a Mohawk brave in "full war costume," sang songs of his people.[27] Yet Libbie's manuscript notes indicate that she still held certain stereotypical views of Indians: "All are like children, so sensitive. Suspicious, so quickly roused to anger and often pouting and morose."[28]

Nonetheless, by the twentieth century Libbie could publicly admit that the Indians had been in the right at the Little Bighorn. It was her enmity toward those she considered truly responsible for her husband's death—President Grant and Major Reno—that remained unchanged. In 1885 she wrote a newspaper article on Grant's funeral parade without referring to him by name.[29] As for Reno, she never altered her opinion that he was "a coward who lost all control on [the] battlefield and took revenge on a soldier who could not reply."[30]

Libbie's voluminous papers are full of notes for a projected book on Custer in the Civil War, but it is clear from these notes that in spite of intending to do such a book for many years, she never got it well underway. The few episodes she committed to paper she rewrote many times, always returning to her memories of Stevensburg, her first army camp, and to the shock of transition from a protected girlhood to a situation that demanded maturity and courage.

When her last book was published in 1890, Libbie was only forty-eight years old, a woman of physical and mental vitality and a writer whose success should have given her every incentive to go on writing. Why, then, did she fail to do the Civil War book?

One reason may have been her own absence from the scene for all but the final fourteen months of the war, for even if she always cast herself in a subordinate role, Libbie was strongest as a writer of what she herself had observed. Furthermore, although she seems to have shared Custer's love of military ceremony, she had no interest in the battlefield except as a theater of human drama: strategy and tactics failed to move her pen, and she shrank from suffering and death. For the Custers' life on the Plains, where battles had been infrequent, this lack of interest was immaterial; for the Civil War, when Custer had been engaged in one fight after another, it was a serious flaw. Alternatively, Libbie could have treated the book as a record of her own experience during the war, which would have been both fascinating and historically valuable, but she was incapable of intentionally making herself the central figure in her writing. This inhibition, combined with her inability to truly describe Custer's battlefield experience, probably accounted for her failure to produce a fourth book.[31]

For the remainder of her life, however, Libbie behaved as if she was in the process of writing about Custer in the Civil War. She continued to solicit material from veterans who had served with him at that time and often spoke of it in letters as a book in progress, never abandoning the idea entirely. No doubt to have done so would have seemed like a betrayal of her husband's memory and a loss of connection with him.

24

Monuments

We add to our own honor by doing honor to Custer.
—Motto of the Michigan Custer Memorial Association

Your interest is inspired by a loyal devotion to a loved one's memory and is more personal than others can feel.
—Colonel George G. Briggs, Michigan Cavalry Brigade Association, to Libbie Custer

Libbie wanted the world to admire and honor her late husband as she did, and she also wanted to control this process as absolutely as possible. One of the first testimonies to the public's grief and outrage over the Battle of the Little Bighorn was the *New York Herald*'s immediate creation of a fund for a monument to the general.[1] A Custer Monument Committee was established with General Sheridan as president, and contributions poured in. The *Herald*, always an enthusiastic supporter of Custer, gave an initial sum of $1,000. The prominent and the obscure rushed to contribute according to their means—Judge Henry Hilton donated $1,000, the Grand Duke Alexis gave $500, and a schoolgirl sent in ten cents with a touching letter about Custer: "My heart was filled with pity when I read the other night for mother the account in your paper of the awful slaughter done by the Indians on General Custer & his army. . . . I would have given the world to have had one look at the fearless General Custer; and then he was so young and, as the papers say, so handsome. I could cry tears over his sad fate."[2]

One dissenting voice belonged to Colonel Samuel D. Sturgis, the commanding officer of the Seventh Cavalry whose son Jack had been with the Seventh only a short time when he accompanied Custer to the Last Stand. Colonel Sturgis blamed Custer for his son's death, and only two weeks after learning of it his anguish was still raw. The *New York Times* of that day reported his emotional reaction to the *Herald*'s proposal: "If a monument is to be erected to General Custer for God's sake let them hide it in some dark valley, or veil it, or put it anywhere the bleeding hearts of the widows, orphans, fathers and mothers of the men so uselessly sacrificed to Custer's ambition, can never be wrung at the sight of it."[3] Ultimately, that is exactly what did happen to it, although ironically the moving spirit to remove it from sight was none other than the general's devoted widow.

Oddly enough, despite Libbie's known interest in perpetuating the memory of her husband, the *New York Herald* failed to involve her in the process of establishing the monument. Men were accustomed to making such decisions in the public sphere, and it was assumed that she would naturally approve of such a splendid and permanent tribute to her husband. It was further assumed that the most fitting site for the monument would be West Point, where the general had expressed a wish to be interred. Though he had not been a distinguished student there, Custer had become a more than distinguished graduate, and one who retained a fondness for the place and for his classmates throughout his life.

After the initial spurt of generosity, donations stagnated for a year or so until the campaign was brought back to life by Custer's burial at West Point on October 10, 1877, with great pomp and circumstance. To the $4,051.20 contributed immediately after the battle, almost another $3,000 was added, so that when the committee decided to solicit designs for a statue, it had about $7,000 in hand. This modest amount ruled out an equestrian statue, and only two designs were submitted. The one selected was proposed by J. Wilson MacDonald, a self-taught sculptor of heretofore modest achievement. On August 24, 1878, a private showing of his model for the Custer statue was held for the press.

Libbie, clearly piqued at her complete exclusion from the project, wrote to the committee chairman and former friend of her husband, the New York banker August Belmont, asking who had selected the design. Belmont's reply made it clear that the decision was irrevocable: the committee had made the selection, the work was nearly done, and the sculptor had already received some payment.[4] None of these circumstances in and of themselves indicated that the statue would be of poor quality; nevertheless, Libbie chose not to attend its unveiling on August 30, 1879. In doing so, she denied herself what would ordinarily have been a great pleasure: an elaborate ceremony attended by almost three thousand people gathered to honor her husband, and at which she assuredly would have been the recipient of much attention and homage. Such military luminaries as General Schofield, commandant of West Point, and General Nathaniel P. Banks, a renowned orator, extolled the dead hero, while others read an ode to Custer and performed music written especially for the occasion.

The public reception of the statue was overwhelmingly favorable. The reporter from the *Detroit Free Press* praised its site as "the finest in West Point," and the statue itself as "of heroic size and very striking in appearance."[5] The *New York Herald* described it as "an accurate likeness of the dead soldier."[6] John Bulkley, who had grown up with Libbie and Autie in Monroe, and remained the Custers' devoted friend, was well pleased. He wrote to Libbie that the statue was "as satisfactory as any statue could be made—from one point of view especially, the left front, the likeness is excellent and the attitude very fine."[7]

Rarely was anything concerning Custer uncontroversial, however, and the *Free Press* reporter also had this to say:

> Strange as it may seem the officers at West Point, at least many of them, were rather lukewarm in their manner of celebrating the day. Several of them sneered at the statue and said it was a ridiculous one. That no soldier ever held a sword and a pistol in that way and that Custer was a hero made by the newspapers and said that military men did not look on his as did the general public.[8]

How many officers expressed such opinions was not clear from the article: the iconoclastic opinion, so often attractive to journalists, is all but irresistible at the moment an icon is being displayed for admiration. Custer had been a notable figure, and the unveiling took place only a few months after the court of inquiry had exonerated Major Marcus Reno of wrongdoing at the Battle of the Little Bighorn. Those well-publicized proceedings had undoubtedly revived arguments among military officers about Custer's role in the disaster.

Whether or not Libbie learned of these less than generous opinions, she heard others that hardened her heart against the West Point monument, however impressively sited and warmly received by cadets. Her main objections, made repeatedly in letters, were two: Custer was portrayed incorrectly in terms of dress and accoutrements (the sword and pistol) and "the face of the McDonald [*sic*] statue is said to be that of a man sixty years old."[9] Said by whom? It seems unlikely that any friend or acquaintance would have said such a thing to Custer's widow unless she had first made it clear that she wanted to hear criticism of the statue.

Libbie was in fact furious, writing to Vinnie Ream, a sculptor who had done a bust of Custer in 1866, "I cannot think the statue else than a great insult to Autie's memory." Just as tellingly, she burned with resentment over the slight to herself as the final arbiter on all things pertaining to her husband: "I was never consulted and did not even know about it until it was done. The bitter disappointment I feel is such a cross [for] me to bear, it seems to me I cannot endure it."[10]

When Libbie learned that a movement was afoot to have the statue reproduced and erected in Washington, she wrote to Ream that her blood boiled "at the thought of that wretched statue being repeated."[11] An odd conjunction of pro- and anti-Custer forces defeated the plan. The MacDonald Bill was reported unfavorably from committee with the explanation that Mrs. Custer had written against it *and* a petition signed by citizens in Detroit, Michigan, and Rochester, New York, had protested "against any measures being taken by Congress for the erection of a monument to General Custer on account of his alleged departure from the rules of organized warfare."[12]

The threat of reproducing the statue removed, Libbie set her sights on getting rid of the statue itself. Not long after writing in this vein to Robert Todd Lincoln, the secretary of war, she met him unexpectedly. Lincoln politely acknowledged her letter and diplomatically agreed that she "was right in desiring the removal of the statue as every one pronounced it outrageous."[13] He also told her that he had talked with General Howard, the commandant of West Point, about removing it but had found him to be adamantly opposed.

Lincoln perhaps thought that this perfunctory effort—expressing sympathy but doing nothing—would be enough to calm the widow's feelings. Instead, she applied herself to another powerful figure, the army's ranking general, William Tecumseh Sherman. Her account of the problem to General Sherman relied on a typical Libbie strategy, contempt phrased as innocence: "I was amazed to find that the Secretary of War looked for assistance from the Commandant at West Point. I had an idea he would direct what he wished and the commandant would obey." Revealingly, she continued, "It frightens me dear General Sherman, because . . . this vital matter to me rests so much in other hands, I have little hope."[14] The hands in which Libbie preferred Custer's reputation to rest were her own, even if it meant that there would be no statue of Custer in the nation's capital or at West Point.

Libbie's appeal was likely to move the gallant old soldier, whose vision of war as realpolitik had been shared by her husband: "What hope I now have rests in you, the kindest and truest of friends to me, when I so need all that they can do to make my sad life endurable."[15]

Sherman responded immediately. He not only told Libbie "I sympathize with every pulsation of your wounded heart," he instructed her in some detail about writing a more effective letter to him insisting on her rights, "a short, strong letter *demanding* as the widow of Custer, the *sole* and *exclusive* right to make the grave of your husband." Characterizing her first letter as "an appeal," he now asked her to provide him with an ultimatum. "Possessed of such a letter from you," he told her, "I will present it to the Secretary endorsed with my judgment that the widow had this unqualified right."[16]

When Libbie produced the letter conforming to his specifications, Sherman forwarded it to Lincoln with his own note of support, "an expression of earnest sympathy for Mrs. Custer now toiling with her own hands to eke out a sum of support in addition to the pension she receives and her heart torn when she thinks of that awful statue of Gen. Custer at West Point."[17]

After this, Secretary Lincoln pursued the matter more seriously. As he wrote to Leonard Swett, his former law partner, whom Libbie had also interested in the case: "If it [the statue] had been put up by the government of course there would be no difficulty, but I understand that it was erected by the contributions of a number of prominent citizens, who presumably take great pride in it, and with whom it would be difficult to consult."[18]

Another letter from Lincoln to Swett indicates that Libbie had made another suggestion:

> I do not think it practicable to comply with Mrs. Custer's request that the statue be removed to the battlefield of the Big Horn for two reasons: First the basis for its removal from its

> pedestal at West Point is that it is devoid of artistic merit and is offensive to the eye. Both of these reasons would be inconsistent with an order directing it to be set up in any public place. Secondly, in 1878, Congress made an appropriation of a number of bronze cannon to assist in the erection of the statue of Gen. Custer at West Point. . . . It would be of doubtful propriety for me to order a statue thus made, the location of which was fixed in an act of Congress to be set up in a new position without congressional action.[19]

Libbie had evidently proposed banishing the statue to the remote corner of southeastern Montana where her husband had died as a plan to insure its virtual invisibility: in 1884 she could have had no idea that the twentieth century would see increasing numbers of people visiting the battlefield.

If Secretary Lincoln did not feel authorized to place the statue elsewhere, he apparently did feel that he could have it removed from view entirely without consulting Congress, and he so directed the superintendent of West Point, Custer's old Civil War rival Wesley Merritt. Possibly, in view of that rivalry, Merritt was happy enough to rid West Point of a Custer statue: he acted with alacrity to have the statue removed "without unnecessary publicity."[20] From Libbie's point of view this was an even better outcome than her proposal to place it on the battlefield.

The public seems not to have been disturbed by the statue's disappearance, but on June 20, 1906, Libbie wrote to the then superintendent of West Point, A. L. Mills, suggesting—rather surprisingly—that the head and shoulders could be salvaged and placed on public view. He promptly replied that the cutting of the statue had been done, and it would be displayed as soon as an appropriate place was decided upon.[21] This never happened, nor have later efforts to find any pieces of the Custer statue been successful.[22]

When the *Herald* began its campaign for a monument right after the battle, a similar effort was undertaken independently in Monroe, Michigan, Libbie's hometown and the place where a number of Custers, including her husband's parents, still lived. When it became clear that West Point was the place agreed upon, the fund-raisers of Monroe contributed the thousand dollars they had collected to the New York fund. Some citizens of Michigan remained convinced that their state should have a Custer monument, not because of the Custer family's residence there but because Custer had led the famed Michigan Cavalry Brigade to glory during the Civil War. Eventually they recovered from being rejected as the site for the first monument and took up the cause with renewed enthusiasm.

Heralding a notable difference between the nineteenth and the twentieth centuries, when the movement got underway again in 1907 it was determined to have the government foot the bill. Colonel George G. Briggs of the Michigan Cavalry Brigade Association wrote to Libbie that he would contact every member of the brigade to lobby his own representative in the legislature, "urging such representative to favor the appropriation."[23] On March 20, 1907, a Monroe booster, Charles E. Greening, wrote to Libbie from the Michigan Custer Memorial Association on impressive letterhead that prominently displayed the association's motto, "We add to our own honor by doing honor to Custer." Greening urged Libbie to write to Charles E. Ward, speaker pro tem of the Michigan House of Representatives, soliciting his support for the monument.[24]

These political efforts were successful, and although one faction had favored placing the statue in Lansing, the state capital, Monroe ultimately won out. A commission was chosen consisting of James H. Kidd, Frederick A. Nims, and Briggs—all veterans of the Michigan Brigade, Custer worshipers, and friends of Libbie. Briggs made it clear that Libbie would have the deciding voice in any commission deliberations: "Certainly no model will be decided upon without your inspection and approval," he wrote to her.[25] Greening, who had evidently expected to be on the commission, was excluded by virtue of its restriction to veterans of the Michigan Brigade. He continued to have a proprietary interest in the project and kept up an energetic correspondence about it with Libbie.

So, it seemed, did every sculptor in the land. Briggs was more than prophetic when he told Libbie, "You will certainly have many trials in listening to all the whims and suggestions of the artists whom you meet."[26]

The first trial was especially painful for Libbie: a barrage of letters from the Washington sculptor Vinnie Ream, who had done the bust of the general that both Custers liked so much. Although they had not seen each other for many years, Ream had reason to believe that Libbie would favor her selection. Not long after Custer's death, Libbie had followed up her frank letters to Ream about the hated statue at West Point by offering to buy Ream's bust of Custer. A partial and undated letter to the sculptor from Libbie, probably from the early 1880s when they were in frequent communication, closes effusively: "With very good wish for you both [Vinnie had married] and always a heart full of gratitude for your kindness and friendship and tender never dying sympathy."[27] About the bust, Libbie wrote: "I do not know how to use sufficiently forcible language to prove to you how excellent I think the likeness is, that you have made of General Custer as I have seen it in the clay. I thank you with all my heart for having preserved by your genius such a speaking face."[28]

Libbie could not think of actually acquiring the bust of her husband until she was settled in her own home. When this happened in 1881, she wrote to Ream, "And now if I could only have the bust of General Custer that you have so faithfully made from his own features, I would think my home so blessed. . . . I have so set my heart on having the bust you have made I cannot think with calmness of going to anyone else to get what I must have."[29] Ream was more than accommodating: their correspondence indicates that she did not allow Libbie to contribute to any of the costs but simply made a present of the bust to the eager widow.

Libbie's later coldness to someone she had unburdened herself to, albeit more than twenty years before, is puzzling: Ream was a serious and experienced artist who had not only seen Custer in his glory days but had already produced a sculpture of him that Libbie adored. As the only sculptor with personal acquaintance of the subject, Ream would have logically been a strong candidate for such a project, but it may be that she offended Libbie by presuming too strongly upon their friendship and by interfering in a matter that Libbie already had under control: in her great desire to win the commission, Ream had officiously written to the governor of Michigan, asking him to put Custer's widow on the selection committee. Then she wrote forthrightly to Libbie, "You know how ambitious I am to make the equestrian statue of Genl Custer . . . and I invoke your warm friendship in this matter."[30] Evidently, Libbie did not reply in kind: Ream's next letter reproaches Libbie for a response "so conventional, so unsympathetic, with no kind word even or mention of my likeness of the brave Genl Custer."[31]

More threatening, perhaps, to Libbie's control over the memory of her husband was the sculptor's own sense of proprietorship, a sense that is all too apparent even when she is insisting upon Libbie's rights: "I would not want even to make the statue unless you, his wife, his well-beloved, were not anxious for me to do so. Then indeed it would be a pleasure for I feel Genl Custer would like to have me make it, for *no other* sculptor could be inspired as I would be, with the memory of that brave soldier who died in his prime, a friend who was mourned for by my family and myself as for a Brother."[32] Moreover, Custer had once paid the sculptor a graceful compliment: "Your victories are lasting and unlike mine are not purchased at the expense of the lifeblood of fellow creatures, leaving sorrow and desolation in their track."[33]

In her first enthusiastic letter to Libbie, Ream had, perhaps unwisely, reminded Custer's widow that she had spent hours with Custer in the intimacy of her studio:

> I feel . . . I have Genl Custer's likeness in my heart. You felt so yourself when you saw the bust I had made of him from sittings from life—yes he even worked on it himself and helped with the wide hat, the shoulder straps, neck-tie and all. Remembering how you appreciated it and knowing how it brings Genl Custer right before me, every time I enter my studio now, I feel that no one can reproduce him in bronze more carefully, more truthfully, more faithfully than I can.[34]

Libbie could not allow anyone else to flourish this kind of possessiveness, however innocently meant. And Ream's relationship with Custer may not have been so innocent. At the time she had been an extremely attractive single woman who clearly enjoyed the attention of men, and Custer's flirtatiousness was all too well known to Libbie.[35]

Ream's nostalgic effusions, coupled with undisguised pleas for support, were awkward for Libbie. In what came to be a habit during the period when the prize was yet to be assigned, she sent the problematic correspondence to Briggs for his advice. In this case he commonsensically suggested that she refer Ream, and other applicants as well, to the commission.

Ream was difficult because of past history, but Libbie's time was soon taken up by sculptors not previously known to her who set out to capture her good opinion. Many lived in New York or the nearby area: she was invited to their studios and their country homes; their wives—all other candidates were men—joined them in penning gracious notes about how pleasant these visits had been. A good guest, Libbie invariably presented the sculptors with copies of her book *"Boots and Saddles,"* which occasioned more thank-you notes. Finally, in December of 1907, Briggs wrote of his pleasure in learning that "after the long search for the right man, you are convinced he can be found in the person of either [*sic*] Mr. Potter, Mr. Proctor, Mr. [H. M.] Shrady, Mr. Solon Borglum or Mr. Brush-Brown."[36] G. Borglum, who went on to fame as the sculptor of Mount Rushmore, was eliminated because of reports of "unprofessional and dishonorable acts."[37]

Now that the moment for a decision approached, Briggs reiterated that it was Libbie's alone to make, but he did seek to influence her opinion. Evidently the two had originally agreed upon a posture of action for the statue, but then Briggs changed his mind and lobbied for a statue in repose: "The figure in repose possesses a dignity, and often a dramatic quality, that is not found where action is represented."[38] Libbie was convinced.

Meanwhile, Charles E. Greening, who never wrote to Libbie without reminding her of his (unfair) exclusion from the commission, had nothing better to do on the day after Christmas, 1907, than write her another upsetting letter. "The members of the Old Custer Brigade are dying off fast," he wrote—complaining about the two years projected to complete the statue—"and we would want to have as many as possible to attend the dedication."[39] Libbie sent the letter on to Briggs, who promptly reassured her, not about the alarming death rate of the Civil War veterans, but about the wisdom of Greening's exclusion from the commission: "If anything was needed to prove his unfitness for a place upon the Commission his letter supplies it. . . . Since reading his letter to you the man himself no longer interests me."[40]

By early February when Briggs came to New York to meet with Libbie, both felt that Edward Potter was their strongest candidate. He had especially impressed Libbie by writing that nothing should be decided until "the Sculptor and Committee have been on the spot where the Statue is to stand."[41] While Potter was certainly right about the importance of siting a work of art carefully, in view of the sculpture's later history of removal and relocation, it is more than a little ironic that this concern was decisive in winning Potter the commission.

Since it was clear that they had no need to tour more studios, take tea with more sculptors' wives, or distribute more copies of *"Boots and Saddles,"* Libbie canceled an appointment made for her and Briggs with

F. W. Ruckstuhl and his assistant, Tholenaar. Ruckstuhl was highly irate. He wrote to Libbie that "for him [Briggs] to leave us in the lurch, as if we were the dregs of the earth, instead of two distinguished artists, paralyzed us with astonishment."[42] The sculptor was not too paralyzed to be scathing, however. What a pity, he went on to say, since they would have been able to do the work for two thousand dollars less than offered and to exhibit it in the Paris salon! Once again, the sensitive Libbie referred the letter to Briggs, who showed himself equal to the sculptor's indignation: "It is not worthy a moment's consideration, as its contents stamps the writer as an ill-tempered, ill-mannered and impertinent individual."[43]

On February 21, 1908, Potter's selection was officially announced, eliciting a new batch of courteous notes from the unsuccessful candidates. Both Proctor and Shrady wrote to praise the choice of Potter, Shrady adding that "the pleasure of meeting you has more than compensated for my disappointment."[44] To Vinnie Ream Libbie wrote untruthfully that she and Margaret Custer Calhoun had "held firmly to our resolution not to attempt to influence the committee."[45] She further told Ream, at rather suspicious length, that the committee had insisted on someone who had already done an equestrian statue.

In his usual fashion Briggs provided reassurance that Libbie had made the right choice: "You and I know that Mr. Potter was selected for the reason, and no other, that we believed him to be the best man for our work. The fact of his being a brother-in-law of the clerk of the Supreme Court of Michigan had no weight whatever with the Commissioners."[46]

Fulfilling Greening's worst expectations, the monument was not ready to be revealed to the world until June 4, 1910. The occasion was big enough, however, to overcome all of his past carping, and he threw himself into preparations for Monroe's biggest day: to the already fancy letterhead of the Custer Memorial Association with its list of the association's four officers and twenty-four members, and its inspirational Custer motto, was added the announcement "Unveiling of Custer Statue June 4th, 1910. President Taft will be here. Everybody Invited."

It was in all respects a magnificent event for the small town, replete with important political and military figures, marching bands, and veterans from the Civil War Michigan Cavalry Brigade and the postwar

Seventh Cavalry. There were speeches, music, and the reading of a poem by William Carlton, described in the program as "the poet of the day."[47] That evening Greening's Custer Memorial Association gave an elaborate banquet in honor of the unveiling. After beginning with oxtail soup with croutons, followed by radishes and pickles, the diners proceeded to baked white fish à la Custer with Saratoga potatoes, fried spring chicken à la Greening with mashed potatoes and wax beans, pineapple sherbet, shrimp salad, wafers, vanilla ice cream, cake, and coffee. For those still able to stay awake after consuming such a feast, there was an ambitious after-dinner program, including a number of speeches and musical selections. The featured address was on patriotism, given by the Honorable Burton A. Parker. The banquet was such a success that a First Anniversary Celebration was held a year later.[48]

Most of all, it was Libbie Custer's day, undoubtedly one of the most satisfying—as well as one of the most stressful—of her widowhood. She noted her impressions of it in an unpublished twenty-eight-page essay, supposedly written for family and friends who were unable to attend but more convincing as a record of the experience for herself.

The account began with a justification for remaining away from Monroe for so long, as if she sensed that the occasion required some such explanation: "Instead of going to Monroe when I was tired with work and my nerves exhausted from constant endeavor to perpetuate my husband's memory, I have gone to the other side [Europe], where I would meet people and see sights that had nothing to do with my past. Dear, yes precious, as my life work is, I have to drop it all occasionally."[49]

Libbie's private writings often refer to the physical and psychological toll of her work; paradoxically, happy occasions like the unveiling produced their share of painful feelings as well as the pleasure associated with honoring her husband. She was surrounded by veterans who wanted to speak with her individually, but her nieces sent her off to recover from the mounting emotional strain. She could hear veterans at the door of the room where she was resting presenting their cases for personal interviews to her niece Clara, arguing, sometimes for as long as fifteen minutes, against being turned away: "Each one saw a reason which he thought would bring me out of my room. I did not remember any of them." One who wanted his grandchild "to see Mrs. Custer" told Clara that "10,000 men would have married her. I don't doubt she could have married a thousand men." But, he concluded, "she was content to be Mrs. Custer."

A previous soldiers' reunion had unnerved Libbie so much that she did not recover from it for months in spite of a regimen of "hydropathy, osteopathy, and Kneipe herbs for six weeks." This event was far worse, "for there was everything in the music, the speeches, the recitations, to call from the depths of the heart all the pathos and emotion in one's being." As she constantly did on her lecture tours, Libbie drew sustenance from the approval of others. She noted General George Spaulding's comment, "we loved him but we adore her," and reported that it was followed by "thunderous applause." Knowing from this response that "they hold me in affection, in honor, and worthy to bear the name of their beloved Commander, made me most grateful, and gave me courage to go through such an ordeal as I can never endure again."

Her account of the event repeatedly brought up both her need for constant reassurance and her usual self-deprecation. Even a simple "God bless you!" from a veteran elicited an unusually effusive expression of gratitude:

> I told them how I needed such words, and it was a sincere rejoinder for the inevitable result of those who try always to go smiling through life, and put up a bluff of perpetual content, that only a few—the nearest, dearest or the most discerning and sympathetic—ever know that the hours that one sees people and keeps up the farce of perpetual happiness are few compared with the neverending hours when one is alone with the past, and all those who were nearest have "gone to the country from which no traveller returns."

Like her lecture tours, the activities of the day were both a respite from those "neverending hours" of lonely remembrance and a reminder of them, a lavish measure of praise and attention that always invoked Libbie's concern that her devotion had fallen short of the measure. Yet a moment after her usual musings on her failings, she recalled her effectiveness in another situation two years before: "I had, by being able to face a blizzard, reached the telegraph office on foot in the Catskills, in time to defeat the attempt of a congressman who had eighty votes promised which were withdrawn on the receipt of my despatch. He claimed to have my consent. His efforts to have the statue placed in the Capitol [Lansing] nearly succeeded." Once again Libbie's heroic efforts had achieved her goal, but to what purpose? She had the dubious success of seeing her wishes fulfilled and the statue of her husband erected in a small town rather than in the state capital!

Nonetheless, to Libbie this was a triumph, and yet she followed her account of it in a spirit less than triumphant: "I was inwardly conscious of my shortcomings, of my *rooted belief* [my emphasis] that another woman would have done so much more for her husband's memory." Why, in the face of demonstrable achievements, was her sense of personal inadequacy "a rooted belief"? Not because she was inadequate in her efforts to memorialize her husband—she clearly was not. Possibly, then, her self-doubt stemmed from believing she had failed in the central requirement of patriarchal marriage: she had not borne a son to carry on her husband's illustrious name, and she had compounded this failure by resisting her husband's desire to adopt his nephew Autie Reed. Custer had deferred to her wishes—as he said he would do in his letter broaching the topic of adoption—but she lived with the knowledge that he had wanted a son, and she had stood in the way.

Once back in New York after the festivities, Libbie dutifully wrote to every official from the president on down, thanking them for their participation in the ceremonies. Intriguingly, after her violent reaction to a statue she never saw, Libbie said nothing specific about the statue she unveiled. Of course, she had approved in advance the sculptor, the sketch, the location—everything of importance. Seeing it today one recalls a word of advice that Frederic Remington offered to Briggs early on: "Whoever does it, don't let him make the mistake of sticking it away up in the air where one viewing it sees only the horse's belly & the General's boot heels. I regard this as one of the weak points of too many equestrian statues and hope it will appeal to your reason."[50] Evidently, what appealed more was the towering pedestal Remington warned against, from which Custer is portrayed sighting the enemy on the third day of the battle of Gettysburg, July 3, 1863. Veterans told Libbie that every detail of Custer's portrayal was accurate, and she remained satisfied that the statue rendered her husband as the ideal warrior "he really was, 'sans peur et sans reproche.'"[51]

Libbie's satisfaction (like that of the supporters of the Custer statue at West Point) was not destined to endure. The equestrian Custer had been erected in the center of Monroe's busiest intersection, where its imposing bulk eventually began to be perceived as an obstacle to the increasing traffic. Prompted by an accident in 1922 in which a drunk driver slammed into it, a group of citizens brought pressure on the city council to move the statue to another location. The issue stirred up the usual pro- and anti-Custer sentiments, with the faction in favor of moving arguing that traffic vibrations were weakening the monument and making it dangerous, and the opposing faction intimating that the real reason was political—no longer did everyone want to honor Custer with the central location, and, in addition, the horse's rear disrespectfully faced one of the community's churches.

While some parishioners may have been offended by the equine backside, the political issue probably weighed more. There was some indication that veterans of the Spanish-American War and World War I felt slighted. The Custer family continued to live in Monroe, but they were not among the town's most prosperous or influential citizens. In spite of the governor's attempt to stop the move, the disgruntled prevailed, and the statue was relocated in a swampy peripheral area, to what outrage on the part of the eighty-one-year-old Libbie can be imagined. She had sent a succinct and restrained telegram of protest before the move: "Have learned of proposed removal of General Custer's statue from present excellent situation to river bank. Should feel very great regret if change was made."[52] Libbie never visited Monroe again.

Ten years later the town of New Rumley, Ohio, erected a statue on the site of Custer's birthplace. The program expressed regret that "Mrs. Elizabeth B. Custer, 71 Park Ave., New York City, aged widow of the brilliant General, and who accompanied him on his western campaigns, is unable to attend these ceremonies. A great regret was felt on the pronouncement to the effect she was unable to withstand the trip. However, she will be an interested listener to the ceremonies which will be disseminated over the radio." According to the program, the unveiling would be done by Mrs. May Custer Elmer of Brooklyn, inaccurately described as the "Favorite Niece of General Custer." Mrs. Elmer represented Libbie's graciousness well, having been instructed by her aunt to "shake hands with every one present."[53] By this time it was obligatory on such occasions for the band—in this case the Tenth U.S. Infantry Band from Fort Thomas, Kentucky—to play the Seventh Cavalry favorites, "Garryowen" and "The Girl I Left Behind Me." At this event, the band also played a contemporary piece entitled "Custer's Last Fight."[54]

The Ohio Custer is portrayed on foot, stepping forward, weapon in hand. After a while, some bushes planted to provide surrounding foliage grew apace, and before long Custer appeared to be stepping out of the underbrush, more like a scout than a commanding officer.

Libbie never gave up hope that the monument of Monroe's most famous son would be restored to a more central location. Her will specified five thousand dollars or as much as it would take to pay for such a move. Only much later, in 1955, did the town move the statue yet again, back to a more central location. At the ceremony, attended by Michigan governor G. Mennen Williams, Custer's grandnephew Colonel Brice Custer unveiled the statue, and the Fifth Army Band was on hand to play "Garryowen." Another grandnephew, Lieutenant Colonel Charles Custer, remarked that "the City of Monroe now keeps faith with the devoted wife and widow of General Custer."[55] And with its churchgoers: the statue's rear now faces a large parking lot.

25

Aging

'Tis my sincere desire that you get married for will it not be terrible when you are old and all by yourself?

—Libbie to James W. Forsyth, January 25, 1867

On February 15, 1869, the twenty-one-year-old Kansas volunteer David L. Spotts wrote admiringly in his diary of the joint Custer-Crawford campaign, "Gen. Sheridan has been with us ever since we left Camp Supply and had his headquarters with us, camping in a tent when the weather was fair or foul, marching at our head in snow and rain, enduring all the hardships of wind and weather. He is not a young man either, between 35 and 40 years old."[1] Sheridan was, in fact, thirty-seven at the time he shared the discomforts of this field campaign.

The battlefield has always been a place that demands the physical and psychological resilience of youth. Only the young, with their sense of invulnerability and immortality still intact, can be expected to energetically and enthusiastically hurl themselves into battle, suffer and inflict unspeakable horrors, take and lose life. In the young it is not unusual to find an idealistic and self-sacrificing patriotism of the sort that inspired Custer to write to his sister when he was still a West Point cadet, "If it is to be my lot to fall in the service of my country and my country's rights I will have no regrets."[2]

If the battlefield requires the qualities we associate with youth, the military as a profession has always had its share of "grizzled veterans," a cliché that connotes both age and experience. There are few references to the special problems of aging men in the service, although Elizabeth Burt, a frontier army wife in the 1860s and 1870s, appears to have been unusually observant on the subject. When General Henry Wessels visited her on his way to Fort Fetterman, "his white hair and delicately built frame made me feel that he ought not to be required to make that march." Observing the beginning of General Crook's winter campaign against the Sioux, her "heart ached for General Reynolds braving the winter elements on this march planned to surprise the Indians. His gray hairs proclaimed that such hardships were better suited to a younger man."[3]

Aging was a sensitive issue in the military. When the one-armed veteran commander General Oliver Otis Howard failed to pursue the Nez Percé with vigor, General Sherman wrote to him, "If you are tired, give the command to some young energetic officer." Howard replied indignantly, protesting his unparalleled vigor and causing Sherman to respond hastily: "Have every possible faith in your intense energy, but thought it probable you were worn out, and sometimes I think men of less age and rank are best for Indian warfare."[4] Howard was forty-seven.

For many a man who had spent his life in the army, and had been vigorous in his prime, the effects of growing old were a challenge that the holder of a sedentary job did not face. Frederick Benteen, who loved the army and had been much admired for his leadership, must have raged against the growing physical incapacity that led to his medical discharge. Conducting his own court-martial defense the year before he left the army, Benteen gave a rhetorical closing speech suggesting that he had earned the privileges of age: "Gentlemen," he addressed the court, "the quarter of a century that I have given to the service . . . are more than sufficient to offset the few months of my life that my detractors can speak of. . . . Now, at the age of 53 yrs, with my locks snowy white, gotten in the service of my country, it is just a little severe to be court-martialed for not falling into line with a Post Trader & Contractor."[5] The court was unsympathetic.

When Libbie Custer was still young, she expressed an uncharacteristically extreme aversion to the aged on several occasions. In *Tenting on the Plains* she described an encounter with General Winfield Scott, who, in 1865, happened to be staying in the same New Orleans hotel as the Custers. The old war hero remembered his brief meeting with Lieutenant Custer at the beginning of the war, and he generously complimented the younger man on his military exploits. General Scott then politely asked to meet Libbie, begging Custer to explain that because of his infirmity, he would be forced to sit in Libbie's presence. But as Libbie would later write,

> It was too much for his etiquettical instincts, and, weak as he was, he feebly drew his tall form to a half-standing position, leaning against the lounge as I entered. Pictures of General Scott, in my father's home, belonged to my earliest recollections. He was a colossal figure on a fiery steed, whose prancing forefeet never touched the earth. . . . And now this decrepit, tottering man—I was almost sorry to have seen him at all, except for the praise that he bestowed upon my husband, which, coming from so old a soldier, I deeply appreciated.[6]

This casual encounter resonates, for Libbie was looking back on herself at age twenty-three when she wrote years later, after her husband had died in his prime, himself preserved forever as "a colossal figure on a fiery steed." Unlike General Scott, Custer would never become decrepit and tottering, a shadowy invocation of an earlier heroic self, but Libbie, then in her early forties, knew that she was inexorably aging, drawing farther and farther away from the twelve years of their life together. By the publication date of *Tenting on the Plains*, in which she recalled her reaction to Scott, she had already been a widow for a longer period than she had been married.

Libbie recorded a far more developed episode in her final book of memoirs, *Following the Guidon*. At Fort Hays in 1869 Custer insisted on taking his reluctant wife to see the Indians he had captured on the Washita. These were women prisoners with whom the Seventh Cavalry officers had amicable—some say too amicable—relations. Custer undoubtedly felt that there was no danger whatsoever in going among them and refused to take Libbie's fears seriously, reassuring her "over and over again." The Indian women crowded around the two, touching and fondling them, admiring the softness of Libbie's kid gloves, which they stroked.

In Libbie's telling the undifferentiated crowd of women and children gave way to "old hags" and "antique ones," who frightened and repelled her: "[I] hid my tremors and my revulsion, but inwardly I wished with all my heart that the younger and prettier women had been detailed as a reception committee." What seemed to horrify Libbie most were signs of age:

> The old women were most repulsive in their appearance. The hair was thin and wiry, scattering over their shoulders and hanging over their eyes. Their faces were seamed and lined with such furrows as come from the hardest toil, and the most terrible exposure to every kind of weather and hardship. . . . The dull and sunken eyes seemed to be shrivelled like their skins. The ears of these hideous old frights were punctured with holes from the top to the lobe, where rings once hung, but torn out, or so enlarged as they were by years of carrying the weight of heavy brass ornaments, the orifices were now empty, and the ragged look of the skin was repugnant to me.[7]

In all of Libbie's writings there are few comparable episodes where she brings so much sharply rendered physical detail to bear on the construction of a scene. The physical decline that approached and threatened to engulf her, unmitigated by the evasions and concealments of her own culture, created a strong, almost nightmarish memory. Other than references to her husband's enemies, it is the one time in her published writing when she is completely unsympathetic—this woman who could weep easily over the tribulations of enlisted men, the melodramas that she and Custer saw at the theater, and the death of puppies.

Libbie's reaction was not only unsympathetic but unrestrained: once again a quality unique in Libbie's books and rare in her private writings. The torrent of words describing the old women seems to be unmediated feeling. While the women were handling her gloves, marveling that any animal could have a skin so soft, she was fixated upon the weathered hardness of their skin and its unsightly mutilation. Moving on to the younger women and their babies, she recovered her usual tone and demeanor, her own tears answering the tears of an Indian woman widowed at the Washita.

In the same period that she was committing these memories to paper Libbie had some photographs taken by a friend to be presented to the girls' club with which she was involved. Seeing the photos of her forty-five-year-old self was a shock, as she wrote to a close friend: "I keep feeling that I don't want those girls to see such a wreck, and compare a truthful likeness of me with Autie's portrait painted in his prime. . . . You see, being alone, I don't realize how I change—what *ravages* old age makes in me!—and truthfully, I care little—whereas if A were here I would protest every wrinkle!" She went on to blame her pride for seeking to conceal her image from the girls: "I know that I am showing a very vacillating side but I *may* reconcile myself to my real self if I put one of the photographs on my bureau and get accustomed to the fearful record of antiquity that the camera remorselessly depicts."[8]

This sense of juxtaposition to her husband's eternal thirty-six years may explain Libbie's sensitivity on the subject of her age, a curious foible in a woman who wanted only to be known as her husband's widow. In the journal that she kept of her lecture tour of 1892–93, she recorded a number of flattering comments made about her appearance, some of which she elicited by representing herself as "a war worn veteran brown and rough and antiquated." Such self-deprecations, of which there were many, invariably called forth protests from her well-disposed audience. The fifty-year-old Libbie *did* look good and enjoyed hearing it. "They were all good enough to say very nice things about my looks," she wrote on one occasion, "wondering how I had been thro' so much and still did not seem to show it, and would hardly believe that I dated back to the war."[9]

For years Libbie and John Burkman, Custer's striker, played a harmless game in which he would ask how old she was, and she would reply that "the General did not think it proper for a lady to tell her age." At the dedication of the equestrian statue of Custer in Monroe in 1910 Burkman asked his usual question, saying this time that the other veterans had deputed him to ask. The sixty-eight-year-old Libbie gave her customary answer but in recounting the incident said that she had thought of replying "'as old as I look,' relying on the dotted veil to help me drop a few years."[10]

It may not have been vanity or affectation that prompted Libbie's thoughts so much as cherishing the past in which she had been young with Custer. That image had also been preserved by the veterans who attended the ceremony, and she wanted them to recognize in her the woman they had last seen so many years ago. Their memories were another link with a past that inexorably receded.

In fact Libbie aged gracefully. In what seems to be more than the usual gallantry paid to a person of her estate, interviewers never failed to comment on her pleasing and youthful appearance—the soft white curls, alert eyes, animated expression, and undiminished zest for life that late photographs attest to. Libbie confided to Custer's niece Frances Elmer that she had feared "the inertia of old age," but at the age of eighty-five had not yet experienced it: "I dreaded it so but so far I cannot hold on to myself because of the dynamo inside me."[11] She remained a model of vigorous old age until the end. On the fifty-third anniversary of the battle, the eighty-seven-year-old widow told an interviewer, "I am an antique, but I do enjoy myself. I have a delightful time."[12]

In a letter to the Western photographer David Barry, written when Libbie was eighty-eight, she remarked that it was natural for people to give up "everything that is not really necessary" as they aged: "Most people call it 'the lassitude of old age' and when I hear that I find that I work at my desk more persistently than ever!"[13] Although she became increasingly incapacitated by arthritis in her eighties, she never became too old or too infirm to abandon her efforts to preserve her husband's memory or defend his reputation by writing herself or arranging for a rebuttal from some military figure. Until it was absolutely impossible she continued to make scores of appearances at veterans' reunions, at other military functions, and at dedications honoring her late husband—nothing involving Custer was too small to be neglected.

The increasingly well-publicized and celebrated battle anniversaries usually added to her burden of correspondence. While Libbie could never bring herself to visit the scene of Custer's death, superintendents of the battlefield were happy enough to invoke her prestige in the ceremonies, consulting her on appropriate events to be held and eliciting a statement to be read on the occasion. For the forty-fifth commemoration she praised Godfrey's revised article on the battle as authoritative, then went on to hope that the words spoken on the anniversary day would "dispel any last, lingering doubt or criticism that might ever tend to dim the glory of that band of heroes and their beloved general."[14]

The volume of correspondence was steady, and sometimes tremendous. In conjunction with the most significant milestones, letters would pour in from veterans, scouts, and civilians who had had some contact with Custer, strangers who had written poems about him—a heterogeneous group of admirers whose lives had been in some way touched by Custer. There were constant requests for information and memorabilia from historical collections and for photographs from veterans' posts named after Custer. Libbie's own advertisements in veterans' publications requesting reminiscences of Custer for her Civil War book brought in a large number of letters.

To Frances Elmer, Libbie confessed some flagging of her energy for the task toward the end: "I am almost thru with the strangers, veterans and antiques from way back, who write of your Uncle Autie. . . . How many years I have been at it—carrying bundles of 'unanswereds' about with me from place to place."[15] She came to regret not the task of answering but her own scrupulous, even superstitious insistence on conducting this heavy correspondence by hand: "I hope from now on what time is left me, I can keep in touch more with my own personal friends. I regret that in the years and years of writing to veterans, frontiers men—admirers of my husband in private and public life—that I have not made shorter work of answering the letters by using a typist. I have been afraid that I would hurt their feelings by a printed reply."[16]

At the same time, the letters were such reinforcement of Libbie's own worship of Custer that she most likely took a deep pleasure in the more personal and time-consuming method of answering them by hand. It was routine for her correspondents to write in the most extravagant terms of Custer and of herself. A former Confederate, General Reuben Gaines, wrote to assure Libbie that *no* Union cavalry leader had been her husband's equal. More than that, he claimed, "of all the gallant leaders on the Union side with whom I came in contact, not one had the quality of audacity which Custer possessed. His valor was peerless, and will confer upon his name an immortality of honor and renown." Thomas Cheney wrote to tell Libbie "what a wonderfully brave woman I think you have been all these many years. I am sure if the General could know how bravely you have carried on, notwithstanding the great cross you have had to bear, he would be very much pleased."[17]

Elizabeth Bacon Custer died on April 6, 1933. Her niece by marriage, May Custer Elmer, and her friend Agnes Bates Wellington remained close to Libbie until her death, then assumed their appointed tasks as executors of her substantial estate. The will instructed them to select some article of furniture or ornament for themselves as compensation.

Between the drawing up of Libbie's will on November 18, 1926, and the addition of a codicil on August 23, 1929, her plans for the disposition of her property underwent a radical change. For many years she had wanted to do something for girls raised in the army, whose schooling was apt to be inferior because of frequent moves. Her original intention had been to "build and equip a home for army girls," but when it appeared that she would not have enough for that purpose, she decided to leave the bulk of her estate to Vassar College to establish scholarships in the name of her late husband for the daughters of army officers.[18]

With the codicil she revoked that project, however, and instead required that the estate be distributed among the surviving Custer kin, strictly apportioned according to degree of kinship to her husband: four shares to members of the third generation, two shares to the fourth, one share to the fifth. It turned out to be a notable sum in 1933 dollars: securities valued at $99,203.22 actually brought in $123,969.82.[19]

Of personal possessions Libbie left nothing exceptional: almost no jewelry of value, a few pieces of nice but inexpensive furniture, and clothing valued at $25. Most of her bequests were concerned with perpetuating the Custer name: $5,000 to the Monroe library for a "Custer room," $5–10,000 to the Monroe Hospital for another Custer room, $5,000 to the Children's Museum of Brooklyn for a Custer memorial similar to "the Washington and Lincoln Exhibits in that place." General Custer's picture was to be delivered and hung in the Monroe Armory. Even—should the town one day change its mind—$5,000 to move the Custer statue again. Libbie gave $1,000 to the Presbyterian Church, where she and Custer had been married, and in addition, $1,000 each to two Methodist churches that the Custer family had attended. Similar bequests to the Infants Hospital and to the Welcome Home for Girls, both in Brooklyn, reflected her own interests. She left another thousand for a bronze tablet in the Monroe Court House honoring her father.

In the end, then, Libbie's identification with the Custer name was stronger than any purely charitable impulse, no matter how worthy or logical. Of the people who in 1933 inherited the money that she herself had earned, few had ever known George Armstrong Custer or had a great deal of contact with Libbie herself: after the exile of the equestrian statue in 1923, she did not return to Monroe. Letters indicate her fondness for several Custer descendants, and some of the younger generation had become military men, but neither group was singled out for special favor by her will—which simply distributed shares of the property according to the nearness of blood relationship to her husband.

In 1893 a collateral relation of Custer's had written to Libbie about seeing her on one of her lecture tours. He praised her performance extravagantly as well as confided that his father, a first cousin of the general, had brought up his children "to almost worship his memory." Libbie replied on her black-edged mourning stationery: "Though the letter you sent me last winter needs no answer I am going to take the first leisure I have had to assure you that I deeply appreciated your saying the Custers think I do honor to the name and that they are proud of me." Then she added the almost reflexive comment, "I suffer from self-depreciation and no woman ever needed such words of commendation as you so generously [gave] me."[20]

It was perhaps feelings such as these that lay behind the revision of Libbie's will in favor of the Custers, not for any affection toward them as particular individuals but in recognition of their relationship to her husband. She had once said, "I have but two regrets, my husband's death and the fact that I had no son to bear his honored name."[21] To compensate, Libbie had ceaselessly glorified her dead husband: she must have ultimately felt that if she could not be the mother of a Custer line, she could be the benefactor of those who bore "his honored name."

Epilogue

Custer Forever

> Their the Bravest General of Modder times met his death with his two Brothers Brotherinlaw and Nephew not 5 yards apart Surrounded by 42 Men of E Company. Oh what a slaughter . . . eavery one of them were Scalped and otherwise Mutilated but the General he lay with a smile on his face the indians eaven respected the great Chief.
>
> —*I Buried Custer: The Diary of Pvt. Thomas W. Coleman, 7th U.S. Cavalry*

> It was the real old folks who had spirit and wisdom to give us. The grandfathers and grandmothers who still remembered a time when Indians were Indians, whose own grandparents or even parents had fought Custer gun in hand, people who for us were living links with a great past.
>
> —Mary Crow Dog

At some point in the twentieth century Little Big Horn became Little Bighorn, a current spelling I have reluctantly used. It seems anomalous, not only because everyone at the time of the battle and long afterward thought of it and wrote it as three words—Little Big Horn—but because the sharp polarity of the two contiguous and equal words—Little Big—emphasizes their opposition in a way appropriate to the difference between the magnitude of the battle and its reputation. Little/Big: the dichotomy applies to so many disparities here, beginning with the contrast between an insignificant stream in southeastern Montana and an event that publicized its name far and wide. That the site was otherwise undistinguished was not unusual: most of the great Civil War battles also took place on ordinary terrain—farmland, country roads, gently rolling hills, wilderness. But there is so much more that is both little and big about this particular battle: its size versus its notoriety, the scrutiny it has received versus its importance, and most notably, its place in history versus its place in myth.

If history tries to tell us what happened, and to make sense of it empirically, myth tells us what we as a people *need* to believe happened to fulfill some deep-seated collective desire.[1] The transformation of the Battle of the Little Bighorn into myth began immediately after the event and continues to flourish today, although efforts of historical recuperation have discredited many of the battle's mythic accretions.

On a different level of awareness myth replaces history. While history attempts to make sense of events, its efforts, constrained as they are by hard realities, may not entirely fulfill the human need for structure and meaning. Since history cannot explain the debacle of the Little Bighorn well enough to satisfy the popular imagination, myth must do so. In every case, the mythic version—whether as supplement to or contravention of fact—creates a greater and more widely accepted meaning.

The preponderance of firsthand observation agrees that Custer's body was neither scalped nor otherwise mutilated, but no matter how many Indians have asserted that they had no idea who was attacking them—that, if anything, they assumed it was the same army they had fought at the Rosebud on June 17—the idea has persisted that Custer's body was singled out for special treatment because he was recognized and honored by his foe as a great warrior. An unauthorized story also exists that he *was* mutilated because he was recognized as the notorious Long Hair. In either case it is mythically crucial for the warrior to assert his individuality, to be acknowledged by his foe as himself and no other, to die for who he is rather than anonymously and without special significance. Thus did the Greek warrior Odysseus risk his life and bring a curse upon himself when, instead of retiring in safe anonymity from the island of the Cyclops, he insisted upon claiming his identity:

Kyklops,
If ever mortal man inquire
how you were put to shame and blinded, tell him

Odysseus, raider of cities, took your eye:
Laërtes' son, whose home's on Ithaka![2]

And thus did Sitting Bull inappropriately ask a committee of senators visiting the Standing Rock reservation, "Do you know who I am?"—incredulous that they should not recognize him as the great chief he still believed himself to be.[3] His question reverberates ironically against General Sheridan's offhand revelation that for many years *after* the Battle of the Little Bighorn he thought that Sitting Bull was simply a generic term rather than an individual.[4] It also produces a nice symmetry: whites did not know who Sitting Bull was; the Indians fighting at the Little Bighorn did not recognize Custer.

Another random battlefield event later endowed with intentionality, the severe mutilation of Tom Custer, was long attributed to Rain-in-the-Face, who supposedly sought to avenge his arrest at Tom's hands. A noted warrior, Rain-in-the-Face did not mind the attribution, but his comment to Dr. Charles Eastman during his last illness has the ring of truth. After telling Eastman that no one knew who killed Custer, he added: "Why, in that fight the excitement was so great that we scarcely recognized our nearest friends! Everything was done like lightning. After the battle we young men were chasing horses all over the prairie, while the old men and women plundered the bodies; and if any mutilating was done, it was by the old men."[5] For the warriors, live horses were of greater consequence than those dead white men.

Myth requires that the nature of the hero's death be consistent with the rest of his mythic identity. In a novel "intended primarily for young Americans," two survivors of the battle, one white and one Indian, meet in later life. The Indian, who has become a doctor, speaks of what his people have learned—farming—as a notable lesson. His white friend responds: "And if we Americans can learn the wisdom of caution, the loyalty to duty, and the lesson of heroism that we may gather from that sad but immortal story of Custer's last rally and his ride into fame, then I don't know as he died in vain."[6] On the other hand, if Custer is regarded as a rash and foolhardy commander, these are the qualities that must be seen in every critical decision that led to the annihilation of his command: in his rejection of the Gatling guns and extra troops, in his failure to obey Terry's instructions, in his decision to divide his slender forces. In either case, because the image of Custer imprinted on the national consciousness in the Civil War had long hair and brandished a saber, despite the fact that he had cut his hair and left his saber behind, at the Little Bighorn Custer must go down clutching a saber, his yellow curls streaming.

So it is in the most popular version of the event, the Otto Becker–Cassilly Adams painting of the battle that Anheuser Busch distributed as lithographs to some 150,000 client establishments.[7] The teetotaler Custer, with his long hair and saber, thus became a familiar icon in barrooms across America. Although the painting gives a good sense of the terrain where the battle took place, it is by no means the best or most realistic rendition of the struggle; on the contrary, approaching the once omnipresent barroom scene without other knowledge of the battle, you could be forgiven for imagining that the cavalry won the day after a hard fight.[8] In the face of history, myth will have its way.

The most persistent Custer myth is the idea that some mysterious knowledge of the Last Stand was withheld, either out of deference to the grieving widow or because of her influence. Those who knew were "honor bound" not to tell the real story of the battle "so long as the brave little woman who shared many of the vicissitudes of frontier life with her illustrious husband should live."[9] This secret knowledge, understood to be unfavorable to Custer, was then lost to posterity because Libbie Custer outlasted all those who might have possessed it: "If there was a 'conspiracy of silence' to defer attacks on him until she died, it was a futile conspiracy, for she outlived all the conspirators."[10] Like a ritualized charm, this formula has been automatically passed down from one generation of historians to the next, yet it is patently absurd. Since all of the battle's white survivors were some four miles away from the area where the five companies commanded by Custer met their death, it is unlikely that any of them could have shed further light on the Last Stand. As for criticism of Custer, it began immediately after the battle with President Grant's forthright condemnation and was never silenced.[11]

A newspaper article of 1927 hailed Libbie as "a heroic figure for the last half century. Since the Battle of the Little Big Horn where she lost five members of her family she has fought for the record of the regiment she loved and the brave husband who was its leader."[12] Certainly Libbie did devote her best energies to her husband's memory, but the power that historians have attributed to her has been greatly exaggerated. She may have succeeded in getting a statue of her husband removed from

West Point because of her personal pique at being ignored by the selection committee, but this was of relatively minor consequence and hardly to the advantage of perpetuating his memory. In the far more significant matter of the court of inquiry into Major Reno's conduct, Libbie was bitterly disappointed. The official army verdict exonerated Reno's actions on the battlefield of the Little Bighorn, which, by implication, condemned her husband's. And although Custer had numerous defenders of his conduct as well as critics, a single powerful voice that might have definitively quelled all opposition never spoke. Nor could it: the mysteries left behind by the Last Stand were bound to be stronger than any efforts at censorship.

Perhaps overly encouraged by General Sherman's gallant deference, or merely impelled by her own zeal, Libbie wrote to President Grover Cleveland in 1885:

> If you knew how year after year the sorrow of my life has been intensified by the knowledge that I, as a woman, could do nothing to establish the proof that my husband did not go to his death rashly, you would realize how earnest is my appeal, now that the opportunity has come, before you.
>
> For nine years I have only been able to hear the unjust accusations against my husband's name by the hope that a friend would sometime be raised up, brave and loyal enough to defend him against the charge of his rashness on the day of the Battle of the Little Big Horn in which he lost his life.[13]

These words were prelude to Libbie's request that General Nelson Miles be transferred to St. Paul, Minnesota, where he could work on constructing a view of the battle favorable to Custer! There is no record of the president's response to this amazing petition, but he did not see fit to alter the scheduled posting of General Miles to Arizona. The mantle of defender eventually fell upon Edward Settle Godfrey, a first lieutenant at the battle who progressed through the ranks to general without becoming well known outside the army.

If Libbie failed to control history, she probably did influence the opinion of a number of ordinary citizens who heard her lecture about her life with Custer, or read her books commemorating their life together. Moreover, she devoted countless hours throughout her widowhood to corresponding with those who were already her husband's admirers—or professed to be such for the privilege of receiving a gracious and grateful letter from Custer's well-known widow. As the forty-fifth anniversary of the battle approached, Libbie's cousin Rebecca wrote to her, "You certainly have accomplished your heart's desire, and kept the memorial fires burning down to the third generation, and I congratulate your persistence and devotion. They have placed in our National History a tragically romantic figure which can never be duplicated on account of changed conditions. Brava!!"[14]

With a few notable exceptions, Custer has not attracted the attention of prominent academic historians. For all of his panache, controversy, and mysterious death, the general was not—from a historical perspective—an important figure. As Ray Billington has observed, somewhat unfairly, "George Custer did less toward hurrying the occupation of western America than the little-known commanders who won rather than lost engagements with the Indians."[15] In fact, none of the commanders who opposed the Indians did as much damage as the relentless pressure of European immigration, the railroads, or the buffalo-hide hunters. Writing to Libbie, General Sherman gave her husband credit for opening the West to civilization; when he was writing to intimates, he gave the credit to the advance of the railroads and the disappearance of the buffalo.[16]

Billington was exasperated that "thousands of pages have been wasted on . . . the Battle of the Little Bighorn, while few other than serious students of the West are aware of the importance of the tides of immigration that swept civilization toward the Pacific."[17] Yet it is hardly surprising that "few other than serious students" would want to read about anonymous tides of humanity and impersonal forces, or that most would find charismatic individuals and catastrophic battles more persuasive than lifetimes of hard and uneventful toil. The climactic clash of cultures represented by groups of fighting men is a more riveting and comprehensible spectacle than the thousands of small events that lead up to it.

Even so, the passion and enduring interest aroused by Custer and the Battle of the Little Bighorn seem extraordinary. Arguments over any aspect of the event can become heated exchanges, as if a creed or way of life is at stake—and in a way it is. To commit yourself to Custerphilia is to embrace a number of other beliefs as well: first and foremost, the idea of the hero—the man on horseback waving a sword—an anachronism for which we can find no perfect equivalent in contemporary society. The hero embodies admirable values, and he dies defending them, to be remembered with satisfaction as having fought the good fight. To be a Custerphile is to be a romantic, to cherish the gallant gesture—as Custer himself did—and to affirm the possibility of meaningful individual action. It is to subscribe to the American dream of self-creation—the poor boy who rises to fame, if not to fortune, and beyond that, to the Western ideal of democratic individualism. Custer was, after all, the man who even within the rigidity of the military often managed to go his own way and leave his own special stamp on events.

Oddly enough, Custerphobes are not always the other side of the coin, that is, they do not necessarily reject the qualities ascribed to the figure of Custer. Many tend to applaud all the virtues and possibilities Custerphiles associate with Custer and simply disagree that Custer exemplified them. They believe that he was, instead of a hero, an egomaniac without talent. Sometimes the Custerphobe is a disillusioned Custerphile. "I began my work thirty-five years ago with some streaks of hero-worship in my own constitution," one Custerphobe wrote to a Custerphile, "but a few years study showed me some very ordinary individuals and some others that revealed a wonderful capacity for whiskey-drinking, poker games, and debauchery so that the 'christian gentlemen' of Capt. Fred Whittaker [Custer's first biographer] strangely faded away."[18]

Whatever the side taken, intense commitment is a hallmark of the Custer or Last Stand buff. In an interview with the *Denver Post*, John William Husk, a self-described "history hater," told a reporter how a visit to the battlefield had changed his life: "It was the end of the day, the sun was going down, and we were the only people up there. It was the loneliness and the dead silence that did it."[19] Since that occasion, Custer and the Last Stand have become Husk's "all-consuming hobby." The article went on to relate how he has made repeated pilgrimages to the battlefield, accumulated a library of more than 250 books, and joined two national organizations of Custer buffs. At meetings of these groups, he said, "we stay up to the wee hours of the night, arguing over different theories of what occurred that day."[20]

The battlefield seems to have exerted its own magnetic pull from the very beginning, with each succeeding generation producing a cadre of buffs who haunt its environs and retrace each segment of the June 25 journey, pondering once again its whys and wherefores. One such story is that of Charles Kuhlman, a retired professor of history. Depressed over his wife's death and his own deafness, he was "coaxed into a Sunday afternoon visit to the Custer battlefield. Intrigued and at the same time vexed by what he had seen, his attention was soon channeled into untangling the web of visual and circumstantial evidence that shrouded the truth."[21] Needless to say, Kuhlman, who was already "afflicted with a lifelong fascination" for warfare, soon found himself specifically afflicted by the arguments that have been going strong since the Battle of the Little Bighorn was fought.[22]

Fifty years after the battle, and long before Kuhlman or Husk, E. A. Brininstool wrote to a fellow Custerphobe that at the fiftieth anniversary of the battle "there was darn near more than one fist fight."[23] Writing to another kindred spirit, R. G. Carter, on May 31, 1932, Brininstool referred to Custerphile William J. Ghent as "that imitation historian" and "a double-crosser of the worst sort." Like other buffs, Brininstool asserted a proprietary claim for his views: "I have made a special study for over 40 years of the Little Big Horn affair, and I ought to be pretty well acquainted with every feature of it."[24]

Ghent wrote to Carter several weeks later, announcing that he had intended to ignore "Mr. Brininstool's raving abuse" but then tearing into him: "As I have rarely found any of his statements of professed fact dependable, it is quite impossible that I should ever have asked him for data."[25]

Brininstool's claim to authority is hardly exceptional in battle annals: many have staked out special territories of expertise. General Hugh L. Scott maintained that although he had not been present during the fight, "I believe that I have greater opportunities for arriving at the truth than anybody else."[26] For his part, Ghent wrote that the movement of the scouts at the battle "is one to which I have devoted a great deal of study, and I doubt that any other living person has examined the data as thoroughly as I have."[27] Some preferred to let their résumés speak for themselves. Walter Camp wrote to Libbie that he had studied the battle for twenty years and visited the battlefield in nine different years. He had followed the trail from the Yellowstone to the Little Bighorn five times, and from the Wolf Mountains to the battlefield eight times. He had also interviewed more than sixty white participants in the battle and more than one hundred fifty Indian survivors.[28]

Thomas B. Marquis, an eccentric doctor who lived next door to the battlefield in Hardin, Montana, attempted to establish his credentials with Libbie more impressionistically. He wrote that in addition to having studied "all writings of the Little Bighorn conflict," he had spent much time on the battlefield: "Over and over, scores of times, I have gone there alone and walked meditatively about the entire field, hour after hour. To me, there is no place in this world that holds so fascinating an interest."[29] Whatever Libbie thought of this, and her annotation of his letter indicates that she referred him to General Godfrey, Custer buffs would be bound to agree.

Another figure introduced into the Brininstool-Ghent controversy was Theodore Goldin, an enlisted man who claimed to have brought a last message from Custer to Reno, and who became the recipient of a number of reminiscent letters from Frederick Benteen during the last decade of Benteen's life. Brininstool charged that Ghent regarded Goldin as "a faker or a liar" (a view generally held today),[30] to which Ghent indignantly replied: "I do not believe Mr. Goldin to be either a faker or a liar. I believe him to be senile and demented." Brininstool, he continued, "can think only in terms of pro-Custer or anti-Custer. Of a fact as an objective entity he seems to have no more comprehension than a grasshopper. To his primitive psychology anything that supports his opinion or prejudice is good, and anything that confutes it is bad; and his reasoning processes can go no further."[31] Actually this is a fairly good description of many of the participants in the Custer controversy, including, of course, Ghent himself.

What this exchange lacks in subtlety, it makes up for in virulence, a virulence all too common in the annals of Custer studies. The truth of the matter, or rather one truth of the matter, is that both Brininstool and Ghent are staunchly committed to something other than the truth—Brininstool anti- and Ghent pro-Custer—but each earnestly asserts that his position is an objective appraisal of the facts.

When writing about Custer, neutral ground is elusive. What should Custer have done at any of the critical junctures that rapidly presented themselves, each now the subject of endless speculation and rumination? There will always be a variety of opinions based upon what Custer knew, what he did not know, and what he could not have known, but one thing is clear: had he known as much as the army of Little Bighorn buffs, even the decisive Custer would have become paralyzed by information overload. On the other hand, had he had as many cavalrymen as battle buffs, his force would have overwhelmed his foe.

One can understand and share the exasperation of the Montana rancher cum battle buff who wrote, "It doesn't take long for a person to become very confused, especially when you can read three or four reports about the exact same incident or place, none of which agree. What really makes it tough is that many of these reports come from supposedly very reliable sources. SO, WHO DO YOU BELIEVE? It becomes downright discouraging."[32] But then, as Husk observed, "I don't believe anybody really wants to know what happened—there wouldn't be anything to discuss or debate."[33]

Mystery, in the end, has literally proven itself larger than life: "The true inside history . . . I believe will never be known, as no man of the entire command came out alive to tell of the fierce struggle and deeds of heroism performed on that bloody day."[34] William Ahern's formulation is classic, involving as it does blood, death, struggle, heroism, and—above all—mystery. Because no white soldier survived, the "true inside history" will never be known, yet no such obstacle prevents Ahern's certainty that there was a "fierce struggle" and "deeds of heroism."

Belief in the existence and essential endurance of Custer's mystery is all but universal, even among sources presumably above the fray, like the *New York Times*. In a 1986 article headlined "Custer's Defeat: A 110-Year Mystery," the writer asserts that "the new discoveries will not answer the old arguments between those who regard Custer as a hero and others who blame him for leading his men to their deaths."[35] In an argument based on evidence, "new discoveries" might very well settle such issues. There is a strong desire, however, to preserve the Last Stand as a locus of mystery, a battleground of the spirit where one can commune with imponderables and never arrive at resolution. Like Keats's Grecian urn, the battlefield might be addressed: "Thou, silent form! dost tease us out of thought as doth eternity."

While Custer's reputation has been volatile, in death as in life, that of his wife has remained constant, with the important qualification that his is far more in the public domain than hers. In her unceasing efforts to preserve Custer's memory, and through her tangible bequests and memorials, Libbie became a monument of wifely devotion. Tributes by latter-day writers suggest that the dedication of her long widowhood to serving her husband's memory strikes many as the perfection of feminine devotion. John M. Carroll, an indefatigable Custer buff, thought of Libbie as "America's sweetheart." At a time when he himself was no longer young he wrote, "If she were alive today I would have serious competition from Larry Frost [another middle-aged Custerphile], but I would pursue her hand with all the fervor of a twenty-year-old."[36] Another writer dedicated his book "to Elizabeth Custer, whose love for her husband is exceeded only by my wife Frankie's love for me."[37]

Feminine fidelity has traditionally been so prized that Libbie Custer's devotion has pleased even those who consider her husband a villain, as if fidelity to such a man has even greater merit than it would to a more deserving spouse.[38] To historian Stephen Ambrose, Libbie was "one of the most remarkable American women of the nineteenth century," although he never justifies this sweeping statement, remarking only that she had "unbounded energy" and was "as courageous as Custer himself." Both characterizations are nonsense.[39] Libbie was never known for feats of endurance on a par with her husband's, and she was so fearful of thunderstorms, for example, that she would crawl under the bed. Custer's energy and courage were both widely acknowledged as exceptional.

Ambrose, evidently thinking in terms of late-twentieth-century career women, further belittled the worth of Libbie's chosen life's work serving Custer and his memory: "Had Libbie been a boy, given the good start in life a child of Judge Bacon would have enjoyed and the talents and energy Libbie had, she would probably have gone right to the top of the American scene in any one of a number of fields. As it was, she was fated to be known only as a wife and then as a widow."[40] Underneath this speculative enhancement, Ambrose is unfairly dismissive of the real Libbie Custer and the meaning of her life. Aside from her obviously intense psychological investment in the memory of her husband, she made an enlightened choice in devoting her long widowhood to memorializing him. It *was* a career, and a remunerative one. Contrary to Ambrose's expansive view, without the support of Custer she was plagued by an almost pathological sense of inadequacy; without seeing her work as a tribute to him, it seems likely that she would never have written the books or given the lectures that brought her financial independence and public acclaim.

Perhaps the public Libbie may be suspected of calculation in skillfully manipulating her husband's image and extracting sympathy for her brokenhearted widowhood. Her correspondence is full of the kind of appeals for sympathy that impelled General Sherman to exclaim that he sympathized "with every pulsation" of her "wounded heart." More important, he did as she wished, accompanying his letter to the secretary of war on her behalf with a moving description of the desolate widow.[41]

One of Libbie's literary friends left behind a revealing anecdote of her widowhood. In London, upon hearing talk of the approaching durbar, she decided that she would like to go to India to see this impressive colonial ceremony. She accordingly appeared one day at the War Office to see about obtaining passage on a British transport. Told that this was only for the families of British officers, she thanked the functionary for his politeness, but then reiterated her desire to go, "like a child who had to stay home from a party." As she was reluctantly leaving, the officer looked at her visiting card more closely and asked if she was related to the famous general. When she identified herself as Custer's widow, he excitedly called several other officers to meet her. It turned out that the rules could be bent for the widow of the famous general, and Libbie did indeed travel on a British transport to India.[42]

The incident is paradigmatic: typically, Libbie was gentle and feminine, but insistent on what she wanted. Nevertheless, without the cachet of Custer's name, her charm would not have been so powerful. Just as everyone had felt sorry for Libbie's motherless condition when she was twelve, even Custer's detractors responded sympathetically to her widowhood.

The private Libbie, however, was equally obsessed with Custer. When General Sherman wrote to her that "the nation owes a debt of gratitude to his widow," she crossed out "his widow" and substituted "him."[43] Libbie could never allow herself center stage: she never even considered writing a memoir of her life after Custer's death, although it was an exceptional life, certainly as groundbreaking in its way as her life at Custer's side.

Through the attention of the press, the American public came to see Libbie as she saw herself and to marvel at and take satisfaction in her steadfast devotion. "Mrs. Custer has marked out a unique career among the remarkable women of America," a reporter for the *Detroit Journal* wrote. "She has lived for Gen. Custer. 'The general' to Mrs. Custer is manifestly the one grand subject. . . . the 12 years of their married life, spent in fields and fortresses, still hold all the beauty of life to her, and she has been 34 years a widow."[44] The admiration is palpable.

For most of us there is a middle course between forgetting and remembering, with intense grief over a loss followed by a gradual resumption of ordinary life. Both of Custer's parents were widowed early in life, but after a proper interval they remarried and began anew, as Libbie might have done as a young widow. She was attractive and sought after: perpetual widowhood was her own choice, and one she never regretted. As she told her literary executor, Marguerite Merington, "One gets so lonely. But I always felt I should be committing adultery if I were to wake up one morning, and see any head but Autie's on the pillow by me."[45]

Among Libbie's papers is a poem entitled "A Mourner," whose emphatic message is the refusal to pity a bereaved woman. It begins: "'Pity her?' Nay, not so! / She sounded Life's whole secret in her day; She hath had all things, having Love." The conclusion restates the theme that Libbie undoubtedly applied to her own life: "Nay, unto you who pity, I aver / Hers is Love's loveliest story!"[46]

The object of this long devotion was neither great nor ordinary, a man who had a brief period of heroic grandeur in which his gifts conspired with the moment to produce dazzling success. The talent he so conspicuously revealed at that time should neither be diminished nor inflated: from a contemporary vantage point we can see its dimensions clearly and recognize both its special excellence and its limitations. Even as military ability goes, Custer's talent was narrow, but its effect—for all that it was breathtaking and crowd pleasing—was also substantive. He could lead a cavalry charge with as much courage and verve as any commander ever had, and he could act and react quickly in battle, modifying a plan as the exigencies of the fight demanded. In an army where too many leaders approached the enemy and then temporized, he never held back, never lost heart. In battle after battle during the Civil War he inspired his men with the desire to fight as he did, to follow him into even the grimmest situation and, almost always, to win.

After that supreme moment, history did not cooperate to produce further occasions for glory, and in the professional role that had given him his triumphs, he performed erratically—often competently, just as often self-indulgently. During the Civil War he clearly derived satisfaction not only from his performance on the battlefield, but from a concern for his troops, whom he perceived as men like himself, fellow Michiganders or other northerners who were motivated as he was and worthy of his leadership. After the war, he lost this quality, but his sin was not so much the harsh discipline he sometimes imposed and sincerely believed in as it was a general neglect and lack of concern for his troops. Had there been opportunities for great military exploits on the frontier, Custer would still have felt that the soldiers he commanded there were inferior: they were not the best men of their society, fighting for an ideal like the Union, but more like the dregs, earning a miserable wage because they were unfit for better. After the Civil War, Custer rarely felt challenged by his military assignments: the tidal wave of history receded, taking away the thousands of eager soldiers he had led to victory and leaving him on a barren strand with a mere regiment.

Once glory was no longer within his everyday reach, disappointment almost unbalanced him until he recovered and turned his attention to personal goals with typical enthusiasm. As long as he had Libbie's loyally reflecting mirror, he could maintain his equilibrium.

His unusual energy and zest for life raised him above the ordinary without qualifying him for genuine distinction. Men of power would continue to hail him as a Civil War hero, but he himself did not walk the corridors of power. He was too self-willed to be politically successful, with a willfulness that seems much like the less attractive side of the boyish exuberance that could be so appealing. His testimony at the House hearings on post traderships was analogous to his letters to Libbie about other women: however impolitic, he would not be denied the satisfaction of speaking as he pleased, as if his own perceived innocence was bound to make everything all right—with Libbie and with the world as well.

Certainly, as Vine Deloria, Jr., wrote, Custer died for the sins of white America against its native inhabitants, since the people he attacked were on land that even the United States government had acknowledged to be their own.[47] He was following orders, but inasmuch as he embraced his country's values and expansionist policies, and was wholeheartedly willing to fight for them, he was not an innocent victim. He had the rare privilege of dying for what he believed in, and dying as a military leader might wish and expect to die—in battle, surrounded by his men.

The meanings that Americans have given to Custer since his death, and because of his death, speak to the contradictory needs of the national psyche more than to the contradictory realities of his life—to our desire in a less self-reflective era for the sharply etched image of the hero charging into battle and more recently to our critical reassessment of the violent conquest of our country. If Custer lives on to encapsulate our ambivalent feelings about our nation's past, it is because the fire that touched him, the fire of deep and significant collective experience, spread from the Civil War to the frontier. It is still burning.

Acknowledgments

Robert M. Utley's body of work on frontier military history is an invaluable source for any scholar writing about Custer; my admiration for the numerous other writers whose work on Custer has inspired and aided my own must be reflected in the text itself. Here I wish to acknowledge the many people and institutions who generously helped me research and write this book. The Research Council of Rutgers University enabled me to make research trips to Washington, D.C., and West Point, New York. Kitty Deernose and John Doerner of the Little Bighorn Battlefield National Monument were unfailingly patient in answering my frequent questions, as were Carl Katafiaz of the Monroe County Library System and Jennifer Barner, formerly of the Monroe Historical Museum. William Lindt (now retired) and Michael Meier in the Military Reference Department of the National Archives admirably scouted that unfamiliar territory for me. The staffs of the many depositories of primary materials where I worked or with whom I corresponded—too large a number to be listed individually—were helpful without exception, but I wish to particularly express my gratitude to the staff of the Bancroft Library of the University of California at Berkeley, where I spent a pleasurable eight months reading secondary sources. Mary Shelly and Andrew Gulati of the Inter-Library Loan Service of Franklin and Marshall College filled my frequent and often difficult requests graciously and efficiently. Robert Aldrich kindly made his and the late John M. Carroll's private collection available to me, while

Deborah Gardner, Glenna Matthews, and Shirley A. Leckie gave the term "community of scholars" deeper meaning for me with their most generous help. Gerry McCauley and Darcy Tromanhauser gave me excellent professional advice and encouragement. Over the long haul my brother, Stephen Kennamer, was a faithful and much appreciated reader, as was my husband, Robert J. Barnett, who could always be relied on to untangle my prose. Needless to say, those faults that remain in my writing are my own.

To my two sons—Robert Nicholas and Gregory Richard Barnett—and their partners, Laura Robinson and Sylvia Ouelette, I give thanks for inspiration and emotional support.

Notes

ABBREVIATIONS

In notes George Armstrong Custer and Elizabeth Bacon Custer will be referred to as GAC and EBC (or EB before her marriage). I have silently corrected the infrequent spelling errors in the correspondence.

AGO	Adjutant General's Office
BC	Bates Collection
BCWCC	Brice C. W. Custer Collection
BP	Edward Brininstool Papers
CarC	Carnegie Collection
CenC	Century Collection
CC	Custer Collection
CMC	George Armstrong Custer Manuscript Collection
CrC	Crook Collection
CP	Camp Papers
CPP	Christiancy-Pickett Papers
CRP	Crook Papers
DP	Daniel O. Drennan Papers
EBCC	Elizabeth Bacon Custer collection of manuscript materials at the Little Bighorn National Monument (Where I have examined an actual manuscript, the number will be given. Otherwise, I will cite the microfilm reel number.)
EBCMC	Elizabeth Bacon Custer Manuscript Collection, Western Americana Collection, Beinecke Rare Book and Manuscript Library, Yale University
FC	Lawrence A. Frost collection

GFP	Godfrey Family Papers
GP	Edward Settle Godfrey Papers
HC	Francis L. Hagner Collection
HP	Harper and Brothers Papers
IP	Papers of Bernard John Dowling Irwin
LR	Letters Received
LS	Letters Sent
McCP	William S. McCaskey Papers
MMP	Marguerite Merington Papers
MP	Nelson A. Miles Papers
OR	*The War of the Rebellion: A Compilation of the Official Records of the Union and Confederate Armies.* Ser. 1, 128 vols. (Washington, D.C., 1880–1901).
RG	Record Group
SC	Stedman Collection
ShP	Sherman Papers
SP	Sheridan Papers
USMA	United States Military Academy Archive
VP	Van De Water Papers
VRHP	Vinnie Ream Hoxie Papers

INTRODUCTION

1. GAC to Judge Kidder, August 23, 1867, cited in Bruce A. Rosenberg, *Custer and the Epic of Defeat* (University Park, Penn.: Pennsylvania State University Press, 1974), p. 233.
2. *Phobe,* meaning "fear of," is not technically correct. I use it to mean "having an aversion to."
3. For the extremes see the first biography of Custer's life, a hagiographic treatment, Frederick Whittaker, *A Complete Life of General George A. Custer* (New York: Sheldon and Co., 1876); the most impressive revisionist treatment is Frederic F. Van De Water, *Glory-Hunter: A Life of General Custer* (1934; reprint, New York: Argosy-Antiquarian, 1963). See also Thomas Berger, *Little Big Man* (New York: Dial Press, 1964).
4. Elbert Hubbard, *Hartford Lunch Company Brochure* (Hartford, Conn.: privately printed, 1917), pp. 6, 37.
5. Andrew Ward, "The Little Bighorn," *American Heritage* 43:2 (April 1992): 76.
6. Brian W. Dippie, ed., *Nomad: George A. Custer in Turf, Field and Farm* (Austin: University of Texas Press, 1980), pp. xii–xiii.
7. See Susan Wabuda, "Elizabeth Bacon Custer in Japan, 1903," *Manuscripts* 35 (winter 1983): 12–18; and Lawrence A. Frost, *General Custer's Libbie* (Seattle: Superior Publishing Co., 1975), p. 308.

8. *Monroe Evening News*, April 5, 1933.
9. Henry James, "The Altar of the Dead," in *The Complete Tales of Henry James,* ed. Leon Edel, 12 vols. (Philadelphia: Lippincott, 1961–64) 9:231–71.

CHAPTER 1: EARLY DAYS

1. Recollection of Nevin Custer, EBCC, reel 5.
2. GAC to Judge Bacon, October 1863, in Marguerite Merington, ed., *The Custer Story: The Life and Intimate Letters of General George A. Custer and His Wife Elizabeth* (1950; reprint. Lincoln: University of Nebraska Press, 1987), p. 67.
3. Maria Custer to GAC, n.d., ibid., p. 6.
4. "Libbie's Tribute to Emmanuel Custer," December 11, 1892, FC, box 1, folder 2.
5. Ibid.
6. Emmanuel Custer to GAC, October 25, 1863, FC, box 1, folder 20.
7. Emmanuel Custer to GAC, September 22, 1864, ibid.
8. Emmanuel Custer to EBC, February 3, 1887, cited in EBC, *Tenting on the Plains, or General Custer in Kansas and Texas* (New York: Charles L. Webster, 1887), pp. 287, 290.
9. EBC, *Tenting*, p. 291.
10. Ibid., p. 158; EBC, *Following the Guidon* (New York: Harper and Brothers, 1890), p. 6.
11. EBC, *Tenting*, pp. 476, 162–63.
12. *Irrepressible* was the word that occurred to a friend of Emmanuel's, John Giles, when he recalled Custer as a child. Henry Howe, *Historical Collections of Ohio* (Norwalk, Ohio: Laning Printing Company, 1896), 1:899, cited in Charles B. Wallace, *Custer's Ohio Boyhood: A Brief Account of the Early Life of Major General George Armstrong Custer* (Freeport, Ohio: Freeport Press, 1978), p. 9.
13. Mary Custer, cited in L. Milton Ronsheim, *The Life of General Custer* (Cadiz, Ohio: Cadiz Republican, 1929), unpaged pamphlet.
14. Wallace, *Custer's Ohio Boyhood*, p. 9.
15. Ibid.
16. GAC to Emmanuel Custer, n.d., in Merington, *Custer Story*, p. 6.
17. Mrs. Rachel Cochran, cited in Ronsheim, *Life of Custer*; Alfred P. Sheriff to EBC, March 24, 1906, EBCC, no. 6400. Sheriff's letter contains the reminiscence of Sarah McFarland, a pupil of Custer's from November 1856 to March 1857.
18. Ronsheim, *Life of Custer*.
19. Hopedale, Ohio Teacher's Class Notebook, 1856, FC, box 3, folder 22.
20. Wallace, *Custer's Boyhood*, p. 64.

21. Hon. John A. Bingham, *Reminiscences*, cited in Merington, *Custer Story*, pp. 7–8.
22. GAC to his sister Lydia Ann Reed, n.d., in Merington, *Custer Story*, p. 9.
23. GAC, "From West Point to the Battlefield," in *The Custer Reader*, ed. Paul Andrew Hutton (Lincoln: University of Nebraska Press, 1992), p. 43.
24. A Custer partisan has been at pains to point out that he was dead last in only three subjects: philosophy in his third year; ethics and chemistry in his fourth. John M. Carroll, "Was Custer Really the 'Goat' of His Class?" *Four on Custer by Carroll* (Guidon Press, 1976), p. 13.
25. Joseph Pearson Farley, *West Point in the Early Sixties* (Troy, N.Y.: Pafraets Book Company, 1902), p. 22.
26. Tobias Wolff, *In Pharoah's Army: Memories of the Lost War* (New York: Alfred A. Knopf, 1994), p. 58.
27. Stephen Ambrose, *Duty, Honor, Country: A History of West Point* (Baltimore: Johns Hopkins University Press, 1966), pp. 129–30.
28. Jay Monaghan, *Custer: The Life of General George Armstrong Custer* (1959; reprint, Lincoln: University of Nebraska Press, 1971), p. 22.
29. Ibid., pp. 31, 35.
30. In addition to Grant and Sheridan, Stonewall Jackson, Joe Johnson, Hooker, Hancock, Crook, and Early were Civil War generals who finished close to the bottom of their respective classes at West Point. Lawrence A. Frost, *The Custer Album: A Pictorial Biography of General George A. Custer* (Seattle: Superior Publishing Co., 1964), n.p.
31. Ulysses S. Grant, *Personal Memoirs of U. S. Grant*, ed. E. B. Long (New York: Da Capo Press, 1982).
32. Cited in Richard O'Connor, *Sheridan the Inevitable* (Indianapolis: Bobbs-Merrill, 1953), p. 32.
33. GAC to Augusta Frary, December 13, 1859, Rochester Public Library.
34. T. Harry Williams, *Lincoln and His Generals* (New York: Alfred A. Knopf, 1952), p. 4.
35. Ibid.
36. Catherine S. Crary, *Dear Belle: Letters from a Cadet and Officer to His Sweetheart, 1858–1865* (Middletown, Conn.: Wesleyan University Press, 1965) p. 41.
37. "West Point before the War," unidentified magazine article in EBCC, nos. 7786–90.
38. Crary, *Dear Belle*, p. 239.
39. EBCC, reel 5.
40. Merington, *Custer Story*, p. 8.
41. Morris Schaff, *The Spirit of Old West Point, 1858–1862* (Boston: Houghton Mifflin, 1907), p. 159.
42. Handwritten fragment, no name or date, EBCC, reel 3.
43. USMA.

44. Retired Brigadier General Evan A. Andruss to EBC, September 27, 1905, EBCC, no. F1729.
45. GAC, extract from "War Memories," seven-page typescript, EBCC, reel 6. This same statement appears in his *Galaxy Magazine* article, "From West Point to the Battlefield," reprinted in Hutton, *The Custer Reader*, p. 43.
46. Frazier Hunt, *Custer, The Last of the Cavaliers* (New York: Cosmopolitan Book Corp., 1928), p. 20.
47. "Was the Battle of Bull Run a National Disaster?" in John M. Carroll, ed., *Custer in the Civil War: His Unfinished Memoirs* (San Rafael, Calif.: Presidio Press, 1977), p. 101.
48. Carroll, *Custer in the Civil War,* p. 74.
49. Ambrose, *Duty, Honor, Country,* p. 157.
50. *Register of Delinquencies, 1849–1854, 1853–54, 1856–61*, USMA.
51. Letter of August 22, 1869, GAC Letters in West Point Special Collections, USMA.
52. See Ambrose, *Duty, Honor, Country*, p. 129.
53. Farley, *West Point*, p. 58.
54. USMA.
55. The following account is taken from RG 153, Records of the Office of Judge Advocate General, National Archives.
56. GAC, "From West Point to the Battlefield," p. 45.
57. Ibid., p. 42.

CHAPTER 2: LIBBIE BACON, LIBBIE BACON

1. EB to GAC, January 1864, Merington, *Custer Story*, p. 80.
2. Libbie's Day-Book, October 2, 1860 (April 8, 1852–December 31, 1860), EBCMC.
3. EB, postscript to father's letter to GAC (January 1864), Merington, *Custer Story*, p. 81.
4. Libbie's Day-Book, August 27, 1854.
5. Merington, *Custer Story*, p. 38.
6. Libbie's Day-Book, August 27, 1854.
7. Libbie was six years old when Eddie died.
8. Daniel Bacon to EBC, FC, box 1, folder 1.
9. EB to Mrs. Sabin, June 1862, in Merington, *Custer Story*, p. 44.
10. Letter of June 1862, Merington, *Custer Story*, p. 43.
11. "Libbie Bacon's Journal No. 2 (1861–1864)" BCWCC, cited in Lawrence A. Frost, *General Custer's Libbie* (Seattle: Superior Publishing Co., 1975), p. 38.
12. Letter of 1862 in Merington, *Custer Story*, p. 48.

13. "Libbie's Journal," cited in Frost, *Custer's Libbie*, p. 38.
14. Ibid., p. 39. Frost identifies the man as a "Mr. Ball."
15. Ibid., p. 40.
16. Ibid.
17. Ibid., p. 72.
18. Ibid., pp. 40, 41.
19. Frost, *Custer's Libbie*, p. 44.
20. EBCC, reel 5.
21. Frost, *Custer's Libbie*, p. 73.
22. Letter of 1862, in Merington, *Custer Story*, p. 49.
23. Libbie's Day-Book, EBCMC.
24. Cited in Frost, *Custer's Libbie*, p. 31.
25. Libbie's Day-Book, EBCMC.
26. McCrea wrote to his cousin, "He [Custer] is a handsome fellow, and a very successful ladies' man. Nor does he care an iota how many of the fair ones break their hearts for him. What a monster! methinks I hear you say." Letter of August 12, 1863, in Crary, *Dear Belle*, pp. 214–15.
27. Frost, *Custer's Libbie*, p. 58.
28. "Libbie Bacon's Journal," cited ibid., p. 63.
29. Ibid., pp. 60–61.
30. Ibid., p. 61.
31. Ibid., p. 74.
32. Ibid., p. 76.
33. Daniel Bacon to GAC, December 12, 1863, FC, box 1, folder 1.
34. EB to Daniel Bacon, January 8, 1859, BCWCC, in Frost, *Custer's Libbie*, p. 31.
35. EB to GAC, October 1863, in Merington, *Custer Story*, p. 74.
36. Daniel Bacon to sister, April 13, 1864, ibid.
37. See Janice L. Krupnick and Fredric Solomon, "Death of a Parent or Sibling during Childhood," in *The Psychology of Separation and Loss: Perspectives on Development, Life Transitions, and Clinical Practice,* ed. Jonathan Bloom-Feshbach, Sally Bloom-Feshbach, and Associates (San Francisco: Jossey-Bass, 1987), pp. 345–71; the citation is from the editors, p. 346.

CHAPTER 3: "THE HONORABLE AND GLORIOUS PROFESSION OF ARMS"

1. James. M. McPherson, *Ordeal by Fire: The Civil War and Reconstruction* (New York: Knopf, 1982), p. 210.
2. Ibid., p. 285.
3. W. C. King and W. P. Derby, comps, *Camp-Fire Sketches and Battlefield Echoes* (Springfield, Mass.: King, Richardson, 1888), p. 397.

4. McPherson, *Ordeal by Fire*, p. 149.
5. GAC, "From West Point to the Battlefield," pp. 46–47.
6. Minnie Dubbs Millbrook, "Cadet Custer's Court-Martial," in *Custer and His Times*, ed. Paul Andrew Hutton (El Paso, Tex.: Little Big Horn Associates, 1981), p. 80.
7. Cited in Carroll, *Custer in the Civil War*, p. 1.
8. Civil War notes, EBCC, reel 5.
9. EBC, *Tenting on the Plains*, p. 7.
10. George B. McClellan, *McClellan's Own Story* (New York: Charles L. Webster, 1887), p. 123.
11. Ibid.
12. Carroll, *Custer in the Civil War*, p. 143.
13. Nelson A. Miles to EBC, March 16, 1877, EBCC, no. 3372.
14. Captain Biddle to EBC, May 2, 1892, EBCC, reel 5. See also James Scrymser, who has a highly embellished version of Custer's Chickahominy exploit. *Personal Reminiscences of James A. Scrymser* (New York: privately printed, 1915), pp. 20–21.
15. Theodore Lyman to his wife, June 2, 1864, in George R. Agassiz, ed., *Meade's Headquarters, 1863–1865: Letters of Colonel Theodore Lyman from the Wilderness to Appomattox* (Boston: Atlantic Monthly Press, 1922), p. 139.
16. Gen. A. B. Nettleton, commander of the "Fighting Second Ohio," cited in Whittaker, *Complete Life of Custer*, p. 612.
17. Monaghan, *Custer*, p. 61.
18. GAC to parents, March 26, 1862, EBCC, reel 1.
19. Elliot Wright to EBC, April 30, 1888, EBCC, reel 2.
20. McClellan, *Own Story*, p. 123.
21. *Letter of the Secretary of War: Organization of the Army of the Potomac*, 38th Cong., 1st Sess., Ex. Doc. no. 15, House of Representatives (Washington, D.C.: Government Printing Office, 1864), p. 100: "A very dashing and successful reconnoissance was made near New bridge on the 24th of May, by Lieutenant Bowen [*sic*], topographical engineers, escorted by the 4th Michigan volunteers and a squadron of the United States cavalry, commanded, respectively, by Colonel Woodbury and Captain Gordon."
22. Monaghan, *Custer*, p. 121.
23. Adams to his mother, May 12, 1863, Worthington Chauncey Ford, ed., *A Cycle of Adams Letters, 1861–1865*, 2 vols. (Boston: Houghton Mifflin, 1920), 2:8. Three of Adams's four references to Pleasonton in his letters label him a "humbug." For other criticisms of Pleasonton see Stephen Z. Starr, *The Union Cavalry in the Civil War: From Fort Sumter to Gettysburg, 1861–1865* (Baton Rouge: Louisiana State University Press, 1979), 1:313–14.

24. Merington, *Custer Story*, p. 55.
25. This brigade, composed of the First, Fifth, Sixth, and Seventh Regiments, constituted Custer's first command as a brigadier general.
26. Photocopy of GAC to Judge Christiancy, July 26, 1863, CPP.
27. George B. Sanford, *Fighting Rebels and Redskins: Experiences in Army Life of Colonel George B. Sanford, 1861–1892,* ed. E. R. Hagemann (Norman: University of Oklahoma Press, 1969), p. 317.
28. Charles A. Page, *Letters of a War Correspondent* (Boston: L. C. Page, 1899), p. 294; Whittaker, *Complete Life*, p. 222.
29. Whittaker, *Complete Life*, p. 222.
30. Sanford, *Fighting Rebels*, p. 225.
31. Ibid., p. 284.
32. Cited in Edward J. Stackpole, *Sheridan in the Shenandoah: Jubal Early's Nemesis* (Harrisburg, Penn.: Stackpole Company, 1961), p. 121.
33. Frank A. Burr and Richard J. Hinton, *"Little Phil" and His Troopers: The Life of Gen. Philip H. Sheridan* (Providence, R.I.: J. A. and R. A. Reid, 1888), p. 30.
34. Grant to J. R. Young, "Grant's Words: Quotations from his Speeches and Conversations," in King and Derby, *Camp-Fire Sketches*, p. 231.
35. Horace Porter, *Campaigning with Grant* (New York: Century Company, 1897), p. 308.
36. Cited in Stackpole, *Sheridan*, p. 123.
37. Sanford, *Fighting Rebels*, p. 222.
38. Joshua L. Chamberlain, *The Passing of the Armies* (Dayton: Morningside Book Shop, 1974), pp. 153–54, cited in Starr, *Union Cavalry*, 2:452.
39. Porter, *Campaigning with Grant*, p. 441.
40. George F. Price, *Across the Continent with the Fifth Cavalry.* (New York: D. Van Nostrand, 1883), p. 104.
41. Cited in Charles D. Rhodes, *History of the Cavalry of the Army of the Potomac* (Kansas City, Mo.: Hudson-Kimberly Publishing Co., 1900), p. 142.
42. Cited in C. J. Woods, *Reminiscences of the War* (1880), p. 212; Testimony of Major General Alfred Pleasonton, March 7, 1864, United States Report of the Joint Committee on the Conduct of the War, 38th Cong. 2d sess. (1865), p. 365.
43. W. H. Beebe to EBC, June 18, 1910, EBCC, no. C1758.
44. Roger Hannaford, cited in Stephen Z. Starr, "The Last Days of Rebellion," *Cincinnati Historical Society Bulletin* 35 (1977): 9–11.
45. G. G. Benedict, *Vermont in the Civil War*, 2 vols. (Burlington, Vt.: Free Press Association, 1886–88), 2:660–61; Henry Norton, *Deeds of Daring, or History of the 8th New York Volunteer Cavalry* (Norwich, N.Y.: Chenango Telegraph Printing, 1889), p. 93.

46. Gregory J. W. Urwin, *Custer Victorious: The Civil War Battles of General George Armstrong Custer* (Rutherford, N.J.: Fairleigh Dickinson University Press, 1983), p. 276.
47. O. L. Hein, *Memories of Long Ago* (New York: Putnam, 1925), p. 37.
48. See Starr, *Union Cavalry*, 2:503; Utley, *Cavalier in Buckskin: George Armstrong Custer and the Western Military Frontier* (Norman: University of Oklahoma Press, 1988), p. 35.
49. EBCC, reel 5.
50. Carroll, *Custer in the Civil War*, p. 74. The fullest accounts of these battles are in Urwin and Monaghan. Starr places Custer within the context of the entire cavalry operation.
51. William E. Miller, "The Cavalry Battle Near Gettysburg," *Battles and Leaders* 3:404.
52. Henry Edwin Tremain, *Last Hours of Sheridan's Cavalry* (New York: Bonnell, Silver and Bowers, 1904), p. 216.

CHAPTER 4: LIBBIE'S WAR

1. Unless otherwise indicated, citations are taken from Libbie Custer's voluminous but completely disorganized manuscript notes in EBCC, reel 5. The notes represent various stages of composition and generally are undated, although most were written between 1890, when her last book of Plains reminiscences appeared, and 1920.
2. Libbie crossed out "Montana" and substituted "Dakota." I have restored the correct original. Libbie never visited the battlefield where her husband was killed, hence her mistaken identification of the hilly terrain as a "plain."
3. Starr, *Union Cavalry* 2:63–67.
4. OR 33:187–88.
5. Bruce Catton, *A Stillness at Appomattox* (Garden City, N.Y.: Doubleday, 1953), pp. 17–18.
6. Theodore Lyman to Elizabeth Lyman, March 5, 1864, in Agassiz, *Meade's Headquarters*, p. 79.
7. EBC, *Tenting on the Plains*, p. 340.
8. EBCC, reel 4. When Libbie first came to camp, Custer's commander was General Alfred Pleasonton, but he was replaced with Sheridan, Grant's choice, in April of 1864.
9. In 1892, when she gave a lecture in Cincinnati, a man who introduced himself as Colonel Schoonmacher of Pittsburgh told her about the first time he had seen her. It was at Winchester, and he remembered Libbie, on the verge of one of those painful departures from camp, in tears.
10. GAC to Lydia Ann Reed, August 24, 1864, EBCC, reel 1.

11. GAC to Lydia Ann Reed, September 17, 1864, ibid.
12. GAC to EBC, April 23, 1864; June 1864, in Merington, *Custer Story*, pp. 92, 103.
13. GAC to EBC, June 21, 1864, Merington, *Custer Story*, p. 105. The ellipsis is Merington's. (Unfortunately, she edited the letters heavily, and most of the originals are no longer available.)
14. EBC to GAC, June 1864, ibid., pp. 105–6.
15. Karen Lystra, *Searching the Heart: Women, Men, and Romantic Love in Nineteenth-Century America* (New York: Oxford University Press, 1989), p. 75.
16. GAC to EBC, July 3, 1864; EBC to GAC, July 1864, Merington, *Custer Story*, p. 112.
17. EBC to GAC, October 1864, ibid., p. 124.
18. William W. Blackford, *War Years with Jeb Stuart* (New York: Charles Scribner's Sons, 1945), p. 242.
19. Libbie Bacon Journal, 26 April 1863, cited in Shirley A. Leckie, *Elizabeth Bacon Custer and the Making of a Myth* (Norman: University of Oklahoma Press, 1993), p. 27.
20. GAC to Lydia Ann Reed, June 8, 1863, GAC Letters in West Point Special Collections, USMA.
21. Warren Lee Goss, *Recollections of a Private: A Story of the Army of the Potomac* (New York: Thomas Y. Crowell, 1890), p. 9.
22. James L. Bowen, "The Citizen Soldier," in King and Derby *Camp-Fire Sketches,* pp. 473–74.
23. Mason Whiting Tyler, *Recollections of the Civil War*, ed. William S. Tyler (New York: G. P. Putnam's Sons, 1912), p. 36.
24. J. H. Kidd, *Personal Recollections of a Cavalryman: With Custer's Michigan Cavalry Brigade in the Civil War* (1908; reprint, Grand Rapids, Mich.: Black Letter Press, 1969), p. 73.
25. McPherson, *Ordeal by Fire*, p. 387.
26. See Virginia Jean Laas, *Wartime Washington: The Civil War Letters of Elizabeth Blair Lee* (Urbana: University of Illinois Press, 1991), pp. 158–59, for Elizabeth Blair Lee's desire to be a nurse. Although she knew herself to be too frail, her conscience was nevertheless "restless when so many need help" (p. 158).
27. EBC to Daniel and Rhoda Bacon, April 3, 1864, MMP.
28. Libbie writes "at commanding the 7th Cavalry," but this is clearly a mistake.
29. Sheridan to EBC, April 10, 1865, in Merington, *Custer Story*, p. 159.

CHAPTER 5: KNIGHT SANS PEUR ET SANS REPROCHE

1. Urwin, "The Civil War Years," p. 24, concludes that "from the numerous accolades found in the memoirs, letters, and diaries left by his followers, Custer was one of the most popular generals in the Army of the Potomac."
2. Sanford, *Fighting Rebels,* p. 316.
3. E. D. Woodsbury to EBC, February 9, 1924, EBCC, reel 3. Woodsbury writes "h—l" in deference to Mrs. Custer's sensibilities.
4. Cited in Monaghan, *Custer*, p. 219.
5. "Sheridan against Stuart," in King and Derby, *Camp-Fire Sketches*, p. 409.
6. "The Cavalry Raid into Virginia," front page, *New York Herald*, March 3, 1864.
7. Official Report of the Battle of Gettysburg, August 22, 1863, cited in Jno. Robertson, ed. *Michigan in the War*, rev. ed. (Lansing: W. S. George, 1882), p. 583.
8. Cited in Starr, "Last Days of Rebellion," 9.
9. William Lanier Washington to EBC, July 10, 1909, EBCC, reel 3.
10. GAC to Lydia Ann Reed, May 15, 1862, in Merington, *Custer Story*, p. 30.
11. All the particulars of this anecdote are taken from Harlan Page Lloyd, a captain of the New York Volunteer Cavalry who served under Custer. "The Battle of Waynesboro," in Hutton, *The Custer Reader*, pp. 79–80.
12. "Custer at the Surrender," *Southern Bivouac* (July 1885), cited in John M. Carroll, "The Custer Image in Confederate Journals," *Research Review* 1:4 (1984): 10.
13. Tremain, *Last Hours*, p. 231.
14. L. E. Tripp, in "With Custer at Yellow Tavern and in the Raid around Richmond," in King and Derby, *Camp-Fire Sketches*, p. 250.
15. A. J. McLaren to EBC, June 8, 1913, EBCC.
16. July 16, 1876, in James W. Wengert, *The Custer Dispatches: The Words of the "New York Herald" Correspondents in the Little Big Horn Campaign of 1876*, pt. 1 (Manhattan, Kans.: Sunflower University Press, 1987), p. 145.
17. J. R. Young, "Grant's Words: Quotations from His Speeches and Conversations," in King and Derby, *Camp-Fire Sketches*, p. 231.
18. Monaghan, *Custer*, p. 131.
19. O'Connor, *Sheridan the Inevitable*, p. 36.
20. To Roland H. McCrea, December 12, 1858, in Crary, *Dear Belle*, p. 30.
21. Williams, *Lincoln and His Generals*, p. 107.
22. Among those critics who accuse Custer of loving war are Frederic Van De Water; Stephen E. Ambrose, *Crazy Horse and Custer: The Parallel Lives of Two American Warriors* (Garden City, N.Y.: Doubleday, 1975), p. 155; Paul Andrew Hutton, *The Custer Reader*, p. 3; and Karol Asay, *Gray Head and Long*

Hair: The Benteen-Custer Relationship (New York: Mad Printers of Mattituck, 1983), p. 20.

23. GAC to Ann Reed, April 26, 1861, EBCC, reel 1.
24. GAC to Augusta Frary, October 3, 1862, Rochester Public Library.
25. GAC to Lydia Ann Reed, April 20, 1862, in Merington, *Custer Story*, p. 29.
26. GAC to Lydia Ann Reed, October 25, 1863, EBCC, reel 1.
27. EBCC, reel 4.
28. Kidd, *Personal Recollections*, p. 129.
29. Lyman to his wife Elizabeth, September 17, 1863, in Agassiz, *Meade's Headquarters*, p. 17.
30. Tully McCrea to Belle McCrea, August 12, 1863, in Crary, *Dear Belle*, p. 215.
31. See Francis A. Lord, *Uniforms of the Civil War* (New York: Thomas Yoseloff, 1970), p. 35: "Despite the explicit detail of the Army Regulations, Federal generals showed their individuality in dress."
32. S. E. Whitman, *The Troopers: An Informal History of the Plains Cavalry, 1865–1890* (New York: Hastings House, 1962), p. 190; see also Robert M. Utley, *Frontier Regulars: The United States Army and the Indian, 1866–1891* (New York: Macmillan, 1973), p. 74: "Officers presented a dazzling array of gold cords, tassles, epaulettes, and a double row of brass buttons."
33. Whitman, *The Troopers*, p. 190; Col. John Esten Cooke, "General Stuart in Camp and Field," in *The Annals of the War Written by Leading Participants North and South* (Philadelphia: Times Publishing Company, 1879), p. 665.
34. Cited in Walter Prescott Webb, *The Great Plains* (New York: Ginn and Company, 1931), p. 493.
35. OR ser. 1, vol. 46, pt. 1, p. 134.

CHAPTER 6: POSTWAR DOLDRUMS

1. Only three of this number would survive as major generals in the regular army. John D. Bergamini, *The Hundredth Year: The United States in 1876* (New York: G. P. Putnam's Sons, 1976), p. 57.
2. GAC to EBC, April 17, 1866. She also told him he would die a natural death. MMP.
3. This is mentioned in the Civil War manuscript notes and also in EBC, *Tenting on the Plains*, p. 312.
4. GAC to EBC, October 2, 1868, EBCC, reel 4.
5. Grant, *Personal Memoirs*, p. 583.
6. George W. Cullum, *Biographical Register of the Officers and Graduates of the U. S. Military Academy at West Point, New York*, 3d ed., 9 vols. (Boston: Houghton Mifflin, 1891), 2:843.
7. Sherman to Sheridan, March 9, 1879, SP, reel 17.

8. Introduction to Sanford, *Fighting Rebels*, p. 4.
9. William Wordsworth, *The Prelude*, book 11.
10. Charles Hofling, *Custer and the Little Big Horn: A Psychobiographical Inquiry* (Detroit: Wayne State University Press, 1981).
11. EBC, *Tenting on the Plains*, pp. 433–34.
12. Carroll, *Custer in the Civil War*, p. 112.
13. Sheridan to Custer, May 7, 1865, EBCC, reel 2. See John M. Carroll, ed., *Custer in Texas: An Interrupted Narrative* (New York: Sol Lewis, Liveright, 1975) for a collection of primary documents on this period and a favorable view of Custer's actions.
14. See William L. Richter, *The Army in Texas during Reconstruction, 1865–1870* (College Station: Texas A & M University Press, 1987), pp. 12–13, 23–24.
15. Cited in Robert J. Ege, *Curse Not His Curls* (Fort Collins, Colo.: Old Army Press, 1974), p. 29.
16. GAC to EBC, Letter of January 2, 1869, EBCC, reel 4.
17. Richter, *Army in Texas*, p. 19.
18. Thomas S. Cogley, *History of the Seventh Indiana Cavalry Volunteers* (LaPorte, Ind.: Herald Company, 1876), p. 164.
19. Grant, *Personal Memoirs*, p. 577.
20. Charles Lothrop, *A History of the First Regiment Iowa Cavalry Veteran Volunteers* (Lyons, Iowa: Beers and Eaton, 1890), p. 224.
21. Emmet C. West, *History and Reminiscences of the Second Wisconsin Cavalry Regiment* (Portage, Wisc.: n.p., 1904), p. 28.
22. Dale had been brought to court-martial for making deprecating remarks about President Lincoln at the time of his assassination. A lawyer in civilian life, Dale defended himself and was found guilty of conduct unbecoming an officer and a gentleman; however, his sentence was light: to be reprimanded by his commander, Major General Cadwalder C. Washburn. Court-martial of Lt. Col. N. H. Dale, Second Regiment Wisconsin Cavalry Volunteers, Department of Military Justice, National Archives.
23. Cited in West, *Wisconsin Cavalry*, p. 29.
24. Ibid.
25. Cited in Lothrop, *Iowa Cavalry*, p. 228.
26. Ibid., p. 222. General Orders no. 15 are reproduced pp. 246–49.
27. Ibid.
28. Citations from General Orders no. 15, Military Division of the Gulf, August 7th, 1865, are reproduced in full in Lothrop, *Iowa Cavalry*, pp. 246–49.
29. Lothrop, *Iowa Cavalry*, p. 249.
30. Special Orders no. 2, Alexandria, Louisiana, June 24, 1865, reproduced ibid., pp. 244–45. The citation is on p. 244.

31. Ibid., p. 222. Lothrop reproduces Special Order no. 2 in its entirety, pp. 244–45.
32. Deposition of October 31, 1890, sworn to before a notary public, cited ibid., p. 280.
33. Cogley, *Indiana Cavalry*, p. 165.
34. EBC, *Tenting on the Plains*, p. 110.
35. Ibid., p. 114.
36. EBC to Rebecca Richmond, November 17, 1865, EBCC, no. 3551.
37. EBC to Mrs. Kingsley, January 6, 1887, CC.
38. EBC, *Tenting on the Plains*, p. 133.
39. EBC to her parents, October 22, 1865, in Merington, *Custer Story*, p. 171.
40. Lothrop, *Iowa Cavalry*, p. 241.
41. Ibid., p. 245.
42. West, *Wisconsin Cavalry*, p. 31.
43. General Custer's statement, Headquarters 2d Division Cavalry, Military Division of the Gulf, October 26th, 1865, is reproduced in Lothrop, *Iowa Cavalry*, pp. 262–66.
44. Cited ibid., p. 272.
45. Ibid., p. 265. Custer's entire statement of October 26th, 1865, addressed to Major George Lee, Acting Adjutant General, Military Division of the Gulf, is reproduced.
46. Ibid., p. 271.
47. McQueen, cited ibid., p. 251. Such foolish practices of food distribution were not confined to Custer's march to Texas. In 1872 an officer who had led a scout in Texas requested that hard bread be issued on such expeditions instead of flour. "Not knowing the country or water stations," he wrote, "it is often necessary to make long and tedious marches, in order to obtain water, grass and wood, and thus the men are compelled to bake Bread before they can have their suppers, and it is frequently badly baked and results in dissatisfaction and sickness." N. B. McLaughlin's Report of Scout, April 27–May 13, 1872, letter to Post Adjutant, May 15, 1872, *Ranald S. Mackenzie's Official Correspondence Relating to Texas 1871–1873*, ed. Ernest Wallace (Lubbock: West Texas Museum Association, 1967), p. 68.
48. See Starr, *Union Cavalry*, 2:504: "Such orders invariably resulted in ill feeling between officers and enlisted men, protests, a wave of desertions, the threat of mutiny, and the enlistment of whatever influence, military or political, the regiment could muster, to obtain its discharge from the service."
49. Sheridan to GAC, November 13, 1865, EBCC, no. 1861.
50. Cited in Minnie Dubbs Millbrook, "Custer's March to Texas," *Prairie Scout* 1 (1973): 56.
51. Sheridan to GAC, November 13, 1865, EBCC.

52. *The Papers of Ulysses S. Grant*, ed. John Y. Simon, May 1–December 31, 1865 (Carbondale: Southern Illinois University Press, 1988), 15:432. I have corrected Washburn's misspelling "Custar."
53. Ibid., p. 431.
54. Philip H. Sheridan to Ulysses S. Grant, letter of December 15, 1865, DP, box 11, p. 371. Also reproduced in Grant, *Papers*.
55. Grant to Matias Romero, May 16, 1866, in *Papers*, 16:202.
56. Sheridan to Brevet Major General John A. Rawlins, April 15, 1868, ibid. 18:373.

CHAPTER 7: JOINING THE FRONTIER ARMY

1. The *Chicago Inter-Ocean,* August 17, 1874.
2. Fred S. Kaufman, *Custer Passed Our Way* (Aberdeen, S.D.: North Plains Press, 1971), p. 167.
3. Utley, *Frontier Regulars*, p. 170.
4. Don Rickey, Jr. *Forty Miles a Day on Beans and Hay: The Enlisted Soldier Fighting the Indian Wars* (Norman: University of Oklahoma Press, 1963), p. 22, notes that between 1865 and 1890 "the unemployed constituted about one-half of all Indian Wars recruits." Most were unskilled laborers (p. 19).
5. Anson Mills, "The Organization and Administration of the United States Army" (1897), in *My Story*, ed. C. H. Claudy (Washington, D.C.: Byron S. Adams, 1918), p. 371.
6. "The Honor of the Soldier" (1904), King Papers, Wisconsin State Historical Society Library, cited in Oliver Knight, *Life and Manners in the Frontier Army* (Norman: University of Oklahoma Press, 1978), p. 222.
7. Douglas D. Scott et al., *Archaeological Perspectives on the Battle of the Little Bighorn* (Norman: University of Oklahoma Press, 1989), p. 250.
8. Rickey, *Forty Miles*, p. 143; Utley, *Frontier Regulars*, p. 86.
9. "Report of the Surgeon-General," October 1, 1874, in *Report of the Secretary of War*, 42d Congress, 3d Sess., House of Representatives, Ex. Doc. 1, pt. 2 (Washington, D.C.: Government Printing Office, 1874) 1:232, 233. James Calhoun observed of the Seventh Cavalry that "comparatively few of the men can swim a stroke." *Some Observations on the Yellowstone Expedition, 1873*, ed. Lawrence A. Frost (Glendale, Calif.: Arthur H. Clark, 1981), p. 71.
10. Utley, *Frontier Regulars*, pp. 80–81.
11. John Ryan, "Ten Years with General Custer among the Indians," *Town Crier* (Newton Centre, Mass.), February 5, 1909.
12. Henry C. Dwight, "Feeding an Army," in King and Derby, *Camp-Fire Sketches*, p. 112. The Civil War soldier made sixteen dollars a month.

13. GAC to EBC, October 26, 1868, cited in Frost, *Custer's Libbie*, p. 177.
14. Letter of October 28, 1868, in Robert M. Utley, ed., *Life in Custer's Cavalry: Diaries and Letters of Albert and Jennie Barnitz, 1867–1868* (New Haven: Yale University Press, 1977), p. 203.
15. Cited in Kittie Dale, *Echoes and Etchings of Early Ellis* (N.p.: Big Mountain Press, 1964), p. 224.
16. EBC, *Tenting on the Plains*, pp. 656–57.
17. Whitman, *The Troopers*, p. 163.
18. An account of this episode is given by Theodore R. Davis, "With Generals in their Camp Homes: General George A. Custer," *Westerners Brand Book, 1945–46* (Chicago, 1947): 129–30. Davis was with Custer at the time.
19. *Junction City Weekly Union*, July 8, 1871, cited in Joseph G. Rosa, *They Called Him Wild Bill: The Life and Adventures of James Butler Hickok*, 2d rev. ed. (Norman: University of Oklahoma Press, 1974), p. 135; Ryan, July 16, 1909, September 24, 1909. The wife of a Hays City hotel keeper told an army wife that "shooting scrapes were common, but that she never could get used to them." *An Army Wife on the Frontier: The Memoirs of Alice Blackwood Baldwin, 1867–1877*, ed. Robert C. Carriker and Eleanor R. Carriker (Salt Lake City: University of Utah, Tanner Trust Fund, 1975), p. 93. William Elsey Connelley writes, "There was no more lawless town on the border than Hays." *Wild Bill and His Era: The Life and Adventures of James Butler Hickok* (New York: Press of the Pioneers, 1933), p. 126.
20. *The Newton Circuit*, November 19, 1909, EBCC, reel 7.
21. Louis Laurent Simonin, *The Rocky Mountain West in 1867,* trans. Wilson O. Clough (Lincoln: University of Nebraska Press, 1966), p. 71.
22. Letters of April 25 and [May 11], 1876, Edward S. Luce, ed. "The Diary and Letters of Dr. James M. DeWolf," *North Dakota History* 25 (1958): 64, 68.
23. Lawrence Frost, *Custer's 7th Cav and the Campaign of 1873* (El Segundo, Calif.: Upton and Sons, 1986), p. 119.
24. Ryan, "Ten Years with General Custer."
25. Merington, *Custer Story*, p. 9.
26. Whitman, *The Troopers*, p. 95.
27. Teresa Griffin Viele, *"Following the Drum": A Glimpse of Frontier Life* (Lincoln: University of Nebraska Press, 1984), p. 231.
28. *Town Crier*, February 12, 1909. An army wife, Alice Baldwin, describes without feeling or comment seeing two deserters with half their heads shaved drummed out of camp to the tune of "The Rogue's March." Robert C. Carriker, *Fort Supply Indian Territory: Frontier Outpost on the Plains* (Norman: University of Oklahoma Press, 1970), p. 66.
29. Mrs. Orsermus Bronson Boyd, *Cavalry Life in Tent and Field* (New York: J. Selwin Tait and Sons , 1894), p. 52.

30. George Bird Grinnell, "Portraits of Indian Types," *Scribner's Magazine* 37:3 (March 1905): 267.
31. Mills, "Organization and Administration," *My Story*, p. 366. Custer remarked that "the gulf which separated cadets from commissioned officers seemed greater in practice than that which separated enlisted men from them. Hence it was rare indeed that a cadet ever had an opportunity to address or be addressed by officers." "From West Point to the Battlefield," p. 47.
32. *Private Theodore Ewert's Diary of the Black Hills Expedition of 1874*, ed. John M. Carroll and Dr. Lawrence A. Frost (Piscataway, N.J.: CRI Books, 1976), p. 25.
33. Anni Frank Mulford, *Fighting Indians! In the Seventh United States Cavalry, Custer's Favorite Regiment* (Fairfield, Wash.: Ye Galleon Press, 1972), p . 57.
34. *Annual Report, Secretary of War, 1891* 52nd Cong., 1st sess. (Washington, D.C.: Government Printing Office, 1892), 1:93.
35. Vielé, "*Following the Drum*," 168.
36. Roger Darling, *Custer's Seventh Cavalry Comes to Dakota: New Discoveries Reveal Custer's Tribulations Enroute to the Yellowstone Expedition* (El Segundo, Calif.: Upton and Sons, 1989), p. 151.
37. Ewert, *Diary*, pp. 50–51.
38. Calhoun, *Observations*, p . 52.
39. Jack D. Foner, *The United States Soldier between Two Wars: Army Life and Reforms, 1865–1898* (New York: Humanities Press, 1970), p. 1.
40. Robert G. Athearn, *William Tecumseh Sherman and the Settlement of the West* (Norman: University of Oklahoma Press, 1956), p. 347.
41. Robert M. Utley, "The Frontier and the American Military Tradition," *Soldiers West: Biographies from the Military Frontier*, ed. Paul Andrew Hutton (Lincoln: University of Nebraska Press, 1987), p. 4.
42. *Report of Delos B. Sackett*, May 8, 1866, House Exec. Doc. No. 23, 39th Cong., 2d sess., pp. 24, 33.
43. *Report of the Secretary of War*, 42d Cong., 3d sess., House Exec. Doc. 1, pt. 2 (Washington, D.C.: Government Printing Office, 1874) 1:v.
44. Penciled notes, ca. 1927, EBCC, no. 3532.
45. Frances C. Carrington, *My Army Life and the Fort Phil Kearney Massacre* (Philadelphia: Lippincott, 1910), p. 184.
46. *The Management of the War Department: Report No. 799*, House Committee on Expenditures in the War Department, 44th Cong., 1st sess., 1875–76, 9 vols., ser. 1715. (Washington, D.C.: Government Printing Office, 1876), 7:163.
47. *Annual Report of the Post of Fort Buford*, Brevet Brig. Gen. Henry A. Morrow, commanding, November 18, 1869, ibid.; Robert G. Athearn, *Forts of the Up-*

per Missouri (Englewood Cliffs, N.J.: Prentice-Hall, 1967), p. 248; see also, Robert W. Frazer, *Forts of the West: Military Forts and Presidios and Posts Commonly Called Forts West of the Mississippi River to 1898* (Norman: University of Oklahoma Press, 1965), p. 110.

48. SP, reel 81.
49. *Frontier Scout*, Fort Union, July 14, 1864, cited by Athearn, *Forts*, p. 143.
50. Letter of July 16, 1867, *The Sherman Letters: Correspondence between General and Senator Sherman, from 1837 to 1891*, ed. Rachel Sherman Thorndike (New York: Charles Scribner's Sons, 1894), p. 291.
51. Ibid.
52. Samuel J. Barrows, New York *Tribune*, cited in Frost, *Custer's 7th Cavalry*, p. 84. For Frost's identification of the correspondent, see p. 208n.
53. Hall to Sherman, September 24, 1868, *Sherman Letters*.

CHAPTER 8: FRONTIER ARMY WIVES

1. Letter of May 26, 1861, Crary, *Dear Belle*, p. 237.
2. "A Winter on the Plains," *Harper's New Monthly Magazine* 39 (June 1869): 25. See also Henry Eugene Davies, *Ten Days on the Plains* (New York: Crocker and Co., [1871]), p. 24: "To the ladies who are willing to share their husbands' fortunes on the frontier, existence must be dreary indeed."
3. Patricia Y. Stallard, *Glittering Misery: Dependents of the Indian Fighting Army* (San Rafael, Calif., and Fort Collins, Colo.: Presidio Press and Old Army Press, 1978), p. 13.
4. Davis, "Winter," p. 25.
5. Dee Brown, *The Gentle Tamers: Women of the Old Wild West* (New York: Putnam, 1958), p. 45.
6. Martha Summerhayes, *Vanished Arizona: Recollections of the Army Life of a New England Woman* (1908; reprint, Glorieta, N.M.: Rio Grande Press, 1976), p. 22.
7. Ibid., p. 24.
8. Ibid., p. 98.
9. Baldwin, *An Army Wife*, p. 45.
10. Frances M. A. Roe, *Army Letters from an Officer's Wife, 1871–1888* (New York: D. Appleton, 1909), pp. 66–69.
11. EBC, "Where the Heart Is: A Sketch of Woman's Life on the Frontier," in John M. Carroll, ed., *Another Libbie Custer Gallimaufry!* (Bryan, Tex.: privately printed, 1978), p. 21.
12. Baldwin, *An Army Wife*, pp. 72–73.
13. Lydia Spencer Lane, *I Married a Soldier, or Old Days in the Old Army* (Albuquerque, N.M.: Horn and Wallace, 1964), p. 48.

14. EBC Diary (1890), CC, box 6, folder 13.
15. Roe, *Army Letters*, p. 81.
16. Ibid., p. 80.
17. "Home-Making in the American Army," in John M. Carroll, ed., *A Libbie Custer Gallimaufry* (Bryan, Tex.: privately printed, 1978), p. 4.
18. Alice to Benjamin Grierson, August 7, 1877, in Shirley A. Leckie, ed., *The Colonel's Lady on the Western Frontier: The Correspondence of Alice Kirk Grierson* (Lincoln: University of Nebraska Press, 1988), p. 108.
19. Vielé, *"Following the Drum,"* p. 168; Carrington, *Army Life,* p. 86.
20. Summerhayes, *Vanished Arizona*, p. 43, 65.
21. Margaret Carrington, 1831–79, was the first wife of Colonel Henry Carrington. After her death, he married Frances Grummond, the widow of an officer killed in the Fetterman massacre. The second Mrs. Carrington then wrote her own account of life at Fort Phil Kearny when she was there as Mrs. Grummond.
22. Margaret Carrington, *Ab-Sa-Ra-Ka: Home of the Crows* (Philadelphia: Lippincott, 1868), p. 43.
23. Ibid., p. 65.
24. Henry B. Carrington, *The Indian Question: An Address* (Boston: DeWolfe and Fiske, 1884), p. 9.
25. M. Carrington, *Ab-Sa-Ra-Ka*, pp. 176–77.
26. "Memoirs of Marian Russell," *Winners of the West* 21:3 (March 28, 1944): 5.
27. Lane, *I Married a Soldier*, pp. 134–35.
28. Merrill J. Mattes, *Indians, Infants and Infantry: Andrew and Elizabeth Burt on the Frontier* (Denver: Old West Publishing Co., 1960), p. 103.
29. Roe, *Army Letters*, p. 44.
30. Ellen McGowan Biddle and Libbie Custer both had this last experience, one in Texas, the other in Dakota. See *Reminiscences of a Soldier's Wife* (Philadelphia: J. B. Lippincott, 1907), p. 64; *"Boots and Saddles,"* or *Life in Dakota with General Custer* (Norman: University of Oklahoma Press, 1961), p. 69.
31. Summerhayes, *Vanished Arizona*, p. 89.
32. Sandra L. Myres, "Romance and Reality on the American Frontier: Views of Army Wives," *Western Historical Quarterly* 13 (1982): 425, observes that "the army authoresses were an elite, eastern-oriented, and somewhat exclusive group, and their circumstances were different from those of other nineteenth-century western women."
33. Mary Carr cited in James T. King, ed., "Fort McPherson in 1870: A Note by an Army Wife," *Nebraska History* 45 (March 1964): 101.
34. Baldwin, *An Army Wife*, pp. 25, 39.
35. Summerhayes, *Vanished Arizona*, pp. 78–79.
36. M. Carrington, *Ab-Sa-Ra-Ka*, p. 198.

37. Biddle, *Reminiscences*, p. 148, heard General Sherman tell the story, but it was in wide circulation.
38. Lane, *I Married a Soldier*, pp. 25, 42, 45, 44, 190.
39. EBC, *Tenting on the Plains*, p. 486.
40. F. C. Carrington, *Army Life*, p. 99.
41. Mattes, *Indians, Infants, and Infantry*, p. 196.
42. Biddle, *Reminiscences*, p. 89.
43. Summerhayes, *Vanished Arizona*, p. 223.
44. M. Carrington, *Ab-Sa-Ra-Ka*, p. 51.
45. EBC Journal, 1891–92, EBCC, p. 20, no. 5671.
46. See Brian Pohanka, "A Summer on the Plains, 1870: From the Diary of Annie Gibson Roberts," in *Custer and His Times*, ed. Paul A. Hutton (El Paso, Tex.: Little Big Horn Associates, 1981), pp. 7–56, for a good description of heavy socializing on a frontier post.
47. Ibid., p. 22.
48. Rebecca Richmond to her mother, March 16, 1870; Rebecca Richmond to her parents, March 21, 1870, EBCC, reel 2.
49. Robert M. Utley, "Arizona Vanquished: Impressions and Reflections Concerning the Quality of Life on a Military Frontier," *American West* 6:6 (November 1969): 21.
50. EBC, *Tenting on the Plains*, pp. 463–65.
51. EBC, "*Boots and Saddles*," p. 141.
52. Summerhayes, *Vanished Arizona*, p. 61.
53. Rebecca Richmond to her mother, March 16, 1870, EBCC, reel 2.
54. Sandra L. Myres, ed., *Cavalry Wife: The Diary of Eveline M. Alexander, 1866–1867* (College Station, Tex.: Texas A & M University Press, 1977), pp. 87, 89.
55. Ibid., p. 36.
56. Glenda Riley writes: "If women had any doubts regarding the brutal natures of the American Indian population, they were quickly dissipated by the climate of prejudicial opinion that enveloped women throughout the nineteenth century." *Women and Indians on the Frontier, 1825–1915* (Albuquerque: University of New Mexico Press, 1984), pp. 15–16.
57. Roe, *Army Letters*, p. 10.
58. Ibid.
59. EBC, *Tenting on the Plains*, p. 356.
60. Fitzgerald to Aunt Annie, September 20, 1876, in Abe Laufe, ed., *An Army Doctor's Wife on the Frontier: Letters from Alaska and the Far West, 1874–1878* (Pittsburgh: University of Pittsburgh Press, 1962), p. 207.
61. This view was shared by both sexes. See Katherine Weist, "Beasts of Burden and Menial Slaves: Nineteenth Century Observations of Northern Plains Indian Women," in *The Hidden Half: Studies of Plains Indian Women*, ed. Patri-

cia Albers and Beatrice Medicine (Lanham, Md.: University Press of America, 1983), pp. 29–62. Weist observes: "The descriptions of Indian women as beasts of burden do not appear to alter over time, for both early and late writers employ very similar images."

Tribes varied, but as Marla N. Powers writes of the Oglala, the roles of the two sexes were complementary. Each was valued for its contributions to society. *Oglala Women: Myth, Ritual, and Reality* (Chicago: University of Chicago Press, 1986), pp. 5–6.

62. Mattes, *Indians, Infants, and Infantry*, p. 89.
63. EBC, "*Boots and Saddles*," p. 196.
64. MS headed Stevensburg [18]64 and dated 1918, EBCC, reel 5.
65. *Tabeau's Narrative of Loisel's Expedition to the Upper Missouri,* ed. Annie Heloise Abel, trans. Rose Abel Wright (Norman: University of Oklahoma Press, 1939), p. 148. An editorial note, p. 148n, says that "this was the almost universal observation made by white men."
66. Calhoun, *Some Observations*, p. 55.
67. Cited in Bayard H. Paine, *Pioneers, Indians, and Buffaloes* (Curtis, Neb.: Curtis Enterprise, 1935), p. 113.
68. Lane, *I Married a Soldier*, p. 142.
69. Ibid., p. 80.
70. Summerhayes, *Vanished Arizona*, p. 43.
71. Ibid., pp. 95, 108.
72. Ibid., pp. 162, 170–71.
73. Ibid., pp. 234, 154, 158.
74. Roe, *Army Letters*, pp. 7–8.
75. Baldwin, *An Army Wife*, p. 49.
76. Carrington, *Army Life*, p. 20. Ironically, in addition to being a free spirit, Annie Sokalski may also have been a battered wife. Stallard writes of Sokalski's husband that "even though he reportedly had beaten and verbally abused her, she stood by him to the end." *Glittering Misery*, p. 108.
77. Mattes, *Indians, Infants, and Infantry*, p. 159.
78. EBC, *Tenting on the Plains*, p. 622.
79. Vielé, "*Following the Drum*," p. 256.
80. Summerhayes, *Vanished Arizona*, p. 303.

CHAPTER 9: THE PLAINS INDIANS

1. Merrill E. Gates, Address at Lake Mohonk Conference, 1896, from *Proceedings of the Fourteenth Annual Meeting of the Lake Mohonk Conference of Friends of the Indian*, pp. 8–13, in *Americanizing the American Indians: Writings by the "Friends of the Indian," 1880–1900*, ed. Francis Paul Prucha (Cambridge: Harvard University Press, 1973), p. 332. Even that severe critic of Cooper,

Mark Twain, confessed that before he had acquired frontier experience, he had viewed the Indian "through the mellow moonshine of romance." Samuel L. Clemens, *Roughing It* (New York: Harper and Brothers, 1913), 1:132.

2. GAC, *My Life on the Plains, or Personal Experiences with Indians* (Norman: University of Oklahoma Press, 1962), p. 19. See p. 13 for Custer's critique of Cooper.
3. O. G. Libby, ed., *The Arikara Narrative of the Campaign against the Hostile Dakotas, June 1876* (New York: Sol Lewis, 1973), p. 77. "Arikara" will in future be referred to by the commonly used "Ree."
4. John Gibbon, *Gibbon on the Sioux Campaign of 1876*, facsimile ed. (Bellevue, Nebraska: Old Army Press, 1969), p. 14.
5. Leslie Tillett, *Wind on the Buffalo Grass: The Indians' Own Account of the Battle at the Little Big Horn River, and the Death of Their Life on the Plains* (New York: Thomas Y. Crowell, 1976), p. 127, account of the Crow scout Goes Ahead.
6. GAC to EBC, June 21, 1876, in EBC, *"Boots and Saddles,"* p. 275.
7. Libby, *Arikara Narrative*, pp. 73–74.
8. Ibid., p. 73.
9. Henry Benjamin Whipple, *Lights and Shadows of a Long Episcopate* (New York: Macmillan, 1912), p. 319.
10. Samuel J. Crawford, *Kansas in the Sixties* (Chicago: A. C. McClurg, 1911), p. 263.
11. Cited in Alban W. Hoopes, *The Road to the Little Big Horn and Beyond* (New York: Vantage Press, 1975), p. 33. Robert Winston Mardock, *The Reformers and the American Indian* (Columbia: University of Missouri Press, 1971), p. 87, claims that most people on the frontier favored extermination.
12. Teresa Viele, *"Following the Drum,"* p. 121.
13. Tillett, *Wind on the Buffalo Grass,* p. 96.
14. Stanley Vestal, *Sitting Bull: Champion of the Sioux* (Boston: Houghton Mifflin, 1932), p. 196. The letter was written by the tribe's adopted son, Big Leggins Brughière, who was half Indian, half white. Letter of Sherman to John Sherman, September 23, 1868, ShP, vol. 23, reel 13.
15. "Remarks of General Nelson A. Miles at Banquet of the Order of Indian Wars of the U.S., March 2, 1917," *The Unpublished Papers of the Order of Indian Wars*, ed. John M. Carroll, 10 vols. (New Brunswick, N.J.: privately published, 1977), 1:8.
16. January 7, unpaged typescript, EBCC, reel 6.
17. Cited in Robert G. Athearn, *Forts*, p. 280.
18. *The Autobiography of Benjamin Franklin: A Restoration of a "Fair Copy" by Max Farrand* (Berkeley: University of California Press, 1949), p. 149.
19. Cited in Thomas F. Gossett, *Race: The History of an Idea in America* (Dallas: Southern Methodist University Press, 1963), p. 230.

20. Speech to the Order of Indian Wars in *The Unpublished Papers of the Order of Indian Wars* 1:20.
21. Letter of June 25, 1875, cited in George W. Kingsbury, *History of Dakota Territory: South Dakota, Its History and Its People*, ed. George Martin Smith, (Chicago: S. J. Clarke, 1915), 1:902.
22. George E. Hyde, *Life of George Bent Written from His Letters*, ed. Savoie Lottinville (Norman: University of Oklahoma Press, 1967), p. 257.
23. Stanley Vestal, *New Sources of Indian History, 1850–1891* (Norman: University of Oklahoma Press, 1934), p. 263.
24. Nelson A. Miles to Alfred Terry, Letter of October 28, 1876, MP, box 2.
25. E. A. Brininstool, "Chief Crazy Horse, His Career and Death," *Nebraska History Magazine* (December 1929): 38.
26. This is what most Indians believe, according to William Powers, professor of Anthropology at Rutgers University and a speaker of the Lakota language.
27. Paul I. Wellman, *Death on Horseback: Seventy Years of War for the American West* (Philadelphia: Lippincott, 1947), p. 164.
28. John Bourke, *On the Border with Crook* (New York: Charles Scribner's Sons, 1891), p. 414.
29. Vestal, *New Sources*, p. 225.
30. E. S. Godfrey, *General George A. Custer and the Battle of the Little Big Horn* (New York: Century Company, 1921), p. 29. This pamphlet consists of Godfrey's 1908 edition of "Custer's Last Battle," originally published in the *Century Magazine* 43:3 (January 1892), 358–384, here reprinted with added material.
31. Thomas B. Marquis, *Custer on the Little Bighorn*, 2d. rev. ed. (Algonac, Mich.: Reference Publications, 1986), p. 49.
32. Libby, *Arikara Narrative*, pp. 257–58.
33. Francis B. Taunton argues persuasively that even a great victory in the Sioux Wars would not have catapulted Custer to the kind of national prominence necessary to be seriously considered as a presidential candidate. The timing was off in any case: the Battle of the Little Bighorn took place while the Democrats were in convention. What Custer must have hoped for was a Democratic victory followed by his promotion. *"Sufficient Reason?" An Examination of Terry's Celebrated Order to Custer* (London: English Westerners' Society, 1977), p. 91.
34. W. O. Taylor to EBC, April 5, 1922, EBCC, reel 3.
35. Marquis, *Custer on the Little Bighorn*, p. 114.
36. According to the Sioux physician, Dr. Charles Eastman, cited in Wellman, *Death on Horseback*, p. 128n.
37. *The Poems of Alexander Pope*, ed. John Butt (New Haven: Yale University Press, 1963), p. 508; see Robert Taft, *Artists and Illustrators of the Old West,*

1850–1900 (New York: Charles Scribner's Sons, 1953), pp. 300–301, for an extensive discussion of this phrase. The earliest reference to it he has found is in the *New York Weekly Tribune*, December 30, 1843.

38. Gossett, *Race*, p. 229.
39. *Times and Conservative*, June 20, 1869.
40. Sarah Winnemucca (Hopkins) *Life among the Piutes: Their Wrongs and Claims*, ed. Mrs. Horace Mann (Boston, 1883), p. 20, cited in Sandra L. Myres, *Westering Women and the Frontier Experience, 1800–1915* (Albuquerque: University of New Mexico Press, 1982), p. 66.
41. Ewert, *Diary*, p. 67.
42. Annual Report, Nov. 25, 1876, *Report of the Secretary of War, Executive Documents 1, Part 2, Messages and Documents Communicated to the Two Houses of Congress at the Beginning of the Second Session of the 44th Congress* (Washington, D.C.: Government Printing Office, 1876), 1:447.
43. According to Edward S. Ellis, *The History of Our Country from the Discovery of America to the Present Time*, 8 vols. (Cincinnati: Jones Brothers, 1900), 6:1483, what Sheridan actually said to an Indian who identified himself to the general as a "good Indian," was this: "The only good Indians I ever saw were dead." In time, Dee Brown writes, these words "were honed into an American aphorism: *The only good Indian is a dead Indian.*" *Bury My Heart at Wounded Knee: An Indian History of the American West* (New York: Holt, Rinehart and Winston, 1970), p. 172.
44. Prucha, *Indian Policy in the United States: Historical Essays* (Lincoln: University of Nebraska Press, 1981), pp. 180–97, argues that "Indian policy of the post–Civil War decades continued the optimism and doctrines of Indian perfectibility" (p. 194). Officially, yes, but this policy was notoriously ineffective in assimilating Indians into the dominant culture, both during this period and long afterward.
45. Gossett, *Race*, pp. 144, 244.
46. Second Annual Message, December 2, 1878, Gov. Doc. 3265, in James D. Richardson, comp., *A Compilation of the Messages and Papers of the Presidents, 1789–1897* (Washington, D.C.: Government Printing Office, 1897–98) 7:503.
47. Patricia Nelson Limerick, *The Legacy of Conquest: The Unbroken Past of the American West* (New York: W. W. Norton, 1987), p. 199.
48. Herman Melville, *Billy Budd, Sailor (An Inside Narrative)*, ed. Harrison Hayford and Merton M. Sealts, Jr. (Chicago: University of Chicago Press, 1962), p. 114.
49. EBC, "*Boots and Saddles*," pp. 186–89.
50. Francis Paul Prucha, *The Great Father: The United States Government and the American Indians*, 2 vols. (Lincoln: University of Nebraska Press, 1984), 1:586–89, recapitulates the many failed efforts to break up the Indian ring.

See also, George H. Phillips, "The Indian Ring in Dakota Territory, 1870–1890," *South Dakota History* 2 (fall 1972): 345–76.

51. Sheridan to Grant, January 19, 1869, DP.
52. Crook to Hayes, Nov. 28, 1871, CrP.
53. O. C. Marsh, *A Statement of Affairs at Red Cloud Agency, Made to the President of the United States, July 10, 1875*. Collected in Bancroft Library Pamphlets on North American Indians, University of California at Berkeley, vol. 3, p. 5.
54. Ibid., p. 4.
55. The interpreter Louis Reshaw, quoted by Marsh, *Statement*, p. 18.
56. The same situation obtained in Texas. A correspondent of the *New York Herald* traveling with Ranald Mackenzie when he captured a Comanche village remarked on finding there some reservation blankets "which it is interesting to note, are about four feet by three in size, obliging them to run two together to make one of ordinary size." *Ranald S. Mackenzie's Official Correspondence Relating to Texas, 1873–1879* (Lubbock: West Texas Museum Association, 1968), pp. 117–18.
57. Cited in Marsh, *Statement*, p. 36.
58. Ibid., p. 37.
59. George E. Hyde, *Red Cloud's Folk: A History of the Oglala Sioux Indians* (Norman: University of Oklahoma Press, 1957), p. 236.
60. James C. Olson, *Red Cloud and the Sioux Problem* (Lincoln: University of Nebraska Press, 1965), p. 195.
61. Cited ibid., p. 184; agent Savile was removed in early 1876. Loring B. Priest, *Uncle Sam's Stepchildren* (New Brunswick, N.J.: Rutgers University Press, 1942), p. 67.
62. Paine, *Pioneers, Indians and Buffaloes*, p. 109.
63. Ibid., p. 114.
64. Evan S. Connell, *Son of the Morning Star: Custer and the Little Bighorn* (New York: Harper and Row, 1985), p. 146.
65. The most recent archaeological investigation of the Little Bighorn battle site confirms that the Indians had an array of effective weapons, although a number of these had been acquired either in the Battle of the Rosebud on June 17 or in the first fighting with Reno's men on June 25. See Douglas D. Scott and Richard A. Fox, Jr., *Archaeological Insights into the Custer Battle: An Assessment of the 1984 Field Season* (Norman: University of Oklahoma Press, 1984), pp. 112–13.
66. Letter of June 13, 1870, SP, container 39, vol. 1.
67. Bergamini, *The Hundredth Year*, p. 44.
68. George E. Hyde, *Spotted Tail's Folk: A History of the Brulé Sioux* (Norman: University of Oklahoma Press, 1974), p. xii.
69. As Thomas C. Leonard notes, "Protestant American culture . . . had never achieved a clear vision of the red man's future." "Red, White and the Army

Blue: Empathy and Anger on the American West," *American Quarterly* 26 (May 1974): 177.

70. Robert Wooster, *The Military and United States Indian Policy, 1865–1903* (New Haven: Yale University Press, 1988), p. 4.
71. Lowie, *Indians of the Plains*, p. 106. Lowie also cites J. R. Swanton: "[Warfare] was a social institution and warlike exploits a necessary means of social advancement" (p. 111).
72. Samuel Bowles, *Our New West: Records of Travels between the Mississippi River and the Pacific Ocean* (New York: J. D. Dennison, 1869), p. 158; Mardock, p. 100.
73. George A. Forsyth, *The Story of the Soldier* (New York: D. Appleton, 1900), p. 74.
74. Nelson A. Miles, *Serving the Republic: Memoirs of the Civil and Military Life of Nelson A. Miles* (New York: Harper and Brothers, 1911), p. 164.
75. Typescript of GAC essay, "The Red Man," EBCC, reel 6.
76. *New York Times*, May 23, 1871.
77. Eugene V. McAndrews, ed., "An Army Engineer's Journal of Custer's Black Hills Expedition, July 2, 1874–August 23, 1874," *Journal of the West*, 13:1 (January 1974): 84.
78. Thomas Henry Tibbles, *Buckskin and Blanket Days: Memoirs of a Friend of the Indians* (Chicago: Lakeside Press, 1985), p. 188.
79. Interview with Sitting Bull, *New York Herald*, November 16, 1877. Lowie, *Indians of the Plains*, p. 113, writes that "a great man could maintain his status best by lavish generosity to the poor. Such liberality, next to a fine war record, was the basis for high standing."
80. Helen Hunt Jackson, *A Century of Dishonor* (New York: Harper and Brothers, 1881).
81. President Grant's first choice as commissioner of Indian affairs, his former staff member, the Senecan Indian Ely Parker, was ineffective. By 1871 Parker had resigned.
82. Cited in Hoopes, *Road to Little Bighorn*, p. 151.

CHAPTER 10: INDIAN FIGHTING

1. George Armstrong Custer, "On the Plains," October 26, 1867 (published November 9, 1867), in *Nomad: George A. Custer in Turf, Field and Farm*, ed. Brian W. Dippie (Austin: University of Texas Press, 1980), p. 20.
2. Telegram of September 24, 1868, SP, reel 81. Such appeals from territorial political figures were often hyperbolic.
3. Judge Charles E. Flandrau, in Wellman, *Death on Horseback*, p. 35; see also Vestal, *New Sources*, p. 133. On the other hand, an experienced Indian fighter

could develop an immunity to this aspect of Indian warfare. Lieutenant Charles Larned, describing a fight on the Yellowstone Expedition of 1873, reported somewhat matter-of-factly: "On they came . . . screaming and yelling as usual." He went on to say that the cavalry countered by having the band play "Garryowen" and beginning to yell themselves. "Camp on the Musselshell River," *Chicago Inter-Ocean*, August 19, 1873."

4. Talcott E. Wing, *History of Monroe County, Michigan* (New York: Munsell and Company, 1890), p. 58.
5. Russell F. Weigley, *The American Way of War: A History of United States Military Strategy and Policy* (New York: Macmillan, 1976), p. 19.
6. Abe Laufe, ed., *An Army Doctor's Wife on the Frontier: Letters from Alaska and the Far West 1874–1878* (Pittsburgh: University of Pittsburgh Press, 1962), p. 204.
7. Tremain, *Last Hours*, pp. 155–56.
8. GAC to Lydia Ann Reed, September 27, 1862, EBCC, reel 1.
9. Letter of February 2, 1863, Tyler, *Recollections*, p. 75.
10. Cited in *The Fighting Norths and Pawnee Scouts: Narratives and Reminiscences of Military Service on the Old Frontier* (Lincoln, Neb.: Robert Bruce, 1932), p. 21.
11. General Orders no. 8, Camp Robinson, Nebraska, October 24, 1876, quoted by Captain O. C. Applegate in a letter to *Winners of the West* 4:4 (January 30, 1926): 3. Promotion depended upon seniority, and brevets for Indian engagements were not given until 1890.
12. Cited in Charles F. Lummis, *General Crook and the Apache Wars* (Flagstaff, Ariz.: Northland, 1966), p. 17.
13. Michael V. Sheridan, *Personal Memoirs of Philip Henry Sheridan*, 2 vols. (New York: D. Appleton, 1904) 2:51–52. When Custer had fired only a few houses he received a change of orders.
14. *Washington Post*, August 11, 1902.
15. According to Harry Turney-High, "the primitive warrior butchered the civilians because he was incapable of conceptualizing such a status." *Primitive War: Its Practice and Concepts*, 2d ed. (Columbia: University of South Carolina Press, 1971), p. 264.
16. Ibid., p. 104.
17. See Thomas W. Dunlay, *Wolves for the Blue Soldiers: Indian Scouts and Auxiliaries with the United States Army, 1860–90* (Lincoln: University of Nebraska Press, 1982), pp. 201–5, for a discussion of differences between white and Indian warfare. As Dunlay concludes, most whites "preferred to believe . . . that they were different from savage warriors" (205). See also Utley, *Frontier Regulars*, pp. 45–46: "In the end, army men found it nearly impossible to approve of any of the Indians' fighting practices that differed from their own."
18. GAC, "On the Plains," p. 28.

19. Turney-High, *Primitive War*, p. xiii, uses the term "civilized war" descriptively to mean the warfare practiced by societies that have writing, metal smelting, organized commerce, civil government, etc.
20. Report of W. T. Sherman, November 7, 1877, *Annual Report of the Secretary of War*, 45th Cong., 2d sess., *House Executive Document No. 1, Part II (Serial 1794)*.
21. W. T. Sherman to EBC, January 24, 1889, EBCC, no. 3352.
22. George Bird Grinnell, *The Cheyenne Indians*, 2 vols. (New Haven: Yale University Press, 1923), 2:7.
23. As Turney-High, *Primitive War*, p. 147, writes: "Among almost all American Indians . . . war existed to bring glory to the individual."
24. Report No. 7, The Shenandoah Valley Campaign, September 28, 1864, in Carroll, *Custer in the Civil War*, p. 38.
25. "Late Indian Outrages," *Harper's Weekly* 11:552 (July 27, 1867): 468.
26. Kate Bighead, "She Watched Custer's Last Battle," in *The Custer Reader*, ed. Paul Andrew Hutton (Lincoln: University of Nebraska Press, 1992), p. 371.
27. Jan Augusta Gunn, *Memorial Sketches of Doctor Moses Gunn, by His Wife* (Chicago: W. T. Kenner, 1889), p. 136.
28. See Thomas B. Marquis, *Keep the Last Bullet for Yourself: The True Story of Custer's Last Stand* (New York: Two Continents, 1976), for a number of anecdotes on this subject.
29. Vestal, *Sitting Bull*, pp. 61, 62.
30. Rhodes, *History of the Cavalry*, p. 148.
31. M. Sheridan, *Personal Memoirs*, pp. 374–75.
32. George A. Forsyth, *Thrilling Days in Army Life* (New York: Harper and Brothers, 1900), p. 168.
33. Theodore Davis, "A Summer on the Plains," *Harper's New Monthly Magazine* 36:2 (February 1868): 296.
34. Turney-High, *Primitive War*, p. 94. Bernard Mishkin, *Rank and Warfare among the Plains Indians* (Seattle: University of Washington Press, 1940), p. 39, gives the hierarchy of battle exploits for the Kiowa. More significant than killing an enemy were counting first coup, covering a retreat, rescuing a fallen member of the party during a retreat, and charging the enemy's leading warrior alone before the fight had begun.
35. Marquis, *Wooden Leg: A Warrior Who Fought Custer* (Lincoln: University of Nebraska Press, 1931), p. 264.
36. Mishkin, *Rank and Warfare*, p. 61, remarks that "Plains warfare contains an element of the game in it."
37. Grinnell, "Portraits of Indian Types," p. 260. This incident, which took place near Plum Creek Station, Nebraska, is also described by George Bent in Hyde, *Life of George Bent*, pp. 276–77.

38. John Stands in Timber and Margot Liberty, *Cheyenne Memories* (New Haven: Yale University Press, 1967), pp. 208–209.
39. GAC to EBC, October 10, 1864, in Merington, *Custer Story*, p. 122: "I am now arrayed in Genl. Rosser's coat." See also, EBC, "*Boots and Saddles*," p. 72; H. E. Eaton to EBC, July 20, 1896, EBCC, reel 3: "Gen. Custer just for the joke of it, for several months wore Rosser's sombrero and overcoat." According to Eaton, on December 21, 1864, this coat enabled him to pass through confederates who, during the night, had surrounded the house he had slept in.

CHAPTER 11: NADIR

1. Custer believed that blacks were an inferior race, but his primary motivation in requesting a white command was undoubtedly his career: commanding black troops was simply not as prestigious. His most definitive statement on blacks occurs in a letter to his Bacon in-laws, October 5, 1866, cited in Merington, *Custer Story*, p. 175: "I am in favor of elevating the negro to the extent of his capacity and intelligence, and of our doing everything in our power to advance the race morally and mentally as well as physically, also socially. But I am opposed to making this advance by correspondingly debasing any portion of the white race. As to trusting the negro of the Southern States with the most sacred and responsible privilege—the right of suffrage—I should as soon think of elevating an Indian Chief to the Popedom of Rome. . . . I regard the solution of the negro problem as involving difficulty and requiring greater statesmanship than any political matter that has arisen for years."
2. Monaghan, *Custer*, p. 272.
3. *New York Tribune*, September 14, 1866.
4. Letter of March 1, 1867, Records of GAC, RG 9, National Archives.
5. Hancock was commander of the Department of the Missouri within the Division of the Missouri commanded by General Sherman.
6. EBC to Rebecca Richmond, October 13, 1867, MMP.
7. See Minnie Dubbs Millbrook, "The West Breaks in General Custer," *Kansas Historical Quarterly*, 36:2 (summer 1970): 113–48, for the most detailed treatment of this subject and of Custer's 1867 expedition in general.
8. GAC to EBC, cited in *Tenting on the Plains*, p. 528.
9. Ibid., p. 561.
10. Ibid., p. 571.
11. Ibid., p. 578.
12. EBC to GAC, April 26, 1867, ibid., pp. 543–44.
13. EBC to GAC, April 22, 1867, ibid., p. 540.
14. EBC to GAC, April 18, 1867, ibid., p. 538.

15. GAC, *My Life on the Plains or, Personal Experiences with Indians* (Norman: University of Oklahoma Press, 1962), p. 57. This is a restrained, "literary" version compared to the more horrific account he gave Libbie: "The flesh was roasted and crisped from their faces and bodies, and altogether it was one of the most horrible sights imaginable." GAC to EBC, April 20, 1867, *Tenting on the Plains*, p. 570.
16. GAC to EBC, April 22, 1867, *Tenting on the Plains*, p. 571.
17. GAC to EBC, April 30, 1867, ibid., p. 574.
18. Ibid.
19. GAC to EBC, May 2, 1867, EBC, *Tenting on the Plains*, pp. 576–77.
20. Davis, "With Generals in Their Camp Homes," 119.
21. Ibid., p. 120
22. Special field order directing the destruction of the village, cited by Custer in *My Life*, p. 57. Custer's first account of this episode had been quite different. Bitter over his court-martial, he had wanted to blame Hancock for the inept campaign, and had suggested in an article for *Turf, Field and Farm* that the Indians responsible for the Smoky Hill violence could not have been those of the deserted village, intimating that Hancock's destruction of the village was an impulsive and gratuitous act: "Gen. Hancock's rage at finding himself baffled and outwitted by the Indians was so great that he ordered all the lodges and other Indian property to be collected and burned." "On the Plains," in Dippie, *Nomad*, pp. 25–26; for similar revisions in Custer's account of the campaign, see pp. 124–33.
23. Henry M. Stanley, *My Early Travels and Adventures in America and Asia*, 2 vols. (New York: Charles Scribner's Sons, 1895), 1:v.
24. Cited in William H. Leckie, *The Military Conquest of the Southern Plains* (Norman: University of Oklahoma Press, 1963), p. 154.
25. Davis, "Summer on the Plains," p. 298.
26. Stanley, *Early Travels*, p. 86.
27. Robert M. Utley, ed., *Life in Custer's Cavalry: Diaries and Letters of Albert and Jennie Barnitz, 1867–1868* (New Haven: Yale University Press, 1977), p. 51.
28. GAC to Winfield Scott Hancock, April 6, 1867, photocopy in catalog of Joseph Rubinfine, list 94, American Historical Autographs, West Palm Beach, Florida.
29. Letter of February 24, 1867, ShP, reel 11. Sherman concluded his assessment of Custer with the remark, "I have no excuse to offer for his attempt to act a political part," probably a reference to Custer's appearance as a delegate at the convention of the National Union party in August of 1866. Custer's involvement with the party was brief.
30. Blaine Burkey, *Custer, Come at Once! The Fort Hays Years of George and Elizabeth Custer, 1867–1870* (Hays, Kans.: Thomas More Prep, 1976), p. 26.

31. Court-Martial Proceedings, September 16, 1867, Records of the Office of Judge Advocate General, RG 153, National Archives, pp. 152–153.
32. GAC, *My Life*, p. 190.
33. Ibid., p. 84. A more critical view is provided by George Bent: "The Indians had no difficulty in avoiding Custer's command, and the raids went on." George Hyde, *Life of George Bent*, p. 272.
34. Hyde, *Life of George Bent*, p. 276.
35. Samuel Carter III, *The Last Cavaliers: Confederate and Union Cavalry in the Civil War* (New York: St. Martin's Press, 1979), p. 196.
36. Cited in Gregory J. W. Urwin, *Custer Victorious: The Civil War Battles of General George Armstrong Custer* (Rutherford, N.J.: Fairleigh Dickinson University Press, 1983), p. 252.
37. Utley, *Custer's Cavalry*, pp. 46, 50–51.
38. Letter of June 27, 1867, EBC, *Tenting on the Plains*, p. 548.
39. GAC, *My Life*, p. 88.
40. GAC to EBC, June 22, 1867, cited in EBC, *Tenting on the Plains*, p. 582.
41. Ibid., p. 548.
42. GAC, *My Life*, p. 90; EBC, *Tenting on the Plains*, p. 626. Millbrook, *The West Breaks in General Custer*, 127n., seems justified in doubting that Libbie was ever at Fort Wallace. There is no evidence that she was there other than her own, possibly faulty, recollection.
43. EBC, *Tenting on the Plains*, p. 626. It may be that General Hancock forbade her to go to Fort Wallace from Fort Hays, and this is the disappointment she remembered so keenly.
44. Ibid., pp. 671–72.
45. Monaghan, *Custer*, p. 295, gives this figure. Custer, *My Life*, p. 103, says "upwards of forty."
46. Telegram of January 14, 1867, MMP.
47. Davis, "Summer on the Plains," p. 306.
48. GAC, *My Life*, p. 112.
49. Letter of August 15, 1867, in Millbrook, T*he West Breaks in General Custer*, p. 140n.
50. GAC, *My Life*, p. 117.
51. Testimony of Sergeant James Connelly, General Court Martial Orders no. 93, Fort Leavenworth, September 16, 1867, in Records of GAC, RG 9, National Archives, p. 77. Further court-martial citations will be to this source.
52. Testimony of Captain Louis Hamilton, Court Martial, p. 60.
53. It seems clear from the court-martial testimony that Captain Hamilton had reported two deaths to Custer at the time although Sergeant Connelly, who had been in the party attacked, insisted that he had told Hamilton that one man was wounded and he did not think the Indians had seen him dismount. Court Martial, p. 85.

54. Interview with Walter M. Camp, October 19, 1910, CP, box 6, folder 5. Harold B. Lee Library.
55. Frederick Benteen, in his annotations to Custer's book, noted that Custer had received such a letter. John M. Carroll, *Custer: From the Civil War to the Big Horn* (Bryan, Tex.: John M. Carroll, 1981), p. 7. E. G. Mathey had a similar story. Mathey Interview, October 19, 1910, CP, p. 323.
56. Libbie's recent biographer, Shirley A. Leckie, believes that Custer was motivated by concern over Weir, but that nothing more than an innocent flirtation had occurred, possibly inspired by Libbie's desire to "settle old scores with her husband for past attentions to other women." *Elizabeth Bacon Custer and the Making of a Myth* (Norman: University of Oklahoma Press, 1993), pp. 102–3.
57. T. A. Weir to GAC, August 14, 1876, FC.
58. Millbrook, *The West Breaks in General Custer*, p. 143, says that since Libbie had come with Custer to Fort Harker, Colonel Smith remanded Custer to Fort Riley so that she would not be exposed to the cholera outbreak at Harker.
59. John D. Billings, *Hardtack and Coffee, or The Unwritten Story of Army Life* (Boston: George M. Smith, 1887), p. 180. Billings estimated that only 10 percent of deaths of horses during the Civil War were due to battle wounds.
60. At the height of the cavalry campaign in the Shenandoah, the Cavalry Corps needed an average of one hundred and fifty replacement horses each day. Stackpole, *Sheridan in the Shenandoah*, p. 131.
61. Not that this particular would have necessarily altered Custer's plans. He might well have been equally willing to allow Captain Carpenter to see about a wounded man as well as a dead one.
62. Court-Martial, p. 210; a contemporary article in the *Army and Navy Journal* (August 5, 1871) makes the same point: "A bold front will cause Indians to be wary of you; the least sign of timidity emboldens them; turn to run from them, and you are lost." Cited in Ernest Lisle Reedstrom, *Bugles, Banners and War Bonnets* (Caldwell, Idaho: Caxton Printers, 1977), p. 193.
63. Merington, *Custer Story*, pp. 205–6.
64. Testimony of Second Lieutenant Henry Jackson, Court-Martial, p. 145.
65. Testimony of Dr. Coates, ibid., p. 120.
66. Ibid., pp. 122–23.
67. Ibid., pp. 212–13.
68. To Mr. Walker, September 1867, Merington, *Custer Story*, p. 212.
69. Court-Martial, p. 200.
70. Since "pay proper" was only basic salary, Custer would continue to receive government paychecks for various allowances during his period of suspension.
71. November 20, 1867, Records of GAC, RG 9, National Archives.
72. *The Papers of Ulysses S. Grant*, ed. John Y. Simon (Carbondale: Southern Illinois University Press, 1991) 18:372–73.

73. Sheridan to Brevet Major General John A. Rawlins, April 15, 1868, Grant, *Papers*, p. 373.
74. *Military Life in Dakota: The Journal of Philippe Régis de Trobriand*, trans. and ed. Lucile M. Kane (St. Paul: Alvord Memorial Commission, 1951), pp. 64–65, 63.

CHAPTER 12: VICTORY ON THE WASHITA

1. GAC, *My Life*, p. 183. The campaign alluded to in Sheridan's telegram was planned by the general as a reprisal for Indian raids on the Santa Fe road. An excellent detailed account of the situation is given in Donald J. Berthrong, *The Southern Cheyennes* (Norman: University of Oklahoma Press, 1963), 289–317.
2. Letter of October 8 [1868], Miscellaneous Correspondence, 1850–1870, IP.
3. Letter of October 4, 1868, EBCC, reel 4. *I* is not capitalized in the MS and *judgment* is spelled *judgement*.
4. Letter of October 7, 1868, ibid. Custer wrote "78," an obvious error.
5. Letter of November 22, 1868, ibid. As usual, Custer misspells *judgment*.
6. Office of the Adjutant General, LR, Records of the War Department, National Archives.
7. Utley, *Custer's Cavalry*, p. 205.
8. GAC, *My Life*, pp. 193–98.
9. Ibid., p. 379.
10. Holdout Johnson, cited by Joe E. Milner and Earle R. Forrest, *California Joe: Noted Scout and Indian Fighter* (Caldwell, Idaho: Caxton Printers, 1935), p. 282. Charles P. Jordan, an Indian trader, claimed to have captured Joe's assassin, a man he identified as "Texas Tom." Jordan to EBC, July 9, 1910, EBCC, reel 3.
11. V. T. McGillycuddy to Joe E. Milner, April 8, 1927, cited in Milner and Forrest, *California Joe*, p. 280. Because Joe was a civilian at the time of his death on a military post, his killer could be held only four days. Johnson, in his account, says that a "terrific blizzard" delayed the officers who went to inform the Holt County sheriff (p. 282).
12. Joseph K. Griffis to EBC, June 2, 1910, EBCC, no. 4278.
13. Cited by Carl Coke Rister, *Border Command: General Phil Sheridan in the West* (Norman: University of Oklahoma Press, 1944), p. 92.
14. Samuel J. Crawford, *Kansas in the Sixties* (Chicago: A. C. McClurg, 1911), p. 320.
15. Proclamation of October 11, 1868, cited in James Albert Hadley, "The Nineteenth Kansas Cavalry and the Conquest of the Plains Indians," *Collections of the Kansas State Historical Society,* 10 (1908): 430n.
16. "John McBee's Account of the Expedition of the 19th Kansas," ed. William E. Connelley, *Collections of the Kansas State Historical Society*, 17 (1928): 362.

17. Hadley, "Nineteenth Kansas," p. 441.
18. GAC, *My Life*, p. 216.
19. Ibid., p. 214.
20. *New York Sun*, May 14, 1899, transcript in GP.
21. EBCC, reel 5.
22. S. L. A. Marshall, *Crimsoned Prairie: The Wars between the United States and the Plains Indians during the Winning of the West* (New York: Charles Scribner's Sons, 1972), p. 107.
23. Fred Dustin, *The Custer Tragedy: Events Leading Up To And Following the Little Big Horn Campaign of 1876* (Ann Arbor, Mich.: Edwards Brothers, 1939), p. 26, n.5.
24. C. P. Godfrey, "General Edward S. Godfrey," *Ohio Archaeological and Historical Quarterly* 43:1 (1934): 83.
25. Report No. 4, Mine Run, Virginia, November 26, 1863, in Carroll, *Custer in the Civil War*, p. 15.
26. Civil War notes, EBCC, reel 5.
27. Donald F. Danker, *Man of the Plains: Recollections of Luther North, 1856–1882* (Lincoln: University of Nebraska Press, 1961), p. 184.
28. Sherman's instructions to Hazen were absolutely clear. On October 13, 1868, he had directed Hazen "to go to Fort Cobb, and to make provision for all the Indians who come there to keep out of the war. . . . I will approve and justify any expense, or anything you may do to encourage Indians to come on to the reservation, there to remain at peace." Cited by Morris Schaff, "The Indian: What We Should Do with Him," *Harper's Monthly* 40:4 (1870) 737.
29. Fort Cobb, November 20, 1868, Statement taken by Hazen from Black Kettle, SP, reel 81.
30. Ibid.
31. Sheridan to Brevet Major General W. A. Nichols, December 2, 1868, SP, reel 81. Sheridan consistently expressed such views. His endorsement of Ranald Mackenzie's letter of June 4, 1872, to the assistant adjutant general, Department of Texas, asseverated that "to defend the long line of Northern Texas against Indians who are supplied with food, arms and ammunition at the reservations seems to me ridiculous." 2545 AGO 1872 filed with 1582 AGO 1872 RG94.
32. Unless otherwise specified, details of the march and battle are taken from Custer's account in *My Life*.
33. *My Life*, p. 233.
34. Field report of November 28, 1868, SP, reel 81.
35. Ben Clark interview with Walter Camp, CP, Lilly Library.
36. Pickens to EBC, letter of June 29, 1921, EBCC Reel 3.

37. E. S. Godfrey, "Some Reminiscences, Including the Washita Battle, November 27, 1868," *Cavalry Journal*, galleys with Godfrey's corrections in the EBCC, reel 6.
38. Ibid., p. 248.
39. Custer to Sheridan, November 28, 1868, Copybook in which are transcribed reports of various expeditions and operations conducted within the military division, 1868–76, p. 103, Military Division of the Missouri Papers, Military History Institute. There is an interesting detail omitted from Custer's later account of the battle in *My Life*: "Even driving the women from the village with little or no clothing." He recorded elsewhere that the temperature at the time was below freezing.
40. General Field Orders no. 6, November 29, 1868; Sheridan to EBC, November 29, 1868, EBCC, reel 2.
41. Hadley, "Nineteenth Kansas," p. 443.
42. Ibid.
43. David Spotts, *Campaigning with Custer and the Nineteenth Kansas Volunteer Cavalry*, ed. E. A. Brininstool (Los Angeles: Wetzel, 1928), pp. 67, 68.
44. Entry of Monday, December 7, 1868, ibid., p. 79.
45. Charles M. Harvey to William James Ghent, June 21, 1935, GP.
46. Copybook NA, p. 115.
47. GAC to EBC, December 6, 1868, EBCC, reel 4.
48. DeB. Randolph Keim, *Sheridan's Troopers on the Borders: A Winter Campaign on the Plains* (London: George Routledge and Sons, 1885), pp. 149–50.
49. Godfrey, "Some Reminiscences," 4.
50. Letters of October 3, 1933, and November 29, 1933, VP.
51. *Army and Navy Journal* (January 20, 1877). Frederick Whittaker, *The Complete Life of Gen. George A. Custer* (New York: Sheldon and Company, 1876), is an extremely partisan view of Custer. Whittaker blamed both Benteen and Major Marcus Reno for not coming to Custer's aid in the Battle of the Little Bighorn.
52. Interview in *New York Sun*, May 14, 1899; clipping in GP, Box 31. Interview with Walter Camp, ca. 1910, CP, Lilly Library.
53. D. L. Spotts to W. J. Ghent, May 26, 1933, GP, box 31.
54. Spotts, *Campaigning with Custer*, p. 67.
55. Horace L. Moore, "The Nineteenth Kansas Cavalry," *Transactions of the Kansas State Historical Society, 1897–1900* (Topeka: W. F. Morgan, 1900), 6:41.
56. *New York Times*, February 14, 1869.
57. GAC to EBC, December 19, 1868, EBCC, reel 4.
58. Cited in Keim, *Sheridan's Troopers*, p. 103.
59. Sheridan to Brevet Major General W. A. Nichols, December 2, 1868, SP, reel 81.

60. Sheridan to W. A. Nichols, January 1, 1869, SP, reel 81.
61. *Executive Documents Printed by Order of the House of Representatives during the Second Session of the Forty-first Congress, 1869–'70*, 14 vols. (Washington, D.C.: Government Printing Office, 1870), 3:48.
62. Murphy to N. G. Taylor, December 4, 1868, cited in Brill, *Conquest of the Southern Plains*, p. 316.
63. Wynkoop to N. G. Taylor, January 26, 1869, cited ibid., p. 315.
64. George W. Manypenny, *Our Indian Wards* (Cincinnati: Robert Clarke, 1880), p. 247.
65. Custer's most recent and thorough biographers, Jay Monaghan and Robert Utley, both describe Custer's men finding damning evidence in the Indians' tepees, but neither cites a source. See *Custer*, p. 318; *Cavalier in Buckskin*, p. 69.
66. Citation of Sheridan's General Field Orders no. 6, November 29, 1868, *My Life*, pp. 266, 251.
67. Marvin E. Kroeker, *Great Plains Command: William B. Hazen in the Frontier West* (Norman: University of Oklahoma Press, 1976), p. 73.
68. Murphy to Taylor, December 4, 1868, cited in Brill, *Conquest of the Southern Plains*, p. 318.
69. House Exec. Doc. 1, 41st Cong., 2 sess.; 45, cited in Carriker, *Fort Supply*, p. 13; Manypenny, *Our Indian Wards*, p. 217.
70. Grierson to Asst. Adjutant General, Headquarters, Department of the Missouri, SP, reel 81.

CHAPTER 13: SAVE THE LAST BULLET FOR YOUR WIFE

1. *New York Tribune*, December 3, 1868.
2. EBC, *Tenting on the Plains*, pp. 628–29.
3. Edwin L. Sabin, *On the Plains with Custer* (Philadelphia: Lippincott, 1913), p. 140.
4. EBC, "*Boots and Saddles*," pp. 56–57.
5. Whitman, *The Troopers*, p. 148, writes that most officers wives "carried pocket derringers, and every last one of them had drilled into them the fact that if threatened with imminent capture by Indians they were to kill themselves. Children present were to be shot first."
6. Nellie Snyder Yost, *Buffalo Bill: His Family, Friends, Fame, Failures, and Fortunes* (Chicago: Swallow Press, 1979), p. 14.
7. Carrington, *Army Life*, pp. 153–54.
8. Biddle, *Reminiscences*, p. 160.
9. Summerhayes, *Vanished Arizona*, p. 123.
10. Fairfax Downey, *Indian-Fighting Army* (New York: Scribner's, 1941), p. 99. Cyrus Brady refers to captives as "poor women whose fate cannot be de-

scribed or dwelt upon." *Indian Fights and Fighters* (1904; reprint, Lincoln: University of Nebraska Press, 1971), p. 157. A captive belonged to the man who had captured her, who might keep her for his own use or prostitute her. Randolph B. Marcy, one of the earliest army officers to explore the southern plains, remarked that "the prairie Indians . . . invariably compel the females to submit to their lewd embraces." *Adventure on Red River: Report on the Exploration of the Headwaters of the Red River by Captain Randolph B. Marcy and Captain G. B. McClellan*, ed. Grant Foreman (Norman: University of Oklahoma Press, 1968), p. 169; see also, Lonnie White, "White Women Captives of Southern Plains Indians, 1866–1875," *Journal of the West* 8:3 (July 1969), 351.

11. GAC, *My Life*, pp. 61–62.
12. Lane, *I Married a Soldier*, pp. 73–74.
13. "Indian Barbarities—The Box Family," *Harper's Weekly* 10 (December 22, 1866): 806–7.
14. Ray Mattison, ed., "An Army Wife on the Upper Missouri: The Diary of Sarah E. Canfield, 1866–1868," *North Dakota History* 20 (October 1953): 217.
15. Mary Manley Parmalee, "A Child's Recollections of the Summer of '76," *Teepee Book* 1 (June 1915): 128.
16. EBC manuscript notes, EBCC, reel 5.
17. Spotts, *Campaigning with Custer*, p. 159. Anna Morgan was nineteen, in fact.
18. EBC, *Following the Guidon* (New York: Harper and Brothers, 1890), pp. 56–57.
19. Report of Operations of Troops operating South of the Arkansas, Brevet Major General George A. Custer, Commanding, from March 2d, 1869, to March 21st, 1869, SP, reel 81.
20. EBC, *Following the Guidon*, p. 60.
21. When the Kiowa chiefs Satanta and Big Tree were tried, the district attorney, S. W. T. Lanham, referred to their having "carried off our women into captivity worse than death." J. W. Wilbarger, *Indian Depredations in Texas* (Austin: Pemberton Press, 1967), p. 564.
22. Richard Irving Dodge, *The Plains of the Great West and Their Inhabitants* (New York: G. P. Putnam's Sons, 1877), p. 395. J. P. Dunn, *Massacres of the Mountains: A History of the Indian Wars of the Far West* (New York: Harper and Brothers, 1886), pp. 427–29, is clearly derivative of Dodge in his similar descriptions of this practice. He asserts that "no white woman has ever been known to escape this treatment at the hands of plains Indians" (p. 429).
23. Dodge, *Plains*, p. 398.
24. Richard Irving Dodge, *Our Wild Indians* (Hartford, Conn.: A. D. Worthington, 1883), p. 531.

25. Carl Coke Rister, *Border Captives: The Traffic in Prisoners by Southern Plains Indians, 1835–1875* (Norman: University of Oklahoma Press, 1940), p. 101. An entry in the Newberry Library catalog of Indian captivities makes the point tersely. *An authentic and thrilling narrative of the captivity of Mrs. Horn and her two children, with Mrs. Harris, by the Comanche Indians, and the murder of their husbands and travelling companions* (Cincinnati, 1853) is annotated with the following comment: "Both Mrs. Horn and Mrs. Harris died very shortly after their liberation, as also did Mrs. Rachel Plummer, another Texas victim of the Comanche Indians." *Narratives of Captivity among the Indians of North America* (Chicago: Newberry Library, 1912), p. 45.
26. Wilbarger, *Indian Depredations*, p. 3. Rena Maverick Green, ed. *Memoirs of Mary A. Maverick* (1921; reprint, Lincoln: University of Nebraska Press, 1989), p. 38, describes Matilda Lockhart in a similar fashion: "Her head, arms and face were full of bruises, and sores, and her nose actually burnt off to the bone—all the fleshy end gone, and a great scab formed on the end of the bone. Both nostrils were wide open and denuded of flesh. . . . She was very sad and broken hearted."
27. Fanny Kelly, *My Captivity among the Sioux Indians* (1871; reprint, Secaucus: Citadel Press, 1973), pp. 43–44. Some women did choose death. "The Sand Creek Massacre," *Report of the Secretary of War, Senate Executive Document No. 26, 39th Congress, 2d Session (1867)*, p. 44, reports that the mother of Isabel Ewbanks, "a child of four or five years old," tore her dress into strips and hanged herself in captivity.
28. Letter to Junction City (Kansas) *Weekly Union*, April 10, 1869.
29. Abigail Gardner-Sharp, *History of the Spirit Lake Massacre and Captivity of Miss Abbie Gardner*, facsimile of 1885 edition (Spirit Lake, Iowa: Dickinson County Historical Society, 1990), pp. 280–81. Ten years later she added an epilogue attributing her recovery of health to Christian Science.
30. Spotts, *Campaigning with Custer*, p. 210.
31. State of Kansas, *Applications for Admissions to State Hospitals*, vol. C (subseries II), January 7, 1899–February 19, 1905, records the date of her admission; an obituary in the *Delphos Republican*, July 18, 1902, gives her death as July 11, 1902.
32. EBC, *Following the Guidon*, p. 62.
33. Spotts's memoir of the 1868 campaign was published in 1928. In a letter of November 11, 1932, to General Godfrey's widow he enclosed more complete histories of the captive women. Unless otherwise indicated, further citations from their stories are taken from this document in GP, box 31.
34. Spotts to General Edward S. Godfrey, March 19, 1927, in GP, box 31; see Emily Haines Harrison, "Reminiscences of Early Days in Ottawa County," *Kansas Historical Collections* 10 (1907–8): 627–28, for a somewhat different version of Anna Morgan's story.

35. Spotts, *Campaigning with Custer*, p. 213.
36. Spotts to Godfrey, April 27, 1929, GP, box 31.
37. Spotts to Godfrey, October 9, 1931, ibid.
38. Rister, *Border Captives*, p. 157.
39. GAC, *My Life*, p. 290.
40. Wilbarger, *Indian Depredations*, p. 4.
41. Rister, *Border Captives*, p. 113.
42. Lee Heron, "Battle of Little Coon Creek," typescript, EBCC, reel 6.
43. Minnie Dubbs Millbrook, "The Jordan Massacre," *Kansas History* 2:4 (winter 1979); 219–30, tells the complete story of Mary Jordan and her family.
44. Kittie Dale, *Echoes and Etchings of Early Ellis* (N.p.: Big Mountain Press, 1964), p. 115.
45. Ibid.
46. Sheridan to Sherman, November 30, 1872, SP, box 8.
47. Davis, "A Summer on the Plains," p. 296.
48. GAC, *My Life*, p. 254.
49. LR, File 4805-AGO-1872 Office of the Adjutant General, *Records of the War Department*, National Archives.
50. Millbrook, "Jordan Massacre," p. 227.
51. Dale, *Echoes and Etchings*, pp. 117, 118.
52. Ibid., p. 117.
53. Letter of John D. Miles, Cheyenne and Arapaho Indian Agency, to Edward A. P. Smith, Commissioner of Indian Affairs, September 29, 1873, Records of Bureau of Indian Affairs, "Letters Received—Upper Arkansas Agency," H968-1873, RG No. 75, National Archives.
54. Dale, *Echoes and Etchings*, p. 99.
55. Cited by Donald J. D'Elia, "The Argument over Civilian or Military Indian Control, 1865–1880," *Historian*, 24:2 (February 1962), 219.
56. Sheridan to Sherman, March 18, 1870, SP, box 91.
57. Commissioner of Indian Affairs, *Annual Report*, 1866, p. 281.
58. Ibid.
59. MS filed with Lieutenant General Sherman's Annual Report, 1868, subcaptioned "Transmitting his Annual Report, together with the Reports of Subordinate Commanders."
60. Dunlay, *Wolves for the Blue Soldiers*, writes that "men of many Plains tribes are known to have raped captive women, probably as an expression of hatred and contempt" (202).
61. *Report of the Secretary of War {1869}* 1:47–48.
62. Letter of February 28, 1870, SP, Box 91.
63. Manypenny, *Our Indian Wars*, p. 247.
64. One of the articles in treaties made with the Kiowa, Comanche, Cheyenne, and Arapaho at Medicine Lodge Creek in 1867 specified that these tribes

"will never capture or carry off from the settlements white women or children." Charles J. Kappler, Treaty with the Kiowa and Comanche, 1867, and Treaty with the Cheyenne and Arapaho, 1867, *Indian Affairs, Laws and Treaties* 2:980, 988.

65. Commissioner of Indian Affairs, *Annual Report*, 1866, p. 218.
66. Cited in Wellman, *Death on Horseback*, p. 29.
67. Rister, *Border Captives*, p. vii.
68. Catherine M. Haun, "A Woman's Trip across the Plains, from Clinton, Iowa, to Sacramento, California, by Way of Salt Lake City (1849)," Huntington Library, San Marino, California, cited in Riley, *Women and Indians*, p. 99.
69. Cited ibid., p. 106.
70. EBC, *Tenting on the Plains*, p. 559.
71. GAC to EBC, April 20, 1867, ibid., p. 570. His contemporaneous description for the reading public of *Turf, Field and Farm* was more restrained: "Their remains were completely charred . . . [wolves] had removed much of the flesh, leaving but grim, unsightly skeletons." "On the Plains," December 15, 1867 (published January 4, 1868) in *Nomad*, p. 38.
72. EBC, *Following the Guidon*, p. 225.
73. Ibid., p. 222.
74. Ibid., pp. 223–24.
75. EBC, "*Boots and Saddles*," p. 133.
76. Ibid., p. 225.
77. Riley, *Women and Indians*, pp. 95ff.
78. Letter of April 5, 1867, cited in EBC, *Tenting on the Plains*, p. 536.
79. Joanna L. Stratton, *Pioneer Women: Voices from the Kansas Frontier* (New York: Simon and Schuster, 1981), p. 111.
80. Dale, *Echoes and Etchings*, p. 117.
81. Elizabeth Hampsten, *Read This Only to Yourself: The Private Writings of Midwestern Women, 1880–1910* (Bloomington: Indiana University Press, 1982), pp. 40–41.
82. Riley, *Women and Indians*. Riley refers to "tragic misunderstanding" in her explanation of the "horror stories" that were endemic in mid-nineteenth-century Texas (p. 156), but the conflict along the Texas frontier was not the result of misunderstanding: it was a consequence of the struggle of two different cultures over the land.
83. Letter of July 19, 1873, appendix, EBC, "*Boots and Saddles*, p. 233.
84 Walter Prescott Webb, *The Great Plains* (New York: Ginn and Company, 1931), p. 505.
85. The degree of women's independence on the frontier is the subject of controversy among historians today. As Lee Chambers-Schiller writes in *Liberty, a Better Husband* (New Haven: Yale University Press, 1984), p. 218n: "Much work has pictured women on the frontier as being the reluctant, sometimes

coerced, participants in a venture largely initiated by and for men." Julie Roy Jeffrey, *Frontier Women: The Trans-Mississippi West, 1840–1880* (New York: Hill and Wang, 1979), pp. xv–xvi, "hoped to find that pioneer women used the frontier as a means of liberating themselves from stereotypes and behaviors which I found constricting and sexist. I discovered that they did not." My own work tends to support this view.

CHAPTER 14: LIBBIE AND AUTIE

1. Miss [Sallie] Tallmadge, quoted by Frank Tallmadge, "Buffalo Hunting with Custer" *Cavalry Journal* 33 (1924): 10.
2. She told the *Detroit Free Press* on June 3, 1910, that "official jealousy is one of the terrible drawbacks to happiness in military life." Manuscript notes in her papers proclaim that "there is so much jealousy, rivalry, and implacable hatred among officers that they put each other in arrest for trifles to take out their spite or take revenge." EBCC, reel 4.
3. Charles W. Larned, Letter to his Mother, June 26, 1873, "Expedition to the Yellowstone River in 1873: Letters of a Young Cavalry Officer," ed. George Frederick Howe, in *The Custer Reader*, ed. Paul Andrew Hutton (Lincoln: University of Nebraska Press, 1992), p. 191.
4. Annie Roberts Yates, "General Custer's Home Life" 8 pp. typescript, EBCC, reel 6, p. 4. Annie married one of the Seventh's officers, George Yates, and became part of the Custer circle.
5. Ibid., pp. 2–3. Indeed, Libbie seemed to exemplify what Barbara Welter has called the "ideal woman of midcentury," characterized by four qualities: piety, purity, submissiveness, and domesticity." "The Cult of True Womanhood, 1820–1860," *American Quarterly*, 18:1 (spring 1966): 152.
6. Yates, "Custer's Home Life," p. 4; see also EBC, "*Boots and Saddles*," p. 193.
7. GAC to EBC, April 23, 1864, in Merington, *Custer Story*, p. 92.
8. Daniel Scott Smith, "Family Limitation, Sexual Control, and Domestic Feminism in Victorian America," in *Clio's Consciousness Raised: New Perspectives on the History of Women*, ed. Mary S. Hartman and Lois Banner (New York: Harper and Row, 1974), p. 120.
9. See Erna Olafson Hellerstein, Leslie Parker Hume, and Karen M. Offen, eds., *Victorian Women: A Documentary Account of Women's Lives in Nineteenth-Century England, France, and the United States* (Palo Alto, Calif.: Stanford University Press, 1981), p. 127: "Motherhood was central to the identities of most nineteenth-century women." See also Mary P. Ryan, *The Empire of the Mother: American Writing about Domesticity, 1830–1860* (New York: Haworth, 1982), p. 97: "The 1850s saw two icons—the isolated home and the imperial mother—installed at the center of popular discourse."

10. EBC to GAC, June 10, 1864, in Merington, *Custer Story*, p. 102.
11. EBC to GAC, October 30, 1864, cited in Frost, *General Custer's Libbie*, p. 121.
12. Merington, *Custer Story*, p. 102.
13. Charles Rosenberg, "Sexuality, Class and Role in Nineteenth Century America," *American Quarterly* 25:2 (May 1973): 146.
14. For James Marion Sims (1813–83) see James Reed, *The Birth Control Movement and American Society: From Private Vice to Public Virtue* (Princeton: Princeton University Press, 1984), pp. 28–29.
15. Ibid., p. 67.
16. Benteen to Theodore Goldin, letter of October 20, 1891, in *The Benteen-Goldin Letters on Custer and His Last Battle*, ed. John M. Carroll (New York: Liveright, 1974), p. 197.
17. Charles Meigs, *Females and Their Diseases* (Philadelphia: D. G. Brinton, 1879), p. 55, cited in Carroll Smith-Rosenberg, "Puberty to Menopause: The Cycle of Femininity in Nineteenth-Century America," in Hartman and Banner, *Clio's Consciousness Raised*, pp. 32–33.
18. Leckie, *The Colonel's Lady*, p. 134.
19. GAC to EBC, October 31, 1868, cited in Frost, *General Custer's Libbie*, p. 178.
20. It seems to have been a family custom to refer to the Reed children by their mother's maiden name.
21. GAC to EBC, October 28, 1868, cited in Frost, *General Custer's Libbie*, p. 177.
22. According to John Doerner, Park Service, Little Bighorn Battlefield National Monument.
23. Nineteenth-century women were typically involved in childbearing for the greater part of their adult life. Hellerstein, Hume, and Offen, *Victorian Women*, p. 454. Marcus Reno's biographers write of Libbie, "Having no child upon whom she might bestow part of her affection, she poured all of it on Autie." John Upton Terrell and Colonel George Walton, *Faint the Trumpet Sounds: The Life and Trial of Major Reno* (New York: David McKay, 1966), p. 102.
24. GAC to EBC, letter of July 19, 1873, appendix, *"Boots and Saddles,"* p. 234.
25. EBC, *Tenting on the Plains*, p. 255.
26. EBC, *"Boots and Saddles,"* p. 88.
27. Frost, *General Custer's Libbie*, p. 300; John M. Barry, *Evening Post*, May 28, 1910.
28. Katherine Gibson Fougera, *With Custer's Cavalry* (1940; reprint, Lincoln: University of Nebraska Press, 1986), p. 110.
29. EBC, *Tenting on the Plains*, p. 252.
30. GAC, "The Hunt on the Plains, November 8, 1869" (published November 19, 1869) in *Nomad*, p. 63; Don Schwarck discovered these plagiarisms. "Campaigning in Kansas with Maida and Blucher: General Custer's Staghounds," *Research Review: The Journal of the Little Big Horn Associates* 6:2 (June 1992): 15.

31. EBC, *Following the Guidon*, p. 10.
32. GAC to EBC, July 19, 1873, cited in EBC, "*Boots and Saddles*," p. 234.
33. Libbie tells Johnnie's story in *Tenting on the Plains*, pp. 477–83. Through Custer's recommendation Johnnie had obtained a position with the Wells-Fargo Express Company. Eventually, "in a courageous defense of the passengers and the company's gold, when the stage was attacked, he had been killed by the Indians" (p. 483). Her manuscript notes on the Civil War mention that someone asked Fought if General Custer had a son, and Fought responded: "No, I was all he had." EBCC, reel 5.
34. William Eleroy Curtis, *Chicago Inter-Ocean*, July 19, 1874.
35. Cited in Frost, *General Custer's Libbie*, p. 177.
36. Lystra, *Searching the Heart*, p. 79, notes that "purity was a central theme in Victorian public life, often applied . . . to women who were supposed by nature to be purer than men in body as well as mind. Purity was also regularly used in private correspondence to praise a woman's character, a relationship, or love itself." See also Mary P. Ryan, *Womanhood in America: From Colonial Times to the Present* (New York: New Viewpoints, 1975), p. 160, which describes nineteenth-century middle-class women as inundated "with the value of female purity." A popular nineteenth-century textbook, *The American Reader*, described women as "guardians of purity." Joseph Richardson, 2d ed. (Boston: Lincoln and Edmands, 1813), p. 23.
37. *The Tragedy of Othello, The Moor of Venice*, ed. George Lyman Kittredge (New York: Ginn and Company, 1941), p. 63: "I had rather be a toad / And live upon the vapour in a dungeon / Than keep a corner in a thing I love / For others' uses" (3.3.270–73).
38. GAC to EBC, July 1871 in Merington, *Custer Story*, p. 235.
39. GAC to EBC, October 28, 1868, cited in Frost, *General Custer's Libbie*, p. 177.
40. GAC, *My Life*, p. 282.
41. Custer also used two other women as go-betweens, the elderly Mahwissa, sister of the late chief Black Kettle, and a friend of Mahwissa's who is not named.
42. Rayna Green, "The Pocahontas Perplex: The Image of Indian Women in American Culture," *Massachusetts Review* 16 (1975): 703, remarks that "the only good Indian [of either sex] . . . rescues and helps white men."
43. GAC, *My Life*, pp. 366, 378.
44. Frederick Benteen to Theodore Goldin, February 17, 1896, in Carroll, *The Benteen-Goldin Letters*, p. 271. Benteen's annotations of Custer's book make a similar statement next to Monahseetah's name: "Custer took up with her from that time till summer of 1869, when, his wife coming to camp, the squaw had to get with other prisoners." *Custer: From the Civil War to the Little Big Horn*, ed. John M. Carroll (Bryan, Tex.: n.p., 1981), p. 14 (annotation of *Wild Life on the Plains* [1891], p. 228).

45. See Bighead, "She Watched Custer's Last Battle," p. 364; Marquis, *Custer on the Little Bighorn*, pp. 35, 43; Mari Sandoz, *Cheyenne Autumn* (New York: McGraw-Hill, 1953), xvii, passim; Brill, *Conquest of the Southern Plains*, pp. 22, 45–46; David Humphreys Miller, *Custer's Fall: The Indian Side of the Story* (New York: Duell, Sloan and Pearce, 1957), pp. 67–68. John Stands in Timber and Margot Liberty are an important exception: they regard the story of a liaison as merely a tale. *Cheyenne Memories*, p. 193n.
46. Interview with Ben Clark, c. 1910, CP, Lilly Library.
47. GAC to EBC, January 14, 1869, in EBC, *Following the Guidon* p. 49. Cheyenne tradition has credited Monahseetah with bearing Custer's child, but this event—if it occurred at all—could have taken place only in the fall of 1869. When Monahseetah gave birth in January, she had known Custer for less than two months. Monaghan, *Custer*, p. 328, has a useful reprise of the evidence for such a child.
48. EBC, *Following the Guidon*, p. 94.
49. Ibid., pp. 95–96.
50. Ibid., p. 96.
51. Bighead, "She Watched Custer's Last Battle," p. 364, says that Monahseetah waited for Custer to come back, but after his death married a white man named Isaac and had several children. Leslie Tillett, *Wind on the Buffalo Grass: The Indians' Own Account of the Battle at the Little Big Horn River, and the Death of Their Life on the Plains* (New York: Thomas Y. Crowell, 1976), p. 27, says that she died in January of 1921 in Oklahoma.
52. See S. Leckie, *Elizabeth Bacon Custer*, p. 117 and Utley, *Cavalier in Buckskin*, p. 107. As both writers comment, the Cheyenne oral tradition, made use of by such writers as Charles Brill, Thomas Marquis, and Mari Sandoz, among others, adopts the same view. Brown, *The Gentle Tamers*, p. 72, refers to this episode as Custer's "one serious extramarital adventure." I would rephrase this as Custer's one extramarital adventure for which we have significant sources.
53. GAC to EBC, BCWCC, cited in Leckie, *Elizabeth Bacon Custer*, p. 95.
54. In 1869 he had gone to Monroe to settle Judge Bacon's estate, but it is not clear why Libbie did not accompany him.
55. The letter consists of several fragments divided between two manuscript collections. Leckie, *Elizabeth Bacon Custer*, pp. 125–26 and 343 n. 46, recognized that these fragments belonged to one letter. Internal evidence indicates that the letter was written in December of 1870: in October of that year the Custers had gone to St. Louis, where they had stayed at the Southern Hotel. The letter mentions the trip as a recent occurrence. Custer left for the East in November, and he refers to his birthday having passed (December 5).

No one has ever disputed Custer's propensity to gamble, including Custer himself. Writing about this time, Benteen describes him as "a persistent bucker of Jayhawker Jenison's faro game." Benteen to Theodore Goldin, February 17, 1896, in Carroll, *Benteen-Goldin Letters*, 262. Faro is the one game mentioned by name in Custer's letter.

56. GAC to EBC, December 20, 1870, MMP.
57. Ibid., CMC.
58. CMC.
59. Fragment in MMP.
60. Considering Custer's notoriety, it is surprising that there are so few contemporary references to possible sexual misbehavior on his part. Another Seventh Cavalry wife, Jennie Barnitz, said that "we all talk very freely about other people." Cited in Edward M. Coffman, *The Old Army: A Portrait of the American Army in Peacetime, 1784–1898* (New York: Oxford University Press, 1986) p. 92. On the other hand, Sherry L. Smith, *The View from Officers' Row: Army Perceptions of Western Indians* (Tucson: University of Arizona Press, 1990), p. 78, asserts that "nineteenth-century officers were exceedingly discreet about all sexual liaisons"—which may explain the absence of documentary evidence.
61. Frederick Benteen to Theodore Goldin, February 17, 1896, *Benteen-Goldin Letters*, p. 262. Benteen seems to be writing about 1868 or shortly thereafter, dates consistent with the crisis in the Custer marriage.
62. Typescript of questionnaire completed by Libbie Bacon Custer, April 3, 1870, in Topeka, Kansas, in Monroe County Library, Monroe, Michigan. Custer also filled out the questionnaire, but his answers are clearly lighthearted; for example, he listed his "idea of misery" as being hungry and his "dream" as apple pie and cream.
63. Ibid.
64. Composition book dated 1891–92, p. 12, EBCC, no. 5671.
65. EBC to Rebecca Richmond, August 29 (1866), EBCC, no. 3560.
66. GAC to EBC, 20 December 1870, cited in Leckie, *Elizabeth Bacon Custer*, p. 127.
67. GAC to EBC, December 16, 1869, MMP.
68. EBC to GAC, n.d., EBCC, no. 3548. During the period Custer was stationed in Elizabethtown, 1871–73, Libbie was frequently alone.
69. Ibid. A suspicious person might wonder about the circumstances or demeanor that prompted women to take the initiative with Custer. Moreover, an incident in which Custer followed one such woman obviously portrays him in the role of pursuer, however he might describe the activity as "sport." See chap. 15, "The Great Buffalo Hunt," p. 212.
70. GAC to Mary Holland, January 1, 1859, CMC.

71. Letter of April 20, 1866, BCWCC, cited in Frost, *General Custer's Libbie*, p. 147.
72. EBC to William S. McCaskey, September 3, 1876, McCP.
73. EBC to Vinnie Ream Hoxie, January 2, 1882, VRP, box 2.
74. F. W. LaRouche, "Mrs. Custer Liked to Tell Stories of Civil War Days," Monroe *Evening News*, April 6, 1933.
75. Pohanka, "A Summer on the Plains," pp. 24, 26.
76. EBCC, reel 6.
77. EBC to Katie (Gibson), pencil draft, October 15 (n.d.), EBCC, no. 4862.
78. *The Journal of Elizabeth B. Custer for the Years 1892–93*, transcribed by Arlene Reynolds Killian (Hardin, Mont.: Magpie Traveling Players, 1992), p. 79.
79. Fragment of letter, GAC to EBC, MMP.
80. GAC to EBC, July 1873, in Merington, *Custer Story*, p. 259.
81. EBC to GAC, June 21 (1876), MMP.

CHAPTER 15: THE GREAT BUFFALO HUNT

1. EBC to Mrs. Calhoun (Margaret Custer), 1871, in Merington, *The Custer Story*, p. 241.
2. *The Grand Duke Alexis in the United States of America* (New York: Interland, 1972), pp. 102–4.
3. Quoted in Paine, *Pioneers, Indians and Buffaloes*, p. 158.
4. *The Grand Duke Alexis*, p. 151.
5. EBC manuscript notes on the Grand Duke's hunt, EBCC, reel 4. The following account of the hunt will be based on these notes unless otherwise indicated.
6. *The Grand Duke Alexis*, p. 159.
7. EBC to Rebecca Richmond, October 16 (1870), EBCC, reel 1.
8. Earl Pomeroy, *In Search of the Golden West: The Tourist in Western America* (New York: Alfred A. Knopf, 1957), p. 75.
9. Sheridan, *Personal Memoirs*, 2:485–86. Sheridan died before finishing his memoirs. The citations in this chapter come from the account of the hunt written by his brother, who completed the work.
10. January 6, 1872, cited in Paine, *Pioneers, Indians and Buffaloes*, p. 159.
11. Miguel Antonio Otero, *My Life on the Frontier, 1864–1882* (New York: Press of the Pioneers, 1935), p. 53.
12. Russell, p. 86, thinks that Cody's .50-caliber Springfield rifle was named after Victor Hugo's play *Lucretia Borgia*, which was popular at that time.
13. William McDonald interview in *North Platte Telegraph-Bulletin*, January 13, 1958, quoted in Yost, *Buffalo Bill*, p. 452 n. 8. The scrupulous Yost points out that the same menu is reproduced in Cody's posthumously published au-

tobiography of 1920 as the menu for Sheridan's New York hunting party of September 1871. There may be a confusion of remembering, as she suggests, both accounts being well after the fact, but it is also possible that the same sumptuous menu was served to both groups. Henry Eugene Davies, who was one of Sheridan's guests on the 1871 hunt, reproduced a dinner menu in his book *Ten Days on the Plains*, p. 53. His more detailed menu describes the fish as broiled Cisco and fried Dace, and includes sweet potatoes, mashed potatoes, and green peas, with tapioca pudding for dessert.

14. Sheridan, *Personal Memoirs* 2:490.
15. The Hunkpapa leader often warned his people about abandoning their way of life for a few material things. "If you set your hearts upon the goods of the white man," he supposedly said before the Battle of the Little Bighorn, "it will prove a curse to the nation." Vestal, *Sitting Bull*, p. 153.
16. Sheridan, *Personal Memoirs* 2:490.
17. Letter of April 15, 1911, EBCC, reel 3.
18. *Daily State Journal* of February 16, 1872, cited in Paine, *Pioneers, Indians and Buffaloes*, p. 176.
19. Sheridan, *Personal Memoirs* 2:491.
20. GAC to EBC, 1871, in Merington, *Custer Story*, p. 237.
21. Manuscript in EBCC, reel 4.
22. Ibid.
23. It may have had good buffalo hunting, but describing Kit Carson a few months before, in October 1871, the army wife Frances Roe said "the whole place is horrible, and dismal beyond description." *Army Letters*, p. 1.
24. Marshall Sprague, *A Gallery of Dudes* (Boston: Little, Brown, 1966), p. 114.
25. Ibid.
26. James Hadley, "A Royal Buffalo Hunt," pp. 572–73.
27. Ibid., p. 578.
28. Paine, p. 160.
29. Ibid.
30. Monaghan, *Custer*, p. 216.
31. Letter of March 25, 1877, MMP, Box 4.
32. Cody considered his Wild West to be an "exhibition." Don Russell, *The Wild West, or A History of the Wild West Shows* (Ft. Worth, Tex.: Amon Carter Museum, 1970), p. 5. In other words, like the royal hunt, it was a contrived performance that sought the stamp of authenticity.
33. EBC, *Tenting on the Plains*, p. 46.
34. J. W. Boddam-Whetham, *Western Wanderings: A Record of Travel in the Evening Land* (London: Richard Bentley and Son, 1874), p. 363
35. John Brinckerhoff Jackson, *American Space: The Centennial Years, 1865–1876* (New York: W. W. Norton, 1972), p. 167.

36. Cited in Dale, *Echoes and Etchings*, p. 222.
37. Ray Allen Billington, *Westward Expansion: A History of the American Frontier*, 4th ed. (New York: Macmillan, 1974), p. 579.
38. Frank B. Linderman, *Pretty-Shield: Medicine Woman of the Crows* (New York: John Day, 1972), p. 250.
39. Testimony of the Secretary of the Interior, January 10, 1874, U.S. House Committee on Military Affairs. *Report to Accompany the Bill (H.R. 2546) . . .*, House Report 384 (Washington, D.C.: Government Printing Office, 1874), p. 99.
40. Ibid., pp. 169, 171.
41. Robert M. Utley, *The Indian Frontier of the American West, 1846–1890* (Albuquerque: University of New Mexico Press, 1984), p. 227. The second quotation is cited by Utley from the *New York World*, April 26, 1891.
42. Chalkley M. Beeson, "A Royal Buffalo Hunt," *Transactions of the Kansas State Historical Society* 10 (1907–8): pp. 579–80.

CHAPTER 16: HEROES OF THE PLAINS

1. Mishkin, *Rank and Warfare*, p. 36; Bighead, "She Watched Custer's Last Battle," p. 377.
2. M. Helen Moss to EBC, July 30, 1912, EBCC, no. 2253.
3. [S. D. Bruce?], GAC, editorial note in *Turf, Field and Farm*, September 24, 1869, cited in GAC, *Nomad*, p. 52.
4. M. Helen Moss, EBCC, n. 2253.
5. Manuscript notes, EBCC, reel 4; Scott et al., *Archaeological Perspectives*, p. 250. Charles Varnum, Custer's chief of scouts on the Little Bighorn march, supposedly told a neighbor of his, T. M. Coughlin, that Custer was 5'10. Coughlin to Frederic Van De Water, letter of March 31, 1934, VP. John F. Finerty, who also knew Custer, described him as "almost six feet." *War-path and Bivouac, or The Conquest of the Sioux* (Chicago: Donohue and Henneberry, 1890), p. 425.
6. Sanford, *Fighting Rebels and Redskins*, p. 225.
7. GAC to EBC, December 14, 1869, BCWCC, cited in Frost, *General Custer's Libbie*, p. 186: "I have not been so *fleshy* for a long time. I weighed 143 last summer. I now weigh 164. Everybody says I look better than for years."
8. Kidd, *Personal Recollections of a Cavalryman*, p. 129.
9. R. H. McKay, *Little Pills: An Army Story* (Pittsburg, Kans.: Pittsburg Headlight, 1918), pp. 9–10.
10. EBC, *Tenting on the Plains*, pp. 398–99.
11. Thomas McLean Newson, *Thrilling Scenes among the Indians* (New York and Chicago: Butler Brothers, 1889), pp. 76–77. Fred Dustin, *The Custer*

Tragedy, p. 203, repeats Newsom's comments verbatim without benefit of citation.

12. Van De Water, *Glory-Hunter*, p. 129.
13. George Ward Nichols, "Wild Bill," *Harper's New Monthly Magazine* 34 (February 1867): 274, 277, 282.
14. Rosa, *They Called Him Wild Bill*, p. xi.
15. H. Stanley, *My Early Travels* 2:4. GAC, *My Life*, p. 44.
16. EBC, *Following the Guidon*, pp. 161, 162.
17. Theodore Davis, "Henry M. Stanley's Indian Campaign in 1867," *Westerners Brand Book, 1945–46* (1947): 105–6.
18. George Henry Kingsley, *Notes on Sport and Travel* (London: Macmillan, 1900), p. 134.
19. General Nelson Miles, Interview, *Washington Herald*, February 27, 1923, p. 6.
20. Yost, *Buffalo Bill*, p. 195.
21. Don Russell, *The Lives and Legends of Buffalo Bill* (Norman: University of Oklahoma Press, 1960), p. 432.
22. Colonel George Armes, *Ups and Downs of an Army Officer* (Washington, D.C.: n.p., 1900), p. 272.
23. Davies, *Ten Days on the Plains*, p. 25.
24. Ibid., p. 26.
25. Russell, *Lives and Legends*, p. 477.
26. EBCC, reel 5.
27. William F. Cody, *An Autobiography of Buffalo Bill* (New York: Cosmopolitan Book Corp., 1920), p. 100.
28. Milner and Forrest, *California Joe*, p. 246.
29. Letter of Andrew Platner to author, cited in Connelley, *Wild Bill*, p. 9.
30. Robert A. Kane, *Outdoor Life* (June 1906), cited in Connelley, *Wild Bill*, p. 9.
31. GAC, *My Life*, p. 44.
32. EBC, *Following the Guidon*, p. 146.
33. Charles Stewart Stobie Diary, 1902, cited in Russell, *Lives and Legends*, p. 430.
34. Beeson, "A Royal Buffalo Hunt," p. 576.
35. W. F. Cody, *Story of the Wild West and Campfire Chats* (Chicago: R. S. Peale, 1888), p. 595.
36. Letter of July 16, 1880, cited by John M. Carroll, "Cavalry Scraps: Letters on the Seventh Cavalry," in *Custer and His Times*, ed. Paul A. Hutton (El Paso: Little Big Horn Associates, 1981), p. 160. Custer had appointed Cooke leader of the sharpshooters' squad he established in the fall of 1868.
37. *The Passing of the Great West: Selected Papers of George Bird Grinnell*, ed. John F. Reiger (New York: Winchester Press, 1972), p. 99.
38. Coffman, *The Old Army*, pp. 278–79. Coffman remarks that there was no

target practice because soldiers were allotted so little ammunition that few of them were particularly good marksmen.

39. Edward S. Luce, "Diary and Letters of James M. DeWolf," p. 81.
40. Calhoun, *Some Observations*, p. 47.
41. Grinnell, *Two Great Scouts and Their Pawnee Battalion* (Cleveland: Arthur H. Company, 1928), pp. 241–42.
42. Reiger, ed., *Passing of the Great West*, p. 105.
43. Ewert, *Diary*, p. 59; the experienced hunter and scout Luther North confirmed that the bear was a grizzly. Danker, *Man of the Plains*, p. 187.
44. "That Missing Apology" (typescript), EBCC, reel 6.
45. James William Buel, *Heroes of the Plains* (Philadelphia: Historical Publishing Company, 1891), pp. 153–54.
46. Cited in Rosa, *They Called Him Wild Bill*, p. 183.
47. Cody considered his Wild West to be an "exhibition." Russell, *Wild West*, p. 5.
48. C. D. O'Kieffe, cited in Robert Phipps, "Nebraska Scene," *Omaha World-Herald Sunday Magazine* (March 19, 1950), p. 2C.
49. Russell, *Wild West*, p. 21.
50. Anonymous letter of June 1935, BP.
51. Marquis to EBC, December 23, 1929, EBCC, n. 3879.
52. Anne Chamberlin, "Bad Day Ahead for the Army's Greatest Loser," *Saturday Evening Post* 239:18 (August 27, 1966): 71.
53. The *Chicago Inter-Ocean*, August 17, 1876, describes McCall as cross-eyed, as does the letter of February 25, 1877, from his sister to the marshal of Yankton when McCall was awaiting execution there. Joseph G. Rosa, *Alias Jack McCall: A Pardon or Death?* (Kansas City, Mo.: Kansas City Posse of the Westerners, 1967), p. 26. Allison Hardy, *Wild Bill Hickok: King of the Gun-Fighters* (Girard, Kans.: Haldeman-Julius Publications, 1943), p. 21.
54. Edward L. Senn, *"Wild Bill" Hickok: "Prince of Pistoleers"* (Deadwood, S.D.: n.p., 1939), p. 14.
55. Hardy, *Wild Bill*, p. 21.
56. Hickok to Agnes Lake Hickok, July 17, 1876, cited in GAC, *Wild Life on the Plains and Horrors of Indian Warfare*, ed. Frederick Whittaker (St. Louis: Pease-Taylor Publishing Co., 1891), p. 433.
57. Jesse Brown and A. M. Willard, *The Black Hills Trails: A History of the Struggles of the Pioneers in the Winning of the Black Hills*, ed. John T. Milek (Rapid City, S.D.: Rapid City Journal Company, 1924), p. 410.
58. James B. Meriwether and Michael Millgate, eds., *Lion in the Garden: Interviews with William Faulkner* (Lincoln: University of Nebraska Press, 1980), p. 139.
59. Cited in Robert M. Snyder, Jr., "The Kansas City Days of 'Wild Bill,'" *Kansas City Star Magazine* 3:4 (August 15, 1926): 3–4.

CHAPTER 17: FARTHER WEST

1. EBC, *"Boots and Saddles,"* pp. 4–5.
2. Roger Darling, *Custer's Seventh Cavalry Comes to Dakota: New Discoveries Reveal Custer's Tribulations Enroute to the Yellowstone Expedition* (El Segundo, Calif.: Upton and Sons, 1989), p. 84. I am indebted to this admirable book, the only text to treat this period of Custer's life in meticulous detail.
3. April 19, 1873, Custer's Dakota Records, cited ibid., p. 87.
4. Custer's Dakota Records; W. W. Foster letter, April 23, 1873, cited ibid., p. 114.
5. Ibid., p. 114.
6. Ibid., pp. 183–84.
7. Charles W. Larned to Mary Hobbes Larned, April 19, 1873, in Larned, "Expedition to the Yellowstone River," p. 184.
8. Letter of April 30, 1873, ibid., p. 185.
9. Edgar I. Stewart, *Custer's Luck* (Norman: University of Oklahoma Press, 1955), p. 163. Stewart notes that Custer's Civil War record was superior to that of Sturgis, and that the two men did not get along, although other interpretations of their relationship are possible; see also, Burkey, *Custer, Come at Once!* p. 81. Burkey states that after his victory on the Washita, Custer had expected the promotion. Moreover, Sheridan had promised to push his cause.
10. Judson Elliott Walker, *Campaigns of General Custer in the North-West and the Final Surrender of Sitting Bull* (New York: Jenkins and Thomas, 1881), p. 42.
11. Darling, *Custer's Seventh*, p. 145n, suggests that Custer's retaining command indicates that Sturgis found nothing wrong.
12. S. E. Sturgis to GAC, July 10, 1875, EBCC, reel 2.
13. This is the suggestion of Darling, *Custer's Seventh*, p. 177.
14. Charles Larned to Mary Hobbes Larned, May 24, 1873, Larned Family Collection, cited in Darling, *Custer's Seventh*.
15. Darling, *Custer's Seventh*, p. 178, 144n.
16. Larned to Mary Hobbes Larned, "Expedition," p. 187.
17. Ibid., p. 185.
18. *Yankton Press*, May 7, 1873, cited in Darling, *Custer's Seventh*, p. 134.
19. Ibid., p. 173.
20. Charles King, "Esprit de Corps," in *The Army of the United States*, ed. Theodore F. Rodenbough and William L. Haskin (New York: Maynard, Merrill, 1896), p. xi.
21. John C. Ewers, "Intertribal Warfare as the Precursor of Indian-White Warfare on the Northern Great Plains," *Western Historical Quarterly* 6 (October 1975): 407, 399.

22. Meriwether Lewis, *Original Journals of the Lewis and Clark Expedition, 1804–1806*, ed. Reuben Gold Thwaites, 16 vols. (New York: Dodd, Mead, 1905) 6:98.
23. Jean Claude Allouez, "Father Allouez's Journey to Lake Superior, 1665–1667," in *Early Narratives of the Northwest, 1634–1699*, Louise Phelps Kellogg, ed. (New York: Charles Scribner's Sons, 1917), p. 132.
24. Ewers, "Intertribal Warfare," p. 407.
25. Richard White, "The Winning of the West: The Expansion of the Western Sioux in the Eighteenth and Nineteenth Centuries," *Journal of American History* 65 (September 1978): 321.
26. Frank B. Linderman, *Plenty-Coups: Chief of the Crows* (Lincoln: University of Nebraska Press, 1962), p. 154.
27. Henry A. Boller, *Among the Indians: Eight Years in the Far West, 1858–1866*, ed. Milo Milton Quaife (Chicago: R. R. Donnelley and Sons, 1959), p. 176.
28. White, "Winning of the West," p. 325.
29. Boller, *Among the Indians*, p. 176; *Chicago Inter-Ocean*, August 10, 1873. The Sioux were particularly singled out among the Plains tribes for physical beauty. Sandra L. Myres observes that travelers generally thought the Sioux "a handsome people, much more what they envisioned as a noble savage than the Pawnees or other tribes they had encountered." *Westering Women*, p. 55.
30. EBC, "*Boots and Saddles*," pp. 47, 46.
31. Charles Larned to Mary Hobbes Larned, June 11 and 17, 1873, cited in Darling, *Custer's Seventh*, p. 198.
32. Charles Larned to Mary Hobbes Larned, June 11, 1873, Larned Family Collection, cited in Darling, *Custer's Seventh*, p. 199.
33. EBC, "*Boots and Saddles*," p. 70.
34. George W. Kingsbury, *History of Dakota Territory: South Dakota, Its History and Its People*, ed. George Martin Smith (Chicago: S. J. Clarke Publishing Co., 1915), 1:880.
35. GAC, "Battling with the Sioux on the Yellowstone," in *The Custer Reader*, ed. Paul Andrew Hutton (Lincoln: University of Nebraska Press, 1992), p. 204.
36. Ibid., p. 204.
37. GAC to EBC, June 1873, in Merington, *Custer Story*, p. 252.
38. Entry of June 29, 1873, in Calhoun, *Some Observations*, p. 48n.
39. Calhoun, *Diary*, entry of July 6, ibid., p. 49n.
40. Lawrence A. Frost, *Custer's 7th Cavalry*, p. 26.
41. See Pomeroy, *In Search of the Golden West*. Pomeroy writes, p. 74: "The hunter-tourist seems to appear on every hand in the trans-Mississippi West. He is almost a regular fixture of the Western Army post . . . occasionally by special permission he follows a military expedition in the field."
42. It might not have been coincidental that Fred Calhoun was the brother of Custer's brother-in-law James Calhoun, an officer under Custer's command.

43. Special Order no. 19, cited in Frost, preface to Calhoun, *Some Observations*, p. 27.
44. Ibid., p. 28.
45. Ibid., p. 29.
46. Ibid., p. 30.
47. Ibid., p. 27.
48. General Custer's original letter book for the expedition, in Frost's personal collection, cited in Calhoun, *Some Observations*, p. 32.
49. D. S. Stanley, *Report on the Yellowstone Expedition of 1873* (Washington, D.C.: Government Printing Office, 1874), p. 5.
50. Ibid., p. 4.
51. Ibid., p. 7.
52. Ibid., p. 5.
53. Calhoun, *Some Observations*, p. 61.
54. Ibid., p. 68.
55. Custer's Report on the Yellowstone Expedition, August 15, 1873, in Calhoun, *Some Observations*, p. 123.
56. Ibid., pp. 68–69.
57. Review of "*Boots and Saddles*," *Christian Register* (Boston, May 1885), cited in Frost, *Custer's 7th Cavalry*, p. 86.
58. Calhoun, *Some Observations*, p. 76.
59. GAC, "Battling with the Sioux on the Yellowstone," p. 212.
60. Arthur R. Bingham to EBC, September 16, 1921, EBCC, no. 3110. Bingham was in the Pioneer Company of the Twenty-second Infantry. The sutler, August Baliran, whom Stanley had wanted to send back, was one of these men; the other was the expedition veterinarian, Joseph Honsinger. A young trooper was killed in a separate incident.
61. Frost, *Custer's 7th Cavalry*, p. 96.
62. Calhoun, *Some Observations*, p. 57.
63. W. A. Falconer, "Sketches of Bismarck's Early History," *North Dakota Good Roads Magazine* (1922): 22–24.
64. Rosa, *Wild Bill*, p. 137.
65. Falconer, "Sketches of Bismarck," p. 24.
66. Frost, *Custer's 7th Cavalry*, p. 118.
67. Grinnell, *Passing of the Great West*, p. 84. Grinnell (1849–1938), who became the great authority on the Cheyenne, was at the very beginning of his distinguished career in the 1870s. He accompanied Custer's expedition to the Black Hills in 1874 as a substitute for one of his Yale professors.
68. James Calhoun noted in his record of the Yellowstone expedition that "after each shot the distance would be measured and the record preserved." *Some Observations*, p. 47.
69. Danker, *Man of the Plains*, p. 185.

70. Letter of September 28, 1873, "*Boots and Saddles*," p. 258.
71. Another well-known Indian fighter and avid hunter, General George Crook, similarly took up taxidermy.
72. "*Boots and Saddles*," pp. 143–49; quotation, p. 149.
73. Ibid., p. 118.
74. Ibid.
75. G. Collins to EBC, n.d., EBCC, no. 3481.
76. Walker, *Campaigns of General Custer*, pp. 33, 36.

CHAPTER 18: PRELUDE

1. GAC to EBC, July 1873 in Merington, *Custer Story*, p. 254.
2. GAC to EBC, August 2 and 15, 1874, in EBC, *"Boots and Saddles,"* pp. 264, 265.
3. Cited in McPherson, *Ordeal by Fire*, p. 12.
4. Cited in Claude G. Bowers, *The Tragic Era: The Revolution after Lincoln* (Cambridge, Mass.: Houghton Mifflin, 1929), p. 415.
5. Cited in Dee Brown, *The Year of the Century: 1876* (New York: Charles Scribner's Sons, 1966), p. 199.
6. Bergamini, *Hundredth Year*, p. 334.
7. Letter of March 3, 1876, cited in Robert V. Bruce, *Alexander Graham Bell and the Conquest of Solitude* (Boston: Little, Brown, 1973), p. 175.
8. Some commentators have questioned Custer's account on the basis of a letter General J. W. Forsyth wrote to Belknap about the visit. Forsyth, who had been a member of the Belknap party, agreed that Custer had not met the secretary at the steamboat landing, but added that he had sent the excuse that he was ill. Forsyth could recall no lack of politeness in the ensuing brief visit. Custer had said that he refused to serve champagne furnished by the post trader for the secretary's visit; Forsyth says that no one expected wine because it was well known that Custer did not drink. There is no contradiction in these accounts: Custer had not said that he insulted Belknap in any direct manner. It should be noted, however, that in spite of Custer's status as a nondrinker, he was willing to serve wine to guests. For Forsyth's letter see Earl K. Brigham, "Custer's Meeting with Secretary of War Belknap at Fort Abraham Lincoln," *North Dakota History* 9:2 (August 1952): 130–31.
9. Clara Morris, cited in Bowers, *Tragic Era*, p. 257.
10. Ibid.
11. *Centennial Campaign: The Sioux War of 1876* (Ft. Collins, Colo.: Old Army Press, 1976), p. 62. If Hazen was indeed the source of Custer's subpoena, it was not the first time, nor would it be the last, that he played a role in Custer's life. Hazen was the lieutenant who apprehended Custer for not stop-

ping a fight at West Point, resulting in his court-martial there. Hazen was also the Cheyenne and Arapaho agent at Fort Cobb when Custer met the Indians on the Washita, and later they engaged in a heated dispute in print over the value of the northern plains for settlement.

12. *New York Times*, March 30, 1876.
13. Van De Water, *Glory-Hunter*, p. 279.
14. *The Management of the War Department: Report No. 799*, House Committee on Expenditures in the War Department, House of Representatives, 44th Cong., 1st Sess., 1875–76, 9 vols., ser. 1715 (Washington, D.C.: Government Printing Office, 1876), 7:155.
15. Ibid., p. 156.
16. Ibid.
17. Ibid., p. 154.
18. Ibid., p. 158.
19. Ibid., p. 155.
20. Ibid., p. 159.
21. See Edgar Stewart, ed., *Penny-an-Acre Empire* (Norman: University of Oklahoma Press, 1968), pp. 15–16: Hazen had appeared before the House Committee on Military Affairs in 1872 to testify on an entirely different subject. He had agreed to speak about the corrupt dealings of post traders only under the cloak of confidentiality. When his confidential testimony was leaked to the *New York Tribune*, he was transferred to Fort Buford.
22. William S. McFeely, *Grant: A Biography* (New York: W. W. Norton, 1981), p. 435, writes that Julia Grant sent notes to all the cabinet members and "in tears, pleaded with them in person to call on Mrs. Belknap."
23. Cited in Charles E. Merkel, Jr., *Unravelling the Custer Enigma* (Enterprise, Ala.: Merkel Press, 1977), p. 94.
24. May 6, 1876, cited in Monaghan, *Custer*, p. 368.
25. Davis, "With Generals in Their Camp Homes," p. 119.
26. GAC to Col. D. B. Sackett, Inspector General, U.S. Army, December 30, 1872, LS, Elizabethtown, Ky., National Archives.
27. Glendolin Damon Wagner, *Old Neutriment* (New York: Sol Lewis, 1973), pp. 92–93.
28. Emmanuel Custer to GAC, September 20, 1864, FC, box 1, folder 20.
29. Frost, *General Custer's Libbie*, p. 147.
30. Whittacker, *A Complete Life of Custer*, p. 477.
31. See S. Leckie, *Elizabeth Bacon Custer*, p. 128; Richard Slotkin, *Fatal Environment: The Myth of the Frontier in the Age of Industrialization, 1800–1890* (New York: Atheneum, 1985), p. 405; and Utley, *Cavalier in Buckskin*, p. 109.
32. Letter of March 5, 1871, Records of George Armstrong Custer, RG 94, National Archives.

33. Frost, *General Custer's Libbie*, p. 191.
34. GAC to EBC, April 8, 1871, BCWC Collection, cited in Frost, *General Custer's Libbie.*
35. Jarius Hall to GAC, September 23, 1872, EBCC, reel 2.
36. Hall to GAC, August 19, 1874, ibid.
37. Hall to GAC, April 1, 1875, ibid.
38. Hall to GAC, June 3, 1875, ibid.
39. See Frank Fossett, *Colorado: Its Gold and Silver Mines, Farms and Stock Ranges, and Health and Pleasure Resorts* (New York: C. G. Crawford, 1879), pp. 400–401; see also the Bureau of Mines Scrapbooks, vol. 10, p. 130, item 640 in the Manuscript Collection of the Colorado Historical Society.
40. *Justh v. Holliday* [*sic*], 7 May 1883, *1906 Decennial Edition of the American Digest: A Complete Table of American Cases from 1658 to 1906, G–L* (St. Paul, Minn.: West Publishing, 1912), 23:346–47. The note is part of the records of the Monroe County Probate Court, Monroe, Michigan.
41. "First Account of Libbie B. Custer, Executrix under Last Will and Testament of George A. Custer, deceased," Monroe County Probate Court, gives the value of Custer's assets as $2,915.75 and his liabilities as $13,291.06.
42. *Justh v. Holliday* [*sic*], pp. 355–56.
43. Ibid., p. 349.
44. Ibid., p. 355.
45. He is also a somewhat sinister figure of the Gilded Age, close to various scandals but never indicted. According to Ben Holladay's biographer, Holladay's son believed that Ingalls had poisoned Holladay's widow in order to gain complete control of the Holladay estate. Ellis Lucia, *The Saga of Ben Holladay: Giant of the Old West* (New York: Hastings House, 1959), pp. 350–51.
46. *Justh v. Holliday* [*sic*], p. 356.
47. Ibid., p. 358.
48. John Tipple, "The Robber Baron in the Gilded Age: Entrepreneur or Iconoclast?" in *The Gilded Age: A Reappraisal*, ed. H. Wayne Morgan (Syracuse, N.Y.: Syracuse University Press, 1963), p. 34.
49. John Steele Gordon, *The Scarlet Woman of Wall Street: Jay Gould, Jim Fisk, Cornelius Vanderbilt, the Erie Railway Wars, and the Birth of Wall Street* (New York: Weidenfeld and Nicolson, 1988), p. xviii.
50. H. L. Martin, *The New York Stock Exchange* (New York: n.p., 1919), p. 81, makes a useful distinction between gambling and speculation: "In gambling value passes from one party to the other but no value is passed back; the law of supply and demand has had no part in the transaction."
51. Cited in ibid., p. 129.
52. Ibid., p. 139.
53. Ingalls to GAC, letter of August 22, 1875, EBCC, no. 3093.

54. Richard Slotkin, "And Then the Mare Will Go!: An 1875 Black Hills Scheme by Custer, Holladay, and Buford," *The Journal of the West* 15:3 (July 1976): 73. By the time he reprised this material in his book, *The Fatal Environment*, pp. 421–24, Slotkin presented it in a far less tentative light. In the later text, instead of being merely "capable of" or "not adverse to," Custer is characterized as "angling to acquire . . . an Indian agency and to purchase . . . a post tradership." Moreover, he was "willing to countenance an attempt to defraud his own branch of the service" (p. 424). Yet between the publication of the article and the book, no additional evidence was offered for this conclusion.

    The Buford in the above title was Abraham Buford, a Kentucky civilian who Slotkin misidentified as the author of the letter to Custer. In 1995, in *Montana: The Magazine of Western History* 45 (spring 1995), 93, Slotkin finally admitted his mistake, but by then it had been repeated, along with the idea of Custer as an "unscrupulous wheeler-dealer," by James Welch in *Killing Custer: The Battle of the Little Bighorn and the Fate of the Plains Indians* (New York: W. W. Norton, 1994), pp. 215–17.

55. See Lucia, *Ben Holladay*, especially pp. 67–186, for Holladay's early career in first stagecoach routes and then steamboats.
56. By 1875 Holladay, once prosperous, had suffered irreversible losses. He never regained the fortune that he lost in the Panic of 1873. See *The Dictionary of American Biography*, 20 vols. (New York: Charles Scribner's Sons, 1929), 9:141–42.
57. Benteen's annotations of his copy of GAC, *Wild Life on the Plains* (1891 edition) in John M. Carroll, ed., *Custer: From the Civil War to the Little Big Horn* (Bryan, Tex.: privately printed, 1981), 10. See Utley, *Cavalier in Buckskin*, 153, for a summation of Benteen's charges against Custer.
58. Marie Cook Gorgas and Burton J. Hendrick, *William Crawford Gorgas: His Life and Work* (Philadelphia: Lea and Febiger, 1924), p. 56.
59. Slotkin, *The Fatal Environment*, p. 424.
60. GAC to Tom Custer, January 1876, in Merington, *Custer Story*, p. 277.
61. *The Sherman Letters: Correspondence between General and Senator Sherman from 1837 to 1891*, ed. Rachel Sherman Thorndike (New York: Charles Scribner's Sons, 1894), p. 321.
62. Letter of September 28, 1867, ibid., p. 296.
63. See Harry H. Anderson, "A Challenge to Brown's Sioux Indian Wars Thesis," *Montana* 12 (January 1962): 40–49, reprinted in *The Great Sioux War, 1876–77: The Best from "Montana, the Magazine of Western History,"* ed. Paul L. Hedren (Helena: Montana Historical Society Press, 1991): 39–52, for a good recapitulation of this argument.
64. Quoted by Herbert Krause and Gary D. Olson, eds., *Prelude to Glory: A Newspaper Accounting of Custer's 1874 Expedition to the Black Hills* (Sioux Falls, S.D.:

Brevet Press, 1974), p. 3; cf. Donald Jackson, *Custer's Gold: The United States Cavalry Expedition of 1874* (New Haven: Yale University Press, 1966), p. 120: "As carried out by Custer, the expedition was a treaty violation in spirit if not in fact."

65. Eugene V. McAndrews, ed., "An Army Engineer's Journal of Custer's Black Hills Expedition, July 2, 1874–August 23, 1874," *Journal of the West* 13:1 (January 1974): 84. See also, Sherman to Sheridan, September 26, 1872: "I think our interest is to favor the undertaking of the Road [the North Pacific railroad], as it will help to bring the Indian problem to a final solution." Sherman-Sheridan Correspondence, Vol. 1, SP.
66. Finerty, *War-path and Bivouac*, p. 41.
67. Entry of June 23, *With Custer in '74: James Calhoun's Diary of the Black Hills Expedition*, ed. Lawrence A. Frost (Provo, Utah: Brigham Young University Press, 1979), p. 10.
68. Walter P. Jenney, *The Mineral Wealth, Climate and Rain-Fall, and Natural Resources of the Black Hills of Dakota* (Washington, D.C.: Government Printing Office, Dept. of the Interior, Office of Indian Affairs, 1876), p. 56.
69. Doane Robinson, *History of the Dakota or Sioux Indians* (Aberdeen, S.D.: News Printing Company, 1904), p. 421.
70. Ambrose, *Crazy Horse and Custer*, p. 364n.
71. Charles Francis Bates, "The Red Man and the Black Hills," *Bronxville Review*, August 20, 1927, p. 16.
72. Cited in Tillett, *Wind on the Buffalo Grass*, p. 96.

CHAPTER 19: THE LITTLE BIGHORN

1. *House Executive Document No. 184,* cited in Taunton, *"Sufficient Reason?"* p. 15.
2. Sherman to Sheridan, February 21, 1877, SP, reel 17.
3. EBC, "*Boots and Saddles*," p. 218. Such mirages, as they were called, were not uncommon on the Plains.
4. EBC to GAC, June 21 (1876), MMP.
5. Letter of May 19, 1876, and letter of May 25, 1876, in Luce, "The Diary and Letters of Dr. James M. DeWolf," pp. 73, 75.
6. Cited in Gray, *Centennial Campaign*, p. 75.
7. LR, RG 393, Department of Dakota, 1868–1911, no. 3953, National Archives.
8. James H. Bradley, *The March of the Montana Column: A Prelude to the Custer Disaster*, ed. Edgar I. Stewart (Norman: University of Oklahoma Press, 1961), p. 101.

9. *With the Indian and the Buffalo in Montana, 1870–1878: Edward J. McClernand's Narrative, 1870–1878, and Journal (1876)* (Glendale, Calif.: Arthur H. Clark, 1969), p. 45.
10. Bradley, *Montana Column*, p. 105.
11. Ibid.
12. Holmes O. Paulding, letter to his mother, June 14, 1876, in Thomas R. Buecker, ed., "A Surgeon at the Little Big Horn: The Letters of Dr. Holmes O. Paulding," in *The Great Sioux War, 1876–1877*, ed. Paul L. Hedren (Helena: Montana Historical Society Press, 1991), p. 130.
13. Bradley, *Montana Column*, p. 126.
14. Barry C. Johnson, "Dr. Paulding and His Remarkable Diary: A Jaundiced Look at Gibbon's Montana Column of 1876," in *Sidelights of the Sioux Wars*, ed. Francis B. Taunton (London: English Westerners' Society, 1967), p. 57.
15. Bradley, *Montana Column*, p. 41.
16. Hein, *Memories of Long Ago*, pp. 91–92.
17. John Bourke, "General Crook in the Indian Country," *Century Magazine* 41 (March 1891): 652–53.
18. Whitman, *The Troopers*, p. 225, emphasis removed.
19. Oliver Knight, *Following the Indian Wars: The Story of the Newspaper Correspondents among the Indian Campaigners* (Norman: University of Oklahoma Press, 1960), p. 168.
20. Bourke, *On the Border with Crook*, p. 89.
21. Ibid., p. 109.
22. It also fits other well-known Indian fighters such as Eugene Carr, Nelson Miles, and Ranald Mackenzie. To succeed on the frontier required these qualities.
23. Finerty, *War-path and Bivouac*, p. 26.
24. Stewart, *Custer's Luck*, p. 196.
25. H. R. Lemly, "The Fight on the Rosebud," in *The Papers of the Order of Indian Wars*, ed. John M. Carroll (Ft. Collins, Colo.: Old Army Press, 1975), p. 14.
26. A. Mills, *My Story*, p. 405.
27. Cited in J. W. Vaughn, *With Crook at the Rosebud* (Lincoln: University of Nebraska Press, 1956), p. 51.
28. A. Mills, *My Story*, p. 406.
29. Finerty, *War-path and Bivouac*, p. 135.
30. Charles King, "Custer's Last Battle," *Harper's* 81 (August 1890): 381.
31. A. Mills, *My Story*, p. 408.
32. Cited in Grace Raymond Hebard, *Washakie* (Cleveland: Arthur H. Clark, 1930), p. 197. According to Hebard, p. 189, on June 17 Washakie "was a close riding companion" of Crook for the entire day.

33. Cited in Vaughn, *With Crook at the Rosebud*, p. 162. The fierce Apache were scarcely "indolent," but some explanation was needed for Crook's success in one arena and failure in another.
34. Letter of February 17, 1877, SP, reel 17.
35. Luce, *Diary and Letters of DeWolf*, letter of April 3, 1876, p. 51.
36. *The Terry Letters: The Letters of General Alfred Howe Terry to His Sisters during the Indian War of 1876*, ed. James Willert (La Miranda, Calif.: James Willert, 1980), p. 8.
37. *The Field Diary of General Alfred H. Terry: The Yellowstone Expedition, 1876* (Bellevue, Nebr.: Old Army Press, 1969), p. 3.
38. Roger Darling, *A Sad and Terrible Blunder: Generals Terry and Custer at the Little Big Horn. New Discoveries* (Vienna, Va.: Potomac-Western Press, 1990), p. 20.
39. William Falconer, "Early Notes and Comments," typescript, January 16, 1934, p. 8, VP.
40. *Terry Letters*, p. 3.
41. Sheridan to Terry, May 16, 1876, SP, box 58.
42. *Terry Letters*, p. 9.
43. Luce, *Diary and Letters of DeWolf*, letter of June 21, 1876, p. 81.
44. James Willert, *Little Big Horn Diary: Chronicle of the 1876 Indian War* (La Miranda, Calif.: James Willert, 1977), p. xxi.
45. GAC to EBC, May 30, 1876, cited in EBC, "*Boots and Saddles*," p. 268.
46. Gray, *Centennial Campaign*, p. 137. Elsewhere, Gray conjectures that Reno departed from the precise route of Terry's instructions "because Mitch Boyer told him about the big village seen on the Rosebud." *Custer's Last Campaign: Mitch Boyer and the Little Bighorn Reconstructed* (Lincoln: University of Nebraska Press, 1991), p. 189.
47. *Terry Field Diary*, p. 7.
48. A letter of June 21, 1876, that Terry wrote to his family is now missing. Hughes quoted from it as follows: "To my great surprise I received a note from Colonel Reno which informed me that he had flagrantly disobeyed my orders, and he had been on the Rosebud, [in] the belief that there were Indians on that stream and that he could make a successful attack on them which would cover up his disobedience. . . . He had not the supplies to go far and he returned without justification for his conduct unless wearied horses and broken down mules would be that justification. Of course, this performance made a change in my plans necessary." *Terry Letters*, p. 47. This account omits the salient fact that the plans were changed for the better.

    Charles G. duBois, *Kick the Dead Lion: A Casebook of the Custer Battle* (El Segundo, Calif.: Upton and Sons, 1987), p. 101n, describes another suspicious instance concerning the orders Terry gave to Custer: "Shortly after the battle someone close to General Terry, probably a member of his staff, changed these words [sufficient reason] to read, *'absolute necessity,'* in an effort to strengthen the case against General Custer. Fortunately . . . the original copy written by General Terry was located in a warehouse at Fort Snelling, Minnesota, which proved that the phrase, 'sufficient reason,' was the correct version. . . . It is not known which of Terry's officers were guilty of this forgery, but Col. Hughes, who had both motive (as Terry's brother-in-law) and opportunity (as aide de camp), ranks high on the list of suspects."

49. *Report of the Secretary of War, Executive Documents 1, Part 2*, 45th Cong., 2d sess. (Washington, D.C.: Government Printing Office, 1878), 1:465.
50. Ibid.
51. *General Custer and the Battle of the Little Big Horn*, p. 15.
52. Evan S. Connell, *Son of the Morning Star: Custer and the Little Bighorn* (New York: Harper and Row, 1984), 258.
53. Cited in Darling, *Sad and Terrible Blunder*, p. 74.
54. Bradley, *Montana Column*, p. 143.
55. Charles Varnum in an interview with Charles Bates, *I Varnum: The Autobiographical Reminiscences of Custer's Chief of Scouts*, ed. John M. Carroll (Glendale, Calif.: Arthur H. Clark, 1982), pp. 22–23.
56. "Our Last Camp on the Rosebud," manuscript, EBCC, reel 6.
57. Varnum to Camp, April 14, 1909, cited in *Custer in '76: Walter Camp's Notes on the Custer Fight*, ed. Kenneth Hammer (Provo, Utah: Brigham Young University Press, 1976), pp. 60–61.
58. Letter, *Winners of the West* 4:4 (January 30, 1926): 2.
59. *New York Tribune*, July 23, 1876, cited in W. A. Graham, *The Custer Myth: A Source Book of Custeriana* (Harrisburg, Penn.: Stackpole, 1953), p. 237.
60. *Report of the Secretary of War* 1:479. Roger Darling, *Benteen's Scout-to-the-Left: The Route from the Divide to the Morass (June 25, 1876)* (El Segundo, Calif.: Upton and Sons, 1987), is the best source of information on this part of the battle. Darling comments, tellingly, that Benteen never sent the expected message to Custer: "Benteen's later denigration of the scout as a wild goose chase was an effort to minimize his failure to send information back to Custer, to make it seem unimportant" (p. 32).
61. Charles Windolph, "The Battle of the Big Horn," *Sunshine Magazine* 11 (September 1930): 8.
62. Frederick Benteen, typescript of "An Account of the Little Big Horn Campaign," GP, box 26.
63. Reno's Report, July 5, 1876, *Report of the Secretary of War* 1:32.
64. *The Official Record of a Court of Inquiry*, 2 vols. (Pacific Palisades, Calif.: W. A. Graham, 1951) 1:520.
65. Ibid., 2:34.
66. Ibid.
67. Darling, *A Sad and Terrible Blunder*, p. 209. Emphasis removed.

68. *Court of Inquiry* 1:163.
69. Ibid., 1:243.
70. duBois, *Kick the Dead Lion*, p. 14.
71. *Court of Inquiry* 2:522.
72. "Sergeant Martin's Story," in Graham, *Custer Myth*, p. 291.
73. This message, written by Adjutant William Cooke at Custer's direction, is now in the museum of the United States Military Academy at West Point.
74. *Court of Inquiry* 2:380.
75. Camp, *Custer in '76*, p. 101; see John M. Carroll and Robert Aldrich, "Some Custer and Little Big Horn Facts to Ponder" for a discussion of *skedaddle. English Westerners Society Talley Sheet* 40:3 (summer 1994): 112.
76. Praise for Benteen was universal. George Herendeen said that "in desperate fighting Benteen is one of the bravest men I ever saw." Graham, *Custer Myth*, p. 259. French was characterized by, among others, Private William C. Slaper, in the account he gave E. A. Brininstool in 1920, in *Troopers with Custer* (Harrisburg, Penn.: Stackpole, 1952), p. 53.
77. Unpublished essay, p. 14, GP, box 26.
78. Edgerly typescript, p. 9, EBCC, reel 6.
79. Godfrey to John G. Neihardt, letter of January 6, 1924, typescript in HC.
80. Reno's Report 1:33.
81. Typescript, GP, box 22.
82. *Court of Inquiry* 1:123, 136, 2:393.
83. Edgerly interview in Camp, *Custer in '76*, p. 56.
84. Kanipe interview, ibid., pp. 92–93.
85. Martin's interview, ibid., p. 100.
86. Ibid., p. 101.
87. Some Indian accounts maintain that the command did reach the river; archaeological evidence is not clear on this point. The fact that footprints from many shod horses were found in the vicinity means nothing since the Indians captured a number of cavalry mounts. No army artifacts or bodies of dead cavalry horses were found at the river. See Richard Allan Fox, Jr., *Archaeology, History, and Custer's Last Battle: The Little Big Horn Reexamined* (Norman: University of Oklahoma Press, 1993), p. 139.
88. Scott and Fox, *Archaeological Insights*, pp. 112–13.
89. Cited in Robertson, *Michigan in the War*, p. 583.
90. Ibid., p. 124. See also Fox, *Archaeology*, pp. 135–221 and passim.
91. GAC, "Battling with the Sioux on the Yellowstone," p. 218.
92. GAC to Judge Kidder, letter of August 23, 1867, cited in Rosenberg, *Custer and the Epic of Defeat*, p. 233.
93. James McLaughlin, *My Friend the Indian* (Boston: Houghton Mifflin, 1910), p. 123.

94. Lowie, *Indians of the Plains*, p. 105.
95. Vestal, *Sitting Bull*, p. 179.
96. McClernand, "The Fight on Custer Hill," *Cavalry Journal* (January 1927): 40, 38.
97. Scott and Fox, *Archaeological Insights*, p. 45. At the same time, there is also evidence of disintegration and rout. See Fox, *Archaeology*, pp. 135–221, passim.
98. A good discussion of this possibility is found in Taunton, *"Sufficient Reason?"* p. 79. Taunton asserts that "there can be little doubt that his [Custer's] army career would have ended."
99. Letter of July 2, 1876, ESGP.
100. Cited in Carroll, "Cavalry Scraps," pp. 167–68.
101. Cited in Robert M. Utley, *Custer and the Great Controversy: The Origin and Development of a Legend* (Los Angeles: Westernlore Press, 1962), pp. 63–64.
102. E. S. Godfrey, *An Account of Custer's Last Campaign and the Battle of the Little Big Horn* (Palo Alto, Calif.: Lewis Osborne, 1968), p. 33. Reprint of article in *Century Magazine* (January 1892).
103. Letter of July 25, 1876, *Helena Herald.*
104. EBCC, Reel 6.
105. Report of July 4, 1864, in Jno. Robertson, *Michigan in the War*, p. 596.
106. W. A. Graham, *The Story of the Little Big Horn* (New York: Century Company, 1926), p. 96.
107. Captain Theodore Allen, cited in John P. Langellier, Kurt Hamilton Cox, and Brian C. Pohanka, eds., *Myles Keogh* (El Segundo, Calif.: Upton and Sons, 1991), p. 79; Keogh to Tom Keogh, letter of June 1, 1869, cited in Francis B. Taunton, "The Man Who Rode Comanche," in *Sidelights of the Sioux Wars* (London: English Westerners' Society, 1967), p. 76.
108. Taunton, "The Man Who Rode Comanche," p. 77.
109. Hyde, *Life of George Bent*, p. 325.
110. Mills, *My Story*, p. 410.
111. Cited by Gray, *Centennial Campaign*, p. 198.
112. "Report of the General of the Army," *Report of the Secretary of War, Executive Documents 1, Part 2*, 44th Cong. 2d sess. (Washington, D.C.: Government Printing Office, 1876), 1:27.
113. Ibid., p. 29.
114. Homer W. Wheeler, *Buffalo Days: Forty Years in the Old West*, 2d ed., rev. (Indianapolis: Bobbs-Merrill, 1925), p. 172; W. J. Ghent typescript of Godfrey's notes on *Buffalo Days*, p. 2, GFP, box 16.
115. Copy of Charles Francis Roe, *Custer's Last Battle* (New York: Robert Bruce, 1927), p. 8, in GFP.
116. Knight, *Following the Indian Wars*, p. 162.
117. Charles Edmund Deland, "The Sioux Wars," vol. 15 of *South Dakota Historical Collections* (Pierre, S.D.: Hipple Printing Company, 1930), p. 430.

118. Hughes stated that Ludlow had written to Terry after the Sioux expedition ended. However, neither the Terry Papers at Yale nor the records of the Department of the Dakota, RG 393, contain such a letter.
119. Cited in M. V. Sheridan, *Personal Memoirs*, 1:169–70.
120. Stan Hoig, *The Battle of the Washita: The Sheridan-Custer Indian Campaign of 1867–1869* (Garden City, N.Y.: Doubleday, 1976), pp. 123–24.
121. Col. T. M. Coughlin, "The Battle of the Little Big Horn: A Tactical Study," *Cavalry Journal* (January–February 1934): 19.
122. Jay Smith, "What Did Not Happen at the Battle of the Little Big Horn," *Research Review* 6:2 (June 1992): 13.
123. Roger Darling, *General Custer's Final Hours: Correcting a Century of Misconceived History* (Vienna, Va.: Potomac-Western Press, 1992), pp. 9–14, has brought the distinction between the two villages to light.
124. Camp, *Custer in '76*, p. 53.
125. Jay Smith, "A Hundred Years Later," *Custer and His Times*, ed. Paul Andrew Hutton (El Paso, Tex.: Little Bighorn Associates, 1981), p. 104. Smith uses a ratio of 18 to 1 for the Custer fight, but this seems too high in light of recent information about the number of Indians present.
126. DeLand, *Sioux Wars*, p. 322, observes: "This theory—of keeping the Indians from running away—is everywhere seen to have been in mind all through this campaign."
127. George Bird Grinnell, *The Fighting Cheyennes* (Norman: University of Oklahoma Press, 1956), p. 356.
128. *Biographical Annals of Lancaster County, Pennsylvania* [McCaskey's birthplace] (Chicago: J. H. Beers, 1903), p. 124, reports: "We have heard him say that the hardest thing he has ever had to do was to tell Mrs. Custer and the ladies of the post the awful news of the disaster."
129. See Frost, *General Custer's Libbie*, p. 227: "Libbie, shivering in the sweltering, humid air, sent for a wrap."
130. MMP, box 3.
131. A letter sent from Fort Lincoln and reprinted in the *Army and Navy Journal* (July 29, 1876) says that there were twenty-four widows and "twice that number of children." This may be an approximation: when names are specified, the total is thirty-two. See Edgar I. Stewart, "The Custer Battle and Widow's Weeds," *Montana* 22 (1972): 52–59.
132. Parmelee, "A Child's Recollections," 128–29.
133. Joseph Mills Hanson, *The Conquest of the Missouri: Being the Story of the Life and Exploits of Captain Grant Marsh* (Chicago: A. C. McClurg, 1916), p. 314.
134. Cited in Virginia Weisel Johnson, *The Unregimented General: A Biography of Nelson A. Miles* (Boston: Houghton Mifflin, 1962), p. 87.
135. Letter of July 27, 1876, GP, box 36.

136. EBC, *Following the Guidon*, p. 291.
137. Parmelee, "A Child's Recollections," p. 129.
138. EBCC, reel 3.

CHAPTER 20: SURVIVORS

1. Out of the total, which includes 6 packers, the newspaperman Mark Kellogg, and the civilians Autie Reed and Boston Custer—as well as scouts and interpreters—210 were killed at the Last Stand and 53 elsewhere. Appendix B in John Gray, *Custer's Last Campaign*, pp. 406–7.
2. Letter of July 8 in *St. Paul and Minneapolis Pioneer-Press and Tribune*, reprinted in the *New York Herald*, July 11, 1876.
3. Clipping in FC, box 1, folder 2. John M. Carroll, *They Rode with Custer: A Biographical Directory of the Men that Rode with General George A. Custer*, rev. ed. (Mattituck N.Y.: John M. Carroll, 1993), p. 113, says that Harrington's wife was "found in a small town in Texas suffering from amnesia and pneumonia" after being missing for two years.
4. *Detroit Evening Journal*, December 2, 1887. Reno's testimony before the court of inquiry simply indicated that Harrington was missing and believed dead. Moreover, even with field glasses Reno probably could not have seen as far as the village, and although the Indians were noisily celebrating their victory, they always denied having taken or tortured any of the soldiers.
5. Hugh Lenox Scott, *Some Memories of a Soldier* (New York: Century Company, 1928), p. 29.
6. *Official Record of a Court of Inquiry* 1:iii–iv.
7. *New York Herald*, August 21, 1876.
8. *Personal Recollections and Observations of General Nelson A. Miles* (New York: DaCapo Press, 1969), p. 290.
9. Camp, *Custer in '76*, p. 238.
10. Ibid., p. 239.
11. Jesse M. Lee to EBC, letter of June 27, 1897, EBCC, reel 3.
12. *Official Record* 2:356.
13. Ibid. 1:256.
14. Ibid. 2:492.
15. Ibid. 1:300, 206.
16. Ibid. 2:497.
17. Others who were not there who agreed with Gibbon were Benteen, James S. Brisbin (commanding the Second Cavalry unit in the Gibbon-Terry army), and Nelson Miles, who was part of the reinforcement brought to the campaign against the Sioux after the Battle of the Little Bighorn.

18. An especially thorough analysis of Gibbon's part in the Sioux campaign can be found in John S. Gray, "Bradley Finds and Gibbon Loses the Sioux," in *Custer's Last Campaign*, pp. 150–63.
19. Marcus A. Reno (R314 CB 1865), reel 3, National Archives.
20. Ibid.
21. The account that follows is taken from the original transcript of the court-martial, CM QQ87, box 1839A, National Archives.
22. Captain Benteen described her flatly as a "nymphomaniac." Benteen to Theodore Goldin, letter of March 19, 1896, John M. Carroll, ed., *The Benteen-Goldin Letters on Custer and His Last Battle* (New York: Liveright, 1974), p. 290. Elsewhere he wrote, "Is it within the bounds of possibilities that 'Maj. B.' could or did not scent out the musky mis-steps of Madam? I, for one have my doubts on it! The affairs—from Dame Rumor's accts. have been too oft." Benteen to Goldin, March 10, 1896, p. 285.
23. Letter of May 17, 1877, in John M. Carroll, *Camp Talk: The Very Private Letters of Frederick W. Benteen of the 7th U.S. Cavalry to His Wife, 1871 to 1888* (Mattituck, N.Y., and Bryan, Tex.: J. M. Carroll, 1983), p. 64. "Scrouging" is an archaic word for "squeezing."
24. Letter of May 15, 1878, to President Hayes, Reno ACP File.
25. The account that follows is taken from the transcript of the General Court Martial Proceedings in the case of Major Marcus A. Reno, November 24–December 8, 1879, CM-QQ-1554, National Archives.
26. John Upton Terrell and Colonel George Walton, *Faint the Trumpet Sounds: The Life and Trial of Major Reno* (New York: David McKay, 1966), p. 299.
27. Unknown correspondent to E. D. Townsend, August 19, 1869, reel 3, NA.
28. *The Diary of Cyrus B. Comstock*, ed. Merlin E. Sumner (Dayton, Ohio: Morningside House, 1987), p. 183.
29. Frazier Hunt and Robert Hunt, *I Fought with Custer: The Story of Sergeant Windolph, Last Survivor of the Battle of the Little Big Horn* (New York: Charles Scribner's Sons, 1953), p. 50.
30. Luce, "Diary and Letters of Dr. James M. DeWolf," p. 72.
31. Garlington to Frederic Van De Water, letter of January 16, 1934, VP.
32. Scott, *Some Memories*, p. 29.
33. *The Field Diary of Edward Settle Godfrey*, ed. Edgar I. Stewart and Jane R. Stewart (Portland, Ore.: Champoeg Press, 1957), p. 37.
34. See Brininstool, *Troopers with Custer;* Dustin, *Custer Tragedy*; Van De Water, *Glory-Hunter*.
35. Department of the Army, Army Board for Correction of Military Records, Case of Marcus A. Reno, 3 May 1967, p. 75.
36. Ibid.

37. Brian Pohanka, "In Hospital at West Point: Medical Records of Cadets Who Later Served with the Seventh Cavalry," *Little Big Horn Associates Newsletter* 23:6 (July 1989): 5–7.
38. James B. Wyngaarden and Lloyd H. Smith, Jr., *Cecil Textbook of Medicine* (Philadelphia: W. B. Saunders, 1985) 2:1656, cited in Pohanka, "In Hospital," p. 6.
39. Death certificate, Vital Records no. 65938, cited in Pohanka, "In Hospital," p. 6.
40. T. M. Coughlin, interview with Charles Varnum, November 27, 1933, VP, reports that Varnum never heard Custer say anything against Reno or vice versa.
41. Lieutenant Richard E. Thompson, Camp, *Custer in '76*, p. 235.
42. Annotation on p. 108, Carroll, *Custer*, p. 7.
43. See discussion in chapter 12, pp. 160–63.
44. Annotation of p. 187, in Carroll, *Custer*, p. 11.
45. Annotation of p. 153, ibid., p. 10.
46. Annotation of picture, p. 28, ibid., p. 4. All of these accusations were made in the 1890s, long after the fact. Karol Asay, *Gray Head and Long Hair: The Benteen-Custer Relationship* (New York: Mad Printers of Mattituck, 1983), pp. 32–33, believes that Benteen changed significantly at that time, becoming more extreme in his feelings against Custer.
47. Cyrus Townsend Brady, *Indian Fights and Fighters: The Soldier and the Sioux* (Lincoln: University of Nebraska Press, 1971), p. 404.
48. Graham, *The Custer Myth,* p. 247.
49. Scott, *Some Memories*, p. 454.
50. Benteen, Frederick William, Official Court-Martial Transcript, 1887, Old Army Branch RR 2327, NA, cited in Charles K. Mills, *Harvest of Barren Regrets: The Army Career of Frederick William Benteen, 1834–1898* (Glendale, Calif.: Arthur H. Clark, 1985), p. 351.
51. Hunt and Hunt, *I Fought with Custer*, pp. 2–3.
52. John M. Carroll, ed., *The Court Martial of Frederick W. Benteen, Major 9th Cavalry, or Did General Crook Railroad Benteen?* (Bryan, Tex.: privately printed, 1981), p. 100.
53. W. T. Sherman, *Memoirs of General W. T. Sherman, Written by Himself*, 4th ed., rev., 2 vols. (New York: Charles L. Webster, 1891), 2:414.
54. General P. H. Sheridan, *Record of Engagements with Hostile Indians within the Military Division of the Missouri, from 1868 to 1882* (Chicago: Military Division of the Missouri, 1882), p. 119.
55. *The Annual Report of the Board of Indian Commissioners for the Year 1879* (Washington, D.C.: Government Printing Office, 1880), p. 12.
56. Brown, *Bury My Heart at Wounded Knee*, p. 298, says that the commission to buy the Black Hills included several members who were "old hands at stealing Indian lands."

57. *Annual Report of the Commissioner of Indians Affairs, 1875*, pp. 184–85.
58. Major D. H. Brotherton, who accepted the surrender, described the condition of Sitting Bull's band as "starving" in a communiqué sent to General Terry, July 14, 1881, in Walker, *Campaigns of General Custer in the North-West*, p. 74.
59. Cited in Robert M. Utley, *The Lance and the Shield: The Life and Times of Sitting Bull* (New York: Henry Holt, 1993), p. 232.
60. I have taken the particulars of Sitting Bull's death from Utley, *Lance and Shield*, pp. 291–307.
61. Loring Benson Priest, *Uncle Sam's Stepchildren: The Reformation of United States Indian Policy, 1865–1887* (New Brunswick, N.J.: Rutgers University Press, 1942), pp. 64–65.
62. Commissioner of Indian Affairs, 1889, in Paul Francis Prucha, ed., *Americanizing the American Indians: Writings by the "Friends of the Indian," 1880–1900* (Cambridge: Harvard University Press, 1973), p. 1.
63. Merrill E. Gates, Address at Lake Mohonk Conference, 1896, *Proceedings of the Fourteenth Annual Meeting of the Lake Mohonk Conference of Friends of the Indian* (1896), pp. 8–13, cited in Prucha, *Americanizing the Indian*, p. 334.
64. McLaughlin, *My Friend the Indian*, p. 161.
65. Ben Clark, *New York Sun*, May 14, 1899.
66. *The Economist* 325:7790 (December 19, 1992): 29. More recently, an article about the Bureau of Indian Affairs, "The Worst Federal Agency," *U.S. News and World Report* 117:21 (November 28, 1994): 63, stated that Native Americans are the most impoverished Americans: "less than 20 cents of each dollar [of federal funds] trickles down to the reservations."
67. James Creelman, *On the Great Highway: The Wanderings and Adventures of a Special Correspondent* (Boston: Lothrop, 1901), p. 301.
68. GAC, *My Life on the Plains*, pp. 21–22.
69. Marshall, *Crimsoned Prairie*, p. 155.
70. Herbert E. Smith, "Comanche Still Lives," *Recruiting News* (November 15, 1926): 36, describes how Comanche received his name. The postbattle fame of Comanche has obscured the fact that he was not Captain Keogh's only, or necessarily favorite, horse. Scott, *Some Memories*, p. 47, reports that "Captain Nowlan was a close friend of Captain Keogh, both Irishmen, and he loved the government horse Paddy, ridden by Keogh up to the fight, when he changed to Comanche."
71. It was not true that Comanche was the only surviving horse: he was the only one found on the battlefield deemed worthy of being saved rather than destroyed. See Elizabeth Atwood Lawrence, *His Very Silence Speaks: Comanche—the Horse Who Survived Custer's Last Stand* (Detroit: Wayne State University

Press, 1989), and Edward S. Luce, *Keogh, Comanche and Custer* (Ashland, Ore.: Lewis Osborne, 1974). Lawrence's is the fuller treatment, but both books refer to the works of literature and art that Comanche has inspired.

72. Cited in Luce, *Keogh, Comanche and Custer*, pp. 82–83.
73. Ibid., pp. 82–92.
74. Cited in Lawrence, *His Very Silence Speaks*, p. 148.
75. Now the copious description surrounding Comanche focuses on other matters than the battle; for example, the involved process of preparing his body for exhibition, how he received his name, and so forth.
76. Herman Melville, *Moby-Dick* (New York: W. W. Norton, 1967), p. 264.
77. Brian W. Dippie, *Custer's Last Stand: The Anatomy of an American Myth* (Missoula: University of Montana Press, 1976), p. 76. See also, Dippie, "Why Would They Lie? or Thoughts on Frank Finkel and Friends," in *Custer and His Times*, ed. Paul Andrew Hutton (El Paso, Tex.: Little Big Horn Associates, 1981), pp. 209–28. Theodore Roosevelt said that he had met or heard of fifty "solitary survivors" of Custer's defeat. Appendix E, *The Winning of the West*, 4 vols. (New York: G. P. Putnam's Sons, 1903) 1:340.
78. Reprinted in *Winners of the West* 15:2 (February 1938): 3.

CHAPTER 21: MYSTERY

1. E. V. Westrate, *Those Fatal Generals* (New York: Knight Publications, 1936), p. 238.
2. Don Russell, "How Many Indians Were Killed? White Man versus Red Man: The Facts and the Legend," *American West* 10:4 (1973): 62. The problem of obtaining accurate statistics of Indian deaths is reflected in Robert E. Morris's conjecture that the Indians involved in the Wagon Box fight lost between twelve and one thousand men. "Custer Made a Good Decision," *Journal of the West* 16 (1977): 6.
3. Urwin, *Custer Victorious*, p. 167. Westrate, p. 239, says that Grant's army lost sixty thousand men in thirty days—or two thousand a day.
4. Gray, *Centennial Campaign*, p. 1.
5. Gray, *Custer's Last Campaign*.
6. Paulding to his mother, July 15, 1876, in Thomas R. Buecker, ed., "A Surgeon at the Little Big Horn," p. 147.
7. Cited in Graham, *The Custer Myth*, pp. 116, 117.
8. *McClellan's Own Story*, p. 65. Cf. Sherman's remark, *New York Herald*, July 11: "With the information he had, we do not see how he could have acted otherwise. Had he let Sitting Bull escape after so much pains to find him, he would have incurred the indignant censure of every army officer and of the whole country. . . . If he had waited and given the Indians an opportunity to

run away, what would have been said of him? Wengert, *The Custer Dispatches*, p. 19.

9. Wellman, *Death on Horseback*, p. 140n.
10. Readers will find plausible answers to these and other such questions in Gray's two books, *Centennial Campaign* and *Custer's Last Campaign*.
11. Fifty-four years after the battle Edward Godfrey made public the story that he had obtained from a reluctant Frederick Benteen. Remarks of Brigadier General Edward S. Godfrey at Annual Dinner of Order of Indian Wars, January 25, 1930, GFP, box 19.
12. Cited in Carroll, *Four on Custer by Carroll*, p. 47. In Fougera, *With Custer's Cavalry*, p. 269, the letter has been altered as follows: "We heard Custer's command fighting about five miles off in our front, *and we tried repeatedly, but in vain, to join him*."
13. *Bismarck Tribune*, July 6, 1876.
14. Walter Camp, "Interview with John Martin," in *Custer in '76*, p. 101.
15. Godfrey, *Field Diary*, pp. 8–9.
16. See Ward, "The Little Bighorn," pp. 76–86, for a description of a convention of Custer buffs.
17. *New York Herald*, July 17, 1876.
18. See also the *Chicago Times* for July 9, 13, and 14, 1876.
19. Clipping in USMA archive.
20. Lucy Heath to "Uncle John," November 8, [18—], FC.
21. See John M. Carroll, ed., *The Sitting Bull Fraud* (Bryan, Tex.: privately published, n.d.).
22. Fred White, Jr., Catalogue #28, cited in the Introduction, ibid., n.p.
23. Interview with Sitting Bull, *New York Herald*, November 16, 1877, in Graham, *The Custer Myth*, p. 67.
24. Report of July 5, *Report of the Secretary of War, Executive Documents 1, Part 2, Messages and Documents Communicated to the Two Houses of Congress* (44th Cong.) (Washington, D.C.: Government Printing Office, 1876), 1:33.
25. "Kill Eagle's Story of His Stay with the Hostiles," *New York Herald*, September 24, 1876, in Graham, *Custer Myth*, pp. 54, 56.
26. Graham, "The Story of the Little Big Horn," *The Cavalry Journal* 35 (July 1926): 359n.
27. Cited in A. J. Donnelle, *Cyclorama of General Custer's Last Fight against Sioux Indians, or The Battle of the Little Big Horn, with Grand Musée of Indian Curios* (Boston: Boston Cyclorama Company, 1889), p. 24.
28. McClernand, *With the Indian and the Buffalo in Montana*, p. 52.
29. Gibbon, *Gibbon on the Sioux Campaign of 1876*, pp. 23, 26.
30. Marquis, *Custer, Cavalry & Crows: The Story of William White as Told to Thomas Marquis* (Ft. Collins, Colo.: Old Army Press, 1975), p. 66.

31. Richard A. Roberts, "Custer's Last Battle: Reminiscences of General Custer," typescript, EBCC, reel 6.
32. Godfrey, *General George A. Custer*, p. 33. This pamphlet reprints Godfrey's 1908 revision of "Custer's Last Battle," originally published in the *Century Magazine* 43 (January 1892): 358–84, and adds additional material, primarily the testimony of Indian participants in the battle.
33. Frederick E. Hoxie, *A Final Promise: The Campaign to Assimilate the Indians, 1880–1920* (Lincoln: University of Nebraska Press, 1984), p. 86.
34. Reel 4, EBCC.
35. "Recollections of Army Life," Ms., FC, box 3, folder 4.
36. *Ellis County Star*, June 29, 1876, p. 4.
37. Carrington, *Army Life*, p. 119.
38. Ibid.
39. Cited in Edward Lazarus, *Black Hills, White Justice: The Sioux Nation versus the United States, 1775 to the Present* (New York: HarperCollins, 1991), p. 39.
40. Records of U.S. Army Mobile Units, 7th Cavalry, Det. 1867–68, LS, National Archives. Cf. George Armstrong Custer, *My Life*, p. 184, for a description of the same practice.
41. GAC, "Battling with the Sioux on the Yellowstone," pp. 216–17.
42. Godfrey, *Field Diary*, p. 10.
43. May 17, 1876, clipping reel 6, EBCC.
44. Runs the Enemy, cited in Joseph K. Dixon, *The Vanishing Race: The Last Great Indian Council* (New York: Doubleday, Page, 1913), p. 176; Donnelle, *Cyclorama*, p. 25.
45. Stands in Timber and Liberty, *Cheyenne Memories*, p. 209.
46. Bighead, "She Watched Custer's Last Battle," p. 376.
47. Fox, *Archaeology, History, and Custer's Last Battle*, p. 138.
48. Ibid.; interestingly, the Native activist Vine Deloria, Jr., reports that even now, "when an Indian gets too old and becomes inactive, people say he is 'too old to muss the Custer anymore.'" *Custer Died for Your Sins* (Norman: University of Oklahoma Press, 1988), p. 150.
49. Marquis, *Keep the Last Bullet for Yourself*.
50. W. A. Falconer to E. A. Brininstool, November 30, 1934, VP.
51. See Carroll, *The Benteen-Goldin Letters on Custer and His Last Battle*, p. 32: "We had quite a number of dismounted recruits who were left at the supply camp at Powder River." The best discussion of the recruit issue, reprising earlier research, is Joe Sills, "The Recruits Controversy: Another Look," *Greasy Grass: Annual for the Battlefield Dispatch* (May 1989): 2–8. Sills concludes that the regiment did not have a large number of recruits and that the recruits "did not significantly affect either the outcome of the battle or any of its segments" (8).

52. Scott and Fox, *Archaeological Insiqhts*, p. 70. For an analysis of the miles covered on the march, see Gray, *Centennial Campaign*, p. 170.
53. Gray's persuasive conclusion, *Centennial Campaign*, p. 183: "Custer's decisions, judged in the light of what he knew at the time, instead of by our hindsight, were neither disobedient, rash, nor stupid. Granted his premises, all the rest follows rationally. It was what neither he, nor any other officer, knew that brought disaster."
54. Norman Maclean, *Young Men and Fire* (Chicago: University of Chicago Press, 1992), p. 63.
55. Van De Water, *Glory-Hunter*. For an excellent treatment of Custer as a twentieth-century antihero, see Dippie, *Custer's Last Stand.*
56. Deloria, *Custer Died for Your Sins*, p. 148, notes that "the most popular and enduring subject of Indian humor is, of course, General Custer. There are probably more jokes about Custer and the Indians than there were participants in the battle."
57. Graham, *Custer Myth*, p. 290.
58. *Los Angeles Times*, August 14, 1993.

CHAPTER 22: "I LONGED TO DIE"

1. GAC to EBC, December 20, 1870, MMP.
2. See Mary P. Ryan, *Womanhood in America: From Colonial Times to the Present* (New York: New Viewpoints, 1975), 137–91, and *The Empire of the Mother: American Writing about Domesticity, 1830–1860* (New York: Haworth, 1982), 1–70, 97–141, for a discussion of this period's rigorous confinement of middle-class women to the domestic sphere.
3. Ruth Miller Elson documents the message of nineteenth-century American schoolbooks that women belonged in the home, without other interests or ambitions. She describes the "ideal woman" portrayed in these schoolbooks as "a model of self-abnegation; her only role in life, her only fulfillment comes in helping the male fulfill his ambition." *Guardians of Tradition: American Schoolbooks of the Nineteenth Century* (Lincoln: University of Nebraska Press, 1964), p. 303. Libbie fit this description perfectly.
4. EBC to GAC, October 1864, in Merington, *Custer Story*, p. 121. Two years later she professed herself thankful for "a husband who is so far superior to me in judgment and in everything else." EBC to GAC (March 1866), BCWCC, cited in Leckie, *Elizabeth Bacon Custer*, p. 82. This was a typical view of the time; cf. Rebecca Richmond's opinion that "those whom we women cannot honor as superiors, are not worthy the name—'man.'" Entry for April 2, 1868, "Rebecca Visits Kansas and the Custers: The Diary of Re-

becca Richmond," ed. Minnie Dubbs Millbrook, *Kansas Historical Quarterly* 42 (1976): 387.

5. Manuscript notes, EBCC, reel 5.
6. See Stewart, "The Custer Battle and Widow's Weeds," pp. 52–59.
7. In 1908 the amount paid to an Indian war widow was *raised* to twelve dollars a month. William H. Glasson, *Federal Military Pensions in the United States*, ed. David Kinley (New York: Oxford University Press, 1918), p. 115.
8. Letter of August 8, 1876, FC, box 1, folder 15.
9. Letter of June 18, 1877, Margaret Calhoun to EBC, FC, box 2, folder 4.
10. Milan S. Harmon to Rev. and Mrs. William Jenkins, July 27, 1876, GP.
11. Letter of June 14, 1877, FC, box 2, folder 4.
12. Letter of June 5, 1877, ibid.
13. Letter of September 3, 1877, ibid.
14. Letter of July 1, 1877, ibid.
15. As Alice Kessler-Harris writes about this period, "The only sanctioned occupations for 'respectable' women were teaching and, when genteel poverty struck, dressmaking—done in the privacy of the home." *Women Have Always Worked: A Historical Overview* (Old Westbury, N.Y.: Feminist Press, 1981), pp. 62–63.
16. Letter of March 26, 1877, FC, box 1, folder 18.
17. Letter of April 5, 1877, ibid.
18. Frost, *General Custer's Libbie*, p. 239.
19. Letter of April 22, 1877, FC, box 1, folder 18.
20. Kessler-Harris, *Women Have Always Worked*, p. 963, notes that "a talented and lucky few might earn their livings at writing."
21. *Winners of the West* 15:5 (April 1938): 6; Terri L. Premo, *Winter Friends: Women Growing Old in the New Republic, 1785–1835* (Urbana: University of Illinois Press, 1990), p. 25. Women had similar reasons for remaining single, as Lee Virginia Chambers-Schiller discusses in *Liberty, A Better Husband.*
22. Benteen uses this expression in two letters to the Western photographer David Barry. On August 29, 1895, he wrote, "I am of the opinion that Mrs. Custer would approve of almost anything that would keep the fame of Custer to the fore—that being her capital stock in trade." In a letter of March 29, 1897, he says that Libbie "believes in having Custer stock hold up. . . . it has been her whole stock in trade." EBCC.
23. Undated letter, EBCC, no. 4110.
24. Letter of May 3, 1877, FC, box 2, folder 3. Further citations of Margaret Calhoun's letters will be from this source, including folder 4.
25. Letter of August 31, 1877, Margaret Calhoun to EBC.
26. Letter of August 15, 1877.

27. Candace Wheeler, *Yesterdays in a Busy Life* (New York: Harper and Brothers, 1918), pp. 210, 218.
28. Ibid.
29. EBC to Kingsley, February 13, 1886, CC, box 6, folder 6. The "noble woman" referred to is probably Rebecca Richmond.
30. Ibid.
31. EBC to Kingsley, February 13, 1886, EBCMC.
32. EBC to C. C. Buel, October 23, 1891, CenC.
33. EBC, *Tenting on the Plains*, p. 24.
34. Edward S. Godfrey, "Custer's Last Battle," *Century Illustrated Monthly Magazine* 43 (January 1892): 373.
35. See her letter to C. C. Buel, Thanksgiving Day 1891, CenC.
36. *Detroit Free Press*, June 4, 1910.
37. Composition book, 1891–92, EBCC, typescript, p. 7.
38. EBC to Carnegie, February 5, 1890, CarC.
39. EBC to Carnegie, July 8, [n.d.], CarC.
40. Springfield [Mass.], April 1892, Diary, EBCC, p. 33; no. 5671.
41. Rebecca Richmond to EBC, July 11, 1876, cited in Frost, *General Custer's Libbie*, p. 234.
42. EBC note [1930], EBCC, n. 3492.
43. Sidney Zisook, Stephen Shuchter, Marc Schuckit, "Factors in the Persistence of Unresolved Grief among Psychiatric Outpatients," *Psychosomatics* 26:6 (1985): 497.
44. Sidney Zisook and Richard DeVaul, "Unresolved Grief," *The American Journal of Psychoanalysis* 45:4 (1985): 373.
45. John B. Kennedy, "A Soldier's Widow," *Collier's* (January 29, 1927): 41.
46. EBC to Edmund Clarence Stedman, July 19, 1905, SC.
47. EBCC, reel 5.

CHAPTER 23: LITERARY CAREERS

1. EBC to Kingsley, February 13, 1886; n.d. [1886?]; January 6, 1887, CC, box 6, folder 6. Leckie, *Elizabeth Bacon Custer*, pp. 243–45, has a valuable discussion of the Custer-Kingsley relationship.
2. EBC to Kingsley, January 6, 1887, n.d., ibid.
3. EBC to Kingsley, February 13, 1886, ibid.
4. J. M. Wright, "West Point before the War," clipping in EBCC, reel 8.
5. GAC to EBC, April 17, 1876, in Frost, *General Custer's Libbie*, pp. 290–91. A slightly different account of this exchange appears in EBC, "*Boots and Saddles*," p. 125.
6. *Detroit Journal*, May 31, 1910.

7. Whittaker to EBC, March 31, 1877, FC, box 1, folder 15.
8. Rossiter Johnson, review of *Tenting on the Plains, Chicago Dial*, May 1888, in *Tenting on the Plains* scrapbook, CC, box 7.
9. August 1888, ibid.
10. Review of *"Boots and Saddles," Albany Times*, April 4, *"Boots and Saddles"* scrapbook, CC, box 7.
11. Review of *"Boots and Saddles," Harper's Monthly*, in *"Boots and Saddles"* scrapbook, ibid.
12. So Libbie wrote in a letter to Kingsley dated September 7, 1889, CC, box 6, folder 6.
13. EBC to Edmund Clarence Stedman, February 6 [1895], SC. On February 21, 1895, Frederick J. Hall signed a document assigning the rights to *Tenting on the Plains* from the publishing house of Charles L. Webster to Harper's. Hall was Webster's partner. HP.
14. Kent Ladd Steckmesser, *The Western Hero in History and Legend* (Norman: University of Oklahoma Press, 1965), p. 175, considers GAC, *My Life on the Plains* "an important historical and literary document [that] helped to transform the dreary 'American Desert' into a land of romance." This applies equally well or more so to Libbie's books.
15. EBC, *Tenting on the Plains*, p. 30.
16. Libbie's anecdotes about Eliza and imitation of Eliza's speech were always popular when she gave lectures. On one occasion she wrote in her diary that "so many wished . . . that I might have brought Eliza." March 6 [1893], Albany, *The Journal of Elizabeth B. Custer for the Years 1892–3*, transcribed by Arlene Reynolds Killian (Hardin, Mont.: Magpie Traveling Players, 1992), p. 63. Although Eliza had eventually been dismissed for insolence, Libbie brought her to New York to contribute her recollections to *Tenting on the Plains*.
17. EBC, *Tenting on the Plains*, p. 640. All the particulars in this account are taken from this source.
18. Ibid., pp. 640–44. See chap. 7, "Joining the Frontier Army," p. 77.
19. Providence, February 19 [1893], *Journal*, p. 52.
20. See Glenna Matthews, *The Rise of Public Woman: Woman's Power and Woman's Place in the United States, 1630–1970* (New York: Oxford University Press, 1992), pp. 3–11.
21. EBC, *Journal*, pp. 54–55.
22. In Camden, March 10, ibid., p. 68.
23. In Newark, November 14, ibid., p. 24.
24. In Cincinnati, [January 1893], ibid., pp. 47–48.
25. In Cincinnati, May 13, ibid., p. 6.
26. In Springfield, Ohio, January 21, ibid., pp. 43–44.
27. Barnard Club program, New Year's Day 1918, EBCC, no. 5783.

28. EBCC, reel 4.
29. Unidentified clipping, September 19 [1885], CC, box 7.
30. Annotation, dated 1924, of "Major Reno and the Custer Massacre," Part 2, 357, unidentified article in EBCC, 3052x.
31. Michael L. Tate, "The Girl He Left Behind: Elizabeth Custer and the Making of a Legend," *Red River Valley Historical Review* 5 (winter 1980): 19, believes that "letter writing became such an obsession and so time consuming that her attempts to complete a book on Autie's Civil War years proved futile." The correspondence, which had not prevented Libbie from writing her earlier books, seems to me a rationalization rather than a genuine cause.

CHAPTER 24: MONUMENTS

1. See *New York Herald* editorial, July 10, 1876, only three days after the story broke in the news on July 7.
2. Ibid., July 13, 1876.
3. *New York Times*, July 25, 1876.
4. Belmont to EBC, April 3, 1879, EBCC, reel 2.
5. *Detroit Free Press*, August 31, 1879.
6. *New York Herald*, August 31, 1876.
7. Quoted by Minnie Dubbs Millbrook, "A Monument to Custer," *Montana: The Magazine of Western History* 24 (spring 1974): 18–33, reprinted in *The Custer Reader*, ed. Paul Andrew Hutton (Lincoln: University of Nebraska Press, 1992), p. 276.
8. *Detroit Free Press*, August 31, 1876.
9. Letter to Vinnie Ream, September 26, 1879, VRHP.
10. Ibid.
11. Letter of March 15, 1879, ibid.
12. *Congressional Record*, 46th Cong., 2nd sess. (Washington, D.C.: Government Printing Office, 1880), vol. 10, pt. 3, 2629; vol. 10, pt. 4, 3264. Millbrook, "A Monument to Custer," p. 278, assumes that the protest refers to Custer's actions at the Washita, but this is not necessarily the case. His flogging men on the 1865 march to Texas, after flogging had been prohibited in the military, or any of the actions in Kansas that he was court-martialed for in 1867, could have been the subject.
13. EBC to William T. Sherman, October 15, 1882, ShP.
14. Ibid.
15. Ibid.
16. William T. Sherman to EBC, October 17, 1882, cited in Frost, *General Custer's Libbie*, p. 254.
17. Photocopy of Sherman's note of January 3, 1882, Custer file, USMA.

18. Robert Todd Lincoln to Honorable Leonard Swett, April 25, 1884, EBCC, reel 2.
19. Lincoln to Swett, November 28, 1884, ibid.
20. Correspondence in Custer file, USMA. Lincoln's letter to Merritt, November 28, 1884, indicates that he had received letters from prominent subscribers to the statue fund who concurred with Mrs. Custer's wishes. Evidently Lincoln had never seen the statue, but the campaign he had been subjected to had convinced him: "So far as any expression has come to me it is unanimous that the statue does discredit to General Custer, and disfigures the public grounds." Merritt may have been glad enough to have a statue of Custer consigned to oblivion. He gave the order the following day, November 29, 1884.
21. Correspondence cited in Millbrook, "A Monument to Custer," p. 281.
22. Ibid., p. 281, records the efforts of cadet John Byers to locate the statue in 1951.
23. Letter of July 2, 1906, FC, box 1, folder 7.
24. Letter of Greening to EBC, ibid.
25. Briggs to EBC, August 16, 1907, ibid., box 1, folder 18.
26. Briggs to EBC, September 27, 1907, ibid.
27. Correspondence, VRHP, box 2.
28. Letter of February 22, 1879, ibid.
29. Letter of June 12, 1881, EBC to Ream, ibid.
30. Vinnie Ream Hoxie to EBC, July 12, 1907, FC, box 1, folder 14.
31. Hoxie to EBC, July 25, 1907, ibid.
32. Ibid.
33. GAC to Ream, February 13, 1871, cited in Gordon Langley Hall, *Vinnie Ream: The Story of the Girl Who Sculptured Lincoln* (New York: Holt, Rinehart and Winston, 1963), p. 104.
34. Hoxie to EBC, July 12, 1907, ibid.
35. In the 1870s, when Ream also saw Custer on his visits to Washington, she began a correspondence with General Sherman that suggests, if it does not confirm, an intimate relationship between them. See John F. Marszalek, *Sherman: A Soldier's Passion for Order* (New York: Free Press, 1993), pp. 418–19.
36. Briggs to EBC, December 21, 1907, FC, box 1, folder 10.
37. Ibid. These acts are not specified in extant documents, but Borglum had a history of quarreling with clients.
38. Letter of December 21, 1907, FC, box 1, folder 10.
39. Letter of December 26, 1907, ibid.
40. Briggs to EBC, January 2, 1907, ibid., box 1, folder 11.
41. Potter to EBC, December 24, 1907, FC, box 1, folder 10. Lawrence A. Frost, *Custer Slept Here* (Monroe, Mich.: Garry Owen Publishers, 1974), p. 14, adds

that "no other contestant" had suggested coming to Monroe to examine the site.

42. F. W. Ruckstuhl to EBC, February 20, 1908, FC, box 1, folder 10.
43. This note was written on the back of Ruckstuhl's letter.
44. H. M. Shrady to EBC, March 14, 1908, FC, box 1, folder 10.
45. EBC to Hoxie, March 8 [1908], VRHP, box 2.
46. Briggs to EBC, March 8, 1908, FC, box 1, folder 11.
47. Program, FC, box 3, folder 14.
48. Ibid., box 3, folder 15.
49. Account of Monument Unveiling, FC, box 3, folder 8. Further citations in the text will be to this account.
50. Frederic Remington to George G. Briggs, October 31, 1907, FC, box 1, folder 9.
51. S. Leckie, *Elizabeth Bacon Custer*, p. 288; EBC cited in Lawrence A. Frost, *Boy General in Bronze: Custer, Michigan's Hero on Horseback* (Glendale, Calif.: Arthur H. Clark, 1985), p. 153.
52. *Monroe Evening News*, June 16, 1923.
53. C. B. Galbreath, "George Armstrong Custer," *Ohio Archaeological and Historical Quarterly* 41:4 (October 1932): 632.
54. Program, FC, box 3, folder 15.
55. *Monroe Evening News*, September 3, 1955; Frost, *Custer Legends* (Bowling Green, Ohio: Bowling Green University Popular Press, 1981), p. 34.

CHAPTER 25: AGING

1. Spotts, *Campaigning with Custer*, p. 110.
2. Letter of May 1861, in Merington, *Custer Story*, p. 10.
3. Mattes, *Indians, Infants and Infantry*, pp. 104, 209.
4. Sherman to Howard, August 24 and August 28, 1877, cited in Wooster, *The Military and United States Indian Policy*, p. 69.
5. Cited in Barry C. Johnson, "Benteen's Ordeal at Fort Du Chesne: A Narrative with Background," in Barry C. Johnson and Francis B. Taunton, *Benteen's Ordeal and Custer's Field: Two Papers* (London: Johnson-Taunton Military Press, 1983), pp. 42–43.
6. EBC, *Tenting on the Plains*, pp. 42–43.
7. EBC, *Following the Guidon*, pp. 84, 87.
8. Letter of July 1, 1887, to "Dora" [Mrs. Boudinot Keith, the daughter of Libbie's friend Candace Wheeler], EBCC, no. 4080. Libbie wrote "remorsefully" instead of remorselessly.
9. EBC, *Journal*, pp. 25, 5–6.
10. "Account of Monument Unveiling," FC, box 3, folder 8, p. 10. For Burkman's account see Wagner, *Old Neutriment*, p. 46.

11. "Account of Monument Unveiling," p. 10.
12. *Monroe Evening News*, April 5, 1933.
13. EBC to David Barry, January 30, 1930, EBCC, no. 5248.
14. Draft of 45th Anniversary Speech, EBCC, no. 3566.
15. EBC to Frances Elmer, February 28, 1925, FC, box 1, folder 16.
16. EBC to Frances Elmer, December 25, 1926, ibid.
17. General M. Gaines to EBC, November 12, 1906, EBCC, no. C1753; Thomas C. Cheney to EBC, July 25, 1927, EBCC, no. 2224.
18. EBC to Katie, September 16, 1923, EBCC, no. 4859. The correspondent is probably Katie Gibson, the wife of an officer in the Seventh Regiment.
19. References to Libbie's will are taken from the copy in CC, box 6, folder 15.
20. Levitt E. Custer to EBC, January 31, 1893, and EBC to Levitt E. Custer, April 9, 1893, CC, box 6, folder 5.
21. Kennedy, "A Soldier's Widow," p. 41.

EPILOGUE: CUSTER FOREVER

1. *Myth* has many definitions, but posing history and myth as opposites, as I do here, is inevitably to regard myth as a form of fiction. At the same time, even as a secular narrative, myth emulates the sacred in its claim to significant collective meaning. Most applicable to my use of the term is Lauri Honko's definition of myth as a mirror of culture or social structure that "may reveal values which would otherwise be difficult to detect." "The Problem of Defining Myth," *Sacred Narrative: Readings in the Theory of Myth*, ed. Alan Dundes (Berkeley: University of California Press, 1984), p. 47.
2. Homer, *The Odyssey*, trans. Robert Fitzgerald (New York: Doubleday Anchor, 1963), p. 160.
3. *Senate Reports*, 48th Cong., 1st sess., no. 283, serial 2164, 80–81.
4. Annual Report, November 25, 1876, *Report of the Secretary of War, Executive Documents 1, Part 2, Messages and Documents communicated to the two houses of Congress at the beginning of the second session of the 44th Cong.* (Washington, D.C.: Government Printing Office, 1876) 1:447.
5. Charles A. Eastman, "Rain-in-the-Face: The Story of a Sioux Warrior," *Outlook* (October 27, 1906): 512.
6. Elbridge S. Brooks, *The Master of the Strong Hearts: A Story of Custer's Last Rally* (New York: E. P. Dutton, 1900), pp. iii, 313.
7. Don Russell, *Custer's Last, or The Battle of the Little Big Horn in Picturesque Perspective* (Ft. Worth, Tex.: Amos Carter Museum of Western Art, 1968), p. 35.
8. Some sense of the variety of pictorial representations of the Last Stand can be obtained in Russell, *Custer's Last*, and in Harrison Lane, "Brush, Palette and the Little Big Horn," *Montana* 23 (summer 1973): 66–80.
9. Brill, *Conquest of the Southern Plains*, p. 18.

10. Utley, *Cavalier in Buckskin*, p. 8.
11. The president was quoted in the *New York Herald*, September 2, 1876: "I regard Custer's Massacre as a sacrifice of troops, brought on by Custer himself, that was wholly unnecessary—wholly unnecessary."
12. *The Bronxville Review*, August 20, 1917, BC, box 13, folder 13.
13. Letter of July 13, 1885, BC, box 13, folder 159.
14. Rebecca Richmond to EBC, June 10, 1921, EBCC, reel 3.
15. Ray Billington, "The New Western Social Order and the Synthesis of Western Scholarship," *The American West: An Appraisal*, ed. Robert G. Ferris (Santa Fe: Museum of New Mexico Press, 1963), p. 12.
16. Sherman to EBC, January 24, 1889, EBCC, no. 3352; to Grenville Dodge, the Union Pacific's chief engineer of construction, Sherman wrote as early as January 18, 1867: "I regard this Road of yours as the solution of 'our Indian affairs.'" Grenville Dodge Papers, 14, State Department of History and Archives, Des Moines, Iowa, cited in Robert G. Athearn, "War Paint against Brass: The Army and the Plains Indians," *Montana: The Magazine of Western History* 6 (summer 1956): 20. This was a sentiment repeated many times. See Sherman to Sheridan, September 26, 1872, *The Sherman Letters*, vol. 1: "I think our interest is to favor the undertaking of the Road [Northern Pacific railroad], as it will help to bring the Indian problem to a final solution."
17. Billington, "The New Western Social Order," p. 12.
18. Fred Dustin to W. J. Ghent, January 15, 1932, GP, box 2.
19. John Aloysius Farrell, "Closeup: History Hater Loves Quest of Custer's Last Stand," *Denver Post*, July 3, 1985.
20. Ibid.
21. Robert J. Ege, "*Settling the Dust*" (Sheridan, Wyo.: Quick Printing Co., 1968), p. iv.
22. Ibid.
23. Brininstool to Frederic Van De Water, letter of September 30, 1933, VP.
24. Brininstool to R. G. Carter, letter of May 31, 1932, "A Debate of Authors on the Custer Fight," *Westerners Brand Book*, 30:6 (August 1973): 44, 45.
25. Letter of June 19, 1932, ibid., p. 47.
26. "Custer's Last Fight: Notes by General Scott," *New York Times*, January 6, 1935: 2.
27. Ghent to Harvey A. Olson (battlefield superintendent), March 5, 1936, GP.
28. Walter M. Camp to EBC, October 31, 1917, EBCC, reel 3.
29. Thomas B. Marquis, M.D., to EBC, letters of September 16 and December 23, 1929, EBCC, nos. 3878 and 3879.
30. For the most decisive analysis of Goldin's lack of credibility see Graham, *The Custer Myth*, pp. 267–78.
31. Letter of June 19, 1932, "A Debate of Authors on the Custer Fight," pp. 47–48.

32. Henry Weibert, *Sixty-six Years in Custer's Shadow* (Billings, Mont.: Bannack, 1985), p. 93.
33. Farrell, "Closeup."
34. William Ahern, "Detroit Indian Fighters Rally to Custer Guidon," *Winners of the West* 16:3 (April 1939): 5.
35. *New York Times*, June 26, 1986, A18.
36. Carroll, *An Elizabeth Custer Gallimaufry*, p. i.
37. Richard Upton, *The Custer Adventure* (Fort Collins, Colo.: Old Army Press, 1975).
38. "The love his wife bore him and he bore her may be George Armstrong Custer's most intrinsically sound fame"—so wrote one of Custer's most severe critics, Frederic Van De Water, *Glory-Hunter*, p. 123.
39. Stephen E. Ambrose, *Crazy Horse and Custer*, p. 168; see also Ambrose, "Sidesaddle Soldier: Libbie Custer's Partnership in Glory," *Timeline* 3:2 (April–May 1986): 2–13.
40. Ambrose, *Crazy Horse and Custer*, pp. 168–69.
41. See chap. 24, p. 377.
42. Robert Underwood Johnson, *Remembered Yesterdays* (Boston: Little, Brown, 1923), p. 499.
43. Sherman to EBC, January 24, 1889, EBCC, reel 2.
44. Charles D. Cameron, "Life in Light of a Memory," *Detroit Journal*, June 3, 1910.
45. "Army Lady: Mrs. Custer, Wife, Widow of General George Armstrong Custer," typescript, MMP, box 3.
46. EBCC, reel 6.
47. Vine Deloria, Jr., *Custer Died for Your Sins*, p. 148. Actually, the land on which the battle was fought belonged to the Crows rather than to the Sioux; my point is that it was not at that time considered to be land open to white settlement.

Bibliography

COLLECTIONS OF MANUSCRIPTS AND PERSONAL PAPERS

Brininstool, Edward. Papers. Military History Institute, Carlisle Barracks, Carlisle, Pennsylvania.

Camp, William M. Papers. Harold B. Lee Library, Brigham Young University, Provo, Utah; Lilly Library, Indiana University, Bloomington, Indiana.

Carnegie Papers. New York Public Library, New York City.

Century Collection. New York Public Library, New York City.

Christiancy-Pickett Papers. U.S. Army Military History Institute, Carlisle Barracks, Carlisle, Pennsylvania.

Crook, George. Papers. Rutherford B. Hayes Presidential Library, Fremont, Ohio.

Custer, George A., and Elizabeth B. Western Americana Collection. Beinecke Rare Book and Manuscript Library, Yale University; Little Bighorn Battlefield National Monument, Crow Agency, Montana.

Custer Collection. Monroe County Historical Museum, Monroe, Michigan.

Drennan, Daniel 0. Papers. Library of Congress, Washington, D.C.

Frost, Lawrence A. Collection. Monroe County Historical Museum, Monroe, Michigan.

Ghent, William J. Papers. Library of Congress, Washington, D.C., and New York Public Library, New York City.

Godfrey Family Papers. U.S. Army Military History Institute, Carlisle Barracks, Carlisle, Pennsylvania.

Hagner, Francis R. Collection. New York Public Library, New York City.

Harper and Brothers Papers. Rare Books and Manuscripts, Butler Library, Columbia University, New York City.

Hoxie, Vinnie Ream. Papers. Library of Congress, Washington, D.C.
Irwin, Bernard John Dowling. Papers. Library of Congress, Washington, D.C.
McCaskey, William S. Papers. U.S. Army Military History Institute, Carlisle Barracks, Carlisle, Pennsylvania.
Merington, Marguerite. Papers. New York Public Library, New York City.
Military Division of the Missouri. Papers. U.S. Army Military History Institute, Carlisle Barracks, Carlisle, Pennsylvania.
Monroe County Library System. Ellis Reference and Information Center, Monroe, Michigan.
Order of the Indian Wars Papers. U.S. Army Military History Institute, Carlisle Barracks, Carlisle, Pennsylvania.
Scott, Hugh L. Papers. U.S. Army Military History Institute, Carlisle Barracks, Carlisle, Pennsylvania.
Sheridan, Philip H. Papers. Library of Congress, Washington, D.C.
Sherman, William T. Papers. Library of Congress, Washington, D.C.
Stedman Family Papers. Rare Books and Manuscripts, Butler Library, Columbia University, New York City.
United States Military Academy Archives. West Point, New York.
Van De Water, Frederic F. Papers. New York Public Library, New York City.

GOVERNMENT PUBLICATIONS AND OFFICIAL DOCUMENTS

Adjutant General. Letters Received, 1869–70. Records of the War Department. National Archives.
Board of Indian Commissioners. *Annual Report . . . 1875–1879.* Washington, D.C.: Government Printing Office, 1876–80.
Bureau of Indian Affairs. Records. 1873. RG 75. National Archives.
Congressional Record, 46th Cong., 2d sess. Washington, D.C.: Government Printing Office, 1880.
Custer, George Armstrong. Records. RG 9, 94. National Archives.
Department of the Army. Army Board for Correction of Military Records. Case of Marcus A. Reno. National Archives.
Department of Dakota. Records. RG 393. National Archives.
Executive Documents, House of Representatives, 40th Cong., 3d sess., 1868–69. Vol. 3 of 14 vols. Washington, D.C.: Government Printing Office, 1869.
House Committee on Military Affairs. *Report to Accompany the Bill (H.R. 2546) . . .* House Report 38. Washington, D.C.: Government Printing Office, 1874.
Judge Advocate General. Records of the Office. RG 153. National Archives.
McClellan, George B. *Letter of the Secretary of War: Organization of the Army of the Potomac.* 38th Cong., 1st sess., Ex. Doc. no. 15. Washington, D.C.: Government Printing Office, 1864.

The Management of the War Department: Report No. 799. House Committee on Expenditures in the War Department, 44th Cong., 1st sess., 1875–76. 9 vols., Ser. Washington, D.C.: Government Printing Office, 1876, 7:163.

Monroe County Probate Court Records. Monroe, Michigan.

Reno, Marcus A. ACP file. R314 CB 1865. National Archives.

Richardson, James D., comp. *A Compilation of the Messages and Papers of the Presidents, 1789–1897*. Vol. 7. Washington, D.C.: Government Printing Office, 1897–98.

Secretary of the Interior. *Annual Report of the Commissioner of Indian Affairs, 1866–76*. Washington, D.C.: Government Printing Office, 1867–77.

———. Commissioner of Indian Affairs. *Annual Report of the Commissioner of Indian Affairs, 1846*. Washington, D.C.: Ritchie and Heiss, 1846.

———. *Report to Accompany the Bill (H.R. 2546) . . .* House Report 384. January 10, 1874, U.S. House Committee on Military Affairs. Washington, D.C.: Government Printing Office, 1874.

Secretary of War. *Annual Report of the Secretary of War for the Year{s} 1864–1891*. Washington, D.C.: Government Printing Office, 1867–1892.

Senate Reports. 48th Cong., 1st sess., no. 283. Washington, D.C.: Government Printing Office, 1884.

7th Cavalry, 1867–68. Records. Letters Sent. National Archives.

Sherwood, Isaac R. "The Horse—A Vital Force in War and in the Evolution of the Human Race." *Speech of Hon. Isaac R. Sherwood of Ohio in the House of Representatives, January 24, 1918*. Washington, D.C.: Government Printing Office, 1918.

State of Kansas, *Applications for Admissions to State Hospitals*, vol. C, subser. 2, January 7, 1899–February 19, 1905.

The War of the Rebellion: A Compilation of the Official Records of the Union and Confederate Armies. 20 vols. ser. 1. Washington, D.C.: Government Printing Office, 1902.

BOOKS AND ARTICLES

Agassiz, George R., ed. *Meade's Headquarters, 1863–1865: Letters of Colonel Theodore Lyman from the Wilderness to Appomattox*. Boston: Atlantic Monthly Press, 1922.

Ahern, William. "Detroit Indian Fighters Rally to Custer Guidon." *Winners of the West* 16:2 (March 1939): 1,4.

Allouez, Jean Claude, "Father Allouez's Journey to Lake Superior, 1665–1667." In *Early Narratives of the Northwest, 1634–1699*, edited by Louise Phelps Kellogg. New York: Charles Scribner's Sons, 1917.

American Digest System. *1906 Decennial Edition of the American Digest: A Complete Table of American Cases from 1658 to 1906, G–L*. Vol. 23. St. Paul, Minn.: West Publishing, 1912.

Ambrose, Stephen E. *Crazy Horse and Custer: The Parallel Lives of Two American Warriors.* Garden City, N.Y.: Doubleday, 1975.

———. *Duty, Honor, Country: A History of West Point.* Baltimore: Johns Hopkins University Press, 1966.

———. "Sidesaddle Soldier: Libbie Custer's Partnership in Glory." *Timeline* 3:2 (April–May 1986): 2–13.

Anderson, Harry H. "A Challenge to Brown's Sioux Indian Wars Thesis." *Montana* 12 (January 1962): 40–49. Reprinted in *The Great Sioux War, 1876–1877: The Best from "Montana, the Magazine of Western History,"* edited by Paul L. Hedren (Helena: Montana Historical Society Press, 1991): 39–52.

The Annals of the War Written by Leading Participants North and South. Philadelphia: Times Publishing Company, 1879.

Armes, Colonel George A. *Ups and Downs of an Army Officer.* Washington, D.C.: n.p., 1900.

Asay, Karol. *Gray Head and Long Hair: The Benteen-Custer Relationship.* New York: Mad Printers of Mattituck, 1983.

Athearn, Robert G. *Forts of the Upper Missouri.* Englewood Cliffs, N.J.: Prentice-Hall, 1967.

———. "Warpaint against Brass: The Army and the Plains Indians," *Montana: The Magazine of Western History* 6 (summer 1956): 11–22.

———. *William Tecumseh Sherman and the Settlement of the West.* Norman: University of Oklahoma Press, 1956.

Baldwin, Alice Blackwood. *An Army Wife on the Frontier: The Memoirs of Alice Blackwood Baldwin, 1867–1877.* Edited by Robert C. Carriker and Eleanor R. Carriker. Salt Lake City: University of Utah, Tanner Trust Fund, 1975.

Battles and Leaders of the Civil War. 4 vols. New York: Century Company, 1884.

Beeson, Chalkley M. "A Royal Buffalo Hunt." *Transactions of the Kansas State Historical Society* 10 (1907–8): 574–80.

Benedict, G. G. *Vermont in the Civil War.* 2 vols. Burlington, Vt.: Free Press Association, 1886–88.

Bergamini, John D. *The Hundredth Year: The United States in 1876.* New York: G. P. Putnam's Sons, 1976.

Berger, Thomas. *Little Big Man.* New York: Dial Press, 1964.

Berthron, Donald J. *The Southern Cheyennes.* Norman: University of Oklahoma Press, 1963.

Biddle, Ellen McGowan. *Reminiscences of a Soldier's Wife.* Philadelphia: Lippincott, 1907.

Bighead, Kate. "She Watched Custer's Last Battle," as told to Thomas B. Marquis. In *The Custer Reader,* edited by Paul Andrew Hutton. Lincoln: University of Nebraska Press, 1992.

Billings, John D. *Hardtack and Coffee, or The Unwritten Story of Army Life.* Boston: George M. Smith, 1887.

Billington, Ray. "The New Western Social Order and the Synthesis of Western Scholarship." In *The American West: An Appraisal*, edited by Robert G. Ferris. Santa Fe: Museum of New Mexico Press, 1963.

———. *Westward Expansion: A History of the American Frontier*. 4th ed. New York: Macmillan, 1974.

Biographical Annals of Lancaster County, Pennsylvania. Chicago: J. H. Beers, 1903.

Blackford, William W. *War Years with Jeb Stuart*. New York: Charles Scribner's Sons, 1945.

Boddam-Whetham, J. W. *Western Wanderings: A Record of Travel in the Evening Land*. London: Richard Bentley and Son, 1874.

Boller, Henry A. *Among the Indians: Eight Years in the Far West, 1858–1866*. Edited by Milo Milton Quaife. Chicago: R. R. Donnelley and Sons, 1959.

Bourke, John G. "General Crook in the Indian Country." *Century Magazine* 41 (March 1891): 643–60.

———. *On the Border with Crook*. New York: Charles Scribner's Sons, 1891.

Bowers, Claude G. *The Tragic Era: The Revolution after Lincoln*. Cambridge, Mass.: Houghton Mifflin, 1929.

Bowles, Samuel. *Our New West: Records of Travels between the Mississippi River and the Pacific Ocean*. New York: J. D. Dennison, 1869.

Boyd, Mrs. Orsemus Bronson. *Cavalry Life in Tent and Field*. New York: J. Selwin Tait and Sons, 1894.

Bradley, James H. *The March of the Montana Column: A Prelude to the Custer Disaster*. Edited by Edgar I. Stewart. Norman: University of Oklahoma Press, 1961.

Brady, Cyrus Townsend. *Indian Fights and Fighters: The Soldier and the Sioux*. 1904. Lincoln: University of Nebraska Press, 1971.

Brigham, Earl K. "Custer's Meeting with Secretary of War Belknap at Fort Abraham Lincoln." *North Dakota History* 9:2 (August 1952): 129–31.

Brill, Charles J. *Conquest of the Southern Plains: Uncensored Narrative of the Battle of the Washita and Custer's Southern Campaign*. Oklahoma City, Okla.: Golden Saga, 1938.

Brininstool, E. A. "Chief Crazy Horse: His Career and Death." *Nebraska History Magazine* (December 1929): 38.

———. *Troopers with Custer*. Harrisburg, Penn.: Stackpole, 1952.

Brooks, Elbridge S. *The Master of the Strong Hearts: A Story of Custer's Last Rally*. New York: E. P. Dutton, 1900.

Brown, Dee. *Bury My Heart at Wounded Knee: An Indian History of the American West*. New York: Holt, Rinehart and Winston, 1970.

———. *The Gentle Tamers: Women of the Old Wild West*. New York: G. P. Putnam's, Sons, 1958.

———. *The Year of the Century: 1876*. New York: Charles Scribner's Sons, 1966.

Brown, Jesse, and A. M. Willard. *The Black Hills Trails: A History of the Struggles of the Pioneers in the Winning of the Black Hills*. Edited by John T. Milek. Rapid City, S.D.: Rapid City Journal Company, 1924.

Bruce, Robert V. *Alexander Graham Bell and the Conquest of Solitude.* Boston: Little, Brown, 1973.

Buecker, Thomas R., ed. "A Surgeon at the Little Big Horn: The Letters of Dr. Holmes O. Paulding." In *The Great Sioux War, 1876–1877*, edited by Paul L. Hedren. Helena: Montana Historical Society Press, 1991.

Buel, James William. *Heroes of the Plains.* Philadelphia: Historical Publishing Company, 1891.

Burkey, Blaine. *Custer, Come at Once! The Fort Hays Years of George and Elizabeth Custer, 1867–1870.* Hays, Kans.: Thomas More Prep, 1976.

Burr, Frank A., and Richard J. Hinton. *"Little Phil" and His Troopers: The Life of Gen. Philip H. Sheridan.* Providence, R.I.: J. A. and R. A. Reid, 1888.

Calhoun, James. *Some Observations on the Yellowstone Expedition, 1873.* Edited by Lawrence A. Frost. Glendale, Calif.: Arthur H. Clark, 1981.

———. *With Custer in '74: James Calhoun's Diary of the Black Hills Expedition.* Edited by Lawrence A. Frost. Provo, Utah: Brigham Young University Press, 1979.

Camp, Walter. *Custer in '76: Walter Camp's Notes on the Custer Fight.* Edited by Kenneth Hammer. Provo, Utah: Brigham Young University Press, 1976.

Canton, Frank. *Autobiography of Frank M. Canton.* Edited by Edward Everett Dale. Norman: University of Oklahoma Press, 1966.

Carriker, Robert C. *Fort Supply Indian Territory: Frontier Outpost on the Plains.* Norman: University of Oklahoma Press, 1970.

Carrington, Frances C. *My Army Life and the Fort Phil Kearney Massacre.* Philadelphia: Lippincott, 1910.

Carrington, Henry B. *The Indian Question: An Address.* Boston: DeWolfe and Fiske, 1884.

Carrington, Margaret. *Ab-Sa-Ra-Ka: Home of the Crows.* Philadelphia: Lippincott, 1868.

Carroll, John M. "Cavalry Scraps: Letters on the Seventh Cavalry." In *Custer and His Times*, edited by Paul A. Hutton. El Paso, Tex.: Little Big Horn Associates, 1981.

———. "The Custer Image in Confederate Journals." *Research Review* 1:4 (1984): 3–19.

———. *Custer in Texas: An Interrupted Narrative.* New York: Sol Lewis, Liveright, 1975.

———. *Four on Custer by Carroll.* Guidon Press, 1976.

———, ed. *Another Libbie Custer Gallimaufry!* Bryan, Tex.: Privately printed, 1978.

———, ed. *The Benteen-Goldin Letters on Custer and His Last Battle.* New York: Liveright, 1974.

———, ed. *Camp Talk: The Very Private Letters of Frederick W. Benteen of the 7th U.S. Cavalry to His Wife, 1871 to 1888.* Mattituck, N.Y., and Bryan, Tex.: J. M. Carroll, 1983.

———, ed. *The Court Martial of Frederick W. Benteen, Major, 9th Cavalry, or Did General Crook Railroad Benteen?* Bryan, Tex.: Privately printed, 1981.

———, ed. *Custer: From the Civil War to the Little Big Horn*. Bryan, Tex.: Privately printed, 1981.

———, ed. *Custer in the Civil War: His Unfinished Memoirs*. San Rafael, Calif.: Presidio Press, 1977.

———, ed. *A Libbie Custer Gallimaufry*. Bryan, Tex.: Privately printed, 1978.

———, ed. *The Sitting Bull Fraud*. Bryan, Tex.: Privately printed, n.d.

———, ed. *They Rode with Custer: A Biographical Directory of the Men that Rode with General George A. Custer*. Rev. ed. Mattituck, N.Y.: J. M. Carroll, 1993.

Carroll, John M., and Robert Aldrich. "Some Custer and Little Big Horn Facts to Ponder." *English Westerners Society Tally Sheet* 40:3 (summer 1994): 102–15.

Carter, Samuel III. *The Last Cavaliers: Confederate and Union Cavalry in the Civil War*. New York: St. Martin's Press, 1979.

Catton, Bruce A. *A Stillness at Appomattox*. Garden City, N.Y.: Doubleday, 1953.

Chamberlin, Anne. "Bad Day Ahead for the Army's Greatest Loser." *Saturday Evening Post* 239:18 (August 27, 1966): 70–73.

Chambers-Schiller, Lee Virginia. *Liberty, a Better Husband*. New Haven: Yale University Press, 1984.

Clemens, Samuel L. *Roughing It*. 2 vols. New York: Harper and Brothers, 1913.

Cody, William F. *An Autobiography of Buffalo Bill*. New York: Cosmopolitan Book Corp., 1920.

———. *The Life of Hon. William F. Cody*. Lincoln: University of Nebraska Press, 1978.

———. *Story of the Wild West and Campfire Chats*. Chicago: R. S. Peale, 1888.

Coffman, Edward M. *The Old Army: A Portrait of the American Army in Peacetime, 1784–1898*. New York: Oxford University Press, 1986.

Cogley, Thomas S. *History of the Seventh Indiana Cavalry Volunteers*. LaPorte, Ind.: Herald Company, 1876.

Comstock, Cyrus B. *The Diary of Cyrus B. Comstock*. Edited by Merlin E. Sumner. Dayton, Ohio: Morningside House, 1987.

Connell, Evan S. *Son of the Morning Star: Custer and the Little Bighorn*. New York: Harper and Row, 1985.

Connelley, William Elsey. *Wild Bill and His Era: The Life and Adventures of James Butler Hickok*. New York: Press of the Pioneers, 1933.

Coughlin, T. M. "The Battle of the Little Big Horn: A Tactical Study." *Cavalry Journal* (January–February 1934): 19.

Crary, Catherine S. *Dear Belle: Letters from a Cadet and Officer to His Sweetheart, 1858–1865*. Middletown, Conn.: Wesleyan University Press, 1965.

Crawford, Samuel J. *Kansas in the Sixties*. Chicago: A. C. McClurg, 1911.

Creelman, James. *On the Great Highway: The Wanderings and Adventures of a Special Correspondent*. Boston: Lothrop, 1901.

Crook, George. *General George Crook: His Autobiography*. Edited by Martin F. Schmitt. Norman: University of Oklahoma Press, 1946.

Crow Dog, Mary, and Richard Erdoes. *Lakota Woman*. New York: G. Weidenfeld, 1990.

Cullum, George W. *Biographical Register of the Officers and Graduates of the U.S. Military Academy at West Point, New York*. 3d ed. 9 vols. Boston: Houghton Mifflin, 1891.

Custer, Elizabeth B. *"Boots and Saddles," or Life in Dakota with General Custer*. 1885. Norman: University of Oklahoma Press, 1961.

———. *Following the Guidon*. New York: Harper and Brothers, 1890.

———. *The Journal of Elizabeth B. Custer*. Edited by Arlene Reynolds Killian. Hardin, Mont.: Magpie Traveling Players, 1992.

———. *Tenting on the Plains, or General Custer in Kansas and Texas*. New York: Charles L. Webster, 1887.

Custer, George Armstrong. "Battling with the Sioux on the Yellowstone." In *The Custer Reader*, edited by Paul Andrew Hutton. Lincoln: University of Nebraska Press, 1992. First published in *Galaxy Magazine* 22 (July 1876): 91–102.

———. "From West Point to the Battlefield." In *The Custer Reader*, edited by Paul Andrew Hutton. Lincoln: University of Nebraska Press, 1992. First published in *Galaxy Magazine* 21 (April 1876).

———. *My Life on the Plains, or Personal Experiences with Indians*. 1875. Norman: University of Oklahoma Press, 1962.

———. *Nomad: George A. Custer in Turf, Field and Farm*. Edited by Brian W. Dippie. Austin: University of Texas Press, 1980.

———. *Wild Life on the Plains and Horrors of Indian Warfare*. Edited by Frederick Whittaker. St. Louis: Pease-Taylor Publishing Co., 1891.

Dale, Kittie. *Echoes and Etchings of Early Ellis*. N.p.: Big Mountain Press, 1964.

Danker, Donald F. *Man of the Plains: Recollections of Luther North, 1856–1882*. Lincoln: University of Nebraska Press, 1961.

Darling, Roger. *Benteen's Scout-to-the-Left: The Route from the Divide to the Morass (June 25, 1876)*. El Segundo, Calif.: Upton and Sons, 1987.

———. *Custer's Seventh Cavalry Comes to Dakota: New Discoveries Reveal Custer's Tribulations Enroute to the Yellowstone Expedition*. El Segundo, Calif.: Upton and Sons, 1989.

———. *General Custer's Final Hours: Correcting a Century of Misconceived History*. Vienna, Va.: Potomac-Western Press, 1992.

———. *A Sad and Terrible Blunder: Generals Terry and Custer at the Little Big Horn. New Discoveries*. Vienna, Va.: Potomac-Western Press, 1990.

Davies, Henry Eugene. *Ten Days on the Plains*. New York: Crocker and Co., [1871].

Davis, Theodore. "Henry M. Stanley's Indian Campaign in 1867." *Westerner's Brand Book, 1945–46* (1947): 101–14.

———. "A Summer on the Plains." *Harper's New Monthly Magazine* 36 (February 1868): 292–307.

———. "A Winter on the Plains." *Harper's New Monthly Magazine* 39 (June 1869): 22–34.

———. "With Generals in Their Camp Homes: General George A. Custer." *Westerner's Brand Book, 1945–1946* (1947): 115–30.

"A Debate of Authors on the Custer Fight." *Westerner's Brand Book* 30:6 (August 1973): 41–48.

DeLand, Charles Edmund. *The Sioux Wars*. Vol. 15 of *South Dakota Historical Collections*. Pierre, S.D.: Hipple Printing Company, 1930.

D'Elia, Donald J. "The Argument over Civilian or Military Indian Control, 1865–1880." *Historian* 24:2 (February 1962): 207–25.

Deloria, Vine, Jr. *Custer Died for Your Sins*. Norman: University of Oklahoma Press, 1988.

Dictionary of American Biography. 20 vols. New York: Charles Scribner's Sons, 1928–1936.

Dippie, Brian W. *Custer's Last Stand: The Anatomy of an American Myth*. Missoula: University of Montana Press, 1976.

———. "Why Would They Lie?, or Thoughts on Frank Finkel and Friends." In *Custer and His Times,* edited by Paul Andrew Hutton. El Paso, Tex.: Little Big Horn Associates, 1981.

Dixon, Joseph K. *The Vanishing Race: The Last Great Indian Council.* New York: Doubleday, Page, 1913.

Dodge, Richard Irving. *Our Wild Indians*. Hartford, Conn.: A. D. Worthington, 1883.

———. *The Plains of the Great West and Their Inhabitants*. New York: G. P. Putnam's Sons, 1877.

Donnelle, A. J. *Cyclorama of General Custer's Last Fight against Sioux Indians, or The Battle of the Little Big Horn, with Grand Musée of Indian Curios*. Boston: Boston Cyclorama Company, 1889.

Downey, Fairfax. *Indian-Fighting Army*. New York: Charles Scribner's Sons, 1941.

duBois, Charles G. *Kick the Dead Lion: A Casebook of the Custer Battle*. El Segundo, Calif.: Upton and Sons, 1987.

Dunlay, Thomas W. *Wolves for the Blue Soldiers: Indian Scouts and Auxiliaries with the United States Army, 1860–1890*. Lincoln: University of Nebraska Press, 1982.

Dunn, J. P. *Massacres of the Mountains: A History of the Indian Wars of the Far West*. New York: Harper and Brothers, 1886.

Dustin, Fred. *The Custer Tragedy: Events Leading Up to and Following the Little Big Horn Campaign of 1876*. Ann Arbor, Mich.: Edwards Brothers, 1939.

Eastman, Charles A. "Rain-in-the-Face: The Story of a Sioux Warrior." *Outlook* (October 27, 1906): 507–12.

Ege, Robert J. *Curse Not His Curls*. Fort Collins, Colo.: Old Army Press, 1974.

———. *"Settling the Dust."* Sheridan, Wyo.: Quick Printing Co., 1968.

Ellis, Edward S. *The History of Our Country from the Discovery of America to the Present Time*. 8 vols. Cincinnati: Jones Brothers, 1900.

Elson, Ruth Miller. *Guardians of Tradition: American Schoolbooks of the Nineteenth Century*. Lincoln: University of Nebraska Press, 1964.

Ewers, John C. "Intertribal Warfare as the Precursor of Indian-White Warfare on the Northern Great Plains." *Western Historical Quarterly* 6 (October 1975): 397–410.

Ewert, Theodore. *Private Theodore Ewert's Diary of the Black Hills Expedition of 1874*. Edited by John M. Carroll and Dr. Lawrence A. Frost. Piscataway, N.J.: CRI Books, 1976.

Falconer, W. A. "Sketches of Bismarck's Early History." *North Dakota Good Roads Magazine* (1922): 22–24.

Farley, Joseph Pearson. *West Point in the Early Sixties*. Troy, N.Y.: Pafraets Book Company, 1902.

Fern, Fanny [Sara Parton]. *Ruth Hall {1854} and Other Writings*. Edited by Joyce W. Warren. New Brunswick, N.J.: Rutgers University Press, 1990.

The Fighting Norths and Pawnee Scouts: Narratives and Reminiscences of Military Service on the Old Frontier. Lincoln, Neb.: Robert Bruce, 1932.

Finerty, John F. *War-path and Bivouac, or The Conquest of the Sioux*. Chicago: Donohue and Henneberry, 1890.

Foner, Jack D. *The United States Soldier between Two Wars: Army Life and Reforms, 1865–1898*. New York: Humanities Press, 1970.

Ford, Worthington Chauncey, ed. *A Cycle of Adams Letters, 1861–1865*. 2 vols. Boston: Houghton Mifflin, 1920.

Forsyth, George A. *The Story of the Soldier*. New York: D. Appleton, 1900.

———. *Thrilling Days in Army Life*. New York: Harper and Brothers, 1900.

Fossett, Frank. *Colorado: Its Gold and Silver Mines, Farms and Stock Ranges, and Health and Pleasure Resorts*. New York: C. G. Crawford, 1879.

Fougera, Katherine Gibson. *With Custer's Cavalry*. 1940. Lincoln: University of Nebraska Press, 1986.

Fox, Richard Allan, Jr. *Archaeology, History, and Custer's Last Battle: The Little Big Horn Reexamined*. Norman: University of Oklahoma Press, 1993.

Franklin, Benjamin. *The Autobiography of Benjamin Franklin: A Restoration of a "Fair Copy" by Max Farrand*. Berkeley: University of California Press, 1949.

Frazer, Robert W. *Forts of the West: Military Forts and Presidios and Posts Commonly Called Forts West of the Mississippi River to 1898*. Norman: University of Oklahoma Press, 1965.

Frost, Lawrence A. *Boy General in Bronze: Custer, Michigan's Hero on Horseback*. Glendale, Calif.: Arthur H. Clark, 1985.

———. *The Custer Album: A Pictorial Biography of General George A. Custer*. Seattle: Superior Publishing Company, 1964.

———. *Custer Legends*. Bowling Green, Ohio: Bowling Green University Popular Press, 1981.

———. *Custer's 7th Cavalry and the Campaign of 1873*. El Segundo, Calif.: Upton and Sons, 1986.

———. *Custer Slept Here*. Monroe, Mich.: Garry Owen Publishers, 1974.

———. *General Custer's Libbie*. Seattle: Superior Publishing Co., 1975.

Galbreath, C. B. "George Armstrong Custer." *Ohio Archaeological and Historical Quarterly* 41:4 (October 1932): 623–33.

Gardner-Sharp, Abigail. *History of the Spirit Lake Massacre and Captivity of Miss Abbie Gardner*. Facsimile of 1885. Spirit Lake, Iowa: Dickinson County Historical Society, 1990.

"General Custer in Wall Street." *Army and Navy Journal* 20:51 (July 21, 1883): 1146.

Gibbon, John. *Gibbon on the Sioux Campaign of 1876*. Facsimile ed. Bellevue, Neb.: Old Army Press, 1969. Reprinted from *American Catholic Quarterly Review* (April and October 1877).

Glasson, William H. *Federal Military Pensions in the United States*. Edited by David Kinley. New York: Oxford University Press, 1918.

Godfrey, C. P. "General Edward S. Godfrey." *Ohio Archaeological and Historical Quarterly* 43:1 (1934): 83.

Godfrey, E. S. *An Account of Custer's Last Campaign and the Battle of the Little Big Horn*. Palo Alto, Calif.: Lewis Osborne, 1968. Reprint of "Custer's Last Battle," *Century Magazine* 43:3 (January 1892): 358–84.

———. *The Field Diary of Lieutenant Edward Settle Godfrey*. Edited by Edgar I. Stewart and Jane R. Stewart. Portland, Ore.: Champoeg Press, 1957.

———. *General George A. Custer and the Battle of the Little Big Horn.* New York: Century Company, 1921. Revision of "Custer's Last Battle."

———. "Some Reminiscences, Including the Washita Battle, November 27, 1868." *Cavalry Journal*, annotated galleys.

Gordon, John Steele. *The Scarlet Woman of Wall Street: Jay Gould, Jim Fisk, Cornelius Vanderbilt, the Erie Railway Wars, and the Birth of Wall Street*. New York: Weidenfeld and Nicolson, 1988.

Gorgas, Marie Cook, and Burton J. Hendrick. *William Crawford Gorgas: His Life and Work*. Philadelphia: Lea and Febiger, 1924.

Goss, Warren Lee. *Recollections of a Private: A Story of the Army of the Potomac*. New York: Thomas Y. Crowell, 1890.

Gossett, Thomas F. *Race: The History of an Idea in America*. Dallas: Southern Methodist University Press, 1963.

Graham, W. A. *The Custer Myth: A Source Book of Custeriana*. Harrisburg, Penn.: Stackpole Company, 1953.

———. *The Story of the Little Big Horn*. New York: Century Co., 1926.

———. "The Story of the Little Big Horn," *Cavalry Journal* 35 (July 1926): 295–369.

The Grand Duke Alexis in the United States of America. 1872. Reprint. New York: Interland, 1972.

Grant, Ulysses S. *The Papers of Ulysses S. Grant*. Edited by John Y. Simon. 20 vols. Carbondale: Southern Illinois University Press, 1988.

———. *Personal Memoirs of U.S. Grant.* Edited by E. B. Long. New York: Da Capo Press, 1982.

Gray, John S. *Centennial Campaign: The Sioux War of 1876*. Fort Collins, Colo.: Old Army Press, 1976.

———. *Custer's Last Campaign: Mitch Boyer and the Little Bighorn Reconstructed*. Lincoln: University of Nebraska Press, 1991.

Greeley, Horace. *The American Conflict: A History of the Great Rebellion*. 2 vols. Hartford, Conn.: O. D. Case and Co., 1864.

Green, Rayna. "The Pocohontas Perplex: The Image of Indian Women in American Culture," *Massachusetts Review* 16 (autumn 1975): 698–714.

Green, Rena Maverick, ed. *Memoirs of Mary A. Maverick*. 1921. Reprint. Lincoln: University of Nebraska Press, 1989.

Grinnell, George Bird. *The Cheyenne Indians*. 2 vols. New Haven: Yale University Press, 1923.

———. *The Fighting Cheyennes*. 1915. Reprint. Norman: University of Oklahoma Press, 1956.

———. *The Passing of the Great West: Selected Papers of George Bird Grinnell*. Edited by John F. Reiger. New York: Winchester Press, 1972.

———. "Portraits of Indian Types." *Scribner's Magazine* 37:3 (March 1905): 258–73.

———. *Two Great Scouts and Their Pawnee Battalion*. Cleveland: Arthur H. Clark Company, 1928.

Gunn, Jan Augusta. *Memorial Sketches of Doctor Moses Gunn, by his Wife.* Chicago: W. T. Kenner, 1889.

Hadley, James Albert. "The Nineteenth Kansas Cavalry and the Conquest of the Plains Indians." *Collections of the Kansas State Historical Society* 10 (1908): 428–56.

———. "A Royal Buffalo Hunt." *Transactions of the Kansas State Historical Society, 1907–1908* 10 (1908): 564–80.

Hall, Gordon Langley. *Vinnie Ream: The Story of the Girl Who Sculptured Lincoln.* New York: Holt, Rinehart and Winston, 1963.

Hampsten, Elizabeth. *Read This Only to Yourself: The Private Writings of Midwestern Women, 1880–1910.* Bloomington: Indiana University Press, 1982.

Hanson, Joseph Mills. *The Conquest of the Missouri: Being the Story of the Life and Exploits of Captain Grant Marsh*. Chicago: A. C. McClurg, 1916.

Hardy, Allison. *Wild Bill Hickok: King of the Gun-Fighters*. Girard, Kans.: Haldeman-Julius Publications, 1943.

Harrison, Emily Haines. "Reminiscences of Early Days in Ottawa County." *Kansas Historical Collections* 10 (1907–8): 627–28.

Hebard, Grace Raymond. *Washakie*. Cleveland: Arthur H. Clark, 1930.

Hein, O. L. *Memories of Long Ago*. New York: G. P. Putnam's Sons, 1925.

Hellerstein, Erna Olafson, Leslie Parker Hume, and Karen M. Offen, eds. *Victorian Women: A Documentary Account of Women's Lives in Nineteenth-Century England, France, and the United States*. Palo Alto, Calif.: Stanford University Press, 1981.

Hofling, Charles K. *Custer and the Little Big Horn: A Psychobiographical Inquiry*. Detroit: Wayne State University Press, 1981.

Hoig, Stan. *The Battle of the Washita: The Sheridan-Custer Indian Campaign of 1867–1869.* Garden City, N.Y.: Doubleday, 1976.

Holmes, Oliver Wendell. *The Occasional Speeches of Justice Oliver Wendell Holmes*. Cambridge: Harvard University Press, 1962.

Homer. *The Odyssey*. Translated by Robert Fitzgerald. New York: Doubleday Anchor, 1963.

Honko, Lauri. "The Problem of Defining Myth." In *Sacred Narrative: Readings in the Theory of Myth*, edited by Alan Dundes. Berkeley: University of California Press, 1984.

Hoopes, Alban W. *The Road to the Little Big Horn—and Beyond*. New York: Vantage Press, 1975.

Hoxie, Frederick E. *A Final Promise: The Campaign to Assimilate the Indians, 1880–1920.* Lincoln: University of Nebraska Press, 1984.

Hubbard, Elbert. *Hartford Lunch Company Brochure*. Hartford, Conn.: privately printed, 1917.

Hunt, Frazier. *Custer: The Last of the Cavaliers*. New York: Cosmopolitan Book Corporation, 1928.

Hunt, Frazier, and Robert Hunt. *I Fought with Custer: The Story of Sergeant Windolph, Last Survivor of the Battle of the Little Big Horn*. New York: Charles Scribner's Sons, 1953.

———. *Phil Sheridan and His Army*. Lincoln: University of Nebraska Press, 1985.

Hyde, George E. *Life of George Bent Written from His Letters*. Edited by Savoie Lottinville. Norman: University of Oklahoma Press, 1967.

———. *Red Cloud's Folk: A History of the Oglala Sioux Indians*. Norman: University of Oklahoma Press, 1957.

———. *Spotted Tail's Folk: A History of the Brulé Sioux*. Norman: University of Oklahoma Press, 1974.

"Indian Barbarities—The Box Family." *Harper's Weekly* 10 (December 22, 1866): 806–7.

Jackson, Donald. *Custer's Gold: The United States Cavalry Expedition of 1874*. New Haven: Yale University Press, 1966.

Jackson, Helen Hunt. *A Century of Dishonor*. New York: Harper and Brothers, 1881.

Jackson, John Brinckerhoff. *American Space: The Centennial Years, 1865–1876*. New York: W. W. Norton, 1972.

James, Henry. *The Complete Tales of Henry James*. Edited by Leon Edel. 12 vols. Philadelphia: Lippincott, 1962–64.

Jeffrey, Julie Roy. *Frontier Women: The Trans-Mississippi West, 1840–1880*. New York: Hill and Wang, 1979.

Jenney, Walter P. *The Mineral Wealth, Climate and Rain-Fall, and Natural Resources of the Black Hills of Dakota*. Washington, D.C.: Government Printing Office, Department of the Interior, Office of Indian Affairs, 1876.

Johnson, Barry C. "Dr. Paulding and His Remarkable Diary: A Jaundiced Look at Gibbon's Montana Column of 1876." In *Sidelights of the Sioux Wars*, edited by Francis B. Taunton. London: English Westerners' Society, 1967.

Johnson, Barry C., and Francis B. Taunton. *Benteen's Ordeal and Custer's Field: Two Papers*. London: Johnson-Taunton Military Press, 1983.

Johnson, Robert Underwood. *Remembered Yesterdays*. Boston: Little, Brown, 1923.

Johnson, Virginia Weisel. *The Unregimented General: A Biography of Nelson A. Miles*. Boston: Houghton Mifflin, 1962.

Kappler, Charles J. *Indian Affairs, Laws and Treaties*. 2 vols. Washington, D.C.: Government Printing Office, 1904.

Kaufman, Fred S. *Custer Passed Our Way*. Aberdeen, S.D.: North Plains Press, 1971.

Keim, DeB. Randolph. *Sheridan's Troopers on the Borders: A Winter Campaign on the Plains*. 1870. Reprint. London: George Routledge and Sons, 1885.

Kelly, Fanny. *My Captivity among the Sioux Indians*. 1871. Reprint. Secaucus, N.J.: Citadel Press, 1962.

Kennedy, John B. "A Soldier's Widow." *Collier's* (January 29, 1927): 10, 41.

Kessler-Harris, Alice. *Women Have Always Worked: A Historical Overview*. Old Westbury, N.Y.: Feminist Press, 1981.

Kidd, J. H. *Personal Recollections of a Cavalryman: With Custer's Michigan Cavalry Brigade in the Civil War*. 1908. Reprint. Grand Rapids, Mich.: Black Letter Press, 1969.

King, Charles. "Custer's Last Battle." *Harper's* 81 (August 1890): 378–87.

King, James T., ed. "Fort McPherson in 1870: A Note by an Army Wife." *Nebraska History* 45 (March 1964): 99–107.

King, W. C., and W. P. Derby, comps. *Camp-Fire Sketches and Battlefield Echoes*. Springfield, Mass.: King, Richardson, 1888.

Kingsbury, George W. *History of Dakota Territory: South Dakota, Its History and Its People*. Edited by George Martin Smith. Vol. 1. Chicago: S. J. Clarke Publishing Co., 1915.

Kingsley, George Henry. *Notes on Sport and Travel*. London: Macmillan, 1900.

Knight, Oliver. *Following the Indian Wars: The Story of the Newspaper Correspondents among the Indian Campaigners*. Norman: University of Oklahoma Press, 1960.

———. *Life and Manners in the Frontier Army*. Norman: University of Oklahoma Press, 1978.

Krause, Herbert, and Gary D. Olson, eds. *Prelude to Glory: A Newspaper Accounting of Custer's 1874 Expedition to The Black Hills*. Sioux Falls, S.D.: Brevet Press, 1974.

Kroeker, Marvin E. *Great Plains Command: William B. Hazen in the Frontier West*. Norman: University of Oklahoma Press, 1976.

Krupnick, Janice L., and Fredric Solomon. "Death of a Parent or Sibling during Childhood." In *The Psychology of Separation and Loss: Perspectives on Development, Life Transitions, and Clinical Practice*, edited by Jonathan Bloom-Feshbach, Sally Bloom-Feshbach, and Associates. San Francisco: Jossey-Bass, 1987.

Laas, Virginia Jeans, ed. *Wartime Washington: The Civil War Letters of Elizabeth Blair Lee*. Urbana: University of Illinois Press, 1991.

Lane, Harrison. "Brush, Palette and the Little Big Horn." *Montana: The Magazine of Western History* 23 (summer 1973): 66–80.

Lane, Lydia Spencer. *I Married a Soldier, or Old Days in the Old Army*. 1893. Reprint. Albuquerque, N.M.: Horn and Wallace, 1964.

Langellier, John P., Kurt Hamilton Cox, and Brian C. Pohanka, eds. *Myles Keogh*. El Segundo, Calif.: Upton and Sons, 1991.

Larned, Charles W. "Expedition to the Yellowstone River in 1873: Letters of a Young Cavalry Officer." Edited by George Frederick Howe. In *The Custer Reader*, edited by Paul Andrew Hutton. Lincoln: University of Nebraska Press, 1992.

"Late Indian Outrages." *Harper's Weekly* 11:552 (July 27, 1867): 468.

Laufe, Abe, ed. *An Army Doctor's Wife on the Frontier: Letters from Alaska and the Far West, 1874–1878*. Pittsburgh: University of Pittsburgh Press, 1962.

Lawrence, Elizabeth Atwood. *His Very Silence Speaks: Comanche—The Horse Who Survived Custer's Last Stand*. Detroit: Wayne State University Press, 1989.

Lazarus, Edward. *Black Hills, White Justice: The Sioux Nation versus the United States, 1775 to the Present*. New York: HarperCollins, 1991.

Leckie, Shirley A. *The Colonel's Lady on the Western Frontier: The Correspondence of Alice Kirk Grierson*. Lincoln: University of Nebraska Press, 1988.

———. *Elizabeth Bacon Custer and the Making of a Myth*. Norman: University of Oklahoma Press, 1993.

Leckie, William H. *The Military Conquest of the Southern Plains*. Norman: University of Oklahoma Press, 1963.

Leland, Charles Godfrey. *Memoirs*. London: William Heinemann, 1894.

Lemly, H. R. "The Fight on the Rosebud." In *The Papers of the Order of Indian Wars*, edited by John M. Carroll. Fort Collins, Colo.: Old Army Press, 1975.

Leonard, Thomas C. "Red, White and the Army Blue: Empathy and Anger in the American West." *American Quarterly* 26 (May 1974): 176–90.

Lewis, Meriwether. *The Original Journals of the Lewis and Clarke Expedition, 1804–1806*. Edited by Reuben Gold Thwaites. 16 vols. New York: Dodd, Mead, 1904–5.

Libby, O. G., ed. *The Arikara Narrative of the Campaign against the Hostile Dakotas, June 1876*. New York: Sol Lewis, 1973. First published in North Dakota Historical Collections, vol. 6, Bismarck, 1920.

Liddic, Bruce, ed. *I Buried Custer: The Diary of Pvt. Thomas W. Coleman, 7th U.S. Cavalry*. College Station, Tex.: Creative Publishing, 1979.

Limerick, Patricia Nelson. *The Legacy of Conquest: The Unbroken Past of the American West*. New York: W. W. Norton, 1987.

Linderman, Frank B. *Plenty-Coups: Chief of the Crows*. Lincoln: University of Nebraska Press, 1962.

———. *Pretty-Shield: Medicine Woman of the Crows* (originally published as *Red Mother*). New York: John Day, 1972.

Lloyd, Harlan Page. "The Battle of Waynesboro." In *The Custer Reader*, edited by Paul Andrew Hutton. Lincoln: University of Nebraska Press, 1992.

Lord, Francis A. *Uniforms of the Civil War*. New York: Thomas Yoseloff, 1970.

Lothrop, Charles H. *A History of the First Regiment Iowa Cavalry Veteran Volunteers*. Lyons, Iowa: Beers and Eaton, 1890.

Lowie, Robert H. *Indians of the Plains*. New York: McGraw-Hill, 1954.

Luce, Edward S., ed. "The Diary and Letters of Dr. James M. DeWolf." *North Dakota History* 25 (1958): 33–81.

———. *Keogh, Comanche and Custer*. 1939. Reprint. Ashland, Ore.: Lewis Osborne, 1974.

Lucia, Ellis. *The Saga of Ben Holladay: Giant of the Old West*. New York: Hastings House, 1959.

Lummis, Charles F. *General Crook and the Apache Wars*. Flagstaff, Ariz.: Northland, 1966.

Lystra, Karen. *Searching the Heart: Women, Men, and Romantic Love in Nineteenth-Century America*. New York: Oxford University Press, 1989.

Mackenzie, Ranald Slidell. *Ranald S. Mackenzie's Official Correspondence Relating to Texas, 1873–1879*. Edited by Ernest Wallace. Lubbock: West Texas Museum Association, 1968. Reprinted from *Museum Journal* 10 (1966): 1–241.

Maclean, Norman. *Young Men and Fire*. Chicago: University of Chicago Press, 1992.

McAndrews, Eugene V. "An Army Engineer's Journal of Custer's Black Hills Expedition, July 2, 1874–August 23, 1874," *Journal of the West* 13:1 (January 1974): 78–85.

McBee, John. "John McBee's Account of the Expedition of the 19th Kansas." Edited by William E. Connelley. *Collections of the Kansas State Historical Society* 17 (1928): 361–74.

McClellan, George B. *McClellan's Own Story*. New York: Charles L. Webster, 1887.

McClernand, Edward J. "The Fight on Custer Hill." *Cavalry Journal* (January 1927).

———. *With the Indian and the Buffalo in Montana, 1870–1878: Edward J. McClernand's Narrative, 1870–1878, and Journal (1876)*. Glendale, Calif.: Arthur H. Clark, 1969.

McFeely, William S. *Grant: A Biography*. New York: W. W. Norton, 1981.

McKay, R. H. *Little Pills: An Army Story*. Pittsburg, Kans.: Pittsburg Headlight, 1918.

McLaughlin, James. *My Friend the Indian*. Boston: Houghton Mifflin, 1910.

McPherson, James M. *Ordeal by Fire: The Civil War and Reconstruction*. New York: Alfred A. Knopf, 1982.

Manypenny, George W. *Our Indian Wards*. Cincinnati: Robert Clarke, 1880.

Marcy, Randolph B. *Adventure on Red River: Report on the Exploration of the Headwaters of the Red River by Captain Randolph B. Marcy and Captain G. B. McClellan*. Edited by Grant Foreman. Norman: University of Oklahoma Press, 1968.

Mardock, Robert Winston. *The Reformers and the American Indian*. Columbia: University of Missouri Press, 1971.

Marquis, Thomas B. *Custer, Cavalry and Crows: The Story of William White as Told to Thomas Marquis*. Fort Collins, Colo.: Old Army Press, 1975.

———. *Custer on the Little Bighorn*. 2d ed., rev. Algonac, Mich.: Reference Publications, 1986.

———. *Keep the Last Bullet for Yourself: The True Story of Custer's Last Stand*. New York: Two Continents, 1976.

———. *Wooden Leg: A Warrior Who Fought Custer*. Lincoln: University of Nebraska Press, 1931.

Marsh, O. C. *A Statement of Affairs at Red Cloud Agency, Made to the President of the United States, July 10, 1875*. Collected in Bancroft Library Pamphlets on North American Indians, University of California at Berkeley. Vol. 3.

Marshall, S. L. A. *Crimsoned Prairie: The Wars between the United States and the Plains Indians during the Winning of the West*. New York: Charles Scribner's Sons, 1972.

Marszalek, John F. *Sherman: A Soldier's Passion for Order*. New York: Free Press, 1993.

Martin, H. S. *The New York Stock Exchange*. New York: n.p., 1919.

Mattes, Merrill J. *Indians, Infants and Infantry: Andrew and Elizabeth Burt on the Frontier*. Denver: Old West Publishing Company, 1960.

Matthews, Glenna. *The Rise of Public Woman: Woman's Power and Woman's Place in the United States, 1630–1970*. New York: Oxford University Press, 1992.

Mattison, Ray, ed. "An Army Wife on the Upper Missouri: The Diary of Sarah E. Canfield, 1866–1868." *North Dakota History* 20 (October 1953): 217.

Melville, Herman. *Billy Budd, Sailor (An Inside Narrative)*. Edited by Harrison Hayford and Merton M. Sealts, Jr. Chicago: University of Chicago Press, 1962.

———. *Moby-Dick*. Edited by Hershel Parker. New York: W. W. Norton, 1967.

Merington, Marguerite, ed. *The Custer Story: The Life and Intimate Letters of General George A. Custer and His Wife Elizabeth*. 1950. Reprint. Lincoln: University of Nebraska Press, 1987.

Meriwether, James B., and Michael Millgate, eds. *Lion in the Garden: Interviews with William Faulkner*. Lincoln: University of Nebraska Press, 1980.

Merkel, Charles E., Jr. *Unravelling the Custer Enigma*. Enterprise, Ala.: Merkel Press, 1977.

Miles, Nelson A. *Personal Recollections and Observations of General Nelson A. Miles*. 1896. Reprint. New York: Da Capo Press, 1969.

———. *Serving the Republic: Memoirs of the Civil and Military Life of Nelson A. Miles*. New York: Harper and Brothers, 1911.

Millbrook, Minnie Dubbs. "Cadet Custer's Court-Martial." In *Custer and His Times*, edited by Paul Andrew Hutton. El Paso, Tex.: Little Big Horn Associates, 1981.

———. "Custer's March to Texas." *Prairie Scout* 1 (1973): 75–95.

———. "The Jordan Massacre." *Kansas History* 2:4 (winter 1979): 219–30.

———. "A Monument to Custer." *Montana: The Magazine of Western History* 24 (spring 1974): 18–33.

———. "Rebecca Visits Kansas and the Custers: The Diary of Rebecca Richmond." *Kansas Historical Quarterly* 42 (winter 1976): 366–402.

———. "The West Breaks in General Custer." *Kansas Historical Quarterly* 36:2 (summer 1970): 113–48.

Miller, David Humphreys. *Custer's Fall: The Indian Side of the Story*. New York: Duell, Sloan and Pearce, 1957.

Mills, Anson. *My Story*. Edited by C. H. Claudy. Washington, D.C.: Byron S. Adams, 1918.

Mills, Charles K. *Harvest of Barren Regrets: The Army Career of Frederick William Benteen, 1834–1898*. Glendale, Calif.: Arthur H. Clark, 1985.

Milner, Joe E., and Earle R. Forrest. *California Joe: Noted Scout and Indian Fighter*. Caldwell, Idaho: Caxton Printers, 1935.

Mishkin, Bernard. *Rank and Warfare among the Plains Indians*. Seattle: University of Washington Press, 1940.

Monaghan, Jay. *Custer: The Life of General George Armstrong Custer*. 1959. Reprint. Lincoln: University of Nebraska Press, 1971.

Moore, Horace L. "The Nineteenth Kansas Cavalry." *Transactions of the Kansas State Historical Society* 6 (1900): 35–52.

Morris, Robert E. "Custer Made a Good Decision." *Journal of the West* 16 (1977): 6.

Mulford, Ami Frank. *Fighting Indians! In the Seventh United States Cavalry, Custer's Favorite Regiment*. Fairfield, Wash.: Ye Galleon Press, 1972.

Myres, Sandra L. "Romance and Reality on the American Frontier: Views of Army Wives." *Western Historical Quarterly* 13 (1982): 409–27.

———. *Westering Women and the Frontier Experience, 1800–1915*. Albuquerque: University of New Mexico Press, 1982.

———, ed. *Cavalry Wife: The Diary of Eveline M. Alexander, 1866–1867*. College Station: Texas A & M University Press, 1977.

Narratives of Captivity among the Indians of North America. Chicago: Newberry Library, 1912.

Newson, Thomas McLean. *Thrilling Scenes among the Indians*. New York: Butler Brothers, 1889.

Nichols, George Ward. "Wild Bill." *Harper's New Monthly Magazine* 34 (February 1867): 273–85.

Norton, Henry. *Deeds of Daring, or History of the 8th New York Volunteer Cavalry*. Norwich, N.Y.: Chenango Telegraph Printing, 1889.

O'Connor, Richard. *Sheridan the Inevitable*. Indianapolis: Bobbs-Merrill, 1953.

The Official Record of a Court of Inquiry. 2 vols. Pacific Palisades, Calif.: W. A. Graham, 1951.

Olson, James C. *Red Cloud and the Sioux Problem*. Lincoln: University of Nebraska Press, 1965.

Otero, Miguel Antonio. *My Life on the Frontier, 1864–1882*. New York: Press of the Pioneers, 1935.

Page, Charles A. *Letters of a War Correspondent*. Boston: L. C. Page, 1899.

Paine, Bayard H. *Pioneers, Indians and Buffaloes*. Curtis, Neb.: Curtis Enterprise, 1935.

Parmelee, Mary Manley. "A Child's Recollections of the Summer of '76." *Tepee Book* 1 (June 1915): 123–30.

Phillips, George H. "The Indian Ring in Dakota Territory, 1870–1890." *South Dakota History* 2 (fall 1972): 345–76.

Phipps, Robert. "Nebraska Scene." *Omaha World-Herald Sunday Magazine* (March 19, 1950): 2c.

Pohanka, Brian. "In Hospital at West Point: Medical Records of Cadets Who Later Served with the Seventh Cavalry." *Little Big Horn Associates Newsletter* 23:6 (July 1989): 5–7.

———. "A Summer on the Plains, 1870: From the Diary of Annie Gibson Roberts." In *Custer and His Times*, edited by Paul Andrew Hutton. El Paso, Tex.: Little Big Horn Associates, 1981.

Pomeroy, Earl. *In Search of the Golden West: The Tourist in Western America*. New York: Alfred A. Knopf, 1957.

Pope, Alexander. *The Poems of Alexander Pope*. Edited by John Butt. New Haven: Yale University Press, 1963.

Pope, James L. *Custer and His Dogs*. Plover, Wisc.: Phoenix Proprietary Publications, 1990.

Porter, Horace. *Campaigning with Grant*. New York: Century Company, 1897.

Powers, Marla N. *Oglala Women: Myth, Ritual, and Reality*. Chicago: University of Chicago Press, 1986.

Premo, Terri L. *Winter Friends: Women Growing Old in the New Republic, 1785–1835*. Urbana: University of Illinois Press, 1990.

Price, George F. *Across the Continent with the Fifth Cavalry*. New York: D. Van Nostrand, 1883.

Priest, Loring Benson. *Uncle Sam's Stepchildren: The Reformation of United States Indian Policy, 1865–1887*. New Brunswick, N.J.: Rutgers University Press, 1942.

Prucha, Paul Francis. *The Great Father: The United States Government and the American Indians*. 2 vols. Lincoln: University of Nebraska Press, 1984.

———. *Indian Policy in the United States: Historical Essays*. Lincoln: University of Nebraska Press, 1981.

———, ed. *Americanizing the American Indians: Writings by the "Friends of the Indian," 1880–1900*. Cambridge: Harvard University Press, 1973.

Reed, James. *The Birth Control Movement and American Society: From Private Vice to Public Virtue*. Princeton: Princeton University Press, 1984.

Reedstrom, Ernest Lisle. *Bugles, Banners and War Bonnets*. Caldwell, Idaho: Caxton Printers, 1977.

Rhodes, Charles D. *History of the Cavalry of the Army of the Potomac*. Kansas City, Mo.: Hudson-Kimberly Publishing Co., 1900.

Richardson, James D., comp. *A Compilation of the Messages and Papers of the Presidents, 1789–1897*. Vol. 7. Washington, D.C.: Government Printing Office, 1897–98.

Richardson, Joseph. *The American Reader*. 2d ed. Boston: Lincoln and Edmands, 1813.

Richter, William L. *The Army in Texas during Reconstruction, 1865–1870*. College Station: Texas A & M University Press, 1987.

Rickey, Don, Jr. *Forty Miles a Day on Beans and Hay: The Enlisted Soldier Fighting the Indian Wars*. Norman: University of Oklahoma Press, 1963.

Riley, Glenda. *Women and Indians on the Frontier, 1825–1915*. Albuquerque: University of New Mexico Press, 1984.

Rister, Carl Coke. *Border Captives: The Traffic in Prisoners by Southern Plains Indians, 1835–1875*. Norman: University of Oklahoma, 1940.

———. *Border Command: General Phil Sheridan in the West*. Norman: University of Oklahoma Press, 1944.

Robertson, Jno., ed. *Michigan in the War*. Rev. ed. Lansing, Mich.: W. S. George, 1882.

Robinson, Doane. *A History of the Dakota or Sioux Indians*. Aberdeen, N.D.: News Printing Co., 1904.

Rodenbough, Theodore F., and William L. Haskin, eds. *The Army of the United States*. New York: Maynard, Merrill, 1896.

Roe, Charles Francis. *Custer's Last Battle*. New York: Robert Bruce, 1927.

Roe, Frances M. A. *Army Letters from an Officer's Wife, 1871–1888*. New York: D. Appleton, 1909.

Ronsheim, L. Milton. *The Life of General Custer*. Cadiz, Ohio: *Cadiz Republican*, 1929.

Roosevelt, Theodore. *The Winning of the West*. 4 vols. New York: G. P. Putnam's Sons, 1903.

Rosa, Joseph G. *Alias Jack McCall: A Pardon or Death?* Kansas City, Mo.: Kansas City Posse of the Westerners, 1967.

———. *They Called Him Wild Bill: The Life and Adventures of James Butler Hickok*. 2d ed. rev. Norman: University of Oklahoma Press, 1974.

Rosenberg, Bruce A. *Custer and the Epic of Defeat*. University Park: Pennsylvania State University Press, 1974.

Rosenberg, Charles. "Sexuality, Class and Role in Nineteenth Century America." *American Quarterly* 25:2 (May 1973).

Russell, Don. *Custer's Last, or The Battle of the Little Big Horn in Picturesque Perspective*. Ft. Worth, Tex.: Amos Carter Museum of Western Art, 1968.

———. "How Many Indians Were Killed? White Man versus Red Man: The Facts and the Legend." *American West* 10:4 (July 1973): 42–47, 61–63.

———. *The Lives and Legends of Buffalo Bill*. Norman: University of Oklahoma Press, 1960.

———. *The Wild West, or A History of the Wild West Shows*. Ft. Worth, Tex.: Amos Carter Museum, 1970.

Russell, Marian. "Memoirs of Marian Russell." *Winners of the West* 21:3 (March 28, 1944): 5–6.

Ryan, John. *Ten Years with General Custer among the American Indians and Other Writings*. Edited by John M. Carroll. Bryan, Tex.: privately published, 1980.

Ryan, Mary P. *The Empire of the Mother: American Writing about Domesticity, 1830–1860*. New York: Haworth Press, 1982.

———. *Womanhood in America: From Colonial Times to the Present*. New York: New Viewpoints, 1975.

Sabin, Edwin L. *On the Plains with Custer*. Philadelphia: Lippincott, 1913.

Sandoz, Mari. *The Buffalo Hunters: The Story of the Hide Men*. New York: Hastings House, 1954.

———. *Cheyenne Autumn*. New York: McGraw-Hill, 1953.

Sanford, George B. *Fighting Rebels and Redskins: Experiences in the Army Life of Colonel George B. Sanford, 1861–1892*. Edited by E. R. Hagemann. Norman: University of Oklahoma Press, 1969.

Schaff, Morris. "The Indian: What We Should Do with Him." *Harper's Monthly* 40:4 (1870): 737.

———. *The Spirit of Old West Point, 1858–1862*. Boston: Houghton Mifflin, 1907.

Schwarck, Don. "Campaigning in Kansas with Maida and Blucher: General Custer's Staghounds." *Research Review: The Journal of the Little Big Horn Associates* 6:2 (June 1992): 14–22, 30.

Scott, Douglas D., and Richard A. Fox, Jr. *Archaeological Insights into the Custer Battle: An Assessment of the 1984 Field Season.* Norman: University of Oklahoma Press, 1987.

Scott, Douglas D., Richard A. Fox, Jr., Melissa A. Connor, and Dick Harmon. *Archaeological Perspectives on the Battle of the Little Bighorn.* Norman: University of Oklahoma Press, 1989.

Scott, Hugh Lenox. *Some Memories of a Soldier.* New York: Century Company, 1928.

Scrymser, James A. *Personal Reminiscences of James A. Scrymser.* New York: privately printed, 1915.

Senn, Edward L. *"Wild Bill" Hickok: "Prince of Pistoleers."* Deadwood, S.D.: n.p., 1939.

Shakespeare, William. *The Tragedy of Othello, the Moor of Venice.* Edited by George Lyman Kittredge. New York: Ginn and Company, 1941.

Sheridan, Michael V. *Personal Memoirs of Philip Henry Sheridan.* 2 vols. New York: D. Appleton, 1904.

Sheridan, P. H. *Record of Engagements with Hostile Indians within the Military Division of the Missouri, from 1868 to 1882.* Chicago: Military Division of the Missouri, 1882.

Sherman, W. T. *Memoirs of General W. T. Sherman, Written by Himself.* 4th ed., rev. 2 vols. New York: Charles L. Webster, 1891.

The Sherman Letters: Correspondence between General and Senator Sherman from 1837 to 1891. Edited by Rachel Sherman Thorndike. New York: Charles Scribner's Sons, 1894.

Sills, Joe. "The Recruits Controversy: Another Look." *Greasy Grass: Annual for the Battlefield Dispatch* (May 1989): 2–8.

Simonin, Louis Laurent. *The Rocky Mountain West in 1867.* Translated by Wilson O. Clough. Lincoln: University of Nebraska Press, 1966.

Slotkin, Richard. *The Fatal Environment: The Myth of the Frontier in the Age of Industrialization, 1800–1890.* New York: Atheneum, 1985.

———. ". . . & Then the Mare Will Go! An 1875 Black Hills Scheme by Custer, Holladay, and Buford." *Journal of the West* 15:3 (July 1976): 60–77.

Smith, Daniel Scott. "Family Limitation, Sexual Control, and Domestic Feminism in Victorian America." In *Clio's Consciousness Raised: New Perspectives on the History of Women.* Edited by Mary S. Hartman and Lois Banner. New York: Harper and Row, 1974.

Smith, Herbert E. "Comanche Still Lives." *Recruiting News* (November 15, 1926): 36.

Smith, Jay. "A Hundred Years Later." *In Custer and His Times*, edited by Paul Andrew Hutton. El Paso, Tex.: Little Bighorn Associates, 1981.

———. "What Did Not Happen at the Battle of the Little Big Horn." *Research Review* 6:2 (June 1992): 6–13.

Smith, Sherry L. *The View from Officers' Row: Army Perceptions of Western Indians.* Tucson: University of Arizona Press, 1990.

Smith-Rosenberg, Carroll. "Puberty to Menopause: The Cycle of Femininity in Nineteenth-Century America." In *Clio's Consciousness Raised: New Perspectives on the History of Women*, edited by Mary S. Hartman and Lois Banner. New York: Harper and Row, 1974.

Snyder, Robert M., Jr. "The Kansas City Days of 'Wild Bill.'" *Kansas City Star Magazine* 3:4 (August 15, 1926): 3–4.

Spotts, David L. *Campaigning with Custer and the Nineteenth Kansas Volunteer Cavalry*. Edited by E. A. Brininstool. Los Angeles: Wetzel, 1928.

Sprague, Marshall. *A Gallery of Dudes*. Boston: Little, Brown, 1966.

Stackpole, Edward J. *Sheridan in the Shenandoah: Jubal Early's Nemesis*. Harrisburg, Penn.: Stackpole Company, 1961.

Stallard, Patricia G. *Glittering Misery: Dependents of the Indian Fighting Army*. San Rafael, Calif., and Fort Collins, Colo.: Presidio Press and Old Army Press, 1978.

Stands in Timber, John, and Margot Liberty. *Cheyenne Memories*. New Haven: Yale University Press, 1967.

Stanley, D. S. *Personal Memoirs of Major-General D. S. Stanley.* Cambridge: Harvard University Press, 1917.

———. *Report on the Yellowstone Expedition of 1873*. Washington, D.C.: Government Printing Office, 1874.

Stanley, Henry M. *My Early Travels and Adventures in America and Asia*. 2 vols. New York: Charles Scribner's Sons, 1895.

Starr, Stephen Z. "The Last Days of Rebellion." *Cincinnati Historical Society Bulletin* 35 (1977): 7–30.

———. *The Union Cavalry in the Civil War*. Vol. 1, *From Fort Sumter to Gettysburg, 1861–1863*, and vol. 2, *The War in the East: From Gettysburg to Appomattox, 1863–1865*. Baton Rouge: Louisiana State University Press, 1979 and 1981.

Steckmesser, Kent Ladd. *The Western Hero in History and Legend.* Norman: University of Oklahoma Press, 1965.

Stewart, Edgar I. "The Custer Battle and Widow's Weeds." *Montana* 22 (1972): 51–59.

———. *Custer's Luck*. Norman: University of Oklahoma Press, 1955.

———, ed. *Penny-an-Acre Empire in the West*. Norman: University of Oklahoma Press, 1968.

Stratton, Joanna L. *Pioneer Women: Voices from the Kansas Frontier*. New York: Simon and Schuster, 1981.

Summerhayes, Martha. *Vanished Arizona: Recollections of the Army Life of a New England Woman*. 1908. Facsimile reprint of 2d ed. Glorieta, N.M.: Rio Grande Press, 1976.

Tabeau, Pierre Antoine. *Tabeau's Narrative of Loisel's Expedition to the Upper Missouri.* Edited by Annie Heloise Abel, translated by Rose Abel Wright. Norman: University of Oklahoma Press, 1939.

Taft, Robert. *Artists and Illustrators of the Old West, 1850–1900.* New York: Charles Scribner's Sons, 1953.

Tallmadge, Frank. "Buffalo Hunting with Custer." *Cavalry Journal* 33 (1924): 6–10.

Tate, Michael L. "The Girl He Left Behind: Elizabeth Custer and the Making of a Legend." *Red River Valley Historical Review* 5 (winter 1980): 5–22.

Taunton, Francis B. "The Man Who Rode Comanche." In *Sidelights of the Sioux Wars.* London: English Westerners' Society, 1967.

———. *"Sufficient Reason?" An Examination of Terry's Celebrated Order to Custer.* London: English Westerners' Society, 1977.

Terrell, John Upton, and Colonel George Walton. *Faint the Trumpet Sounds: The Life and Trial of Major Reno.* New York: David McKay, 1966.

Terry, Alfred H. *The Field Diary of General Alfred H. Terry: The Yellowstone Expedition, 1876.* Bellevue, Nebr.: Old Army Press, 1969.

———. *The Terry Letters: The Letters of General Alfred Howe Terry to His Sisters during the Indian War of 1876.* Edited by James Willert. La Miranda, Calif.: James Willert, 1980.

Thompson, Peter. *Peter Thompson's Narrative of the Little Bighorn Campaign, 1876.* Edited by Daniel O. Magnussen. Glendale, Calif.: Arthur H. Clark, 1974.

Tibbles, Thomas Henry. *Buckskin and Blanket Days: Memoirs of a Friend of the Indians.* Chicago: Lakeside Press, 1985.

Tillett, Leslie. *Wind on the Buffalo Grass: The Indians' Own Account of the Battle at the Little Big Horn River, and the Death of Their Life on the Plains.* New York: Thomas Y. Crowell, 1976.

Tipple, John. "The Robber Baron in the Gilded Age: Entrepreneur or Iconoclast?" In *The Gilded Age: A Reappraisal*, edited by H. Wayne Morgan. Syracuse: Syracuse University Press, 1963.

Tremain, Henry Edwin. *Last Hours of Sheridan's Cavalry.* New York: Bonnell, Silver and Bowers, 1904.

Trobriand, Philippe Régis de. *Military Life in Dakota: The Journal of Philippe Régis de Trobriand.* Translated and edited by Lucile M. Kane. St. Paul: Alvord Memorial Commission, 1951.

Turney-High, Harry Holbert. *Primitive War: Its Practice and Concepts.* 2d ed. Columbia: University of South Carolina Press, 1971.

Tyler, Mason Whiting. *Recollections of the Civil War.* Edited by William S. Tyler. New York: G. P. Putnam's Sons, 1912.

The Unpublished Papers of the Order of Indian Wars. 10 vols. New Brunswick, N.J.: privately published, 1977.

Upton, Richard. *The Custer Adventure.* Fort Collins, Colo.: Old Army Press, 1975.

Urwin, Gregory J. W. "Custer: The Civil War Years." In *The Custer Reader*. Edited by Paul Andrew Hutton. Lincoln: University of Nebraska Press, 1992.

———. *Custer Victorious: The Civil War Battles of General George Armstrong Custer*. Rutherford, N.J.: Fairleigh Dickinson University Press, 1983.

Utley, Robert M. "Arizona Vanquished: Impressions and Reflections Concerning the Quality of Life on a Military Frontier." *American West* 6:6 (November 1969): 16–22.

———. *Cavalier in Buckskin: George Armstrong Custer and the Western Military Frontier*. Norman: University of Oklahoma Press, 1988.

———. *Custer and the Great Controversy: The Origin and Development of a Legend*. Los Angeles: Westernlore Press, 1962.

———. "The Frontier and the American Military Tradition." In *Soldiers West: Biographies from the Military Frontier*, edited by Paul Andrew Hutton. Lincoln: University of Nebraska, 1987.

———. *Frontier Regulars: The United States Army and the Indian, 1866–1891*. New York: Macmillan, 1973.

———. *The Indian Frontier of the American West, 1846–1890*. Albuquerque: University of New Mexico Press, 1984.

———. *The Lance and the Shield: The Life and Times of Sitting Bull*. New York: Henry Holt, 1993.

———, ed. *Life in Custer's Cavalry: Diaries and Letters of Albert and Jennie Barnitz, 1867–1868*. New Haven: Yale University Press, 1977.

Van De Water, Frederic F. *Glory-Hunter: A Life of General Custer*. 1934. Reprint. New York: Argosy-Antiquarian, 1963.

Varnum, Charles. *I, Varnum: The Autobiographical Reminiscences of Custer's Chief of Scouts*. Edited by John M. Carroll. Glendale, Calif.: Arthur H. Clark Co., 1982.

Vaughn, J. W. *With Crook at the Rosebud*. Lincoln: University of Nebraska Press, 1956.

Vestal, Stanley. *New Sources of Indian History, 1850–1891*. Norman: University of Oklahoma Press, 1934.

———. *Sitting Bull: Champion of the Sioux*. Boston: Houghton Mifflin, 1932.

Vielé, Teresa. *"Following the Drum": A Glimpse of Frontier Life*. Lincoln: University of Nebraska Press, 1984.

Wabuda, Susan. "Elizabeth Bacon Custer in Japan, 1903." *Manuscripts* 35 (winter 1983): 12–18.

Wagner, Glendolin Damon. *Old Neutriment*. 1934. Reprint. New York: Sol Lewis, 1973.

Walker, Judson Elliott. *Campaigns of General Custer in the North-West and the Final Surrender of Sitting Bull*. New York: Jenkins and Thomas, 1881.

Wallace, Charles B. *Custer's Ohio Boyhood: A Brief Account of the Early Life of Major General George Armstrong Custer*. Freeport, Ohio: Freeport Press, 1978.

Ward, Andrew. "The Little Bighorn." *American Heritage* 43:2 (April 1992): 76–86.

Watson, Elmo Scott, and Don Russell. "The Battle of the Washita or Custer's Massacre?" *Brand Book* 15:1 (October 1972): 1–16. Reprint from *Chicago Westerners Brand Book* 5:9 (November 1948).

Webb, W. E. *Buffalo Land*. Cincinnati: E. Hannford, 1872.

Webb, Walter Prescott. *The Great Plains*. New York: Ginn and Company, 1931.

Weibert, Henry. *Sixty-six Years in Custer's Shadow*. Billings, Mont.: Bannack Publishing Co., 1985.

Weigley, Russell F. *The American Way of War: A History of United States Military Strategy and Policy*. New York: Macmillan, 1976.

———. *Towards an American Army: Military Thought from Washington to Marshall*. Westport, Conn.: Greenwood Press, 1962.

Weist, Katherine. "Beasts of Burden and Menial Slaves: Nineteenth Century Observations of Northern Plains Indian Women." In *The Hidden Half: Studies of Plains Indian Women*, edited by Patricia Albers and Beatrice Medicine. Lanham, Md.: University Press of America, 1983.

Welch, James. *Killing Custer: The Battle of the Little Bighorn and the Fate of the Plains Indians*. New York: W. W. Norton, 1994.

Wellman, Paul I. *Death on Horseback: Seventy Years of War for the American West*. Philadelphia: Lippincott, 1947.

Welter, Barbara. "The Cult of True Womanhood, 1820–1860." *American Quarterly* 18:1 (spring 1966): 151–74.

Wengert, James W. *The Custer Dispatches: The Words of the "New York Herald" Correspondents in the Little Big Horn Campaign of 1876*. Part 1. Manhattan, Kans.: Sunflower University Press, 1987.

West, Emmet C. *History and Reminiscences of the Second Wisconsin Cavalry Regiment*. Portage, Wisc.: n.p., 1904.

Westrate, E. V. *Those Fatal Generals*. New York: Knight Publications, 1936.

"What Hope for Pine Ridge?" *The Economist* 325:7790 (December 19, 1992): 29.

Wheeler, Candace. *Yesterdays in a Busy Life*. New York: Harper and Brothers, 1918.

Wheeler, Homer W. *Buffalo Days: Forty Years in the Old West*. 2d ed., rev. Indianapolis: Bobbs-Merrill, 1925.

Whipple, Henry Benjamin. *Lights and Shadows of a Long Episcopate*. New York: Macmillan, 1912.

White, Lonnie. "White Women Captives of Southern Plains Indians, 1866–1875." *Journal of the West* 8:3 (July 1969): 327–54.

White, Richard. "The Winning of the West: The Expansion of the Western Sioux in the Eighteenth and Nineteenth Centuries." *Journal of American History* 65 (September 1978): 319–43.

Whitman, S. E. *The Troopers: An Informal History of the Plains Cavalry, 1865–1890*. New York: Hastings House, 1962.

Whittaker, Frederick. *A Complete Life of General George A. Custer*. New York: Sheldon and Co., 1876.

Wilbarger, J. W. *Indian Depredations in Texas*. 1889. Vol. 1 in Brasada Reprint Series. Austin, Tex.: Pemberton Press, 1967.

Willert, James. *Little Big Horn Diary: Chronicle of the 1876 Indian War*. La Mirada, Calif.: James Willert, 1977.

Williams, T. Harry. *Lincoln and His Generals*. New York: Alfred A. Knopf, 1952.

Windolph, Charles. "The Battle of the Big Horn." *Sunshine Magazine* (September 1930): 8–9.

Wing, Talcott E. *History of Monroe County, Michigan*. New York: Munsell and Company, 1890.

Wolff, Tobias. *In Pharoah's Army: Memories of the Lost War*. New York: Alfred A. Knopf, 1994.

Woods, C. J. *Reminiscences of the War*. 1880.

Wooster, Robert. *The Military and United States Indian Policy, 1865–1903*. New Haven: Yale University Press, 1988.

"The Worst Federal Agency." *U.S. News and World Report* 117:21 (November 28, 1994): 61–64.

Yost, Nellie Snyder. *Buffalo Bill: His Family, Friends, Fame, Failures, and Fortunes*. Chicago: Swallow Press, 1979.

Zisook, Sidney, and Richard DeVaul. "Unresolved Grief." *American Journal of Psychoanalysis* 45:4 (1985): 370–79:

Zisook, Sidney, Stephen Shuchter, and Marc Schuckit. "Factors in the Persistence of Unresolved Grief among Psychiatric Outpatients." *Psychosomatics* 26:6 (1985): 497–500.

NEWSPAPERS

Bismarck Tribune (North Dakota)
Bronxville Review (New York)
Cadiz Republican (Ohio)
Chicago Inter-Ocean
Chicago Times
Delphos Republican (Kansas)
Denver Post
Detroit Evening Journal
Detroit Free Press
Detroit Journal
Ellis County Star (Kansas)
Helena Herald (Montana)
Junction City Weekly Union (Kansas)
Leavenworth Times and Conservative (Kansas)
Los Angeles Times
Monroe Evening News (Michigan)

Newton Centre Town Crier (Massachusetts)
Newton Circuit (Massachusetts)
New York Evening Post
New York Herald
New York Sun
New York Times
New York Tribune
Omaha World Herald (Nebraska)
St. Louis Democrat
Washington Herald

Index